THE TEACHING OF PSYCHOLOGY

Essays in Honor of Wilbert J. McKeachie
and Charles L. Brewer

THE TEACHING OF PSYCHOLOGY
Essays in Honor of Wilbert J. McKeachie and Charles L. Brewer

Edited by

Stephen F. Davis
Professor Emeritus
Emporia State University

William Buskist
Kulynych/Cline Family
Distinguished Professor
Appalachian State University

LAWRENCE ERLBAUM ASSOCIATES, PUBLISHERS
2002   Mahwah, New Jersey   London

Senior Editor:	Debra Riegert
Editorial Assistant:	Jason Planer
Cover Design:	Kathryn Houghtaling Lacey
Textbook Production Manager:	Paul Smolenski
Full-Service & Composition:	TechBooks
Text and Cover Printer:	Hamilton Printing Company

This book was typeset in 10/12 pt. Times, Italic, Bold, and Bold Italic.
The heads were typeset in Americana and Americana Bold.

Lawrence Erlbaum Associates, Inc., Publishers
10 Industrial Avenue
Mahwah, New Jersey 07430

Library of Congress Cataloging-in-Publication Data

The teaching of psychology : essays in honor of Wilbert J. McKeachie and Charles L.
   Brewer / edited by Stephen F. Davis, William Buskist.
      p.   cm.
   Includes bibliographical references and index.
   ISBN 0-8058-3953-4 (casebound : alk. paper) – ISBN 0-8058-3954-2 (pbk. : alk. paper)
   1. Psychology—Study and teaching (Higher)   2. Psychology—Study and teaching
(Graduate)   I. McKeachie, Wilbert James, 1921–   II. Brewer, Charles L.   III. Davis,
Stephen F.   IV. Buskist, William.

BF77 T435   2001
150′.71′1—dc21   2001053227

Books published by Lawrence Erlbaum Associates are printed on
acid-free paper, and their bindings are chosen for strength and durability.

Printed in the United States of America
10 9 8 7 6 5 4 3 2 1

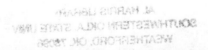

For Virginia Chancey, Al North, and Jack Strange,
who taught me that psychologists can be
scientists, teachers, and real people.

(SD)

For Hal Miller, who showed me the way,
and for Peter Harzem, who illuminated the path.

(WB)

Contents

Preface

Academic disciplines rarely celebrate teaching or their best teachers. Psychology, however, is clearly unique: It is the only academic discipline at the college/ university level that has gone to great lengths to emphasize the importance of high-quality teaching in sustaining, even growing, the discipline. For example, the Society for the Teaching of Psychology (Division Two of the American Psychological Association [APA]), which boasts over 2,500 annual members, publishes a widely known and highly respected journal, *Teaching of Psychology*. It also sponsors a vibrant series of invited addresses, symposia, panel discussions, and poster sessions that focus exclusively on teaching at each APA annual meeting. In addition, there is a separate 3-day National Institute on the Teaching of Psychology (NITOP) held each year in St. Petersburg Beach, Florida, a teaching institute that accompanies the annual meetings of the American Psychological Society (APS), and several annual regional meetings devoted to the teaching of psychology (e.g., SETOP, MACTOP, SWTOP).

That the teaching of psychology has evolved as such a highly visible and significant aspect of academic psychology is due largely to the efforts of two pioneers in this field: Wilbert J. McKeachie, whose book, *Teaching Tips*, now in its 10th edition, set the standard for excellence in college and university teaching; and Charles L. Brewer, whose high standards of scholarship played the pivotal role in establishing *Teaching of Psychology* as a premier academic journal within psychology. Together these two individuals have emerged as undeniable champions of the teaching of psychology.

We have centered this book around their masterful work to recognize their seminal contributions to the teaching of psychology. The major aim of this book is to provide comprehensive coverage and analysis of the basic philosophies, current trends and issues, basic mechanics, and important contextual variables related to effective teaching in psychology. We hope that you, our readers, find our efforts rewarding.

We extend special thanks to a special group of individuals—our authors, who are among the very best college and university teachers in psychology today. Without their exemplary contributions, this volume would not be possible. Lawrence Erlbaum and Debra Riegert at Lawrence Erlbaum Associates (LEA) also deserve no small measure of commendation for their support of this project. They shared our vision from the outset. Special thanks, too, to Jason Planer at LEA, who masterfully kept the channels of communication open and crystal clear between New Jersey and Kansas and between New Jersey and Alabama. Jim Goodwin and his students deserve special commendation for preparing the academic geneaologies for Wilbert McKeachie and Charles Brewer. Finally, we wish to thank our wives, Kathleen Davis and Connie Buskist—two incredibly patient women—for their support, encouragement, and good humor throughout the editing of this book.

—Stephen F. Davis, Emporia, KS
—William Buskist, Boone, NC

List of Contributors

Virginia Andreoli Mathie
School of Psychology
James Madison University

Drew C. Appleby
Department of Psychology
Indiana University Purdue
    University Indianapolis

Scott A. Bailey
Department of Psychology
Texas Lutheran University

Lewis Barker
Psychology Department
Auburn University

John Batson
Department of Psychology
Furman University

Bernard C. Beins
Department of Psychology
Ithaca College and
American Psychological
    Association

Ludy T. Benjamin, Jr.
Department of Psychology
Texas A&M University

Daniel Bernstein
Psychology Department
University of Nebraska–Lincoln

Douglas Bernstein
Department of Psychology
University of South Florida

Charles L. Brewer
Department of Psychology
Furman University

Tanya Buckley
Psychology Department
Auburn University

William Buskist
Psychology Department
Auburn University

Stephen F. Davis
Psychology Department
Emporia State University

Gilles O. Einstein
Department of Psychology
Furman University

James Freeman
Psychology Department
University of Virginia

Peter J. Giordano
Department of Psychology
Belmont University

C. James Goodwin
Department of Psychology
Western Carolina University

Jane S. Halonen
School of Psychology
James Madison University

Diane F. Halpern
Psychology Department
Claremont McKenna College

Elliott Hammer
Department of Psychology
Xavier University

Elizabeth Yost Hammer
Department of Psychology
Loyola University

Maureen P. Hester
Psychology Department
Holy Names College

G. William Hill, IV
Academic Affairs
Kennesaw State University

Reed Hunt
Department of Psychology
University of North
    Carolina–Greensboro

Matthew T. Huss
Department of Psychology
Creighton University

David E. Johnson
Psychology Department
John Brown University

James Kalat
Department of Psychology
North Carolina State University

Stephen Kaplan
Department of Psychology
University of Michigan

James H. Korn
Department of Psychology
Saint Louis University

Nina Kunzer
Psychology Department
University of Wisconsin–Oshkosh

R. Eric Landrum
Department of Psychology
Boise State University

Neil Lutsky
Psychology Department
Carleton College

Margaret Matlin
Department of Psychology
State University of New York–Geneseo

Lee I. McCann
Psychology Department
University of Wisconsin–Oshkosh

Susan H. McFadden
Psychology Department
University of Wisconsin–Oshkosh

Thomas V. McGovern
Department of Integrative Studies
Arizon State University West

Wilbert J. McKeachie
Department of Psychology
University of Michigan

Barbara F. Nodine
Psychology Department
Arcadia University

Baron Perlman
Psychology Department
University of Wisconsin–Oshkosh

Howard R. Pollio
Psychology Department
University of Tennessee–Knoxville

Debra L. Ponec
Department of Education
Creighton University

Thomas P. Pusateri
Department of Psychology
Loras College

Bryan K. Saville
Psychology Department
Auburn University

Jason Sikorksi
Psychology Department
Auburn University

Randolph A. Smith
Department of Psychology
Ouachita Baptist University

Mark E. Ware
Department of Psychology
Creighton University

Kenneth A. Weaver
Psychology Department
Emporia State University

Wayne Weiten
Psychology Department
Santa Clara University

Lonnie Yandell
Department of Psychology
Belmont University

About the Editors

Stephen F. Davis is Professor Emeritus at Emporia State University. He received his Ph.D. in Experimental Psychology from Texas Christian University. He is the author of one of the leading Introductory Psychology books published by Prentice-Hall. He has served as President of APA Division 2 and Psi Chi. He has received several teaching awards including the American Psychological Foundation Distinguished Teaching in Psychology Award and the APA Division 2 Teaching Excellence Award.

William Buskist is Kulynych/Cline Family Distinguished Professor at Appalachian State University. He received his Ph.D. in Experimental Psychology from Brigham Young University in 1982. He has co-authored four books, two introductory texts and two books on preparing for graduate study in psychology (one of these books is published by LEA). He too has received several teaching awards including the 2000 Society for the Teaching of Psychology's Robert S. Daniel Award.

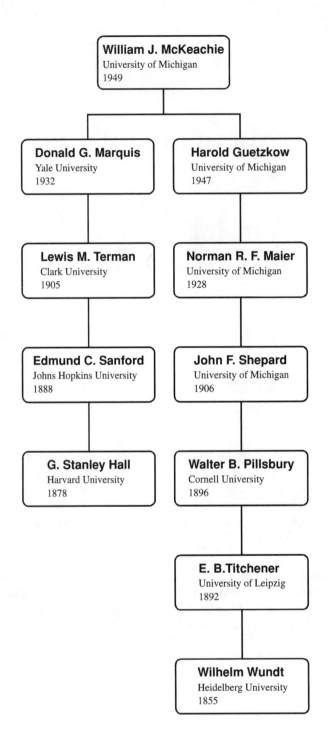

Academic Genealogy—William J. McKeachie

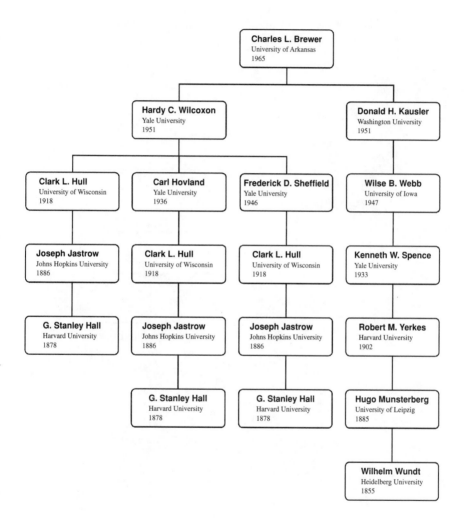

Academic Genealogy—Charles L. Brewer

I

Portraits of Excellence

1

More Than Just Luck: A Brief Biography of Wilbert J. McKeachie

R. Eric Landrum
Boise State University

How do you summarize the life's work of one person in one chapter of a book? For a person of the stature of Wilbert J. McKeachie, the task is impossible. Something will have to be left out. Will it be his seven honorary degrees, his love of sports, his 10-year stint as department chair, his international influence and reputation, his twice weekly singing at the First Baptist Church, 10 editions of *Teaching Tips*, his role as husband to Ginny and father to two girls, his APF Gold Medal award for Distinguished Teaching in Psychology, or his service to the American Psychological Association? How do you tell the story of a man who arguably is the most influential person in the teaching of psychology in the history of the discipline?

Bill McKeachie found that perfect balance between being an active, engaging researcher and excelling at teaching. In most of our classes, we teach our students about the theories of Skinner, Maslow, Bandura, and Festinger. Bill was friends with Fred Skinner and Abe Maslow, knows Al Bandura, and occasionally debated with Leon Festinger. He is clearly a Renaissance man—someone who can talk about any topic while having the humility and grace to never let on how much he really knows.

How did Bill McKeachie come to have this competence, this passion for teaching, and the good fortune to make substantial contributions to the roles of teaching

3

and learning in higher education? The story starts in 1921 in Clarkston, Michigan, 40 miles from Ann Arbor, the home of the University of Michigan. Perhaps part of Bill's passion for teaching was sparked because both of his parents were teachers. The year before Bill's parents married, his mother was a school teacher. It seemed to Bill that she was always teaching in some form or another. She taught piano lessons to children and taught various arts and crafts to women in her neighborhood. Bill's father was his teacher for the first eight grades in a one-room schoolhouse. His father influenced Bill's passion for sports. As a child, Bill would go with his Dad to a Detroit Tigers baseball game once a year; they saw Ty Cobb and Babe Ruth play baseball. Bill and his classmates were unable to afford baseball gloves, so they played softball. Bill would retain his passion for softball for the rest of his life.

As a teenager, Bill became active in a local Presbyterian church. He was the secretary-treasurer of the Sunday School, where he calculated the average collection of 77 cents (checking the date on each penny in case he wanted to make a trade for a penny in his own collection). One Sunday he read in his Sunday School paper, *Young People*, a half-page article about psychology, and from then on he thought psychology was fascinating (*Psychology Today*, 1972). Bill was always a voracious reader—a trait that would be helpful in working 80-hour weeks.

In high school, Bill lettered in baseball, and he played one season of semiprofessional baseball before injuring his knee. After this incident, he could no longer wear cleats, so he went back to wearing sneakers and playing softball.

Unusual for the time and locale, Bill enrolled in Michigan State Normal College (MSNC; now Eastern Michigan University) in Ypsilanti in 1938. He chose MSNC because it was cheaper than the University of Michigan. To attend college, he had help from his family and also won a $30 per year scholarship to help pay for tuition. He chose mathematics as a major. To earn money for clothes and personal expenses, he worked one summer on the assembly line at General Motors Truck and Coach, and he also played piano and sang with bands in bars. During his senior year at MSNC, he met Virginia (Ginny) Mack, whom he would later marry. He graduated with his bachelor's degree in mathematics in 1942.

Bill fondly recalls stories from his college days. When I asked him about this time in his life, here is what he said:

> I helped support my college expenses (about $200 a year) by teaching violin, piano, and cello at 50 cents a lesson and playing piano in small groups—e.g., for square dancing and round dancing in a barn. (The farm kids danced on the barn floor and we were playing from the top of the granary about 8 feet above them.) I also played in a beer garden (the Pal-O-U gardens) for a similar group and sang some of the ballads. When I left to play in the barn for more money, two of the older ladies said that it was as if they had hung black crepe on the door. My senior year I played in the largest bar in Oakland county (Ben's Inn) with a floor show Friday and Saturday nights with jugglers, magicians, exotic dancers, etc. Patrons would tell the bartender to set up a round of drinks for the band, and I would sometimes have 4 or 5 cokes lined up on my piano.

This was 1941–1942. After World War II Kate Smith's song "God Bless America" was popular. One night we played it and started a major riot which was finally broken up by the state police. Apparently one guy at the bar said to another, "take off your hat. They're playing the national anthem." The second guy said "that's not the national anthem!" Fisticuffs started and before long the whole place was bedlam with fists flying among people who had no idea what the fight was about. We played the "Star Spangled Banner" but nobody paid any attention until the police arrived and cleared the place out.

Bill continued to have the desire to teach and to become a minister. After graduation, he drove his 1936 Ford to the Upper Peninsula (UP) of Michigan and served as the minister for the Trout Lake and Hulbert Methodist churches. To earn more income, he also taught math, geography, English, history, and science at Trout Lake school (*Psychology Today*, 1972). While working in the UP, he corresponded with Ginny. He realized that to be a good minister he needed to be able to help people, and that perhaps a background in psychology would be helpful in that regard (Halonen, 1992).

The context of the war was inescapable, however; he would have continued his education in math if not for the war. Bill appreciated the symmetry and explanatory power that mathematics could provide. He carefully considered whether he was a conscientious objector or should join the Navy. Undecided, he chose the ministerial route. This decision was not easy for Bill, as he once said, "I had little doubt that the Nazis and Japanese were the bad guys, but I was not convinced that war was morally justifiable" (*Psychology Today*, 1972, p. 63). Notwithstanding his indecision, Bill's draft board decided that he had become a minister too late, so he joined the Navy. One day prior to joining the Navy, however, he married Ginny.

During World War II, Bill served as a Deck and Radar Officer (Lieutenant) on the U.S.S. Guest (DD 472) in the Pacific Theater. While on board, he became fascinated by the individual differences of his crewmates. He also held shipboard religious services when not in combat. He wrote to Ginny and told her that if he survived the war, he would like to go to graduate school in psychology. He was fortunate to survive the war, and later remarked, "war is not a pleasant thing. If you have actually participated in it, I don't think you would think it is a good thing to have wars" (Halonen, 1992, p. 222).

Bill entered the clinical psychology program at the University of Michigan in 1945. He earned his master's degree in 1946 and his doctorate in 1949. Not unexpectedly, his graduate training experiences shaped his career interests. As a graduate student, he served as a teaching fellow for Harold Guetzkow. These formative experiences with Guetzkow (such as the weekly dinners with teaching fellows) helped to foster his passion and interest in teaching. When his students had teaching concerns, Guetzkow encouraged his teaching fellows to answer these questions empirically. How did McKeachie land the position of teaching fellow? Because most of the veterans were not released until 1946, practically everyone entering graduate school in 1945 was offered a teaching fellowship. During the summer of 1947, when the students beat the faculty in a softball game at the departmental picnic, it was ruled thereafter that teaching fellows were part of the faculty so that Bill could pitch for the faculty team.

When Bill completed his PhD in 1949, the Chair of the Psychology Department at the University of Michigan, Don Marquis, asked him to stay and teach the introductory psychology course and train graduate teaching fellows. Bill accepted the offer despite offers from Northwestern University and Yale University. By staying at Michigan, he also accepted the challenge of revamping the undergraduate psychology curriculum. During 8 weeks in the summer of 1951, Bill and five other psychologists worked to develop a model curriculum (the "Cornell Conference") that achieved the most important liberal arts goals they had identified (McGovern, 1993). His interest in national curriculum issues has remained steady, as he co-hosted the Michigan Conference in 1960 with John Milholland and was also a participant in the St. Mary's Conference in 1991.

Even in his early days of college teaching, Bill emerged as a talented educator. He received his first teaching award in 1955, the Alumni Award for Distinguished Teaching at the University of Michigan. Bill credits Don Marquis as the most significant person in the development of his teaching style. In addition to providing opportunities for Bill (such as the teaching fellowship, curriculum redesign), Marquis offered practical advice as well such as, when lecturing do not try to communicate more than three points.

In 1951, Bill became the first teacher of psychology on video, participating in live broadcasts. On Sunday afternoons, the Detroit News Station (Channel 4) would broadcast the University of Michigan Hour, where Bill would teach the introductory psychology course. Bill later remarked that he helped to boost TV sales in Michigan because many of his relatives went out and bought TV sets just so that they could see him. Because of this widespread exposure, Bill was elected president of the Michigan Psychological Association.

Bill became a full professor at Michigan in 1960, and in 1961 he became the Chair of the Department of Psychology. Lowell Kelly, the Department Chair before Bill, was asked by President Kennedy to become the Director of Selection for the Peace Corps. Bill became Acting Chair of the Department for a year, and when Kelly decided to stay in Washington, DC, another year, Bill became Chair. He served as Chair until 1971. During this period, the psychology faculty grew from 70 to 200 members. With this many faculty members, Bill was known to remark, "so I had a new problem every half hour" (Halonen, 1992, p. 242). He was also clear about his dealings with administrators: "When you move across the street to the administration building, it is as if the head of a nunnery had moved across the street to a house of prostitution" (Halonen, 1992, p. 243). In true McKeachie style, however, he found the good in the position and was able to put a positive spin on the demands of the job:

> An academic man is not supposed to enjoy the role of department chairman. It is often perceived as being onerous and unrewarding. For me, however, it was a real

opportunity to feel that I could have some impact upon the field. Moreover, the department chairmanship met my personal needs. I enjoyed talking to psychologists in all areas. I heard about new findings and hot ideas long before they were generally known. I liked the sense of being a real *general* psychologist. (*Psychology Today*, 1972, p. 67; italics in original)

Throughout Bill's career he was a good teacher and a good learner. He credits Don Marquis with important lessons about how to be an effective Department Chair:

1. Listen to everyone and use the elected executive committee for most decisions, leaving only major policy issues for the monthly faculty meeting.
2. Give nontenured faculty equal power as tenured.
3. Never hire someone unless you are pretty sure he or she will make tenure and that he or she is the best psychologist in the United States in his or her cohort and specialty.
4. Try to participate in hiring psychologists needed by other departments and schools of the university and give them joint appointments in the psychology department so that we can be proud of every psychologist in the university even if their salaries were paid by medicine, law, engineering, social work, natural resources, political science, sociology, the Institute of Social Research, the Mental Health Research Center, or other interdisciplinary center. (personal communication, March 12, 2001)

His love of sports continued throughout his academic career. Bill was the first recipient of the Intramural Department Award for Outstanding Faculty Athletes. Although Bill served as President of the APA, he was particularly proud of his 22–0 fast-pitch softball record that same year. In fact, in a fast-pitch softball career that lasted from 1933 to 1989, he pitched over 30 no-hit games, including one perfect game. His overall career record in pitching was approximately 900 wins and 300 losses, with a lifetime batting average about .300. Sports provided an important balance for Bill. In fact, he once remarked, "in any case I like the fact that my office has almost as much space for volleyball and softball trophies as for books. I wouldn't trade my 31 no-hit games for 31 publications" (*Psychology Today*, 1972, p. 62).

Those persons who knew Bill McKeachie as an instructor in those early days remember him fondly. Cliff Fawl, an undergraduate student of Bill's, recalls this about him:

First, his bright smile. When I think of Bill McKeachie, I picture a smiling person. That was true 50 years ago; it is still true today. Another snapshot comes from the year 1961 when Bill was a presenter at the Nebraska Symposium on Motivation. I invited Bill to have dinner at our home. My memory is of the two of us doing dishes following the meal. Doing dishes. That somehow seems right. It's the kind of thing Bill McKeachie would do as a guest.

Another snapshot goes back to my undergraduate days at Michigan. This snapshot is embarrassing, for I wish that I could replay my part in it. Most of you know that Bill pitches softball. The Psychology Department had a softball team and Bill was the pitcher. It was composed of faculty and graduate students, but for reasons I do not recall I was asked to play shortstop in a game. I did so and made an error. I had played a lot of baseball by then, and I knew what baseball players do when they make an error: they curse. I did so reflexively and with intensity. But no sooner had I done so than I remembered with humiliation that the pitcher was a minister. Bill, of course, made no comment nor even seemed to notice. (personal communication, February 1, 2001)

A biography of Bill McKeachie's life would not be complete without some mention of his contributions in the areas of teaching, research, and service to psychology. His impact as a teacher is clear and evidenced in many ways. In talks Jane Halonen has given about being a professor in the postmodern age, she has defined five categories of college teachers: (a) the energetic (first and second year), (b) the monomaniacal (pretenure), (c) the relaxed (early posttenure), (d) the vigorous (late posttenure who get back on the path), and (e) Bill McKeachie (personal communication, January 31, 2001). She rightfully puts Bill McKeachie in a teaching category all his own.

His impact as a teacher is seen not only through the thousands of students he taught at Michigan (or the hundreds he trained as teaching assistants), but also through his 10 editions of *Teaching Tips*, which has been translated into Chinese, Portuguese, Arabic, Japanese, and Spanish. Many of today's prominent teachers of psychology were influenced by *Teaching Tips*. Diane Halpern wrote:

> When I was in graduate school, Bill's book was the first and only one that I read on college teaching. I didn't even know that anyone had ever written about it until I found Bill's book. I still use it. Bill has defined the field for us and has made it 'okay to care about teaching.' I love him! (personal communication, January 31, 2001)

Jim Korn wrote:

> At an APA convention several years ago, Bill gave a talk on what makes a good teacher great. In his usual data-based style he reviewed the literature on good teaching and drew some reasonable conclusions. Then, at the end of his talk he became choked up as he talked about the importance of teaching and concluded that there is greatness in all of you.
>
> I also have been impressed with his willingness to write and talk about spiritual values in teaching. He does that in the last chapter of *Teaching Tips*. He describes himself as a religious person who believes strongly that love and respect for other human beings is a universal value that should guide the behavior of all human beings at all times. The concluding sentence in that chapter follows a quotation from St. Augustine: "Hope has two lovely daughters, anger and courage. Anger at the way things are, and courage to see that they need not remain as they are." Let us have hope. (personal communication, February 2, 2001)

Bill was thoughtful about the learning process as described here:

> I have argued elsewhere that all learning and memory involves transfer; we never use learning in exactly the same situation in which learning occurred. If the new situation is a little different from the original ones we describe the outcome as *near transfer*; if it is more different, we call it *far transfer*; . . . if the situation is still more different, we speak of *problem solving*; and if the new situation bears little resemblance to the situations in which relevant previous learning occurred, we talk about *creativity*. (McKeachie, 1994, pp. 343–344; italics in original)

Indeed, one of Bill's most important legacies is *Teaching Tips* and the role it continues to play for teachers new and old alike.

When asked about his teaching style, Bill revealed some of the secrets of teaching. What would students say about his teaching style? "I think informality. I'm trying to think of student ratings I've gotten. Generally they are quite favorable. I think they see me as being concerned about their learning. I think people will forgive a lot if they really feel that you are trying" (Halonen, 1992, p. 238). Two concepts are evident in this response. First, humility—yes, I would imagine that Bill McKeachie's teaching evaluations are *quite* favorable. The second nugget that emerges is the importance of communicating to students what you are trying to accomplish and why. Let students get to know you and what you are about. Bill made this abundantly clear when he recently said, "I believe that respect and concern for students is fundamental to teaching" (Herman, 2000, p. 9).

Bill's commitment to students is well known. Bill McKeachie served as Scott VanderStoep's dissertation co-chair in 1992, one of the last dissertation committees that Bill chaired before retirement. Scott wrote:

> His commitment to his students extends far beyond the classroom. I think of him playing on the graduate student fast-pitch softball team (Bill's competitive softball pitching career spanned *seven* decades!). I think of the events he and Ginny would host at their house. I think of how he has shown great care for me and my family over the years. And I think of how he offered to buy coffee for his *entire* class of Learning to Learn students ($n = 80$) at a coffee shop after class one day (not all of them came, fortunately!). His vita on being gracious and charitable is as impressive as his professional vita. (personal communication, February 3, 2001)

As an aside, others have noticed his humility as well. Jane Halonen wrote

> His humility is both exceptional and humbling. Not so long ago, I got an e-mail from him that was truly keeping in his character. He had heard a speech that I had given and an off-hand reference to a teaching strategy that had captured his attention. Would he be able to make it work in his classroom? As far as I know, Bill's thirst for improving ways to motivate his students knows no equal. (personal communication, January 31, 2001)

Bill's contributions to the research literature on teaching and learning are just as impressive as his contributions in teaching. A complete review of his research interests is not possible here, but a brief mention is required. Pintrich, Brown, and Weinstein (1994) in a festschrift honoring Bill summarized his five basic areas of research: (a) the development of models and methods for understanding the cognitive structures of students; (b) understanding student motivation and, in particular, the role of test anxiety (Bill's first journal article, published in 1950, discussed college student anxiety); (c) interactions among student motivation, cognition, and instructional and classroom characteristics; (d) improving college classroom instruction; and (e) teaching students to become self-regulated learners, as in his "Learning to Learn" course at the University of Michigan.

These research interests have merged with his service activities. For example, Bill served as the Director of the University of Michigan's Center for Research on Learning and Teaching as well as serving as the Associate Director of the National Center for Research to Improve Postsecondary Teaching and Learning. In fact, Pintrich et al. (1994) reflected the interrelatedness of Bill's various professional activities when they indicated that "Bill McKeachie's legacy lies in his scholarly work, the work he has stimulated others to do, the thousands of students he has trained, the thousands of college teachers he has helped, and the lives he has touched with his wisdom, warmth, and support" (p. 11).

Amazingly to others (although typical for Bill), his record of service is just as impressive as his contributions to teaching and research. Here is a listing of his *Presidencies*: APA Division Two (then called) Division on the Teaching of Psychology, 1956–1957; APA Division One, General Psychology, 1972–1973; APA Division 15, Educational Psychology 1975–1976; National President of the American Psychological Association, 1976–1977; National President, American Association for Higher Education, 1978–1979; and National President, American Psychological Foundation, 1980–1982. Bill has served at the top of the governance structure of APA; as President, member of the Council of Representatives; and on the Board of Directors. Ray Fowler tells a story about how Bill kept getting elected to high offices without being a politician. Once when Ray told Bill that he had lost an election to the Board of Directors by one vote, Bill's reply was, "Gee, if I had known that, I might have voted for myself." (personal communication, February 16, 2001)

Charles Brewer and Bill McKeachie often work together in professional capacities. At a symposium honoring Bill McKeachie at the 2000 APA convention, Charles commented that

> at numerous meetings, we have eaten enough stale Danish pastry to sink a battleship. Always prepared for the task at hand, Bill is astute, compassionate, diplomatic, evenhanded, generous, gentle, incisive, knowledgeable, soft-spoken, unflappable, unpretentious, and kind. I have never heard Bill say an unkind word about anybody, and I have never heard anybody say an unkind word about Bill, which may be unique in my experience with vocal bipeds. (personal communication, January 31, 2001)

In addition, Bill's vita lists the numerous service commitments to his university, professional societies, other associations, editorial boards, community service, and consultantships. With regard to university service, Bill indicates that "I have chaired the Academic Senate, been president of the University chapter of AAUP, and have served on, or chaired, most of the major committees in the University, particularly those having to do with athletics, curriculum, economic policy, budget, and searches for President, deans and faculty." Only a Renaissance man could be well versed in all those areas, complete an impressive program of research, and be a world-class teacher/scholar simultaneously.

In his interview with Jane Halonen (1992), Bill mentioned two special awards that he had received—the American Psychological Foundation's Distinguished Teaching in Psychology Award (received in 1985) and the APA Education and Training Board Award for Distinguished Career Contributions to Education and Training in Psychology (received in 1987). Since that time, Bill has also received the Gold Medal Award for Enduring Contributions to Psychology in the Public Interest from APA (received in 1998). His citation from that award reads:

> Wilbert J. McKeachie truly embodies what is meant by psychology in the public interest. Since the beginning of his career, he has been involved in research, innovation, and promotion to improve teaching in psychology, attract students' interest, and motivate students to succeed in their courses and apply what they have learned toward improving the human condition and advancing human welfare. (American Psychological Association, 1998, p. 872)

When you ask Bill McKeachie about the impact he has had on so many others during his career, he answers characteristically with humility: "I think each of us has to follow our own propensities and do the best he or she can, getting help from colleagues, working hard, not getting discouraged if things don't go well for a time, and taking advantage of lucky breaks when they come" (Herman, 2000, p. 10). A similar theme emerged when Halonen (1992) asked him about what would happen if he had the chance to start his career again. His response was, "I can't imagine it being better. Everything worked out better than I had any right to expect. Al Bandura makes a big deal of chance, and I think he's right. I've just been very lucky. In my marriage. In my career. In everything" (p. 256).

What has driven Bill McKeachie to live a life of service to others, to study and help understand fellow human beings? When I asked him this, he said:

> I don't know any special insights. I'm a humanist and have been an active American Baptist for over 50 years. I take literally the statement "god is love"—a value, rather than a supernatural being. Most of the members of our church have more conventional Christian beliefs, but I believe the Anabaptist tradition is that no one knows ultimate truth; so one should respect others' beliefs and try to work together to put religion into practice both in everyday life and in church programs for the homeless, poor people in other countries, and so on, as well as in social policy nationally. (personal communication, March 12, 2001)

In the final analysis, it is both psychology students and psychology educators who have been lucky. We are lucky that at age 14 Bill McKeachie read a half-page article about psychology in Sunday school. We are lucky that, because in the course of World War II, Bill's interests changed from mathematics to psychology. We are lucky that Bill chose to serve the public at the University of Michigan, teach others how to learn, and conduct important research in the arena of instructional psychology. We are lucky that Bill chose to dedicate himself to 80-hour workweeks, and we are lucky that Ginny McKeachie was willing to make sacrifices as well. It is not that Bill McKeachie was lucky; it is that we are lucky to know Bill McKeachie, that we are lucky that his legacy lives on in his students, in his colleagues, in his writings and body of research, and in his life as a scholar and a gentleman. On behalf of teachers and learners everywhere, thank you, Bill McKeachie.

ACKNOWLEDGMENTS

I wish to acknowledge the generous help and support of Bill McKeachie throughout this project. The materials he shared with me and the e-mail correspondence between us has been invaluable in shaping this chapter. As with his usual grace and style, he helped immensely. I am also grateful to all the individuals who communicated with me about Bill McKeachie. Their words make this chapter much richer and bring Bill's legacy to life.

I also want to thank Bill Buskist and Steve Davis for (a) the opportunity to write the opening chapter in this important book, and (b) their thoughtful and incisive feedback about earlier drafts of this chapter—their combined editorial skills lead to significant improvements. Also, I wish to thank Lisa Nelsen for her careful proofreading of multiple drafts of this chapter—her efforts greatly improved its readability.

REFERENCES

American Psychological Association. (1998). Gold Medal Award for Enduring Contributions to Psychology in the Public Interest. *American Psychologist, 53,* 872–874.

Halonen, J. S. (1992). "I was just lucky": An interview with model teacher Wilbert J. McKeachie. In A. E. Puente, J. R. Matthews, & C. L. Brewer (Eds.), *Teaching psychology in America: A history* (pp. 219–257). Washington, DC: American Psychological Association.

Herman, W. E. (2000). An interview with Wilbert (Bill) J. McKeachie. *Newsletter for Educational Psychologists, 24*(1) [Special Insert], 7–10.

McKeachie, W. J. (1994). Concluding remarks. In P. R. Pintrich, D. R. Brown, & C. E. Weinstein (Eds.), *Student motivation, cognition, and learning: Essays in honor of Wilbert J. McKeachie* (pp. 343–357). Hillsdale, NJ: Lawrence Erlbaum Associates.

McGovern, T. V. (1993). Introduction. In T. V. McGovern (Ed.), *Handbook for enhancing undergraduate education in psychology* (pp. 3–15). Washington, DC: American Psychological Association.

Pintrich, P. R., Brown, D. R., & Weinstein, C. E. (1994). Preface. In P. R. Pintrich, D. R. Brown, & C. E. Weinstein (Eds.), *Student motivation, cognition, and learning: Essays in honor of Wilbert J. McKeachie* (pp. 9–15). Hillsdale, NJ: Lawrence Erlbaum Associates.

Psychology Today. (1972, September). Academician Wilbert J. McKeachie. *Psychology Today,* pp. 63–67.

2

"I Can't Ever Remember not Wanting to be a Teacher": A Brief Biography of Charles L. Brewer

John D. Batson
Gilles O. Einstein
Furman University

Charles L. Brewer has tirelessly devoted his career to improving the teaching of psychology at all educational levels. With inimitable style and verve, Charles has touched countless lives by working with and on behalf of high school psychology teachers, mentoring undergraduates, helping departments in the discipline shape psychology curricula, and serving on innumerable committees and boards. Charles's labor of love, the editorship of Teaching of Psychology, *has resulted in a pedagogical journal second to none in quality and influence. For his commitment to and accomplishment for teachers of psychology, we honor Charles L. Brewer. (American Psychological Association, 1996, p. 345)*

So reads the citation from the American Psychological Association (APA) Award for Distinguished Career Contributions to Education and Training. Over a career spanning four decades of teaching, Charles Brewer has demonstrated that he is one of this nation's true teaching talents. In an era when teaching is sometimes denigrated and viewed as an impediment to research, Charles proudly devotes his energies to teaching, undergraduate education, and pedagogical scholarship.

He is a person with broad interests, unusual abilities, and remarkable dedication to the profession. He is a Fellow of APA Divisions 1 (General Psychology), 2 (Teaching of Psychology), 26 (History of Psychology), and 52 (International), and he is a Charter Fellow of the American Psychological Society. He has been President of Divisions 1 and 2 of the APA, President of the Southeastern Psychological Association, President of the Council of Undergraduate Psychology Departments, Chair of the APA's Committee on Undergraduate Education, a member of the APA's Board of Educational Affairs, a member of the APA's Council of Representatives, and a member of APA's Board of Directors. His impact on students, colleagues, and the profession has been broad and deep, and we highlight some of these contributions later in this chapter. Before we do so, however, we present a brief biographical sketch.

BIOGRAPHICAL SKETCH

Charles L. Brewer was born on May 10, 1932, in Pine Bluff, Arkansas. For those not familiar with the area, Charles quickly points out that Pine Bluff is not far from the hamlet of Toadsuck, Arkansas. Charles' early experiences suggest that nature endowed him with a powerful predisposition to be a teacher. Even before he enrolled as a student, he was imprinting on the teaching profession. Miss Laverne Kennaway, a friend of the family, taught third grade at Watson Chapel School, which was directly across the street from Charles' house. When he was 4 years old, he often spent mornings in the back of Miss Kennaway's class. His parents may have viewed this as nothing more than convenient child care, but Charles fell in love with the classroom. Its oiled wooden floors and Miss Kenneway's writing on the blackboard were both alluring and mysterious.

In first grade, when most young boys in those days were dreaming of becoming cowboys, firemen, and policemen, even his playtime revolved around teaching. After school and on weekends, he would set up a blackboard on an easel in the sun porch at his home and cajole his sister, brother, and neighborhood kids into playing school. Of course, Bo (as Charles was called back then) was *always* the teacher, and the neighborhood kids were *always* the students. By all accounts, he was a gifted teacher, although a bit overdemanding even then. In those days, before he had a captive audience, he had to restrain his penchant for rigor for fear that the neighborhood kids would not return.

Charles was a well-rounded student throughout his public school years. He not only excelled in the classroom, but was also a campus leader at Watson Chapel School, serving as president of the student body in his senior year. Charles was also an excellent athlete as he played on the football team and captained the basketball team his junior and senior years. Charles' love of football continues unabated. He attends the Furman Paladins' home games with a passion that approaches religious fervor.

Beyond valuing what he learned in his courses, Charles keenly observed, compared, and absorbed different pedagogical styles. He knew that he wanted to be a teacher, and he saw the classroom as a stage. Thus, while taking courses, he reflected on the techniques and demands that were most effective in his own learning. The only unanswered questions for Charles were at what level he would teach and what subject.

Answers to these questions came not long after enrolling at Hendrix College, a private liberal arts college in Conway, Arkansas, with a strong reputation and an enrollment of about 600 students at the time. Charles' life changed in his sophomore year when he enrolled in an introductory psychology course taught by Dr. John P. Anderson. Dr. Anderson earned his Ph.D. from Columbia University, and he taught the course in the liberal arts tradition. This broadly based course stimulated Charles' Renaissance-like interests in a variety of areas (such as history, philosophy, biology, statistics, etc.). Moreover, Dr. Anderson was a marvelous lecturer who had an unusual knack for weaving stories into lectures and illustrating key points with engaging examples. He was theatrical in class and effectively used voice modulation, such as speaking softly, to accentuate important points. He was the toughest teacher that Charles had ever encountered, but Charles loved him. Dr. Anderson was urbane, suave, sophisticated, and known for his sartorial splendor. In Dr. Anderson's course, Charles often found himself reflecting on how "nice it would be to do what he does." Although Charles is unique, it is interesting to notice the similarities between Charles and Dr. Anderson.

Unless you think that he was too serious as an undergraduate, Charles heartily satisfied his impish nature during these years. Hendrix College was in a dry county. Believing that certain libations were important for the relaxation of college students, Charles and his cohorts would often drive across the county line to buy beer. They kept their refreshments in a cooler in their dorm room and bribed the campus policeman to keep quiet by offering him his fill of beer. It is no wonder that Charles and his dormitory room were quite popular at Hendrix.

Another influential teaching model in Charles' life was Emily Penton. After graduating from Hendrix College, Charles participated in a Ford Foundation-sponsored internship program designed to attract people to the teaching profession. Through this program, Charles taught at Little Rock Central High School, which a few years later would be a nationally visible site of civil rights protests. Emily Penton, a dynamic and dignified teacher, supervised and inspired Charles. She was confident in manner, had outstanding command of the course material, and simply told students, in a theatrical and exciting manner, how it was.

Charles then obtained his M.Ed. in counseling from the University of Arkansas. He spent the next 2 years in the army, during which he was the Chief of the Southeast Asia Desk for the U.S. Army Psychological Warfare Center in Tokyo, Japan. While there, he was also an instructor in psychology for the University of Maryland extension at the Tokyo Education Center.

After his stint in the army, Charles returned to the University of Arkansas where he obtained his master's degree in psychology in 1959. He then taught for 2 years at The College of Wooster, where he met Marjorie Constance Suhs, a young assistant professor in the music department and his future wife. Marjorie had attended a one-room school in Waupaca, Wisconsin. Because there was simultaneous instruction in several grades, Marjorie advanced more rapidly than other students and skipped two grade levels. She graduated from Carroll College and, as a graduate student at the Eastman School of Music, taught undergraduates who were older than she was. Marjorie is a master pianist and a gourmet cook. Charles reports that at Wooster, Marjorie "snared me with rhubarb pie and coconut cake." They were married in 1962. Daughter Stephanie was born in 1966.

Teaching at The College of Wooster confirmed his love of the profession, and he enrolled at the Indiana University to obtain his Ph.D. in psychology. While there, he worked with Lloyd Peterson and Isidore Gormezano. Things were going well at Indiana until Charles had an epiphany emanating from a severe medical experience. While recovering from a ruptured appendix, Charles decided that he wanted to become a teacher of psychology first and a researcher second.

Thus, he decided to enroll again at the University of Arkansas where he could get a broad-based foundation in psychology. Charles' important mentors at the University of Arkansas were Donald Kausler, who was extremely bright, knowledgeable, articulate, organized, and demanding; and Hardy Wilcoxon, who was also very demanding and who used the Socratic method to great effect. Charles obtained his Ph.D. from the University of Arkansas in 1965. A common characteristic of all Charles' mentors was that they knew how to motivate their students. They understood Emerson's belief that "our greatest want in life is for someone to make us do what we can."

Charles taught at Elmira College (in Elmira, New York) for 3 years before being lured to Furman University in 1967, where as you might imagine he hit the ground running. He was the first winner of the Alester G. Furman Meritorious Teaching Award a year after he arrived, and he chaired the department from 1972 to 1984.

A TEACHER OF UNDERGRADUATES

Coincident with winning the Meritorious Teaching Award were grand rumors among Furman undergraduates about this new professor. As Charles would be proud to proclaim, these rumors were of a mixed, but intense nature. It has always been Charles' belief that the best teachers are those who stir up the students or, as he is wont to say, "jostle some folkways." Thus, some students avoided Charles' classes by changing their major from psychology to something else in their senior years, but many others flocked to his classes and became devoted psychology majors.

By the time I (JB) was a freshman at Furman in 1970, Charles' teaching was often discussed among the students. I will never forget how often the name *Brewer* surfaced in students' conversations or how enthusiastic so many of my classmates were about his General Psychology course. It was perfectly clear that this was a teacher who simply should not be missed. I eventually enrolled in every course that he taught.

Although I did not realize it at the time, I was not only learning some psychology from him, but I was storing memories of what makes for inspired teaching—a profession to which only later was I committed. Some of the more salient traits that continue to make Charles one of the most dynamic teachers today include his passion for scientific psychology, his demand for hard work by students, his articulate lectures, his eagerness to help students, and his humor.

Perhaps the first thing that is evident when you hear Charles lecture is his overwhelming passion for his subject matter. To hear him in a General Psychology class, you would think that there is no other subject in the world as inherently interesting or as important as the science of psychology. All teachers at least occasionally spend class time on topics that are less interesting to them than other topics, but to hear Charles talk you would think he has spent his life devoted to the study of personality, development, neuroscience, statistics, or whatever he happens to be talking about that day. One lesson that all teachers should learn is to be passionate about what they teach or, as Charles might prefer to advise, first find what you are passionate about and then devote yourself to teaching it passionately.

Students in Charles' classes are often overwhelmed with the workload. He demands not only their attendance and attention in class, but their dedication to course goals outside of the classroom. In an interview in the 1971 Furman yearbook, Charles indicated very simply his expectations of undergraduates in his classes: Students should be familiar with "the burning of midnight oil." It has been interesting to hear students complain about his course requirements and the difficulty of his tests and then a few years after graduation (or even a few weeks after the course) hear these same people boast about how they learned so much. As he does in so many other ways, Charles puts psychological research to practice, including a principle from cognitive dissonance theory: Students often learn to love what they have to suffer through.

Charles is a master of the English language, and this mastery becomes apparent to anyone listening to him speak. Students sometimes keep running lists of words, literary allusions, and maxims that he sprinkles in his lectures, and thus often learn a lot more from lectures than about psychology alone. Indeed, many of his faculty colleagues continue to add to their own vocabulary by having a 30-minute lunch with Charles. Generations of students can never forget a number of distinctive phrases, or *Brewerisms* as some call them, including the advice to students as they write research reports: "Write with clarity, conciseness, and felicity of expression." In advising students who are planning to conduct research, Charles warns that "things always take longer than they do."

For probably his entire career as a teacher, whenever students asked "What are your office hours," Charles has had the same simple, effective answer: "Seven to seven, seven days a week." Although this is somewhat exaggerated (in recent years, Charles actually does not spend much time in his office on Sundays), it is his way of saying to students, "You tell me when you want to see me and I'll be there." His time with individuals outside of class often resembles private tutoring sessions, where he and the student review specific material or tests. The hours he devotes each week to individual students has made the difference in countless lives.

There is one more attribute that is at the core of Charles Brewer: his ability to use humor to reinforce lecture material. In General Psychology many years ago, for example, he taught the Freudian principle of sexual fixations and then asked the class what Freud would say about him owning a large Volkswagen van. When teaching about successive approximation, he once crawled on all fours on top of the desk and oinked like a pig in response to students' reinforcing his behavior. Charles endears himself to students with these vivid and memorable antics. Other examples of his lighter side are described toward the end of this chapter.

Of the scores of undergraduates with the privilege of taking his classes, there are many former students who are now teaching their own students. In speaking with some of these teachers, we hear the same type of comments: Charles was then and continues to be an inspiration and a model. For many teachers, he continues to teach about teaching, always encouraging the development of their individual styles, always with insight and sagacious advice. Indeed, these teachers speak of him much like he speaks of Dr. Anderson.

A TEACHER OF TEACHERS

Because of his commitment to the classroom, scholarship, the editing of *Teaching of Psychology*, and service to the APA, one might expect Charles to be the kind of person who cuts back on interactions with students and colleagues. Nothing could be further from the truth. His door is always open, and when you are in his office he gives you his undivided attention. Having come to Furman as neophyte professors, we have often benefited first hand from his wise advice. In fact, in our first few years of teaching, we spent countless hours in his office, and he was an immeasurable source of help to us, both in terms of advice and encouragement. Perhaps this attitude is borne out of deep respect and appreciation for his own mentoring.

In at least one of our cases, the beginning instincts as a new teacher were all wrong. The tendency for a new teacher is to want to be as familiar as possible with the students and to be loved. Charles patiently taught me (GE) in the very beginning that it is important to be demanding, set rigorous standards, be warm and equitable with your students, but also maintain an appropriate distance. Indeed, his influence on us has been so thorough that it is at times difficult to know where his mentoring ends and where our independent proclivities and judgments begin. His opinion is highly valued by both novice and experienced teachers in many academic departments. Regardless of the issue, be it stylistic, content, or philosophical, Charles loves to talk about teaching.

As Charles is often fond of pointing out, it is difficult to know where a teacher's influence ends. In his case, the geometric progression produces a span of influence that is nearly infinite. There is not a student who has taken psychology during the last 34 years at Furman University who has not in some way, either directly or indirectly, been influenced by Charles. His mentoring extends far beyond the psychology department as he willingly shares his remarkable insights about teaching with high school and college teachers from all over the world. It is clear in these discussions about teaching with Charles that he shares these ideas with the caveat that individuals are unique and must evaluate his suggestions in light of their own teaching styles.

DEVELOPING THE CURRICULUM AT FURMAN

When Charles arrived at Furman in 1967, the psychology department courses were designed to develop students' interest in service almost exclusively in what we today call *social work* and *pastoral counseling*. With Charles' broader perspective on psychology as an empirical discipline, the entire curriculum was rapidly modernized to reflect more accurately the current state of the science. Although this change was difficult for many students in the midst of their undergraduate work, it formed the foundation for what soon became not only one of the strongest and most vibrant majors in the university, but also for what is often today considered to be one of the strongest undergraduate majors in liberal arts colleges. His insistence on laboratory experiences with modern laboratory equipment (much of which came from funded equipment grant proposals he wrote) made it possible for students to have meaningful hands-on experience in empirical science, which of course helped generate more excitement in students for what they were reading in their books. His legacy in today's department includes faculty who have continued to equip labs through funded grants, as well as faculty whose individual research grants make it possible for still more undergraduates to be involved in original, publishable research.

Throughout his career at Furman, Charles has always been concerned about curricula. As the following section reveals, his accomplishments in developing outstanding and up-to-date educational goals and courses have had a major impact at a national level.

CURRICULUM

Charles is probably this country's leading expert on undergraduate psychology curricula. He has written extensively on the topic (Brewer, 1997; Brewer et al., 1993; Lloyd & Brewer, 1992), and he frequently serves as an outside evaluator for psychology departments across the country. He has also worked tirelessly with the APA's Education Directorate for Teachers of Psychology in Secondary Schools to help develop recommendations for precollege psychology courses. In 1991, Charles chaired the curriculum group sessions at the APA-sponsored St. Mary's Conference, the purpose of which was to reassess the undergraduate psychology curriculum and develop a set of recommendations. These recommendations were published in a chapter of the *Handbook for Enhancing Undergraduate Education in Psychology* in 1993. This chapter serves today as the authoritative guide for developing and evaluating undergraduate psychology curricula.

He resisted the popular temptation in the 1960s and 1970s to abandon requirements and to strive for relevance in a psychology major. Instead, he has persistently and eloquently promoted the view that the primary aim of an undergraduate psychology major is to "teach students to think as scientists about behavior and experience" (Brewer, 1997, p. 439).

Those readers who do not know Charles Brewer may not realize that he has a wonderful knack for drama and flair in both his written and spoken language. For example, when writing about the difficulty of developing curriculum recommendations from the large and diverse curriculum group at the St. Mary's Conference, Charles wrote, "Our working sessions were characterized by catharsis, contentiousness, controversy, confrontation, cooperation, conciliation, camaraderie, and—at the end—collapse" (Brewer, 1997, p. 438). In evaluating the outcome of the St. Mary's Conference, he wrote, "Eventually this resolution led to the most unusual and most comprehensive analyses of and recommendations about undergraduate psychology since bipeds appeared on the evolutionary totem pole" (Brewer, 1997, p. 438). Literary creativity of this sort captivates both students and colleagues.

PROFESSIONAL ACTIVITY

In addition to his expertise in the undergraduate curriculum, Charles is also a recognized authority on John B. Watson. Charles began to study Watson's life soon after coming to Furman, knowing that he was in a unique position to investigate the famous behaviorist who had grown up in the shadow of, and later attended, Furman University. Much of what is generally known today of Watson's personal life derives from Charles' interviews of people who had known Watson and his family. Some of his research efforts are represented in an acclaimed biography of Watson (Buckley, 1989). Some rather touching and intimate remembrances of Watson's son James would never have been published (Brewer, 1991) without Charles' efforts.

Charles was editor of the APA Division 2 journal, *Teaching of Psychology*, from 1985 to 1996. The journal's founding editor was Robert Daniel, another dedicated teacher. It is fitting for Charles to have been the second editor of the journal that best represents the passion and science of teaching of psychology, and for him now to be recognized as Editor Emeritus. He imposed his high standards and clear and dynamic writing style in this journal. Indeed, many authors believe that the quality of their papers as well as their writing improved substantially through the review process. During his tenure as editor, the *Teaching of Psychology* was featured along with two other journals in *Change* (Weimer, 1993) magazine as the best journals of any kind devoted to teaching.

PROFESSIONAL STYLE

Any serious attempt to characterize Charles Brewer would be incomplete without some mention of his warm nature and clever and ever-present sense of humor. He is neither shy nor modest, and he is the kind of person who enlivens a gathering.

For example, several years ago the Furman Psychology Department moved from a dingy and cramped basement into the second floor of a beautiful and spacious new building. The psychology majors decided that we should celebrate this monumental shift in venue with a New Orleans style jazz funeral march. The students persuaded a trumpeter to lead us. We marched out of the old space to the tune of slow, mournful music. As we exited the building, the mood quickly changed as our musician belted out a rousing rendition of "When the Saints Go Marching In." Most of us were dancing at this point in broad daylight in the middle of campus albeit in an understandably hesitant manner. That is, all of us except Charles. Grand Master Charles, who was completely unrestrained, indecently gyrated his way through all of the buildings on our way to our new home. He even dragged the reserved and slightly embarrassed trumpeter through the administration building and through the board room—with a Board of Trustees meeting in session.

In a 2000 talk to the general faculty of Furman, Charles gave tips on good teaching. In these modern times, when computers are used in nearly every human activity, Charles warned that technology should be used to enhance good teaching without letting it become the showpiece of the classroom. A memorable comment was, "I have seen a lot of PowerPoint presentations that had a lot of power, but very little point."

Charles' ability to react playfully to a situation is legendary. Every year his students surprise Charles during class with a birthday party. Sometimes they hold a contest to see who can best mimic his teaching and personal affectations. When they do a particularly good job of imitating him, he comes back to the department smiling and saying, "That damn student. He can do Brewer better than Brewer can do Brewer." Sometimes the students get a bit more exotic. One year they hired a belly dancer to perform in his Methods course. After warming up a bit, she exposed her midriff and revealed one of his favorite phrases—"Keep your Eyeballs on the Data"—written on her belly. Charles then attempted to belly dance with her, matching wiggle for wiggle, all the while keeping his eyeballs on the data. His sense of humor wonderfully balances a keen intellect and distinguished manner.

CONCLUSION

Charles Brewer is one of a kind: a master teacher, an expert in the psychology curriculum, an effective advocate for undergraduate education, and a wise and generous advisor. His legacy will live long among those who have been fortunate to know him personally, including students and teachers. His impact on undergraduate psychology will continue to be felt for decades to come. To paraphrase the title of one of his papers (Brewer, 1996), Charles has bent many twigs and greatly affected eternity.

NOTE

Order of authors was determined alphabetically.

REFERENCES

American Psychological Association. (1996). Awards for distinguished education and training contributions. *American Psychologist, 51,* 345–347.

Brewer, C. L. (1991). Perspectives on John B. Watson. In G. A. Kimble, M. Wertheimer, & C. White (Eds.), *Portraits of pioneers in psychology* (pp. 171–186). Hillsdale, NJ: Lawrence Erlbaum Associates.

Brewer, C. L. (1996, Spring). A talk to teachers: Bending twigs and affecting eternity. *Platte Valley Review, 24,* 12–23.

Brewer, C. L. (1997). Undergraduate education in psychology: Will the mermaids sing? *American Psychologist, 52,* 434–441.

Brewer, C. L., Hopkins, J. R., Kimble, G. A., Matlin, M. W., McCann, L. I., McNeil, O. V., Nodine, B. F., Quinn, V. N., & Saundra (1993). Curriculum. In T. V. McGovern (Ed.), *Handbook for enhancing undergraduate education in psychology* (pp. 161–182). Washington, DC: American Psychological Association.

Buckley, K. W. (1989). *Mechanical man: John Broadus Watson and the beginnings of behaviorism.* New York: Guilford.

Lloyd, M. A., & Brewer, C. L. (1992). National conferences on undergraduate psychology. In A. E. Puente, J. R. Matthews, & C. L. Brewer (Eds.), *Teaching psychology in America: A history* (pp. 263–284). Washington, DC: American Psychological Association.

Weimer, M. (1993, November/December). The disciplinary journals on pedagogy. *Change,* pp. 44–51.

II

Essential Qualities and Skills of Effective Teachers

3

Elements of Master Teaching

William Buskist
Jason Sikorski
Tanya Buckley
Bryan K. Saville
Auburn University

If only we knew exactly what makes a master teacher. We would require a course for all future teachers that would instantly transform them into master teachers. We might develop *pep pills* to provide these aspiring teachers with enthusiasm for their subject matter and their students. Would it not be glorious? The days of unprepared instructors with their dreary lectures would be a thing of the past. Instead, the teachers of the new millenium would be dynamic classroom teachers who model scholarship, seek the company of their students, and teach life's most essential lessons. Students of this new breed of teacher would experience the unadulterated joys of learning, and our culture would flourish. The cycle would be self-perpetuating as these students become the master teachers of tomorrow.

With regret, we report that there is no such protocol or chemistry available that magically turns ordinary teachers into master teachers. Thus, our vision of a teaching and learning utopia must remain just that—an imaginary world where students everywhere would sit in inspiring classes led by the likes of Bill McKeachie and Charles Brewer.

Master teaching at the college and university level has been an enduring and passionate interest of many members of the academy, including psychologists. Educational researchers, philosophers, and teachers have long written about the qualities possessed by master teachers. What we currently know about master teaching is derived from a blend of the musings of experienced and astute teachers with a dash of formal research. This chapter reviews what we know about master teachers based on these methods and describes a new approach to understanding what it is that makes master teachers so good at what they do. Our review is not exhaustive. Instead, it focuses on a representative sample of that literature.

MASTER TEACHERS
ON MASTER TEACHING

The past two decades have witnessed the publication of several books authored by master teachers on the art, craft, and science of teaching. These books summarize the most important lessons learned by each author over a lifetime of college and university teaching. Each author testifies that the road to becoming a master teacher is often long and arduous with plenty of wrong turns and dead ends, although rich rewards invariably accrue to those persons who merge onto and travel along this road. The authors of these books share three common themes about what they believe to be the qualities of master teachers: knowledge, personality, and classroom management skills.

Knowledge

Master teachers are well versed in the content of their courses. They present the current state of what research can tell us about their subject matter. They also come to class prepared to offer anecdotal information that may facilitate student learning (Eble, 1983). Their presentations are well organized (Gill, 1998).

Master teachers teach students that their discipline is not an island unto itself. The content of their courses is often distilled from several disciplines reflecting the oft-heard adage of Charles Brewer (1982) that "everything is related to everything else." Master teachers share with their students new discoveries and how new knowledge complements and extends older knowledge. More important, master teachers model how to think critically about what we know.

Personality

There is likely no single personality type that enables teachers to be successful in the classroom. Master teachers use their own unique personal strengths to engage students in the learning process, and they are willing to alter their personal style and tailor their teaching tactics to different and unique teaching environments (Eble, 1983, 1984).

Master teachers are approachable, genuine, and humorous (Vargo, 1997). They respect their students and expect the same in return (Beidler, 1997). These characteristics contribute to the development of rapport between student and teacher similar to that formed in psychotherapy between therapist and client (Lowman, 1995). Rapport facilitates trust, which in turn leads to the kind of approachability in which students feel that their questions are welcomed (Brookfield, 1990).

Perhaps the most often talked about personality characteristic of master teachers is passion, sometimes referred to as *enthusiasm* (see e.g., Brookfield, 1990). Passion in this case means an excitement for the subject matter, enthusiasm for sharing that subject matter with students, and enjoyment of teaching. Simply put, the teaching process *turns on* master teachers. Master teachers convey that excitement in their classroom demeanor and their interactions with students outside of class.

Classroom Management Skills

Master teachers know how to deal with problem students and difficult situations by invoking well-developed problem-solving and decision-making skills (Boice, 1996; Eble, 1983; McKeachie, 1999). These teachers promote student cooperation. They communicate high expectations and devote time—in and out of the classroom—to helping students succeed (Hatfield, 1995).

Master teachers often control their classrooms through active learning techniques that help motivate students to become more personally invested in their own learning. Master teachers downplay the authority inherent in their positions and create an atmosphere of participation, sharing, and playful learning (Eble, 1983; Gill, 1998).

In addition to knowledge, personality, and classroom management skills, authors of many teaching books agree that master teaching involves many other characteristics and tendencies. Some of these qualities include: flexibility, common sense, sense of humor, thoughtfulness, recognition that learning how to teach is a life-long quest, desire to stay current in their subject matter, strong work ethic, well-developed listening and speaking skills, creativity, and rigorous academic standards for their students (Baiocco & DeWaters, 1998; Lowman, 1995; Roth, 1997).

QUALITIES OF AWARD-WINNING TEACHERS

Another approach to understanding master teaching involves the analysis of the characteristics of award-winning teachers. For example, Baiocco and DeWaters (1998) recently surveyed presidents of the American Association of University Professors (AAUP) in New York State, Delaware, and Massachusetts to determine their perceptions of the selection processes used to honor outstanding teachers.

One question in Baiocco and DeWaters' (1998) survey asked respondents to identify the characteristics of the award winners with respect to their teaching. In order, Baiocco and DeWaters found the following 10 characteristics to be ascribed to award-winning teachers: (a) work ethic and commitment, as represented, for example, by campus leadership, reputation, and quality service; (b) positive affect, including enthusiasm and pleasantness; (c) excellent communication skills, as typified by sensitivity to students and a willingness to listen to them; (d) classroom creativity, for example, involving students in the learning process; (e) concern for students; (f) intelligence and knowledge, including the love of the subject matter; (g) demeanor toward students; (h) humanistic values; (i) high standards for student work; and (j) popularity among students.

In an earlier study, Lough (1997) surveyed recipients of the National Professor of the Year award, which is bestowed annually on a single professor by the Council for the Advancement and Support of Education (CASE) and the Carnegie Foundation for the Advancement of Teaching. Lough's survey queried CASE winners regarding biographical information; age; teaching experience; professorial rank; scholarly contributions to their disciplines; summer activities; and, of most relevance to this chapter, specific aspects of the winners' teaching as reflected on their syllabi.

In general, CASE winners constructed syllabi that laid out the day-to-day schedule of their courses and described highly specific policies for attendance, office hours, and grading. In most cases, CASE winners required attendance in their courses and were available to students for 20 or more hours a week for office visitations. They described grading standards in clear and detailed ways, such as listing the number of points earned through various class activities and providing a grading scale that specified the minimum number of points necessary to earn a particular grade.

Similarly, Pittenger (1992) examined the attributes of winners of the American Psychological Foundation's (APF) Award for Distinguished Teaching in Psychology, the American Psychological Association's (APA) highest teaching award. Pittenger's study was markedly broader than Lough's examination of CASE winners. He used nine categories to catalog the contributions of APF award winners: (a) development of new teaching methods and materials, (b) development of new courses and curricula, (c) contributions to a psychological subfield, (d) noteworthy departmental leadership as chair, (e) teaching of minority students and women, (f) extraordinary teaching and training of teachers, (g) teaching at smaller institutions, (h) provision of a forum for teaching enhancement, and (i) authorship of outstanding texts.

Pittenger (1992) noted that each APF honoree contributed to some degree in all nine categories. However, he stressed that these individuals shared four characteristics. First, each individual was an author, either of textbooks and text ancillaries or items that facilitated the training of teachers. Second, each individual was a rock-solid classroom teacher. Third, award winners were exemplars of creative thinking with respect to the role that psychology plays in everyday life. Fourth, award winners portrayed the teaching of psychology as a scholarly endeavor.

STUDENT PERCEPTIONS
OF MASTER TEACHERS

A third approach to investigating master teaching entails examination of student evaluations. Although the problems associated with assessing teacher performance using student evaluations has been well documented (see Davis, 1993, for a brief review), student evaluations nonetheless offer us another perspective on what is involved in master teaching.

In an early study, Feldman (1976) found that students prefer instructors who are stimulating, enthusiastic, prepared, organized, clear, comprehensive, and fair. More recently, Lowman (1995) used confirmatory factor analysis in an attempt to reveal the underlying structure of student perceptions of their teachers. His results point to two broad factors that separate the best teachers from ordinary ones. First, students believe that the best teachers present material both clearly and enthusiastically. They tend to use concrete examples that stimulate thinking. Second, students like instructors who are warm, understanding, and concerned for them as individuals.

WHAT IS A MASTER TEACHER?

This question is a difficult one to answer, and so far we have escaped defining the term. We all know master teachers. Some of us may even be master teachers. Nonetheless, most of us are hard pressed to put into words exactly what distinguishes master teachers from ordinary, run-of-the-mill teachers. One way, albeit tenuous, is to summarize what the three approaches reviewed before—writings of master teachers, analyses of the qualities of award-winning teachers, and examinations of student evaluations of faculty—tell us about master teaching. Table 3.1 provides a summary of 40 different qualities found across the three approaches. The "General Writings" category contains 22 qualities. The "Analyses of the Credentials of Award Winning Teachers" sources contain 14 qualities, with only 5 qualities overlapping with the former category. Finally, "Analyses of Student Evaluations" sources produced only 10 qualities. Interestingly, passion/enthusiasm is the only quality to appear on each of the three lists given in Table 3.1. No doubt this commonality underscores the critical importance of a teacher's excitement about the topic, the students, and teaching.

It is unlikely that possessing just 1 or even a few of the 40 qualities makes an individual a master teacher. It is equally unlikely that an individual must possess all of these qualities to be a master teacher. Rather, master teachers are likely to come in all shapes and sizes, so to speak, and represent different combinations or blends of these qualities. What makes Bill McKeachie a master teacher is not exactly the same as what makes Charles Brewer a master teacher, although there may be some overlap in the personal qualities and penchants relevant to teaching

TABLE 3.1
A Summary of the Qualities of Master Teachers Based
on a Brief Review of the Literature

General Writings	Analyses of Credentials of Award Winning Teachers	Analyses of Student Evaluations
Approachable	Commitment to field	Caring
Creative	Concern for students	Clear
Current in field	Creative	Comprehensive
Establishes rapport	Enthusiastic	Enthusiastic
Flexible	Good classroom teacher	Fair
Genuine	High standards for student work	Stimulating
Good listener	Humanistic	Understanding
Trusting	Intelligent	Warm
Passionate	Knowledgeable	Well organized
High expectations for students	Popular among students	Well prepared
Humorous	Scholarly	
Knowledgeable	Strong communication skills	
Models critical thinking	Strong work ethic	
Promotes cooperation	Write about their fields	
Respectful		
Stresses life-long learning		
Strong speaking skills		
Strong work ethic		
Thoughtful		
Uses active learning methods		
Uses common sense		
Uses interdisciplinary approach		

that each possesses. Thus, for those of us who train others to become teachers, we must be careful not to fashion our protégés from the same mold. Master teachers are as unique as teachers as they are as human beings.

Nonetheless, master teachers seem to be able to do four things to a greater extent than ordinary teachers: (a) instill in their students a desire to learn, (b) help their students actually learn something about the subject matter, (c) help their students discover that what they are learning is interesting, and (d) demonstrate to their students that learning in and of itself is enjoyable. It is quite possible that possessing some critical combination of the qualities listed in Table 3.1 enables master teachers to provide the context for accomplishing each of these processes.

WHAT ABOUT TEACHER BEHAVIOR?

As can be seen, these approaches to the study of master teaching reveal the person-ality characteristics and traits of persons believed to be master teachers. A problem with these approaches is that they beg the questions of (a) how a person acquires such qualities, and (b) what specific behaviors reflect such characteristics. If a person wishes to teach another individual how to become a more effective teacher, as is the case in many graduate teaching assistantship training programs (see Davis & Huss, chap. 11, this volume), a person is more likely to be successful by training a range of specific behaviors as opposed to more ambiguous personality characteristics such as *creativity, concern,* or *demeanor.* Obvious questions arise: What do I do to become more creative? How can I demonstrate that I am concerned? How do I develop an appropriate demeanor?

The remainder of this chapter describes an alternative approach for examining the basic elements of master teaching. Our aim in developing this approach was to identify a broad range of personality qualities and their attendant behaviors that appear to exist in master teachers. In addition, we sought to compare undergraduates and faculty with respect to which of these qualities/behaviors they believe are the most important to effective college and university teaching.

THE BEHAVIOR OF MASTER TEACHERS

Our research involved two phases. In Phase 1, we asked 114 undergraduates to list at least three characteristics that they believed were central to a person being a master teacher at the college and university level. This process produced a list of 47 characteristics. We presented this list to 184 other undergraduates whom we instructed to "list or otherwise indicate up to three *specific* behaviors that reflect these qualities and characteristics." These students were then given the following example as a guide:

An Example of a Teacher Quality: *Sense of Humor.*
An Example of Teacher Behavior That Reflects This Quality: *Tells funny stories or makes witty remarks in class and kids around or jokes with students.*

Three researchers met subsequently to compare behaviors that these participants listed for each quality. In many cases, the behaviors students assigned to particular qualities overlapped with behaviors they assigned to other qualities. Thus, some categories of qualities were collapsed, resulting in a list of 28 qualities and the behaviors that students said reflected them (see Table 3.2). (It is likely that some of the qualities listed in Table 3.1 also overlap considerably, and if we asked students or faculty to assign behaviors to these qualities, this list, too, would be much condensed.)

In Phase 2, we gave the list of 28 qualities/behaviors to 916 undergraduate students enrolled in a large introductory psychology course and 118 Auburn University faculty members. The undergraduates included 413 men and 503 women; 717 of these students were freshmen or sophomores and 199 were juniors or seniors. The faculty members included 89 men and 29 women whose names were selected

TABLE 3.2
The 28 Qualities and Behaviors as Derived from Undergraduates

Quality	Behaviors
Accessible	Posts office hours, gives phone number and e-mail address
Approachable/personable	Smiles, greets students, initiates conversations, invites questions, responds respectfully to student comments
Authoritative/confident	Establishes clear course rules, maintains classroom order Speaks loudly, makes eye contact, and answers questions correctly
Creative/interesting	Experiments with teaching methods; uses technological devices to enhance lectures; uses interesting, relevant, and personal examples
Effective communicator	Speaks clearly, uses precise English, gives clear, compelling examples
Encourages/cares for students	Provides praise for good student work, helps students who need it, offers bonus points/extra credit, knows student names
Enthusiastic about teaching	Smiles during class, prepares interesting class activities, uses gestures and expressions of emotion to emphasize important points
Establishes goals	Prepares and follows a syllabus, outlines goals for each class meeting at beginning of period
Flexible/open minded	Changes calendar of course events when necessary, will meet at times outside of office hours, pays attention to students' opinions, accepts criticism, allows students to do make up work when appropriate
Good listener	Does not interrupt students while they talk, maintains eye contact, replies respectfully to student comments, asks questions about points students make
Happy/positive/humorous/ humble	Smiles, tells jokes and funny stories, laughs with students, admits mistakes, never brags, does not take credit for others' successes
Knowledgeable about topic	Easily answers students' questions, does not read straight from book or notes, uses clear and understandable examples
Prepared	Brings necessary materials to class, provides outlines of class discussion
Presents current information	Relates topic to current, real life situations; uses recent videos, magazines, newspapers to highlight points; talks about current topics, uses new or recent texts
Professional	Dresses nicely (neat and clean shoes, slacks, blouses, dresses, shirts, ties), no profanity
Promotes class discussion	Asks controversial or challenging questions during class, gives points for class participation, involves students in group activities during class
Promotes critical thinking	Asks thoughtful questions during class, uses essay questions on tests and quizzes, assigns homework, holds group discussions/ activities
Provides constructive feedback	Writes comments on returned work, answers students' questions, gives advice on test-taking
Manages class time	Arrives to class on time/early, dismisses class on time, presents relevant materials in class, leaves time for questions, keeps appointments, returns work in a timely way

TABLE 3.2
(Continued)

Quality	Behaviors
Rapport	Makes class laugh through jokes and funny stories, initiates and maintains class discussions, knows student names, interacts with students before and after class
Realistic expectations/fair	Covers material to be tested during class, writes relevant test questions, does not overload students with reading, teaches at an appropriate level for the majority of students in the course, curves grades when appropriate, provides extra credit work
Respectful	Does not humiliate or embarrass students in class, is polite to students (says thank you and please, etc.), does not interrupt students while they are talking, does not talk down to students
Sensitive/persistent	Makes sure students understand material before moving to new material, holds extra study sessions, repeats information when necessary, asks questions to check student understanding
Strives to be a better teacher	Requests feedback on his/her teaching ability from students, continues learning (attends workshops, etc. on teaching)
Technologically competent	Knows now to use a computer, knows how to use e-mail, knows how to use overheads during class, has a Web page for classes
Understanding	Accepts legitimate excuses for missing class or coursework, is available to answer questions, does not lose temper at students, takes extra time to discuss difficult concepts

at random from the university phone directory. These faculty represented numerous disciplines across campus. We instructed both students and faculty to select "the 10 qualities/behaviors that are most important to master teaching at the college and university level." Thus, every student and faculty member casts 10 votes apiece—one vote for each of the categories they believed represented the top 10 qualities/behaviors of master teaching. Following data collection, all participants' responses were analyzed for similarities and differences. Analyses of differences among participants in both groups did not reveal any appreciable differences in rankings: Male and female students rated items similarly regardless of year in school as did male and female faculty members.

Table 3.3 compares faculty and students with respect to their ordering of the importance of each of the 28 qualities/behaviors. The qualities/behaviors are listed in descending order according to student tallies of all 28 items. The shaded numbers in the far right column indicate each of the top 10 categories for faculty. Interestingly, students and faculty agreed on 6 of the top 10 qualities/behaviors, although the specific order of these items differed between the two groups. These

TABLE 3.3

Comparison of Student and Faculty Ratings of the 28 Qualities/Behaviors

	Students			Faculty		
Quality/Behavior Category	n	%	rank	n	%	rank
Realistic Expectations/Fair	587	64	1	55	47	9
Knowledgeable About Topic	558	61	2	107	91	1
Understanding	554	60	3	27	23	21
Approachable/Personable	543	59	4	62	53	5
Respectful	488	53	5	59	50	7
Creative/Interesting	469	51	6	58	49	8
Happy/Positive/Humorous	453	49	7	7	6	27
Encourages/Cares for Students	452	49	8	44	37	12
Flexible/Open Minded	450	49	9	43	36	13
Enthusiastic About Teaching	448	49	10	86	73	2
Rapport	387	42	11	8	7	26
Accessible	358	42	12	48	41	11
Provides Constructive Feedback	349	38	13	40	34	14
Sensitive/Persistent	347	38	14	25	21	22
Master Communicator	323	35	15	61	52	6
Confident	310	34	16	34	29	17
Strives to be a Better Teacher	268	29	17	39	33	15
Good Listener	244	27	18	31	26	20
Promotes Class Discussion	225	25	19	35	30	16
Prepared	208	23	20	72	61	4
Humble	179	20	21	7	6	27
Presents Current Information	166	18	23.5	55	47	9
Manages Class Time	165	18	23.5	33	28	18
Establishes Goals	165	18	23.5	32	27	19
Promotes Critical Thinking	164	18	23.5	75	64	3
Authoritative	145	16	26	22	19	23
Technologically Competent	79	9	27	13	11	24
Professional	76	8	28	12	10	25

six qualities/behaviors were (a) realistic expectations/fairness, (b) knowledge-ableness, (c) approachable/personable, (d) respectful, (e) creative/interesting, and (f) enthusiasm. With respect to the 4 remaining top 10 items, students and faculty differed markedly, with faculty emphasizing specific elements of classroom instruction (effective communication, prepared, current, and critical thinking) and students favoring aspects of the student–teacher relationship (understanding, happy/positive/humorous, encouraging, flexible). In a similar study, Wann (2001) obtained highly congruent results using a sample of students and faculty at a medium-sized midwestern college.

Thus, students and teachers do not view the teaching enterprise all that differently. Where they differ perhaps reflects what is most central to the educational process from their unique perspectives. Teachers wish to transmit well-prepared and up-to-date knowledge effectively and stimulate students to think critically about it. Students desire to learn such knowledge within the context of a personal, empathetic, and supportive relationship. Perhaps the ideal approach to teaching includes both perspectives. Teachers who are able to convey the essence of a content domain clearly to students within the context of a supportive emotional environment are likely to be judged by students as the most effective and interesting teachers—that is, master teachers.

Our data overlap considerably with those derived data from the three approaches described earlier ("General Writings," "Analyses of the Credentials of Award Winning Teachers," and "Analyses of Student Evaluations"). Like these approaches, our approach showed the quality/behavior of enthusiasm to be associated with master teaching. In fact, each of 14 qualities/behaviors found in the combined "Top 10" lists for faculty and students in our study also appears in the results generated by the three previous approaches (see Tables 3.1 and 3.3). More specifically, 12 of the qualities/behaviors identified in our study overlap with the qualities identified through "General Writings" (approachable, creative, current in field, establishes rapport, flexible, good listener, passionate, humorous, knowledgeable, models critical thinking, respectful, and strong speaking skills), 4 overlap with "Analyses of Credentials of Award Winning Teachers" (creative, enthusiastic, knowledgeable, and strong communication skills), and 5 overlap with "Analyses of Student Evaluations" (caring, enthusiastic, fair, understanding, and well prepared). Finally, our approach uncovered 12 qualities/behaviors not previously identified in these three approaches (accessible, provides constructive feedback, sensitive/persistent, confident, strives to be a better teacher, promotes class discussion, humble, manages class time, establishes goals, authoritative, technologically competent, and professional).

BECOMING A MASTER TEACHER

At some point in their careers, persons who are serious about teaching ask themselves, in one way or another, "How can I become a more effective teacher?" The question is simple, but its answer is complex. As Brookfield (1990) so clearly noted, teaching is messy business.

Perhaps the best way to answer the question is by attempting to incorporate some of the behaviors given in Table 3.2 into one's existing repertoire. For example, if you feel that your teaching would be enhanced by being more creative and interesting, then you might attempt to experiment with novel teaching methods; incorporate more technology in the classroom; and use more interesting, relevant, and personal examples during class presentations. Likewise, if student or peer reviews of your teaching suggest that you lack rapport with the class, you might try learning your students' names and talking to them students before and after class. In addition, you might consider telling a funny story every now and then or involving the class in more discussion of the subject matter.

Knowing which specific behaviors to adopt to augment one's approach to teaching is certainly advantageous in that much of the guess work is removed from wondering how to go about becoming a better teacher. To the extent that we implement the behaviors listed in Table 3.2 into our teaching, the more likely we are to provide contexts that favor student learning. Most of these behaviors are relatively easy to acquire and pay huge dividends in terms of how students view us. Being on time to class, smiling during our lectures, knowing our students' names, stopping every now and then in the hallways to chat with our students, and so on show students we respect and care for them. In other words, such actions on our part establish the foundation for the kind of student–teacher relationships that seem likely to motivate students to come to our classes, pay attention and participate in class discussions, study in earnest outside of class, and, most important, discover that learning psychology is interesting, worthwhile, and just plain fun.

Keep in mind, too, that the student–teacher relationship is a two-way street. By incorporating any or all of the behaviors given in Tables 3.2 and 3.3 into our teaching, we are likely to have a positive influence on our students' motivation to come to class and study; their academic performance; and their attitude toward our subject matter, us, and, for that matter, higher education in general. In turn, students are apt to behave positively toward us—enhancing our motivation to come to class prepared and well organized and our attitude toward them and our teaching. The student–teacher relationship, like all human relationships, is at its core an exchange relationship characterized by intertwining positive and negative feedback loops. Clearly, however, as teachers we set the tone for what happens in this relationship through our actions. Our behavior matters.

REFERENCES

Baiocco, S. A., & DeWaters, J. N. (1998). *Successful college teaching: Problem solving strategies of distinguished professors.* Needham Heights, MA: Allyn & Bacon.

Beidler, P. G. (1997). What makes a good teacher? In J. K. Roth (Ed.), *Inspiring teaching: Carnegie professors of the year speak* (pp. 2–12). Bolton, MA: Anker.

Boice, R. (1996). *First order principles for college teachers: Ten basic ways to improve the teaching process.* Bolton, MA: Anker.

Brewer, C. L. (1982, August). *Gladly learn and gladly teach.* Paper presented at the annual meeting of the American Psychological Association, Washington, DC.

Brookfield, S. D. (1990). *The skillful teacher.* San Francisco: Jossey-Bass.

Davis, B. G. (1993). *Tools for teaching.* San Francisco: Jossey-Bass.

Davis, S. F., & Huss, M. T. (2002). Training graduate teaching assistants. In S. F. Davis & W. Buskist (Eds.), *The teaching of psychology: Essays in honor of Wilbert J. McKeachie and Charles L. Brewer.* Mahwah, NJ: Lawrence Erlbaum Associates.

Eble, K. E. (1983). *The aims of college teaching.* San Francisco: Jossey-Bass.

Eble, K. E. (1984). *The craft of teaching.* San Francisco: Jossey-Bass.

Feldman, K. A. (1976). The superior college teacher from the student's view. *Research in Higher Education, 5,* 243–288.

Gill, V. (1998). *The 10 commandments of good teaching.* Thousand Oaks, CA: Corwin Press.

Hatfield, S. R. (1995). *The seven principles in action: Improving undergraduate education.* Bolton, MA: Anker.

Lough, J. R. (1997). The Carnegie Professors of the Year: Models for teaching success. In J. K. Roth (Ed.), *Inspiring teaching: Carnegie Professors of the Year speak* (pp. 212–225). Bolton, MA: Anker.

Lowman, J. (1995). *Mastering the techniques of teaching* (3rd ed.). San Francisco: Jossey-Bass.

McKeachie, W. J. (1999). *Teaching tips: Strategies, research, and theory for college and university teachers* (10th ed.). Boston: Houghton Mifflin.

Pittenger, D. J. (1992). A brief history of the American Psychological Foundation's award for distinguished teachers of psychology. In A. E. Puente, J. R. Matthews, & C. L. Brewer (Eds.), *Teaching psychology in America: A history* (pp. 153–170). Washington, DC: American Psychological Association.

Roth, J. K. (Ed.). (1997). *Inspiring teaching: Carnegie Professors of the Year speak.* Bolton, MA: Anker.

Vargo, J. W. (1997). Stretching minds: Personal and academic aspects of teaching. In J. K. Roth (Ed.), *Inspiring teaching: Carnegie Professors of the Year speak* (pp. 13–23). Bolton, MA: Anker.

Wann, P. D. (2001, January). *Faculty and student perceptions of the behaviors of effective college teachers.* Poster session presented at the National Institute for the Teaching of Psychology, St. Petersburg Beach, FL.

4

Classroom Presence

Jane S. Halonen
James Madison University

There are predictable revealing moments in the lives of teachers that set the stage for a discussion of *presence* in the college classroom. Consider the following examples:

- How do you cope with the strain of the minute before you begin your first class?
- How much attention do you pay to protocol in your syllabus?
- Do you encourage e-mail contact and religiously observe your office hours?
- When you overhear your students describe you as *tough*, are you pleased or put off?
- Do you fuss with your appearance or wear whatever is handy or clean?
- How do you respond to suspect excuses for students' failure to perform?
- Do you strive to stay current with pop culture and language?
- How do you feel when a student asks a question that you cannot answer?

THE ESSENCE OF PRESENCE

What does it mean to have presence in the classroom and how does presence contribute to the success or failure of learning? Each teacher brings a distinctive self to the classroom. Nearly everyone has had the unfortunate experience of being in the presence of a toxic teacher, whose teaching style becomes an impediment to learning. To realize the learning objectives of the course, the student may have to ignore or strive in other ways to neutralize the negativity felt in the presence of such a teacher. In contrast, the magical teacher makes learning compelling and meaningful (Halonen, 2000). Such a teacher does not make learning effortless, but does make the effort worthwhile.

Enter the wild card: What is toxic teaching for some students may be just the right sort of teaching for others. This point accounts for the puzzling polar teaching evaluations that occur even for the most gifted of teachers and certainly complicates understanding teacher presence. Therefore, I begin with a fundamental fact. A teacher's presence may create an overall climate that may appear to be homogeneous, but in truth the teacher's presence may have a distinctive, variable impact on each individual student. The teacher's presence can strongly influence not just individual student success, but how the student feels about the class content and the process by which the student learns as well as whether the teacher can be deemed toxic, magical, or somewhere in between.

Let us focus for a moment on the presence of the two individuals for whom this volume has been developed. Their classroom presence could not be more differentiated. Charles Brewer is a paragon of classroom expertise. His opening strategy for a class or lecture is legendary. He braces himself against the podium, slowly sweeps the room with a pointed gaze as conversations diminish, and when the time is right . . . begins. He maintains high standards and can validly make the remarkable claim that no student has ever turned in a paper after deadline during his career. He establishes his own authority in the classroom vigorously and demands that students invest their intellectual energies to meet his high standards. He assiduously promotes adherence to APA format to generate high-quality research projects. In his demand for "clarity, conciseness, and felicity of expression," Charles Brewer has become one of the most beloved of teachers and colleagues in psychology.

In contrast, Bill McKeachie offers a softer, gentler classroom presence that is arguably as endearing, engaging, and inspiring. Bill eschews most outward vestiges of authority. For example, he routinely allows his introductory honors students to choose their own textbooks, which then means that the class operates out of four or five different books. He requires extensive in-class activities—primarily discussion and writing—to maximize student engagement with the material. Bill feels most successful when all of his students master understanding of the concepts he has to present, sometimes engendering distress among students who expect to break the class curve to prove their intellectual worth. He continually works to incorporate new strategies to promote collaboration and renew his quest for more meaningful ways to help students learn and remember. For him, the course content is important, but it is less important than the changes that transpire in the learner. His kindness, humanity, and humility ring true as central features of his classroom presence.

How do we account for the extraordinary impact of such very different individuals in creating positive presence? In contrast, how can we also address the characteristics of teachers that drain the life from class and potentially alienate students from the joy of learning?

A FRAMEWORK FOR EXPLORING PRESENCE

The purpose of this chapter is to explore the dimensions of teacher presence. I propose a framework for understanding the impact of teacher presence that benefits from an application of the five-factor theory (Costa & McRae, 1994), a two-decade career in teaching, and the help of some astute college students.

I invited my senior students in a capstone course at James Madison University on the History of Psychology to identify the qualities that constituted both positive and negative teacher presence in the classroom. I asked them to respond in writing to capture five characteristics that produced positive presence in the classroom and five characteristics that contributed negative presence. I distilled some general categories of teacher presence from the various characteristics they described. The categories include expressive personality variables, behaviors that demonstrate receptivity to and concern for students, pedagogical practices that facilitate or impede learning, and physical/sociocultural characteristics. Their contributions are highlighted in Tables 4.1 and 4.2.

How might the "big five" personality factors explain success in the classroom? Costa and McRae (1994) proposed that there are five key stable dimensions on which personality can be assessed, including introversion/extraversion, neuroticism, agreeableness, openness to experience, and conscientiousness. There appears to be a natural overlap between the characteristics in their first three categories cited by my students and the five-factor model proposed by Costa and McRae. In the first section, we explore expressive personality factors, including introversion/extraversion. Next we examine agreeableness and neuroticism as the foundation for behaviors that demonstrate receptivity to students. Sound pedagogical practices reflect conscientiousness as well as openness to experience.

Expressive Personality Factors

According to my students, enthusiasm is the most potent of all elements that determines positive teacher presence. Enthusiasm may be enhanced or constrained by the teacher's degree of introversion or extraversion.

TABLE 4.1
Twelve Perspectives on Positive Presence*

What are the Five Most Important Qualities for Positive Presence in the Classroom?

Expressive Personality Characteristics
10   energy/excitement/enthusiasm for subject, students, and life

Behaviors That Show Connection to Student
3   understands students' needs/views, makes effort to remember names and personal detail, caring and compassionate, shows interest in talking to students
2   available, willing to share to facilitate student growth, patient, emotional proximity
1   demonstrates relevance to students lives, signals willingness to go extra steps to help students understand, encouraging, uses positive reinforcement, admits when they do not know something, friendly, shows commitment, dedication, engaging voice, eye contact, physical proximity

Pedagogical Practices
5   fosters full involvement/interactivity
3   reliability/consistency/keeps word, fair test of ability, competence in material, engages attention through variable activity, creative, casual, laid-back style
2   use of visual aids, appropriate pacing of material
1   prompt return of assignments, strong preparation, maintain control of class, making effort to make the class fun

Physical/Sociocultural Characteristics
1   nice dress

---

*12 students in a history of psychology class responded to the question. The numbers represent the frequency with which the item was identified among the 12 students.

Enthusiasm.   W. H. Auden once defined a *professor* as "one who talks in someone else's sleep." According to my students, the deadliest teaching sin of all is absence of enthusiasm. Students were most unforgiving about teachers who evince little interest in what they are teaching, particularly if the result culminates in a monotonous delivery.

In my experience, most students come to a course with all the expectancy of a first date. They hope the match is an excellent one. At a minimum, they hope that their time will not be wasted. If they are lucky, the enthusiasm of the professor can open news doors and the students can extract from the course larger life lessons than even the content can purvey. When their hopes are met with a flat emotional response, students feel alienated from the discipline and distanced from the teacher.

Introversion/Extraversion.   Unfortunately, introverted teachers may be at a higher risk for engendering boredom because of their discomfort in self-expression. Teachers differ in the extent to which they feel comfortable in the classroom. Little (2000) proposed that classes may be a comfortable fit for teachers who are by

TABLE 4.2
Twelve Perspectives on Negative Presence

What are the Five Most Important Qualities for Positive Presence in the Classroom?

Expressive Personality Characteristics
6 monotone delivery
1 lack of energy, absence of emotion, does not enjoying teaching

Behaviors That Show Connection to the Student
4 shows no interest in getting to know students, indifferent to students
2 crude or insulting comments, boring, pompous, selfish, self-absorbed
1 dismisses efforts made, unresponsive to students' needs, unapproachable, no open doors to students, no capacity for friendship, treats students as inferior, physical distance (podium as barrier), insists that students should suffer in the same manner they had to, judgmental, angry, prideful, complacent, mean, impatient, would obviously rather teach people who already *know* the subject, overformal/dictatorial, standing still, distracting mannerisms

Classroom Practice
3 incompetence with material
2 unfair, treats people unequally, inconsistent, wishy-washy rules lecturing straight from notes, ambiguous tests, instructions
1 more into knowledge than teaching, tangential commentary keeping students beyond class limits, improper pacing (way too fast), exaggerated expectations, assigning work that has no useful purpose, racing through PowerPoint, unfair grading policy, teachers who wing their classes hoping things will fall into place, no class interaction, invariable predictable activity in class, calling on someone to talk

Physical/Sociocultural Characteristics
  None reported

nature extroverts. Intense scrutiny by the members of the class is not disturbing to extroverts. These teachers see a class as a perfect vehicle by which they can relax and connect with their students. For them, there is a seamless connection between the self that they experience in the classroom and the self in other contexts; class is simply a comfort zone.

In contrast, introverts may find themselves so uncomfortable in the classroom spotlight that they must adopt the teacher's role as if they were performing theatrically. They must act at being outgoing at a high cost of experiencing excessive arousal. Little (2000) suggested that they have to develop some strategies for coping with such excess stimulation if they are to survive their chosen occupation. For those teachers who do not manage to transform their anxieties, powerful inhibiting forces may result in a wooden delivery that is unlikely to translate to attributions that the teacher has enthusiasm for the subject, students, or anything else. Clearly, more expressive and extroverted faculty members are at an advantage in student evaluations if the demands of the spotlight suit the positive narcissistic needs of the faculty member.

Teachers should find avenues to show their enthusiasm whether it is naturally expressed or orchestrated. If we cannot muster any of the passion and communicate that driving force to our students, the toll will be seemingly endless classes, eyeball rolling from disaffected students, and recurrent daydreams about easier ways to make a living. I add one caveat from another psychology teaching legend, David Myers (1992). He endorses the importance of enthusiasm in high-quality teaching, but suggests that we are likely to become heartbroken if we ever expect our students to be as excited about our discipline as we are. Our students do not have to mirror our joys of discovery for them to benefit from the adventure we have to offer.

Behaviors That Show Receptivity to Students

Students want to make a strong connection with their teachers. Agreeability, absence of neurosis, welcoming behavior, empathy, and empowerment facilitate this outcome.

Agreeability. Washington Irving suggested that "an inexhaustible good nature" was critical to survive life's challenges. He could easily have been addressing another fundamental characteristic that gives teachers positive presence. Students want teachers who clearly enjoy the profession that they have chosen and who demonstrate that enjoyment by being pleasant and friendly.

My students highlighted a variety of ways that teachers alienate them through disagreeable characteristics. These aversive qualities included being complacent, prideful, pompous, self-absorbed, and just plain mean.

Neuroticism. Ralph Waldo Emerson insisted that "Sanity is very rare; every man almost, and every woman, has a dash of madness." (I forgive Emerson his sexism and believe he almost got it right.) Because both teaching and learning can be emotionally and intellectually challenging, it is easy to see why classes might provide a reasonable context in which madness can be made visible. Although students may have had experiences with neurotic teachers during their education, most students assume reasonable mental health on the part of their teachers until temper displays, irrationalities, or other peculiarities prove otherwise. When students discern unresolved adjustment problems in their professors, they are likely to focus on self-protection rather than learning.

Several of my students stressed the importance of their teachers having patience. Teachers who are low in neuroticism are much less likely to jump to conclusions or respond negatively when frustrated. When it comes to negotiating a break or requesting a clarification on an assignment or test question, students feel intimidated when they have observed that the teacher has a short fuse and can predict their inquiry might prompt an explosion.

Welcoming Attitude. Generous eye contact, smiling, and remembering personal details are strong indicators of teachers with positive presence, according to my students. Hiding behind the podium and objectifying students sends the opposite message.

Chickering and Gamson (1987) identified frequent faculty–student contact as a fundamental principle of good teaching practice. Not every student requires individual attention from a faculty member, but teachers differ in how seriously they respond to making themselves available. Cues for accessibility can typically be found in the syllabus. Office hours can be listed with an encouraging note that might help some students overcome their anxieties about professor contact and engage the professor electronically or in person.

Many professors religiously observe their office hours—regardless of whether students take advantage of them. They use e-mail efficiently to establish even stronger bonds with their students. In effect, they conduct office hours ad libitum. Some teachers develop memory tricks to encode names of students quickly as a signal of their intent to make students feel welcome. For example, I like to collect personal information about my students on a survey at the outset of a class to help jog my memory regarding their distinctiveness and also to give me some rich material from which to draw examples.

Empathy. Students gravitate toward faculty members who project concern and compassion about the lives of their students. Positive teachers strive to remember about the confusions of college life—to remember that heartaches and compelling social obligations sometimes may take priority over even the best of academic intentions. The magical teacher uses such dilemmas as teachable moments to enhance the larger lessons that college has to offer. They share sufficient personal detail with students, carefully chosen for its relevance to the dilemmas that the students face, so that students can see the humanity beyond the teacher's role.

In contrast, toxic teachers purposefully create distance between themselves and their students. They do not see empathy as an obligation and act as if time spent with students is a distraction or intrusion. They choose to tell personal stories for narcissistically driven reasons that are likely to be less effective in helping students gain relevant insights about the personal or academic problems they are trying to solve.

Empowerment. Michaelangelo stated, "I saw the angel in the marble and carved until I set him free." In this regard, the role of the professor is to glimpse possible futures for their students and help students see a positive possibility as a likely outcome. I think the best professors are inclined to see the glass as three-quarters full especially as it applies to their students and what their students can become. That optimism encourages them to promote positive outcomes for their students. According to my students, teachers with positive presence acknowledge hard work even when it does not necessarily lead to the desired outcome. They help students imagine beyond the immediate context.

In contrast, teachers with negative presence may not see themselves as integrally related to the students' future. It simply may not be a priority, which encourages an attitude of marking time with students.

Pedagogical Practices

Students fare best in the presence of teachers who comfortably and appropriately demonstrate their disciplinary expertise, show conscientiousness about the chores of teaching, promote full engagement of diverse learners, and exude sufficient authority and rigor to facilitate a civil atmosphere.

Disciplinary Competence. Students tend to trust from the outset of their course that their teachers have sufficient disciplinary expertise or they would not have been hired to do the job. However, they are quick to revise their judgment if given sufficient provocation by teachers who lack confidence, distort known truths, or pretend to know things when they do not.

Some beginning students have an expectation, clarified through William Perry's (1970) work on cognitive development, that the teacher should be an all-knowing authority. As such, teachers need to take special care to help students accept that teachers are still in the process of learning as well. Students are far more tolerant of admission of an unknown when followed up with a promise to find out. However, they are intolerant of bluffing.

One insightful student suggested that disciplinary competence sometimes can become an obstacle. Teachers can be alienating if they clearly communicate that they care more about the discipline than the students whom they are teaching.

Conscientiousness. Although my students did not highlight this concept from five-factor theory directly, they emphasized many qualities that would constitute conscientious. For example, students expect to be treated equitably. Although students undoubtedly learn the lesson many times over that life may not be fair, students should have the right to expect fair treatment in their classes, in- cluding grading practices. The syllabus should provide a comprehensive set of expectations. When teachers have laid out the expectations properly, students want teachers to stay the course. Assignments and tests should be straightforward and facilitate learning rather than become adventures in decoding. If students ask for clarification, the teacher should assume that the clarity of what is written needs improvement rather than being angry with the student for challenging the exist- ing text. Students believe that teachers should try hard to keep their promises and be predictable. When teachers violate such expectations, students feel unsafe, distracted, and angry.

Royse (2000) recommended some specific strategies to reinforce student per- ceptions of teacher conscientiousness. He emphasized prompt return of homework and exams preferably as soon after these items are submitted as possible. He also recommended offering detailed feedback on written work. To enhance positive impact, I recommend that your feedback should highlight as many positive features as developmental comments.

My students also discussed some mechanics of teaching as relevant to presence. They strongly prefer well-organized and goal-oriented classroom experiences to class sessions that feel disorganized, chaotic, or unstructured. They expect to see evidence of preparation that takes into account the difficulty of the material and their interests as learners. Course experiences should be paced so students do not feel like they have inadvertently entered a transcribing marathon. Assignments should have a strong link to course outcomes and should be returned promptly to maximize students gains.

Students also expressed appreciation for teachers who make a point to appeal to a broad range of learning styles. The liberal use of visual aids, the incorporation of learning strategies that encourage participation and reflection, and other learner-centered practices (cf. McKeachie, 1999) can help students stay connected to the important ideas offered by teachers.

Openness to Experience. My students focused on the importance of teachers' striving to present new and different experiences in the classroom to help them stay motivated and interested. Some students specifically pointed to the effectiveness of classroom strategies that reflected innovation and creativity to make class more engaging and vigorous. Students clearly favor faculty who embrace innovation and variety to help them stay engaged.

Teachers differ in the comfort with which they can abandon a strategy they have planned for a class. However, many teachers report that these moments of spontaneity—changing a plan at the last minute or following up on an expected development as the class unfolds—can lead to greater satisfaction than slavishly adhering to the outline as planned.

My students also complained that some class experiences feel so routine that it is obvious why the teacher shows little enthusiasm. Aging lecture notes or out-dated assignments give hints that recent classroom preparation has not been a priority. One student complained that a teacher might choose to require a rigorous assignment for the sake of academic tradition—to promulgate suffering for the sake of academic tradition—as opposed to work that might produce greater impact or fulfillment. This insight reinforces Schoenfeld and Magnan's (1992) explanation for poor-quality teaching: Teachers simply teach the way they were taught. Thus, legacy and long-suffering tradition converge to create deadly classroom experiences.

E. M. Forster suggested, "Spoon feeding in the long run teaches us nothing but the shape of the spoon." Students cited reading from lecture notes as among the most negative of teaching practices. Teachers who incorporate novelty stay motivated and interested in the material. Involving students in discussion and other active learning strategies sends a message that their presence matters as an active ingredient in the class. They work at the course material to help students understand the relevance in their own lives. When the teacher figures out ways to make the class fun, the students find that learning may not require as much sweat equity.

Authority. Ralph Ellison stated, "Power doesn't have to show off. Power is confident, self-assuring, self-starting and self-stopping, self-warming and self-justifying. When you have it, you know it." The teacher is the formal authority in the classroom, and students benefit from the benign exercise of that authority. Although my students identified a preference for a casual, laid-back atmosphere as an important ingredient of positive presence, they do not want the atmosphere to be so casual that the sense of control is gone in the classroom.

Although there are intriguing discussions about the reported relation between laxness and student evaluations of teaching performance (McKeachie, 1997), serious students appreciate teachers who set and maintain high standards. Rigor should apply both to student and teacher expectations and performance. Students show little patience with teachers who *wing* their classes with an expectation that things will simply fall into place.

Many campuses report increases in campus incivility and disregard of classroom authority (Kauffman & Burbach, 1997). Language can be harsh and crude. Students show disrespect through inappropriate jokes and provocative behaviors that seem to be getting more and more outlandish. For example, in a recent campus consultation on civility, one professor complained to me that she had a male student who stripped to the waist in her computer lab complaining that he "was hot." It may be a challenge for teachers to stay an optimistic force when students' behavior in the classroom violates fundamental assumptions about how people should relate.

Teachers communicate expectations about the nature of the civility responses that they expect to have in the classroom, whether they do so explicitly or implicitly (Halonen, 1999). Some faculty make their expectations about civility explicit by writing up "rules of conduct," posting them in the syllabus, and reviewing them as part of the first day's activities. Others assume that traditional classroom civility should prevail without necessarily seeing it as an obligation to teach this conduct.

Remarkably, some faculty members engage in disrespectful, uncivil behavior. For example, students have sometimes disclosed to me that their teachers have embarrassed them in class by demeaning comments. They find opportunities to reinforce the students' sense of inadequacy by belittling their abilities or making them the target of inappropriate sarcasm. Even when disappointed with the quality of a student's response, there is little justification for the kind of faculty presence that can poison the student's interest and motivation not just in the current course, but for the entire higher education enterprise.

Physical Characteristics

H. L. Mencken speculated, "One may no more live in the world without picking up the moral prejudices of the world than one will be able to go to hell without perspiring." Few of my students commented on physical characteristics as part of teacher presence perhaps because it is impolite and socially undesirable to admit that physical appearance influences our judgment. For example, only one student emphasized the importance of attractive attire as part of a teacher's positive presence. However, these physical dimensions link to prejudices (sometimes subtle and sometimes not so subtle) that can influence whether a teacher and student can make a strong connection.

Physical Attractiveness.   During a recent observation of a new faculty member, I scanned the class of 70 juniors and experienced a shock of recognition that the students were physically remarkable. There were no glasses. No blemishes. Weights were moderate to emaciated. It was a startling moment that left me with the realization that the array of new means of enhancing attractiveness (laser surgery, antibiotics, plastic surgery) may allow students to achieve their physical ideals. Students' investment in this pursuit not only suggests the prominence of this value, but might also suggest that we would be foolhardy not to think that our own physical attractiveness may have an impact on students with this value system.

Several years ago, I conducted a survey about psychology teachers in general across several colleges. In general, the students were quite complimentary about the teaching prowess of their respective psychology faculties, but the comments of one very sincere sophomore stood out. She suggested that she would relate much better to her psychology instructor if the instructor "didn't dress like such a geek." I do not think her comment suggests that teachers need to be devotees of *Vogue* or *Gentlemen's Quarterly*. However, like it or not, students clearly pay attention to our clothing tastes and may feel alienated if our tastes are too off the mark. Bizarre, disheveled, or controversial attire simply produces one more obstacle that may interfere with the development of mutual respect and trust.

Gender.   Gender has taken center stage in psychology in the last few years. Early in psychology's history, women were systematically excluded from psychology classes and clubs (Goodwin, 1999). More recently, the balance of majors has dramatically shifted so that female students outnumber male students by as much as 5 to 1 on some campuses. A departmental colleague of mine reported that an advanced class in learning theory had nearly 40 women and no men.

This shift has been a remarkable one to watch. When I began graduate school in 1973, I was the only woman in my 10-person class. During my graduate education, I had little exposure to female faculty members, and some of those faculty were employed outside the tenure track. Although I believe I was treated fairly in my graduate program, I pined for role models whose life patterns could help me figure out the puzzle of my future.

Once I became a faculty member, my experiences about gender in the classroom have been instructive. I have taught in both single-gender and co-ed contexts. I found it relatively easy to relate to my all-female classes to develop examples that fit female experience. I was dismayed to discover the degree to which my own gender-based explanations became obvious when I moved to a co-ed setting. In contrast, I recently observed a gifted male faculty member who consistently offered engaging examples that he conspicuously labeled as examples that came from the *male perspective*.

Depending on the student's comfort level with the gender of the teacher, the student may feel a stronger or weaker sense of connection to the teacher and possibly to the discipline that the teacher represents. Teachers with positive presence strive to include examples that will draw in their students, but gender-sensitive teachers also recognize the extent to which their own experiences may not naturally connect to students in the classrooms of the opposite gender.

Age. Our students seem to look younger each year, but the sad truth is that *their* ages are relatively constant (Halonen, 1997). As the chronological chasm grows between you and your students, it may be harder to make a strong connection with them. You may not share their popular culture interests, so in informal moments you may strain to find common ground.

Our culture is ageist. Therefore, we would be unwise not to recognize that our students approach the gray-haired among us with some expectations that we will have to prove to them that we are not in the full bloom of "geezerhood," but somehow manage sufficient "cool" to be worthy sources of learning. Some faculty simply compensate for that distance in years by bolstering their formal authority. Others may strive, and some in vain, to adopt language, customs, humor, and media habits that give them some venues in which to engage.

Virginia Woolf suggested a solution to this dilemma. She noted, "One of the signs of passing youth is the birth of a sense of fellowship with other human beings as we take our place among them." I propose that it is our good fortune to be able to have fellowship with our aging colleagues. However, it is fellowship with students—those who can help us continuously relive the joys of youth and feel relief that we do not have to relive the despairing moments so directly—that constitutes one of the true rewards of the work that we do.

Race. We are disastrously short of minority faculty members in psychology. Not only does this situation diminish the wealth of our collective faculty talent, but having few minority faculty members produces a disincentive for students of color to gravitate toward psychology as a major. Minority professors provide an important role model for students just as exposure to more women faculty members would have been helpful for me. Similarly, minority professors may have dramatically different experiences teaching in historically African-American institutions versus settings that are more multicultural. They may confront in their students some racist expectations that can sour the environment and complicate studying sensitive topics in psychology.

Fortunately, the zeitgeist has changed dramatically such that open prejudicial reactions hardly would be supported by the majority of students' peers. However, we need to recognize that some students will make negative attributions when the authority figure in front of them in the class does not conform to their expectations about how power should be distributed in the world.

Regionalism.   A current graduate student recently reminded me of the power of this kind of sociocultural given in assessing the impact of presence. A clinical practitioner from North Carolina, she shared in her lyrical southern accent that a prospective client had once asked to be transferred from her care because her accent "sounded uneducated." Although clearly such an inference is outrageous, it does remind us that subtle—and not so subtle—biases may be activated if the teacher's accent contrasts in noticeable ways with those of the region in which he or she is teaching.

There is little we can do to make changes in the category of physical and socio-cultural characteristics to change how students respond to us. However, teachers who wish to enhance positive presence need to be aware of the potential obstacles for making strong connections with their students. As we know from a strong tradition of research in social psychology, working with individuals who are different from us over time can often produce a shift in attitude if there are no additional incidents that reinforce the original prejudice.

A CHILD'S EYE VIEW

The conclusions of my college seniors are instructive for the comprehensive view of what makes for most effective teaching presence. Their contributions to our framework are perhaps not so remarkable given how quickly students may be able to form a critical eye about high-quality teaching. For example, a 7-year-old student named Allison (Burke, 1996) suggested a catalog of characteristics of what she thought made a teacher effective. In a list that she entitled "Stuff for a Good Teacher," Allison listed the following:

1. Loves her kids.
2. Helps you out.
3. Always has a smile.
4. Is fair with her kids.
5. Is full of surprises.
6. Takes good care of us.

7. Has smart brains.
8. Tries her best.
9. Likes to laugh.
10. Listens to her heart.

Although the language is somewhat more primitive, the points Allison makes are eerily similar to the list developed by my seniors.

CONCLUSION

By the time students reach the college classroom, they have amassed countless hours of instruction from a variety of teachers. Students can learn from anyone. However, the question remains whether the lesson is what we intend. Kahlil Gibran reflected, "I have learnt silence from the talkative, toleration from the intolerant, and kindness from the unkind; yet strange, I am ungrateful to these teachers." Although Gibran was not talking about teachers per se, he did capture the difficulties about the life lessons that can be learned from teachers with negative presence.

In contrast, teachers with positive presence transcend the confines of the classroom. When the minutiae of the discipline have fallen into disrepair in the brain's attic, such teachers occupy a special place in their students' memory for the larger lessons their teachers have been able to convey.

ACKNOWLEDGMENTS

I am enormously indebted to both Wilbert J. McKeachie and Charles Brewer. They represent teachers with positive presence in their truest and finest sense. I cannot be in their company without learning something new, and I hope to grow up to be just like them.

I also owe a debt of gratitude to my undergraduate students who assisted me with the conceptualization of this chapter and who had not really made that bargain when they registered to take history of psychology with me. They include Cassandra L. Beltz, Stephen Dee, Kristi Gochenour, Katie Herrington, John Herron, Michelle Hicks, Meghan Kenealy, Amy Lu, Jared McCutchen, Heidi Petway, Julie Tobin, and Greg Voigt.

I am blessed to have teaching colleagues whose shared experiences shaped my observations for this chapter. I acknowledge the contributions of Jim Benedict, Charles Lockett, and Kay Huskins for enriching my ideas about teaching with their helpful examples.

In addition, I thank Sam, Penny, Rachel, and Graham Halonen for locating Allison's perspective on teaching. I appreciate their "smart brains" put to good and generous use.

Finally, I wish to thank Bill Buskist and Steve Davis for their creative energies in assembling this tribute—a volume whose time has really come.

REFERENCES

Burke, N. (1996). *Teachers are special: A tribute to those who educate, encourage, and inspire.* New York: Gramercy Books.

Chickering, A. W., & Gamson, Z. F. (1987). Seven principles for good practice in undergraduate education. *AAHE Bulletin, 39,* 3–7.

Costa, P. T., & McRae, R. R. (1994). "Set like plaster"? Evidence for the stability of adult personality. In R. Heatherton & J. Weinberger (Eds.), *Can personality change?* Washington, DC: American Psychological Association.

Goodwin, C. J. (1999). *A history of modern psychology.* New York: Wiley.

Halonen, J. S. (1997, August). *Struggling against the undertow: Staying student-centered over time.* Ruth Hubbard Cousin Distinguished Lecture for Psi Beta, American Psychological Association Convention, Boston, MA.

Halonen, J. S. (2000, August). *Teaching as alchemy.* American Psychological Foundation Distinguished Teaching Address/Society for the Teaching of Psychology Presidential Address, American Psychological Association Convention, Washington, DC.

Halonen, J. S. (1999, January). *Uncivil liberties: Managing challenging classroom dynamics.* National Institute for the Teaching of Psychology, St. Petersburg, FL.

Little, B. (2000, October). *Professing out of character: Free traits and the immortal profession.* Keynote Address at the Eastern Conference on the Teaching of Psychology, James Madison University, Harrisonburg, VA.

Kauffman, J. M., & Burbach, H. J. (1997). On creating a climate of classroom civility. *Phi Delta Kappan, 79,* 320–325.

McKeachie, W. J. (1997). Student ratings: The validity of use. *American Psychologist, 52,* 1218–1225.

McKeachie, W. J. (1999). *Teaching tips: Strategies, research, and theory for college and university teachers* (10th ed.). Boston: Houghton-Mifflin.

Myers, D. (1992). A quarter century professing psychology: Lessons I have learned. *Contemporary Social Psychology, 16,* 44–49.

Perry, W. G., Jr. (1970). *Forms of intellectual and ethical development in the college years: A scheme.* New York: Holt, Rhinehart & Winston.

Royse, D. (2000). *Teaching tips for college and university instructors: A practical guide.* Needham Heights, MA: Allyn & Bacon.

Schoenfeld, A.C., & Magnan, R. (1992). *Mentor in a manual.* Madison, WI: Magna.

5

Lecturing

Ludy T. Benjamin, Jr.
Texas A&M University

When American consumers are surveyed about what cheese they especially like, they name cheddar, American, gouda, Swiss, mozzarella, parmesan, or, perhaps, gorgonzola. Yet they almost never mention the leading selling cheese in America, the cheese that outsells every other cheese by a substantial margin. That cheese is, of course, Velveeta. Apparently in a world of increasing culinary sophistication, it would be gauche, if not high-society list suicide, to admit a preference for a cheese of such low social standing. So the millions of Velveeta eaters remain in the closet, but the sales figures do not lie.

The lecture is the Velveeta of teaching methods. It is the most maligned of teaching techniques, yet it is the method of choice for better than 80% of college instructors today. How do we explain this apparent paradox? How can we account for the incredible longevity of this teaching method whose demise has been predicted on multiple occasions in centuries past and whose imminent death is ensured by today's technology clairvoyants? When printed books first appeared in the 16th century, it could be argued that the principal justification for the lecture as a means of imparting knowledge no longer existed, a claim made in James Boswell's (1791/1946) biography of Samuel Johnson, in which Johnson was quoted as saying, "I cannot see that lectures can do so much good as reading the books from which the lectures are taken" (p. 315). The more modern version of this view has been expressed by Maryellen Weimer (1988):

> We are at a point in history where we can say emphatically, if the lecture exists to transmit information, then the lecture has no real purpose. Information in published forms and databases can be far more current, far more comprehensive, and far more convenient than any lecture. (p. 1)

Now, 14 years later at the beginning of the 21st century, after several new generations of personal computers and an explosive growth of the Internet, we can surely make that statement even more emphatically. However, as Weimer and others know, the lecture continues to thrive because it does something more than just impart information. That "something more" is not always easy to define, which gives lecture bashers and lecture supporters plenty to debate.

In this chapter, it would be impossible to give a comprehensive overview of the lecture method in terms of dos and don'ts and certainly not a review of the extant scientific literature on lecturing. Such coverage already exists and for that the reader is encouraged to refer to Brown (1978), Davis (1993), Eble (1988), Banner and Cannon (1997), McKeachie (1999), and Tierney (1996). Instead, this chapter explores selected issues endemic to lecturing that are often problematic for the novice lecturer. I hope that by the end of this chapter you may have a fresh idea or two about the lecture and understand something of the reasons for the lecture's popularity and longevity.

LECTURE STYLE

Much has been written about the importance of lecture style, an admittedly ambiguous term related to personal characteristics of the lecturer (sense of humor, friendliness, optimism, honesty, creativity, etc.) and the manifestation of those characteristics in the delivery of the lecture. As the story goes, when the novice teacher asked the master, what are the three most important components of the lecture, the master replied, "delivery, delivery, delivery."

In the same way that personal characteristics of the psychotherapist are important in predicting patient recovery, regardless of method used, so too are such traits important in determining teaching effectiveness or at least teacher popularity as determined by student ratings. Beginning teachers often wrestle with their teaching style, or what Banner and Cannon (1997) called *teaching personality*. They pointed out a problem that can be disastrous:

> A trap young teachers often fall into is that of assuming "teaching personalities" that are not their own. . . . Acting may be an important technique of successful teachers, but the adoption of roles must always be deliberate and temporary—and always for good

effect. Teachers who assume permanent masks without realizing what they are doing are guilty of a kind of hypocrisy particularly offensive to the young, who show a remarkable talent for unmasking such deception. The classroom is not a stage, and those who feel obliged to assume different characters in order to be effective in it should probably not be teachers in the first place. (pp. 108–109)

I have observed such transformations in faculty members—one, for example, who is soft spoken outside of class but displays a classroom lecture style that borders on the histrionic. For a few teachers this Jekyll and Hyde strategy may work, but for most it signals certain failure.

Lectures are performances, and they should star you as you. I recall reading a newspaper article about a university in the Los Angeles area that was dismayed that its chemistry department faculty were getting poor teaching evaluations from students who often commented that the faculty lacked a sense of humor. Someone in the university administration decided to hire Hollywood comedy writers to provide some jokes for the chemistry professors to use in their classes (aren't college administrators hilarious?). I never read a follow-up to that story, but, like you, I think I know the outcome. In her discussion of the lecture, Weimer (1988) summarizes this issue quite well:

> The most effective "performing" is not a contrived act, but a genuine, authentic presentation of the person involved. If the "role" to be played *is the person you are*, you don't need to fear being false or not being up to the part. (p. 1)

Teachers need to be aware of their own traits and how they can be used to advantage in the classroom. Ultimately such self-knowledge is a critical variable in determining the cognitive strategies one would use in delivering a lecture (Weinstein & Meyer, 1991).

PASSION

Passion is sometimes included among those variables associated with lecture style or teaching personality. However, I have separated it because of its importance and because I view it to be independent of lecture style. That is, you could envision a number of lecture styles, any one of which might or might not involve passion as a component. Some writers (e.g., Weimer, 1993) prefer the term *enthusiasm* to *passion*, but whatever the term, the message is the same: It is critical for good lecturing.

Perhaps, it is this dimension that separates the adequate lecturers from the good and really great ones. I recall an anthropology professor from my undergraduate years who was enormously popular (his classes filled the first day of registration) despite that he rarely gave As in his classes. I took both of his undergraduate courses, made Bs in both of them, and sat in the front row (I had been told by another student to do that) every day, spellbound by his lectures. He was in his 60s, near retirement, and had taught those same two courses for more than 30 years. He had long since ceased his program of scholarly work, but he had not lost his passion for the subjects that he taught. He made us laugh and cry, and once I remember him crying, facing the board with his back to the class, his body trembling, and in a weak voice saying, "class dismissed," after which we filed out in silence, compassion, and awe for the humanity and integrity of this man. Mostly he made us think, and he made us care about issues beyond our own lives. I still think about some of those lectures today, almost 40 years later, and realize how they changed my life. It was his passion for his subject that made those lectures so memorable. As someone remarked about another great teacher, clearly students were "willing to venture the work for the sake of the zest" (Benjamin, 1991, p. 132).

It is difficult to imagine a lecture delivered with genuine passion (or enthusiasm) that would not be exciting to students. The flip side is that it is difficult to envision a lecture delivered without passion that would be interesting. I cannot imagine passion being faked in the classroom. Perhaps a few rare individuals could muster such a ruse, but for most lecturers the task is an impossible one.

Passion is not a personality trait; it is a feeling that is domain-specific. One might be passionate about baseball but wonder why sports pages bother to publish hockey scores. We all know introductory psychology instructors who omit assigning chapters in their text (and thus the accompanying lectures) that they deem uninteresting or unimportant, whereas they may expand the lecture coverage of those topics about which they are passionate. Such selection (unless carried to extremes) is desirable. Faculty should lecture on those topics about which they are most enthusiastic. Camille Wortman has done just that in her introductory psychology course:

> I knew at some level, that if I was not lecturing about something that was vital and involving for me, the lectures would not have high interest value for students. At that point, I decided that I would not try to cover the entire field of psychology in my lectures. I reasoned that this was why I had assigned a textbook. I began to see my job in the lectures as that of supplementing the textbook by covering topics that I wholeheartedly believed the students should know about. (Wortman & Smyth, 1997, p. 166)

Of course some faculty (e.g., those who teach six to eight preparations in a year) may not be able to exhibit genuine passion for all, or even most, of those subjects, as compared with faculty members who teach a few courses each year that are typically related to their research interests.

Presumably everyone has some subjects or issues about which they are passionate. Know what yours are and find ways to feature them in your lectures. You need to care about what you are teaching. Displaying that passion in your lectures leads to greater satisfaction for you and your students.

IDENTIFY CLEAR GOALS
FOR THE LECTURE

One of students' chief complaints about lectures is that the lecture objectives are never made clear. Weimer (1987) suggested that, "At the beginning of the lecture tell students outright where you are headed and how you intend to get there" (p. 5). I would add why you are going there.

Teachers should have overarching goals for their courses, and each class meeting should be planned to mesh with one or more of those goals. The goals for the course might include teaching content, teaching critical thinking, using writing to learn exercises, and connecting textbook content to everyday life experiences. Class days differ in which goals get covered and how much coverage they receive, but those overarching goals should be paramount in helping the instructor plan for each day.

As Weimer (1987) encouraged, begin the lecture with a clear statement of your goals for that day, ideally on the board or screen. You should spend a few minutes going over each one of them. Do not assume that the students know why you are covering the material that you have selected. Tell them why. That is, give them the rationale for your lesson plan. Explain briefly why you are going to cover the topics you have selected for that day. Proselytize for your goals of the day.

In her book on how to give effective lectures, Elizabeth Tierney (1996, quoting Andrew Grove) reminded us that, "How well we communicate is determined not by how well we say things, but by how well we are understood" (p. 10). To achieve that for your students, give them a context for the day's lesson. They will understand and enjoy the presentation more if you have shared with them your plan for what you hope to accomplish in the lecture as well as your reasons for the day's content and methods.

REMEMBER THAT LESS IS MORE

In observing beginning teachers over the years and in talking with colleagues who have taught for a decade or more, there are some evident changes in teaching practice that come with experience. One of the most obvious is a substantial reduction in the number of ideas the teacher chooses to present in lecture. Instead of covering acquisition, extinction, spontaneous recovery, generalization, discrimination, and 10 other conditioning concepts in a single lecture, you might use the lecture to show how reinforcement and punishment procedures are used in therapy, industry, or parenting. In this approach, you teach only a few concepts, perhaps two to four, and you elaborate on those concepts with multiple examples.

Some faculty assume that they cannot devote their lectures to such depth at the sacrifice of breadth. Like Camille Wortman, my assumption is that textbooks exist to provide breadth. Second, I assume that college students can and will read the book on their own. Making those assumptions allows me to use class time for whatever topics I (or the students) might choose (see Bernstein, 1997). I have a daily reading list for all of my classes and communicate the expectations that (a) I expect the reading to be done prior to class, (b) I will lecture on some topic related to the reading for that day, and (c) the reading will typically be important background in understanding the material to be covered in lecture.

To understand why less is better than more, think about a 20-page term paper you might assign. The best papers are always those that take a small topic and cover it in real depth. For the students who choose to tackle topics too large for the page limit, their papers seem superficial. There is no room for the kind of integration and analysis of ideas needed to make sense of the topic—in reading the paper you will be unable to determine whether the student understands the topic.

Lectures work the same way. Cover too much material in the allotted time and students take away very little from the class. Narrow the coverage, create a real focus for the lecture, elaborate on the ideas you are presenting—especially with examples that make sense in the lives of your students—and your students understand the ideas better and retain the information longer. As Casey Stengel said, "you could look it up." It is in the cognitive psychology literature.

The sad reality is that, even among experienced teachers, lectures are still packed with more than can be covered in the allotted hour—a fact that leads to hurried deletions, poor explanations, holding students beyond the ending time for the class, and failing to provide any summary for the lecture (more on this last issue later).

All topics are by definition too large for the class time available. The "lecturer's specific task, like the scholar's task at large, is to bring some part of knowledge too big in its unselected vastness . . . into a manageable form" (Eble, 1988, p. 75). The task is to select. As Eble (1988) noted, "wisdom is in part learning what to leave out" (p. 73). If you feel that you have to communicate to students all that you know about your discipline, you are in for a life of disappointment.

THE NEED FOR SPONTANEITY

Clearly, planning is important for lectures. Successful lecturers typically put in many hours of preparation for their classes. Beginning teachers sometimes write out their lectures in full, a few, perhaps, reading them in class. Such presentations, despite the planning, are not usually successful, nor are those rare teachers who write out their complete lectures and then memorize them for later recitation. Most teachers work from some kind of outline that seems to get abbreviated over the years to a few notecards of prompts for particular points to be made in the lecture.

"Preparing the lecture is important, but it must accommodate spontaneity as well as planning" (Eble, 1988, p. 72). Instructors must be willing to let go of some of their planning. Think about the message you send when you say to a student, "Well, that's an interesting question and it certainly relates to what we're talking about today, but we don't have time to go into that because I have other material I have prepared that I have to cover." As I said earlier, my experience with textbooks is that they tend to be encyclopedic; that is, they certainly cover the breadth of the subject. My class time is mine and the students to do as we please. If a digression prevents me from covering 75% of the lecture I had planned for that day, so be it.

There may be times when departures from the plan may not be desirable or feasible—for example, the class period before the exam that contains questions you have yet to cover. On the whole, however, good lecturers are willing and able to alter their plans when the need arises (see Benjamin, 1999). Be willing to take risks in class, to relinquish some of the control that a thoroughly scripted lecture may imply. Research has shown that such spontaneity is highly valued by students and associated with teachers whose students do well (Boice, 1996).

DO NOT LECTURE ALL THE TIME

In his book on teaching, Eble (1988) recalled that, in his student days in graduate school, he had "only two highly effective lecturers" (p. 69). I would echo that exact figure for my 4 undergraduate years. Like Eble, I do not remember most of the others (who probably performed adequately), and the few that I do recall were truly awful lecturers. If we can generalize these anecdotal data more broadly, they would suggest that most of us in college teaching are not maestros of the lectern. That may be a good reason to look for supplements (not necessarily replacements) to the lecture method, but it is not the only reason.

There is interesting research on student attention span and the lecture. When the lecture begins, most students are paying close attention unless previous experience with a particular lecturer has encouraged students to tune out early. Indeed, it is the time of optimal attention for the class in terms of the percentage of students attending. If they are going to be reached, the start of class is when it can best happen. According to research, for most students that attention lasts for about 10 minutes (McKeachie, 1999). Most readers can validate that finding from their own experience as listeners at conventions and departmental colloquia. Interestingly, it is paying attention that causes many students to shift their attention elsewhere. They listen to the lecturer who, after a short while, triggers an association for the listener who then gets carried away on a path of reverie elicited by that association. After that initial departure, students cycle in and out of the lecture, paying attention from time to time but drifting away frequently as well. At any one time, less than 50% of the class is likely attending to the lecture. So what can the lecturer do? The answer is to break up the lecture in ways that encourage students to maintain attention.

There are countless ways to break up a lecture, including brief demonstrations, activities, problem posting on the board, 1-minute writing assignments, video segments, small student discussion groups, and in-class Internet searches (perhaps to demonstrate how to get information for a question raised in class). The active learning literature in psychology is probably better than any other field, consisting of probably more than 1,000 published activities, including two series of psychology activities handbooks published by the American Psychological Association and Lawrence Erlbaum Associates (Benjamin & Lowman, 1981; Benjamin, Nodine, Ernst, & Blair-Broeker, 1999; Makosky, Sileo, Whittemore, Landry, & Skutley, 1990; Makosky, Whittemore, & Rogers, 1987; Ware & Johnson, 2000a, 2000b, 2000c). Thus, there should be one or more appropriate activities regardless of your lecture topic.

In addition to the use of various activities as ways to break up long lectures, think about constructing your lectures as mini-lectures, or what Hoover (1980) called *lecturettes*. Lecturettes might be 10 to 20 minutes in length. They can be used to foster discussion, writing, or other in- or out-of-class activities. Some of the topics for the lecturettes can even be student generated, with enough time, of course, for the instructor to prepare. I have developed a number of these for my classes over the years based on student questions: How is a child's understanding of humor related to its cognitive development? What happens to the nature of dream imagery in persons who suddenly lose their sight?

Robert Boice (1996) proposed breaking lectures into brief sections, with each section having a clear beginning and ending, perhaps separated by discussion or some other activity. He suggested that if you have three main ideas for a lecture, you might consider three mini-lectures, perhaps followed by a still shorter fourth mini-lecture that would integrate the ideas of the other three. In summary, the lesson is that unless you are one of those rare lecturers who can hold an audience spellbound, you would be wise to pace your lectures in some way that enhances student attention.

THE NEED FOR A SUMMARY

Earlier I talked about the importance of beginning the lecture with a clear exposition of the main ideas that would be covered and some explanation for why those particular ideas had been selected. The end of the lecture is a great place to remind students of what they should have learned. This obviously crucial component to any good lecture is about as common in the classroom as bluefin tuna are in the Missouri River. Why is this so? Likely you know the answer. My guess is that we do not offer a lecture summary because we are too busy at the end of class trying to mention the last critical idea or two that we did not get to cover. It does not take a genius to see the loss in such a misguided pedagogical practice. You have 3 minutes left in the class when you finish covering the second of your four points for the day. Your decision is either to spend those minutes summarizing the key points to be remembered from the main ideas already presented or rapidly cover the remaining two ideas. Surely that decision should be a "no brainer," but apparently not.

If you do not regularly provide a summary in your lectures, start now. Such a capstone is critical in maximizing learning in the lecture. If students come to expect such regular summaries of key ideas, they will be attentive at the end of the lecture knowing the importance of such integration for their own understanding, not to mention better grades.

WHY LECTURE?

Perhaps because so few lecturers are truly great ones, Eble (1988) wondered if "The best general advice to the teacher who would lecture well is still, 'Don't lecture' " (p. 68). But it is not the advice that Eble would give.

McKeachie (1999) asked this basic question: What are lectures good for? He cited the research evidence that shows that when measures of knowledge are used, the lecture is as efficient as other teaching methods. However, when the dependent variables are

> measures of retention of information after the end of a course, measures of transfer of knowledge to new situations, or measures of problem solving, thinking, or attitude change, or motivation for further learning, the results show differences favoring discussion methods over lecture. (McKeachie, 1999, p. 67)

Lectures can be very effective devices for communicating certain kinds of information, as McKeachie (1999) noted. They can provide integrative and evaluative accounts (the fruits of the lecturer in reducing that "unselected vastness to a manageable form") that may not be available in any printed or electronic version. Lectures can be models of critical thinking and problem solving that can teach students higher cognitive skills. Further, lectures have motivational functions. By challenging students' beliefs, lectures can motivate students to pursue further learning (McKeachie, 1999).

For years educators justified the lecture as a means of providing the maximum amount of information in the shortest amount of time. Whereas the invention of books did not seem to seriously challenge that claim, recent developments in computer technology have. I doubt that the current challenge will differ much from the earlier ones that forecast the end of the lecture. After World War II, some education specialists predicted that the lecturer would be replaced by films, later by teaching machines and programmed instruction, still later by computer-assisted instruction, and most recently by personal computers and the Internet. Although the current claim of imminent doom is yet to be tested, the fate of the earlier dire predictions suggest that this one, too, is overstated (Benjamin, 1988).

Eble (1988) argued that the lecture has persisted because "human beings remain responsive to all forms of intercourse with other consenting humans" (p. 69). Books and television and computers all lack a critical element as information devices, they lack "face-to-face confrontation with other talking, gesturing, thinking, feeling humans" (Eble, 1988, p. 69).

Of course the lecture is not the only teaching method that involves the students and teacher in face-to-face interactions. Other techniques, such as discussion methods, do that as well. But the lecture is unique in defining the role of teacher and student. The one-directional nature of this method (information flowing from teacher to student)—the characteristic that draws criticism from those who want students to play a more active role in their educational experiences—is arguably, and paradoxically, its strength. The lecture clearly acknowledges the scholarly authority of the teacher—an authority that most college students feel they have paid to see. It offers the teacher the best chance to illustrate the creativity, magic, and insight that are components of great lectures. It offers faculty the opportunity to inspire and students the opportunity to be moved, enlightened, or changed in dramatic ways.

Eble (1988) noted that "teachers everywhere enter into lecturing too lightly, pay too little attention to what good lectures might accomplish. They are even more remiss in failing to consider what makes up the skills of a really good lecturer" (p. 70). Because the lecture will likely continue as the dominant mode of instruction in higher education, at least for the foreseeable future, it is incumbent on faculty to take this activity more seriously. With the authority attached to the lecturer comes the awesome responsibility of stimulating the intellectual growth of students. So if you lecture, learn to do it well; if you do it well, learn to do it better. There are plenty of resources to help you, and the references in this chapter provide a good start.

REFERENCES

Banner, Jr., J. M., & Cannon, H. C. (1997). *The elements of teaching*. New Haven, CT: Yale University Press.

Benjamin, Jr., L. T. (1988). A history of teaching machines. *American Psychologist, 43,* 703–712.

Benjamin, Jr., L. T. (1991). *Harry Kirke Wolfe: Pioneer in psychology*. Lincoln: University of Nebraska Press.

Benjamin, Jr., L. T. (1999). A platform disaster: Harry Hollingworth and the psychology of public speaking. *Nebraska History, 81,* 67–73.

Benjamin, Jr., L. T., & Lowman, K. D. (Eds.). (1981). *Activities handbook for the teaching of psychology* (Vol. 1). Washington, DC: American Psychological Association.

Benjamin, Jr., L. T., Nodine, B. F., Ernst, R. M., & Blair-Broeker, C. (Eds.). (1999). *Activities handbook for the teaching of psychology* (Vol. 4). Washington, DC: American Psychological Association.

Bernstein, D. A. (1997). Reflections on teaching introductory psychology. In R. J. Sternberg (Ed.), *Teaching introductory psychology: Survival tips from the experts* (pp. 35–47). Washington, DC: American Psychological Association.

Boice, R. (1996). *First-order principles for college teachers: Ten basic ways to improve the teaching process*. Bolton, MA: Anker.

Boswell, J. (1946). *The life of Samuel Johnson.* Garden City, NY: Doubleday & Co. (Original work published in 1791).

Brown, G. (1978). *Lecturing and explaining.* New York: Methuen.

Davis, B. G. (1993). *Tools for teaching.* San Francisco: Jossey-Bass.

Eble, K. E. (1988). *The craft of teaching: A guide to mastering the professor's art* (2nd ed.). San Francisco: Jossey-Bass.

Hoover, K. H. (1980). *College teaching today: A handbook for postsecondary education.* Boston: Allyn & Bacon.

Makosky, V. P., Sileo, C. C., Whittemore, L. G., Landry, C., & Skutley, M. L. (Eds.). (1990). *Activities handbook for the teaching of psychology* (Vol. 3). Washington, DC: American Psychological Association.

Makosky, V. P., Whittemore, L. G., & Rogers, A. M. (Eds.). (1987). *Activities handbook for the teaching of psychology* (Vol. 2). Washington, DC: American Psychological Association.

McKeachie, W. J. (1999). *Teaching tips: Strategies, research, and theory for college and university teachers* (10th ed.). Boston: Houghton-Mifflin.

Tierney, E. P. (1996). *How to make effective presentations.* Thousand Oaks, CA: Sage.

Ware, M. E., & Johnson, D. E. (Eds.). (2000a). *Handbook of demonstrations and activities in the teaching of psychology: Vol. 1. Introductory, statistics, research methods, and history* (2nd ed.). Mahwah, NJ: Lawrence Erlbaum Associates.

Ware, M. E., & Johnson, D. E. (Eds.). (2000b). *Handbook of demonstrations and activities in the teaching of psychology: Vol. 2. Physiological-comparative, learning, cognition, and development* (2nd ed.). Mahwah, NJ: Lawrence Erlbaum Associates.

Ware, M. E., & Johnson, D. E. (Eds.). (2000c). *Handbook of demonstrations and activities in the teaching of psychology: Vol. 3. Personality, abnormal, clinical-counseling, social* (2nd ed.). Mahwah, NJ: Lawrence Erlbaum Associates.

Weimer, M. (1987). Changing complaints about lectures into compliments. *The Teaching Professor, 1*(2), 5.

Weimer, M. (1988). Lecturing: Performing or being? *The Teaching Professor, 2*(3), 1–2.

Weimer, M. (1993). *Improving your classroom teaching.* Newbury Park, CA: Sage.

Weinstein, C. E., & Meyer, D. K. (1991). Cognitive learning strategies and college teaching. In R. J. Menges & M. D. Svinicki (Eds.), *College teaching: From theory to practice* (pp. 15–26). San Francisco: Jossey-Bass.

Wortman, C. B., & Smyth, J. M. (1997). Using one's own passion and undergraduate TAs to transform the large-lecture introductory psychology course. In R. J. Sternberg (Ed.), *Teaching introductory psychology: Survival tips from the experts* (pp. 163–180). Washington, DC: American Psychological Association.

6

Humor and College Teaching

Howard R. Pollio
The University of Tennessee

A long time ago, Charles Osgood (1952) invented the semantic differential, a procedure designed to capture the meaning of all sorts of things in terms of adjectives such as *good–bad*, *active–passive*, and *strong–weak*. Over the years, Osgood's theory of semantic differentiation has been replaced by newer conceptions of meaning, although researchers still use semantic differential scales to describe people, objects, situations, and so on. To come now to the present case, suppose someone told you that he or she had ratings for individuals in some specific occupation and that the major defining adjectives were *wise*, *articulate*, *good*, *spontaneous*, *honest*, and *powerful*. Suppose he or she told you these adjectives also agreed with a more conceptual analysis of traits required for success in that profession. Now suppose he or she asked you to guess the profession: "Let's see, *articulate*, *wise*, *spontaneous*, *good*, *powerful*, and *honest*—why, that's me—a college professor in all of my academic virtue and glory."

Actually, these six adjectives do not describe college professors, but professional comedians, and each adjective derives from a different theory of comic art (Pollio & Theg-Talley, 1991). From psychoanalytic theory, comedy is about honesty and morality (good–bad); from existential theory, it is about spontaneity and flexibility; from cognitive theory, it is about being articulate and wise; and from social-comparison theory, it is about power and superiority. Although each theory assumes one or two principles as crucial, comedy seems better construed as a patterned gestalt capable of revealing one or another facet in specific performance situations. In fact, it is also only within comedy that a word like *fast* can refer to intellect, morality, spontaneity, and power.

Is it an accident that these adjectives apply both to standup comics and college professors? On the side of comedy, there is no problem. Comedians regularly describe themselves as teachers, doctors, or priests—in short, as individuals accepting the sacred task of confronting ignorance and immorality on the basis of a personally unique perspective on culture and its foibles (see Fisher & Fisher, 1982, for more on comedians' self-perceptions). If this is the case for comedy, why do some professors (and deans and legislators) find it disturbing that there might be a close affinity between teaching and humor?

Part of the answer, from the side of the professor, might be that we have a general distrust of humor and play and prefer the serious work of universities to be done by serious people—us. Play and humor are seen as distracting to intellectual activity, and comedy can be only a foil to the more intellectual matters of the classroom. A second reason might be that we do not know much about the role of humor in education. Although we have some information, it always seems suspect to take humor too seriously in any context, higher education included.

To evaluate what you know about humor in the college classroom, I have prepared an eight-item multiple-choice test. If you answer all of the following questions correctly, you definitely have a much higher "HQ" than most of your colleagues.

1. How many times per hour does the average class laugh?

   (a) 0   (b) 1–2   (c) 3–4   (d) 5–7   (e) 8 or more

2. What are favorite topics for humorous remarks?

   (a) clever word play   (b) hostility   (c) sex
   (d) a and b   (e) all of the above

3. What percentage of humorous remarks made by professor have a specific target?

   (a) 0–10%   (b) 11–20%   (c) 21–30%
   (d) 31–40%   (e) 41% and more

4. When they target, who do professors target most frequently?

   (a) themselves   (b) someone else in the class
   (c) someone not in the class   (d) a and b   (e) a and c

5. What percentage of classroom humor does not relate to the content of the lecture?

   (a) 0%   (b) 1–5%   (c) 6–15%   (d) 16–25%   (e) 26% or more

6. What percentage of classroom humor contributes to the major point of the lecture?

(a) 85%   (b) 65%   (c) 45%   (d) 25%   (e) 5%

7. Does humor help students remember classroom material?

(a) Yes!   (b) Yes   (c) Maybe   (d) No   (e) No!

8. Are funny students creative or just annoying?

(a) annoying   (b) creative   (c) neither   (d) both a and b

HOW MANY TIMES PER LECTURE DOES YOUR CLASS LAUGH?

If you selected three to four per lecture, you chose the average value for college professors teaching at a large state university (Bryant, Comisky, & Zillmann, 1979). This number does not tell the whole story. Some 20% of professors provoked no laughter, and 13% made the class laugh seven or more times. The largest single value was 16 per hour.

When Bryant and associates (1979) looked at what sorts of things we do to get laughs, they found 39% involved funny stories, followed by humorous remarks (18%), jokes (17%), puns (8%), and riddles (1%). To give you an idea of what your colleagues do in the classroom, consider the following examples:

Funny Story: A botany professor told the following anecdote. Dr. W. C. Coker, the famous botanist, was walking in the woods with one of his small nieces. Suddenly he stopped, picked up a mushroom, and gave it to the child as a snack. After a time, he asked how she felt. The child reported feeling fine. At this time, Dr. Coker remarked: "Good, we have another edible mushroom."

Humorous remark: The next specimen was contributed by a professor of anatomy: "The Pratt Museum has a Miocene shark jaw you could drive a Volkswagen bus through."

Joke: A professor of advertising produced the following gem: Two ulcers stopped to exchange greetings on Madison Avenue. Sighed one, "I feel terrible. I must be getting an advertising man."

Pun: A professor of English told the following story: It seems Shakespeare suddenly felt an unusual chill and asked a friend to check the seat of his trousers. Upon closer inspection, the colleague reported, "No holes, Bard."

Riddle: A physicist told this one: "What weighs the same no matter what size it is?" Answer: "A hole."

With these examples mercifully behind us, let us move to the safer confines of numbers and ask how frequently laughter occurs in other teaching/learning contexts. Goodrich, Henry, and Goodrich (1954) examined humorous comments during psychiatric training sessions at a teaching hospital. Within this context, there were seven or so humorous remarks per each 75-minute session, or four to five per 50 minutes. Sociologist Rose Coser (1960) also evaluated case presentations in a didactic medical setting and recorded about five laughs for each of twenty, 50-minute sessions.

As a point of comparison, Scogin and Pollio (1980) recorded laughter-eliciting events in natural settings ranging from senior citizens playing pool to participants in a college growth group. Some rates, per 50 minutes, were as follows: 20.5 for pool playing, 44.0 for growth groups, and 38.0 for college students solving problems in a laboratory. It seems clear that three or four laughs per 50-minute lecture hour is less than any of these values. Could it be: (a) professors are not funny, (b) professors do not value laughter, (c) laughter is not a welcome guest in the college lecture hall, or (d) all of the above?

WHAT ARE FAVORITE TOPICS
FOR CLASSROOM HUMOR?

Bryant et al. (1979) reported that 13% of all lecture humor is sexual in nature. As an example, consider the following anecdote by a history professor concerning (false) stories told about Abraham Lincoln: "Mr. Lincoln attended a charity bazaar and tendered a twenty-dollar bill in payment for a bunch of violets. Receiving no change, he reached over the counter to pat the woman's breasts. 'What are these my dear?' he requested. 'Why, Mr. Lincoln, they're breasts.' 'I'm relieved,' he replied, 'everything is so high around here, I thought they might be your buttocks.'

Hostile humor accounted for 32% of responses, including the following remark by a public health instructor: "He never has a hangover, he stays drunk." Thus, some 45% of lecture humor is not innocent, playful, or nice. Although 55% of humorous remarks do involve word play, it seems fair to conclude that sex and hostility, combined with word play, are the major topics for humor in the college classroom. Although you can take humor to college, you cannot make it behave more than 50% of the time.

DOES CLASSROOM HUMOR
HAVE A TARGET?

A number of years ago, Scogin and Pollio (1980) found that laughter-producing remarks could be coded into two categories having little to do with content: whether the remark did or did not have a specifiable target. After recording humorous events in six different natural settings involving over 1,300 events, targeted remarks varied from 39% to 89%, with an overall average of 70%. What initially interested us was that the largest number occurred in situations in which participants knew one another and the smallest number when they were strangers. Although the latter finding makes some sense (people who do not know one another are not likely to target each other), the finding for friends was interpreted to mean that what looks like a targeted put-down to an outside observer might not be experienced as such when it takes place between two friends.

There is one situation, however, in which people know one another and in which the targeting remark is a put-down: settings having a clear social hierarchy. The best study of such a setting was reported by Coser (1960), who evaluated the origin and target of humor in psychiatric training sessions. Of 90 remarks having a target, Coser found that 53 were made by senior medical staff, 33 by junior medical staff, and 4 by paramedical staff. This result occurred despite that junior staff spoke more often than anyone else because most sessions concerned case presentations by them.

Who were the targets of these remarks? Of 53 senior staff remarks, 22 were directed at junior staff, 4 at themselves, 4 at other senior staff, and 14 at no one in the situation. Of the 33 junior staff remarks, 14 were directed at patients, 12 at themselves, 2 at senior staff (but only when the person was absent), and 5 were untargeted. Thus, persons at the top of the hierarchy use humor more often than persons below them and tend to target themselves and their peers much less frequently than persons lower in the hierarchy. Although witty remarks may do many positive things, they are nowhere near as benign in hierarchical groups as in less hierarchical ones.

How do these results compare with directed remarks made in college and university lectures? Table 6.1 presents results from a number of contexts, including the lecture hall. The top row presents values for lectures; the bottom row presents a variety of other teaching and nonteaching contexts. The first significant result concerns the total proportion of directed remarks. Starting from the right, we note that college lecture humor did not have a specifiable target in 14% of the cases in comparison with 30% for other contexts. For two of the three target groups—self and

TABLE 6.1
Comparison of Targets: Colleges Lectures and Other Contexts

	Nature of Target									
	Self*			Other in Situation			General Other			Non-Targeted	Total Number of Incidents
Setting	+	−	Σ	+	−	Σ	+	−	Σ		
College lectures	.09	.26	.35	.03	.12	.15	.12	.24	.36	.14	234
Other contexts	.07	.14	.21	.11	.20	.31	.04	.13	.17	.30	1312

*Note. + means positive, − means negative.

general other—college lectures lead by a wide margin. For the category other-in-situation, however, values are reversed: Here lecturers target people in the lecture hall about half as often as in other contexts. When we examined whether targeted remarks were positive or negative across all settings, negative remarks predominated by a margin of 2:1. Although professors may be in a superior position vis-à-vis students, negatively targeted student put-downs account for only 12% of humorous remarks in the lecture hall. The majority of negatively targeted remarks, however, was aimed at the self or some person, idea, or concept not in the present setting, suggesting humor is used in a more self-effacing way in the classroom than elsewhere. Although college lecture humor may deflate many things, only infrequently is it the student.

WHAT PERCENT OF HUMOR RELATES TO LECTURE CONTENT AND WHAT PERCENT CONTRIBUTES TO ITS EDUCATIONAL POINT?

Of 234 laughter-evoking events studied by Bryant et al. (1979), 54% were judged to be *extremely related* to content and 18% as *not at all related*. Although 45% of such remarks were seen as contributing to the educational point and only 6% as distracting from it, fully 49% were judged as neither contributing to nor distracting from the educational point.

As one example of related humor, consider the following story used by Ziv (1988) to illustrate that correlation between two variables does not mean one causes the other:

> On a planet whose inhabitants had just discovered earth and who were invisible to earthlings, experts decided to study the behavior of humans. One of them planned to conduct a study on differences between fat and thin people. He went to a cafeteria and watched and noted the coffee-drinking patterns of those coming in. He noted carefully the behavior, calculated correlations on his data, and found a positive significant relation. He reported: "There is a positive correlation between coffee drinking and body weight. Fat people mostly drink coffee with 'Sweet and Low,' thin people mostly with sugar. Conclusion: Sugar makes humans thin, while 'Sweet and Low' fattens them." (p. 9)

Building on this point and other anecdotes and cartoons carefully related to lecture content, Ziv (1988) developed a teaching-with-humor approach involving three steps: (a) the teacher first presents the concept in a relatively straightforward way; (b) the concept is then illustrated by a preselected cartoon or anecdote; and (c) after laughter subsides, the teacher paraphrases the concept presented in steps (a) and (b). Teaching teachers to use humor in this way, Ziv (1988) was able to demonstrate significant differences in learning between students taught by this procedure and students not taught in this way. The absolute difference in final exam score was impressive—on the order of 10 points—suggesting that humor, used judiciously, does improve student learning and recall.

Although Ziv (1988) was careful to use only related humor, we are still left with spontaneously produced humor: What role does it play in the college classroom? Perhaps the best way to think about such remarks concerns the fact that college lectures are multilevel events. Not only are they designed to transmit information, but they also are sociopersonal events very much in the present tense. Two of the more obvious ongoing issues in any class concern whether the material is understood and whether the student (or professor) is bored. Even when students try to be polite, there are tell-tale signs (fidgeting, reading the paper, etc.) that let us know when a threshold of either misunderstanding or boredom has been exceeded.

There are clear ways to deal with misunderstanding. For example, the student or lecturer asks a question. Although there are many ways to signal boredom, there are only a few ways to dispel it, humor being one of the best. Hence, a laughter-eliciting remark may be seen as an attempt to handle a problematic aspect of the lecture, and laughter is the students' response of having understood, and of accepting, the lecturer's attempt to change tone. Many years ago, Bergson (1928/1990) noted that "Laughter always implies a kind of secret freemasonry, or even complicity, with other laughters" (p. 4), and both the student and lecturer give evidence of such social connection every time they share a moment in laughter.

DOES HUMOR HELP STUDENTS LEARN AND RECALL COURSE CONTENT?

Part of the reason (so we tell ourselves) for using humor is to increase attention, promote learning, and help students recall material better. On the negative side, Singer and Singer (1979) argued that laughter may disrupt the students' rehearsal of material, thereby making it difficult to move information from immediate to long-term memory. Another negative possibility is that students may miss subsequent parts of the lecture if they are still laughing at a humorous remark. Finally, some nay-sayers such as Singer and Singer even suggest that humor may create a frivolous mood incompatible with real college learning.

In response to such unsmiling prophets of educational doom, many researchers have suggested that humor can have positive effects particularly if related to content. For example, Kaplan and Pascoe (1977) played four different video lectures to over 500 undergraduates. One version of the tape used humor directly related to six concepts that would later be tested, a second version contained humor unrelated to these same six concepts, and a third contained humor related only to three of the concepts and unrelated to the remaining three. A final, nonhumor version provided baseline values. In addition, five other items were presented in a nonhumorous way to all four groups. To evaluate differences among groups, two different multiple-choice tests were given: one immediately after the lecture and a second 6 weeks later.

The results from the first test indicate no difference among the four groups on all 11 items, although students in the nonhumor group scored better on nonhumorous items. The second test produced a different pattern: Students showed no difference in recall of the five serious items and significantly better recall for the six humorous ones. Does humor facilitate learning? The answer is "yes" if we look at recall a month and a half after learning. The answer is "no" if we look at recall tested immediately after presentation.

Distraction is the general principle used to make sense of these and other similar results. Humor, especially unrelated humor, is thought to distract students from course content, thereby making it less likely for them to learn material presented in class. For this type of explanation, humor facilitates learning only if it directs students to the material. This conclusion seems reasonable in light of results presented by Ziv (1988), who found significant facilitation for humorous materials used to exemplify concepts when they were embedded in a sequence having direct instruction precede and follow the humorous example. The best answer to whether humor facilitates learning would seem to be: "Yes, maybe, No, It depends."

ARE FUNNY STUDENTS CREATIVE OR ANNOYING?

According to Koestler (1964), humor and creativity both depend on an individual's ability to combine different domains of information or knowledge. For certain creative acts, such as in music and art, relevant combinations are assumed to occur under motivational systems described as self-transcendent. For other creative combinations, such as in humor, they are assumed to occur under motivational systems best described as self-assertive. In both cases, Koestler assumed the core conceptual act is similar.

Starting from a less theoretical perspective, Getzels and Jackson (1962) noted that creative adolescents not only had "a good sense of humor," but also were humorous in dealing with teachers and peers. Compared with students who were judged less creative but of equal or greater IQ, creative adolescents tended to use a good deal of humor in imaginative stories. In agreement with Koestler (1964), such stories contained more aggressive themes than were found in stories written by students of equal intelligence but of lower creative ability.

A small number of studies concerning younger children also report positive relations between humor and creativity. For example, Weisberg and Springer (1961) conducted interviews with fourth graders and their parents and found that having a sense of humor was positively related to scores on standard tests of creativity. In a study of kindergarten children, Lieberman (1977) found that teacher ratings of humor correlated with scores on three different creativity tasks. Hauck and Thomas (1972) reported a positive relation between creativity test scores and peer nominations of funny students in late elementary school children. Finally, McGhee (1976, 1979) found that creativity indexes for 6- to 11-year-old children predicted both teacher and observer ratings of humor.

Although these studies suggest a relationship between humor and creativity, they have two possible limitations: (a) they depend on indirect measures of humor production such as teacher ratings, and (b) they deal with children not yet at the proper intellectual stage to evaluate Koestler's hypothesis. To overcome some of these limitations, Fabrizi and Pollio (1987) observed adolescents in a college-bound 11th-grade high school honors class to determine which students actually made other students laugh. Students in this class also were rated by teachers, peers, and outside observers as to how humorous they thought these students were. In addition, teachers rated students on creative ability, and students completed a test of creative thinking. Students also answered a self-report test to assess self-concept.

Participants in this study agreed as to who was or was not a *funny* student. Teachers agreed with students, and both agreed with counts of how many times specific students made others laugh. When other information concerning these students was considered, results indicated that they got good grades, were popular with peers, and scored well on both self-concept and creativity scales. So far, so good: Funny students are productive, creative, and well liked. Because Fabrizi and Pollio (1987) were interested in developmental issues, they also considered results for seventh graders. Although raters, teachers, and peers were still able to agree on who was (was not) funny, funny 13-year-olds tended to not do well in school, be reprimanded by teachers, show average scores on tests of creativity, and have relatively negative self-concepts. The lack of correlation between humor and creativity for seventh graders and the positive correlation for eleventh graders suggest that being humorous has a different meaning for different age children. Seventh-grade students who are humorous are neither creative nor self-satisfied, whereas eleventh graders who are humorous tend to be both creative and well liked.

The view that humor relates differently to creative ability and self-esteem in students of different ages also finds some support from a study of professional comedians. Fisher and Fisher (1982) noted that being a professional comedian as an adult (or a funny kid when in school) frequently related both to feelings of low self-esteem and to finding school a confining experience. Such experiences occurred even though adult comedians (and comic children) have IQs considerably higher than average. Professional comedians, and their comic child counterparts, seem to embody many of the major issues involved in relating humor to creativity: Being funny may be a sign of creativity in a well-functioning and self-assured person, of acting out in a not so well-functioning or not so self-assured person, or of a potentially creative and bright person in conflict with the demands of his or her contemporary social world.

CONCLUSION

Usually a test ends when the answers are given and explained. This test is a little different because it is meant as much to pose a question as provide an answer, and the question is this: What attitude should I as a college professor take toward humor in the classroom? Should I find it a distracting intrusion or a liberating tonic? As usual, an answer does not come simply from knowledge of the facts. Rather, it depends equally on our attitudes concerning the role and purpose of higher education. It also asks us to consider, at least implicitly, what we consider as uniquely human in our students and ourselves.

These are heavy questions for such a seemingly frivolous topic as humor. The answer each of us provides, however, offers a clue to our views of education and people. Although each person must decide for him or herself, it seems proper to consider two quite respectable and contrasting understandings of the roles laughter and humor play in human life. One understanding comes from Thomas Hobbes, who described laughter in the following terms:

> Sudden glory is the passion which maketh those Grimaces called LAUGHTER (and is caused either by some sudden act of their own, that pleaseth them; or by the apprehension of some deformed thing in another, by comparison whereof they suddenly applaud themselves). And it is incident most to them, that are conscious of the fewest abilities in themselves; who are forced to keep themselves in their own favour, by observing the imperfections of other men. And . . . much laughter at the defects of others, is a signe of Pusillanimity. . . . For of great minds, one of the proper workes is, to help and free others from scorn; and compare themselves only with the most able. (cited in Gruner, 1978, p. 30)

A different understanding derives from Koestler (1964) some three centuries later:

> Humor is the only domain of creative activity where a stimulus on a high level of complexity produces a massive and sharply defined physical response. . . . This paradox enables us to use the response as an indicator for the presence of that elusive quality, the comic, which we are seeking to define. . . . Since the comic is related to other, more exalted, forms of creativity, this backdoor approach promises to yield positive results. We all know that there is only one step from the sublime to the ridiculous; the more surprising that psychology has not considered the possible gains which could result from the reversal of that step. (pp. 31–32)

So now that the facts and some of the theories are in, what do they add up to? First, it seems clear that every classroom has two different types of things going on in it: one concerning its socioemotional climate and the other its content. Usually humor and laughter are assigned to the first category and learning to the second. In the case of related humor, both streams coalesce, and a good joke catches the content and provides a vital image. We all know the pedagogical usefulness of such events, and they show up in empirical studies as facilitating learning and recall.

What about the spontaneously funny event that just happens? Although it is tempting to relate it to the socioemotional stream, and thereby assign it a lesser educational status, there seems to be a more significant possibility—namely, that a spontaneously funny remark models professorial risk—after all, the instructor did not prepare such a remark, but created it on the spot. Risk taking always seems a good value to promote in our classrooms lest students come to the conclusion that everything is prescripted and known. Attempts at funny remarks—even those that fail—indicate a kind of courage in confronting the established order, and it was probably for reasons of this sort that Orwell characterized jokes as *little revolutions*.

A second consequence to spontaneous humor is that it keeps the class alert and offers a bit of presentness to both student and teacher. A long time ago, Edwin Guthrie (1959), in the language of stimulus–response psychology, pointed out that to learn a connection one had to notice it first. What humor does is help both the student and professor note things. It also encourages the student to come to class, confident that his or her professor will also show up, not some disinterested person reciting prepackaged notes. Students have a right to expect us to appear, and humor is one sure way in which we indicate our presence. Student laughter at a humorous remark indicates that they, too, decided to show up, and these conclusions take place in a learning environment made engaging by humorous connection.

What about the professor who is not funny, who does not feel comfortable in being or trying to be funny? He or she would seem to have two options: (a) use cartoons, jokes, or other preplanned events in the manner suggested by Ziv (1988), or (b) seek the virtue of presentness in other ways— compelling enthusiasm for one's discipline, probing questions to which the instructor does not have the answer, or committing to preparation that allows for those wonderful moments in the classroom where we feel so comfortable and good that humor and laughter are not a struggle, but a natural consequence of the delight we feel in our disciplines and our students.

One additional piece of business still remains: If teachers and comedians share a number of personal characteristics, what makes one a professor and the other a comedian? Pollio (1996), in a piece dealing with differences between metaphor and humor (and secondarily between poets and comedians), noted that humor emphasizes the boundary separating two ideas joined by a joke, whereas metaphor seeks to overcome the boundary and provide a new and revealing combination of the ideas joined by the figure. This same conclusion may be applied to professors. Whereas comedy enables us to see a boundary, it is only the poet or professor who seeks to provoke a new understanding. Although perhaps it is too much to expect each and every class to produce a little revolution in thought, it is not too much to expect us to keep this possibility in mind each and every time we step into the sacred precincts of the college classroom.

REFERENCES

Bergson, H. (1928/1990). *Laughter: An essay on the meaning of the comic*. New York: Macmillan.

Bryant, J., Comisky, P. W., & Zillman, D. (1979). Teachers' humor in the college classroom. *Communication Education, 28,* 110–118.

Coser, R. (1960). Laughter among colleagues. *Psychiatry, 23,* 81–95.

Fabrizi, M. S., & Pollio, H. R. (1987). Are funny children creative? *Psychological Reports, 38,* 751–761.

Fisher, S., & Fisher, R. (1982). *Pretend the world is funny and forever*. Hillsdale, NJ: Lawrence Erlbaum Associates.

Getzels, J. W., & Jackson, P. W. (1962). *Creativity and intelligence*. New York: Wiley.

Goodrich, A. J., Henry, J., & Goodrich, D. W. (1954). Laughter in psychiatric staff conferences: A socio-psychiatric analysis. *Journal of Orthopsychiatry, 24,* 175–184.

Guthrie, E. R. (1959). Association by contiguity. In S. Koch (Ed.), *Psychology, a study of a science* (pp. 158–195). New York: McGraw-Hill.

Gruner, C. R. (1978). *Understanding Laugher: The workings of wit and humor*. Chicago: Nelson-Hall.

Hauck, W. E., & Thomas, J. W. (1972). The relationship of humor to intelligence, creativity, and intentional and incidental learning. *Journal of Experimental Education, 40,* 52–55.

Kaplan, R. M., & Pascoe, G. C. (1977). Humorous lectures and humorous examples: Some effects on comprehension and retention. *Journal of Educational Psychology, 89,* 61–65.

Koestler, A. (1964). *The act of creation*. London: Hutchinson.

Lieberman, J. N. (1977). *Playfulness: Its relationships to imagination and creativity*. New York: Academic Press.

McGhee, P. E. (1976). Sex differences in children's humor. *Journal of Communication, 26,* 176–185.

McGhee, P. E. (1979). *Humor: Its origin and development*. San Francisco: W. H. Freeman.

Osgood, C. E. (1952). The nature and measurement of meaning. *Psychological Bulletin, 49,* 197–237.

Pollio, H. R. (1996). Boundaries in humor and metaphor. In J. Mio & A. Ketz (Eds.), *Metaphor: Implications and applications* (pp. 231–253). Mahwah, NJ: Lawrence Erlbaum Associates.

Pollio, H. R., & Theg-Talley, J. (1991). The concepts and language of comic art. *Humor, 4,* 1–22.

Scogin, F. J., & Pollio, H. R. (1980). Targeting and the humorous episode in group process. *Human Relations, 33,* 831–852.

Singer, J. L., & Singer D. G. (1979, March). Comeback, Mr. Rogers, comeback. *Psychology Today, 56,* 59–60.

Weisberg, P. S., & Springer, K. J. (1961). Environmental factors in creative function. *Archives of General Psychiatry, 5,* 64–74.

Zillmann, S. D., & Bryant, J. (1983). Uses and effects of humor in educational ventures. In P. E. McGhee & J. H. Goldstein (Eds.), *Handbook of humor research* (Vol. II, pp. 173–193). New York: Springer.

Ziv, A. (1988). Teaching and learning with humor: Experiment and replication. *The Journal of Experimental Education, 57,* 5–15.

7

Process/Pedagogy

Thomas V. McGovern
Arizona State University West

McKeachie (1987) began his autobiographical narrative "Teaching, Teaching, Teaching, and Research on Teaching" in this way:

> I propose to reflect on my 40 years of teaching and to try to identify what I have learned. I suspect that the things that I have learned are already familiar to many experienced teachers. In fact, I find from time to time that I learn again something that I had learned years ago and forgotten. (p. 135)

In "Valediction from Traveler's Rest," Brewer (1996) launched his reflections in this way:

> What we call the beginning is often the end
> And to make an end is to make a beginning.
> The end is where we start from. (p. 205)

It was the 25th anniversary of my first semester as a teacher of psychology when I wrote this chapter. Turning points are apt moments for reflection, and I took inspiration from what Charles Brewer and Bill McKeachie prompted me to think about over the years. In the first decade of my academic career, Charles

81

taught me how to be more precise in my language and more historical in my perspectives. "Strive for felicity of expression," he always advised. Beginning in the second decade, after reading his research on teaching, I worked with Bill on two undergraduate curriculum projects. He taught me how to link cognitive processes and teaching.

This chapter is about the discovery of pedagogical processes that I can now call my own. What we know, however, about the construction of any autobiographical text is that it is an act of writing fiction, creating unified meanings about choices that become more deliberate in retrospect than they were at the time. What we call *faculty development* means to "learn again something that I had learned years ago and forgotten."

After defining terms, I reflect on my first 10 years at Virginia Commonwealth University (VCU). At that research university with APA accredited doctoral programs in counseling and clinical psychology, I constructed a pedagogy to use with graduate and undergraduate students in a variety of scientific and practitioner courses. Then in 1986, the assessment movement arrived at Virginia universities. I coordinated projects designed to identify learning outcomes for undergraduate general education programs. This assignment changed my focus from faculty pedagogy to student learning. Since 1990, at Arizona State University West (ASU West), I have worked only with undergraduate students in an interdisciplinary studies environment. This context enabled me to examine the cognitive processes of teaching and learning that are common to many disciplinary, interdisciplinary, and multicultural fields of study.

Although this is a personal narrative, its theme is generalizable. Process/pedagogy requires always being an amiable skeptic about teaching and learning.

DEFINITIONS

Process was introduced to the English language between the 12th and 15th centuries. According to *Webster's Ninth New Collegiate Dictionary* (1990), it is "a natural phenomenon marked by gradual changes that lead toward a particular result (synonymous with growth); a series of operations conducing to an end" (p. 937). In 1814, the British made the noun into a verb: "to move in a procession" (p. 938), no doubt in anticipation of Sir Edward Elgar and the strains heard at commencements. *Pedagogy* can be traced to 1583 as "the art, science, or profession of teaching" (p. 866).

The two words are steeped in the rich historical traditions of Renaissance and Reformation. Yet using these two words in departmental meetings evokes responses from arts and sciences colleagues ranging from disdain to vitriol. Why?

Having studied the history of the undergraduate curriculum in America, my hypothesis is that psychology faculty link our discipline's identity to a content-rich knowledge base and particular scientific methods (McGovern & Brewer, 2002).

For academics, discussions about process are more apt for practitioner (subtext = less scientific) meetings. Discussions about pedagogy (subtext = K–12 education) are throwbacks to the first half of the 20th century, when undergraduate psychology was taught as a service for elementary school teachers in training.

At the end of the 20th century, discussions about process/pedagogy returned to higher education. There is a renewed commitment to undergraduate teaching in research universities, with changing definitions of scholarship linked to pedagogy (Halpern et al., 1998). There are continuing demands by accrediting groups and state legislatures for assessment of student learning. Active learning is no longer innovative, but essential, in responding to changing values and learning styles of new generations of adult and technology-literate students. Old-fashioned liberal arts values are important once again to employers of baccalaureates. Academics have responded with renewed scholarly and instructional emphases on writing across the curriculum (Nodine, 1990) and critical thinking (Halpern & Nummedal, 1995) activities.

DEVELOPING PEDAGOGY

For my first 10 years as a teacher, I focused primarily on pedagogy because I knew very little about the content of psychology. Teaching Introductory Psychology for the first time, 12 years after receiving my Ph.D., was a humbling experience.

I was an undergraduate theology and philosophy major trained by the Jesuits at Fordham University and took only one course in undergraduate psychology from Father Henryk Misiak. He welcomed me into his senior year, psychology major, capstone course in History and Systems because I had already taken two seminars and an independent study project on John Dewey. The philosopher/psychologist captured me by his approach to progressive education, art, democracy, and social change; then I read about his reflex arc.

In 1972, I was admitted into an APA accredited program in Counseling Psychology at Southern Illinois University in Carbondale. These were the days before a degree in undergraduate psychology or a core curriculum in scientific psychology was required. I was trained to be a group psychotherapist and vocational counselor within an emotionally and behaviorally demanding, process-oriented, humanistic curriculum. At graduation, my breadth and depth in psychological science warranted the warning label of *Ph.D. light*. My first department chair at VCU was a statistician who liked my enthusiasm for program development and for teaching undergraduates, but judged that my knowledge of psychology content and my research expertise were seriously deficient. He was confident that the Jesuits had taught me how to think, and judicious course assignments and a catholic reading program would solve my problem of a sparse psychological education.

My undergraduate courses included Theories of Personality, Adjustment, and Group Dynamics. My graduate courses included Career Development Theory and

Practice, Group Psychotherapy Theory and Practice, and Ethical Principles. Later, as Director of Undergraduate Studies, I offered a regular practicum for graduate students in Teaching of Psychology and for undergraduate students in Peer Advising. My interdisciplinary interests were satisfied by teaching special topics courses during the summer sessions in Psychology and Religious Experience and Racial Awareness Training Groups. These teaching responsibilities enabled me to craft a pedagogy that effectively synthesized course material with the group therapy principles and counseling skills I learned while in graduate school. In retrospect, two principles were paramount.

Principle 1

I conceptualized the classroom as a space where students learn from the teacher and from one another. In their study of Stanford college students taking experiential learning courses, Lieberman, Yalom, and Miles (1973) recommended that

> leaders abandon a Ptolemaic conception of the process of change. Change does not revolve around the solitary sun of the leader; the evidence is strong that psychosocial relations in the group play an exceedingly important role in the process of change. (p. 428)

In my classrooms, this principle was implemented by what we now label as *active learning* strategies. Students analyzed text material via class discussions and synthesized their understandings via multiple essay assignments that had peer reviews as a critical element.

Principle 2

This same study, as well as Yalom's (1975) insightful work on how learning takes place in group psychotherapy, concluded that the most effective outcomes were linked to four basic leadership functions: caring, emotional stimulation, cognitive meaning-attribution, and executive function. Participants learn most effectively when a leader responds to them with empathy and as unique individuals. It is important to shape an environment that stimulates energetic expression and intellectual reflection in a predictable, structured, and safe manner. For example, in my classrooms and on course-specific evaluation forms, I emphasized the communication of empathy and respect for individual differences, group discussions that fostered conflict and the animated expression of a wide array of opinions, a critical ideas versus exhaustive coverage approach to course content, and setting clear expectations for how we would spend class time or how writing assignments would be evaluated.

These two principles—participants learn from one another and manifesting the four essential leadership functions—were incredibly powerful for me. Adhering conscientiously to them produced excellent student ratings, high enrollments, and

alumni who continued to write to me years after their graduations. These two pedagogical principles remain as touchstones in my annual evaluations and continuing
reflections about faculty development.

Two colleagues at VCU were more scientifically trained. Jack Corazzini was
the Director of University Counseling Services. We fashioned a graduate training
specialization in group counseling and psychotherapy that required course work
on classical group dynamics research, supervised practica, and a design for a
research or evaluation study. Don Forsyth, a social psychologist and outstanding
undergraduate teacher, taught the Group Dynamics seminar and introduced me to
the empirical traditions of group leadership studies. He exposed me to the research
on task versus relationship leadership styles, then to situational leadership theory
in which the developmental stages of a group are taken into consideration when
choosing appropriate interventions. Working on this training sequence helped me
understand the empirical bases for what had been working so well experientially.

ASSESSMENT

When VCU received a mandate from the state to assess undergraduate student
learning, the Provost shrewdly transformed an obligation into an opportunity for
faculty to discuss what they expected from general education courses. An easier
approach would have been to concentrate on major field content knowledge, but
he knew that would allow faculty not to talk to one another across disciplinary and
college boundaries. Instead, assessment became a catalyst to explore common de-
nominators that could be measured and then to identify specific courses to achieve
these outcomes. We started with existing university requirements in writing, mathematics, science, social science, and humanities, and then we added two consensus
areas of general education importance—values and multicultural experiences. The
Provost asked me to coordinate the 50 faculty members who volunteered for this
university-wide project, which I called, "The Varieties of Undergraduate Experience," borrowing somewhat mischievously from William James' classic text on the
psychology of religion. As Project Director, I learned the cultures, assumptions, and
pedagogical practices of the disciplines and professional schools at the university.

During this assessment period, I first met Bill McKeachie. The American
Psychological Association (APA) participated in an Association of American
Colleges (AAC) Project on Liberal Learning, Study-in-Depth, and the Arts and
Sciences Major. Faculty representatives from learned societies in biology,
economics, history, interdisciplinary studies, mathematics, philosophy, physics,
political science, psychology, sociology, religion, and women's studies met over a
2-year period. The reports addressed the characteristics of undergraduate students
in the major, common goals for the curriculum, measurement and evaluation of
major field outcomes, structure of the major field requirements, and nature of student learning and self-evaluation. The APA asked Laurel Furumoto, Diane Halpern,

Greg Kimble, Bill McKeachie, and me to work on this project. I was appointed chair of the group by the APA; the AAC's designation was for me to be the scribe. For 2 years, I listened attentively to Greg argue with Laurel, mediated by Bill, about the philosophical roots of the discipline's methodologies, and to Diane and Bill make elegant connections between cognitive psychology, learning, curriculum, and pedagogy, with feminist, historical commentary provided by Laurel. It was one of the most profound learning experiences for me as a psychologist.

In the final report (McGovern, Furumoto, Halpern, Kimble, & McKeachie, 1991), we identified eight goals for undergraduate psychology: knowledge base, thinking skills, language skills, information-gathering and synthesis skills, research methods and statistical skills, interpersonal skills, history of psychology, and ethics and values. Working with interdisciplinary colleagues on the whole project disposed us to suggest broadly defined goals, important "in spite of the diversity of settings in which the undergraduate degree is completed" (McGovern et al., 1991, p. 601). A fresh look at pedagogy was required, and I suggested the following:

> How does our field look from the point of view of the learner? . . . We want to build a cognitive science upon which teaching is based, and we cannot leave it to the specialists alone, good as they may be. We the teachers, as *clinicians of cognitive science* in our classrooms, need to articulate what we do. (McGovern et al., 1991, p. 603; italics added)

With Bill and the others as tutors, I was beginning to understand more fully what this observation meant.

BEYOND PEDAGOGY TO PROCESS

In his article on the validity of student ratings, McKeachie (1997) said that if asked to consult with a faculty member who received poor marks, he might say:

> Effective teaching is not just a matter of finding a method that works well and using it consistently. Rather, teaching is an interactive process between the students and the teacher. Good teaching involves building bridges between what is in your head and what is in the students' heads. What works for one student or for one class may not work for others. (p. 1224)

At ASU West, I work in a Department of Integrative Studies. We have 10 faculty members with disciplinary backgrounds in astronomy, history and philosophy of science, mathematics, philosophy, and psychology. We share a common commitment to interdisciplinarity and constructed a major field curriculum to implement that commitment. Despite different ethnic experiences and disciplinary educations, our most basic pedagogical practice is to teach a contemporary version of the medieval university *trivium* (grammar, rhetoric, logic or dialectic) and *quadrivium* (arithmetic, music, geometry, astronomy).

This unity among disciplinary diversity prompted me to consider how my courses and approaches to teaching could be connected to my colleagues by more than just cross-disciplinary topics. I had to go beyond a personal pedagogy to synthesize a philosophy of teaching processes to cut across courses and other faculty members' approaches. Moreover, the outcomes of these processes had to be amenable to a student assessment mandate.

What was common to courses with disparate titles such as Adult Career Development, Environmental Philosophy and Policy, Moral Dilemmas, Multicultural Autobiographies, Evolution of Ideas, and the History and Philosophy of Mathematics (or Social Science or Biology) was Bloom, Hastings, and Madaus' (1971) description of cognitive levels. Our faculty identified departmental outcomes and examined ways to structure our in-class writing assignments and a graduation portfolio to demonstrate students' achievement (or not) of increasing levels of cognitive complexity. Using a departmental writing handbook, we defined the nature of different types of assignments (i.e., report, essay, journal, etc.) and tried to state clear expectations for their thinking and writing efforts. For example, we use the following taxonomy so that students and faculty share a common understanding of what is expected:

Thinking Level	Verbs Used to Communicate Assignment
Knowledge	State, list, name, define
Comprehension	Explain, identify, discuss, describe
Application	Apply, demonstrate, illustrate
Analysis	Analyze, compare and contrast, distinguish
Synthesis	Create, hypothesize, design, compose
Evaluation	Evaluate, criticize, judge, value

I designed my class sessions, hand-out materials, and assignments in a sequential fashion that fostered more and more activities at the analysis, synthesis, and evaluation levels as the semester progressed. Although we had the luxury of smaller class enrollments on our campus, even in a large, section of Introductory Psychology, I tried to incorporate more material and increasing proportions of multiple-choice questions that called for the higher levels of thinking in the latter topics of the semester.

For the past 10 years, I have been working on a second approach to process. In the gateway course, Adult Career Development, for upper division courses in our major, my students read Belenky, Clinchy, Goldberger, and Tarule's (1997) *Women's Ways of Knowing. The Development of Self, Voice, and Mind.* These authors' research on college women and women attending educational programs in community mental health agencies resulted in their definition of *epistemological positions.* These positions are labels for how their student respondents described becoming more and more sophisticated in acquiring and working with knowledge. Regardless of age, the respondents talked about changes that took place in their intellectual, emotional, and moral development as they encountered new sources of information and different forms of authority.

In a *received knowledge* position, students trusted others' expertise—faculty and their textbook authors—more than their own. Their task was to absorb and reproduce this knowledge as close to verbatim as possible. In the *subjective knowledge* position, students were more apt to listen to their own intuitions in forming judgments about what to think or do.

Knowledge accumulated during the received phase, then filtered through their own experiences during the subjective phase, established the platform for *procedural knowledge.* Students discovered that some academic problems and tasks required rational strategies and methods and were based on analytical arguments. They also discovered that some problems are more receptive to solutions based on intuitive and qualitative judgments by making connections between problems and problem solvers via empathy and listening. Both separate and connected knowing strategies were legitimate procedures, given the context and nature of the issue being addressed. In a *constructed knowledge* position, the respondents deeply appreciated the complexities of information, sources, and solutions, as well as the strengths and limitations of even their best arguments. Passion for learning was coupled with the humility of never knowing enough.

I now conceptualize this movement from received knowledge positions to procedural sophistication and, ideally, to the constructed epistemological position as the overarching process goal for all my courses. I described teaching an interdisciplinary, multicultural autobiographies class within this framework (McGovern, 2001). Each of our courses separately and the whole of our core curriculum collectively attempts to achieve this movement from authority and knowledge being vested in outside experts, distant from the learner, to one in which students construct, evaluate, and savor the roots and fruits of their knowledge. Although the interdisciplinary environment was ideal for me to arrive at this understanding of process—within and across courses—a traditional disciplinary major (e.g., psychology) could benefit as well from such an understanding of student intellectual development. Moreover, epistemological positions are qualitative benchmarks to evaluate the overall learning taking place on the eight common goals identified for the major by McGovern et al. (1991).

CONCLUSION

At the St. Mary's Conference of Maryland, Charles Brewer chaired the group that focused on curriculum. I have always regarded him as a staunch advocate for teaching the scientific content of our discipline. Yet his description of how the nine psychologists responsible for this area arrived at their outcome characterizes what I find best about process/pedagogy. I hope my classes could be described thus: "Our working sessions were characterized by catharsis, contentiousness, controversy, confrontation, cooperation, conciliation, camaraderie, and—at the end—collapse" (Brewer, 1997).

REFERENCES

Belenky, M. F., Clinchy, B. M., Goldberger, N. R., & Tarule, J. M. (1997). *Women's ways of knowing. The development of self, voice, and mind.* New York: Basic Books.

Bloom, B. S., Hastings, J. T., & Madaus, G. F. (1971). *Handbook on formative and summative evaluation of student learning.* New York: McGraw-Hill.

Brewer, C. L. (1996). Valediction from Traveler's Rest. *Teaching of Psychology, 23,* 205–206.

Brewer, C. L. (1997). Undergraduate education in psychology: Will the mermaids sing? *American Psychologist, 52,* 434–441.

Halpern, D. F., & Nummedal, S. G. (Eds.). (1995). Psychologists teach critical thinking [Special Issue]. *Teaching of Psychology, 22.*

Halpern, D. F., Smothergill, D. W., Allen, M., Baker, S., Best, D., Ferrari, J., Geisinger, K. F., Gilden, E. R., Hester, M., Keith-Spiegel, P., Kiernesky, N., McGovern, T. V., McKeachie, W. J., Prokasy, W. F., Szuchman, L. T., Vasta, R., & Weaver, K. (1998). Scholarship in psychology: A paradigm for the twentyfirst century. *American Psychologist, 53,* 1292–1297.

Lieberman, M. A., Yalom, I. D., & Miles, M. B. (1973). *Encounter groups: First facts.* New York: Basic Books.

McGovern, T. V. (2001). A multicultural autobiographies interdisciplinary course. *Teaching of Psychology, 28,* 215–217.

McGovern, T. V., & Brewer, C. L. (2002). Undergraduate education in psychology: Teaching, scholarship, and service. In D. K. Freedheim (Ed.), Volume 1 of the *Comprehensive handbook of psychology,* Editor-in-Chief: I. B. Weiner. New York: Wiley.

McGovern, T. V., Furumoto, L., Halpern, D. F., Kimble, G. A., & McKeachie, W. J. (1991). Liberal education, study in depth, and the arts and sciences major—Psychology. *American Psychologist, 46,* 598–605.

Merriam-Webster. (1990). *Webster's Ninth New Collegiate Dictionary.* Springfield, MA: Author.

McKeachie, W. J. (1987). Teaching, teaching teaching, and research on teaching. *Teaching of Psychology, 14,* 135–139.

McKeachie, W. J. (1997). Student ratings: The validity of use. *American Psychologist, 52,* 1218–1225.

Nodine, B. F. (Ed.). (1990). Psychologists teach writing [Special issue]. *Teaching of Psychology, 17.*

Yalom, I. D. (1975). *The theory and practice of group psychotherapy.* New York: Basic Books.

8

Teaching for Critical Thinking: A Four-Part Model to Enhance Thinking Skills

Diane F. Halpern

Claremont McKenna College

What are the most important outcomes from a college education? Although there will be some differences in the way different people answer this question, the odds are good that your list, like most, would include the idea that colleges should help students develop their ability to think. Critical thinking is one of the few educational outcomes that people from all corners of the political spectrum can agree on. Both George Bush, Sr. and Bill Clinton supported the enhancement of critical thinking in college students as an important national goal, although it was the only one of the educational goals identified in "Goals 2000," the blue ribbon report on the future of education that was never funded (National Education Goals Panel, 1991). Almost every discussion about the contents of a college-level general education curriculum includes the enhancement of critical thinking skills as an essential component. For example, Lynne V. Cheney, former chair of the National Endowment for the Humanities, was a highly vocal advocate for a common core of knowledge for college students that would consist of "self-knowledge, critical thinking, and community" (Lauer, 1990). College faculty from a variety of academic disciplines list critical thinking (and problem solving) along with communicating, interpersonal skills, and computer literacy as the "the basic competencies or skills that every college graduate [should] have" (Diamond, 1997). Adult workers agree, with 81% of the over 1,000 persons who responded to a national survey reporting that critical thinking, literacy, and communication skills are *very important* (compared with only 50% who rated computer skills as *very important*; The Chronicle of Higher Education, 2000).

News reports from Pakistan and many different countries in Eastern Europe and Asia also document phenomenal growth in the number of college courses designed to help their students become better thinkers (Bollag, 1997; Cohen, 2000; Collett, 1994). Even the virtual universities are on board. At Virtual Online University, for example, all lower division classes require at least two of these three elements: writing, numeracy, and critical thinking (Jacobson, 1994). Why are so many politicians, federal agencies, college faculty, and working adults around the world so concerned with helping students become better thinkers?

THE INFORMATION GLUT MEETS THE KNOWLEDGE ECONOMY

The Internet and other multimedia have created a deluge of information that is capable of flooding every household that has a computer and modem. With only a few clicks, more pages of information are now available, in even the most remote regions of the world, than are held in the libraries of our most prestigious and elite institutions. The Internet may have an effect on how we think, learn, and relate that is more powerful than TV, telephone, airplane, printing press, and steam engine combined because it can quickly and fundamentally alter international communication, democratize the spread of knowledge, and change the nature of education. However, all of that information is of no more use on one's computer screen than it is in an inaccessible institution if it cannot be used intelligently. High-quality, relevant information needs to be identified, selected, comprehended, and applied in meaningful ways. More than ever, today's college students need to be able to judge the credibility of information, recognize and defend against propaganda, reason effectively, use evidence in decision making, and identify and find ways to solve problems if they are to benefit from the wealth of information that is available to them.

The need to help young adults become better thinkers is also a national and international concern. Today's workforce requires more complex skills and abilities at every level of employment, from the very lowest wage earners to the highest corporate executive (Hunt, 1995), making a college diploma the passport for entry into the middle class. Economic forecasters agree that less educated workers will suffer steep declines in their wages in the coming years—a fact that will continue to widen the gap between the rich and the poor:

> The gap in annual wages between those with and without college degrees widens every year. Currently, those who have a college degree earn roughly twice what high school graduates earn. The annual wages of workers without a college education have

actually declined (when adjusted for inflation) over the last 25 years. (The California State University, 1997, p. 25)

National economies are knowledge-based; those countries that have well-educated citizens are enjoying the economic boom that is reflected in a generally strong stock market. With new knowledge being replaced with even newer knowledge at an unprecedented rate, the twin abilities of knowing how to think critically and learn efficiently provide the best education for today's college students.

WHAT IS CRITICAL THINKING?

Fischer and Spiker (2000) recently reviewed the literature on critical thinking and found that most definitions revolved around common themes that included judgment, reasoning, meta-cognition, and reflective questioning. Here is a definition that I have used over the last 20 years: *Critical thinking* is the use of those cognitive skills or strategies that increases the probability of a desirable outcome. It is purposeful, reasoned, and goal directed. It is the kind of thinking involved in solving problems, formulating inferences, calculating likelihoods, and making decisions. Critical thinkers use these skills appropriately, without prompting, and usually with conscious intent in a variety of settings. That is, they are predisposed to think critically. When we think critically, we evaluate the outcomes of our thought processes—how good a decision is or how well a problem is solved. Critical thinking also involves evaluating the thinking process—the reasoning that went into the conclusion we have arrived at or the kinds of factors considered in making a decision (Halpern, 1998).

Instruction in critical thinking is based on two implicit assumptions: (a) that there are critical thinking skills that can be identified and taught to students along with the appropriate circumstances when they should be used, and (b) when students learn and apply these skills in the appropriate contexts, they will become better thinkers. These assumptions now rest on a solid body of evidence that provides support for educators and students who believe that better thinking can be taught and learned. A small sampling of the research is presented here. A more exhaustive review of the literature is beyond the scope of this chapter; additional evidence is reviewed in Halpern (in press).

There is no reason to believe that critical thinking skills cannot be learned in ways that transfer to novel contexts. Most students who take courses in writing or oral communication become better writers or speakers. Similarly, most people who take course work in mathematics are able to apply mathematical principles to a wide range of problems. We now have a sufficiently large body of research that shows that it is possible to teach in ways that help students become better thinkers and that these skills transfer to novel situations when we teach specifically for transfer. However, critical thinking is not necessarily a by-product of standard instruction within the discipline.

Types of Evidence

One of the largest and most ambitious studies of the benefits of instruction designed to improve thinking was conducted in the 1980s in Venezuela. Unlike most other studies, this one used a strong experimental design, including the random assignment of participants to different learning conditions and blind evaluations of the outcomes (Herrnstein, Nickerson, de Sanchez, & Swets, 1986). Students who received the critical thinking instruction were better thinkers than students in the control groups that received standard instruction. Unfortunately, because of a change in the political leadership in Venezuela, there has been no long-term follow-up to determine whether these gains were sustained over time. There are many studies where the dependent measures are student self-reports and self-assessments of how well they can think (e.g., Block, 1985). These studies provide only weak data because the belief that one can think well is not always correlated with actual performance, but it is reassuring to know that students believe that their thinking has improved as a result of instruction designed to improve thinking.

There are many studies that have shown gains in thinking skills when the assessment consists of standardized tests of critical thinking (reviewed in U.S. Department of Education, 2000). However, the validity of the standardized tests is questionable. Although none of these measures is ideal, taken together they do support the idea that critical thinking can be improved with appropriate instruction specifically designed for this outcome. Instructional programs that focus on specific critical thinking skills provide more convincing data. For example, in one study where students explained their thinking and provided reasons for their problem-solving choices as they worked through physics problems, they showed enhancements in their ability to transfer the skills learned to novel problems (Chi, Bassok, Lewis, Reimann, & Glaser, 1989).

A strong case for critical thinking instruction comes from several different studies by Nisbett and his colleagues (Nisbett, 1993). For example, in one study, they phoned students at their homes after the course work was completed under the guise of conducting a survey. They found that students spontaneously applied the thinking skills that they had been taught in school when they encountered novel problems even when the school-related context cues were absent (Fong, Krantz, & Nisbett, 1986). In a different study, college students learned inductive reasoning tasks using realistic scenarios from many different domains. The authors concluded that critical thinking is a transferable skill (Jepson, Krantz, & Nisbett, 1993).

Kosonen and Winne (1995) studied the transfer of critical thinking skills to a novel domain in college students, secondary school students, and middle-school students. Like Nisbett, they found that when students learned general rules about reasoning and practiced these skills with everyday ill-structured problems, the thinking skills transferred to new contexts and different domains. More recently, Lovett and Greenhouse (2000), building on the work of Paas (1992), reported similar results. When students learned to solve multiple problems using varied problem sets during learning, the initial learning took significantly longer, but the students who learned with a variety of examples performed better on transfer problem sets than students who practiced only on similar problems. Thus, it seems that critical thinking skills are learned best and are most likely to transfer to novel situations when they are taught using a variety of contexts. Principles derived from empirical studies like these (and others) show that the successful transfer of critical thinking skills can serve as a model for instructional design for instructors who want to teach for critical thinking.

A FOUR-PART MODEL FOR CRITICAL THINKING INSTRUCTION

Cognitive psychology is the scientific study of how people learn, remember, comprehend, solve problems, and make decisions. Research in cognitive psychology has already generated a considerable body of knowledge that can be used to improve educational methods and outcomes and to guide curricular design and learning activities in ways that will help students become better thinkers. Using these principles, I propose a four-part model for critical thinking instruction. Instructors who want to enhance critical thinking skills in their students should design learning activities that:

1. Explicitly teach the skills of critical thinking
2. Develop the disposition for effortful thinking and learning
3. Direct learning activities in ways that increase the probability of transcontextual transfer (structure training)
4. Make metacognitive monitoring explicit and overt

A Skills Approach to Critical Thinking

In an earlier publication written for the U.S. Department of Education, I proposed a five-part taxonomy of critical thinking skills (Halpern, 1994). The taxonomy is not meant to be an exhaustive list of all possible thinking skills—it is just a starting point for a serious discussion of what is meant by critical thinking skills and how we can best define them so that they are meaningful to a broad audience. I have been working on the development of a test of critical thinking based on this taxonomy because an assessment directly tied to instructional practices and objectives is needed to provide feedback that can link instructional practices to their outcomes (Halpern, in press). Other taxonomies are possible, and a legitimate case can be made for alternative groupings or adding other skills and deleting some of those that are listed. This taxonomy can help decide what we want college graduates entering the workforce to know and be able to do so they can compete and cooperate in the world's market place and function as effective citizens in a complex democratic community.

Here are the five category headings for organizing college-level critical thinking skills:

1. Verbal Reasoning Skills

The skills listed under this rubric include those needed to comprehend and defend against the persuasive techniques embedded in everyday language (also known as *natural language*). Thinking and language are closely tied constructs, and the skills included in this category recognize the reciprocal relationship between language and thought in which an individual's thoughts determine the language used to express them and the language used shapes the thoughts.

2. Argument Analysis Skills

An argument is a set of statements with at least one conclusion and one reason that supports the conclusion. In real-life settings, arguments are complex with reasons that run counter to the conclusion, stated and unstated assumptions, irrelevant information, and intermediate steps between the conclusions and evidence that supports them. Arguments are found in commercials, political speeches, textbooks, and anywhere else where reasons are presented in an attempt to get the reader or listener to believe that the conclusion is true. The skills of identifying conclusions, rating the quality of reasons, and determining the overall strength of an argument should be sharpened in college course work.

3. Skills in Thinking as Hypothesis Testing

The rationale for this category is that much of our day-to-day thinking is like the scientific method of hypothesis testing. In many of our everyday interactions, people function like intuitive scientists to explain, predict, and control the events in their lives. The skills used in thinking as hypothesis testing are the same ones used in scientific reasoning—the accumulation of observations, formulation of beliefs or hypotheses, and use of the information collected to decide if it confirms or disconfirms the hypotheses.

4. Using Likelihood and Uncertainty

Because few events in life can be known with certainty, the correct use of probability and likelihood plays a critical role in almost every decision. Huff's (1954) tiny, popular book, *How to Lie With Statistics*, is still widely quoted because it explains how easy it is to mislead someone who does not understand basic concepts in probability. The critical thinking skills that are subsumed under this heading are an important dimension of a college-level critical thinking taxonomy.

5. Decision-Making and Problem-Solving Skills

In some sense, all of the critical thinking skills are used to make decisions and solve problems, but the ones that are included here involve the use of multiple problems statements to define the problem and identify possible goals, the generation and selection of alternatives, and judging among the alternatives. Many of these skills are especially useful in quantitative reasoning problems.

Taken together, these five categories define an organizational rubric for a skills approach to critical thinking. They have face validity and can be easily communicated to the general public and students. They offer one possible answer to the question of what college students need to know and be able to do when they graduate from college.

Dispositions for Effortful Thinking and Learning

It is important to separate the disposition or willingness to think critically from the ability to think critically. Some people may have excellent critical thinking skills and may recognize when they are needed, but they may also decide not to engage in the effortful process of using them. This distinction calls attention to what people can do and what they actually do in real-world contexts. Good instructional programs help learners decide when to make the necessary mental investment in critical thinking and when a problem or argument is not worth it. Dispositions for effortful thinking and learning include:

- willingness to engage in and persist at a complex task,
- conscious use of plans and suppression of impulsive activity,
- flexibility or open-mindedness,
- willingness to abandon nonproductive strategies in attempts to self-correct, and
- awareness of social realities that need to be overcome so that thought can become actions.

Transfer of Training

In teaching for thinking, the goal is to have students not only understand and successfully use a particular skill when it is being taught, but also to be able to recognize when that skill will be appropriate in a novel situation. This issue is the Achilles' heel of transfer. In the language of cognitive psychology, it is a pattern-recognition problem—recognizing events that should trigger a conscious decision to engage in the hard work of critical thinking and serve as a guide for selecting the appropriate skills. The difficulty in learning thinking skills that are needed in multiple contexts is that there are no obvious cues in the context to initiate the recall of the thinking skill. Students need to create the recall cues from the structural aspects of the problem or argument so that when the structural aspects are present, they can serve as cues for retrieval. A similar point was made by Hummel and Holyoak (1997), who said, "First, thinking is structure sensitive.

Reasoning, problem solving, and learning…depend on a capacity to code and manipulate relational knowledge" (p. 427).

When we teach critical thinking skills so that they transfer appropriately and spontaneously, students learn to focus on the structure so the underlying characteristics become salient instead of the domain-specific surface characteristics. There is an old saying in psychology that "the head remembers what it does." If you want to teach for transfer, it is important to design learning activities so that the skills are encoded in a way that facilitate their recall in novel situations. It is what the learner does that determines what gets learned, not what the teacher does. Thus, the task for the instructor is to design learning activities that enable learners.

Teaching for transfer requires variable conditions at learning, with an emphasis on the structural aspects of the problem or argument. After context-rich information is provided, learners perform certain tasks or answer carefully crafted questions. Here are some examples of relevant tasks and questions that require learners to attend to structure:

- Draw a diagram or other graphic display that organizes the information.
- What additional information would you want before answering the question?
- Explain why you selected a particular multiple-choice alternative. Which is second best? Why?
- State the problem in at least two ways.
- Which information is most important? Which information is least important? Why?
- Categorize the findings in a meaningful way.
- List two solutions for the problem.
- What is wrong with an assertion that was made in the question?
- Present two reasons that support the conclusion and two reasons that do not support the conclusion.
- Identify the type of persuasive technique being used.
- What two actions would you take to improve the design of the study that was described?

Metacognitive Monitoring

Metacognition refers to our knowledge of what we know (or what we know about what we know) and the use of this knowledge to direct further learning activities. When engaging in critical thinking, students need to monitor their thinking process, check whether progress is being made toward an appropriate goal, ensure accuracy, and make decisions about the use of time and mental effort. Students can become better thinkers and learners by developing the habit of monitoring their understanding and judging the quality of their learning. It is the executive or boss function that guides how adults use different learning strategies and make decisions about the allocation of limited cognitive resources. Numerous studies have found that good learners and thinkers engage in more metacognitive activities than poor learners and thinkers. The skills and attitudes of metacognitive activities can be taught and learned so that students can direct their own learning strategies and make judgments about how much effort to allocate to a cognitive task (Nelson, 1996).

A schematic diagram of the critical thinking process, including individual differences and situation variables, is shown in Figure 8.1. Notice how dispositions and attitudes influence the process at multiple points, beginning with recognizing patterns in the environment that may require critical thinking (e.g., a gas gauge pointing to empty or a career decision that needs to be made) and ending with the decision when to end the thinking process. The skills of critical thinking are selected and applied as individuals monitor their progress toward a desirable outcome. Good instruction with structure training will make all of the stages of the process more efficient and more likely to be successful.

EXAMPLES

Here are some examples that may help understand and apply the critical thinking model proposed.

An Example of Teaching for Noncritical Thinking (or Perhaps Not Thinking At All)

Faculty often ask whether the emphasis on critical thinking implies that they have been teaching noncritical thinking. Unfortunately, far too often this interpretation is correct. Examples of noncritical thinking are the rote applications of rules, verbatim memory, or nondirected thinking such as day dreaming. For example, consider the common practice in most courses in developmental psychology to have students learn Piaget's stages of cognitive development and list them in order by name and age on an exam. Certainly Piaget's stages of cognitive development are important content in a class in developmental psychology, and students need to know them, but too often the learning ends there. Students can list the stages in order, along with the related ages for each stage. They can even give the same common example of cognitive developmental milestones, such as the ability to conserve or object permanence. The rote repetition of this information is rewarded with a high grade, but too often the same students cannot understand any implications from Piaget's work, provide or recognize a novel example of a developmental milestone, or use the concepts in any meaningful way. These common practices that teach for and reward rote repetition are not teaching for thinking. If the listing of stages or developmental milestones was accompanied with exercises that required students to make predictions based on Piaget's work or to design an age-appropriate

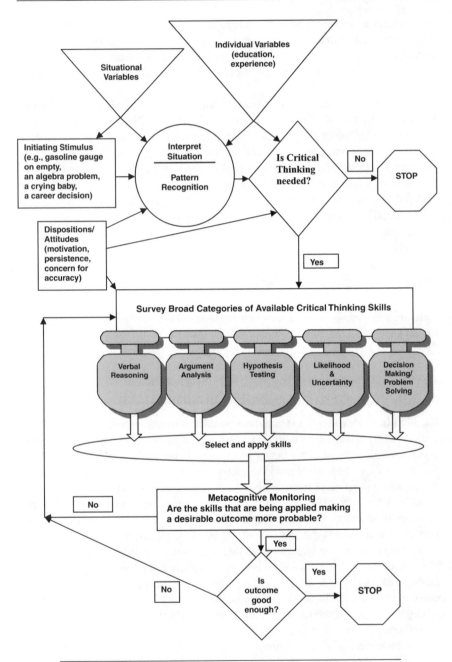

FIG. 8.1. A schematic model of the critical thinking process. Notice how dispositions, individual background variables, and situational variables all influence the way a situation is interpreted

(Continued on next page)

learning plan that incorporated Piaget's ideas, then a rote learning exercise would be transformed into one that results in better retention and more thoughtful learning. However, consider an example that uses the four-part model as a guide for critical thinking instruction.

A Simple, but Powerful Demonstration of a General Skill

Lessons designed to enhance critical thinking skills need to begin with clear objectives—exactly which skills does the instructor want students to learn? How will the skills be taught so they are most likely to transfer to novel situations, without prompting, and be used long into the future (i.e., outside of school and after graduation)? What principles of learning and human cognition will guide the design of the learning activity? This example is taken from a graduate class in cognitive psychology that I taught at Bosphorus University in Istanbul, Turkey. I began the lesson by asking the students to assume the role of commander of a large battleship. I told the class that the story I was about to tell was true. Yet even if they had never heard of the ship or could not identify with the commander of U.S. ship, they could assume that they were in command of a large Turkish ship. (Turkey is a partner in the North Atlantic Treaty Organization [NATO].) I then told the true story of the USS Vincennes, which, in 1988, was patrolling the Persian Gulf not far from the Iranian border (Balles, 1988).

> The U.S. and Iran were not at war, but they were engaged in fierce sea battles in the Persian Gulf. On this hot, sticky day, the Vincennes together with another U.S. ship fired a total of 119 rounds at small, darting Iranian patrol boats. The Iranian gunboats fired at a U.S. helicopter that had taken off from the Vincennes. You are in a windowless command center in the Vincennes, where you are in charge of all of the ship's actions. As captain, you are informed that your advanced radar system just picked up the signal from an aircraft that took off from a nearby Iranian airstrip. Staff in the ship's radar room warn that the airplane is descending in altitude and

---

(Fig. 8.1 caption continued)

and the decision as to whether it requires the effortful process of critical thinking. If critical thinking is needed, then individuals select the critical thinking skills that are most likely to be appropriate for the situation. Good critical thinkers have a large repertoire of critical thinking skills to chose from and are skilled at making selections that are appropriate for the situation. (Critical thinking skills and the selection of the appropriate skill are learned.) Metacognitive monitoring is repeatedly cycled as individuals determine whether the skills they are using are increasing the likelihood of a desirable outcome or if other skills are needed. When a "good enough" outcome is achieved, the process is stopped.

heading toward the Vincennes. You warn the approaching aircraft to change course, but there is no response. An electronic system asks the aircraft to identify itself as friend or foe—still no response. The crew on the aircraft does not respond to repeated requests to change course or provide an identity. Worse yet, crew members in your Combat Information Center identify the plane as an Iranian F-14 fighter.

At this point in the narrative, I asked each student in turn what he or she would do, reminding them that they are not only responsible for their own life, but also every other life on the Vincennes. I also reminded them that a mistake would cost the lives of innocent people and could precipitate a major war. Students were told, "You have only a few minutes before the approaching aircraft is within striking range of the Vincennes."

Every student decided to fire on the F-14. I then told them that they made a BIG mistake—they shot down a commercial airliner, killing 290 innocent passengers—and that the information they received was wrong. The aircraft was ascending, not descending, and the plane was misidentified by the Combat Command Center crew. Like the real captain of the Vincennes, the students never thought to verify the accuracy of the information they received.

After receiving the news that they would have made a disastrous mistake, the class filled with various moans, and the following discussion was lively. I also built on this example, using it to discuss other common biases in thinking, including the confirmation bias (preference for information that confirms a hypothesis that is considered most likely), overconfidence (failure to consider why a decision might be wrong), and others. Although class ended for the day, this was not the end of the lesson. Approximately 1 week later, and with no apparent connection, I posed a seemingly different problem. Students were told to suppose that they have rented a truck that is 11′2″ tall. As they drive along an intercity road, they come to an overpass with a sign posted that says, "Maximum Clearance 11′. " What would you do? The suggested solutions included, "Back up several miles on the road until you come to an exit, then find a way around the overpass," but this is clearly not an ideal solution. As we pondered the problem, one student yelled out, "Verify the information." Perhaps the 11′2″ truck is really closer to 11′ (rounding, imprecision in measurement, and low tire pressure could account for 2″; similarly the underpass could be slightly higher than 11′). By the third time that I posed similar problems to be solved—no matter when or what topic—everyone immediately asked about the quality of the information. In fact, students still send me e-mails telling about times when they spontaneously remembered to check the quality of the information they were provided. They often add that they deliberately use other methods that we practiced in class—for example, listing reasons that a preferred hypothesis might be wrong.

Readers with a good background in cognitive psychology can probably identify many of the principles from cognitive psychology that I applied in this learning activity. Most notable is the fact that I made each student personalize the situation and respond as if he or she were the captain—an obvious application of the self-reference effect, in which material that is directly personalized is recalled with greater accuracy than the same material when it is presented in a nonpersonalized way (Hartlep & Forsyth, 2000; Rogers, Kuiper, & Kirker, 1997). By presenting the same principles spaced over several different class periods, I was able to take advantage of the spaced-practice effect, which shows that material is learned better when the learning is spaced over several sessions than when it is massed in a single learning session (Cull, 2000; Donovan & Radosevich, 1998). I also used a narrative to teach these skills—a strategy used as a mnemonic device to promote retention and recall (Bower & Clark, 1969). The use of different domains—*variability in encoding* is the more technical name for this strategy—promotes transfer (Benjamin, Bjork, & Schwartz, 1998), and the way the exercises were structured, every student had the opportunity to practice recall and receive informative feedback, another cognitive principle known to promote long-term retention (Balch, 1998).

This brief overview of critical thinking instruction is intended to convince readers that critical thinking can be enhanced through deliberate instruction, especially when the instruction is firmly rooted in the principles of human cognition, with careful attention paid to techniques that promote transfer and long-term retention. A thinking citizenry is our greatest hope for the future. The development of critical thinking skills in our students can be one of psychology's greatest contributions to the next generation.

REFERENCES

Balch, W. R. (1998). Practice versus review exams and final exam performance. *Teaching of Psychology, 25,* 181–185.

Balles, J. (1988, December). Vincennes: Findings could have helped avert tragedy, scientists tell Hill panel. *American Psychological Association Monitor,* pp. 10–11.

Benjamin, A. S., Bjork, R. A., & Schwartz, B. L. (1998). The mismeasure of memory: When retrieval fluency is misleading as a metamnemonic index. *Journal of Experimental Psychology: General, 127,* 55–68.

Block, R. A. (1985). Education and thinking skills reconsidered. *American Psychologist, 40,* 574–575.

Bollag, B. (1997, October 31). School-reform effort grows in Eastern Europe. *The Chronicle of Higher Education* [Retrieved December 28, 2000 from the World Wide Web: http://chronicle.com/search97cgi/s97_cgi?].

Bower, G. H., & Clark, M. C. (1969). Narrative stories as mediators for serial learning. *Psychonomic Science, 14,* 181–182.

The California State University. (1997). *The cornerstones report.* Long Beach, CA: Author.

Chi, M. T., Bassok, M., Lewis, M. W., Reimann, P., & Glaser, R. (1989). Self-explanations: How students study and use examples in learning to solve problems. *Cognitive Science, 13,* 145–182.

The Chronicle of Higher Education. (2000, June 23). Survey finds that most Americans want college to prepare them for a job. *The Chronicle of Higher Education* [Retrieved December 28, 2000 from the World Wide Web: http://chronicle.com/search97cgi/s97_cgi?].

Cohen, D. (2000, January 7). With Asian economies on the rebound, the region's colleges are also upbeat. *The Chronicle of Higher Education* [Retrieved December 28, 2000 from the World Wide Web: http://chronicle.com/search97cgi/s97_cgi?].

Collett, P. (1994, April 27). A new university for Pakistan. *The Chronicle of Higher Education* [Retrieved December 28, 2000 from the World Wide Web: http://chronicle.com/search97cgi/s97_cgi?].

Cull, W. L. (2000). Untangling the benefits of multiple study opportunities and repeated testing for cued recall. *Applied Cognitive Psychology, 14,* 215–235.

Diamond, R. M. (1997, August 1). Curriculum reform needed if students are to master core concepts. *The Chronicle of Higher Education* [Retrieved December 28, 2000 from the World Wide Web: http://chronicle.com/search97cgi/s97_cgi?].

Donovan, J. J., & Radosevich, D. J. (1998). A meta-analytic review of the distribution of practice effect: Now you see it, now you don't. *Journal of Applied Psychology, 84,* 795–805.

Fischer, S. C., & Spiker V. A. (2000, December). *A framework for critical thinking research and training* (Report prepared for the Army Research Institute, Fort Leavenworth, KS).

Fong, G. T., Krantz, D. H., & Nisbett, R. E. (1986). The effects of statistical training on thinking about everyday problems. *Cognitive Psychology, 18,* 253–292.

Halpern, D. F. (1994). A national assessment of critical thinking skills in adults: Taking steps toward the goal. In A. Greenwood (Ed.), *The national assessment of college student learning: Identification of the skills to be taught, learned, and assessed* (pp. 24–64). Washington, DC: U.S. Department of Education, National Center for Education Statistics.

Halpern, D. F. (1998). Teaching critical thinking for transfer across domains: Dispositions, skills, structure training, and metacognitive monitoring. *American Psychologist, 53,* 449–455.

Halpern, D. F. (in press). *Thought and knowledge: An Introduction to critical thinking* (4th ed.). Mahwah, NJ: Lawrence Erlbaum Associates.

Hartlep, K. L., & Forsyth, G. A. (2000). The effect of self-reference on learning and retention. *Teaching of Psychology, 27,* 269–271.

Herrnstein, R. J., Nickerson, R. S., de Sanchez, M., & Swets, J. A. (1986). Teaching thinking skills. *American Psychologist, 41,* 1279–1289.

Huff, D. (1954). *How to lie with statistics.* New York: W. W. Norton.

Hummel, J. E., & Holyoak, K. J. (1997). Distributed representations of structure: A theory of analogical access and mapping. *Psychological Review, 104,* 427–466.

Hunt, E. B. (1995). *Will we be smart enough?* New York: Russell Sage Foundation.

Jacobson, R. L. (1994, November 16). Scholars plan a "virtual university." *The Chronicle of Higher Education* [Retrieved December 28, 2000 from the World Wide Web: http://chronicle.com/search97cgi/s97_cgi?].

Jepson, C., Krantz, D. H., & Nisbett, R. E. (1993). Inductive reasoning: Competence or skill? In R. E. Nisbett (Ed.), *Rules for reasoning* (pp. 70–89). Hillsdale, NJ: Lawrence Erlbaum Associates.

Kosonen, P., & Winne, P. H. (1995). Effects of teaching statistical laws on reasoning about everyday problems. *Journal of Educational Psychology, 87,* 33–46.

Lauer, R. M. (1990, January 31). Self-knowledge, critical thinking, and community should be the main objectives of general education. *The Chronicle of Higher Education* [Retrieved December 28, 2000 from the World Wide Web: http://chronicle.com/search97cgi/s97_cgi?].

Lovett, M. C., & Greenhouse, J. B. (2000). Applying cognitive theory to statistics instruction. *The American Statistician, 54,* 196–209.

National Education Goals Panel. (1991). *The national education goals report: Building a nation of learners.* Washington, DC: U.S. Printing Office.

Nelson, T. O. (1996). Consciousness and metacognition. *American Psychologist, 51,* 102–116.

Nisbett, R. E. (1993). *Rules for reasoning.* Hillsdale, NJ: Lawrence Erlbaum Associates.

Paas, F. G. W. C. (1992). Training strategies for attaining transfer of problem-solving skill in statistics: A cognitive-load approach. *Journal of Educational Psychology, 84,* 429–434.

Rogers, T. B., Kuiper, N. A., & Kirker, W. S. (1997). Self-reference and the encoding of personal information. *Journal of Personality and Social Psychology, 35,* 677–688.

U.S. Department of Education, National Center for Education Statistics. (2000). *The NPEC sourcebook on assessment: Volume 1. Definitions and assessment methods for critical thinking, problem solving, and writing* (NCES 2000-172 Prepared by T. Dary Erwin for the Council of the National Postsecondary Education Cooperative Student Outcomes Pilot Working Group: Cognitive and intellectual development). Washington, DC: U.S. Government Printing Office.

9

Writing: Models, Examples, Teaching Advice, and a Heartfelt Plea

Barbara F. Nodine

Arcadia University

Not only do psychology instructors have the difficult task of teaching a complex set of facts and thinking skills, we should also expect to teach students to write about these facts and skills. I claim that writing is the most difficult of the three Rs to master, so teaching writing is that much more difficult than teaching any of the other skills. This chapter explains the conceptions of writing that demonstrate its complex nature and then offers guidance for teaching writing.

The last two decades have seen numerous conceptions and reconceptions of theoretical approaches to writing. An early and seminal work conceptualizing the writing of school children by linguist James Britton and co-authors (Britton, Burgess, Martin, McLeod, & Rosen, 1975) is a perspective I present because I find it most useful for faculty working with students. Britton et al. (1975) considered all writing to be defined by two important concepts, purpose and audience, and categorized writing as one of three kinds. Some teachers might think three classifications of writing types is an oversimplification of all writing, and Britton et al. began their 1975 book with the sentence, "We classify at our peril" (p. 1). The first category of writing is expressive writing, which is written for an audience of the self for the purpose of gaining understanding. This type of writing is exemplified by writers keeping a journal of ideas or writing an exploratory first draft to discover their thinking on a topic. Britton et al. contrasted expressive writing with the category of transactional writing, which is written for a public audience for the purpose of getting something done. The writer of a transactional piece might be trying to persuade the dean of the need for research funds or to inform colleagues of the results of the latest study. The third type of writing is poetic writing, also written for a public audience for the purpose of the aesthetic pleasure of the reader, such as a poem or a story. Britton et al. claimed that expressive writing was an essential part of learning necessarily preceding either transactional or poetic writing. For me, it is this emphasis that informs our teaching—that is, expressive writing is the necessary prerequisite to other writing. As teachers and writers, we should accept the tenet that first we must write to discover our own thinking. When sentences are put on a page to be reviewed, we can then see what it is that we think. This writing is called *writing to learn* in contrast to the other types of writing that are referred to as *learning to write* (Nodine, 1990, 1999). Teachers should help students realize that writing is a discovery process, not a transcription of ideas formed whole in the mind and placed on paper.

I find the Britton et al. definition of all pieces of writing in terms of their purpose and audience to be very useful when teaching students to compose a writing assignment. When teachers can identify flaws in student writing as a violation of the expectations generated for a particular purpose and audience, then they can offer constructive advice, with a rationale for why this advice is not just the teacher's point of view, but is derived from a supposed impact on an audience.

A different theoretical perspective (Hayes, 1996), also obtained by observing writers, is derived from a cognitive psychology approach based on analysis of the protocols of writers thinking aloud as they worked. The early version of the model, developed by Hayes and Flower (1980), offered a first empirical examination of the behaviors of the writer engaged in the problem of composing a piece of text. Behaviors such as planning, generating text, and revising, although identified by composition experts and literary giants, had not been previously studied as an ongoing psychological behavior. Until the Hayes and Flower work, researchers had not examined how a writer actually went about the process of composing an essay. This new emphasis on the writing process, instead of examination of the finished product, gave teachers a new perspective on interactions with their students. Not only did Hayes and Flower identify a means for examining the psychological processes of planning, generating, and revising, but they also identified other important factors in the act of composing. Thus, factors such as the task environment, the writer's long-term memory of stored writing plans, and knowledge of the topic and audience were now seen as impacting the writing process.

Further exploration of the problem and revisions of the theory have led to the model (Hayes, 1996) illustrated in Figure 9.1. Hayes stated that:

> Writing is a communicative act that requires a social context and a medium. It is
> a generative activity requiring motivation, and it is an intellectual activity requiring

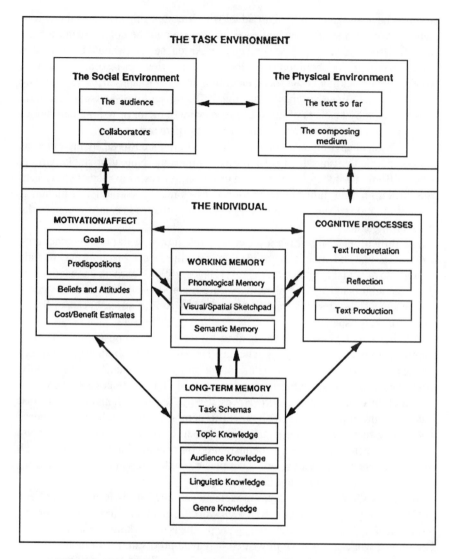

FIG. 9.1. Hayes (1996) model of the cognitive processes in writing. Reprinted by permission of Lawrence Erlbaum Associates.

cognitive processes and memory. No theory can be complete that does not include all of these components. (p. 5)

Space precludes a complete review of this complex model, so I select and emphasize those aspects relevant to the teaching emphasis of this chapter. As shown in Figure 9.1, the task environment includes social and physical environments, both of which have an effect on the individual who is composing. The social environment for writing includes the audience for a piece and the collaborators for the work. Collaboration improves writing quality. As teachers, we should be aware that in the classroom, collaboration could include peer reviews or laboratory partners. Another understanding of the social environment is the traditions of the academic discipline that define the types of writing for that discipline. As I show later, an understanding by teachers of the social environment factor in writing determines the approach taken toward classroom writing assignments.

The physical environment consists of the text produced so far by the writer as well as the medium in which the writer is composing. Not surprisingly, writers behave differently if they are composing on a word processor instead of with a pen. The medium has an influence on those processes mentioned earlier of planning, generating, and revising, as well as how the text produced so far influences the other components.

The difficult task of writing a paper requires the writer to plan by generating ideas for the text and organizing the ideas in an outline or list. Planning may include this outline or actual language for the text (Hayes, 1996). Teachers knowledgeable about the significant role of planning would incorporate this stage in a student assignment. Thus, students might be required to submit an outline or a list of points for their paper.

Another cognitive activity engaged in by the writer is consulting long-term memory for knowledge of the task schemas. These schemas include revision strategies and information about the nature of the finished product. Not surprisingly, extensive practice is essential to developing skill. Thus, novices to a new type of written product show less skill (Hayes, 1996). Teachers should be aware that students confronting the first assignment to complete a research report, a genre with which they are quite unfamiliar, need instruction on the nature of this assignment. Teachers could break the task into components that are easier to teach and learn. Teachers might provide examples of student reports, which look very different from professional journal articles.

An emphasis of the 1996 Hayes model and explorations by Ransdell and Levy (1996) and Kellogg (1996) is on the role of working memory. These researchers inform us that writing quality and fluency are products of working memory capacity. The role of working memory in written language production is to monitor planning, text generation, and evaluative reading. Ransdell and Levy (1996) showed that working memory constraints reflect the efficiency of the writer in allocating resources to the many subtasks of writing. Thus, greater working memory correlates with better quality texts. Their research also shows the relation of working memory's impact on reading comprehension.

Reading ability, which we see in the Hayes model, has an impact on revision processes, and it is also linked to individual differences in working memory capacity. Faculty typically consider writing, reading, and speaking as quite different skills in college students. Hayes (1996) offered us evidence that they are linked in ways that might affect our teaching. Reading text has several connections to writing processes. First, reading source material is related to the writer's generation of content for the writing assignment. Thus, a poor reader may misrepresent or be unable to conceptualize the source material. In addition, readers conceptualize a writer as having a particular persona based on the text. Thus, there is another possibility for misrepresentation of the argument or content of the text. Last, students must read to understand the task required of them. They must know how to argue, analyze, summarize, report, and so on, and there is evidence to suggest that they make mistakes in these reading and writing tasks. The important role of reading in revising text causes poor readers to be handicapped in revising text even if that text is written by them.

TEACHING WRITING

The prior section offers a summary of selected empirically based, theoretical perspectives on writing. Each of these researchers offers direct or indirect advice for instructors practicing the teaching of writing. Useful advice for teachers comes from Kellogg (1994), who, at the end of 10 highly theoretical and empirical chapters, ends his book with 2 pages of tersely worded implications. I select his advice to present here because it most closely agrees with my own perspective and fits well the efforts of those teachers working to enhance the curricular movement called "writing across the curriculum." First, Kellogg pointed out that student writers must have a rich repertoire of content knowledge, including both facts and procedures. Writing instruction must be embedded in specific domains of knowledge (e.g., psychology, biology, history). At the college level, extensive reading in the discipline provides relevant content knowledge and models for composing written work. In fact, Kellogg believes in this disciplinary effect strongly enough that he raised the question of whether multidisciplinary methods (as is typical of college composition courses) can be effective in developing writing skills. I believe that students show the greatest growth as writers when they are working in the area of their major, where they have more knowledge and motivation.

His second guideline is that instructors should use writing as a tool for learning. Putting words on paper, discovering one's own voice for the content, is critical to gaining an understanding of the material and gaining writing skills. The range of activities that fit this guideline is discussed in the next section.

Third, it is important to teach students the general strategies for composing. Students need to be taught processes and activities that they will use as writers. Teachers must assign and teach free writing, brainstorming, consideration of audience and purpose for a piece of writing, and activities of revision.

Fourth, Kellogg (1994) advised that in addition to teaching the general strategies noted in the previous guideline, teaching task-specific procedures is also necessary. Teachers of psychology must identify the various types of writing in the discipline of psychology and teach students how to engage in the processes needed to produce that type of writing.

TEACHING WRITING TO PSYCHOLOGY STUDENTS

The previous section provided guidelines for teaching writing in general. This section builds on the last to review the scholarship on teaching writing in psychology. The types of papers found in the psychology literature are called by different names. I have organized and reviewed the writing assignments by their purpose and audience into five types of papers that might be called a rhetoric for psychology. As did Britton et al. (1975) in an earlier time, I recognize the fallibility of this category system, but present it, believing it is useful to teachers. Following a description of each type of paper is a summary of the literature on teaching these assignments.

Journal Writing

Writing a journal can be construed as expressive writing (Britton et al., 1975), or private writing (Flower, 1981), or *writing to learn* (Nodine, 1990, 1999)—where the purpose is to think about course content in one's own way and with the writer's own words. At one extreme, the entries—at least one per week—would consist of personal reflection on the course and would be shared with no one because the audience should be the self. More typically, teachers make graded assignments read by the instructor and often containing specific instructions on what to write. The constraints of grades and writing instructions make these journal assignments a bit less like expressive writing and more like transactional writing.

Instructors describe various techniques for incorporating some type of journal writing into their courses. Snodgrass (1985) requires and uses journals in the form that Britton et al. (1975) intended. She does not collect or grade them, but allots time in class for personal writing and encourages other specific writing in the journal as preparation for upcoming assignments. I believe this use offers a student the best opportunity to explore ideas without concern for getting it "right"—the way the teacher wants it. Ventis (1990) also did not evaluate the entries, but gave a specific exercise designed to stimulate class discussions and reflection by the student on the discussion. Other faculty (Connor-Greene, 2000; Hettich, 1990) shape the journal writing to fit their beliefs about making it more useful for the student. Hettich (1990) reviewed journals three times during the semester, using grades to encourage depth of thinking and a wider range of examples. He also used the journal to teach Bloom's Taxonomy by having students analyze their own journal entries according to the taxonomy, implicitly encouraging movement to a higher level. Connor-Greene (2000) required journal entries to apply personality theory concepts to characters from the media or students and their friends. Connor-Greene found higher test grades in classes with journals than without journals, inferring more active learning.

I believe that journals should be open to student exploration of their own ideas, so I question the procedure of reviewing or grading journals. I suspect that course instructors are being too conscientious, making the assignment of a journal equated in their minds with a graded assignment. However, in so doing, they put the student in the position of getting it right, which ultimately changes the purpose and audience for this writing activity. However, the instructors noted earlier who ask students to engage in a particular kind of journal writing, either during or outside of class, are teaching students a wider repertoire of writing processes, which will ultimately improve their writing in genres other than the journal.

Summaries/Syntheses

Writing a summary of class notes or text serves the purpose of helping students evaluate the level of importance of the main points of text or notes, in their own words, thus helping them remember the macrostructure, which can then be incorporated into their own knowledge (Knudsen, 1998). Summary writing is an ideal pedagogical means of connecting reading and writing. Radmacher and Latosi-Sawin (1995) described their technique for teaching summary writing by having students make discriminations among variously effective summaries of text material. In a course in which summary writing was a weekly activity, third-year psychology students performed better on exams than those students without required summary writing, although a study by Hinkle and Hinkle (1990) found more ambiguous results. Davis and Hult (1997) did not teach their freshman students how to summarize, but they did require them to write summaries of lecture material. After a fairly long delay, the summary group outperformed the controls on tests of the material. As in the previous study, the authors inferred that students attended better to the main ideas of the lecture. In these studies, writing a summary is viewed by the researchers not as an end in itself, but as a means toward better understanding and remembering of material. After students prepared essay test answers, Madigan and Brosamer (1990) coached them to improve the essays by providing good examples. In an effort to encourage the students to use their own language, not the lecturer's, Blevins-Knabe (1987) had students write about the content for a different audience, such as parents of a young child—an interesting variation of the simple summary.

Although these types of assignments may seem academically low level, no instructor would deny the importance of students being able to summarize their readings and lectures. The essence of what we teach is this synthesis of readings and lectures. In fact, Britton et al. (1975) would probably consider summaries of lectures and readings to be the ideal material of journals or expressive writing. For teachers reluctant to devote much time to this type of writing activity—it would be easy to ask students to share summaries with their seat mates or ask one to volunteer to read theirs aloud, allowing additions or corrections—these types of writing activities might be ideal material for electronic class discussions.

Application Papers

Closely related to the directed journal entries of Hettich (1990) and Connor-Greene (2000) are application papers, in which students prepare a short paper applying a concept from the course to an event. Polyson (1985) had students apply Maslow's peak experience to themselves, and Chrisler (1990) and Hemenover, Caster, and Mizumoto (1999) had students apply concepts from abnormal psychology to characters in a movie or novel.

This type of writing assignment is a favorite of mine. I have students select one concept each week and apply it to their own thinking or behaving. In my courses, these papers are ungraded assignments and might be considered similar to journal assignments. They are assignments that can encourage creativity in student writing. More important for me, they require that the student be thinking all week about how incidents of their own or others' behavior fit concepts in the course, so they must be thinking frequently of the course content.

Review Articles

An important type of writing needed by students of psychology is summarizing and synthesizing psychological literature. Review articles are described as "critical evaluations of material that has already been published" (American Psychological Association, 1994, p. 5). This paper might be what students call *term papers* and can vary from short papers at the level of Introductory Psychology to major work called a *senior thesis*. Bem (1995) offered guidance to professionals submitting articles to *Psychological Bulletin* that could be useful to undergraduates writing their first literature reviews. He noted that an audience of favorite grandmothers should be able to read the broad outlines of the paper, thus establishing an aspect of the writing style. He also offered several organizing strategies for summarizing and integrating the literature for the purpose of presenting the reviewer's perspective. Bem stated that a review should tell a straightforward tale with a single, linear narrative line unobscured by the tangential. He gave the example of an organization beginning with the conclusion and its reasons for acceptance followed by the supporting and nonsupporting data in order of descending weight. Most important, he pointed out that the organization should be by relation not chronology.

Guidance for less sophisticated writers working on their first literature review differs somewhat (Poe, 1990). Breaking the writing task down to subproblems, Poe emphasized individual article summaries with an example and tutorial for accomplishing simple integration of two articles. A model from meta-analysis helps students overcome problems of poorly defined topics, analytic and judgment deficiencies, and lack of integration of articles (Froese, Gantz, & Henry, 1998). Froese et al. (1998) taught solutions to these problems by designing meta-analysis-type exercises for students to apply to articles when writing literature reviews. Torrance, Thomas, and Robinson (1999) described the strategic patterns of processes of students in writing expository essays based on relevant literature. Although they found differences in the strategic application of the processes of reading, outlining, drafting sentences, and reviewing, the different patterns seemed unrelated to the quality of the papers produced.

Whether it is Bem (1995) concerned about professional psychologists or Poe (1990) and Froese et al. (1998) concerned about beginners, the instruction is to break the task down into subproblems, good advice any time one is confronted with a big problem. Hayes (1996) and Ransdell and Levy's (1996) emphasis on working memory's impact on writing described at the beginning of this paper suggests a rationale for these exercises. What is missing from these suggestions is guidance about purpose and audience. Bem's (1995) instruction about writing for one's grandmother, perhaps overstated, surely was meant to encourage professionals to be clearer in their writing. The definition of an audience is meant to define the background knowledge and expectations of that audience. Thus, beginning students should be writing for an audience for which they are able to project the level of knowledge and expectations—their own peers. My experience in coaching seniors in writing their senior theses is that they have great difficulty exerting ownership of the background material they have read. By the time they are seniors, they are comfortable in describing, summarizing, and even integrating the articles of others appropriately for a peer audience. The next level of a literature review—using the writing of others to support or deny a claim of their own—is difficult for them.

Research Proposals and Reports

Although research report papers are written by most undergraduate and graduate psychology students and are difficult for students to learn to write, there are few articles describing techniques for teaching this ubiquitous genre. Nadelman (1990) described a laboratory course in which students struggle to learn the appropriate form, language, and style of research reports. Students readily recognize that introduction, method, results, and discussion are the components of a research report, but they have difficulty composing each of these parts. Lectures, lab exercises, and writing exercises are part of Nadelman's course. The primary teaching techniques she uses for teaching the report are: focus on audience, breaking the report into sections, and successive drafts with comments and opportunities to rewrite. Nadelman presents this course as intertwining thinking and writing about research. Her techniques are good examples of points raised earlier in this paper—techniques for easing working memory constraints.

TEACHING THE PROCESSES OF WRITING IN PSYCHOLOGY

Teaching writing is based on many techniques, the most important of which is teaching students to draft and revise their work. The complexity of the thinking required to write a paper has been shown by the theories described at the beginning of this chapter. In offering advice on teaching writing, Kellogg (1994), in his fourth principle, told us that students should be taught task-specific procedures. How and when should we do this?

Teachers should have clearly in mind which type of paper the students are being assigned to write, as described earlier. Then the student should write a draft of the paper. Our expertise should guide the students' revision by our focus on the nature of the paper, not the grammatical problems. We understand what the ideal paper should be, and we can best guide the student toward that ideal. The method behind that guidance could be (a) offering good models of papers, (b) reading and commenting on drafts (Handelsman & Krest, 1999), or (c) holding peer review sessions with carefully crafted questions for the peers to answer. Which types of guidance you offer in your class are determined by the number of papers to be written, the centrality of the paper to your course goals, and the number of students in your class. Some methods use less faculty time but are still effective in guiding students.

The procedural skills needed to write research reports come from repeated writing experiences and can be supplemented by peer review sessions. Teaching undergraduate sophomores as beginners in the field of psychology may differ little from coaching professional psychologists to improve their writing skills. Drotar (2000) described a writers' workshop seminar for graduate students nearing completion of their dissertation. The seminar is based on verbal and written critique of student writing projects. Although the instructor moderates the seminar, most of the sessions are based on student comments. Common problems prompt general seminar discussion of purpose, organization, or need for cogent hypotheses to enhance the scientific contribution of data. Throughout the seminar, writers return with revisions of manuscripts to go through the review process again, further employing audience response to the work. Although the seminar at one time included lectures on different aspects of writing, Drotar evolved the successful seminar format of active learning—in-class peer reviews of their writing. Rileigh (1998) described a course with a similar goal for beginners in psychology. Because the students are new to psychology, everything about APA style must be taught in lectures and exercises. The parallel to Drotar's seminar is that the students wrote, held peer reviews, and revised their papers. In both of these settings, the revisions reflected the writer's growing skill in the specific genre of a paper in psychology.

In a fine example of a process-based course, Snodgrass (1985) incorporated numerous writing assignments that related to one another and to the course content. Journals were the workbook for the course, offering a place to write about course content and class demonstrations that could lead to working on the other required writing assignments. The fact that she did not evaluate or even look at the journals signaled to the students that the journal was for their own thinking. Thus, students learned that writing is the process to be used for thinking about ideas and other writing assignments. Snodgrass (1985) designed graded assignments so that they built on one another, each with feedback and an opportunity to learn skills needed for the next paper.

An emphasis on peer review and awareness of audience is taught indirectly by Blevins-Knabe (1987) by assigning pairs of students to write together an in-class application paper, which prompts much discussion between the students. Although faculty often pair students in laboratory exercises, they miss an opportunity to engage students in a peer-writing process by having students write individual papers.

The terms *portfolio* and *progressive writing* describe assignments that build on one another. Problem-solving strategies recommend that any large problem should be subdivided into smaller problems with subgoals, each one being solved separately. The role of working memory capacity and its impact on writing quality should lead teachers of writing to consider strategies for reducing the load on novice writers. Writing assignments constitute large problems that would benefit from being subdivided, although students may not come to this strategy unaided. Hemenover et al. (1999) divided an application paper into six steps, each one reviewed by the instructor. Students narrowed and focused a paper topic, summarized text material on their topic, selected and matched a movie to their topic, summarized the movie, and then integrated the sections based on previous comments. Although it was not a long paper, writing it was new to the students, and breaking it into steps allowed them to succeed and learn the skills.

The experience of regular writing assignments that differ in form or processes advance a student's skills. Beers (1985) offered a broad set of writing opportunities (poem, story, autobiography, text analysis, or reflection) restricted only by the requirement that some pieces of writing would be reviewed by the instructor and the student would revise them. Although students could write in a variety of forms, the object was to integrate that writing with course content and to improve on the better pieces. Thus, students gained an appreciation of types of writing they did well and were able to select that type to work on and strengthen. Rickabaugh (1993) similarly required weekly writing, although in a narrower range than Beers (1985). Students made observations and wrote how a theoretical concept could be applied. The advantage of this type of writing assignment is that the format remains the same while the particular concepts in psychology change. Thus, students practice writing with novel psychological content, but also acquire skill in using a format that is well practiced.

Concern for teaching writing skills in psychology has been manifested in each of the prior authors' individual courses. Another approach to teaching the writing process is to examine the psychology major as a whole. Drotar's (2000) seminar was developed in response to developmental expectations and concerns about the skill level of their graduates. Wood (1996) identified the four types of papers (literature review, research proposal, position paper, reflection paper) her department expects graduating seniors to show they have learned to write. Although she did not describe each of these types of papers, she made the point that members of her department recognized these four types. She found that not all seniors had written all four types of papers. Although I or my department members might not agree with the specifics of her seniors' graduation requirement, her approach is exemplary. A department should define what it expects its graduates to be able to do as writers just as we might define what content a student should study. Readers of this chapter have learned about the theoretical models of the writing process and of individual writing assignments. What is not found in the literature is a definition of goals for teaching writing. As departments, we must define the writing expectations we have for our graduates.

FINAL THOUGHTS

Admittedly biased, I have trouble understanding why all psychology faculty are not having students do writing as part of their courses. I have heard many excuses. Either it is too time-consuming to grade many long papers, students cannot write and hate to write, or we faculty are not trained to teach writing. None of these excuses is acceptable! Writing about psychology is thinking and learning about psychology. The reason I presented the many categories of writing assignments is because I want each of you to be able to select one writing task that fits your courses and the constraints and excuses of your class. Some of the writing exercises do not even require grading. Try one new activity in your course—a writing activity! Urge your colleagues to try one new activity. It will make a difference in student learning.

REFERENCES

American Psychological Association. (1994). *Publication manual of the American Psychological Association* (4th ed.). Washington, DC: Author.

Bem, D. J. (1995) Writing a review article for Psychological Bulletin. *Psychological Bulletin, 118,* 172–177.

Blevins-Knabe, B. (1987). Writing to learn while learning to write. *Teaching of Psychology, 14,* 239–241.

Britton, J., Burgess, T., Martin, N., McLeod, A., & Rosen, H. (1975). *The development of writing abilities.* London: Macmillan.

Beers, S. E. (1985). Use of a portfolio writing assignment in a course on developmental psychology. *Teaching of Psychology, 12,* 95–96.

Chrisler, J. (1990). Novels as case-study materials for psychology students. *Teaching of Psychology, 17,* 55–57.

Connor-Greene, P. A. (2000). Making connections: Evaluating the effectiveness of journal writing in enhancing student learning. *Teaching of Psychology, 27,* 44–46.

Davis, M., & Hult, R. (1997). Effects of writing summaries as a generative learning activity during note taking. *Teaching of Psychology, 24,* 47–49.

Drotar, D. (2000). Training professional psychologists to write and publish: The utility of a writers' workshop seminar. *Professional Psychology: Research and Practice, 31,* 453–457.

Flower, L. S. (1981). *Problem-solving strategies for writing.* New York: Harcourt Brace Jovanovich.

Froese, A. D., Gantz, B. S., & Henry, A. L. (1998). Teaching students to write literature reviews: A meta-analytic model. *Teaching of Psychology, 25,* 102–105.

Handelsman, M. M., & Krest, M. (1999). Improving your students' writing: Arts and drafts. In B. Perlman, L. McCann, & S. McFadden (Eds.), *Lessons learned* (pp. 179–184). Washington, DC: American Psychological Society.

Hayes, J. R. (1996). A new framework for understanding cognition and affect in writing. In C. M. Levy & S. Ransdell (Eds.), *The science of writing* (pp. 1–28). Mahwah, NJ: Lawrence Erlbaum Associates.

Hayes, J. R., & Flower, L. S. (1980). Identifying the organization of writing processes. In L. W. Gregg & E. R. Steinberg (Eds.), *Cognitive processes in writing* (pp. 3–30). Hillsdale, NJ: Lawrence Erlbaum Associates.

Hemenover, S. H., Caster, J. B., & Mizumoto, A. (1999). Combining the use of progressive writing techniques and popular movies in introductory psychology. *Teaching of Psychology, 26,* 196–198.

Hettich, P. (1990). Journal writing: Old fare or nouvelle cuisine? *Teaching of Psychology, 17,* 36–39.

Hinkle, S., & Hinkle, A. (1990). An experimental comparison of the effects of focused freewriting and other study strategies on lecture comprehension. *Teaching of Psychology, 17,* 31–35.

Kellogg, R. T. (1994). *The psychology of writing.* New York: Oxford University Press.

Kellogg, R. T. (1996). A model of working memory in writing. In C. M. Levy & R. S. Ransdell (Eds.), *The science of writing* (pp. 57–72). Mahwah, NJ: Lawrence Erlbaum Associates.

Knudson, R. E. (1998). College students' writing: An assessment of competence. *The Journal of Educational Research, 92,* 13–19.

Madigan, R., & Brosamer, J. (1990). Improving the writing skills of students in Introductory Psychology. *Teaching of Psychology, 17,* 27–30.

Nadelman, L. (1990). Learning to think and write as an empirical psychologist: The laboratory course in developmental psychology. *Teaching of Psychology, 17,* 45–48.

Nodine, B. F. (1990). Psychologists teach writing. *Teaching of Psychology, 17,* 4.

Nodine, B. F. (1999). Why not make writing assignments? In B. Perlman, L. McCann, & S. McFadden (Eds.), *Lessons learned* (pp. 167–172). Washington, DC: American Psychology Society.

Poe, R. E. (1990). A strategy for improving literature reviews in psychology courses. *Teaching of Psychology, 17,* 54–55.

Polyson, J. (1985). Students' peak experiences: A written exercise. *Teaching of Psychology, 12,* 211–213.

Radmacher, S. A., & Latosi-Sawin, E. (1995). Summary writing: A tool to improve student comprehension and writing in psychology. *Teaching of Psychology, 22,* 113–115.

Ransdell, S., & Levy, C. M. (1996). Working memory constraints on writing quality and fluency. In C. M. Levy & S. Ransdell (Eds.), *The science of writing* (pp. 93–105). Mahwah, NJ: Lawrence Erlbaum Associates.

Rickabaugh, C. (1993). The psychology portfolio: Promoting writing and critical thinking about psychology. *Teaching of Psychology, 20,* 170–172.

Rileigh, K. K. (1998). Teaching communication skills in psychology. *Teaching of Psychology, 25,* 279–282.

Snodgrass, S. E. (1985). Writing as a tool for teaching social psychology. *Teaching of Psychology, 12,* 91–94.

Torrance, M., Thomas, G. V., & Robinson, E. J. (1999). Individual differences in the writing behavior of undergraduate students. *British Journal of Educational Psychology, 69,* 189–199.

Ventis, D. G. (1990). Writing to discuss: Use of a clustering technique. *Teaching of Psychology, 17,* 42–44.

Wood, M. R. (1996). An advanced writing requirement for psychology majors: Lessons for faculty. *Teaching of Psychology, 23,* 243–245.

10

The Teaching–Advising Connection

Drew C. Appleby
Indiana University Purdue University Indianapolis

When I began my academic career in 1972, I was certain that teaching and advising were mutually exclusive activities. I believed that teaching consisted of giving lectures to groups of students in my classroom and then testing them to determine whether they had accurately assimilated the information from my lectures and their textbook. I believed that advising consisted of meeting individually with my psychology major advisees in my office to help them choose classes for the following semester in a manner that would allow them to graduate in 4 years.

As the years passed, this distinction started to blur as I began to realize that teaching and advising share a great deal in common. For example, my students who did not perform well in my classes often came to my office to seek help in improving their grades. This behavior did not meet my criteria for teaching because we were in my office (not the classroom), and they came alone (not in groups). It also did not meet my criteria for advising because they were my students (not my advisees), and they were concerned about the class in which they were currently enrolled (not about the classes they might enroll in next semester). At this point, I began to realize that I had stumbled into the Twilight Zone where teaching and advising intersect.

Although I had been taught how to teach students in graduate school, I had never been taught how to teach students how to learn what I was teaching them.

As a result, I looked at them seriously and offered platitudes like "Study harder," "Read the book more than once," or "Study with someone who is doing well in the class." They would leave my office, promising to follow my advice, but their grades seldom improved. My solution to this problem was to become a student again by enrolling in a continuing education class entitled "How to Study in College," in which I—and 25 recent high school graduates—learned strategies to listen actively, take useful notes, read a textbook for maximum comprehension, manage study time for optimum efficiency, and prepare for and take different types of tests. Although my graduate education in memory and cognition had provided the rationale for many of these strategies (e.g., the distributed practice effect that indicates studying is more efficient if it is spread out over several sessions, rather than being crammed into one), I had never before heard these principles put to such practical and valuable use in an educational context.

I began to insert the information I learned from this class into my lectures in ways that would help my students realize that a better understanding of their own cognitive processes (i.e., the development of metacognitive skills) could enable them to learn academic material more successfully. At this point, I began to realize that the distinction between teaching and advising was neither as strong nor as valid as I once believed. As my career continued, and I became professionally active in teaching and advising organizations, I started to understand that faculty who make this distinction may be doing so in a manner that is detrimental to their students, their advisees, and their own professional development. With these things in mind, let me pose the four questions that I will answer in this chapter:

1. How do faculty perceive their roles as academic advisors?
2. What is the linguistic relationship between the words teaching and advising?
3. Do effective teachers and effective advisors do the same thing?
4. Can academic advising increase human capital?

HOW DO FACULTY PERCEIVE THEIR ROLES AS ACADEMIC ADVISORS?

Do all my faculty colleagues share my enthusiasm for academic advising? According to a series of national surveys conducted by American College Testing, faculty provide the majority of academic advising in colleges and universities (ACT National Survey on Academic Advising, 1979, 1983, 1988). However, faculty perceptions of their advising roles are far from simple—and often rather disturbing—as characterized by Ware's (1993) unsettling statement that appears in the *Handbook for Enhancing Undergraduate Education in Psychology* (McGovern, 1993a). This statement is: "Although theory, research, and practical applications permeate the advising literature, most academic psychologists appear relatively *uninterested* in advising-related activities and outcomes" (Ware, 1993, p. 47).

Ware (1993) provided a clue to this enigma when he cited Larsen and Brown (1986), who found that when faculty were asked to agree or disagree with statements about "the adequacy of rewards for advising, the consideration of advising when giving merit raises, and the role of advising in promotion and tenure evaluation" (p. 62), 48% to 72% of them disagreed strongly with these statements. Other clues to this puzzle are the dramatic increase of college and university enrollments beginning in the 1950s; an equally striking increase in the demographic heterogeneity of the population of students in higher education; that students rate academic advising as their most used, but one of their lowest rated, campus services; and a dearth of information on advising in the teaching literature. For example, of the 1,790 articles that have appeared in *Teaching of Psychology* since it began publication in 1974, only 12 have the word *advising* or *advisor* in their titles (D. Johnson, personal communication, December 6, 2000).

It is no wonder that faculty have given academic advising such short shrift. It is an activity for which they lack information, are inadequately rewarded, are not always appreciated, and are called on to do in increasing amounts with a rapidly expanding and diversified clientele. McGovern (1993b) lent support to the last of these obstacles when he said, "Understanding developmental issues and teaching problem-solving strategies to students who differ in gender, age, ethnicity, patterns of enrollment, and prior academic and life experiences are significant challenges" (p. 222).

Titley and Titley (1982) put their tongues squarely in their cheeks and produced the following fictitious "advisor's rule," which appears facetious on the surface, but that may unfortunately ring true for many faculty who have served as academic advisors:

> Each faculty member shall be assigned a number of undergraduate students as his or her advisees and shall, with a minimum expenditure of time, effort, and caring, answer whatever trivial questions they might have, inform them of what courses they must take to graduate in whatever major they've chosen (however capricious that choice may be), and be available, if possible, to sign necessary registration forms. The faculty shall also be aware that, for themselves, advising is primarily a perfunctory clerical duty and a minor academic activity relative to teaching, research, and one's own career development, and that there shall be little or no reward or recognition for the performance of advising activities, save for the occasionally expressed appreciation of a grateful, well-advised student. (p. 46)

It was perceptions like these that lead MacLean (1953) to state:

> Advising is a process with a long and dignified history in college and university. At the same time, involving as it often does tedious clerical work combined with hit-and-run conferences with students on curricula, it is a most cordially hated activity by the majority of college teachers. (p. 357)

This affective juxtaposition regarding faculty perceptions of advising echoes in the following student responses to a campus-wide advising evaluation form that asked them to complete this sentence: "Advisors are_____." Their responses were "friends, helpful, uninformed, doing their best, working overtime, necessary, teachers, counselors, knowledgeable, a drag, problem solvers, nervous, listeners, the ones who have all your information but don't remember your name, and too busy" (cited in Crockett, 1978). Perhaps Hardee (1970) said it best when he stated, "Faculty advising is dignified and derided, much desired but often denigrated, done well and done ill" (p. 27).

Does academic advising deserve such vilification from faculty? To begin to answer this question, let us first gain a better understanding of the words *teaching* and *advising*.

WHAT IS THE LINGUISTIC RELATIONSHIP BETWEEN THE WORDS "TEACHING" AND "ADVISING"?

As I prepared this chapter, I decided to augment my review of the professional literature by investigating the linguistic connections between the words *teaching* and *advising*. When I consulted Roget's Thesaurus (1994), I discovered the following: The word *teacher* is synonymous with the words *mentor, guide, confidant, consultant,* and *advisor*. The word *advisor* is synonymous with the words *mentor, guide, confidant, consultant,* and *teacher*. Other words that share synonymous relations with both teacher and advisor are *scholar, instructor, authority, expert, inspirer, persuader, advocate, planner, strategist, mediator, ombudsman, agent,* and *negotiator*.

It appears that—at least within a lexical context—*teaching* and *advising* are words with similar meanings. However, are they as closely related in the way they are perceived in higher education? Reflecting on his experiences during hundreds of developmental advising workshops, Grites (1994) reported his disappointment after asking thousands of faculty to "Write down your synonym(s) for academic advising . . . and never (not once!) receiving teaching as a response" (p. 82). Let me address this puzzling situation by posing my third question.

DO EFFECTIVE TEACHERS AND EFFECTIVE ADVISORS DO THE SAME THINGS?

In her presidential address to the National Academic Advising Association entitled "Advising as Teaching," Ryan (1992) encouraged faculty to regard advising as an integral part of their teaching role. She began her address by citing three experts. The first two are known for their advising expertise and the third for his teaching expertise.

In a ground-breaking article entitled "A Developmental View of Advising as Teaching," Crookston (1972) argued that the facilitation of learning is the duty of both teachers and advisors, and that both of these roles involve working with students to improve their problem-solving and decision-making skills. Kramer (1983) argued that advising is a specific teaching activity during which a student's educational choices are questioned and challenged. In his well-known book *The Craft of Teaching: Mastering the Professor's Art*, Eble (1988) clearly stated that advising is an extension of faculty's teaching role, in which they can demonstrate genuine concern for their students' welfare by being available and approachable outside the classroom.

After introducing the teaching–advising connection in this manner, Ryan (1992) reported the results of a comprehensive search of the ERIC database to identify the characteristics of effective teachers and advisors. She then synthesized these teaching and advising characteristics in such a way that it became clear there is a great deal of overlap between these two activities. Table 10.1 presents the results of Ryan's synthesis, plus seven additional characteristics I gleaned from a review of the recent teaching and advising literature.

After constructing Table 10.1, I came to the same conclusion that Ryan had come to a decade ago: The knowledge, skills, and characteristics displayed by effective teachers are essentially the same as those exhibited by effective advisors. Once teachers become aware of this similarity, they may begin, as Ryan (1992) said, to "perceive their role as advisors differently" (p. 7). Once their perceptions begin to change, they may become more interested in the advising process as a legitimate component of their teaching role. As their interest in advising increases, they may begin to acquire more knowledge of student development theory, sharpen their institutional and departmental knowledge, and perhaps even engage in mentoring pairs where experienced advisors take novice advisors under their wings for a trial period. If they can link these practices to positive outcomes in their advisees, perhaps teachers will no longer share the opinion of Crookston (1972), who stated that most faculty do not view advising as teaching, but rather as an extracurricular, nonteaching burden. After establishing the semantic, affective, and conceptual relations between teaching and advising, it is now time to explore advising from a more analytical perspective by investigating two different approaches to this activity.

IS THERE MORE THAN ONE TYPE OF ACADEMIC ADVISING?

In one of the classic articles in the advising literature, Crookston (1972) introduced the term *developmental advising* by contrasting it with the term *prescriptive advising*. He explained prescriptive advising with the following medical analogy. Patients (advisees) are people who seek the advice of doctors (advisors) when they

TABLE 10.1
A Comparison of the Knowledge, Skills, and Characteristics of Effective Teachers
and Advisors

Knowledge, Skills, and Characteristics of Effective Teachers	Knowledge, Skills, and Characteristics of Effective Advisors
Master their subject matter	Possess accurate information about the policies, procedures, resources, and programs of their departments and institutions
Plan, organize, and prepare materials for classroom presentation	Are well prepared for advising sessions
Engage students actively in the learning process	Enable advisees to participate actively in the advising process by challenging them with new, more demanding learning tasks involving alternative ideas or choices and encouraging them to ask questions to clarify these ideas and explore these choices
Provide regular feedback, reinforcement, and encouragement to students	Provide timely feedback, reinforce learning that has taken place, and applaud student successes
Create an environment conducive to learning	Create a good learning climate within advising sessions
Stimulate student interest in their subject by teaching it enthusiastically	Project enthusiasm for their area of academic expertise and their advisory duties
Help students learn independently	Encourage advisees to become self-directed learners
Teach students how to evaluate information	Help advisees evaluate and reevaluate their progress toward personal, educational, and career goals
Teach students how to express ideas clearly	Use questioning techniques that encourage shy advisees to express themselves
Act as co-learners during the learning process	Set performance goals for themselves and their advisees
Serve as a resource to students	Provide materials to advisees and refer them to others when referral is an appropriate response
Relate course content to students' experiences	Assist students in the consideration of their life goals by helping them relate their experiences, interests, skills, and values to career paths and the nature and purpose of higher education
Provide problem-solving tasks to students	Provide tasks to be completed before the next advising meeting that require the advisee to use information-gathering, decision-making, and problem-solving skills
Personalize the learning process	Help students gain self-understanding and self-acceptance
Deliver information clearly and understandably	Communicate in a clear and unambiguous manner with advisees
Exhibit good questioning skills	Serve as catalysts by asking questions and initiating discussions
Exhibit good listening skills	Listen carefully and constructively to advisees' messages
Exhibit positive regard, concern, and respect for students	Provide a caring and personal relationship by exhibiting a positive attitude toward students, their goals, and their ability to learn

TABLE 10.1

(Continued)

Knowledge, Skills, and Characteristics of Effective Teachers	Knowledge, Skills, and Characteristics of Effective Advisors
Are approachable and available outside the classroom	Provide accessible and responsive advising services
Present themselves to students in an open and genuine manner	Provide a climate of trust in which advisees feel free to ask questions, express concerns, revise ideas, make decisions, and share personal experiences and knowledge
Serve as role models who can help students understand the mission, values, and expectations of the institution	Model the tenets of the university, and demonstrate enthusiasm and knowledge about the goals and purposes of higher education
"Promote effective learning climates that are supportive of diversity" (Puente, 1993, p. 82)	Respect diverse points of view by demonstrating sensitivity to differences in culture and gender
Use outcomes assessment to "make data-based suggestions for improving teaching and learning" (Halpern, 1993, p. 44)	Make changes or add to advising knowledge and skills by assessing the advising process
"Stimulate learning at higher cognitive levels" (Mathie, 1993, p. 185)	Help students move beyond rote memorization or recall (Grites, 1994), help advisees test the validity of their ideas (Hagen, 1994), and "challenge students to confront their attitudes, beliefs, and assumptions" (Laff, 1994, p. 47)
Engage in the "lifelong learning they espouse for their students" (Fretz, 1993, p. 95)	"Participate in training and learn about educational issues that influence advising and about students served" (Frost, 1991, p. 74)
Help students "choose careers that best suit their aptitudes and interests" (Brewer, 1993, p. 171)	Help students explore career goals and choose programs, courses, and co-curricular activities that support these goals
Use professional networks to share ideas, solve problems, provide support, and develop collegiality (Weiten, 1993)	"Learn from each other, share enthusiasm for their duties, and discuss mutual problems" (Frost, 1991, p. 65)
Utilize interactive computer software that promotes active learning (Mathie, 1993)	Utilize institutional technology (e.g., degree audit reports) to augment advising, recommend interactive software (e.g., SIGI PLUS) that can help advisees clarify goals and identify career options (Rooney, 1994), and communicate with advisees via e-mail

Note. All the information in this table has been summarized from Ryan (1992) unless another reference has been provided.

realize they have medical (academic) problems, and doctors are the authorities who prescribe treatments to cure their patients' problems. According to Crookston, a prescriptive advisor assumes that "once advice is given, his responsibility is largely fulfilled; now it is up to the student to fulfill his responsibility to do what is prescribed" (p. 6).

Although the results of prescriptive advising are often successful, it has one major drawback—it fails to help students develop a sense of responsibility for their academic choices. Crookston described this problem when he said, "The decision (prescription) is the advisor's, so if the advice turns out badly, the student doesn't feel responsible; he can place the blame on the advisor" (p. 6). This type of assumption about academic responsibility is particularly damaging to student development if it is made—either implicitly or explicitly—in colleges and universities whose institutional goals include those similar to the following from my former institution: "to support academic freedom with responsibility in order to foster a dynamic community of learners" and "to create a caring and challenging environment in which students, faculty, and staff prepare to be responsible agents of a more humane society" (*Marian College Catalog*, 1997, p. 4).

Crookston used McGregor's (1960) Theory X and Theory Y models of human relations to distinguish between developmental and prescriptive advisors. Prescriptive advisors, like human relations managers who espouse Theory X, believe that people dislike work and seek to avoid it, prefer to be directed, attempt to avoid responsibility, lack ambition, and "must be coerced, controlled, directed, and threatened with punishment to get them to put forth adequate effort toward the achievement of individual objectives" (p. 34). Developmental advisors, like managers who believe in Theory Y, assume that people do not inherently dislike work, are motivated to self-actualize, and behave in ways that demonstrate that external control and the threat of punishment are not the most effective motivators to accomplish goals. It seems obvious that advisors who hold these different views of human nature will construct and use different advising strategies.

Crookston (1972) clearly equated developmental advising with teaching, which he defined as "any experience in the learning community in which teacher and student interact that contributes to individual, group, or community growth and development, and which can be evaluated" (p. 5). He stated that developmental advising is:

> concerned not only with a specific personal or vocational decision but also with facilitating the student's rational processes, environmental and interpersonal interactions, behavioral awareness, problem-solving, decision-making, and evaluation skills. Not only are these "advising" functions but, deriving from the above assumptions, they are essentially "teaching" functions as well . . . based on a negotiated agreement between the student and the teacher in which varying degrees of learning by both parties to the transaction are the product. (pp. 5–9)

Table 10.2 contrasts the assumptions of prescriptive and developmental advisors using 10 dimensions from Crookston's (1972) original article and 19 more dimensions I have identified during my 30 years of advising. Although this table reveals a variety of ways in which these two types of advisors differ, the major thread that runs throughout these differences is that developmental advisors gradually shift the responsibility of the relationship to their advisees and prepare them for this shift by providing them with problem-solving and decision-making skills, challenging them to develop higher order thought processes, and

TABLE 10.2

A Multidimensional Contrast of the Assumptions of Prescriptive and
Developmental Advisors

Crookston's Dimensions	Prescriptive Advisors	Developmental Advisors
Abilities	Focus is on limitations (i.e., the advisor uses student's past performances to predict future obstacles).	Focus is on potentialities (i.e., the advisor uses past performance and current aspirations to anticipate potential).
Motivation	Students are viewed as passive, lazy, irresponsible, and in need of help and prodding.	Students are viewed as competent, striving, and active seekers of information.
Rewards	Students are motivated by grades, credit, income, and parental threats.	Students are motivated by mastery, achievement, recognition, status, and fulfillment.
Maturity	Students are immature, irresponsible, and must be closely supervised.	Students are responsible, maturing, and capable of self-direction.
Initiative	The advisor takes the initiative regarding the fulfillment of requirements; any additional advising is initiated by the student.	Either the advisor or advisee can initiate advising.
Control	The advisor is the authority and is in control.	Control is shared and negotiated.
Responsibility	The advisor's responsibility is to provide advice, and the advisee's responsibility is to act on the advisor's advice.	Responsibility is negotiated and/or shared.
Learning Output	The student learns from the advisor.	Both the student and advisor learn and develop.
Evaluation	The advisor evaluates the advisee's progress.	Evaluation is a collaborative advisor/student effort.
Relationship	A formal relationship exists between advisor (authority) and student (dependent), which is based on status, strategies, games, and a low level of trust.	The advisor/student relationship is informal, flexible, situational, and based on a high level of trust.
Appleby's Dimensions		
Purpose	The purpose of advising is to deliver accurate information to as many students as possible in as efficient a manner as possible.	The purpose of advising is to develop mentoring relationships with students that will enable them to continue to develop personally, academically, and professionally after the formal advisor–advisee relationship has ended.

(Continued)

TABLE 10.2

(Continued)

Appleby's Dimensions	Prescriptive Advisors	Developmental Advisors
Ultimate Goal	The ultimate goal of advising is to enable students to earn diplomas and graduate "on time."	The ultimate goal of advising is to enable students to clarify their future goals, plan strategies to accomplish these goals, and then accomplish them.
Location	Advising takes place in the advisor's office.	Advising can take place anywhere (e.g., in the advisor's office, in the hall, on a campus bench, at a basketball game, in the student union or cafeteria, etc.).
Future	The future refers to next semester.	The future refers to postbaccalaureate opportunities.
Course Rationale	Courses are taken to "get them out of the way."	Courses are taken to develop the knowledge, skills, and characteristics essential to postbaccalaureate success (e.g., graduate school or immediate employment).
Curricular/ Co-Curricular Emphasis	The emphasis is on curricular activities (i.e., classes). Extracurricular activities are deemphasized and seen as extraneous and/or interfering with academic progress.	The emphasis is on both curricular and co-curricular activities (e.g., membership in organizations and volunteer activities) to develop both academic skills and interpersonal capabilities (e.g., leadership, ability to work as a team member, acceptance of diversity, etc.).
Strength/Weakness Emphasis	The emphasis is on hiding weaknesses and using strengths to bolster GPA (i.e., avoiding hard classes and taking easy ones).	The emphasis is on recognizing what skills will be necessary to accomplish future goals, strengthening those that are weak, and continuing to build those that are strong.
Questions Addressed	What courses do I have to take? Who is teaching them? When are they offered? How difficult are they? Will I have to write a paper? Is there a lot of reading?	What can I do with a degree in psychology? Why are statistics and experimental important classes? What classes can I take after English Composition to strengthen my writing skills? What courses will prepare me for graduate school?
Culpability	The advisee assumes the advisor is responsible for negative consequences if errors occur.	Advisees understand that they are responsible for negative consequences if errors in advising occur.

TABLE 10.2
(Continued)

Appleby's Dimensions	Prescriptive Advisors	Developmental Advisors
Delivery System(s)	A single delivery system is used (one-on-one meeting in the advisor's office).	Multiple delivery systems are used (e.g., orientation classes, e-mail, telephone, seminars, workshops, alumni panels, handbooks, and peer advisors).
Curricular Understanding	Students "understand" the curriculum when they know what classes they must take and when to take them.	Students "understand" the curriculum when they realize how they will change as a result of completing classes and how these changes will enable them to accomplish their postbaccalaureate goals.
Stability/Change	The advising process remains constant as the student progresses from freshman to senior.	The advising process changes in response to the developmental needs of students as they progress from freshmen to seniors (i.e., different questions are addressed).
Thinking Skills Involved	*Retention* (e.g., What courses do I have to take? When do I have to take statistics? How many credits do I have to have to graduate?)	*Comprehension* (e.g., Why do I have to take Physiological Psychology? I want to be a counselor, not a biopsychologist.) *Application* (e.g., How can I graduate if I have three semesters of classes to go and only two semesters of financial aid left?) *Analysis* (e.g., How can I satisfy the requirements of General Education, and how do all the requirements fit together?) *Synthesis* (e.g., What electives should I take to help me work with unwed pregnant teenagers after I graduate?) *Evaluation* (e.g., Is clinical psychology an attainable career for me?)
View of Electives	Electives are courses that are easy, fun, can raise GPA, and are offered at convenient times.	Electives are courses that enable students to expand on the knowledge they gain in their required courses and to "construct" themselves as unique individuals who are different from other undergraduates with the same degree.

(Continued)

TABLE 10.2

(Continued)

Appleby's Dimensions	Prescriptive Advisors	Developmental Advisors
Rule Orientation	The advisor attempts to make sure that advisees follow all rules and procedures to the letter.	The advisor will attempt to bend rules and procedures if such accommodations are in the best educational interest of the student.
Appropriate Topics	The advisor sticks to academic advising and avoids giving personal or career advice.	Many topics can be broached and discussed during advising sessions as long as they fall within the competence of the advisor.
Skill Development	Emphasis is on passing skill courses (e.g., Statistics) to "get them out of the way" rather than on actually acquiring and retaining the skills they teach.	The development of skills is stressed in a way that allows advisees to understand the value of the skills they will acquire and how the sequence of the curriculum will require them to retain and build on these skills.
Personal Insight	Personal insight is not stressed after an advisee has decided on a major.	Personal insight is a driving force during all advising sessions (e.g., "Do you still want to be a clinical psychologist?").
Curricular Rationale	It is unnecessary for advisors to explain to advisees why they must take certain classes other than that these classes are required for graduation. (Assumption: Advisees are only interested in what classes they should take, not why they should take them or how they will be changed as a result of taking them.)	One of an advisor's most important roles is to enable advisees to comprehend the rationale behind classes they will take and the way these classes are sequenced. (Assumption: Advisees are more likely to involve themselves in classes they know will enable them to accomplish their goals and will attempt to retain and strengthen the skills these goals require.)

helping them gain clearer insight into their own goals as well as the goals of higher education.

Crookston (1972) said that a developmental advisor views the advising process "as a shared experience and recognizes that the student is not likely to learn from the relationship with the advisor unless the advisor himself is also open to learning" (p. 8). This assumption is in full agreement with teaching's emphasis on professional development as described by Fretz (1993), who admonished teachers to engage in the "lifelong learning they espouse for their students" (p. 95). This active, dynamic interchange, which is the fundamental nature of the developmental advising relationship, produces trust, curiosity, enthusiastic participation, and a sincere desire to learn and grow. This desire to learn and grow is the essence of education, and one of the most important goals of education is to prepare students for their professional futures. Can academic advising enable higher education to accomplish this goal?

CAN ACADEMIC ADVISING INCREASE HUMAN CAPITAL?

Halpern (1993) stated that, "The first and perhaps most persuasive reason for embarking on a nationwide effort to assess educational outcomes in higher education is the concern over a crisis in human capital" (pp. 23–24). This concern was echoed by Shaffer (1997) in his article "A Human Capital Approach to Academic Advising," in which he stated, "Human capital is created when people acquire transferable skills that can be applied in many settings and that can inform many different occupations" (p. 6). He used the phase "investment in human capital" to refer to actions taken by individuals to increase their productivity.

He noted formal education as a prime example of such an investment—in addition to adult education, on-the-job training, health, and geographic mobility—and listed a series of transferable skills that can be acquired during an undergraduate education, which employers indicate are crucial for prospective employees to possess (Carnevale, Gainer, & Meltzer, 1988). This list includes knowing how to learn; reading, writing, and computation; listening and oral communication; creative thinking and problem solving; goal setting; interpersonal skills; and leadership. These attributes are some of the same fundamental skills identified by the U.S. Department of Labor's Secretary's Commission on Achieving Necessary Skills in a 1991 report entitled "What Work Requires of Schools: A SCANS Report for America 2000." According to this report, these skills form the essential foundation for the following complex abilities that American workers need to succeed on the job in the new millennium:

- the ability to utilize resources
- the ability to work effectively with others
- the ability to acquire and use information
- the ability to operate effectively within a system
- the ability to utilize technology to solve problems

Shaffer (1997) emphasized that effective academic advisors and teachers share many of the same qualities, including "actively involving students in identifying their interests, skills, and life goals" (p. 10). When advisors help their advisees think about their education as a way of acquiring the skills and abilities they need to actualize their postbaccalaureate goals, the next logical step is to bring them to the point where they begin to ask themselves the following question when they are faced with educational decisions: "What does this choice contribute to the building of my human capital?" (p. 10). Shaffer was careful to state that this approach should not be adhered to slavishly, but that it is useful for students who must decide among classes that have higher and lower probabilities of helping them increase their human capital (e.g., choosing to enroll in a section of History of the Modern World that involves a substantial writing component rather than in one that requires only memorization of facts to pass objective tests).

Shaffer (1997) concluded his article by saying, "Each time the principle of maximizing human capital is considered, students are actively engaged in considering their futures and the preparatory role of their current educational activities. Such consideration is at the heart of the developmental model of academic advising" (p. 11). Because the average worker now changes careers four to six times during his or her lifetime (Rosenstock, 1991), it is imperative for students to understand they can no longer earn a diploma and assume their education has ended. They must become wise investors in their own human capital if they wish to succeed, and advisors can help them develop this wisdom.

CONCLUDING REMARKS

Thus far, I have attempted to explain (a) how college and university faculty view their role as academic advisors, (b) how teaching and advising are closely related activities, (c) that two types of advising strategies exist, and (d) that developmental advising can enhance human capital. When we teach our students metacognitive skills, we teach them how to think about and understand their own thought processes and how to construct strategies to use their thought processes more effectively. Developmental advising serves the same purpose, but on a much larger scale, because it enables students to understand the purpose of their education, identify their strengths and weaknesses, develop planning and decision-making skills, and tailor their education to their specific postbaccalaureate goals. In other words, developmental advising enables them to form a more meaningful schema of their undergraduate education and to understand how they can use the outcomes of their education to thrive in a world changing faster than ever before.

When developmental advising is delivered in a skillful and caring manner, it provides a cooperative context in which teaching can be maximally effective. Well-delivered developmental advising helps students understand why they are required to take certain classes, why they should take their classes in a certain sequence (e.g., statistics before research methods), what knowledge and skills they can develop in each of their classes (i.e., student learning outcomes [SLOs]), and the connection between the SLOs of their department's curriculum and the knowledge and skills they will be required to demonstrate in graduate school and/or their future careers. When teachers and advisors provide their students with this information, they are empowering them to become motivated and cooperative partners in the teaching–learning process. Two anonymous student responses to a recent survey designed to measure psychology majors' awareness of and ability to accomplish their department's SLOs (Appleby, 2000) illustrate this contention with considerable insight and conviction.

> *Student One*: Give better explanations of *why* students need to know the things they are learning in their classes and not just "You need to know this." For example, in what other classes would the same SLOs be used? Statistics was used again in both my Research Methods and Capstone classes. Students need to know these things!

> *Student Two*: I learned in my cognition class that when people are aware of the purpose of a task they are asked to perform, they usually perform it better. If my teachers would tell me why I am doing the things they want me to do—that is, the department's SLOs and why they are important for me to accomplish—I would be much more enthusiastic about accomplishing them. I am not an animal that must be operantly conditioned. I am a human being who can benefit from knowing the purposes and consequences of the behaviors I am asked to perform.

These student comments are remarkably similar to Lindsay and Norman's (1972) description of the difference between the behaviorist and cognitive models of human learning. "Classical learning theories typically rely on repeated exposure to specific stimuli as the basis of acquiring information," whereas the cognitive model proposes that the human information processing system "learns through an active interaction with its environment, rather than a passive build-up of stimulus-response connections" (p. 431). Twenty-seven years later, Svinicki (1999) took Lindsay and Norman's idea a step further when she declared, "Motivation is based on the learner's perceptions of being in control of his or her own destiny. . . . When learners have choices and believe that their success rides on these choices, they are highly motivated to put forth effort" (p. 22). Well-delivered developmental advising lives out the spirit of the cognitive model by (a) encouraging students to interact dynamically within their educational environments, and (b) providing them with informed choices that give them conscious and purposeful control over their personal, education, and professional destinies.

I conclude this chapter with several noteworthy quotations. The first is from Gordon (1988), one of the foremost experts on the topic of academic advising today. She described three outcomes for advising in this quotation, which summarize much of what I have presented in this chapter. She said that successful advising takes place when students are:

- developing competence, or increasing the intellectual, physical, and social skills that lead to the knowledge that one is capable of handling and mastering a range of tasks;
- developing autonomy, or confronting a series of issues leading ultimately to the recognition of one's independence; and

- developing purpose, or assessing and clarifying interests, educational and career options, and lifestyle preferences and using these factors to set a coherent
direction for life. (p. 109)

I am fond of this quotation because it suggests that successful advising can produce
positive outcomes not only in our students' intellectual and professional lives, but
also in their personal, social, and civic lives as well.

The purpose of higher education is not—and should not be—limited to the
production of employable people. We must constantly remind ourselves that we
have the opportunity to affect our students in a multitude of ways that can help
them become well-rounded human beings. I can think of no better way to explain this well roundedness than to present you with a quotation written nearly
150 years ago by Newman (1852/1947) in his book *The Idea of a University*. In
this volume, he clearly set forth the purpose of higher education by saying the
following:

> University training is the great ordinary means to a great but ordinary end; it aims
> at raising the intellectual tone of society, cultivating the public mind, purifying the
> national taste, supplying true principles to popular enthusiasm and fixed aims to
> popular aspiration, giving enlargement and sobriety to the ideas of the age, facilitat-
> ing the exercise of political power, and refining the intercourse of private life. It is
> the education which gives us a clear and conscious view of our own opinions and
> judgments, a truth in developing them, an eloquence in expressing them, and a force
> in urging them. It teaches us to see things as they are, to go right to the point, to
> disentangle a skein of thought, to detect what is sophisticated, and to discard what
> is irrelevant. It prepares us to fill any post with credit and to master any subject with
> facility. It shows us how to accommodate ourselves to others, how to throw ourselves
> into their state of mind, how to bring before them our own, how to influence them,
> how to come to an understanding with them, and how to bear with them. The edu-
> cated person is at home in any society, has common ground with every class, knows
> when to speak and when to be silent, is able to converse, is able to listen, can ask
> a question pertinently, and gain a lesson seasonably when he or she has nothing to
> impart. (pp. 134–135)

Ramos (1994) asked us to "Think of academic advising as a course offered
to our advisees" (p. 91). He suggested that when we advise, we should think of
ourselves as teachers, our advisees as students, our offices as classrooms, and
student growth—along several dimensions—as the learning outcome of the class.
His words and ideas sum up exactly what I have attempted to communicate in this
chapter—that we should be both teachers and advisors to our students and that the
goal of both our teaching and advising should be to enable our students to become
aware of how and why they must change, to identify the educational strategies
they can use to accomplish these changes, and to have the courage and initiative
to actualize these changes.

It is my sincere hope that this chapter contains information that will enable you to help your students grow within their personal, social, intellectual, civic, and professional dimensions. The two men to whom this book is dedicated—Bill McKeachie and Charles Brewer—have served as teachers and advisors to thousands of undergraduate psychology majors, and it is with their words that I end this chapter. McKeachie (1999) wisely noted that, "Some of your most effective teaching may occur during office hours" (p. 248). Brewer (1993) challenged us to "Provide students with the experience and understanding they will need to make the world a better place in which to lead productive and fulfilling lives" (p. 180). By heeding the advice of these master teacher-advisors, we can facilitate our students' understanding of the nature and value of higher education. Once they have gained this understanding, they can use it to shape the world around them, take their place as professionals in the 21st century, and assume the equally challenging roles of loyal colleagues, faithful friends, loving partners, and devoted parents. It is their accomplishment of these lofty goals that continues to fuel my enthusiasm for the dynamic process of the teaching–advising connection.

ACKNOWLEDGMENTS

I would like to offer my sincere gratitude to Steve Davis and Bill Buskist for inviting me to write this essay and to Bill McKeachie and Charles Brewer for giving them the reason for my invitation. Having colleagues and friends such as these four has been an inspiration to me during my three decades as an academic psychologist. I would also like to thank the G. Stanley Hall Lecture Selection Committee of the American Psychological Association for inviting me to present the lecture from which this chapter is derived, thereby providing me with the motivation and support to research and write about two academic endeavors I truly love: teaching and advising.

REFERENCES

ACT National Survey on Academic Advising. (1979). Iowa City, IA: American College Testing Program.

ACT National Survey on Academic Advising. (1983). Iowa City, IA: American College Testing Program.

ACT National Survey on Academic Advising. (1988). Iowa City, IA: American College Testing Program.

Appleby, D. C. (2000). [Student awareness survey]. Unpublished raw data.

Brewer, C. L. (1993). Curriculum. In T. V. McGovern (Ed.), *Handbook for enhancing undergraduate education in psychology* (pp. 161–182). Washington, DC: American Psychological Association.

Carnevale, A. P., Gainer, L. I., & Meltzer, A. S. (1988). *Workplace basics: The skills employers want.* Washington, DC: U.S. Department of Labor and the American Society for Training and Development.

Crockett, D. S. (Ed.). (1978). *Academic advising: A resource document.* Iowa City, IA: American College Testing Program.

Crookston, B. B. (1972). A developmental view of academic advising as teaching. *Journal of College Student Personnel, 13,* 12–17.

Eble, K. E. (1988). *The craft of teaching: A guide to mastering the professor's art.* San Francisco: Jossey-Bass.

Fretz, B. R. (1993). The compleat scholar: Faculty development for those who teach psychology. In T. V. McGovern (Ed.), *Handbook for enhancing undergraduate education in psychology* (pp. 93–122). Washington, DC: American Psychological Association.

Frost, S. H. (1991). Fostering the critical thinking of college women through academic advising and faculty contact. *Journal of College Student Development, 32,* 356–359.

Gordon, V. N. (1988). Developmental advising. In W. R. Habley (Ed.), *Status and future of academic advising: Problems and promise* (pp. 107–118). Iowa City, IA: American College Testing Program.

Grites, T. J. (1994). From principle to practice: Pain or gain? *National Academic Advising Association Journal, 14,* 80–84.

Hagen, P. L. (1994). Academic advising as dialectic. *National Academic Advising Association Journal, 14,* 85–88.

Halpern, D. F. (1993). Targeting outcomes: Covering your assessment concerns and needs. In T. V. McGovern (Ed.), *Handbook for enhancing undergraduate education in psychology* (pp. 23–46). Washington, DC: American Psychological Association.

Hardee, M. D. (1970). Faculty advising in colleges and universities. *American College Personnel Association Monograph: Student Personnel Services, No. 9.*

Kramer, H. C. (1983). Advising: Implications for faculty development. *National Academic Advising Association Journal, 3,* 25–31.

Laff, N. S. (1994). Reconsidering the developmental view of advising: Have we come a long way? *National Academic Advising Association Journal, 14,* 46–49.

Larsen, M. D., & Brown, B. M. (1986). Rewards for academic advising: An evaluation. In D. S. Crockett (Ed.), *Advising skills, techniques, and resources* (pp. 349–359). Iowa City, IA: American College Testing Program.

Lindsay, P. H., & Norman, D. A. (1972). *Human information processing: An introduction to psychology.* New York: Academic Press.

MacLean, M. S. (1953). Counseling and the Tower of Babel. *Personnel and Guidance Journal, 31,* 357–362.

Marian College Catalog: 1977–1999. (1997). (Available from Marian College, 3200 Cold Spring Road, Indianapolis, IN 46222-1997.)

Mathie, V. A. (1993). Promoting active learning in psychology classes. In T. V. McGovern (Ed.), *Handbook for enhancing undergraduate education in psychology* (pp. 183–214). Washington, DC: American Psychological Association.

McGovern, T. V. (1993a). *Handbook for enhancing undergraduate education in psychology.* Washington, DC: American Psychological Association.

McGovern, T. V. (1993b). Transforming undergraduate psychology for the next century. In T. V. McGovern (Ed.), *Handbook for enhancing undergraduate education in psychology* (pp. 217–238). Washington, DC: American Psychological Association.

McGregor, D. (1960). *The human side of enterprise.* New York: McGraw-Hill.

McKeachie, W. J. (1999). *Teaching tips: Strategies, research, and theory for college and university teachers.* Boston: Houghton-Mifflin.

Newman, J. H. (1852/1947). *The idea of a university.* New York: HoH, Rinehart.

Puente, A. E. (1993). Toward a psychology of variance: Increasing the presence and understanding of ethnic minorities in psychology. In T. V. McGovern (Ed.), *Handbook for enhancing undergraduate education in psychology* (pp. 71–92). Washington, DC: American Psychological Association.

Ramos, B. (1994). O'Banion revisited: Now more than ever. *National Academic Advising Association Journal, 14,* 89–91.

Roget's thesaurus of English words and phrases. (1994). United Kingdom: Longman Group UK Limited.

Rooney, M. (1994). Back to the future: Crookston and O'Banion revisited. *National Academic Advising Association Journal, 14,* 35–38.

Rosenstock, L. (1991). The walls come down: The reunification of vocational and academic education. *Phi Delta Kappan, 72,* 434–436.

Ryan, C. C. (1992). Advising as teaching. *National Academic Advising Association Journal, 12,* 4–8.

Shaffer, L. S. (1997). A human capital approach to academic advising. *National Academic Advising Association Journal, 17,* 5–12.

Svinicki, M. D. (1999). *Teaching and learning on the edge of the millennium: Building on what we have learned.* San Francisco: Jossey-Bass.

Titley, R. W., & Titley, B. S. (1982). Academic advising: The neglected dimension in designs for undergraduate education. *Teaching of Psychology, 9*(1), 45–49.

U.S. Department of Labor: The Secretary's Commission on Achieving Necessary Skills. (1991). *What work requires of schools: A SCANS report for America 2000.* Washington, DC: Author.

Ware, M. E. (1993). Developing and improving advising: Challenges to prepare students for life. In T. V. McGovern (Ed.), *Handbook for enhancing undergraduate education in psychology* (pp. 47–70). Washington, DC: American Psychological Association.

Weiten, W. (1993). From isolation to community: Increasing communication and collegiality among psychology teachers. In T. V. McGovern (Ed.), *Handbook for enhancing undergraduate education in psychology* (pp. 123–159). Washington, DC: American Psychological Association.

11

Training Graduate
Teaching Assistants

Stephen F. Davis
Emporia State University

Matthew T. Huss
Creighton University

The training of graduate teaching assistants (GTAs) is a topic of continuing interest (e.g., Lowman & Mathie, 1993; Meyers et al., 1997; Norcorss, Hanych, & Terranova, 1997; Nyquist, Abbott, & Wulff, 1990; Prentice-Dunn & Rickard, 1994; Sprague & Nyquist, 1990; Weimer, Svinicki, & Bauer, 1990). Two general themes permeate this literature: (a) concern about the availability and use of teaching and training opportunities (Meyers et al., 1997; Norcross et al., 1997), and (b) delineation of the extant procedures for training or supporting GTAs (Lowman & Mathie, 1993; Meyers et al., 1997; Nyquist et al., 1990; Prentice-Dunn & Rickard, 1994; Sprague & Nyquist, 1990; Weimer et al., 1990).

Many of the reports of the availability and implementation of extant training opportunities are based on self-reports from departmental chairs (e.g., Mueller, Perlman, McCann, & McFadden, 1997). Based on these self-reports, Mueller et al. (1997) concluded that GTAs have adequate and consistent training opportunities.

However, others have uncovered a different picture when they surveyed the GTAs (Branstetter & Handelsman, 2000; Meyers, Reid, & Quina, 1998; Prieto & Meyers, 1999). Specifically, Prieto and Meyers (1999) found that 13% of their sample of 176 GTAs received no training or supervision of any kind. Both Branstetter and Handelsman (2000) and Prieto and Meyers (1999) found that 47% received either training or supervision. Similarly, Meyers et al. (1998) surveyed 89 doctoral

141

students at three research universities. These students rated the *level of importance* and their own *level of training* in five general areas: class management, academic life, psychology content, ethical issues, and research training. The participants rated all five areas as important. However, they also rated their level of training as significantly lower in all areas.

Clearly, the graduate students' views of their training and preparation differs from the chairs' perceptions. Such results underscore Prieto and Meyers' conclusion that "These findings support and encourage the training efforts now in place for psychology GTAs and highlight the importance of formally preparing psychology GTAs for their teaching responsibilities" (p. 266). From the GTAs' perspective, there is ample room for improvement.

Turning to the second issue covered in the literature, we find that the nature and specifics of the various training programs vary widely from institution to institution. Table 11.1 shows the various components and activities identified by researchers. The implementation of all these diverse activities and programs require an ongoing year-long GTA training program and substantial commitment by the university.

TABLE 11.1
Representative GTA Training Activities

Activity	Reference
Observe faculty teaching	Mueller et al. (1997), Sharp (1981)
Student evaluations of GTAs	Lowman & Mathie (1993), Mueller et al. (1997), Weimer et al. (1990)
Orientation	Davis & Kring (2001), Lowman & Mathie (1993), Mueller et al. (1997), Sprague & Nyquist (1990), Weimer et al. (1990)
Observation by supervisor	Davis & Kring (2001), Lowman & Mathie (1993), Mueller et al. (1997), Sprague & Nyquist (1990), Weimer et al. (1990)
Teaching workshop	Bray & Howard (1980), Jackson & Simpson (1983), Mueller et al. (1997), Weimer et al. (1990)
Faculty mentor	Mueller et al. (1997), Sprague & Nyquist (1990)
Faculty supervisor	Bray & Howard (1980), Davis & Kring (2001), Lowman & Mathie (1993), Mueller et al. (1997), Sprague & Nyquist (1990), Weimer et al. (1990)
Teaching seminar or class	Buskist et al. (in press), Jackson & Simpson (1983), Mueller et al. (1997), Sprague & Nyquist (1990)
TAs observe their own teaching	Bray & Howard (1980), Lowman & Mathie (1993), Mueller et al. (1997), Weimer et al. (1990)
Preteaching preparation activities	Davis & Kring (2001), Lowman & Mathie (1993)
Regularly scheduled TA meetings	Davis & Kring (2001), Sprague & Nyquist (1990)
Attend teaching conference	Davis & Kring (2001)
Self-evaluation	Davis & Kring (2001), Lowman & Mathie (1993)
Prepare teaching portfolio	Davis & Kring (2001)

COMPONENTS OF AN IDEAL GTA
TRAINING PROGRAM

The difficulties of integrating the various components and activities notwithstanding, in this chapter we attempt to design an ideal GTA training program that can be implemented by any institution that is serious about and willing to commit the needed faculty time and resources to GTA training. We begin by considering the components of the ideal program.

Orientation

At some point during their training, GTAs need to be oriented to both the university and department. Depending on what is covered, these orientation sessions can encompass a morning or afternoon, or 1 or 2 days. At the least, the orientation session(s) should include discussion of:

University policies. This discussion should include sexual harassment, academic dishonesty, appropriate university officials to contact in various situations, and GTA rights.

Departmental policies. This discussion should include posting and keeping office hours, makeup tests, conditions for assigning grades of "incomplete," where to refer students who need remedial help, as well as such mundane, but important, concerns such as use of the telephone and availability of office supplies.

Ethical and professional issues. Ethical and professional expectations of GTAs should be discussed with a clear differentiation between their roles as teacher and student. This discussion may be especially important given recent findings identifying discrepancies between ethical judgments and actual practices among GTAs (Branstetter & Handelsman, 2000).

Teaching resources. The GTAs should be aware of teaching resources, such as handbooks (e.g., Benjamin, Daniel, & Brewer, 1985; Benjamin, Nodine, Ernst, & Broeker, 1999), books (Davis, 1993; McKeachie, 1999; Perlman, McCann, & McFadden, 1999), journals (e.g., *Teaching of Psychology*), and so forth, that are available for use with their classes.

Classroom resources. The orientation session(s) should also include a visit to the classroom(s) in which GTAs are likely to teach. This visit should include a clear and comprehensive demonstration of support equipment and available technology.

Teaching of Psychology Course

According to Buskist, Tears, Davis, and Rodrigue (in press), "Because ... GTA training programs are concerned with the preparation of quality teachers, it seems logical to expect that many such programs would include a graduate course on the teaching of psychology." The results of a national survey conducted by Buskist et al. indicate that several universities currently offer such courses and that the common components of these courses include:

1. Observation of GTAs teaching and providing them with verbal and written feedback (feedback from both supervisor and peers is encouraged),
2. Presentation of microlectures to peers in the teaching of psychology course,
3. Presentation of lectures in the undergraduate classroom,
4. Evaluation of videotapes of the GTA's teaching,
5. Reading a text or selected journal articles (see Buskist et al. [in press] for a list of potential texts for this course).

According to Buskist et al. (in press), the typical teaching of psychology course lasts one academic term, although some courses may last two or three terms. These authors found that many GTAs take this course during the academic term(s) they are actually teaching. Although the typical teaching of psychology course does not involve written assignments (Buskist et al., in press), we believe the inclusion of such assignments (e.g., statement of teaching philosophy) assists GTAs in clarifying their thinking about teaching and provides teachers and supervisors additional opportunities to give feedback.

Regularly Scheduled GTA Meetings

According to Davis and Kring (2001), regularly scheduled GTA meetings can include:

1. A discussion of what has gone well in teaching activities,
2. A discussion of teaching problems and how the GTA and supervisor dealt with them,
3. Presentation of an effective demonstration, and
4. Discussion of a teaching issue (e.g., how to deal with disruptive students, assignment of grades, extra credit, lecture vs. discussion, etc.).

In addition to serving as a source of information, regularly scheduled GTA meetings provide support and feedback from teaching peers. If the GTA training program also includes a teaching of psychology class, then the supervisor may need to adjust the content and frequency of the GTA meetings to avoid duplicating course content.

Interfacing with the Teaching Community

Beginning with the establishment of the Mid-America Conference for Teachers of Psychology in Evansville, Indiana, in 1984, the teaching of psychology community has witnessed the development of several regional conferences for teachers of psychology. These conferences offer GTAs an excellent opportunity to learn more about various aspects of teaching, as well as facilitating the establishment of networks with other persons in the teaching community.

Because most conferences offer a reduced registration fee (which often includes several meals) for graduate students, as well as convention-rate lodging, the cost of arranging for an entire cohort of GTAs to attend such a conference is certainly not prohibitive. Moreover, these regional conferences also offer attendees the opportunity to present teaching-related posters. Here is a perfect opportunity for GTAs to present research results or effective classroom demonstrations.

Development of a Teaching Portfolio

The development of a personal teaching portfolio is fast becoming an established practice for many professionals in higher education (Buskist & Davis, 2001). For junior faculty members seeking tenure or promotion, the teaching portfolio offers an effective and professional means by which teachers can display their credentials. For the GTA, the development of a teaching portfolio can also have pronounced professional consequences. For example, master's-level applicants to Ph.D. programs can use the teaching portfolio to effectively showcase their teaching skills and enhance their chances of admission. Doctoral-level GTAs will find that the teaching portfolio is an outstanding resource to take with them on job interviews.

What should this teaching portfolio contain and how should you assemble these materials? Although there is no standard format for the contents and presentation of the teaching portfolio, some suggestions include (Davis, 2000):

- *Statement of teaching philosophy.* In developing your teaching philosophy, you need to deal with the following questions. Why do you teach? What do you find rewarding about teaching? What principles underlie your teaching? What are your criteria for effective teaching?
- *Statement of teaching goals.* Here are some questions to consider in preparing your statement of teaching goals. What do you want your students to learn? Within what context do you teach? What are your standards?
- *Statement of teaching strategy.* What strategies do you use when you teach? Why do you use these strategies and not others?
- *Statement of expertise in teaching.* What is your specialty area? What courses are you prepared to teach? What new courses would you like to develop? What experience and preparation have you had?
- *Materials that support your excellence as a teacher.* These materials can include syllabi, tests, assignments, student evaluations, peer evaluations, special teaching honors and other recognition, reprints of teaching-related research and papers, student papers and projects, and letters from students.

Assembly. Our recommendation is to place your vita first, followed by the prior sections (in that order, starting with the statement of teaching philosophy).

What about the length of each section? We recommend that the first four sections be one to two pages each.

Packaging. The days of presenting interviewers or evaluation committees with a box (or boxes) full of loosely organized teaching materials are long since past. Hence, the teaching portfolio should be presented as clearly, succinctly, and professionally as possible. We recommend that you assemble your materials in a three-ring binder no more than three-quarter inches wide. Be wary of the "box-of-materials" syndrome; do not give in to the temptation to "graduate" to larger binders as you accumulate additional materials. Be selective with the materials you place in your portfolio. You do not need to include every test and syllabus; representative examples and summaries work just fine.

Additional Reading. Be sure to consult James Korn's chapter on teaching portfolios that appears in this volume (chap. 16). Some additional sources on the preparation of the teaching portfolio that you may want to consult include Edgerton, Hutchings, and Quinlan (1991) and Seldin (1997).

Evaluation

As Davis and Kring (2001) noted, GTA evaluation can take several forms: self-evaluation, peer evaluation, and supervisor evaluation. The following techniques are among the various GTA-evaluation procedures currently in use:

Videotaping and Review. The GTA arranges to have his or her class session videotaped. The videotape is reviewed and critiqued by other GTAs and the GTA supervisor.

Preparation of a Specific Teaching Focus. The GTA prepares a one- or two-paragraph description of a specific teaching issue on which he or she has been working recently. These descriptions are presented to the GTA supervisor at regular intervals (e.g., GTA meetings or teaching class sessions). These specific focus papers easily can become the topic of an excellent teaching class or GTA meeting discussion.

Peer Observation. GTAs routinely observe each other teaching and then write up descriptions of these observations. The description, which should include strengths, weaknesses, and what was learned about teaching, is shared with both the GTA supervisor and the observee.

Student Evaluations. Most, if not all, GTAs are evaluated by their students in the same manner as students evaluate regular faculty. Because such student evaluations typically occur at the end of the academic term and are not effective in promoting change during the current semester, GTAs may want to consider conducting their own evaluations earlier in the semester. These supplementary evaluations can be more focused in their objective(s). For example, the GTA may want to know if a specific class session or special activity/demonstration was effective, if he or she is lecturing too rapidly (or slowly), and so forth.

Self-Evaluations. Once or twice a semester, the GTA completes an extensive self-evaluation that covers all aspects of teaching, as well as the GTA's own intellectual growth and development.[1]

End-of-Term Evaluation. The GTA completes a retrospective, albeit thorough, teaching evaluation at the end of each academic term.[1]

Academic Term Portfolio. Not to be confused with the teaching portfolio described before (although some of the contents overlap), the academic term portfolio contains all the relevant teaching materials that the GTA has accumulated and used during the academic term. Because these portfolios are completed each academic term, the GTA and GTA supervisor can compare portfolios on a term-by-term basis to evaluate growth and development.

End-of-Term Conference. The GTA supervisor reserves a specific time period at the end of the academic term for each GTA to discuss his or her teaching experiences during the term. The GTA's academic end-of-term evaluation and the contents of the term portfolio offer excellent starting points for this discussion. The GTA supervisor should schedule each of these meetings for a minimum of 20 minutes.

IMPLEMENTING COMPONENTS OF THE IDEAL TRAINING PROGRAM

Because each institution faces its own unique situations and needs, it is not possible to describe the *one* best sequence for presenting and implementing the components of the ideal GTA training program. Hence, each institution needs to accommodate its own specific needs. This caveat notwithstanding, there appear to be two general options.

Time to Prepare and Hone Skills

In this option, GTAs have at least one academic term, usually an academic year, to prepare before they actually have their own class to teach. During this time,

---

[1] Copies of these evaluation forms are available from either author.

GTAs can be oriented to the department and university, assist in the classroom, give practice lectures, attend seminars and workshops, attend teaching conferences, give guest lectures in faculty and GTA classes, and enroll in a teaching of psychology class. Under these conditions, the goal of the initial academic term or year is to prepare the GTA to assume responsibility for his or her own class the following term or year. Once the GTA has begun teaching his or her own class, then other activities, such as regularly scheduled GTA meetings, peer observation, and evaluation procedures, can be implemented.

Limited Opportunity to Prepare and Hone Skills

In this option, all GTAs are needed to teach classes. Consequently, no academic term or year is available for training. Under these conditions, it is important that the GTA supervisor be in contact with the GTAs during the summer before the start of the new academic year. New GTAs should use the summer to read the text they will be using in their class(es) and familiarize themselves with the ancillary materials that accompany the text. Additionally, before arriving on campus, they should prepare a rough draft of their syllabus. (The GTA supervisor is well advised to send sample syllabi to incoming GTAs.) The summer also is an excellent time for incoming GTAs to read a basic book on teaching, such as McKeachie's (1999) *Teaching Tips*.

An intensive orientation should precede the start of the fall term. One training model (Davis & Kring, 2001) uses a 3-day orientation. In addition to orienting new GTAs to university and departmental policies, displaying teaching resources, and visiting classrooms, this type of orientation demands additional components. For example, you may want the incoming GTAs to give a short, practice lecture. A good 30-minute lecture can provide information for the GTA supervisor and help bolster confidence to meet that first class. Be sure to use your returning GTAs—they can provide a wealth of information and support.

Because GTAs are not afforded the opportunity to take a teaching of psychology class, practice lecturing, and so forth, before they assume teaching responsibilities for their own class, it is important that the GTA supervisor be available to assist, listen, and counsel. Likewise, the regularly scheduled GTA meetings and the teaching of psychology class are important to beginning GTAs working under these conditions. Of course, additional GTA activities can also be implemented as the supervisor deems appropriate and relevant.

CONCLUSION

The literature suggests that, despite the beliefs of department administrators, GTAs express a lack of preparedness on entering our college classrooms to teach. Given the number of college classes being taught by GTAs, with no decrease evident in the near future, it behooves us to place greater emphasis on preparing GTAs for teaching both in the short and long term. In this chapter, we attempted to outline an ideal training program for GTAs and offered suggestions for implementing such a program. Although the implementation and support of such a program may necessitate a significant commitment to teaching, it is likely to lead to greater rewards in terms of the quality of GTA training and the education of undergraduate students.

REFERENCES

Benjamin, Jr., L. T., Nodine, B. F., Ernst, R. M., & Broeker, C. B. (Eds.). (1999). *Activities handbook for the teaching of psychology* (Vol. 4). Washington, DC: American Psychological Association.

Benjamin, Jr., L. T., Daniel, R. S., & Brewer, C. L. (Eds.). (1985). *Handbook for the teaching of introductory psychology*. Hillsdale, NJ: Lawrence Erlbaum Associates.

Branstetter, S. A., & Handelsman, M. M. (2000). Graduate teaching assistants: Ethical training, beliefs, and practices. *Ethics and Behavior, 10,* 27–50.

Bray, J. H., & Howard, G. S. (1980). Methodological consideration in the evaluation of a teacher-training program. *Journal of Educational Psychology, 72,* 62–70.

Buskist, W., & Davis, S. F. (2001, April). *The teaching portfolio: Packaging your teaching credentials effectively.* Workshop presented at the annual meeting of the Southwestern Psychological Association, Houston, TX.

Buskist, W., Tears, R., Davis, S. F., & Rodrigue, K. (in press). The teaching of psychology course: Prevalence and content. *Teaching of Psychology.*

Davis, B. G. (1993). *Tools for teaching.* San Francisco: Jossey-Bass.

Davis, S. F. (2000, October). *The teaching portfolio: Packaging your teaching credentials effectively.* Teaching enhancement workshop presented at Belmont University, Nashville, TN.

Davis, S. F., & Kring, J. P. (2001). A model for training and evaluating graduate teaching assistants. *The College Student Journal, 35,* 45–51.

Edgerton, R., Hutchings, P., & Quinlan, K. (1991). *The teaching portfolio: Capturing the scholarship in teaching.* Washington, DC: American Association for Higher Education.

Jackson, W. K., & Simpson, R. D. (1983). A survey of graduate teaching assistant instructional improvement programs. *College Student Journal, 17,* 220–224.

Lowman, J., & Mathie, V. A. (1993). What should graduate teaching assistants know about teaching? *Teaching of Psychology, 20,* 84–88.

McKeachie, W. A. (1999). *Teaching tips* (10th ed.). Boston: Houghton-Mifflin.

Meyers, S. A., Prieto, L. R., Fishman, E., Rajecki, D. W., Quina, K., & Massoth, N. (1997, August). *Teaching assistant training in departments of psychology: A national survey.* Paper presented at the annual meeting of the American Psychological Association, Chicago, IL.

Meyers, S. A., Reid, P. T., & Quina, K. (1998). Ready or not, here we come: Preparing psychology graduate students for academic careers. *Teaching of Psychology, 25,* 124–125.

Mueller, A., Perlman, B., McCann, L. I., & McFadden, S. H. (1997). A faculty perspective on teaching assistant training. *Teaching of Psychology, 24,* 167–171.

Norcross, J. C., Hanych, J. M., & Terranova, R. D. (1997). Teaching opportunities for graduate students in psychology: Commonly available but (still) rarely required. *Teaching of Psychology, 24,* 265–266.

Nyquist, J. D., Abbott, R. D., & Wulff, D. H. (1990). *Teaching assistant training in the 1990s.* San Francisco: Jossey-Bass.

Perlman, B., McCann, L. I., & McFadden, S. H. (Eds.). (1999). *Lessons learned: Practical advice for the teaching of psychology.* Washington, DC: American Psychological Society.

Prentice-Dunn, S., & Rickard, H. C. (1994). A follow-up note on graduate training in the teaching of introductory psychology. *Teaching of Psychology, 21,* 111–112.

Prieto, L. R., & Meyers, S. A. (1999). Effects of training and supervision on the self-efficacy of psychology graduate teaching assistants. *Teaching of Psychology, 26,* 264–266.

Seldin, P. (1997). *The teaching portfolio: A practical guide to improved performance and promotion/ tenure decisions* (2nd ed.). Bolton, MA: Anker.

Sharp, G. (1981). Acquisition of lecturing skills by university teaching assistants: Some effects of interest, topic, relevance, and viewing a model videotape. *American Educational Research Journal, 18,* 491–502.

Sprague, J., & Nyquist, J. D. (1990). TA supervision. In J. D. Nyquist, R. D. Abbott, & D. H. Wulff (Eds.), *Teaching assistant training in the 1990s* (pp. 37–56). San Francisco: Jossey-Bass.

Weimer, M., Svinicki, M. D., & Bauer, G. (1990). Designing programs to prepare TAs to teach. In J. D. Nyquist, R. D. Abbott, & D. H. Wulff (Eds.), *Teaching assistant training in the 1990s* (pp. 57–70). San Francisco: Jossey-Bass.

III

Teaching Within the Context of Modern Academic Life

12

Teaching, Research, and Scholarship

David E. Johnson
John Brown University

A discussion about "Teaching Within the Context of Modern Academic Life" would not be complete without mention of one of the most active debates in academia over the last 25 years. What roles do teaching and research play in the academy? What constitutes scholarship and how do we evaluate the utility of faculty members' efforts? In this chapter, I discuss these issues as they might cross disciplinary boundaries, but I also attempt to relate them specifically to psychology where possible.

To most people, teaching and research constitute the primary activities of college and university faculty. Everybody knows that institutions of higher learning exist to produce educated persons and develop new knowledge. To that end, the traditional model of higher education yielded faculty who fit into a teacher-scholar model. Institutions of higher learning promote both research and teaching.

THE PROBLEM

In the 1970s and 1980s, the U.S. educational system came under fire by a number of critics who claimed that, among other things, faculty were teaching less and spending more time on their research. Our institutions no longer emphasized the "basics," but veered off into esoterica that was irrelevant and mind-numbing at best (Bloom, 1987; Sykes, 1988). Some of these critics characterized the professorate as disdainful of teaching and motivated only by protecting their cushy positions and feeding their insatiable egos. Professors wanted to publish their research more than they wanted to profess. After all, institutions, while suggesting that research, teaching, and service are the bases for promotion and tenure, tended to weigh publication more than the other two components. In an attempt to increase the number of publications, critics also claimed that faculty conducted research in increasingly irrelevant content areas. No one actually cared about or read most of the research being published.

Evidence for this publish-or-perish notion at the expense of scientific importance emerged from several studies of scientific citations in journals. For example, statistics collected by the Institute for Scientific Information found that 55% of papers published in the early 1980s in journals indexed by the institute received no citations in the next 5 years after publication (Hamilton, 1990). The study also found that between 5% and 20% of all citations were self-citations and that the number of professional journals increased dramatically in the 20 years before the report. With data such as these, it is little wonder that critics of the academy characterize the work of researchers as irrelevant and self-aggrandizing.

To be fair, this phenomenon is not new. In 1939, Ernst Harms accused many institutions of encouraging greater numbers of publications merely for the sake of numbers:

> Their [faculty] members are expected to produce and produce whether or not they have something to say. This grinding-out of results has degenerated into a sort of publishing competition. Scientific literature no longer stands for a truly important or at least a genuine result of serious work. There is too much talk about...[an] institution appearing with a lot of publications and not enough talk about whether this or that piece of work is important. (p. 325)

Much of modern academic interest in the debate over the relative role of research and teaching emerged with the publication of Ernest Boyer's (1990) *Scholarship Reconsidered: Priorities of the Professorate*. Boyer decried the trend in many academic institutions to disproportionately emphasize research and publication in decisions to hire, compensate, promote, and tenure faculty. Being a scholar essentially meant being a researcher; the barometer of scholarship was the length of the publication section on the vita.

Boyer (1990) concluded that, indeed, many institutions had developed a skewed perspective on what constitutes scholarship and that a new perspective was needed. He characterized scholarship in four ways:

- Scholarship of Discovery, which is virtually synonymous with the term *research*.

- Scholarship of Integration, which involves making connections across disciplines, writing comprehensive review articles within a discipline, and interpreting research for a wider audience.
- Scholarship of Application, which involves applying knowledge to solving real-world problems in new ways.
- Scholarship of Teaching, which involves the professorate being "intellectually engaged" in their discipline and excelling in "transforming" and "extending" the knowledge of that discipline.

Boyer's suggestions struck a cord within the academy, and the tension between research and teaching that had been simmering below the surface now boiled over to be debated widely within the educational community. Just what is the correct balance among research, teaching, and service? What specific actions constitute scholarship aside from publications? How can the institution develop a reward system to reflect a broader view of scholarship? Educators had their work cut out for them. The debate was on—sometimes proponents of differing perspectives became rather strident in their support for their respective positions.

The academy also came under fire from an external source that added insult to injury in the debate over the relevance of research. This source inflamed public attitudes toward the activities of researchers, particularly those researchers who received public funding for their work. In the mid-1970s, Senator William Proxmire of Wisconsin began giving Golden Fleece Awards for, in his words, "wasteful, ridiculous or ironic use of the taxpayers' money." Proxmire often targeted basic research (frequently social science research) funded by organizations such as the National Science Foundation. Ronald Hutchinson received one of the more publicized awards. Hutchinson's research (Hutchinson, 1972, 1982; Hutchinson, Renfrew, & Young, 1971), funded by several government agencies, focused on various animal responses to aggression in an attempt to develop objective measures of emotional behavior (e.g., jaw-clenching). Proxmire ridiculed Hutchinson's research with comments such as:

> The funding of this nonsense makes me almost angry enough to scream and kick or even clench my jaw. Dr. Hutchinson's studies should make the taxpayers as well as his monkeys grind their teeth. In fact, the good doctor has made a fortune from his monkeys and in the process made a monkey out of the American taxpayer. (Irion, 1988, p. 17)

Few people would object to pointing out wasteful governmental spending, but Proxmire's public comments about research that he considered wasteful tended to oversimplify the process, sometimes focusing on small portions of the projects' methodology taken out of context. Hutchinson sued Proxmire for defamation of character and several other charges. The suit eventually made it to the Supreme Court. Proxmire ultimately settled the suit out of court with a small cash payment and an apology to Hutchinson from the Senate floor. In future Golden Fleece Awards, Proxmire did not mention the researchers by name, and the number of awards per year for federally funded research dropped considerably. However, that was little consolation for those whose research was criticized by Proxmire. Michael Domjan, who received an award in 1988, commented, "The fleece hasn't shaken my confidence in the value of my research, but it has affected my confidence in being able to present it in a convincing and effective way. My work was ridiculed in the press, and that can't help but affect me" (Irion, 1988, p. 17).

The Golden Fleece award (given from 1975 through 1988 when Proxmire left the Senate) was recently resurrected by an organization calling themselves Taxpayers for Common Sense. It remains to be seen whether the new award will target basic research as frequently as it did under Proxmire.

What is the relevance of this public assault on basic research to the issue of teaching and scholarship? Proxmire's criticism came at a time when science literacy in the United States was in serious decline. His proclamations fell on public ears that were not attuned to the nature of basic scientific research. Proxmire never attempted to point out that there were potentially important implications for basic research. This oversight only supported the perception that scholars primarily work in their ivory towers on issues of little relevance to the real world and likely served as support for subsequent criticisms of academicians as indifferent to the teaching mission of colleges and universities (Sykes, 1988).

THE RESPONSE

The debate over the roles of teaching, research, and scholarship occupied a prominent place in the professional literature throughout the 1990s. Several organizations, particularly the Carnegie Foundation and the American Association of Higher Education (AAHE), supported a wide array of publications and conferences promoting a dialogue about the roles of teaching, research, and scholarship. In the early 1990s, the Center for Instructional Development at Syracuse University (funded by the Lilly Endowment and the Fund for the Improvement of Postsecondary Education) invited 20 scholarly societies and accreditation organizations to define scholarly work in their disciplines as part of a project to identify similarities and differences in the perception of scholarship among disciplines. The results of deliberations within a variety of disciplines (history, geography, business, chemistry) appeared in *Recognizing Faculty Work: Reward Systems for the Year 2000* (Diamond & Adam, 1995) and bore considerable similarity to each other and to the definitions of scholarship outlined by Boyer (1990).

The Society for the Teaching of Psychology, Division 2 of the American Psychological Association (APA) formed a task force to develop a definition of *scholarship* in psychology and subsequently published it in the *American Psychologist* (Halpern et al., 1998). In many ways, the definitions of scholarship outlined in that article mirrored Boyer's (1990) with one exception: the scholarship of pedagogy. Because psychology includes research on learning and cognition, it is in an ideal position to provide insight into the teaching–learning process. Psychologists also possess methodological competence in assessment of learning and thus make a logical choice for research on learning effectiveness. Finally, many psychology practitioners use the extant research on learning, particularly with persons with disabilities, to suggest potential remedial strategies to improve learning capabilities. In a sense, the scholarship of pedagogy represents the work of psychologists in the service of the other types of scholarship: discovery, application, integration, and teaching.

This broader view of scholarship is not shared by all academicians. Some academicians propose that scholarship and teaching are separate entities and we should not try to equate them. In a response to Halpern et al. (1998), Korn (1999) suggested that teaching and all the activities that go along with it have inherent value as teaching and should not be encumbered by the rhetoric of the research community. Myers and Waller (1999) warned against using the term *the Scholarship of Teaching* as merely a label for the things teachers traditionally do. They suggested that equating teaching and scholarship does not make sense because both are going to be evaluated separately by most institutions.

Some excellent examples of the Scholarship of Teaching (and the Scholarship of Pedagogy outlined by Halpern et al., 1998) exist in several places. At the University of Nebraska–Lincoln, a peer-review program began as part of a national project organized by the American Association for Higher Education (AAHE; see Bernstein, chap. 21, this volume). The program now consists of faculty from five institutions (University of Nebraska–Lincoln, Indiana University, Kansas State University, University of Michigan, and Texas A & M) who are in a process of approaching their teaching as scholarship by writing about their teaching, reflecting on their writing, and critiquing the work of peers (see chap. 21, this volume). The end products of this project are portfolios that are publicly available (see http://www.unl.edu/peerrev/index.html).

The Carnegie Academy for the Scholarship of Teaching and Learning (CASTL) provides another excellent example of interdisciplinary approaches to supporting the scholarship of teaching (see http://www.carnegiefoundation.org/CASTL/index.htm). CASTL supports networking among professionals interested in the scholarship of teaching, as well as contacts among professional organizations. It also supports Carnegie scholars who wish to improve teaching and learning through an intentional process of research and assessment. These goals are achieved in a variety of ways, including offering fellowships in cooperation with the Pew Foundation. CASTL, in conjunction with the AAHE, also supports networking among institutions that wish to expand their perspectives on the Scholarship of Teaching.

Academicians vigorously responded to the challenge of redefining scholarship and its role within the reward system of the academy. However, how could they respond to the public's perceptions of the relevance of scholarly work? Researchers/educators in the sciences acknowledged that one way to change these perceptions required a greater level of science literacy among the general populace. After decades of decreased science requirements in educational institutions and lower achievement scores on indexes of science literacy, the public ironically loved the technology that emerged from basic research, but showed little appreciation for the work on which the technology was based.

The answer to this problem seemed to be in strengthening the science curriculum at all levels of education. Several specific programs developed as a part of this strategy. Three examples are noteworthy. The American Association for the Advancement of Science (AAAS) developed Project 2061 in 1985 (see http://www.project2061.org). Over the last 15 years, the project participants defined science literacy and developed basic standards to be met within the K–12 curriculum. They also compiled resources for the classroom and began a process of evaluating science and mathematics textbooks.

A second initiative—Project Kaleidoscope (PKAL), developed in 1989— focuses on science and mathematics curricula at the undergraduate level (see http://www.pkal.org). Since its inception, participants in PKAL have held conferences and developed a wide variety of materials directed at invigorating undergraduate science education.

Finally, specific to psychology, in 1999 the American Psychological Association approved the Standards for the Teaching of High School Psychology (National Standards, 1999). The Standards set criteria for mastery of the basic content of general psychology and promote an appreciation for understanding behavior and mental processes from an empirical perspective, rather than common sense or intuition.

THE FUTURE?

In the Academy

Academicians have responded vigorously to the challenges put forth by the debate about the relation among teaching, research, and scholarship. What can we expect to see from these responses? What directions can we take to continue progress? What potential pitfalls await us?

It is still too early to tell the extent to which the redefining scholarship initiatives will have a lasting impact on academia. There is some evidence that institutions now place greater emphasis on the importance of teaching as a scholarly endeavor (Diamond & Adam, 1997). For example, the University of Memphis developed a plan to broaden their reward system, which requires all faculty to be evaluated on their teaching and distinguishes between *Teaching* and the *Scholarship of Teaching*:

> Teaching encompasses classroom instruction, course development, mentoring students in academic projects including dissertations, testing, grading, and the professional development of the faculty member as a teacher.

The scholarship of teaching focuses on transforming and extending the knowledge of pedagogy. Examples would include writing an appropriate textbook or educational article in one's discipline. Innovative contributions to teaching, insofar as they are published or presented in a peer-reviewed forum, would also constitute scholarship of teaching. The scholarship of teaching is not equivalent to teaching. Classroom teaching and staying current in one's field are not relevant criteria for evaluating faculty on the scholarship of teaching. (cited in Russell & Pavelich, 1996, p. A270)

Also, many specific disciplines concur that scholarship is not simply publishing basic research (Diamond & Adam, 1995) and that the Scholarship of Teaching can be the basis for promotion, tenure, and salary considerations. However, there is still considerable debate about what constitutes the Scholarship of Teaching. Many academics agree that it is not simply good teaching, but specifically involves the investigation of the teaching process and also meets the following criteria: it is public, can be peer reviewed, can be replicated, can be documented, is innovative, and has impact or significance (Diamond & Adam, 1995; Halpern et al., 1998; Hutchings & Shulman, 1999). Most of these factors are the same as those we use to evaluate disciplinary research. Nevertheless, academics still express concern about whether this scholarship of teaching will be viewed as credible by their colleagues (Hutchings & Shulman, 1999).

To change this situation, professional educational organizations must follow the lead of the AAHE and the Carnegie Foundation by supporting innovative ways to demonstrate scholarship that is relevant to teaching and learning. Part of this process requires that new funding sources be developed. Numerous existing governmental programs focus on funding basic and applied research. Lobbying efforts should be directed toward developing funding sources that explicitly support the Scholarship of Teaching and assessment of that process. Support for endowed chairs or professorships for Teaching Scholars may also serve to highlight the importance of treating pedagogy as a serious object of scholarship.

We must also attempt to foster a broader conception of scholarship within the ranks of graduate students and entry-level faculty—the future generation of teachers. Graduate students typically focus on their content area research in preparation for their academic positions after degree completion. Nevertheless, most students will not take positions in research institutions, and many students will find themselves in situations in which teaching is the primary expectation of their institution. Evidence suggests that graduate programs do not consistently prepare students for this potential situation (Meyers & Prieto, 2000; Prieto & Meyers, 1999). Graduate programs should consider more explicit training—not only in teaching methodologies, but also in the Scholarship of Teaching. Such training may take the form of assembling and evaluating teaching portfolios, conducting research on teaching effectiveness, and development of pedagogical materials.

Possibly one of the biggest challenges facing academicians interested in the Scholarship of Teaching is the development of educational technology. In just a few years, the availability of new technology for classroom presentations and

Internet-based technology grew exponentially. Proponents of technology seemed to suggest that it would prove to be a superior modality for teaching and learning. At present, much of this promise remains unrealized. However, technology provides a rich source of study for those faculty interested in the Scholarship of Teaching. Do new technology-driven methodologies lead to better learning when compared to more traditional methods? What aspects of learning do we augment with technology and which ones result in a deficit in learning? What are the benefits and liabilities of online instruction? It remains to be seen whether technology will lead to enhanced learning, but the Scholarship of Teaching offers a means of providing some answers.

In the Public Forum

Have we made any progress helping the public to have a greater understanding of the work that goes on in the academy? Increasing science literacy among the general populace requires many years of cooperative work by teachers, K–16. Measurable results are likely years in the future. However, one aspect of the scholarship debate may be relevant here. One type of scholarship, the Scholarship of Integration, involves more than just integrating material in review articles published in professional journals or writing coherent textbooks. Writing for public consumption could also be construed as a type of scholarship of integration. Sources of this scholarly work include books, newsletters, and TV. Presenting science to laypersons involves a different approach than presenting to colleagues. Scientists have not always done this well. Joel Widder, an analyst at NSF, suggested that scientists have no one else to blame when the public does not understand their work. "Often scientists are unable to coherently explain the value of a particular project in terms that would make sense to a layperson" (Irion, 1988). Few scientists possess this ability. Carl Sagan was most notable for being well trained and respected in his discipline and for his ability to communicate highly complex astronomical information in ways that the nonscientist could understand. In fact, Sagan almost single-handedly convinced Proxmire to drop his objections to funding the project to search for radio signals from other civilizations in our galaxy. The Search for Extraterrestrial Intelligence project (SETI) was given a Golden Fleece award 3 years earlier. Sagan's universal respect and influence undoubtedly came from his ability to connect to a wide audience in the spirit of the Scholarship of Integration. Scientists should not view this type of scholarship as beneath them. It has the potential not only to educate the public, but also to influence public policy.

The Decade of the Brain, proclaimed by Congress in the 1990s, provides another example of bringing science into public consciousness. President George Bush's proclamation in 1990 specifically stated that this initiative should "... enhance public awareness of the benefits to be derived from brain research." Was this objective accomplished? It is difficult to say, but anecdotally, there does seem to be increased coverage of neuroscience in the various news media. We also see direct advertising of drugs for behavioral disorders on TV and magazines. Public acceptance of neuroscience research seems greater than ever before.

The APA spearheaded the development of a program to play off the Decade of the Brain. Entitled "The Decade of Behavior" (DoB, 2001, http://www.decadeofbehavior.org), APA and over 50 other organizations joined to support the initiative to improve education, health, and safety through behavioral research. The DoB goals include, "Development of a public education campaign to address the compelling need for greater understanding by the general public and state and federal policy makers of behavioral and social science research" (http://www.decadeofbehavior.org). I can think of no better opportunity for behavioral and social scientists to practice the Scholarship of Integration.

CONCLUSIONS

The work of redefining scholarship is not without potential pitfalls. We could easily accept teaching, application (service), and integration as scholarship, then redefine discovery in different terms, bringing us back to where this debate started—discovery being prized more than the other activities. We also may find that the Scholarship of Teaching is more difficult to assess than the Scholarship of Discovery. The latter can be objectively evaluated based on the number of publications in peer-reviewed journals and the awarding of grants to support the research. Documenting the Scholarship of Teaching may be more problematic because it entails a wider variety of activities. Innovative methodologies for this evaluation should be developed (which provides an opportunity to practice the Scholarship of Teaching). In the end, however, we must be careful not to make evaluation of the Scholarship of Teaching a more onerous process than the evaluation of other types of scholarship.

The debate of the relative merits of teaching, research, and service as scholarship has come a long way in the last 10 years. It has the potential to be a divisive debate that yields camps of academicians separated by their perceptions of their primary activities. Alternatively, as this debate continues, it also has the potential to unify academicians in our common goals of producing new knowledge, educating people, and solving real-world problems.

REFERENCES

Bloom, A. D. (1987). *The closing of the American mind: How higher education has failed democracy and impoverished the souls of today's students.* New York: Simon & Schuster.

Boyer, E. L. (1990). *Scholarship revisited: Priorities of the professorate.* Princeton, NJ: Carnegie Foundation.

Decade of behavior. Washington, DC: American Psychological Association (Retrieved January 1, 2001, from the World Wide Web: http://www.decadeofbehavior.org/maininfo.html).

Diamond, R., & Adam, B. (1995). *Recognizing faculty work: Reward system for the year 2000.* San Francisco: Jossey-Bass.

Diamond, R., & Adam, B. (1997). *Changing priorities at research universities (1991–1996).* Syracuse: Center for Instructional Development, Syracuse University.

Halpern, D. F., Smothergill, D. W., Allen, M., Baker, S., Baum, C., Best, D., Ferrari, J., Geisinger, K. F., Gilden, E. R., Hester, M., Keith-Spiegel, P., Kierniesky, N. C., McGovern, T. V., McKeachie, W. J., Prokasy, W. F., Szuchman, L. T., Vasta, R., & Weaver, K. A. (1998). Scholarship in psychology: A paradigm for the twenty-first century. *American Psychologist, 53*, 1292–1297.

Hamilton, D. P. (1990). Publishing by-and-for the numbers. *Science, 250*, 1331–1332.

Harms, E. (1939). Scholarly honesty, textbooks and teaching. *The Educational Forum, 3*, 323–328.

Hutchings, P., & Shulman, L. S. (1999). The scholarship of teaching: New elaborations, new developments. *Change, 31*, 10–15.

Hutchinson, R. R. (1972). The environmental causes of aggression. *Nebraska Symposium on Motivation, 20*, 155–181.

Hutchinson, R. R. (1982). The pain-aggression relationship and its expression in naturalistic settings. *Aggressive Behavior, 9*, 229–242.

Hutchinson, R. R., Renfrew, J. W., & Young, G. A. (1971). Effects of long-term shock and associated stimuli on aggressive and manual responses. *Journal of the Experimental Analysis of Behavior, 15*, 141–166.

Irion, R. W. (1988, December 12). What Proxmire's Golden Fleece did for-and to-science. *The Scientist, 23* (Retrieved January 1, 2000 from the World Wide Web: http://www.the-scientist.com/yr1988/dec/prof_881212.html).

Korn, J. H. (1999). Recognizing teaching as teaching. *American Psychologist, 54*, 362–363.

Meyers, S. A., & Prieto, L. R. (2000). Training in the teaching of psychology: What is done and examining the differences. *Teaching of Psychology, 27*, 258–261.

Myers, D. G., & Waller, J. E. (1999). Reflections on scholarship from the liberal arts academy. *American Psychologist, 54*, 358–361.

National standards for the teaching of high school psychology. (1999). Washington, DC: American Psychological Association.

Prieto, L. R., & Meyers, S. A. (1999). Effects of training and supervision on the self-efficacy of psychology graduate teaching assistants. *Teaching of Psychology, 26*, 264–266.

Russell, A. A., & Pavelich, M. J. (1996). Faculty rewards: Can we implement the scholarship of teaching? *Journal of Chemical Education, 73*, A268–A271.

Sykes, C. J. (1988). *ProfScam: Professors and the demise of higher education.* Washington, DC: Regnery Gateway.

13

Integrating Teaching and Service to Enhance Learning

Virginia Andreoli Mathie
James Madison University

Teaching, research, and service served as the academic triumvirate in North American colleges and universities for most of the 20th century. The primary goals of our institutions of higher education are to generate, disseminate, and apply knowledge, and it is through faculty members' activities as researchers, teachers, and service providers that institutions meet these goals. Although members of academia claim to value all three components of the triumvirate, it is clear that the components are not equal. The disparity between teaching and research has been the source of debate and contention since the early 1900s, resulting in the ironic situation that faculty members are hired to teach but rewarded for their research and scholarship (American Association of University Professors [AAUP], 1994; Amey, 1999; Boyer, 1990; Boyer Commission on Educating Undergraduates in the Research University, 1998; Cuban, 1999). There has been much discussion about the relative importance of teaching and research and which area should be given the most weight in promotion, tenure, and annual evaluations. However, it is only recently that academia has extended this discussion to the service component.

Faculty members are expected to be good citizens and serve their institutions, professions, and communities, yet these activities are seldom rewarded. In some universities, there is outright disdain for service, and colleagues discourage new faculty from engaging in service activities until they get tenure because it interferes with teaching and research. Although peers place little value on service, the pressure to increase service activities is growing as legislators, taxpayers, parents, and students demand institutions of higher education to be more accountable to their communities and constituents and more responsive to their needs (Brand, 2000; Plater, 1995). The result is that there is a growing tension among service, teaching, and research as faculty members strive to satisfy internal expectations and demands of peers to increase research and scholarly productivity as well as external expectations and demands of the public to increase teaching and service to the community. Is this conflict necessary? Is service detrimental to teaching and research? Must service, teaching, and research be mutually exclusive activities that detract from one another? I think not. I believe service has been and continues to be a vitally important component of the faculty role. Furthermore, service need not detract from teaching and scholarly activities. To the contrary, I believe that service can be a scholarly activity that enhances teaching and research and provides direct benefits to students. The goal of this chapter is to provide evidence that this is the case.[1]

THE ROLE OF TEACHING, RESEARCH, AND SERVICE IN THE PROFESSORIATE

Historical Perspective

The tension among teaching, research, and service did not always exist. From the 1600s through the 1800s, the focus of colleges and universities was the education and moral development of students (Boyer, 1990; Cuban, 1999). Teaching was what faculty members in academia did and they were expected to do it well. This is not to say research was completely absent. On the contrary, in 1738, John Winthrop established a laboratory for experiments at Harvard, making him the first American academic scientist. Nonetheless, such laboratories were rare, and instructors were hired to teach the scientific method and the science that was already known, not to create new knowledge.

With the passage of the Morrill Land Grant College Act in 1862 and then the Hatch Act in 1887, a new dimension was added to the work of college faculty (Boyer, 1990). These acts provided funds for colleges to establish laboratories and field stations for agricultural experiments as a way to encourage the nation's institutions of higher education to use their intellectual resources to meet pressing societal needs. Soon service to the community became an important component of faculty life with the scope of service broadening to address manufacturing needs

---

[1]This chapter is an adaptation of the author's Harry Kirke Wolfe Lecture, one of the presentations in the G. Stanley Hall Lecture series, presented at the 2000 meeting of the American Psychological Association, Washington, DC.

as well. This emphasis on service, or *outreach* as it was called, had its critics, but nonetheless the pillars of the university were teaching and service and they complemented each other well.

Obviously this situation was quite different from the state of academia during the last half of the 20th century. What happened? In the mid-1800s, new professors who had studied in Germany brought back to America the German approach to scholarship and research along with the German Ph.D. (Boyer, 1990; Cuban, 1999). The movement grew slowly, but eventually schools like Harvard and Yale added graduate programs in science, with Yale awarding the first American Ph.D. in 1861. When the Massachusetts Institute of Technology (MIT) opened in 1865 and Johns Hopkins in 1876, they were the first universities at which administrators viewed research as the critical component of their institution's mission. Other universities such as Columbia, Princeton, and Chicago soon followed.

Research universities gained stature during the beginning of the 20th century, and then World War II war brought about a new collaboration between government and universities to advance science and set a new agenda for universities. At the same time, higher education became available to the masses. The number of colleges and universities grew rapidly to accommodate the influx of students, and their new professors with Ph.D. degrees established departments similar to the ones they experienced in their graduate training. Most of these new institutions aspired to model themselves after the Harvards of higher education. As a result, research potential and ability became the key criteria for hiring and promoting faculty, and pressure to conduct original research and publish it in prestigious journals became the dominant force in academia (Boyer, 1990; Cuban, 1999).

Data from the 1969 and 1989 Carnegie Foundation for the Advancement of Teaching surveys of faculty at research, doctorate-granting, comprehensive, liberal arts, and two-year colleges reflect these changes (American Association of University Professors, 1994). The percentage of respondents who strongly agreed or agreed with reservations that teaching effectiveness, not number of publications, should be the primary criterion for promotion decreased during this period from 77% to 69%, whereas the percentage of respondents who strongly agreed or agreed with reservations that it was difficult to receive tenure without publishing increased from 41% to 59%.

Strategies to Resolve the Teaching–Research Dilemma: Redefining Scholarship

In the late 1980s, educators began to address the teaching versus research tension to a large extent because they were forced to do so by external constituents. As the cost of higher education skyrocketed and states faced fiscal crises, legislators, taxpayers, and parents questioned what instructors did with their time. They demanded that university instructors spend more time doing what they were hired to do (i.e., teach) and less time pursuing their individual special interests and research. Faculty members found themselves caught between two forces: external constituents who put greater value on teaching and colleagues and administrators who put greater value on research.

One response to this dilemma has been to increase class size, although typically there is no reduction in the pressure to publish or in service assignments. Another approach has been to redefine what qualifies as research or scholarship so that instructors who must cope with larger classes, a more diverse student body, pressures to keep up with new pedagogy and technology, and increasing service demands can earn scholarship credit for these efforts. Boyer (1990) was one of the leaders in this movement with his model of four types of scholarship. The *scholarship of discovery* represents the disciplined pursuit of knowledge for its own sake and for advancing existing knowledge. The *scholarship of integration* occurs when the scholar brings together ideas, theories, and research data and interprets them, gives them new meaning, identifies new connections among them, and fits them into new multidisciplinary contexts. The *scholarship of teaching* requires teachers to be engaged intellectually in their disciplines and to convey their knowledge in such a way that they transform and extend it. In doing so, they stimulate students to think critically and ask questions in their own continual pursuit of knowledge. The *scholarship of application* refers to the application of disciplinary knowledge and professional expertise in a reasonable and responsible way to address community and societal problems. At its best, this application would lead to new questions and knowledge.

Boyer's (1990) work stimulated much discussion and controversy. Some educators were hopeful that teaching would finally be valued for the important and scholarly activity that it is. Others were skeptical that this effort to redefine scholarship would count with those persons who evaluated them. Because faculty members tend to identify with their discipline, many faculty believed efforts to change the definition of scholarship were futile unless the disciplines recognized the change as legitimate. With the support of the Syracuse University project examining scholarship in the disciplines, many professional associations have attempted to redefine scholarship within their disciplines. Leaders from several teaching-related psychology organizations collaborated to represent psychology on this project (Halpern et al., 1998). Building on the work of Boyer (1990), Halpern et al. (1998) proposed five categories of scholarship in psychology: original research, integration of knowledge, application of knowledge, scholarship of pedagogy, and scholarship of teaching. Halpern et al. argued that for activities in these categories to be considered scholarly they must adhere to Diamond and Adam's (1993) six criteria for scholarship. The activities must require a high level of discipline-specific expertise, be innovative, be replicable, be documented, be available for peer review, and have significance and impact. In the realm of teaching, this redefinition of scholarship has encouraged faculty members to reflect on their teaching, share their work with colleagues, and look for more effective teaching strategies. It has also enhanced the status of teaching and led to better teaching. This redefinition has had an impact on service as well.

REDEFINING AND REEVALUATING ACADEMIC SERVICE

Defining Service

The inclusion in Boyer's (1990) model of a category related to the application of disciplinary knowledge and professional expertise has already helped stimulate discussion of the scholarship of service, although this discussion has not received as much attention as the scholarship of teaching. One focus of the discussion has been the distinction among the types of service provided by faculty members and the extent to which these various types represent scholarly activities. Boyer's scholarship of application focused on service to the community and society. Faculty members also do such things as serve on departmental, institutional, and professional organization committees; take leadership roles in professional associations; review journal manuscripts and grant proposals; advise students and write reference letters; give presentations to local community groups and schools; and consult with nonprofit organizations, businesses, and government agencies. Many academic institutions include all of these activities in the service category, although this broad definition of service is rather recent. Historically, what constituted service was quite circumscribed and involved the application of disciplinary expertise to address significant problems for the good of society (Boyer, 1990; Lynton, 1995). Educators striving to elevate the status of service and legitimize it as a scholarly pursuit have distinguished this type of professional service or outreach from citizenship and general community service. A 1994 Carnegie Foundation for the Advancement of Teaching national survey of chief academic officers at four-year institutions revealed that 54% of the respondents reported their institutions were making efforts to distinguish professional service from citizenship (Glassick, Huber, & Maeroff, 1997).

As defined in recent literature, *professional service* requires intellectual engagement and use of one's disciplinary knowledge and expertise to address societal needs. It is demanding work that not only uses knowledge from the discipline, but also contributes new knowledge to the discipline (Boyer, 1990; Braskamp & Ory, 1994; Elman & Smock, 1985; Glassick et al., 1997; Lynton, 1995; Plater, 1995). Fear and Sandmann (1995) used the term *outreach* to refer to a subcategory of professional service that is directly related to the faculty member's institutional responsibilities. Examples of faculty work that might qualify as professional service include conducting program evaluations, consulting in one's area of expertise, or collaborating with schools or agencies to develop policies related to one's area of expertise. *Institutional citizenship* refers to service activities on campus, and *disciplinary citizenship* refers to service to professional associations (Froh, Gray, & Lambert, 1993; Lynton, 1995). The most obvious examples of citizenship activities are service on committees or in leadership roles in the organization. The term *community service* refers to the service faculty members perform for their community but that is not part of their faculty responsibilities and does not make use of their disciplinary expertise (Fear & Sandmann, 1995; Lynton, 1995). Examples of this type of service could include assisting a local charity with fundraising or serving as president for a community service organization.

Sometimes the distinction among the various types of service is fuzzy. For example, some university committees on which I have served required me to draw on my professional knowledge and expertise as a psychologist and produced outcomes that address society's needs by enhancing some aspect of undergraduate or graduate training. Whether colleagues call this activity *institutional citizenship* or *professional service* would depend on whether they focused on the fact that it was a university committee or on the importance of my specific expertise and contribution to meeting a need in the community.

Making distinctions among different types of service activities is not meant to imply that professional service activities are inherently better than citizenship or general community service. Although professional service activities are singled out as scholarship, citizenship and community service activities have just as much potential to result in valuable contributions to the community, the institution, and teaching and learning (American Association of University Professors, 1994; Braskamp & Ory, 1994).

Benefits of Professional Service and Citizenship

Service activities play a critical role in meeting community and society needs, serve as an impetus and implementation vehicle for change in higher education, provide opportunities to test theories in real-life settings, contribute to the disciplinary knowledge base, establish positive university–community relationships, bring recognition to the institution, assist in student recruitment, and stimulate faculty productivity (Altman, 1996; American Association of University Professors, 1994; Elman & Smock, 1985; Lynton, 1995; Seldin, 1998). These outcomes are certainly worthwhile. More important for this chapter, however, are the many ways in which professional service and citizenship enhance teaching and learning.[2]

---

[2]The personal communications I report in this section on benefits of service are the result of an informal survey I conducted for the Harry Kirke Wolfe Lecture. I contacted members of the American Psychological Association Psychology Partnerships Project (P3) Steering Committee, P3 group leaders, and friends in leadership positions in the Society for the Teaching of Psychology (STP) and the Teachers of Psychology in Secondary Schools (TOPSS). Of the 38 people I contacted, 28 responded. My objective was to survey people who were active in the service arena and who demonstrated by their professional activities that they had a passion for teaching to determine how their service had benefited their teaching. Consequently, although the sample was not a random one, it seemed to be an appropriate one.

Professional Service.   Many teachers use their professional expertise to serve their communities in roles such as consultants, program evaluators, or therapists. These activities not only benefit the communities, but also may result in more creative, informative, and engaging teaching. Here are just a few examples to illustrate the ways in which instructors can integrate their professional service into their teaching and thereby enhance teaching and learning.

1. Instructors can more readily transform and extend theories and material in the text by using real-life examples pulled from their service experiences to illustrate concepts and make their teaching materials more applied. The addition of real-life perspectives and examples engages students more fully in the learning process and generates more enthusiasm in the classroom (Boyer, 1990; Rice & Richlin, 1993). Elizabeth Swenson (personal communication, July 25, 2000), a past president of the Society for the Teaching of Psychology (STP), noted that her ability to pull from her professional service activities also increased her own enthusiasm for teaching.

2. Professional service activities help instructors bridge the gap between current practice and their knowledge of theory and thereby update and improve their disciplinary skills (Hirsch & Lynton, 1995). As Jane Halonen (personal communication, July 25, 2000), a past president of the STP and past chair of the Council of Teachers of Undergraduate Psychology (CTUP), pointed out, improving one's applied skills can also improve one's teaching. Instructors who keep their own professional skills current are able to model state-of-the-art practices for their students and mentor their students in the development of these skills.

3. As they engage in professional service in the community, instructors build and strengthen university–community networks. They can tap these connections to provide practicum and internship opportunities for their students. These real-life learning environments are essential to keep Americans competitive and successful players in the global marketplace of the 21st century (Snyder, 1996; Zlotkowski, 2001). Through these experiences, students become active learners and practice applying what they have learned in the classroom, to real life problems and situations. When they reflect on these experiences and bring them back to the classroom, they gain a better understanding of how the theories and research they study in their courses apply to real life. The ability to provide these practical learning environments also allows instructors to assess and evaluate student performance in complex, real-life situations, thereby increasing the authentic nature of the assessment (Lynton, 1995).

4. The connections instructors build through their professional service also facilitate the development of service learning opportunities for students. Students not only learn new skills in these experiences, but they also begin to see themselves as change agents in society; become more aware of the complex nature of society and the problems that exist in communities; gain first-hand experience at identifying, experiencing, and solving societal problems; and learn to work collaboratively (Altman, 1996; Duffy & Bringle, 1998; Jacoby, 1999). Through service learning

opportunities, instructors facilitate the development of what Altman (1996) called *socially responsive knowledge.*

5. By working alongside their students on their service learning projects, instructors can model professional behavior and take advantage of teachable moments that so often occur unexpectedly in the field (Plater, 1995). Modeling desired behavior is an effective teaching strategy. Observing the appropriate behavior tends to have a greater impact on students than simply being told about it.

6. On occasion faculty members are appointed or elected to community agency or government boards because their professional expertise will inform policy and decision making. These activities can have a positive impact on teaching in several ways. Faculty members can incorporate the disciplinary knowledge garnered from these experiences into the content of their classes. Moreover, as they become more familiar with public policy, political reality, and the way community and government agencies work, they can illustrate how these policies and procedures affect their discipline and how their discipline, in turn, can have an impact on these policies and procedures. This knowledge and experience add a new dimension and context to the course content and can lead to thought-provoking discussions. Also, the civic nature of this type of service activity makes faculty members good role models as they try to instill a sense of civic responsibility and citizenship in their students.

Institutional Citizenship. The American Association of University Professors (1994) report contained an apt analogy to highlight the importance of institutional citizenship:

> Service to one's department, college or university is like the portion of the crop held aside to be planted next year, or like the reinvestment of capital so that institutions and academic disciplines may both maintain themselves and change and adapt. Moreover, service is essential to the realization of the ideal of the college or university as a collegial institution, a community of scholars. (p. 46)

Not only is citizenship essential for the maintenance of the institution, but it also provides faculty members with opportunities to enrich their teaching and their students' learning.

1. Participation on university committees can provide unexpected professional development opportunities that sensitize faculty members to educational issues and enrich their teaching. For example, Donna Duffy, a group leader in the Psychology Partnerships Project (personal communication, July 27, 2000), commented that "Some work in committees raises broader dilemmas concerning students—discussion of these dilemmas can then lead to changes in classroom approaches." She cited as examples discussion about issues such as diversity, assessment, and general education requirements.

2. Institutional service often facilitates collaboration between faculty members and student affairs staff, and this collaboration can enhance teaching. Several

commissions addressing changes in higher education—among them the Wingspread Group (1993), the Kellogg Commission on the Future of State and Land Grant Universities (National Association of State Universities and Land Grant Colleges, 1997), and the Boyer Commission on Educating Undergraduates in the Research University (1998)—advocated persuasively for a seamless learning environment on campus in which the learning community transcends the boundaries of the classroom. They stressed the need for partnerships between faculty members and student affairs staff to develop a common set of educational goals and objectives that apply to the entire undergraduate experience. Breaking down the traditional territorial boundaries between academic affairs and student affairs can create a learning community that encompasses all members and all aspects of the institution (Amey, 1999; Fried, 1999; Krahenbuhl, 1998; Kuh, 1996; Schroeder, 1999). In my own case, the opportunity to work with student affairs staff members enriched my teaching in ways I never expected. For example, what I learned from them about students' developmental issues and the emotional and familial problems students often confront has made me a more sensitive and caring teacher in the classroom.

3. Even administrative service can lead to better teaching. Administrators often see teaching, learning, faculty, and students from a different perspective than they did as a faculty member. I know that my tenure as a department head certainly gave me a new perspective on teaching. The responsibility I had as a department head to encourage, model, and reward excellent teaching compelled me to read more extensively and thoughtfully about educational issues, students' needs, and the art of teaching. I learned a great deal from students who came to me with compliments and complaints about their instructors concerning how students view the learning process, what they need from their instructors, and what they most value in teachers they consider inspirational. When I entered full-time teaching again, I found myself reflecting on what I had learned and altering my teaching style in an effort to meet students' needs more effectively.

Disciplinary Citizenship. Involvement in state, regional, and national disciplinary organizations can bring national recognition and awards, but it can also have a direct positive impact on teaching.

1. Active participation in disciplinary organizations facilitates the establishment of a more diverse network of colleagues. These networks can help instructors move beyond their institution's sometimes idiosyncratic way of doing things and incorporate more varied, creative, and effective teaching strategies into their repertoire of skills. David Johnson (personal communication, July 26, 2000), a past president of the STP, said it well: "Working with organizations such as STP puts us in touch with other people who are passionate about teaching. Even though we may be carrying on the business of STP when we attend meetings, I almost always come away from those encounters with new ideas for improving my teaching."

2. Sometimes professional association activities give faculty members opportunities to work with teachers in other academic settings. These partnerships are crucial to enhancing teaching in the 21st century. Consider some statistics. Ernst and Petrossian reported in 1996 that approximately 800,000 students enrolled in a high school psychology course each year. No doubt this figure has increased substantially since then given the increased interest in psychology at the high school level. McClenney (1998) and McGovern and Reich (1996) reported that approximately 50% of all freshmen and sophomores attend community colleges. The total number of students enrolled in public four-year colleges and public two-year colleges is about the same (Hansen, 1998). Approximately 40% of first-time beginning community college students transfer to another institution, with about 50% of these students going to four-year colleges or universities. This transfer between community colleges and four-year institutions will likely increase as tuition at four-year colleges increases and students opt to take their first 2 years at more affordable community colleges. Coordinating curricula, advising, assessment, and faculty development across academic levels is imperative to facilitate students' transition through the levels of psychology education, provide a more seamless educational experience in psychology, and enhance students' learning and preparation for future educational and career pursuits.

3. As Charles Brewer (personal communication, July 26, 2000), a past president of the STP and past editor of the journal *Teaching of Psychology*, noted, participation and leadership in professional organizations give instructors a broader perspective of educational issues in general and of psychology education in particular. Having this big picture view tends to make teachers more sensitive to the teaching context, keeps them on the forefront of activities in their field, and keeps their teaching fresh and current. It can also improve their ability to advise students. For example, George Goedel (personal communication, July 25, 2000), another group leader in the Psychology Partnerships Project, pointed out that his service in the Kentucky Psychological Association increased his knowledge of the problems faced by psychologists in private practice and thus improved his ability to advise students in his professional careers course.

4. Serving the discipline in a consulting capacity can also enhance teaching and benefit students. James Korn (personal communication, July 25, 2000), a past president of the STP, commented that his work as an undergraduate program consultant and an APA accreditation site visitor provided him with current and realistic examples for his teaching of psychology and professional issues graduate courses.

5. Another way to provide service to the discipline is to organize or present professional development workshops. G. William Hill (personal communication, July 25, 2000), the current president of the STP and coordinator of the Southeastern Conference on the Teaching of Psychology, pointed out that this type of service

has had a beneficial impact on his teaching. He said his interaction with the audience gives him new information about the content and teaching of psychology, stimulates new ideas, and provides feedback about his teaching style. He then uses what he learned from this experience to modify and improve his course content and his teaching style.

6. It is important for students to learn how to become informed, active, collaborative contributors to their profession. Modeling this professional behavior for students is a powerful way to teach this lesson. Tonja Ringgold (personal communication, July 25, 2000), a member of the Psychology Partnerships Project Steering Committee, stated that she uses her involvement in professional organizations as an example for her community college students to show them how to get involved in professional organizations and how these organizations can be fulfilling both professionally and personally.

These are just a few of the benefits to teaching that accrue from professional service and citizenship. Undoubtedly, readers can think of many more. Articulating the benefits of professional service and citizenship for teaching and learning is the easy part, however. The challenge is to convince colleagues and administrators that these activities should be rewarded and given greater weight in performance evaluations. Many educators believe the best way to accomplish this objective is to establish service as a scholarly activity and show that it has a favorable impact on teaching and research.

Scholarship of Service

Recall that Diamond and Adam (1993) stipulated that, for an activity to be considered scholarly, it must require discipline-specific expertise, be innovative, be replicable, be documented, be available for peer review, and have significance and impact. Just as Hutchings and Shulman (1999) used these criteria to distinguish among good teaching, scholarly teaching, and the scholarship of teaching, others have used them to distinguish among good service, scholarly service, and the scholarship of service (Lynton, 1995; Sandmann, Foster-Fishman, Lloyd, Rauhe, & Rosaen, 2000). More specifically, *scholarly service* is service informed by the latest relevant theory and research, includes assessment of the effectiveness of the service, is open to peer review, and benefits from faculty members' reflection on the activity. The *scholarship of service* entails making the service public so that it is open to critique and evaluation; provides products others can use; stimulates new questions, theories, and knowledge; and leads to improvement in the profession and the institution or organization. To persuade peers that professional service and citizenship warrant recognition and to ensure that these activities are included in the evaluation process, it is essential that faculty members document and evaluate their service activities.

Documenting Service.   The literature contains several models that highlight the scholarly components of professional service in an organized and comprehensive manner (Braskamp & Ory, 1994; Driscoll & Lynton, 1999; Glassick et al., 1997; Lynton, 1995). The common elements in the proposed documentation include a *personal statement* in which the faculty member describes the project's goals; the activities involved and the rationale for them; how the faculty member's expertise relates to the project; the project's outcome; the project's impact on the faculty member's teaching, the research in the field, the organization, and the academic institution; and a self-evaluation of the activity and its outcomes. The documentation should include high-quality work samples that represent the full scope of the activity, illustrate innovative aspects of the activity, and indicate the extent to which the goals were achieved. External evaluations from clients served by the project, colleagues who collaborated on the activity, and experts in the disciplinary field are also critical components of the documentation.

Assessing Service.   Developing evaluation standards for professional service and citizenship activities is challenging, but the academia has begun to address this issue (Glassick et al., 1997; Lynton, 1995). In the 1994 Carnegie survey of chief administrative officers (Glassick et al., 1997), many respondents reported their institution had developed new methods to evaluate professional service (38%), service to the institution (42%), and service to the discipline (33%). The recommended evaluation criteria include an assessment of the clarity and appropriateness of the goals given the project's resources and constraints; depth and appropriateness of the faculty member's expertise and prior experience; appropriateness of the methods; impact and significance of the outcomes; originality and innovation of the activity; relation of the activity to teaching and research; quality of the presentation of the project; and quality of the faculty member's reflective self-evaluation.

SUMMARY

As I hope this chapter has illustrated, service has been and continues to be a cornerstone of academia. Service activities should not have to compete with teaching and research for time, recognition, and reward. Professional service and citizenship should and can be integrated into the role of faculty members and recognized as vital and worthwhile activities. Furthermore, service does not need to detract from faculty members' roles as teachers and researchers. To the contrary, professional service, institutional citizenship, and disciplinary citizenship provide many unique and important benefits to academia and inform and enhance teaching and learning. It is my hope that, as faculty members become more proficient at documenting and assessing service activities, the contributions of service to teaching and learning will acquire the respect and rewards they deserve.

ACKNOWLEDGMENTS

I am honored to have the opportunity to write a chapter in this book dedicated to Wilbert J. McKeachie and Charles L. Brewer. Both men have had a profound influence on my own teaching and service, and so it is indeed fitting for me to write a chapter on the benefits of integrating teaching and service. Bill was instrumental in my growth as a teacher. I used his book, *Teaching Tips*, as my bible when I began teaching as a graduate student. Since that time, I have always kept a version of his book on the shelf closest to my desk so I can use it when I need it—and I seem to need it often! No matter what the problem is, I always manage to find in Bill's book wise advice about how to deal with it. Without question, Charles is my service mentor. I first met Charles when I was a graduate student and visited a friend who had recently been hired to teach at Furman University. After that I would see Charles at APA conventions and, as he did with so many other young professionals, he encouraged me to become active in APA Division 2. He helped me do so by recruiting me as a reviewer for *Teaching of Psychology*, and since then he has always been there to encourage and support my pursuit of new leadership positions. Thank you, Bill and Charles, for your inspiration, wisdom, encouragement, support, and, above all, friendship. You have been exceptional role models who use your service to improve not only the learning of your own students, but also the professional development of your colleagues and psychology education around the world.

REFERENCES

Altman, I. (1996). Higher education and psychology in the millennium. *American Psychologist, 51,* 371–378.

American Association of University Professors. (1994, January–February). The work of faculty: Expectations, priorities, and rewards. *Academe,* pp. 35–48.

Amey, M. J. (1999). Faculty culture and college life: Reshaping incentives toward student outcomes. In J. D. Toma & A. J. Kezar (Eds.), *Reconceptualizing the collegiate ideal. New directions for higher education #105* (pp. 59–69). San Francisco: Jossey-Bass.

Boyer, E. L. (1990). *Scholarship reconsidered: Priorities of the professoriate.* Princeton, NJ: The Carnegie Foundation for the Advancement of Teaching.

Boyer Commission on Educating Undergraduates in the Research University. (1998). *Reinventing under-graduate education: A blueprint for America's research universities.* New York: The Carnegie Foundation for the Advancement of Teaching.

Brand, M. (2000). Changing faculty roles in research universities: Using the pathways strategy. *Change, 32*(6), 42–45.

Braskamp, L. A., & Ory, J. C. (1994). *Assessing faculty work: Enhancing individual and institutional performance.* San Francisco: Jossey-Bass.

Cuban, L. (1999). *How scholars trumped teachers: Change without reform in university curriculum, teaching, and research, 1890–1990.* New York: Teachers College Press.

Diamond, R. M., & Adam, B. E. (Eds.). (1993). *Recognizing faculty work: Reward systems for the year 2000. New directions for higher education #81.* San Francisco: Jossey-Bass.

Driscoll, A., & Lynton, E. A. (1999). *Making outreach visible: A guide to documenting professional service and outreach.* Washington, DC: American Association for Higher Education.

Duffy, D. K., & Bringle, R. G. (1998). Collaborating with the community: Psychology and service-learning. In R. G. Bringle & D. K. Duffy (Eds.), *With service in mind: Concepts and models for service learning in psychology* (pp. 1–17). Washington, DC: American Association of Higher Education.

Elman, S. E., & Smock, S. M. (1985). *Professional service and faculty rewards: Toward an integrated structure.* Washington, DC: National Association of State Universities and Land-Grant Colleges.

Ernst, R., & Petrossian, P. (1996). Teachers of Psychology in Secondary Schools (TOPSS): Aiming for excellence in high school psychology instruction. *American Psychologist, 51,* 256–258.

Fear, F. A., & Sandmann, L. R. (1995). Unpacking the service category: Reconceptualizing university outreach for the 21st century. *Continuing Higher Education Review, 59,* 110–122.

Fried, J. (1999). Two steps to creative campus collaboration. *AAHE Bulletin, 51*(7), 10–12.

Froh, R. C., Gray, P. J., & Lambert, L. M. (1993). Representing faculty work: The professional portfolio. In R. M. Diamond & B. E. Adam (Eds.), *Recognizing faculty work: Reward systems for the year 2000. New directions for higher education #81* (pp. 97–110). San Francisco: Jossey-Bass.

Glassick, C. E., Huber, M. T., & Maeroff, G. I. (1997). *Scholarship assessed: Evaluation of the professoriate.* San Francisco: Jossey-Bass.

Halpern, D. F., Smothergill, D. W., Allen, M., Baker, S., Baum, C., Best, D., Ferrari, J., Geisinger, K. F., Gilden, E. R., Hester, M., Keith-Spiegel, P., Kierniesky, N. C., McGovern, T. V., McKeachie, W. J., Prokasy, W. F., Szuchman, L. T., Vasta, R., & Weaver, K. A. (1998). Scholarship in psychology: A paradigm for the twenty-first century. *American Psychologist, 53,* 1292–1297.

Hansen, E. J. (1998). Essential demographics of today's college students. *AAHE Bulletin, 51*(3), 3–5.

Hirsch, D., & Lynton, E. (1995). *Bridging two worlds: Professional service and service learning.* Boston: New England Resource Center for Higher Education, University of Massachusetts at Boston.

Hutchings, P., & Shulman, L. S. (1999). The scholarship of teaching: New elaborations, new developments. *Change, 31*(5), 10–15.

Jacoby, B. (1999). Partnerships for service learning. In J. H. Schuh & E. J. Whitt (Eds.), *Creating successful partnerships between academic and student affairs. New directions for student services #87* (pp. 19–35). San Francisco: Jossey-Bass.

Krahenbuhl, G. S. (1998). Faculty work: Integrating responsibilities and institutional needs. *Change, 30*(6), 18–25.

Kuh, G. D. (1996). Guiding principles for creating seamless learning environments for undergraduates. *Journal of College Student Development, 37,* 135–148.

Lynton, E. A. (1995). *Making the case for professional service.* Washington, DC: American Association for Higher Education.

McClenney, K. M. (1998). Community colleges perched at the millennium: Perspectives on innovation, transformation, and tomorrow. *Leadership Abstracts, 11*(8) [Online]. Available: *http://www.league.org/publication/abstracts/leadership/labs0898.htm.*

McGovern, T. V., & Reich, J. N. (1996). A comment on the Quality Principles. *American Psychologist, 51,* 252–255.

National Association of State Universities and Land Grant Colleges. (1997). *Returning to our roots: The student experience.* Washington, DC: Author.

Plater, W. M. (1995). Future work: Faculty time in the 21st century. *Change, 27*(3), 22–33.

Rice, R. E., & Richlin, L. (1993). Broadening the concept of scholarship in the professions. In L. Curry, J. F. Wergin, & Associates (Eds.), *Educating professionals* (pp. 279–315). San Francisco: Jossey-Bass.

Sandmann, L. R., Foster-Fishman, P. G., Lloyd, J., Rauhe, W., & Rosaen, C. (2000). Managing critical tensions: How to strengthen the scholarship component of outreach. *Change, 32*(1), 44–52.

Schroeder, C. C. (1999). Partnerships: An imperative for enhancing student learning and institutional effectiveness. In J. H. Schuh & E. J. Whitt (Eds.), *Creating successful partnerships between academic and student affairs. New directions for student services #87* (pp. 5–18). San Francisco: Jossey-Bass.

Seldin, P. (1998). How colleges evaluate teaching: 1988 vs. 1998. *AAHE Bulletin, 50*(7), 3–7.

Snyder, D. P. (1996). High tech and higher education: A wave of creative destruction is rolling toward the halls of academe. *On the Horizon, 4*(5), 1, 3–7.

Wingspread Group. (1993). *An American imperative: Higher expectations for higher education.* Racine, WI: Johnson Foundation.

Zlotkowski, E. (2001). Mapping new terrain: Service-learning across the disciplines. *Change, 33*(1), 25–33.

14

A Portrait of Teaching Painted by Early Career Faculty

Baron Perlman
Susan H. McFadden
Lee I. McCann
Nina Kunzer
University of Wisconsin–Oshkosh

College teaching is a satisfying and stimulating way of life, but it is a career-long developmental process that we do not understand as well as we should. Faculty need to be asked about their teaching more often, and their colleagues need to listen closely to what is said because in listening to colleagues and participating in meaningful discussions of pedagogy faculty acquire deeper levels of conceptualization about teaching. We present a portrait of teaching by 37 psychology faculty relatively early in their teaching careers (Perlman, Konop, McFadden, & McCann, 1996; Perlman, Marxen, McFadden, & McCann, 1996; Perlman, McFadden, McCann, & Kunzer, 2000) whom we have been studying longitudinally (two waves, 5-year interval). What follows summarizes what they told us in a series of short written responses to questions we asked them to consider. They raise fascinating issues about teaching from which all faculty can learn.

These faculty average 41 years of age and have been teaching an average of 7.7 years. All are tenured or in tenure-track positions and most are now associate professors (64%). They work primarily in public institutions (62%) in departments of 10 or fewer members. Over 70% of their institutions offer graduate degrees, but only 41% work in departments offering graduate education. Their teaching load is typical: an average of six courses per academic year, although 39% teach eight or more undergraduate courses per year.

IMPORTANT TEACHING ISSUES

Teaching Is Time-Consuming

These faculty work almost 61 hours per week with an average of 36 hours a week devoted to teaching (10 hours in class, 7 hours reading, 5.8 hours holding office hours, 5.7 hours writing and grading exams, 2.1 hours talking with colleagues, and 5.2 hours spent on other teaching work). The average time per week spent on teaching has not significantly changed from 5 years ago. As one respondent stated, "I continue to be surprised by how much work it takes to maintain consistently high-quality teaching."

Important Teacher Qualities: Intellectual, Interpersonal, and Affective

We asked participating faculty to list the three most important qualities of good teachers. They were the same for the two waves of data collection: (a) knowledge about class subject matter, (b) approachability—willing to help students in and out of class, and (c) enthusiasm about subject matter. These qualities mirror McFadden and Perlman's (1989) three dimensions of excellent teaching: intellectual, interpersonal, and affective.

Faculty Share Similarities in Why They Became College Teachers

Positive feelings about teaching and making a difference in students' lives are the primary reasons these faculty became teachers. The academic and intellectual lives of a faculty member were other popular reasons. The latter echoes Clark's (1987) finding that "just knowledge itself—creating it, caring for it, teaching or otherwise transmitting it—proved to be the nearest thing to common ideological ground" (p. 131) for the professoriate. One faculty member wrote:

> Intellectual freedom/atmosphere. I enjoy educating those who want to learn ... I like knowing I make a difference in the life of students inspiring them to grow and learn. I strive to help them see the applicability of their knowledge. I still enjoy the academic freedom, I still enjoy reading and preparing lectures. Nothing is as fulfilling as a class that goes well for all involved.

Another stated:

> I teach to have an opportunity to pursue my intellectual interests professionally, to instill in others an appreciation for intellectual inquiry, and to organize and disseminate knowledge in my own field of study.

Seven faculty referred to the ideals of a Liberal Arts education in the initial survey and seven more added it 5 years later. This concern seems an area that becomes more salient as faculty settle into their teaching careers. We found that "Qualities of the Liberally Educated Person" (Diamond, 1998) were reflected in this theme as an emphasis on educating the whole student, in contrast to focusing only on discipline or career-oriented knowledge. The Liberal Arts theme appears clearly in the words of one person:

> I teach because I have found that teaching is one of the few professions through which one can occasionally develop in others both a love of learning and thinking, and a passion for living an examined, beneficial life.

Surprises About Teaching

About two thirds of all faculty report being satisfied or very satisfied with the quality of students on their campuses (Finkelstein, Seal, & Schuster, 1998), yet the most prevalent surprise for our cohort of faculty was students' apathy, negative attitudes, sense of entitlement, poor ability and preparation, and lack of motivation. Typical comments were "too many students resent the fact that the professor expects them to learn," "students who do not want to learn; they view college as a passage which will be of no value to them," and "how little studying many students do." It surprised us that our faculty found unprepared and unmotivated students surprising. Faculty have been complaining about students for centuries; nonetheless, other authors (e.g., Clark, 1987; Rojstaczer, 1999) echo this theme.

The second biggest surprise was their own positive feelings about teaching. Despite that this is the most prevalent reason respondents became college teachers, some were surprised that teaching felt good. One faculty said, "I am surprised how much fun it is. . . . " Another said, "I am surprised by how rewarding it is, how good it feels when I sense that I have had a real impact on a student's understanding."

Respondents also were surprised about time pressures (a theme noted in every study of college teachers) and how much work teaching is. One said, "I am surprised at the necessary preparation time," and another wrote about " . . . how challenging it is to assess student learning."

Intellectual Content May Not Be Most Important

Many faculty said that what they teach is less important than the learning processes students master and how they feel about learning. For many faculty, good lectures and classes are only the starting point in what is most important for a student to learn, not an end, and the affective component (enjoying learning) is as important as the intellectual (the facts).

Faculty want students to gain tools for learning. When asked about "the most important thing a student can learn from you," one faculty member said, "how and why to think critically, creatively, independently, and purposefully." Another group of answers emphasized the affective side of teaching—that learning is fun. This positive response was captured well when one person told us students should "enjoy learning and have fun doing it," and another wrote they should acquire "my joy and love of the subject matter."

Another theme emphasized the intellectual knowledge of psychology, and several faculty discussed the Liberal Arts and the ideal of the good citizen. Student efficacy (capability) was also mentioned.

Mastering the Art and Craft of Teaching

In their busy, full teaching lives, with what do faculty struggle? Almost everyone listed teaching techniques/process/managing the classroom and conveying information. After at least 5 years of teaching, they still sought improvement in basic areas of pedagogy, an indicator of how many faculty may feel they have never mastered the basics of teaching or find there is always more to be learned. It could be that one challenge of teaching well is that as faculty come to understand the complexity of teaching and learning, they continually feel the need to improve.

These faculty are sensitive to students, and many want to make a difference in their lives. However, what it means to relate meaningfully to students is not well understood. Do faculty want more time (time they say they lack) to meet with students, better relationships with students (whatever this means), or a sense that they are *reaching* students? We need to learn more about the student–faculty interaction because it is critical for a sense of community on a campus, student performance, and retention in college (Gardiner, 1996).

Increased enthusiasm was mentioned by several faculty as a needed improvement in their teaching, but again we were uncertain about what this means. Is enthusiasm related to entertaining students, fulfilling an inner need to be excited about their subject matter and communicate this to their students—or as Max Weber hypothesized (as described in Clark, 1987), "... as a prerequisite of inspiration?" (p. 274). Perhaps enthusiasm is the equivalent of zest, an intrinsic reward for the teaching they do and necessary for sustaining themselves.

INFLUENCES ON FACULTY TEACHING

To paint a portrait of faculty early in their teaching careers and to learn about our own teaching in the process, we must arrange the subjects on the canvas in some meaningful way. The lifespan, contextual approach (Baltes, 1987) captures the reality of faculty working in multifaceted environments, and we suggest it as a model for understanding teaching. It emphasizes the context within which faculty teach and recognizes the critical incidents and unexpected events that seem so important in teaching, but are so poorly understood.

Context

The most immediate contextual elements of teaching are students, colleagues, role models and mentors, and department and institution. Also influencing teaching are national pressures and trends such as multiculturalism, technological developments, and economic and political constraints (Finkelstein et al., 1998). Clark's (1987) work and the present data suggest that various types of institutions offer different contexts for teaching and substantively different careers for faculty. One faculty member at a rural institution with mostly first-generation college students wrote that she struggles with whether she wants to be a role model of an independent, female professional. Another said:

> I teach in a rural, working class area, where many students are first generation students who are under-prepared for college and are putting themselves through college, usually working 30–40 hours a week while going to school full time. The impact I can have on these students is phenomenal.

At an institution that emphasizes teaching, another respondent describes how time, emphasis, and identity shift to teaching, with a sense of loss about giving up a program of scholarship.

Teachers' growth and satisfaction with their teaching and careers seem related to their adjustments to contextual issues, many of which are unpredictable. Our observations suggest that, in part because of higher education's changing environment, even senior faculty, who teach a great deal, need more mentoring, collegiality, and support.

Technology provides an example of resistance to contextual influence. The use of technology was not a visible theme in our data. In fact, much of the data conflict with use of technology or distance education. Faculty seem more concerned about high touch—the interpersonal—than high tech. Technology may be an instance where the colossal emphasis on its use, correctly or not, pulls faculty along. If so, it is critical that means be found to retain and nurture the student–faculty relationship and the potential for connection and interaction to the benefit of both students and faculty.

Students

We usually consider education a process where teachers inform, influence, connect with, and reach their students. However, the relationship is bidirectional, and problems and successes occur as students *touch* teachers as well. Some faculty report their most satisfying moments occur when students "get it," when they meet with them outside of class to discuss their lives and problems and when students graduate or complete a course in some way different than they began. One faculty member noted how a kind word at the end of a course can validate a teacher's worth and sustain self-confidence. There are moments when students make it all worthwhile. The obverse is also true. Unpleasant, confrontational, and disappointing experiences with students linger in faculty's psyches.

Personal Characteristics of Faculty

Faculty's personal characteristics and lives must be included in any attempt to understand the world of college teachers (Goodson, 1992). The responsibilities of teaching are omnipresent and weigh heavy on faculty, although they may not be visible to others. For example, the academic role is not a job, but a way of life for most respondents. It is an important reason that faculty became teachers, but personal life may be consumed by this calling. Balancing academic and personal lives can be difficult. As one person said, "it is easy to forget to have a life outside of one's academic job." Another added, "Another area that is becoming more stressful is the years of personal sacrifice ... I cannot manage an academic life as well as a personal life in the number of hours available."

Teachers' Roles and Behavior

Teachers' perceived roles (i.e., the metaphors of teaching that underlie their pedagogy) and how they teach are influenced by and in turn influence students, institutions, and undergraduate education. For example, strong emphasis on affect (caring about the subject matter, enthusiasm, positive and negative feelings toward students) permeated these essays. It seemed as important for faculty to understand their feelings about teaching as their intellectual approach to course content. Many faculty also valued the Liberal Arts perspective that is part of the moral domain of teaching: the desire to inspire students to be thoughtful, responsible citizens.

THE EVOLVING PORTRAIT OF FACULTY WHO TEACH

Stage theories of faculty development that have driven thinking about teaching until recently conclude that certain tasks and problems emerge only during certain periods of a faculty career and are primarily influenced by their current developmental stage (Baldwin & Blackburn, 1981; Weiland, 1994). An often implicit conclusion is that faculty careers move through predictable stages building toward greater wisdom and abilities. However, these conclusions may not be true; there may be no end point to good teaching—a task Palmer (1998) described as never fully mastered. Faculty's greatest achievement may be the ability to cope with ever-present problems and changes in all aspects of their academic life: contexts, students, their own development, and so forth.

There are important implications of a lifespan contextual approach, all of which support the idea that faculty of all ages and experience would benefit from talking with each other about teaching. For example, those faculty nearing retirement probably are different as teachers than 20 years previously, but not necessarily better. Second, faculty at different points in their teaching careers may be more alike than we have believed. Baldwin and Blackburn (1981) found many similarities at different career stages among faculty in liberal arts colleges, such as the percentage of total professional time allocated to teaching and interacting with students and the importance of teaching and contributing to students. Third, the wise teacher as mentor to the mentee (less experienced faculty) may not be the best model for enhancing either group's teaching. A more collaborative, equal relationship based on differences because of age and experience, but not necessarily better teaching, may be more productive.

Additionally, as faculty with different levels of teaching experience explore their pedagogy, they may want to focus on loss. A lifespan contextual model argues that with gains there must be losses. As faculty age and grow in pedagogical experience, what is lost in their teaching? If what is lost is valuable, can it be regained?

It is technique where the faculty we studied believe they need improvement, and undoubtedly good teaching involves mastering a variety of pedagogical techniques. What is unknown is whether this emphasis exists because technique is the easiest place to begin, the most visible to faculty and students alike, or the most important? Is it technique that various educational contexts influence and emphasize the most?

What must not be lost is the awareness that good technique—the good lecture or class—is a starting point, not an ending. Many facets of teaching that contribute to better educated students were seldom mentioned by our faculty. These unattended to aspects of teaching included improving content, teaching critical thinking, or increasing rigor in courses, and no respondent mentioned improving students' ability for cooperative work (Gardiner, 1996), ethics of teaching, use of technology, or connecting with colleagues and mentors. Whether such issues appear later in a teacher's career as areas for pedagogical improvement is unknown.

The place of relationships and affect also should be part of faculty discussions of teaching. For whatever complex reasons, early career faculty struggle with issues of relationship and emotion in their teaching. Are new teachers aware how quickly their teaching moves from the intellectual realm to the world of relationships and emotion? Palmer (1998) provided a good beginning for understanding how teachers' emotional lives influence students, the quality of teaching, and a teacher's nonacademic life. We know that affect—the "challenges and passion" (Clark, 1987, p. 222) of doing academic work—is important. What happens to affect in distance education?

Teachers are exposed to diverse contextual influences. Faculty need to learn more from each other about how contextual factors influence teaching—from who enters and stays in the profession, to how course goals, academic rigor, and day-to-day class activities are altered. For example, what is the influence of fads in teaching and how do teachers distinguish fads from substance?

Most important, the transactional nature of teaching needs to be emphasized in discussions about pedagogy—when the day is done, teachers have to ask whether they touched a student's life and whether their students are learning what they need to learn. Faculty and administrators who attend to teaching would be well served to pause and reflect on what pressures and messages are most salient to both new and experienced teachers. We do not know more about many of the issues addressed in this section because most of the research on college teaching has been cross-sectional and has not attended to the web of contextual factors that affect teachers.

CONCLUSION

Students and teaching matter greatly. Teaching occurs within a dynamic, rapidly changing environment. The time when academia truly was an *ivory tower*, with unlimited time for reading and leisurely conversations with students, is long gone. The portrait painted by our early career faculty is one of teaching as a multi-layered, multifaceted endeavor with multiple meanings. It involves much more than knowledge of the subject matter. In addition to working with a subject's content, faculty must make sense of their teaching and students, what works and what does not, and what to do about it all.

Teaching also includes the power and importance of feelings, surprisingly important to these faculty early in their careers. The faculty in our study want to retain the joy they feel when they teach and to continue to be satisfied with their lives as teachers. We believe these themes would emerge regardless of one's academic discipline, but only further longitudinal research with a larger and more diverse sample will tell us for certain. Until we obtain such data, we continue to believe, with our respondents, that college teaching is a time-consuming task fraught with large and small frustrations, but also immensely satisfying in the lives of individual teachers and their positive, shaping influences on students.

REFERENCES

Baldwin, R. G., & Blackburn, R. T. (1981). The academic career as a developmental process: Implications for higher education. *Journal of Higher Education, 52,* 598–614.

Baltes, P. B. (1987). Theoretical propositions of life-span developmental psychology: On the dynamics between growth and decline. *Developmental Psychology, 23,* 611–626.

Clark, B. R. (1987). *The academic life: Small worlds, different worlds.* Princeton, NJ: Carnegie.

Diamond, R. M. (1998). *Designing and assessing courses and curricula: A practical guide.* San Francisco: Jossey-Bass.

Finkelstein, M. J., Seal, R. K., & Schuster, J. H. (1998). *The new academic generation: A profession in transformation.* Baltimore, MD: Johns Hopkins University Press.

Gardiner, L. F. (1996). *Redesigning higher education: Producing dramatic gains in student learning* (ASHE-ERIC higher Education Report Volume 23, No. 7). Washington, DC: The George Washington University, Graduate School of Education and Human Development.

Goodson, I. F. (Ed.). (1992). *Studying teachers' lives.* New York: Teachers College Press.

McFadden, S. H., & Perlman, B. (1989). Faculty recruitment and excellent undergraduate teaching. *Teaching of Psychology, 16,* 195–198.

Palmer, P. J. (1998). *The courage to teach: Exploring the inner landscape of a teacher's life.* San Francisco: Jossey-Bass.

Perlman, B., Konop, K., McFadden, S. H., & McCann, L. I. (1996). New faculty do want to teach. *Teaching of Psychology, 23,* 232–234.

Perlman, B., Marxen, J. C., McFadden, S. H., & McCann, L. I. (1996). Applicants for a faculty position do not emphasize teaching. *Teaching of Psychology, 23,* 103–104.

Perlman, B., McFadden, S., McCann, L. I., & Kunzer, N. (2000, January). *A longitudinal study of faculty teaching: 5 years after.* Poster session presented at the 22nd annual National Institute on the Teaching of Psychology, St. Petersburg, FL.

Rojstaczer, S. (1999). *Gone for good: Tales of university life after the golden age.* New York: Oxford University Press.

Weiland, S. (1994). Writing the academic life: Faculty careers in narrative perspective. *The Review of Higher Education, 17,* 395–422.

15

Peer Review for Meaningful Teaching Enhancement

Baron Perlman
Lee I. McCann
University of Wisconsin–Oshkosh

Peer review requires collegial conversations about teaching and learning. Peer review promotes examination of our assumptions and rationales for teaching activities. . . . Peer review helps to reinvigorate teaching. (Chism, 1998, p. ix)

In the last decade, teaching has assumed greater importance in faculty discussions and scholarship in all types of institutions across the country. This emphasis on describing, understanding, improving, and better communicating what faculty do when they teach can be of great value. This chapter emphasizes making this attention to teaching more meaningful and useful through better use of peer review. Faculty at many institutions practice some form of peer review of teaching, but many do it as a pro forma evaluative exercise, with little attention to or opportunity for improvement of teaching.

There are several types of peer review. One can visit a colleague's classroom and observe actual teaching, talk with a colleague, or read course materials or a teaching portfolio (Edgerton, Hutchings, & Quinlan, 1991; Seldin, 1997; Seldin & Associates, 1993). Most faculty undergo some type of peer review for personnel purposes, and many voluntarily seek peers for discussion and assistance with their teaching. In both cases, faculty should benefit from thoughtful attention to their teaching. The goals of peer review should always be pedagogical improvement, greater comfort in talking about your teaching, becoming more reflective about your teaching (Dahlin, 1994), and developing relationships with colleagues who share a common interest in teaching.

Our goal is to help faculty get the most out of their discussions and evaluations of teaching, whether colleagues are reviewing teaching as part of peer review done for personnel purposes (summative review) or faculty members consult others voluntarily about some facet of their pedagogy (formative review). We have described the details of implementing and doing peer review in Perlman and McCann (1998), and the work of Bowser (1998), Chism (1998), Helling (1988), Hutchings (1996), Kahn, (1993), Keig and Waggoner (1994), Paulsen and Feldman (1995), Quinlan (1996), Theal and Franklin (1991), Travis (1995), Weimer and Lenze (1991), and Wright and Associates (1995) should prove especially useful to the reader.

Faculty need to be well organized and thoughtful about their teaching if they wish to understand and improve it. Throughout this chapter, we emphasize a formative philosophy–peer review, even when done summatively for personnel purposes, should help faculty reflect on their teaching, maintaining and pointing the way for continuing improvements. Focusing on teaching, the thought and effort put into it, and on ways to improve it should not only serve to meet required personnel rules for teaching assessment, but increase the chances that teaching will be meaningfully discussed and enhanced.

An important aspect of peer review is the encouragement of an open discussion of teaching. This process provides opportunities for major insights into your teaching philosophy and practices while reinforcing small changes in your teaching that over time produce continuing advancements. Public discussion of teaching connects faculty to colleagues in meaningful ways.

BENEFITS OF PEER REVIEW

Done well, peer review can produce the following benefits:

• *Quality of Education Improves.* Attention to the improvement of teaching may be the most important step faculty can take toward improving the quality of education their students receive and the reputation of their college or university.

• *Teaching Becomes "Community Property"* (Hutchings, 1996; Shulman, 1993). Peer review is one step toward making discussion and improvement of teaching more visible in the academic community. Talking about teaching with colleagues creates an environment where teaching can be made public and highlights the realization that others also care about their teaching. This understanding sustains a faculty member in the classroom and in other work with students and enhances the value of teaching within the academic community. It assists both new and established faculty in learning new and different approaches to teaching and in reaching conclusions about what they want to continue or change in their teaching.

• *Faculty Ownership Is Evident.* Pressures beyond the academy are seeking greater accountability and responsibility for teaching. Peer review is one way faculty can document what it is they do as teachers. It allows faculty to "claim ourselves as teachers" (Gillespie, 2000, p. 384), demonstrates concern with and attention to the art and craft of teaching by the professoriate, and assists good teachers to become better. It is a process by which faculty, as much as possible, are in charge of, and active participants in, the assessment and improvement of their own teaching.

• *A Win–Win Process Is Created.* Peer review benefits both the teacher and colleague reviewer, improving both their teaching and morale. Done correctly, it meets institutional or departmental guidelines for personnel review while enhancing faculty teaching. Faculty cannot engage in effective peer review without confronting their own teaching philosophies and practices. Ideas to improve their own teaching typically develop.

• *A Feeling of Pedagogical Community Is Created.* Of all of the advantages and reasons to engage in peer review of teaching, the fact that peer review decreases isolation and increases a sense of community about teaching may be the most important. It is a liberating feeling for faculty to realize that they can choose to attend to their teaching voluntarily. Faculty examine their teaching for many reasons: because they are stale, because they are unhappy with how part of a course is going, or simply because they connect with colleagues when scrutinizing their pedagogy. Although it is fun to *break bread* with colleagues in talking about teaching, there must be room for serious, in-depth explorations of what teaching is, why it can be so difficult, and what skills and abilities are needed with students in a wide variety of courses and learning situations. These discussions should not be just another opportunity to air complaints.

The major theme that emerges in conversations with faculty who regularly use peer review is one of improved fellowship and involvement. These faculty believe that attending to their teaching is important. It is this sense of community—that meeting to talk about teaching is somehow of consequence and perhaps sacred—that allows faculty members to become committed to quality teaching. Stephen Brookfield (1995) stated:

> The importance . . . of belonging to an emotionally sustaining peer learning community cannot be overstated. . . . But the emphasis the members of these groups place on the emotional warmth and psychological security they provide make the term *community* more appropriate, than, say, *network.* The importance of these small communities is that they reassure their members that their private anxieties are commonly experienced. (p. 244)

Thus, the outcome of a good peer review of teaching process is a commitment to teaching and a sense of place within the academy that most faculty neither expect nor predict–shared purpose, a feeling of value, and meaningful relationships. The good feelings that result from attending to one's teaching become their own source of motivation.

TYPES OF PEER REVIEW

We briefly defined summative peer review (for personnel reasons) and its formative counterpart (voluntary improvement of teaching). We now discuss each process in more depth.

Summative Peer Review

Many faculty think of peer review as something required and done to them—part of the process of submitting credentials for tenure, renewal, promotion, or seeking raises in salary. This type of review is typically general, evaluating teaching in a variety of global categories and demonstrates accountability by faculty. More important, evaluation is a powerful means by which faculty learn department, college, or university expectations of teaching, and it can encourage faculty attention to their pedagogy. Additionally, new faculty often need external validation of their teaching.

If carried out with care, summative peer review (with a formative philosophy) can contribute positively to a new faculty's development as a teacher. In fact, we believe that summative review is only useful for improvement of teaching when it is both participatory and collaborative, with the goal of teaching improvement equal in salience and importance to that of evaluation. If formative values and procedures are included within summative requirements, faculty should have greater opportunity and incentive to improve their teaching (and morale).

Summative peer review is most often done with junior faculty. When done in a supportive manner, it may be vital in helping them become better teachers and in retaining them. Junior faculty need to establish competence and a repertoire of effective teaching skills. They need freedom to explore and fail while not being continuously judged by others. Summative peer review with a formative philosophy can facilitate these goals, meet young faculty members' needs for collegiality, and clearly communicate institutional teaching expectations. The summative process must include opportunities for self-improvement. Absent such chances, it is strictly an evaluative and critical process, with the steps needed to improve one's teaching left to inference.

Formative Peer Review

Formative peer review is voluntary teacher development ideally ongoing throughout one's teaching career. The use of such reviews typically focuses on one or two specific behaviors to be examined and perhaps changed (e.g., clarity of lecture, speed of talking) or on specific components of a course such as texts or tests. This focus does not preclude the oftentimes wonderful philosophical discussions of teaching that arise out of peer review, but often serves as a starting point for such reflection and discussion.

Often the faculty working with the teacher do not even give advice, but merely reflect on what they have discussed, experienced in the classroom, or read in portfolios. Formative peer review can be conducted using direct classroom observation, videotaping of classes, evaluation of course materials, assessment of instructor evaluations of the academic work of students, and teaching portfolios. Keig and Waggoner (1994) have an excellent discussion of formative review methods, with examples, including the use of videotape.

GUIDING PRINCIPLES FOR QUALITY PEER REVIEW OF TEACHING

Whether faculty members are untenured and must engage in peer review or established teachers unhappy with some facet of their teaching, the guiding principles for maximizing the process are the same.

• *Be Patient.* Changing unit or institutional culture and climate to encourage and support a systematic peer review process can be slow and difficult. Those persons being reviewed need time to adjust to the process, and those persons doing the reviewing need time to improve their skills and learn how to work with colleagues on teaching-related issues.

From another perspective, senior faculty may struggle in describing what in their teaching they are unhappy with or want feedback on, and their colleagues may need some time before they are satisfied that they are really hearing what is being said, and that their responses are clearly stated and helpful.

• *Peer Review Takes Time.* When done well, the process is often more time-consuming than many faculty realize, especially if they have previously used a *boiler plate* approach. A good peer review involves gathering data, insight by reviewer and teacher, and helpful feedback. Both the reviewer(s) and the reviewee contribute significant time and effort to the process. Nonetheless, avoid peer review procedures that are so extensive they cannot be done well or completed because there is insufficient time available. The sense of contributing to teaching development and working with colleagues usually makes the additional responsibility and time commitment worthwhile.

• *Remember Out-of-Classroom Teaching.* There is more to good teaching than what the teacher does in the classroom. Good teachers advise, supervise, guide, and mentor students. Good teachers talk about teaching with other teachers and administrators and are interested in improvement over time. Summative guidelines must keep this principle in mind.

• *Thinking Behind the Work.* Effective peer review moves beyond technique to the assumptions and decisions that lie behind the teaching. Teachers need to consider their approaches to teaching. Those teachers who know *why* they are using the practices they are, and why these are effective, have a firmer foundation for their teaching than the *natural teachers*, or those who merely stumble onto good teaching practices. Focusing on the *why* adds depth to one's teaching philosophy and work with students.

• *Be Fair.* For summative peer review, the information requested must represent both the criteria used to evaluate teaching (e.g., listed in department documents; e.g., its renewal and tenure policy) and the complexity of the teaching process. It must allow faculty to present all of their teaching efforts and accomplishments. In formative peer review, only the teaching issues that a colleague wants considered are discussed unless, by mutual agreement, both reviewee and reviewer decide to expand their focus and discussions.

Peer review must be credible in content and process. Peer review should focus on teaching behaviors and practices over which the instructor has some control. The information obtained must be comprehensive enough to be reliable, and elements not under the teacher's control (e.g., classroom remodeling, poor classroom acoustics) must be taken into account.

• *No Surprises.* The principle of explicitness is most applicable to summative (personnel purposes) peer review. Faculty must know the use to which a peer review is put. For example, if peer review is required for renewal, tenure, or promotion, everyone in a department must know the process and criteria, which must be clearly set forth. Faculty must know what information is expected from them and how it will be used. Any required summative review process must clearly describe:

1. The purpose of the review being conducted (e.g., required by college, by institution),
2. Sources of information (e.g., talking with faculty member, visiting class, course materials, teaching portfolio), and
3. Who interprets this information (e.g., faculty member, mentor, senior faculty, college committee).

Visit a class, for example, by invitation only. Yes, you may get the teacher's best effort, but because there should be multiple sources for assessing teaching (e.g., student evaluations, portfolio, materials), the department or university will learn if this best effort is representative of the teacher's ability to teach. Further, if there are significant problems with the best effort, you know there are teaching problems to be addressed.

For formative peer review, participants must decide how they will proceed. They can meet biweekly for an entire semester or only once or twice. Faculty members can discuss their teaching without any formal information collection, or they can be very structured, such as deciding to keep logs or journals of their teaching, before and after peer review, learning what works and what does not. They might complete self-rating forms—self-assessments of their teaching using the same questions a student might complete in a student evaluation of teaching, but reworded from the faculty perspective (e.g., Weimer, Parrett, & Kerns, 1988)—or they might visit each other's classes and then talk about what they experienced.

• *Do No Harm.* Peer review can be anxiety provoking and difficult for both reviewer and reviewee. Reviewers may worry that their findings may cause someone to be denied tenure, be made public and cause dissension and disagreement, or that they were not sensitive enough to the self-esteem and feelings of the person reviewed. The person being reviewed, whether for summative or formative purposes, may be concerned about being less than excellent or being treated unfairly or harshly. Trust, working together, and clarity of purpose minimize the potential for harm and maximize positive outcomes such as better teaching. Even when done voluntarily (formative review), confidentiality must be maintained.

• *Tough on the Issues—Tender on the Person.* Faculty need to be told the truth about their teaching. They need to know whether their teaching is good. They need to have any problems identified.

• *Build on Strengths.* It is easy to determine what areas need work. To maximize a colleague's growth as a teacher, anyone acting as a reviewer first needs to identify and communicate what went well and only then offer feedback on what needs work. It is important in peer review to always communicate what it is a teacher did well and to offer suggestions for better teaching in the future.

CRITICAL ELEMENTS OF PEER REVIEW

Three processes in peer review are so critical to its success that we list them separately. These are peer review as an interpersonal enterprise, matters of reflection, and nature of feedback.

Peer Review Is an Interpersonal Enterprise

As noted, the interpersonal nature of peer review is one of its most important elements—two or more professionals working together on teaching; helping and building, not judging; engaging, collaborating, reflecting, describing, and understanding; and dialogue and discourse. In successful peer review, faculty talk with each other about their teaching, reducing their isolation, and making public that which is often private. Reviewers' interpersonal skills can make or break peer review. The idea is to sit beside one another (Braskamp & Ory, 1994) as two peers involved in the reflection on and discussion of teaching. Collaboration is critical even if one faculty is judging the other. The style and context must involve caring about colleagues' teaching.

Bowser (1998) presented characteristics of effective classroom observers that generalize to all forms of peer review. She said effective peer reviewers:

• Are sensitive.
• Reflect on their own teaching.
• Are good listeners.
• Prepare carefully.
• Emphasize teacher development and growth.
• Accept that good teaching can result from widely different methods and styles.
• Give constructive feedback.

Reflection and Reasoned Opinion

Discourse on teaching should be based on reasoned opinions, not personal biases or judgments. An effective peer review requires reflection by both reviewees on their teaching and course materials and by reviewers on what they have read, discussed, and experienced.

The need for reflection and reasoned opinion exists whether teaching portfolios, classroom visits, or submitted course materials are being reviewed. Teachers must step back, formulate, organize, and present what they value and do with students. Talking with others often helps them reflect on their pedagogy. Reading materials on teaching may generate questions, suggest ideas not previously considered, and help organize answers.

Reflection on one's teaching includes questions such as:

• What are my strengths as a teacher?
• What teaching activities do I do best?
• What are my limitations?
• What do students perceive I am good at? Why do they like my courses? (Angelo & Cross [1993] present a superb compilation of techniques for obtaining student feedback.)
• What must I learn to do better?
• What do students perceive I need to do more of or improve?
• What have I done to maintain or improve my teaching?
• Who are the first people I would talk to, and sources I would consult, about a teaching problem?
• What teaching style or methods best fit my strengths and personality?
• What have I read, and what authors and writings influence how I think about teaching?

Feedback

The process of giving feedback is critical to facilitating the improvement of teaching. How information is communicated during a peer review can be more important than the content. Too much information can be overwhelming and confusing, diluting its impact and message. Poorly synthesized and unfocused information is frustrating to the person being reviewed. Brinko (1993) and Carroll and Goldberg (1989) presented guidelines for effective feedback.

Faculty can be anxious, defensive, or eager to learn about their teaching. Any mentor or faculty member serving as a reviewer must be supportive, not rush the time spent with the teacher being reviewed, and emphasize descriptive information with examples. These examples can be heard more readily by faculty being evaluated and have more impact than evaluative comments.

The chances that teaching improvement will occur increase when feedback:

- Comes from a trusted and credible source.
- Is sensitive to the teacher's feelings and self-esteem, what the teacher can control, and the experience level of the teacher.
- Is accurate and specific, with examples.
- Contributes to what the teacher has already thought about (dovetails with self-knowledge).
- Is given in a supportive, nonjudgmental manner.
- Has positives intermixed with areas for growth.
- Provides specific suggestions for teaching that needs change or improvement.
- Is focused.
- Is relevant.
- Reduces teacher uncertainty.
- Allows for discussion and interaction.

Reviewers must provide feedback in a timely and thoughtful manner. For summative review, the reviewer should meet with the faculty member being reviewed to provide this feedback, instead of merely writing a letter. The reviewer can follow this conversation with written feedback for summative review. Regardless of the type of peer review being undertaken, reviewers should remain available for assistance in the future. Their feedback may be needed again at a later date.

A good barometer of successful feedback is that it is solutions-focused. Problems in teaching must never be explicitly identified unless alternative solutions are also presented. Any recommended changes in teaching must be achievable.

COMPONENTS OF CLASSROOM
VISITATION PEER REVIEW

Classroom visitation is the most common and effective form of peer review. When used for summative peer review, it may be very structured, and a department or college's rules may spell out how it is to proceed. Formatively, it may be more informal. Classroom observations provide data that are the closest to actual day-to-day teaching, and the observer sees many of the behaviors to be evaluated and discussed.

Sources helpful in maximizing the classroom visitation process include Braskamp and Ory (1994), Centra, (1975), Ferren and Geller (1983), Helling (1988), Helling and Kuhlmann, (1988), Hilsen and Rutherford (1991), Keig and Waggoner (1994), Millis (1992), and Sorcinelli (1984).

Previsitation Meeting

It is imperative that the reviewer and reviewee meet before the class visitation to talk. During this meeting, the observer gathers information concerning the teacher's goals, the class, students, and any specific problems to be attended to (especially if a formative review). Both the teacher and reviewer must understand and agree on the purpose of the classroom visit, the criteria to be employed, and how information is shared and used afterward (e.g., numerical rating form, qualitative letter). Either before or during this meeting, copies of course materials (e.g., syllabus, handouts, exams) can be given to the observer and/or discussed. The observer needs to learn about specific characteristics of the students (class level, major field), teacher (rank, experience), and the course (size, required or not, prerequisite for other courses). Discussions on the goals of the course, intent of the class period(s) to be observed, teaching methods to be used and why, and how the class relates to previous (and subsequent) ones can be extremely productive.

The Class Visitation

Classroom visits can take various forms. Whether the visitor acts as a student or writes voluminous notes about the process and teaching observed, there are typically major teaching issues to which to attend. These include:

- *Preclass Behavior*—arrive early, talk with students, outline on board?;
- *Time*—does the class start and end on time?;
- *Context*—putting the lecture or discussion in a context, referring to last class period, outlining what will be covered;
- *Mechanics*—voice can be heard, speaks slowly enough, writing can be read, material well paced; atmosphere (active, quiet, questions, deference);
- *Clarity and Organization*—material is presented clearly and in an organized manner;
- *Interpersonal*—respectful of students and questions, answers questions carefully and precisely, is concerned for what the students are learning, communicates enthusiasm, elicits discussion;
- *Content*—the teacher knows what he or she is talking about, true intellectual content, well prepared, can explain concepts clearly, good use of examples;
- *Teacher Behaviors*—use of blackboard, overhead, computer, answering questions; and

- *Student Learning Activities*—for example, taking notes, asking questions, discussion participation, or a small-group activity.

We believe that faculty should know when someone will visit class. We recommend the following for a classroom visit:

- *Be invisible*—try not to affect the teaching–learning process. Sit out of the way and observe.
- *Act like a student*—take notes, listen, try to follow and understand what is taking place.
- *Attend to the big picture*—such as importance and suitability of content, organization, presentation style, clarity, questioning ability, quality and nature of contact with students.
- *Record what takes place*—Either during the class or more desirably after, have materials that serve as templates to organize what you experienced and your comments (see Perlman & McCann, 1998, for examples).

Postvisitation Meeting

Because good peer review is collaborative, more is needed after a classroom visitation than a letter from the reviewer detailing what was observed, the quality of teaching, and so forth. Faculty should meet again. This meeting works best as discussion, not merely the observer giving feedback. Here are some steps that ensure a productive postvisit meeting:

- It is best if the teacher gets the first opportunity to comment before the reviewer does.
- The reviewer should start by discussing what the teacher did well and why.
- The reviewer may ask one or two questions, such as: How do you think the class went? What do you think about your teaching during the class? What went well or not so well? What were your teaching strengths? Weaknesses? What did you like best about this class? What was your best teaching in this class? Did students learn and accomplish what you wanted them to? How do you know? Does your class usually go this well (poorly)? If you had to change one thing that happened in this class, what would it be and why?
- Examples are more useful and powerful than generalities.
- It is common for teachers to suggest concerns and course dimensions on which they would like additional feedback.
- A written appraisal of the observation is most useful. It should contain information about strengths, special teaching behaviors, and suggestions for alternative ways to improve teaching.
- Part of this second meeting should be an evaluation of the effectiveness of the peer review by the participants. How did it go? What was helpful? Were there any barriers or problems that influenced the effectiveness of the peer review?

CONCLUSION

Working with colleagues to understand and improve pedagogy is a powerful tool in the arsenal of any teaching faculty member. Peer review is a life-long habit of good teachers. They enjoy talking with their colleagues about teaching and, despite the uncertainties and anxieties they may experience, they feel responsible for thoughtfully and regularly discussing their teaching. We have summarized what must take place to maximize the outcomes of such collegial discussion and pedagogical processes throughout the chapter. For each reader, we hope that at least one idea serves as a path to better teaching and discussion of teaching with peers.

REFERENCES

Angelo, T. A., & Cross, K. P. (1993). *Classroom assessment techniques: A handbook for college teachers* (2nd ed.). San Francisco: Jossey-Bass.

Bowser, B. (1998). *UNC intercampus dialogues on peer review of teaching, results and recommendations*. http://cte.uncwil.edu/et/prev1.htm.

Braskamp, L., & Ory, J. C. (1994). *Assessing faculty work: Enhancing individual and institutional performance*. San Francisco: Jossey-Bass.

Brinko, K. T. (1993). The practice of giving feedback to improve teaching: What is effective? *Journal of Higher Education, 64,* 574–593.

Brookfield, S. (1995). *Becoming a critically reflective teacher*. San Francisco: Jossey-Bass.

Carroll, J. G., & Goldberg, S. R. (1989). Teaching consultants: A collegial approach to better teaching. *College Teaching, 37,* 143–146.

Centra, J. A. (1975). Colleagues as raters of classroom instruction. *Journal of Higher Education, 46,* 327–337.

Chism, N. V. (1998). *Peer review of teaching: A sourcebook*. Bolton, MA: Anker.

Dahlin, A. (1994). The teacher as a reflective professional. *College Teaching, 42*(2), 57–61.

Edgerton, R., Hutchings, P., & Quinlan, K. (1991). *The teaching portfolio: Capturing the scholarship in teaching*. Washington, DC: American Association for Higher Education.

Ferren, A., & Geller, W. (1983). Classroom consultants: Colleagues helping colleagues. *Improving College and University Teaching, 31,* 82–86.

Gillespie, D. (2000). Claiming ourselves as teachers. In D. DeZure (Ed.), *Learning from change* (pp. 384–386). San Francisco: Jossey-Bass.

Helling, B. (1988). Looking for good teaching: A guide to peer observation. *Journal of Staff, Program, and Organization Development, 6,* 147–158.

Helling, B., & Kuhlmann, D. (1988). The faculty visitor program: Helping teachers see themselves. In K. G. Lewis & J. T. Povlacs (Eds.), *Face to face: A sourcebook of individual consultation techniques for faculty development personnel* (pp. 103–119). Stillwater, OK: New Forums Press.

Hilsen, L., & Rutherford, L. (1991). Front-line faculty development: Chairs constructively critiquing colleagues in the classroom. *To Improve the Academy, 10,* 251–269.

Hutchings, P. (1996). *Making teaching community property: A menu for peer collaboration and peer review*. Washington, DC: American Association for Higher Education.

Kahn, S. (1993). Better teaching through better evaluation: A guide for faculty and institutions. *To Improve the Academy, 12,* 111–126.

Keig, L., & Waggoner, M. D. (1994). *Collaborative peer review: The role of faculty in improving college teaching* (ASHE-ERIC Higher Education Report No. 2). Washington, DC: The George Washington University School of Education and Human Development.

Millis, B. J. (1992). Conducting effective peer classroom observations. *To Improve the Academy, 11,* 189–206.

Paulsen, M. B., & Feldman, K. A. (1995). *Taking teaching seriously: Meeting the challenge of instructional improvement* (ASHE-ERIC Higher Education Report No. 2). Washington, DC: The George Washington Graduate School of Education and Human Development.

Perlman, B., & McCann, L. I. (1998). *Peer review of teaching.* Oshkosh, WI: Authors.

Quinlan, K. M. (1996). Involving peers in the evaluation and improvement of teaching: A menu of strategies. *Innovative Higher Education 20,* 299–307.

Seldin, P. (1997). *The teaching portfolio: A practical guide to improved performance and promotion/ tenure decisions* (2nd ed.). Bolton, MA: Anker.

Seldin, P., & Associates. (1993). *Successful use of teaching portfolios.* Bolton, MA: Anker.

Shulman, L. S. (1993, November/December). Teaching as community property: Putting an end to pedagogical solitude. *Change,* pp. 6–7.

Sorcinelli, M. D. (1984). An approach to colleague evaluation of classroom instruction. *Journal of Instructional Development, 7*(4), 11–17.

Theal, M., & Franklin, J. (Eds.). (1991, Winter). Effective practices for improving teaching. *New Directions for Teaching and Learning, 48.*

Travis, J. E. (1995). *Models for improving college teaching: A faculty resource* (ASHE-ERIC Higher Education Report No. 6). Washington, DC: The George Washington University Graduate School of Education and Human Development.

Weimer, M., & Lenze, L. F. (1991). Instructional interventions: A review of the literature on efforts to improve instruction. In J. C. Smart (Ed.), *Higher education: Handbook of theory and research* (Vol. 7, pp. 294–333). New York: Agathon.

Weimer, M., Parrett, J. L., & Kerns, M. M. (1988). *How am I teaching? Forms and activities for acquiring instructional input.* Madison, WI: Magna.

Wright, W. A., & Associates. (1995). *Teaching improvement practices: Successful strategies for higher education.* Bolton, MA: Anker.

16

Beyond Tenure:
The Teaching Portfolio
for Reflection and Change

James H. Korn
Saint Louis University

If the unexamined life is not worth living, as Plato concluded, then to stay alive as teachers we should be reflecting on the teaching life. We might engage in Zen meditation, spiritual exercises, or guided imagery and thereby gain some insight into the nature and meaning of what we do. My purpose in this chapter is to show that the teaching portfolio, with reflection, can produce that insight and help us make significant changes in our teaching lives.

A teaching portfolio is an organized collection of material that reflects your ideas about teaching, your performance as a teacher, and how your teaching has changed over time. Readers wanting a general introduction to this genre should see Peter Seldin's (1997) basic book on this topic. I describe some elements of a typical portfolio, but this chapter is not a how-to manual. Such a manual would be difficult to write because at this time there is no one agreed-on view of the portfolio. Its content and structure vary with its purpose and the intended audience. Seldin and others suggest a relatively brief narrative with supporting appendixes, but my preference is for a longer document that mixes narrative with supporting information accompanied by a three- to four-page summary.

There is agreement, however, that the portfolio should include a statement of one's philosophy of teaching. This is the heart of the portfolio because it shows who you are as a teacher and provides the rationale for what you do in your courses.

I use this simple model:

Philosophy > Objectives > Methods > Learning > Evaluation > Reflection

Your philosophy (explicit or implicit) of teaching and learning determines the objectives you choose for your courses. These objectives lead to decisions about the most appropriate teaching methods and ways to assess student learning. All of these components are evaluated and modified based on the data you obtain. In reality, our teaching does not develop in this rational, linear manner. At some time during the process, however, we should be able to present the logic of what we do. A well-designed portfolio would show clearly how all these elements are integrated and how our teaching developed over time. In this chapter, I first describe the way portfolios are most often used, which is for academic survival. Then I describe how they could be used throughout one's academic life for reflection on teaching and to promote development as a teacher.

PORTFOLIOS FOR SURVIVAL

In 1994, I began to help graduate students develop teaching portfolios. I would tell them that this would be a great advantage for their academic job search because few other applicants would have one. At least this would be an advantage at institutions where teaching is the primary mission. Now, in 2001, teaching portfolios are more common and I tell students that they may be at a disadvantage if they do *not* have one. Constructing a portfolio that effectively communicates information about teaching gives an advantage for survival in a highly competitive academic marketplace.

Having obtained a teaching position, the next challenge for survival is keeping that position. For promotion and tenure at most colleges and universities, faculty now must submit some version of a teaching portfolio, which usually includes a teaching philosophy, samples of course materials, summaries of student ratings, and other evidence of effectiveness. For this purpose, the portfolio must be designed to impress an audience of senior faculty so the rhetoric of the philosophy is consistent with institutional values. Course designs (syllabi, assignments, etc.) should be well organized and challenging, showing the teacher's scholarship and high standards. Student ratings should be high and show improvement over successive semesters, indicating that the teacher is responsive to students. Like the artist's portfolio, the teaching portfolio is a presentation of the teacher's best work with a preponderance of positive reviews. For survival, the portfolio must show confidence, competence, and commitment.

What happens to that impressive portfolio after the teacher reaches age 35, after tenure? Perhaps it stays in a file cabinet and is pushed farther back in the drawer as the years pass. That happens even when one is actively exploring new directions in teaching and taking on new courses, but then there seems to be no reason to document these changes and write about their effects. Teachers are changed by life events as well as classroom experiences, so they are different teachers at age 50 than at 35. Why should we try to document those changes and who cares? Ask Plato.

THE PORTFOLIO FOR REFLECTION AND CHANGE

One purpose of reflection is discovery. Reflection in spiritual exercises or therapy can lead to discoveries about life, and reflection on one's teaching leads to discovery in that area. To be an instrument of reflection, the portfolio must be more than a container (syllabi, student papers, evaluations, etc.), but must make the reflection visible through narrative writing about the elements of one's teaching life. Transforming our thoughts to the written word can help us discover what we think even when the writing is only for us and not for publication. Reflection, in this sense, is more than meditation. It is a cycle in which we engage in unhurried contemplation, write down the essence of those thoughts, review what we wrote, and revise it. Because this writing is for us, it can be more like a diary or idea book that is unedited and personal.

What is it that one can discover in this process of reflection? My own experience with this process helped me to see what I value most about teaching and what I find most distasteful. I have been able to see more clearly what I have done that makes some learning activities more enjoyable and effective. More generally, I have discovered inconsistencies in what I believe about teaching and what I do, which leads me to change one or the other. There is another benefit of reflection that I have not been able to gain because my portfolio is relatively young, and that is the awareness of how I have developed as a teacher over 35 years.

In the remainder of this chapter, I list the elements of a reflective portfolio and then discuss each of these elements. Before doing so, I want to deny any intent to be overly prescriptive because the teaching portfolio is a personal document that should be unique to every teacher in the same way that one's autobiography is unique. There is some content that is essential, and the organization and writing should be clear because there are occasions when the portfolio may be read by others. Beyond that consideration, there are several ways to organize the material, and we have choices about what and how much to include.

These are the major elements of the reflective portfolio:

- One's teaching philosophy is the centerpiece of the portfolio as both a summary and guide.
- A teaching autobiography describes your development as a teacher. Here even the structured vita can be an object for reflection.

- Course materials are included: a syllabus for each course, perhaps an early version along with the current version, examples of assignments and exercises, samples of student work, course evaluations.
- Developmental experiences: what you learned from teaching conferences and workshops, and how you were influenced by conversations with colleagues.
- The scholarship of teaching: things you have written, regardless of whether they were published.
- A conclusion that relates the contents to the philosophy or an epilog that looks to the future or both.

I can anticipate several reactions to this whole idea of extensive reflection and writing about one's teaching. One reaction might come from someone whose primary commitment is more to research than to teaching and who would say that all this reflection and writing is nonproductive. Then there is the struggling teacher who may want to change, but thinking about all the things that could be wrong makes her anxious, so it might be better just to keep plugging along. Another teacher has been teaching the same courses for many years with good student ratings. He is popular and his students are happy. Why mess with a good thing? All these teachers have legitimate concerns about taking the time and emotional effort required to build a teaching portfolio and to think about it. It takes you away from research, makes you anxious, and leads you to take risks with your success. I hope to show that those concerns are part of an authentic commitment to teaching and one's development as a teacher.

The Teaching Philosophy

I did not compile my first teaching portfolio and write my teaching philosophy until 1997, after I had been teaching for more than 30 years. Before then it had been implicit in what I did as a teacher and in some of the articles that I wrote. I have asked many senior faculty to show me their written teaching philosophy. Most of them (including some authors of chapters in this book) say they do not have one, but they really do in the same implicit way that I had mine. Take, for example, the teachers that this volume honors. Bill McKeachie's teaching philosophy is presented throughout his book, *Teaching Tips* (1999). In his preface, he clearly stated that he is a learner-centered teacher, and many of the chapters that follow show how he practices that approach. His final chapter is on teaching values. It includes an account of how his own deeply felt beliefs affect his teaching. He describes himself as a religious person who believes "strongly that love and respect for other human beings . . . is a universal value that should guide the behavior of all human beings at all times" (McKeachie, 1999, p. 333). The concluding sentence in that chapter follows a quotation from St. Augustine: " 'Hope has two lovely daughters, anger and courage. Anger at the way things are, and courage to see that they need not remain as they are.' Let us have hope" (McKeachie, 1999, p. 344).

Charles Brewer's philosophy is expressed in the titles of two papers that he has presented in various settings over the years: "gladly learn and gladly teach" (Brewer, 1982) and "bending twigs and affecting eternity" (Brewer, 1994). In the former paper, Brewer talked about the importance of teaching principles rather than facts, but this quotation from his other paper may get closer to the core of his philosophy: "...I have decided that authors seldom write about one of the most important traits of good teachers—and that is passion. Good teachers have passion. It is harder to write or talk about passion than it is to practice it, but you must have passion to be a good teacher" (Brewer, 1994, p. 7).

Other award-winning teachers have published statements that I would consider teaching philosophies. Two of my favorites are Douglas Candland's (1980) "Speaking Words and Doing Deeds" and Henry Glietman's (1984) "Introducing Psychology." Few of us will have the opportunity to present our view of teaching to so large an audience, but that is not the point of writing one. Although we carry our philosophy around with us, there are important benefits from making it explicit. First, it provides an important basis for determining course objectives and methods. For example, belief in teaching principles rather than facts may lead a teacher to choose essay rather than multiple-choice examinations. Respect for persons may influence something as mundane as one's attendance policy.

A second benefit is that the philosophy can serve as a guide to classroom research. McKeachie's (1999) *Teaching Tips* contains many examples of studies that tested hypotheses about the effectiveness of various teaching methods, but teachers can do informal studies to collect evidence that will affect their teaching. For example, I believe that students who take part in discussions learn more. I wonder if this holds for electronic discussions as well as those that take place in the classroom.

In addition to these practical benefits, a clearly articulated philosophy gives substance and coherence to the brainstorms and fantasies of reflection. Sometimes reflection should be detached from the data of the classroom and allowed to spring from the imagination. Challenge all the conventional wisdom about teaching and create an ideal learning world. Go where no academic mind has gone before. Then return and translate your most creative thoughts to ideas and ideals that you want to have an influence on your teaching and include those thoughts in your philosophy.

To write the first version of your teaching philosophy, my advice is, "just do it." It is your philosophy, not mine or your mentor's or that of some workshop leader. Begin from experience, perhaps by thinking about good and bad teachers you have known. Reflect on your values and beliefs, not only about teaching, but life. Draw on your favorite psychological theories. After reflecting, engage in some free writing where you write continuously for as long as you can without taking your pen from the page or fingers from the keyboard. When you have transformed this free writing into a relatively coherent first draft, show it to friends who also may have written their philosophies of teaching. You will learn a great deal by talking with someone who has faced the same challenge.

Put this first draft aside for a while. When you return to it, read it critically to search for what it tells you about your assumptions concerning teaching, learning, and students. Do you really believe these things and are they realized in your practice? If the words sound like they come from a stranger, try to figure out who that person is. Perhaps it is someone you want to become or it may be who someone else wants you to be. Then revise the philosophy, trying to find your own voice and discover your true teaching self.

I am now working on the fourth version of my philosophy in the past 5 years. You might think that a person who has been teaching for one third of a century would have this all figured out, but it can be difficult to be honest with oneself. In the first version, I wrote about my passion for teaching and the importance of serving my students. Yet when I sat and thought about it, that was not what I felt. In the last version of my philosophy, I said,

> During the past two years I have come to doubt that [passion] is the feeling that drives my teaching and is most present in it. . . . I am a good teacher, but not passionate. What I do experience is the excellence of desire.

> This excellence of desire means wanting something with all your heart, and continually trying to find it. But what you want is unreachable so it is the wanting, the desire, that is excellent, not some outcome. It is about being and doing; about living the teaching life. It shows itself in teaching most often in the daily work we do, not only in those too rare peak experiences of glory in the classroom, and not in the prizes for excellence that some of us receive. I want to be a good teacher at the mundane level of class preparation, teaching methods, and relationships with students. I *want* this. *That* is the excellence of desire.

I am a bit uncomfortable making this public disclosure of my doubts, but my intention is to provide an example of how reflection based on experience can lead to discovery and change. The word *passion*, which seems so central to Charles Brewer's teaching, sounded good to me, but that word did not quite fit the feeling I usually had when I prepared for class or stood in front of my students. It was my reflection on this dissonance between thought and feeling that turned passion into desire in my written philosophy. The idea that there could be a kind of excellence in desire came from conversations with a colleague.[1] I could not put my feelings into words until we talked about wanting what we will never quite achieve in any of the classes we teach. "Sophia, as true wisdom, is always beyond and ahead of us, drawing us—luring us—into what we are not yet" (Lane, 2000). What gives hope is "not depending on the external response one is able to manipulate from others, but recognizing the teaching process to be a lifelong, endless horizon. It continually draws one forward to what is never fully obtained, but always sought" (Lane, 2000).

---

[1] I thank Belden Lane for helping me find the spiritual side of teaching. He is Professor of Theological Studies at my University and was my mentor when I completed the certificate program in our teaching center.

Course Narratives

Kurt Lewin's maxim that there is nothing as practical as a good theory had its complement, which is that theory is changed by practical application. Theory, or one's philosophy, is put aside while we work our craft. I tinker with my course plan, maybe trying something new. Another set of students appears on the first day and relationships build as they respond, or not, and give you the data of experience. The lectures, exercises, and discussions play themselves out, and students show what they learned through periodic assessments and assignments. The evaluations come in and I review all the data to see what worked and what did not, and how much they liked me.

A teaching philosophy has its most practical application before and after this process. In the design of the course, it provides the rationale for the objectives, which in turn should determine the methods used to implement and assess those objectives. I write a rationale for each course and it serves as the introduction to the section of my teaching portfolio devoted to that course. Soon after the end of the semester, I reflect on what happened, remembering high and low points during the semester, thinking about how various students did on their exams and papers, and I review the data from various sources. Then I write my self-evaluation. This self-evaluation is a personal statement, not the one I submit to my department chair for the annual salary decision. I confess to the sin of pride, express joy and disappointment, reveal my ignorance, although I sometimes hid it from my students, and I promise to do better next time. This reflection continues beyond confession and emotion to discovering what the data show me about the extent to which my philosophy was validated by what I did in the course. The discrepancies tell me that something should change, either the theory or the practice, and I work with the rationale and design of the next edition of that course.

This process promotes change in specific courses and, if carried out regularly, can provide an interesting view of one's development as a teacher. In my portfolio, which at this time is only 4 years old, I keep the materials and rationale for the first version of each course and for the most recent version. I also keep the reflections that I write for all versions. I am now in my 60s so my 4-year portfolio is only a late career slice. I wish I had begun my teaching portfolio as a beginning teacher so I could see the changes over the years. Longevity is another benefit of the teaching portfolio; it can place teaching in the context of one's life cycle.

Autobiography: Stages in the Teaching Life

Developing as a teacher is part of our development as persons. Change continues through life and is affected not only by events in our academic careers, but by our personal lives and events in our culture. For me this happened in 1968, when my first son was born in Pittsburgh 2 days after the assassination of Martin Luther King, Jr. In the morning on the way home, I saw the smoke rising from the city behind the hospital and heard the sharp cracks of sporadic gunfire. I was astonished by the fact that I was alive and had a child and by the awareness that my life would change. The events of that era had profound effects on my generation, and for at least some of us these events led to our commitment to teaching.

Erik Erikson's theory of human development emphasizes this mutual influence of personal life changes with historical moments. An autobiographical section of a reflective teaching portfolio would make us aware of the context of our development as teachers. Each career is unique, but there are similarities in our career paths. Early in our teaching life, we are finding our identity as teachers. This identity is defined by the courses we teach, styles we assume in the classroom, and our relationships with students. Our first statement of a teaching philosophy in our first portfolio may appear during this stage. Survival is the most salient force behind that portfolio, but at this time reflection could be used to gain awareness of one's identity and consider its authenticity. Beginning teachers might reflect on how their dreams of academic heaven are tempered by the reality of a heavy course load or pressures to publish while preparing new courses. A new academic context may provide those new teachers with students who appear as aliens and colleagues who model conflicting values. The portfolio can provide a mirror for who they are becoming as they confront these challenges.

At the next stage, early midcareer, one's teaching reputation is developed. Researchers build their reputations on publications and recognition by the establishment in their specialty area. For most teachers, reputation is local, based mostly on classroom style and influence on their colleagues, but a national reputation also can be developing. Our egos grow through the praise of students and attention of peers, and we may begin to think that we are pretty good. Now reflection gives perspective and gets us to consider whether we are beginning to dig a rut. More positively, reflection shows us how much more there is to learn about teaching.

In later midcareer, teachers assume leadership roles in departments and colleges and perhaps in national organizations. We are beyond tenure, full professors, but full of what? A significant number of us will have experienced life threats from a serious illness such as heart disease or cancer. Those of us who are married with children will be managing adolescents, and some may have gone through divorce. We may wonder what life is for, including our teaching life. The teaching portfolio is not the place to record all these life crises, but our reflection must include life as a context for teaching.

Generativity is our main concern at this time in life, and being a teacher gives us an exceptional opportunity for nurturing and guiding the next generation. In discussing this stage, Erikson (1968) said that we need to be needed and are "guided by the nature of that which must be cared for" (p. 138). Academic survival is no longer an issue, nor is reputation. Reflection now may focus more on how we are helping others to develop, younger colleagues as well as students. We are likely to take on the role of mentor, and reflection may help us see that we do that for ourselves as well as for others.

In his description of human development, Erikson (1968) provided a negative outcome for each stage. The opposite of generativity is a sense of stagnation, which may be expressed for teachers in boredom with our students and courses, cynicism about academic life, and a need to dominate colleagues and pad our reputations. For these teachers, reflection would be painful and thus avoided. They soon will retire in both the traditional and psychological sense, leaving academia to fish and play cards. Perhaps the development of a reflective teaching portfolio could prevent this negative outcome.

Integrity is the word Erikson used to describe the positive resolution of the last stage in life. He described this resolution as the acceptance of one's life and of the people who were important in it, and "acceptance of the fact that one's life is one's own responsibility. It is a sense of comradeship with men and women of distant times and of different pursuits who have created orders and objects and sayings conveying human dignity and love" (Erikson, 1968, p. 139). The word *wisdom* also characterizes this time in life. Reflection would promote acceptance and appreciation of one's teaching life. I can look back with gratitude at how my first courses were modeled after those of my mentor, Keck Moyer, and at the changes in the late 1960s that made those courses "relevant." I see the change over 30 years from stand-up shows to increasing use of small groups. I wonder if I have become a codger when I challenge the value of technology. Then there are the memories of individual students and the emotions of classroom highs and lows. These are the beginnings of late-career reflection, one purpose of which is to begin to gain closure on a teaching life.

I believe that this kind of life-review reflection can be useful for teachers who, in effect, never retire, but like Brewer and McKeachie continue to serve students, colleagues, and the teaching profession. For these teachers, the portfolio could be a legacy that is passed on. It would be an archive of dreams and realities and would show how even the best teachers have days, perhaps even years, of doubt and confusion. The legacy would provide a picture of change with stories of triumph and defeat, some dramatic and others ordinary. What beautiful gifts these legacies would be for the next generation of teachers.

Stages in life, including stages in teaching, are not discrete periods. The young teacher feels some sense of generativity, and the elderly teacher's identity may change in subtle ways. At any time in life, the teaching portfolio can be a means for viewing how the changes taking place within us are being expressed. How does your life shape your teaching and how is teaching changing your life?

THE PORTFOLIO AS SCHOLARSHIP

Reflection leads to discovery, and as the cycle continues over time it also raises questions about teaching and learning. These questions may lead to research conducted in the context of the course and the classroom rather than in the laboratory. The absence of reflection about one's teaching reduces the occasions for questioning, and thus the likelihood that we will learn something about our own teaching and change it. Reflective teachers engage in the scholarship of teaching when they search for answers and evaluate changes. The teaching portfolio can serve as the repository of the results of our inquiry over time. For example, I have hoped that my General Psychology course helps students give thoughtful and informed statements about major issues in psychology, so each semester I give pre- and posttests that include this question: What is the mind? At the end of the semester, I hope to read answers that are of greater complexity than they were at the beginning of the semester, including at least biological, cognitive, behavioral, and psychodynamic views of the mind with awareness of cultural context. This approach is scholarship in the sense of systematic inquiry that can be made public and replicated. Examination of the results reported in my portfolio over time help me to understand the conditions under which I am more or less effective in achieving my course goals.

There is another view of scholarship that is even better suited to the medium of the teaching portfolio. Lee Schulman (summarized in Edgerton, Hutchings, & Quinlan, 1991) believes the scientific approach has "abstracted teaching from particular situations—the fluid, untidy, unstructured realities of classroom life—in which teaching takes place. [This approach neglects] the 'knowing' in teaching that is hard to codify ... but is nevertheless a crucial part of teaching expertise." This expert knowledge is like that of the chess master, "that comes of having been there before, and of which precedents might apply in a new situation.... [These] 'master' teachers know many things that ordinary teachers do not" (p. 2). Perhaps not every portfolio compiled by an experienced teacher would contain this expert wisdom; some portfolios could be full of fantasy and self-delusion. You can imagine, however, a vast hard drive of accumulated experience that would be available to all of us. New teachers could learn from this experience and so could those of us still searching for new ways to approach our teaching.

I use the *hard drive* metaphor not simply for effect, but because electronic, computer-based media are becoming the major sources of our knowledge. Those of us who do have teaching portfolios have them on our personal computers, and from there they could be transferred to Web sites making the documents available on the Internet. These sites could be edited and peer reviewed using criteria that would be developed to evaluate this kind of scholarship. One of the problems with considering teaching portfolios as scholarship would be the physical limits on publishing hard copy versions of the reflections of hundreds of teachers. My current portfolio is about 3 inches thick, but in cyberspace it takes up hardly any room at all.

CONCLUSION

Teaching portfolios can be seen as scholarship, but I do not believe that should be the primary purpose of this activity. The purpose is to keep ourselves in "continual formation" (Brookfield, 1995) as teachers, formed not by passive reactions to changes in our personal lives or academic fads and pressures, but formed by

> continuous and critical study of our reasoning processes and pedagogic actions. We study their origins and their consequences. We also study the extent to which these processes and actions are embedded in investigated experience, as opposed to some external source of authority from which they have been uncritically assimilated. At no time do we ever consider the possibilities for learning and change to be fully closed. (Brookfield, 1995, p. 42)

It takes a significant amount of time and effort to put together your first teaching portfolio, but it is easier to do it early rather than late in one's career. There are strong academic pressures not to take the time for this activity. In a research university, it does not count as scholarship, and in a college where faculty carry teaching loads of four or five courses per semester, maintenance overcomes reflection. I have tried to show the benefits of having a teaching portfolio that is used for reflection, and I believe those benefits far outweigh the costs.

Teachers who are convinced but who also experience those academic pressures could at least begin by writing a draft of a teaching philosophy. Then take just one of your courses and think about how your philosophy is related to what you do in that course. Note any inconsistencies, try to explain them, and then change either your philosophy or methods. If that works, write it down, punch holes in the paper, put the pages in a three-ring binder, and you have the beginning of a reflective teaching portfolio.

REFERENCES

Brewer, C. L. (1982, August). *Gladly learn and gladly teach.* Paper presented at the meeting of the American Psychological Association, Washington, DC.

Brewer, C. L. (1994, April). *A talk to teachers: Bending twigs and affecting eternity.* Paper presented at the meeting of the Southeastern Psychological Association, New Orleans, LA.

Brookfield, S. D. (1995). *Becoming a critically reflective teacher.* San Francisco: Jossey-Bass.

Candland, D. K. (1980). Speaking words and doing deeds. *American Psychologist, 35,* 191–198.

Edgerton, R., Hutchings, P., & Quinlan, K. (1991). *The teaching portfolio: Capturing the scholarship in teaching.* Washington, DC: American Association for Higher Education.

Erikson, E. H. (1968). *Identity: Youth and crisis.* New York: Norton.

Glietman, H. (1984). Introducing psychology. *American Psychologist, 39,* 421–427.

Lane, B. C. (2000). Excellence in teaching and the spirituality of desire. *Horizons: The Journal of the College Theology Society, 27,* 311–321.

McKeachie, W. J. (1999). *Teaching tips: Strategies, research, and theory for college and university teachers* (10th ed.). Boston: Houghton-Mifflin.

Seldin, P. (1997). *The teaching portfolio* (2nd ed.). Bolton, MA: Anker.

17

Representing the Intellectual Work in Teaching Through Peer-Reviewed Course Portfolios

Daniel J. Bernstein
University of Nebraska–Lincoln

Teaching university-level courses is a form of serious intellectual work that can be as challenging and demanding as discovery research. When teaching is undertaken as a form of inquiry into the impact a course has on student understanding, the quality and depth of this work can be revealed through writing that reflects the relation between the process of teaching and its results. This chapter elaborates the basic assertion that teaching is intellectual work, describes a collaborative consultation among professors about their teaching, discusses the value of the products of that collaboration, and considers the place of this representation of teaching in professional life.

TEACHING AS INTELLECTUAL WORK

Offering a college course, like any activity, can be done with varying degrees of investment of time and resources. At the high end, there are initial considerations of the material to be covered and the intellectual goals that learners are to achieve. Even in an introductory course that appears to have a standard outline common to most texts, the instructor decides how broad a set of topics to cover. This decision determines the depth to which each topic can be presented and considered by learners because covering all the topics in a typical text can be a race against the limited time in an academic term. Those teachers who cover fewer topics but in greater depth also have the opportunity to expect deeper understanding from learners, perhaps by including discussions, interactive activities, or supplementary readings. It is also not a trivial matter to identify the conceptual goals for a course: It is necessary to know how the teacher would recognize that a student has acquired the skills and understanding that are intended to be included in the course design. These decisions are contextual in that some instructors assume students are taking a program of courses in a field of study, whereas other instructors use demographic information to identify who their learners are and what place the current course will most likely have in the larger picture of their education. Different conceptual goals would be appropriate depending on the nature of such an analysis of learners and the curriculum.

A second type of intellectual decision is found in the instructional design for a course. It is conventionally acceptable to provide well-crafted lectures that integrate the reading material with ideas and information from the professor's experience. Some teachers seek additional ways of interacting with students, both inside and outside of class, including online activities, group activities, or individual discovery projects. The identification and evaluation of potential instructional components is not easy, and the implementation of the methods selected can be as challenging as the instrumentation of a research project.

A third form of intellectual activity is inherent in designing the activities in which students demonstrate their understanding of the course goals. Sampling from test item pools provided by publishers or written by teaching assistants represents one statement of intellectual goals, whereas designing writing assignments, applications of ideas, or forms of authentic assessment (activities beyond verbal description) would be a different version of goals. This critical step operationalizes what the professor means by a deep understanding of the ideas being taught. In general, professors believe there is more to their field than a set of remembered answers to discrete questions, and the development of opportunities for learners to show a deeper understanding makes a fundamental understanding of the field of study manifest in course design. Teachers need to find creative examples that can exist within the constraints of the time and resources that both students and teachers have available for the course.

A fourth kind of intellectual work is the evaluation of the effectiveness of the course and how well learners achieved the understanding set forth in the goals. The teacher who views a class offering as an inquiry into the best way to generate understanding in students is a high-end version of this perspective. Teachers can examine the evidence of student learning found in the work done in the course, and there are opportunities for reflection on the quality of those achievements. It is even possible that multiple offerings of a course can be considered at one time, resulting in a longitudinal account of the impact of successive attempts to promote understanding. Changing instructional planning and design to improve the learning outcomes of a course involves a variety of intellectual skills ranging from analysis to interpretation to evaluation. The insight needed to improve the effectiveness of iterative offerings of a course is certainly a high-end form of intellectual work.

In many cases, our current professional practices of evaluating teaching do not capture these important dimensions of teaching. Typically, the majority of influence is left with student ratings of their perceptions a course and a teacher. Although the student voice is an essential piece of any view of teaching, it is best suited for those characteristics of teaching that students are in a good position to recognize. Students are the best people to tell us (both teachers and evaluators) whether we are timely, accessible, respectful, open to student perspectives, and complete in our communication. However, there has typically not been an informed voice to offer an opinion of the intellectual quality of the course materials, the appropriateness of the instructional design, or the scope and depth of the student work generated by the course. Some student ratings forms include these dimensions (implicitly or explicitly) in the questions asked, producing information that is likely outside the expertise of the rater. Some units ask teachers to include samples of syllabi and assignments that can be reviewed by evaluators, but it is rare to find reflective writing by teachers about their decisions and goals and the evidence of achieving them. As a result, the intellectual work we do in teaching is largely invisible in our professional lives, both in personnel decisions and for the purposes of growth and development as teachers. A small percentage of teachers do formal research on teaching or put examples of content or class practice in newsletters or journals on teaching, but for most teachers this work is lost with the end of each academic term. Interestingly, all this work is carefully done and completed, but few professors take the time to record what they did, both for their own future practice and the benefit of others.

The present work is designed to help professors take that last step of creating a readable record of the intellectual work in teaching. The project plan offers guides to collaborative practices that are useful in developing several aspects of teaching, and it provides support for professors who reflect on their own practices and identify what can be tried next to further enhance the students' learning experiences. Faculty members at the University of Nebraska are also building a community of readers for this work by identifying like-minded peers who are interested in teaching practices and engaged by offering commentary and reactions to existing work. The peer review of reflective writing (usually in the form of a course portfolio, described later) is useful for both further development of teaching by the author (formative use) and evaluation of teaching at times of accountability (summative use). We believe there are many college and university faculty members who would enjoy the exchange of reflective writing on effective practices in teaching. Organizing a venue for that exchange can help teachers identify a large and eager audience for intellectual work on teaching.

AN EXPANDED AND COLLABORATIVE
PROCESS OF PEER REVIEW
OF TEACHING

Peer review of teaching is often taken to mean a visit to a class by a senior colleague, followed by the filing of a letter evaluating the class visited. The Nebraska
project takes a much broader view that goes well beyond the performance of the
teacher during contact time. Based on Hutchings' (1996) model of peer collaboration and review, the project provides opportunities for professors to exchange
written memos about particular features of a course during the semester in which
it is taught. In the following semester, those separate, shorter memos are integrated into a document that presents a coherent account of the goals, practices,
and achievements of the course connected by the professor's reflections on lessons
learned and future plans for change. Often called a *course portfolio* (cf. Cerbin,
1994; Hutchings, 1998), this document represents activities with the same general
characteristics as other forms of scholarly work (cf. Glassick, Huber, & Maeroff,
1997). The professor describes an intellectual rationale for the work, gives an account of how it was carried out, describes what was discovered, and discusses the
general issues raised as informed by the results of the effort.

Components of the Peer Consultation

Each participating faculty member initially writes three brief memos (two to three
pages each) about an ongoing course, and these memos are presented to three or
four other participating professors in the same field of study (formed into identified
groups by discipline). Each participant also offers and receives brief observations
or comments on the memos from the other faculty members in the same group,
thus we describe the process as three interactions. The first of these interactions
offers an account of the framing of the content and the goals of the course, including
the decisions that were made about what would be the substance of the material
and the goals for student understanding. We provide a simple outline as a starting
point for the memo, with the clear understanding that individual faculty members
have wide discretion in how closely they follow the outline. The outline offers a
way to get started in case the professor is unsure where to begin, but it is not a
required structure. The basic outline for the first interaction is as follows:

Course Goals and Rationale
  - What do want students to learn from your course?
    - What do you want them to know? What do you want them to be able to do?
      What do you want them to understand? What perspectives or attitudes do
      you want them to have?
    - What is important for them to learn about your field? What should they
      learn about themselves as students or contributors to our society?

- Why did you choose the goals you did?
  - Why is it necessary for your students to achieve these goals? What do you know about your students that makes these goals appropriate for their education?
  - What perspectives of your discipline or field shaped your goals for the course? How did you decide between the breadth and depth of content? How is the depth of understanding reflected in your course goals?
- Where are these goals found in the syllabus for your course?
  - What readings or other sources of material are connected with the particular goals of the course? How did your vision of the course influence your selection of topics and resources?
  - Are there any activities for students in the syllabus that are particularly crafted to achieve individual goals of the course?

The second interaction focuses on how the instructor creates a learning environment in which the course goals can be accomplished. It can include peer visits to actual class meetings, which have traditionally been the sole component of a peer review of teaching, but this interaction is intended to capture a broad view of the practices teachers use to promote learning among the students in the class. There can be accounts of lecturing techniques, other in-class activities such as group work or peer teaching, and out-of-class activities done in studios or labs or even outside formal settings altogether. Many instructional design plans now also include work done through online resources that engage learners well outside the boundaries of conventional classroom instruction. The basic outline offered to participants for the second interaction is as follows:

Teaching Methods/Course Materials/Course Activities
- What teaching methods (lecture, group work, question/answer, etc.) are you using during your contact time with students to meet your objectives?
  - How do each of these teaching methods facilitate students' achievement of course objectives?
  - How will you use each of these methods during class time and over the course of the academic term?
- What course materials (textbooks, course notes, etc.) are you using to meet your objectives?
  - What characteristics make these materials useful to students' achievement of the course objectives?
  - How should students use each of the course materials?
- What course activities outside of class (such as projects, computer simulations, Web exercises, practica, or group work) are you using to meet your objectives?
  - Why have you structured your activities in the way that you have?

- What, in particular, do you hope your students will learn from each assignment? What are your expectations?
- What is the rationale for the methods you have chosen?
  - In what ways do you expect your choices for methods, materials, and assignments to assist your students in meeting the goals of your course?
  - What influence has your discipline or field had on your choices?
  - Why do you expect that the methods will be effective in promoting the learning you hope to achieve with these instructional practices?

The third interaction focuses on student performance. Professors are accustomed to offering intellectual rationale for the content of courses to curriculum committees when new courses are proposed, and many units already include some form of class visit by a senior colleague to observe teaching practices as a simple form of peer review. It is much less common for teachers to present examples of student performance and to write about how successfully that student work achieves the stated intellectual goals of the course. In this interaction, faculty members present examples of the assignments they give to provide students opportunities to demonstrate their understanding, along with examples of completed student work with the feedback provided by the teacher to the student. They also show a distribution of achievement scores for the whole class on the assignments—typically a frequency count of how many students achieved in each quality category used in giving feedback. We use the data on achievement in this interaction, not curved grading categories that teachers sometimes derive from class distributions. The written reflection gives the professor a chance to comment on the depth of understanding that students demonstrated, noting how well the original goals were met. The teachers are also encouraged to comment on how many students demonstrated each level of understanding, and they are asked to consider what could be done to help more students achieve in the higher categories. The basic outline provided to guide the third interaction is as follows:

The Nature of Student Understanding
- How solid is learners' fundamental understanding of the ideas and skills you were teaching?
  - Is there evidence of deep understanding in the work samples you received? How does performance on your assignments indicate students have developed an understanding for your field of study that will be retained and that students can apply to new contexts?
  - How does the understanding represented by the work samples you present differ among the students? How do these differences relate to the criteria you use in grading the assignment? How do these criteria relate to the intellectual goals you have set for the class?
- What do your assignments and students' work tell you about how students are constructing the ideas that are central to the course and your teaching goals?

- What misconceptions do they have about these ideas?
- How do you address student errors and misinterpretations?
- Guiding Improvement in Future Offerings
  - Overall, how well did student work meet your intellectual goals for the course? Was the distribution of achievement by students up to your expectations? Was it comparable to previous offerings of the same course?
  - Were there particular parts of the course in which achievement was especially high or low as compared with the rest of the general course goals?
  - What changes could be made to help more students achieve in the higher categories of learning? Are there particular features of the course that you would redesign? How do you think those changes would improve student understanding?

Reflection on the Course as a Whole

After completing the three separate and brief written interactions, the professors take a step back, look at all three pieces together, and reflect on how well the instructional plan they carried out was able to generate student performance that meets the original course goals. We suggest that a good way to start is literally to paste the three interactions together with some sections of connecting prose and attach a conclusions or discussion section to the end. This integrated single document makes a good first draft of a course portfolio, and reading this draft is an excellent prompt to begin the process of refinement and reflection. The root metaphor for this work is that teaching can be conducted as an inquiry into the most effective methods of promoting a rich understanding of the field in students. This inquiry begins with the goal of achieving a deep understanding and it asks this question: What are the best teaching practices that will help the most students reach that goal? At the conclusion of an offering of a course, the teacher has an opportunity to review what was planned and carried out in the course and evaluate the plan by looking at the understanding that was achieved. It is the reflective writing on this question that transforms the three straightforward interactions into a course portfolio. It also becomes an exploration of the successes of the course and a statement of the next iteration of teaching that might be expected to improve the depth or breadth of student learning.

As with the individual written interactions, the course portfolio is shared with other professors participating in the project, and those readers offer comments and suggestions for refining both the course and written analysis of the course in the portfolio document. All of this mutual reading is done in the spirit of making the intellectual work in teaching more public while still under the intellectual control of the course author. The professor gets a local and relatively private audience for the analytic work done to identify the sources of intellectual growth in students, and the feedback received informs further refinement of both teaching and reflection.

Expanding the Audience
for Course Portfolios

Once the course portfolio authors have refined their presentations, the project makes the portfolios available to a wider audience. The professors provide their reflection and the sample of student work to the project staff, and the materials are posted on a password protected Web site accessible only to readers participating in the project. These readers are from the same field of study as the portfolio authors, and in many cases they have taught similar courses at their home institution. Initially the readers will be from a small circle of five institutions participating in the project (Indiana University, University of Nebraska, University of Michigan, Texas A&M University, and Kansas State University), but in principle there is no limit to the locations of the readers given that the portfolios are presented on a Web site. The readers understand that their comments are intended only for the author of the portfolio, and the context for the communication is primarily one of further growth and development of the teacher (in educational parlance, formative review).

The readers have a set of guidelines to frame their comments, although of course all readers are free to offer observations of any kind in addition to or instead of the commentary requested. These guidelines are parallel to the issues raised in the three interactions, and they generally follow the metaphor of an inquiry into successful student understanding. Readers first comment on the intellectual content of the course, including both topics and goals. The guidelines for this component of the review are as follows:

Please evaluate the quality of the course's intellectual content. This evaluation may include but is not limited to:

- appropriateness of course material for both the curriculum and institution,
- intellectual coherence of course content,
- articulation of intellectual goals for learners and congruence of those goals with course content and mission, and
- value/relevance of ideas, knowledge, and skills covered by the course.

Readers next offer comments on the instructional design of the course as represented in the course portfolio. Their focus is on the appropriate use of learners' time both in and out of class, with consideration of how well the teaching methods match the course goals. This segment of a portfolio may include either straightforward data on percentage of class time actually allocated to different activities (routinely collected for our participants) or first-person accounts from a colleague visit to the class. However, the review of course instructional design is not limited to the teacher's live performance in the classroom context, but is intended to include a broader understanding of the decisions teachers make about how the students will spend the time they give to the course. The guidelines for this component of the review are as follows:

Please evaluate the quality of the teaching practices used in the course. This evaluation may include but is not limited to:

- organization and planning of contact time and useful allocation of student time on activities,
- opportunities to engage students actively in the material,
- opportunities (in or out of class) for students to practice the skills embedded in the course goals,
- particularly creative or effective uses of contact time that seem likely to improve student understanding,
- activities scheduled outside of contact time that contribute to student achievement (this may include extracurricular activities, group projects, electronic discussions and assignments, or any other planned course-related assignments or activities), and
- course structures or procedures that contribute especially to the likely achievement of understanding by learners.

Reviewers also comment on the quality and distribution of student performance. They examine both the nature of the opportunities given to learners to demonstrate their understanding and have examples of student work, complete with feedback from the instructor. A portfolio also provides some evidence of how many students achieve at various levels of understanding. The reader can form an independent judgment of the quality of student work by reading graded examples, and those examples give meaning to the typical frequency distributions that show how many students performed in each category of achievement. Because portfolio writers reflect on the success of learners in achieving the intellectual goals of the course, the readers can also comment on how much intellectual achievement the students accomplished. We make a point of using untransformed numbers in preparing the distributions so the reader should know how much of the planned content, understanding, and skills the students in the class mastered. Teachers may use curve grading systems to determine the judgment categories they report for institutional purposes, but the discussion of student learning is focused on the level of achievement represented by the untransformed evaluations made by the teacher. The guidelines for this component of the review are as follows:

Please evaluate the quality of student understanding. This evaluation may include but is not limited to:

- appropriateness of student performance in light of course goals, course level, and institution;
- performance levels that reflect challenging levels of conceptual understanding and critical evaluation of the material appropriate to the level of the course and the students;

- appropriateness of forms of evaluation and assessment given the stated goals of the course;
- creativity in providing students with ways to demonstrate their understanding of and ability to use the ideas and content of the course;
- alignment between the weighting of course assignments in grade calculation and the relative importance of the course goals;
- demonstration that an appropriate percentage of students are achieving competence in the stated course goals or identification of reasons why they might not be reaching these levels of competence; and
- revisions or modifications to the course that could improve performance.

Finally, the readers comment on how the teacher has reflected on the teaching work that has been accomplished. Observations about the intellectual goals achieved and how further learning could be promoted in a future offering of the course are the heart of reflective inquiry into student learning, and readers comment on the insights and plans offered by the portfolio author. The guidelines for this portion of the review are as follows:

Please evaluate the evidence of reflective consideration and development. This evaluation may include but is not limited to:

- substantive reflection by the faculty member on the achievement of the goals for the course,
- identification of any meaningful relations between teaching practice and student performance,
- evidence of insightful analysis of teaching practice that resulted from consideration of student performance, and
- evidence of changed teaching practice over successive course offerings (if present) in reaction to prior student understanding.

Including This Work in Professional Life

Given the consensus that the modern professor is pressed for time due to the growing demands of the academic profession, it is reasonable to ask how faculty members are induced to add this activity to their crowded schedules. The current project offers a modest stipend ($1500 as of 2001) for each participant in the Peer Review Fellowship program, and there is also a pool of funds (currently $2000) to be used by the four participants from each unit to support their academic activities in general (e.g., academic travel, books, research support, or teaching materials). The amounts are not so great as to be a significant incentive that would draw truly unwilling participants, but the support is a nontrivial "thank you" for making room among the priorities for discretionary time around the edges of the academic year.

Prospective participants are encouraged to contact prior peer-review fellows about the benefits of participation for their teaching. Alumni report that their teaching practices are much improved and refined by participation, and they also report enjoying the opportunity to talk about teaching with colleagues in and out of their own field of study. Some alumni report finding new ways to promote student learning beyond what they thought possible in the context of the institution. General participant satisfaction has been an important part of recruiting new fellows.

We have also found that participation is greatly facilitated by a clear structure to the year-long program. There are monthly meetings for discussion of the project and general teaching issues, and there are clear dates for the completion of each component of the interaction process. Participants have readings to accompany each of the interactions, and the issues raised in those readings are discussed at meetings. The proportion of faculty members who complete the planned sequence of activities is much higher when there is a clear structure to the experience. Given the pace of academic life, having an unscheduled set of goals to be done like independent study has not produced successful outcomes by the faculty participants. It is also extremely important that each step of the process is acknowledged by peers in the home unit and by project staff so that professors see this new form of writing as having a meaningful local audience. In one sense, we offer privacy to each author for the beginning stages of this process, whereas we also find that writers gain more from having feedback and comments from an audience than they lose by having their initial and unrefined work seen by other teachers.

Making the Portfolios Accessible

During the initial stages of the project, the individual interactions are exchanged with a small group of colleagues in the same field of study. These professors are organized as a group in a typical Web-based course site, allowing for ready exchange and commentary. We find this is a convenient way to view materials without the hassle of photocopying, and it is also very useful for project staff to keep track of the work. Once the professors get to the stage of presenting student work and commenting on it, we move to a slightly higher level of electronic posting. The central project staff scan selected student work, and the material is posted on a Web site that can be visited by all of that year's participants regardless of field of study. This enhanced visibility was initially made necessary by technical details of posting scanned files, but it turned out to be a desirable change from the perspective of the participating fellows.

Once the integrated portfolio is put into its first completed form, the text and scanned examples of student work are moved onto a professionally maintained Web site dedicated to making this work accessible. It is a password-protected location so only people who are connected with the project (as authors or readers) have access to the materials, and the open format of the site allows for more user-friendly display of both reflections and course materials. In a sense, the professional designer takes the traditional work of the faculty members and presents it in a hypertext format, linking descriptions of student work directly to that work and connecting discussions of classroom practices to materials documenting them. Faculty participants like this format, finding it helpful to see a clear and accessible version of their work. It has also made it much easier for readers from other locations to have quick and easy (but password-protected) access to the portfolios.

THE GENERAL UTILITY
OF COURSE PORTFOLIOS

An organized course portfolio of the sort our participants generate can represent the best features of an effective teacher. When teaching is an intentional program to promote student learning, there is much to be learned from an account of it. The portfolios we support include the key elements of inquiry in them. There are clear goals and preparation, methods of instruction appropriate to the goals and field of study, evidence of the impact of the process on learners, and reflection by the teacher on what was learned from the evidence of learning to refine future teaching. Such a document is especially valuable if it reports multiple offerings of a single course. You can see how a teacher has learned from the experiences of one term, made refinements in subsequent offerings, and evaluated those refinements by looking at their impact on the depth and breadth of student understanding. These features make a course portfolio a good exemplar for the model of scholarly inquiry put forward in *Scholarship Assessed* by Glassick et al. (1997), and the focus on learning is congruent with the emerging consensus that effective teaching is about student understanding rather than merely the teacher's performance.

A critic might question whether there is any reason to make this work available for others to read or comment. The scholarly community is typically not interested in case studies or single examples of any kind of work. It prefers to share findings that have at least some general implications for an understanding of issues in a field. Within the teaching community, there is a similar view (e.g., Richlin, 2001) that a professional should only distribute or publish work that expands on our general understanding of teaching and learning. In contrast, Shulman (1993) argued that there is great benefit to making everyday teaching activities a kind of community property. In addition to avoiding the problem of forgetting the innovations and solutions in teaching from one academic term to the next, written traces of teaching work provide occasions for increased conversations about what works and what does not. These conversations (both live and virtual) provide important feedback that allows for more sophisticated refinement of teaching practices than would likely occur in isolation. Scholars in textual disciplines constantly refer to the importance of audience for the development of excellent writing and thinking skills, and there is every reason to believe that thinking about teaching also benefits greatly from being in constant contact with an interested peer audience.

The repository of electronically shared course portfolios that is the growing product of our project is different from other collections of materials in some important ways. First, a course portfolio focuses on the success of a single course (although it often covers more than one offering of that course). That makes it different from a general teaching portfolio. A typical teaching portfolio includes a statement of teaching philosophy, listings of many courses offered, perhaps some samples of syllabi or assignments from different courses, perhaps a brief teaching-oriented vita, and often a summary of student reactions to being in the courses taught by the professor. It gives a broad view of the range of teaching experiences offered by the professor. In contrast, the course portfolio gives an in-depth account of the effectiveness of a single course through evidence from one or more offerings of that course. The student voice is still present, but it is represented by student work from the course, not by student opinion surveys. Instead of a general statement of teaching philosophy, goals, and practices, the professor's voice is represented by intellectual reflection on the outcomes of teaching the particular course and how that teaching can be modified or improved in the future. A course portfolio would be an excellent item to include as part of a teaching portfolio. Perhaps the ideal teaching portfolio would include several course portfolios, complete with their reflection on effectiveness, in place of the usual pile of syllabi that list only what the teacher planned to present.

Second, a course portfolio is different from what typically appears in journals about teaching—either discipline-specific journals or those devoted to research on teaching. As is appropriate to the tradition of journal publication, articles are printed only when the editors believe that the material makes a substantial contribution of new ideas, understanding, or results that are of interest to a broad range of readers. Most faculty members are unlikely to produce such a product in the course of their everyday teaching, and many faculty would specifically decline to participate in the rigors of experimental design, statistical analysis, and critical review that accompany participation in a journal community. Those same faculty members, however, will teach a course year after year, making ongoing decisions about teaching that are informed by how well students demonstrate understanding. It could be helpful for them to be in contact with other teachers working informally but systematically on the same topics. These teachers are not in search of truth about how all teaching should be done, but they are deeply interested in making informed choices about what to try next in their own teaching. I hope that a community of writers and readers of course portfolios will find it valuable to interact in this middle ground between high science and uninformed guessing.

In addition to the critics from the educational research community, there are also critics from the disciplinary research community who dismiss the intellectual work in teaching as being low level or even trivial. Sometimes teaching is viewed as application of ideas from research or simply the delivery of ideas generated by the much more difficult and advanced process of research into the general nature of things. Having a career that has included much well-funded research, a substantial amount of journal editing, and many kinds of teaching, I can only say that I have found easy and difficult work in both parts of my professional life.

Teaching an advanced seminar to smart Ph.D. students is quite easy work, whereas I have been seriously challenged by trying to create conditions in which lower division undergraduates will embrace the findings of basic research in learning and develop the generalized ability to use those ideas in new contexts. Doing a series of programmatic or parametric basic research studies that follow a well-established trail of procedures and findings is not all that intellectually challenging, but finding a completely new way of framing a research question to resolve a conceptual dispute is more difficult. For me, the range of difficulty in the two domains seems similar, and it is not the case that one is easy and the other hard.

Finally, it is likely that some teachers who create course portfolios and refine them through formative peer review will feel that these documents represent their intellectual work very well. In those cases, at the discretion of the author, the course portfolio could be included in materials used for periodic evaluative review at key points of accountability. When being considered for tenure or promotion, a teacher could ask that a file of refined course portfolios be sent to external readers who are known for their teaching, and letters could be returned with an arm's length view of the quality of the intellectual work represented. This approach is the standard method used to evaluate research work. When a teacher has produced concise documents that represent teaching work, it would be reasonable to adapt that same process. The opinions of independent experts who read our intellectual work has been the standard of judgment in academics for some time, and we can improve the standing of the intellectual work in teaching by giving it the same degree of respect and consideration. Just as not all professors regularly produce written reports of original research, not all professors will produce course portfolios. Those professors who wish to be considered excellent in the teaching portion of their professional work, however, can have the opinions of professional peers to complement the existing student voice in the evaluation of teaching.

CONCLUSION

A program of faculty fellowships has been established to support and guide professors in the creation of course portfolios to represent the intellectual work in their teaching. The program helps faculty identify the decisions and plans they have already made, and it gives support in examining the depth and breadth of student understanding as evidence of the success of teaching. The creation of reflective, integrative electronic documents promotes a community of readers who can provide feedback to guide further refinement of teaching efforts.

To me the most important benefit of creating a community in which course portfolios are regularly created and read is that we no longer lose a great deal of intellectual work that is regularly being done. Talented people find ingenious solutions to problems in learning every academic term, and traditionally most of that work is lost. When people know that there is a community of people who will look at their work, especially the cumulative intellectual work of several offerings of a course, they will be willing to take the modest extra steps of recording and reflecting on what they are already accomplishing as teachers. As a result, there will be a large community of teachers whose decisions about how to teach will be informed by the collective effectiveness of their work.

ACKNOWLEDGMENTS

The peer-review project was supported by grants from the Fund for the Improvement of Postsecondary Education (U.S. Department of Education), the University of Nebraska Teaching Council, the University of Nebraska Pepsi Quasi-Endowment Fund, the Hewlett Foundation, and the Pew Charitable Trusts. Preparation of this chapter was supported by the Pew Charitable Trusts and the Center for New Designs in Learning and Scholarship at Georgetown University. I am especially grateful to Rick Edwards for his continued support and encouragement.

REFERENCES

Cerbin, W. (1994). The course portfolio as a tool for continuous improvement of teaching and learning. *Journal on Excellence in College Teaching, 5,* 95–105.
Glassick, C. E., Huber, M. T., & Maeroff, G. I. (1997). *Scholarship assessed.* San Francisco: Jossey-Bass.
Hutchings, P. (Ed.). (1996). *Making teaching community property.* Washington: AAHE.
Hutchings, P. (Ed.). (1998). *The course portfolio.* Washington: AAHE.
Richlin, L. (2001). Scholarly teaching and the scholarship of teaching. In C. Kreber (Ed.), *The scholarship of teaching: New directions for teaching and learning,* no. 86 (pp. 57–68). San Francisco: Jossey-Bass.
Shulman, L. S. (1993). Teaching as community property: Putting an end to pedagogical solitude. *Change, 25*(6), 6–7.

18

Teaching at a Liberal Arts College: With a Little Help From My Friends

Randolph A. Smith
Ouachita Baptist University

About 25 years ago, as a third-year graduate student in experimental psychology, I began to consider my long-term career possibilities. Texas Tech University had a fairly traditional experimental psychology program with a heavy emphasis on research. Although I had been involved in research for my entire stay there, I did not seriously contemplate a career that involved only research—I knew that I also wanted to teach. Fortunately, I was able to spend 2 years in graduate school as a teaching assistant. My experience consisted only of serving as a lab assistant for an experimental psychology course. I also had the opportunity to give a few guest lectures. To help prepare the graduate students for academic careers, Tech's psychology department offered a teaching seminar to all teaching assistants. Unfortunately, the instructor for the teaching course was one of the department's weaker teachers and taught the seminar as a PSI course. Although it is certainly possible to read a book and extract important information from it, this approach is probably not the best strategy for training new teachers. Thankfully, the main text for the course was Bill McKeachie's (1969) *Teaching Tips*, and I learned many valuable pointers indirectly from Bill.

As I approached my last year of graduate school and thought about employment possibilities, I began to worry about my relative lack of experience in the classroom. Then a serendipitous experience started a chain of events that led me to where I

231

am today. The director of the experimental program at Texas Tech got a phone call from Wayland Baptist College, a small liberal arts college about 50 miles from Lubbock. They needed someone to teach a course in experimental psychology. The director asked me whether I would be interested and I said yes with little hesitation. Here, I thought, was my chance to add some true classroom teaching experience to my vita. I knew next to nothing about small colleges—I had earned my BS from the University of Houston and was attending another large state university for my graduate work. However, I figured that teaching experience was valuable regardless of where I obtained it.

I enjoyed my teaching at Wayland, but it did not really change my career objective. I still planned to find a faculty position at a large university where I could teach and (primarily) carry out my research plans. After all, this approach was the only faculty model I really knew about—I simply drove to and from my class at Wayland without getting to know any faculty there. Still this teaching experience did give me the insight that teaching at a small school might be a viable fallback position. Thus, when I started applying for faculty jobs, I included liberal arts colleges in the mix.

Applying for college teaching jobs in the late 1970s was not fun. The job market was tight and jobs were hard to come by. Rejection letters from the large schools started coming. What interest I did draw came from small liberal arts colleges. First, Wayland offered me a faculty position based (I presume) on my teaching the experimental psychology course there. At that point, I still had applications out at the larger schools and was still optimistic about landing such a position, so I turned down Wayland's offer. However, the rejections continued to mount, so when I got interview opportunities at smaller schools, I accepted them. I applied on the spur of the moment to one such school because I saw an ad for their position in the elevator in the psychology building—a faculty member had died and they were conducting a last-minute search. They offered me the position, but only for 1 year because they were committed to conducting a national search for the position. Despite being strongly attracted to the school because of its location, I turned that position down because of not wanting to go back on the job market after only 1 year. Finally, my job choices came down to two small, private, denominational liberal arts colleges: one in Kentucky and one in Arkansas. I accepted the position at Ouachita Baptist University (OBU) in Arkadelphia, Arkansas, because OBU's psychology department would have three members (rather than two) and because Arkansas was closer to Texas (my ultimate goal for a faculty position) than was Kentucky. At this point, I still envisioned this type of position as a temporary stepping stone to a job at a larger school. I still saw myself doing significant research while I taught. OBU was, and still is, quite teaching oriented. In fact, the teaching load was 15 hours a semester when I started teaching there in 1977. Thinking myself a shrewd negotiator, I swung a deal to teach a 15/12 load, being proud of myself for getting a one-course reduction so that I could carry out my significant research agenda.

I had left Texas Tech ABD, but had already gathered my dissertation data. I figured to finish my dissertation quickly and then begin work on other research projects. Quickly, reality set in. Having taught one course previously did not come close to preparing me to teach five at one time! I was teaching two sections of General Psychology, which must be one of the toughest courses to teach for someone fresh out of a specialized graduate program. I was teaching a course that was probably unique to OBU, Human Processes, which was supposed to combine perception, cognition, and motivation. I was teaching Psychological Testing, a course for which I was totally unprepared given that my sole training was an undergraduate course in the subject. Finally, I was teaching Statistics, a course for which I thought I was prepared given my graduate minor in the subject. Needless to say, I struggled during my first semester. Early in November, I got a call from my graduate advisor, who inquired how my dissertation was coming along. I reported that the dissertation was still sitting in the exact same place on the shelf in my office where I had placed it when I moved in. There was one difference—now the dissertation had about 3 months of dust piled on it. Happily, I did survive that first semester. Even better, during the spring semester, I collected more data for my dissertation and successfully defended it during the summer after my first year at OBU.

I assumed that the first year was going to be the hardest and most time-consuming as far as teaching was concerned and that I would have more free time to devote to research in the coming years. Once again, reality intervened. At OBU, during their first year, new faculty do not serve on faculty committees nor advise majors. Both of those responsibilities quickly began to eat up some of the free time I envisioned. Also, the reality of preparing for class dawned on me—if I wanted to be even an adequate teacher, I needed to work on class presentations on an ongoing basis. However, as I was doing this type of faculty work, I also began to discover that I enjoyed it. As time went on, I enjoyed it more and more. I found working closely with students and colleagues (even from different departments and divisions) to be challenging, invigorating, and fun. I found that OBU would support my activities that were aimed at faculty development and that faculty development encompassed far more than developing a research agenda. I was still interested in conducting research, but the time for it quickly disappeared every day. Over time, I developed guilt feelings about not conducting research as I had been trained to do. I was still involved in research because of my supervision of our majors in our experimental course. We required each student to conduct an original project, and I worked with them outside of class in a one-on-one fashion. Although I enjoyed my job, it was difficult to avoid feeling guilty.

After several years on the job, I had a life-changing experience. I received a brochure advertising a teaching conference in Indiana. Although the conference was well over 500 miles away, I attended the first Mid-America Conference for Teachers of Psychology in 1984. There, I experienced a revelation—there were many people who were similar to me: They taught heavy loads at small colleges and struggled with their identities as research psychologists. It was at this conference that I discovered the journal *Teaching of Psychology*, which has been vital to my development as a teacher. Best of all, I began making friendships at that conference with people who I now count as some of my closest friends and colleagues (even mentors). The common tie among us was an interest in and love for teaching. It was at this point in my career that I realized that teaching was a legitimate form of scholarship, predating Boyer's (1990) report on the scholarship of teaching by several years.

From that conference almost 20 years ago, I identified my main interest in psychology as teaching. I became active in organizations supporting the teaching of psychology at local, regional, and national levels. To be honest, I have gone farther in the discipline of psychology than I ever contemplated as a graduate student. I find myself suffering from the imposter phenomenon when people like the editors of this volume ask me to write a chapter about teaching at a liberal arts college. I am convinced that many, if not all, of my accomplishments have come because I stayed in the small college environment and chose teaching as my pathway. The people I have met and worked with along the way have been helpful in opening doors for me. After hearing horror stories in graduate school about backstabbing and dog-eat-dog competition in research universities, I feel certain that I made the right choice for me.

At a teaching conference or a convention sometime in the past several years, I heard Charles Brewer give a presentation entitled "A Talk to Teachers: Bending Twigs and Affecting Eternity," which was originally his Presidential Address for the Southeastern Psychological Association in 1994. Charles said:

> Despite incredibly hard work, low social status, and vows of poverty (but not chastity), teaching is the most exciting, the most challenging, the most difficult, and the most rewarding thing I have ever done. I simply cannot imagine doing anything else.

This quote has stayed with me since I first heard it. Given the statement, it comes as no surprise to me that Charles has spent his career teaching at small liberal arts colleges. I would not want to imply that a faculty member at a large research institution could not make a similar statement, but I do believe this sentiment would more likely be shared by faculty who teach at institutions similar to Charles's and mine.

At this point in the chapter, I feel rather self-conscious about the amount of space I have devoted to my experiences. To give readers a better sense of what teaching at a small liberal arts school is like, I now turn to the reactions from a group of colleagues such as those I mentioned earlier. I contacted a group of 18 dedicated psychology teachers who teach at liberal arts colleges and who serve as reviewers for the journal *Teaching of Psychology*. My sample included 8 women and 10 men who have taught at liberal arts schools an average of 17.0 years ($SD = 9.0$, range of 1.5–31). Their schools have an average enrollment of about

2,100 students, and their departments average 7.2 faculty (range = 3–15) and 132.2 majors (range = 50–300). I asked them several questions about teaching at small liberal arts colleges.

WHY DID YOU DECIDE TO TEACH AT A LIBERAL ARTS INSTITUTION?

I was curious to know whether my experience in taking a job at a liberal arts college almost by default was a common one. Interestingly, I found a variety of answers to this question. The most common theme was *teaching*, as 11 of the 18 people (61%) mentioned this topic in some fashion. For example, some respondents said that they valued teaching or they were good at teaching:

> "I feel that the greatest impact I can have as a psychologist is as a teacher."
> "Because of the close interaction one can have with students and have a significant impact on their education."

Others knew when they were looking for jobs that they liked teaching.

> "I loved teaching and was delighted to find an institution that valued what I did."
> "I liked the opportunity to teach a variety of courses with relatively small enrollments rather than the same two classes with large enrollments."

Some other respondents had met success in teaching; they were good at it.

> "I was good at and enjoyed teaching as a graduate student."
> "Teaching is my area of strength."

Somewhat surprising to me was the second highest response about why the respondents chose to teach at a liberal arts institution. Seven people (39%) intentionally chose to teach at such a school to avoid research institutions or becoming a narrow specialist. Perhaps their graduate experience had shown them that such a career was simply not right for them.

> "It stemmed from NOT wanting to work at a high-pressure research institution."
> "Because that focus meshed with my own values, interests, and skills, I fled the big university for the small college." (from a respondent who began teaching at a large university)
> "I had eclectic interests and was having trouble narrowing down an area to specialize in."

The next largest category of responses came from five people (28%) who identified with the values of liberal arts colleges. Interestingly, all of these respondents had attended a liberal arts college.

"I think that the liberal arts provide students with a unique set of skills that are
    more difficult to get in pre-professional programs: critical thinking skills,
    good writing skills, and analytical skills."
"I wanted to have close contact with students and to be in a setting where
    teaching plus advising/mentoring would be valued."
"Having been a student at a liberal arts college . . . , I knew firsthand how liberal
    arts institutions take undergraduate teaching as their primary mission."
"I didn't realize it at the time, but as an undergraduate student, I imprinted on
    small, liberal arts institutions."

These three categories accounted for the vast majority of the responses about why these people chose to teach at liberal arts institutions. It is clear that most of my respondents intentionally selected the liberal arts environment for its emphasis on teaching or to avoid what they perceived as the negative aspects of a large university setting. Thus, few of those people surveyed apparently found themselves at liberal arts schools as a second choice. Although I could not have consciously endorsed these values and beliefs fully when I left graduate school (probably because of my limited exposure to liberal arts institutions), I realized subsequently that I share the convictions of my respondents.

WHY HAVE YOU STAYED AT A LIBERAL ARTS INSTITUTION? WHAT ARE THE ADVANTAGES TO TEACHING AT A LIBERAL ARTS SCHOOL?

I originally asked these questions separately. As I studied the responses and attempted to group them, it became clear that there was too much overlap to treat them separately, so I combined the responses.

My decision to stay in a liberal arts environment did not come immediately when I was hired at OBU. Rather, the process was a gradual one in which I came to see the benefits and advantages of the small school with a teaching mission over the large university with a research mission. I was curious to find out from colleagues why they had stayed at their small institutions over the years. Again, there were a variety of responses that I sorted into three categories. Two of the categories were predictable from the responses to the first question: Students and Goals. However, the third category, Community, had not shown up earlier.

Students

Two thirds of the respondents (12 of 18) listed some aspect of working with students as either an advantage to liberal arts schools or as a reason that they have stayed at their institution. As you can see from their comments, these faculty can easily be labeled student-centered. It is reinforcing for a teacher to work with students who are interested in learning. In a similar fashion, it is reinforcing for a teacher to see evidence of his or her influence with students.

> "I have seen that the students who choose this type of environment are more dedicated and involved than those who go to a larger school."
> "I have stayed here because of the close interaction one can have with students and the significant impact on their education."
> "These students are wonderful kids, and it continues to be a pleasure to work with them."
> "Small classes allowed personal interaction, both in and out of class, which enhanced students' learning."
> "... see that you really can make a difference in a student's life."
> "I love the fact that students come first ... "

In their attempts to recruit students, many liberal arts colleges advertise that they have low student/faculty ratios and faculty who care about their students. Prospective students who saw quotes like these might love to enroll at such schools.

Goals

A group of diverse faculty likely has diverse goals. This assumption was certainly true for the 14 respondents (78%) who mentioned some aspect of teaching at a liberal arts institution that I categorized as a goal. By the same token, it was interesting to see a high degree of consensus on one particular goal, as 6 of the 14 (43%) mentioned variety in some fashion. As the quotes show, not all faculty want to become narrow specialists.

> "I like the variety of courses which I have an opportunity to teach."
> "I have been able to offer a wide array of courses."
> "I am able to teach interdisciplinary courses, which combine my interests."
> "I get to be more of a generalist."
> "My setting allowed me greater variability in my life than other settings would do."
> "I have been rewarded for my dual focus on teaching and research."
> "... to grow intellectually and explore new fields, technologies, and techniques."

Of course, my faculty respondents listed other goals. No other goal, however, jumped out at me as did variety.

> "I appreciate the fact that the 'bottom line' for our curriculum is to help students explore psychology as one of the liberal arts."
> "I have the freedom to think and to learn, and then to teach it."
> "I want to continue to develop as a teacher, and these institutions value that."
> "I still find teaching fun and intellectually stimulating."
> "The contributions that I wanted to make coincided with the mission of the school."

By examining these goal-related comments, it is clear that teaching at a liberal arts college has allowed many of these colleagues to meet some important goals in their lives. Some people might be tempted to label these goals as more personal than professional, but it seems that they represent personal preferences about how to handle one's professional life and may be quite important in staying happy in a job.

Community

I strongly believe that one of the factors that was most crucial in changing my feelings about teaching at a small teaching college was the feeling of community that developed over the years. Part of the community feeling deals with students— with only three faculty in my department, we tended to see students in several classes and get to know them well. Combine such frequent contact with close contact (as in supervising research), and close relationships develop.

Another aspect of community was with departmental colleagues. Working in a small department does not guarantee good collegial relationships, but working together is probably much more important than in large departments, which may be prone to factions. I have been fortunate to work with good colleagues in my department, which has led to more close friendships. Indeed, when people have left the department for retirement or other jobs, the feelings of sadness and regret have been as much for the inevitable decline in a friendship as much as for the department's loss.

A third aspect of community has come from working with administration and staff. Because of OBU's smallness and our committee structure, we tend to see administrators fairly frequently. Although there is some of the typical tension that one might expect between faculty and administrators, the relationships are better than I would have predicted. Because we get to know each other better than at larger schools, I believe the sense of trust is probably greater.

The final type of community that I found, for which I was totally unprepared, was the community among colleagues from different departments. Even in retrospect, I find it interesting that this community takes so many different forms. Part of collegial community is friendships—some of the best friends I have at OBU are from different departments. However, a major part of collegial community is continuing education, which takes a variety of forms. We have a brown-bag colloquium series in which faculty from the entire school present their latest research in an informal setting open to all faculty. We have a reading group that meets once a month to discuss a novel the group has read. We have informal gatherings at coffee and lunch where the discussion may range from mundane school business to politics or current events to philosophical issues. OBU has an arrangement whereby faculty can enroll for a class anytime they wish. I have had a historian take my Statistics class and I have taken Western Thought and Culture from a historian and Art in the Humanities from an art faculty member (whose doctorate is in English). I have had the chance to co-lead (with a historian) a group of 15 students on a 3-week study tour of England, France, and Italy for 6 hours credit in humanities.

Because this Community aspect of teaching at a liberal arts college has been so important to me in my career, I was particularly interested to see whether my respondents had had similar experiences or feelings. I was pleased to find that my experience is not a unique one—in fact, it was far from unique, as 14 of 18 respondents (78%) made some comment that I categorized as fitting the Community category.

> "I enjoy the intellectual and cultural opportunities and the close-knit community."
> "Given the diversity in the perspectives faculty from different disciplines bring to the task at hand, I find the experience of collaborating with them stimulating and enriching."
> "The outside-the-classroom activities of the whole community are meaningful to me."
> "I have collaborated with colleagues from our criminal justice, education, social work, and theatre departments over the years on various teaching and research projects."

The following comments, to me, best exemplify the continuing education aspect of teaching at a liberal arts institution. You can almost hear the enthusiasm in the respondents' voices.

> "I've grown to find immense joy in exploring connections among content and colleagues across disciplinary boundaries."
> "Going to lunch and to colloquiums here gives me the liberal arts education I was too busy studying psychology to get when I was an undergraduate."
> "...the cronies I see each day include a theologian, an economist, a political scientist, and a modern American historian (I also regularly chat with a novelist, an English lit professor, and a classicist). In short, my own education has not stopped with graduate school—I learn quite a bit from those who are outside my discipline."

"My interactions go beyond the psychology department and include the entire campus community. As such, I'm having more discussions with historians, economists, political scientists, etc. Even search committees become an opportunity to learn more about a different field. A smaller school is giving me a bigger view of academia!"

WHAT ARE THE DISADVANTAGES OF TEACHING AT A LIBERAL ARTS INSTITUTION?

Lest you think everything is idyllic at liberal arts schools, I did ask my respondents about the negatives at their institutions. Many of the responses were quite predictable. For example, half the respondents mentioned lack of resources, both physical and financial.

"My colleagues are highly motivated in giving students a great education, but we don't always have the money to make our plans a reality."
"Small private colleges have lower salaries than everyone else in academia."

Other respondents gave answers that I categorized as "keeping up." The two types of problems mentioned revolved around staying current in one's field and staying active in research. Although seven respondents (39%) listed these issues as problematic, two of them specifically mentioned e-mail as a vehicle to help with these problems.

"The major disadvantage is the lack of colleagues in my area of expertise."
"I feel less identified with my specific discipline (social psychology)."
"I miss the opportunity to involve graduate students in my teaching and research."

A third of the respondents cited workload issues as a disadvantage. As I read these responses, I recognized some of the complaints and categorized them as "overinvolvement." There seems to be a tendency for strong faculty members at liberal arts schools to take on many roles. Once administrators, other faculty, and students discover that a faculty member is solid, that faculty member gets tapped by various groups to take on additional responsibilities. Such attention can be flattering in that it sends a positive message, but it can also result in large inequities among faculty in terms of workload.

"I don't like wearing so many hats sometimes."
"The smallness can create an atmosphere where faculty can work themselves to death in nonteaching related activities—serving on committees, teams,

task forces, etc. can really chew up the time. . . . It is hard to hide on a small
campus."

"The teaching load can be oppressive, and there is precious little time to pursue
intensive scholarly endeavors."

Although some of the respondents listed overcommitment as a problem, one of
those specifically noted that such commitment was intentional: "My investment
in various activities associated with teaching and the college—by choice I should
state—has made it more difficult to sustain a focused contribution to basic science."

Finally, the last disadvantage of teaching at a liberal arts institution, mentioned
by five respondents (28%), was a factor that I labeled "prestige." This factor involved a recognition by faculty that there is a clear pecking order in terms of the
type of institution at which one teaches.

"For the general public it does not have the same prestige as teaching at a
research university."

"Among some psychologists, these institutions are considered 'just' teaching
jobs."

"Sooner or later it dawns on you that in the hierarchy of academics, you are the
little league."

Thus, as you can see, faculty at liberal arts colleges did perceive some drawbacks
to teaching in that type of environment. The next question provides the reader with
a basis to compare the relative strength of advantages versus disadvantages.

HOW WOULD YOU SAY YOUR
INSTITUTION VALUES TEACHING,
SCHOLARSHIP, AND SERVICE?

I asked respondents to assign percentages to these three traditional academic activities. I had a perception from informal discussions with liberal arts colleagues
at various meetings that several had experienced increased scholarship demands
at their schools over the past few years. Glassick, Huber, and Maeroff (1997) reported that 41% of liberal arts faculty they surveyed believed that research was
more important to their advancement than it was 5 years previously. Unfortunately,
I could find no baseline data with which to compare these data. Still the estimates
of the 18 respondents should provide a snapshot of the state of liberal arts colleges'
weightings of these factors in 2000.

As you might expect, teaching was the most highly valued of the three activities at liberal arts institutions. The respondents' estimates ranged from 25% to
70%, with a mean of 52.9% ($SD = 12.3$; mdn $= 50\%$, mode [$n = 5$] of 50%).

Although teaching is the most valued activity, the range and standard deviation show considerable variability in the respondents' estimates of its value.

Respondents' estimates of the weight their institutions give to scholarship ranged from 10% to 60%, with a mean of 27.9% ($SD = 14.9$; mdn = 25%, modes [$n = 4$] of 10% and 20%). Although respondents estimated that scholarship receives approximately half the weight that teaching does, it is important to again note that there was considerable variability in the estimates. Three respondents gave higher estimates for scholarship than they did for teaching, and one gave equal weight to the two.

Concerning service, respondents gave estimates ranging from 5% to 33%, with a mean of 17.1% ($SD = 7.8$%; mdn = 15%, modes [$n = 5$] of 15% and 20%). Although service was the least valued (and least variable) of the three activities, four respondents weighted it more heavily than scholarship at their institution, and two weighted it equally with scholarship. No one weighted service more heavily than teaching.

Finally, I offered an "other" choice for weighting. Four respondents weighted "other" between 5% and 15%, for an overall mean of 1.7% ($SD = 3.7$%; mdn and mode = 0%). Two respondents defined "other" as collegiality, one as notoriety, and one as having clinical training.

Although teaching is the most important activity at these liberal arts institutions, it is interesting to note that its mean weight is barely over the 50% mark. Both scholarship and service seem to play significant parts of faculty members' roles and responsibilities. The combination of these factors may help contribute to the overcommitment mentioned in the previous section. Although the lack of baseline data makes it impossible to determine whether emphasis on scholarship is increasing, the weight placed on scholarship certainly seems to be more than minimal.

HOW IS SCHOLARSHIP DEFINED
AT YOUR INSTITUTION?

In light of my interest about a possible increasing role for scholarship at liberal arts colleges, I was interested in knowing how these institutions define *scholarship*. As I read respondents' comments, I formed a simple dichotomy to classify the scholarship definitions. One side of the dichotomy was what I defined as "traditional." In this category, I placed responses that emphasized primarily publications. Four of the 18 respondents (22%) gave responses that seemed to fit this category. Interestingly, the mean weight for scholarship estimated by these four respondents was 46.3%, considerably above the 27.9% figure for the entire sample.

"Unfortunately, it's publications in peer-refereed journals."
"For the most part, we still define scholarship in a fairly traditional fashion— publication in refereed journals or 'scholarly' books."

"Generally publication in peer-reviewed journals."
"Scholarship has typically been defined in terms of books, articles, grants, and convention papers/posters."

Eleven of the 18 respondents (61%) gave definitions of scholarship that I categorized as "broad." Four specifically included "the scholarship of teaching" in their response, a phrase made popular by Boyer (1990). Although these respondents did list traditional activities in their definitions of scholarship, they also included some activities that might not carry weight in a research university.

"Scholarship is loosely defined."
"It is broadly defined but has to have application to my teaching performance."
" ... the scholarship of teaching, curriculum development ... "
"Any professional work that enhances one's teaching ... less traditional work of editing, writing instructors' manuals or test banks, reviewing grant proposals."
"Broadly ... an active research program that incorporates undergraduates ... "
" ... editing, reviewing ... preparing new courses ... attending workshops."
"Faculty members whose research focuses on teaching issues are reaching equality with those whose research programs are more discipline-specific."
"We still seem to be emphasizing scholarly teaching and the scholarship of teaching right now."

Lending some support for my notion that definitions of scholarship might be changing at some liberal arts institutions, six respondents (33%) either mentioned that the definition had become more demanding or was under debate at their schools. Not surprisingly, these faculty had been at their institutions long enough that they had the context to perceive such a change (mean of 17 years).

"In recent years the college has made a policy that a faculty member cannot be promoted to full professorship without documenting adequate scholarship via journal articles, books, and other publications."
"Developing new courses or engaging in advanced study used to count, but both have now become an expectation leading to some creation, usually published work."
"There's more of an emphasis now on products, whereas about 30 or so years ago, just 'doing something interesting' was enough."
"Still up for debate."

It appears there is no clear-cut answer as to the full range of activities that might count as scholarship at a liberal arts college. Certainly traditional scholarship fits the bill, but apparently faculty often have some leeway to engage in other types of activities that fit their interests.

IF YOU WERE STARTING OVER, WOULD YOU CHOOSE TO TEACH AT A LIBERAL ARTS INSTITUTION?

One of the most important questions to me dealt with the elusive bottom line. After having the liberal arts faculty compile a list of advantages and disadvantages, I was interested in knowing their overall feeling about teaching at such an institution. I could think of no better question than whether they would pursue the same path if given the opportunity. It was interesting to me that 16 of 18 respondents (89%) said they would choose to teach in a liberal arts setting if they were starting over. The other two respondents were uncertain, but they did not rule out that possibility. Thus, it seems clear, at least for this sample of faculty, that the advantages of teaching at a liberal arts institution far outweigh the disadvantages.

"No doubt whatsoever, I would."
"I would gladly do so and recommend the career to others."
"I can't envision a more satisfying career path."
"Absolutely . . . I am more convinced that this is a good match for me than when I was first on the job market."
"Yes, I would because the emphasis on close student contact and on teaching is what feeds my soul."

CONCLUSION

They say that confession is good for the soul—writing this chapter has been good for my teaching soul. It is easy to get bogged down in the minutiae of the various activities entailed in teaching at a liberal arts college and to forget why you are there. Reading the words of my colleagues has helped me remember why I am here and it has reinvigorated me. If you teach at a similar institution, I hope you have experienced a similar feeling. If you are looking for a teaching job, I hope I have shed some light on the wonderfully indescribable experience of teaching at a liberal arts college. Let me close with an altered version of Charles Brewer's (1994) quote:

> Despite incredibly hard work, low social status, and vows of poverty (but not chastity), teaching *at a liberal arts college* is the most exciting, the most challenging, the most difficult, and the most rewarding thing I have ever done. I simply cannot imagine doing anything else.

ACKNOWLEDGMENTS

I dedicate this chapter to Michael E. Arrington, my good friend and VPAA for many years, for his support and encouragement that played a major role in my professional development. I gratefully acknowledge the help of all my questionnaire respondents: Ruth Ault (Davidson College), Bob Batsell (Kalamazoo College), Andrea Chapdelaine (Albright College), Dana Dunn (Moravian College), Pete Giordano (Belmont University), Christopher Hakala (Lycoming College), Elizabeth Yost Hammer (Loyola University of New Orleans), Neil Lutsky (Carleton College), Janet Matthews (Loyola University of New Orleans), Chandra Mehrotra (College of St. Scholastica), Marianne Miserandino (Arcadia University), Barbara Nodine (Arcadia University), Timothy Osberg (Niagara University), Jack Rossman (Macalester College), Chris Spatz (Hendrix College), Elizabeth Swenson (John Carroll University), Randall Wight (Ouachita Baptist University), and Edythe Woods (Madonna University).

REFERENCES

Boyer, E. L. (1990). *Scholarship reconsidered: Priorities of the professoriate*. Princeton, NJ: Carnegie Foundation for the Advancement of Teaching.

Brewer, C. L. (1994, April). *A talk to teachers: Bending twigs and affecting eternity*. Presidential address at Southeastern Psychological Association, New Orleans, LA.

Glassick, C. E., Huber, M. T., & Maeroff, G. I. (1997). *Scholarship assessed: Evaluation of the professoriate*. San Francisco: Jossey-Bass.

McKeachie, W. J. (1969). *Teaching tips: A guidebook for the beginning college teacher* (6th ed.). Lexington, MA: D.C. Heath.

19

Differences in Teaching in a Liberal Arts College Versus Research University

James E. Freeman
University of Virginia

There are not many psychologists who are as renowned for their contributions to the teaching of psychology as are Charles Brewer and Bill McKeachie. It is noteworthy that they spent their careers in distinctly different academic environments, demonstrating that it is possible to acquire a national reputation for teaching regardless of the type of school at which a person teaches. Charles and Bill are veritable institutions at their respective schools. Charles is at Furman University, a liberal arts college in Greenville, South Carolina. Bill is at the University of Michigan—a Carnegie Research I University.

This chapter is about the differences between these two kinds of academic environments. I comment on the experience of being in each environment, but first a disclaimer. It should be understood that my observations are personal and a bit biased in favor of the liberal arts college side given my 23 years at Denison University compared to 2 years at the University of Virginia (UVa). Denison and Furman, private liberal arts colleges, have more in common with each other than differences, as do the flagship universities of Michigan and Virginia, both public research institutions. Liberal arts colleges are primarily baccalaureate programs (Furman has three master's programs, Denison has none), and research universities have doctoral programs.

RESEARCH

Perhaps the most obvious difference between the two types of institutions is the emphasis of baccalaureate institutions on teaching with research second, whereas the reverse is true at doctoral institutions. According to a committee report for the American Association of University Professors, liberal arts professors spend an average of 8% of their time on research activities, compared with 29% for public research institutions (Rosenthal et al., 1994). The reputation of a university is based, in large part, on the prestige of its faculty's scholarship. Developing a national or even international reputation is expected. Publishing in peer-reviewed journals, writing books, and acquiring large federal grants develop reputations. One faculty member at UVa put it to me this way: "You won't get tenure for excellent teaching and marginal research, but you can get tenure for excellent research and marginal teaching." The AAUP survey of professors at doctoral institutions revealed that 88% agreed with the statement, "It is difficult for a person to receive tenure if he/she does not publish, compared to 39% for liberal arts professors (Rosenthal et al., 1994). Faculties at doctoral granting institutions have more support for research than faculty at other types of institutions. Faculties at doctoral institutions generally have grants from federal agencies to support their research, whereas faculties at liberal arts colleges rely more on internal, institutional support. Also, faculties at doctoral institutions have the support of graduate students. Graduate students serve as apprentices and assist faculty in churning out research. Thus, faculties at doctorial institutions have more institutional support for research than faculties at baccalaureate schools.

Research did not always rule supreme at universities. Research was not a major part of faculty work until after World War II, when there was a large infusion of Ph.D.s into the job market. With decreasing undergraduate enrollments during the early 1970s, faculty began to compete for federal research funds. Diamond and Adam (1983) concluded that the competition for faculty positions enabled academic institutions, doctoral and even baccalaureate schools, to require research productivity of its faculty. A survey revealed that, of liberal arts deans, 40.5% and 30.6% considered research and publication, respectively, a major factor in evaluating faculty, compared with 97.5% for teaching (Seldin, 1998). Scholarship is expected at liberal arts colleges, but the amount and quality vary. High research productivity is essential for tenure at a research university, while moderate productivity is sufficient at a liberal arts college. However a poor teacher is unlikely to be awarded tenure at a liberal arts college than at a research university.

In an effort to promote greater respect for teaching, a definition of the scholarship of teaching has been proposed by an APA task force and others (Halpern & Reich, 1999; Halpern et al., 1998; Hutchings & Shulman, 1999; Peterson & Trierweiler, 1999). Teaching is viewed as scholarly activity in its own right. Girgus (1999), however, exhorted us to recognize the diversity of colleges and universities. She argued that the different institutional missions are valuable, " . . . and it is as important to higher education as it is to the nation as a whole that these differences in emphasis exist and flourish" (p. 357). Still another view, Korn (1999) suggested that teaching "should be honored as teaching, not scholarship" (p. 362) to give it the respect it deserves. Furthermore, he argued that the APA task force report will have no impact on Research I universities. I suspect that Korn's prediction will likely be confirmed.

THE FACULTY

Judging from the advertisements for jobs in *The APA Monitor*, liberal arts colleges seldom hire professors at levels other than assistant professor, and many of those hires are not tenure-track positions. The main reason is fiscal. Hiring new Ph.D.s is cheaper than hiring senior faculty. Although the liberal arts emphasis is on quality teaching, the line is drawn at spending more money for seasoned veterans. With many of the positions within a department already tenured, much of the hiring is for terminal contract positions. Consequently, it is not unusual to find candidates with years of teaching experience relocating from one nontenure-track position to another. The problem with itinerant faculty is they often do not have an investment in the school, have the time to adapt to the culture of the school, or have an opportunity for students to get to know them. Former University of Indiana president Myles Brand (2000) agreed: "Employing part-time faculty members is not inherently bad, but generally they lack the qualifications and standing of regular faculty" (p. 44). Not long after arriving, they have to think about getting a job elsewhere. Graduating students who need letters of recommendation often find that many of their teachers are not at the college anymore, and this situation puts those students at a disadvantage.

Faculty who obtain tenure at a liberal arts college often retire there. There is not much of a job market for senior faculty to move to other liberal arts colleges. The psychology department at UVa does not hire research faculty on nontenure-track contracts, although other universities may be different. Research universities also hire senior faculty. However, there can be a large number of adjunct faculty at research universities, which are similar to the nontenure track faculty at liberal arts colleges. Senior faculty who are highly productive at research universities also have opportunities to move to other, perhaps more prestigious schools. One way for a research university to achieve high status is to hire faculty from other institutions who already have established research reputations (Cuban, 1999).

TEACHING

Given the emphasis of research at universities such as UVa and Michigan compared with liberal arts colleges such as Denison and Furman, differences are reflected in the amount of classes faculty teach at these institutions. At Denison, the standard teaching load is six classes a year, whereas at UVa it is half that—three classes a year. Moreover, at UVa, similar to other research universities, faculty are able to "buy out" of teaching a class with funds from their research grants, thereby reducing the number of classes they teach to two classes a year. This practice rewards faculty who are productive researchers by allowing them to teach fewer classes. The perception that research is more important than teaching is also reinforced by the differences in the average salaries between institutional types, with professors at doctoral institutions earning the most, on the average, followed by comprehensive, baccalaureate, and 2-year institutions, in that order ("What Professors Earn," 2000).

Regardless of how much teaching the faculty does, the public perception often is that it is not enough. Krahenbuhl (1998) suggested, "The popular view is that faculty members are underused in teaching and preoccupied with research" (p. 18). As a result, in recent years, boards of trustees and legislatures have made faculty workload an issue (Plater, 1995). This public relations problem is probably more acute for doctoral institutions where faculty teach the fewest number of classes compared with other academic institutions.

Although research may be the ox that pulls the doctoral institutional cart, this fact does not mean that the faculty give teaching the short shrift. Indeed, several faculty have excellent reputations for attracting majors in psychology and being stimulating in the classroom. However, I miss the informal conversations about pedagogy that blossomed spontaneously at Denison. I suspect this is a common occurrence at other liberal arts colleges. As yet, I do not share much about teaching with my UVa colleagues. For example, my colleagues at James Madison University (JMU) asked me to collaborate with them on the 2000 Eastern Conference of the Teaching of Psychology (ECTOP). It had been previously held at JMU, but we decided to change the venue to UVa to attract more attendees. Besides two speakers I invited from the UVa Psychology Department and myself, no one else from UVa attended. In contrast, several faculty from the psychology department at JMU attended at least 1 day. Although professors from other colleges in the state attended ECTOP, there were also none from the other major research institution in the state—Virginia Tech. This situation is in contrast to Denison, where funds were available from the Provost Office to encourage faculty to attend regional teaching conferences.

Differences in emphasis on research versus teaching are also reflected in how classes are taught at these different institutions. A distinction of baccalaureate colleges is that professors, not graduate teaching assistants (GTAs), teach their classes. GTAs teach some courses at the university level. At UVa, faculty teach all lecture sections, but GTAs teach discussion or lab sections. A select GTA or two may also teach small seminars. At other universities, GTAs may teach some introductory courses.

GTAs are wonderful at doing some of the chores that many of us probably do not enjoy doing (e.g., grading exams and lab reports). GTAs may even conduct review sessions. My research methods class, for example, is divided into several lab sections of no more than 14 students each. A GTA is in charge of each section, but I am in charge of the content of the lab and the guidelines for how assignments are graded. The GTA is responsible for delivery of the content and the grading of the exercises and writing assignments. For the lecture, I write the exams and provide a rubric for the GTA who grades the exams. Large lectures make it difficult to give anything other than multiple-choice exams. My classes, however, are small enough (less than 150) such that I do not have to rely on multiple-choice exams. I am able to write short-answer and essay exams similar to those written at Denison. The lab and lecture grades are combined for the final course grade.

Although I do not have the pleasure of grading my own exams at UVa, I still suffer angst when I make the cutoffs for final grades. With about 25 students, as was the case for a similar course at Denison, it is much easier to find breaks in the successive cutoffs in the distribution of final grades. In a large class, regardless of where the lines are drawn for each grade, there is almost always someone who is just 1 point below the cutoff. If I move the cutoff number to accommodate that person, I encounter yet another person who is 1 point below that cutoff. In a large class, there is higher density in the grade distribution. A 1-point difference between grade levels gives me an unavoidable feeling of arbitrariness.

Classes are invariably larger at research universities than at liberal arts colleges. This differential is probably the most often emphasized distinction in the liberal arts sales pitch. I taught in a large auditorium for the first time at UVa. Most of our undergraduate psychology classes are in lecture halls. Lecture class sizes vary from under 100 to over 300. Fourth-year seminars, however, generally have no more than 25 students. Like many lecture halls, the one to which I was assigned had a floor that sloped up toward the back; I prefer stadium seating in movie theaters, not in my classroom. It was my first teaching experience in which I had to look up toward the back of the room. Additionally, a wireless microphone is available for faculty who do not have the voice to reach the back of the room. Teaching in a large auditorium gave me a feeling of being *on stage* that I did not have before. However, the intimacy of a small class is compensated for by the ego boost of being "the sage on the stage" with a large class.

Teaching larger classes invariably means I do not learn the names of all my students. At Denison I was embarrassed if I forgot the name of a student. At UVa I now get e-mail requests for letters of recommendation from students whose name or face I do not recognize. A student who sits in the back of the lecture hall and does not answer or ask questions can easily fall below my recognition radar. I may know nothing more than the grade a student received; a conference is often required for me to learn who a student is. The opportunity to interact with students in smaller classes, typical for a liberal arts college, is obviously greater; this interaction also makes it much easier to write more informed letters of recommendation for them.

From the student's point of view, both small and large classes have advantages and disadvantages. For the extrovert, smaller classes may be preferred because they offer a greater opportunity to interact with the instructor. Introverted students, however, may not appreciate the additional scrutiny they receive in a small class. They may prefer the comfort of anonymity offered by larger classes. Different kinds of students profit from different kinds of learning environments.

DIVERSITY

Another unforeseen consequence of teaching larger classes became apparent during my first semester at UVa. While shopping at the local supermarket, an African-American woman approached me and introduced herself as one of my students. I did not recognize her. It is not unusual for me to encounter one of my students somewhere on the UVa grounds or while shopping at one of the local stores and not recognize that person. What was disconcerting to me was that at Denison I would always recognize one of my African-American students, past and present, because it was rare to have more than one African-American student in my class. Now I have about a dozen African-American students in my class. However, it is more difficult for private liberal arts schools to attract minority students compared with the larger, public schools. One reason is the difference in cost, but another is that African-American students have a critical mass at many universities. Liberal arts colleges are in a "catch-22" because they do not have the critical mass of students of color necessary to attract additional students of color. I appreciate diversity.

ADVISING

Teaching faculty at UVa are required to advise students just as they are at Denison, but my impression is that the overall competency of advising is lower at UVa. Although the faculty at UVa have more students to advise, on the average, many faculty seem to be unfamiliar with the requirements for graduation or for the major. The advising meetings at UVa are focused primarily on the upcoming academic schedule. There is less time to discuss students' lives and futures and other things that may be affecting students in their university life. As a result, there is an undergraduate committee that is charged with advising students about the requirements for the major. Some faculty try to avoid advising entirely by sending the code needed for registration to their students via e-mail or by posting these codes on their office doors. Both practices are discouraged but difficult to prevent. Moreover, the routine advising period is shorter at UVa compared with what it is at Denison. Rather than the 30-minute schedule customary at Denison for academic advising, the standard at UVa is 15-minute intervals. At Denison, an advising session is longer and covers any topic relevant to the student's life. At

Uva, there is the expectation that students will talk to their academic deans and other support people about personal matters. I do not know how common any of these practices are at other colleges or universities.

GRADUATE STUDENTS

I worry about the opportunities for graduate students to acquire teaching experience. Graduate students complain that they are not trained how to teach at research institutions (Magner, 2000). Politically and pedagogically, it is not good for the university to have GTAs teach too many courses (Brand, 2000). Because GTAs lack the classroom experience, the students may believe that they are not getting the quality of instruction to which they are entitled. Also, many research professors would prefer teaching responsibilities not distract their graduate students from their research duties; time spent teaching is time spent not doing their research. The legacy for research faculty is for their graduate students to go on to universities and establish successful research careers. Teaching experience is not considered a major part of the graduate student's resumé. From conversations I have had with some graduate students who also attended public universities as undergraduates, it is clear that some have no clue what a liberal arts college environment is like. For the brightest graduate students to choose to teach at a liberal arts college would be a disappointment to their faculty mentors. It would be considered a step down compared with going to a research university. Graduate programs are more about training researchers than they are about training teachers.

COMMUNITY

I have found it more difficult to meet faculty outside of my department at UVa compared with Denison. Liberal arts colleges are more like small towns where everybody knows everybody; there simply is less opportunity in the big city. For one, there is no common eating area at UVa; I expect this may be true of other large universities. There are multiple eating places on the university campus and often only one place for faculty to eat on a liberal arts campus. Whereas, at Denison there was a central place to eat. It was easy to find a table in the student union where faculty gathered for coffee in the morning or lunch in the afternoon. There are also school picnics, ice cream socials, an opening convocation, and even dinners at the president's house. These are but a few of the social events where faculty could meet other faculty.

The governance system at liberal arts colleges also fosters opportunities for community. For better or worse, faculty members get to know their colleagues in different departments by participating on committees. At a research university, there is less opportunity to serve on committees with colleagues from other departments.

Over time, I expect to know more people outside of my department, but I do not imagine I will ever feel the level of community common at liberal arts colleges.

PUBLIC VERSUS PRIVATE

Of course another major difference between public and private schools is cost. Private schools cost more than public schools, although most private schools do deep discounting of tuition. The tuition at private colleges and universities is still generally more than the cost for out-of-state students at public universities. The high tuition at private schools can produce a feeling of entitlement on the part of some students. I wish I had a nickel for every student complaint I heard at Denison preceded by the justification, "For the $25,000 (now more than $30,000) my parents are spending (on their tuition plus room and board) we ought to have (something they want the school to provide but do not have which is almost always nonacademic in nature)." I have yet to hear one UVa student whine about being entitled to something because of high tuition.

Although liberal arts colleges tend to be private institutions, universities may be either public or private. State politics can cause more problems for public schools than private schools. For example, a proposal by Governor James S. Gilmore III, of Virginia, would link performance of Virginia universities and colleges to their governmental support (Hebel, 2000). Private schools, on the other hand, are as independent as their endowments allow them to be.

A college or university establishes its national reputation, in part, by the geographical diversity of its students. Public universities have to strike a delicate balance between in-state and out-of-state students because public universities receive state support. For example, occasionally there is political criticism that UVa has too many out-of-state students. Residents of the state expect lower tuition for public colleges and universities than private schools and lower tuition for in-state students than for out-of-state students. Some residents also expect in-state students to have a better chance of being admitted than out-of-state students (Mann, 1997). Compared with public universities, private colleges and universities do not have these problems. A prestigious liberal arts college with a national reputation is one with a low percentage of in-state students. Private colleges and universities enjoy the advantages of greater national diversity, which I think adds to their intellectual and social climate.

COMMENCEMENT

The commencement ceremony at a liberal arts college has a personal touch. There are numerous photo opportunities with faculty, graduates, and family before and after the ceremony. Parents hear their graduate's name read and see him or her shake the hand of the president. The size of the graduating class at most universities makes the intimacy of the liberal arts commencement experience impossible. The challenge is to make the graduation day special for the larger number of graduates and their families. I do not know about other universities, but one solution at UVa is to have separate ceremonies for majors. At the psychology departmental ceremony, the names of majors who are present are read, they are given a psychology diploma, and they shake the hand of the Chair of the Department. The commencement for majors is after the university-wide ceremonies and makes for a longer day compared with a single baccalaureate ceremony. However, the turnout of students and parents suggests that they appreciate it.

SOME FINAL THOUGHTS

Generally, the liberal arts environment is more nurturing of teaching, and good teaching counts more strongly toward promotion and tenure at such institutions (Seldin, 1998). This contention does not mean, however, that teaching is not supported at the university level. At UVa, for example, we have a Teaching Resource Center (TRC), the mission of which is to promote programs for effective teaching strategies, support teaching initiatives, and foster innovative teaching methods. For example, a workshop that the TRC sponsors each summer helps faculty prepare a teaching portfolio. These portfolios are dossiers that documents one's teaching philosophy and evidence of teaching effectiveness. They are subsequently published on departmental Web pages. These workshops are good opportunities for faculty to reflect on their teaching and to brainstorm with other faculty on methods to improve their teaching. Likewise, there are some faculty at liberal arts colleges who really care more about their research than their teaching. This is not surprising if the perception of one liberal arts dean is accurate: "Our professors are paid to teach but are rewarded for their research and publication (Seldin, 1998). A regression analysis of the criteria used by committees to decide pay raises for faculty support this claim (Myers & Waller, 1999).

The two academic environments are different for both teachers and students. I cannot say one is superior to the other from the undergraduate student perspective. It does not seem to make a difference in terms of the chances a student has of getting into a graduate school. A review of the UVa graduate students reveals a diversity of undergraduate academic backgrounds. What is worrisome is that there is scant attention given to teaching during their graduate training. A good graduate student may feel it necessary to do a post-doc for more research experience, but there is no post-doc program devoted to getting more teaching experience. At the least, graduate students need not be made to feel like failures if they pursue careers at liberal arts colleges and not research institutions. Likewise, professors at research schools need institutional support for teaching excellence, not just for being top scholars. Despite what seems like overwhelming advantages listed for the liberal arts college side as a teacher, I still enjoy teaching at a research university. I have enjoyed teaching in both types of academic environments; the differences I have pointed up do not suggest deficiencies.

Notably not included in my discussion are 2-year colleges, where I have no teaching experience. However, 2-year college faculty report the greatest job satisfaction compared with faculty at other academic institutions. A poll conducted by the National Opinion Research Center at the University of Chicago shows that 68.5% of the faculty at 2-year institutions "would 'definitely' pursue an academic career again," compared with 61.3% at private 4-year and 61% at public 4-year schools (Leatherman, 2000). There is an even greater emphasis on teaching at community colleges, and it appears that most who teach there do not regret it.

Recipients of the Teaching Award from the Society for the Teaching of Psychology demonstrate that excellent teaching can thrive in different environments—high schools, community colleges, 4-year colleges, and research universities. Bill and Charles are exemplars of stellar teachers in two of these academic settings.

REFERENCES

What professors earn. (2000, April 14). *The Chronicle of Higher Education, 46,* A21.

Brand, M. (2000, November–December). Changing faculty roles in research universities: Using the pathways strategy. *Change, 32,* 42–45.

Cuban, L. (1999). *How scholars trumped teachers: Change without reform in university curriculum, teaching, and research, 1890–1990.* New York: Teachers College Press.

Diamond, R. M., & Adam, B. E. (Eds.). (1983). Recognizing faculty work: Reward systems for the year 2000. *New Directions for Higher Education #81,* San Francisco: Jossey-Bass.

Girgus, J. S. (1999). Refereeing on different playing fields: Diversity in higher education. *American Psychologist, 54,* 356–357.

Halpern, D. F., & Reich, J. N. (1999). Scholarship in psychology: Conversations about change and constancy. *American Psychologist, 54,* 347–349.

Halpern, D. F., Smothergill, D. W., Allen, M., Baker, S., Baum C., Best, D., Ferrari, J., Geisinger, K F., Gilden, E. R., Hester, M., Keith-Spiegel, P., Kierniesky, N. C., McGovern, T. V., McKeachie, W. J., Prokasy, W. F., Szuchman, L. T., Vasta, R., & Weaver, K. A. (1998). Scholarship in psychology: A paradigm for the twenty-first century. *American Psychologist, 53,* 1292–1297.

Hebel, S. (2000, February 18). Virginia plan offers fiscal stability, but the attached strings worry colleges. *The Chronicle of Higher Education, 46,* A42, A44.

Hutchings, P., & Shulman, L. S. (1999, September–October). The scholarship of teaching: New elaborations, new developments. *Change, 31,* 11–15.

Korn, J. H. (1999). Recognizing teaching as teaching. *American Psychologist, 54,* 362–363.

Krahenbuhl, G. S. (1998, November–December). Faculty work: Integrating responsibilities and institutional needs. *Change, 30,* 18–25.

Leatherman, C. (2000, March 3). Despite their gripes, professors are generally pleased with careers, poll finds. *The Chronicle of Higher Education, 46,* A19.

Magner, D. K. (2000, April 28). Critics urge overhaul of Ph.D. training, but disagree sharply on how to do so. *The Chronicle of Higher Education, 46,* A19.

Mann, J. (1997, April 16). Out-of-state Hoos pay a pretty penny. *The Cavalier Daily,* Opinion page.

Myers, D. G., & Waller, J. E. (1999). Reflections on scholarship from the liberal arts academy. *American Psychologist, 54,* 358–361.

Peterson, R. L., & Trierweiler, S. J. (1999). Scholarship in psychology: The advantages of an expanded vision. *American Psychologist, 54,* 350–355.

Plater, W. M. (1995, May–June). Faculty work: Faculty time in the 21st century. *Change, 27,* 23–33.

Rosenthal, J. T., Cogan, M. L., Marshall, R., Meiland, J. W., Wion, P. K., & Molotsky, I. F. (1994, January-February). The work of faculty: Expectations, priorities, and rewards. *Academe,* pp. 35–48.

Seldin, P. (1998). How colleges evaluate teaching: 1988–1998. *AAHE Bulletin, 50,* 3–7.

20

Lessons From Life:
A Journey in
Lifelong Learning

Mark E. Ware
Debra L. Ponec
Creighton University

Comprehensive descriptions of the process and stages of lifelong learning are available in numerous scholarly books. We examined and evaluated what others had written, but our sense was that such descriptions failed to capture the richness and complexity of what we have experienced. Thus, the contents of this chapter do not model a conventional synthetic approach. We felt challenged to go beyond those more dispassionate accounts and describe our experiences of lifelong learning and extract the commonalities of two professional educators. We wanted to breathe life into the concept of lifelong learning and illustrate how the process twists and turns, involves other people, consists of formal and informal learning, and reflects aspirations or motivations. In this chapter, we expose you to a glimpse of our lives— a slice of our lifelong learning—and we hope you gain some insight from viewing our journey. You might even discover lessons similar to your own experiences.

Insights from our journeys revealed common themes about lifelong learning. Themes included a growth process, varieties of formal and informal education, affective mentors, and motivations that reflect a drive toward achievement or serving others. Our legacy is the discovery that, despite our differences in sex, geography, institutional training, and discipline, we have a high degree of similarity in experiences and views about lifelong learning. We noted only minor dissimilarity in the type of motivation that prompted our aspirations for learning.

Our goal was not to recommend how to inculcate a desire for lifelong learning, but rather suggest strategies for undertaking such a journey of discovery. There are several avenues to consider. First, be honest and open to your experience. Realize that the journey is exploration of the phenomenon *in the moment*, and it changes or is adapted by formal learning and additional life experiences. Although being middle aged and beyond is not a prerequisite, having more extensive life experience might contribute depth to such a venture. Second, be critically reflective. By working independently initially, we found that reflective moments could be enlightening if not difficult to integrate into understanding and self-perceptions. Give yourself an opportunity to grapple with these issues. Third, be willing to share reflections with a peer. Such disclosures proved particularly beneficial to us because it affirmed and clarified our insights. Finally, be optimistic. There were virtually no disadvantages, and in the process we learned a considerable amount about each other and ourselves.

By sharing our journeys, we hope that you gain a personal appreciation for factors contributing to lifelong learning, how it can foster growth—personally and professionally—and how, without such an appreciation, you may be less likely to achieve as high a level of insight and understanding about yourself. Finally, our observations and conclusions may stimulate you to determine how teachers can instill a desire for lifelong learning in students and even colleagues.

To begin our stories, we must set the stage. Currently, we are chairs of different departments in a liberal arts university. We have similar fields of interest—psychology and counseling—but come from vastly different professional experiences. One of us (MW) followed a rather linear path from undergraduate to graduate school and teaching in a university setting. The other (DP) spent more than 15 years in K–12 public and private schools, first as a teacher and then as a school counselor. How did we get to where we are? Separately we describe relevant experiences in our journeys and identify the lessons we learned.

JOURNEY 1 (MW)

Starting in the Present

My effort to grapple with the meaning of lifelong learning begins with the present. For less than 6 months and while writing this chapter, I have been acquiring information and polishing administrative skills for the position of chair of an 11-member department. Information that I could ignore as a faculty member (e.g., procedures and timelines for scheduling classes, conducting evaluations, monitoring and managing an administrative assistant and about two dozen work study students and teaching assistants) now requires diligent attention. Allocating time to talk formally and informally with departmental colleagues has been a necessary and often rewarding part of the job. Service on additional ad hoc committees consumes more hours per week than I could have imagined. There was the serendipity of a one-semester appointment to the university rank and tenure committee. Such an appointment will provide additional insight into the rank and tenure review process, which can be of considerable benefit when advising untenured faculty. Forming an alliance with natural science faculty in planning an addition to and renovation of the current science building has proved particularly strategic for the department and our college while competing with another segment of the university for scarce resources. Oh, and did I mention, I started this job less than 6 months ago.

Some people might think that chairing an academic department within a few years of retirement was the product of disturbed or distorted thinking. I know that some of my psychology colleagues have questioned why I would want to be chair. In the more distant past, I longed to be chair for what may have been the wrong reasons. More recently, I had no desire to relinquish teaching and scholarly activity that kept me in frequent contact with students and generally allowed me to set my own schedule. Why did I agree to serve as chair and what do I hope to accomplish? Answers to those questions may be traced from the fourth grade in a three-room elementary school in a small town in southern Indiana.

Laying the Foundation

During an arithmetic exercise at the chalkboard for fourth-grade students (third- and fifth-grade students were occupied with other tasks), I had a revelation, insight, or epiphany contained in expressions such as "I could do this," "I like this," and "I want to do this." The *this* to which I referred was teaching. I believe that this event was my first experience imagining a career that was not based on fantasy (i.e., cow-boy or fire fighter). At a rudimentary level, I think that I was beginning to make ob-servations and draw inferences about myself that affected the direction of my future.

To what extent the three-room elementary school environment contributed to my interest in teaching, I cannot say for sure. However, some elements of that environment might have contributed. For example, the close, intimate relationship between teacher and students made education a personal experience. Schooling in a setting with younger and older peers fostered a mutual learning environment. Overhearing what one learned in the previous year and what one would learn in the subsequent year reinforced the listener with the familiar and anticipated the new. Seeing one teacher work with multiple grade levels promoted a sense of continuity in education and learning. However, these experiences only partially prepared me for subsequent education.

Expanding Horizons

With high school and college came intellectual and social confrontations. From an elementary school class of maybe a dozen students to classes of 10 to 20 times that number in high school and college, I developed a sense of challenge and isolation. Teachers' expectations and the academic demands of high school and college, along with a greater mass of intellectually gifted and competitive peers, provided novel learning contexts. My memory of teachers was that they knew far more than

I knew or could know and that their critical thinking skills surpassed anything that I could conceive.

A liberal arts college environment, however, was almost emancipating. Exposure to philosophy, fine and performing arts, humanities, and science motivated me to view and interpret the world in ways that had been foreign and mysterious. The intellectual world was strangely comforting and stimulating. Educational institutions were also the contexts in which I developed a variety of social relationships. Learning about boy–girl interactions, adult and peer associations, ethnic relationships—my adolescent and young adult years paralleled the civil rights movement of the 1950s and 1960s—and athletic competitions were integral parts of my coming of age. Learning in and from the classroom paled by comparison to that which occurred outside the classroom.

Finding a niche in psychology was almost serendipity. Initially, I was attracted to chemistry because I associated it with scientific investigation and because of my fantasy for becoming a famous rocket scientist—I entered college in the post-Sputnik era. After a year and a half, I concluded that, although I liked the process of scientific investigation, I found chemistry less than inspiring. My attraction to psychology was the product of (a) a discovery that the psychology department had a laboratory in which students did experiments, and (b) an interest in animal and human behavior. The learning associated with choosing a major consisted of determining what I did not want to do and discovering what I did want to do. I empathize with undergraduate students who also struggle with this two-stage process in making career-related decisions.

Choosing psychology as a major occurred after several false starts. One of those false starts was an extensive exploration and evaluation of teaching natural science and math at the high school level. My first year and a half of college included extensive course work in natural science and math. Once again the inclination or disposition for teaching emerged. However, at an intuitive level, I sensed that working with a high school population of students was not a good fit for me. In retrospect, I realize the wisdom of those feelings. I have neither the patience nor the skills to work with adolescents, but I greatly admire and respect people who do.

From the start as a psychology major, I eschewed the professional practice area. Many years later, while preparing to teach a career development course, I discovered that my personality pattern was more similar to engineers than to psychologists, particularly practice-oriented psychologists. However, with the available choices I had at a small liberal arts college, psychology was the best available match for my personality profile. These experiences taught me that life choices are developmental and often consist of compromises and approximations.

Pursuing Graduate Study

My experiences in graduate school mimicked some of those experiences in high school and college. I found myself surrounded by knowledgeable and intelligent teachers and peers who challenged my cognitive and personal resources. I do not remember a day in graduate school during which I felt caught up with assignments. No class or assignment was easy. To say that graduate school was a challenge is an understatement. Nevertheless, I prevailed and succeeded. I am convinced that my success reflected my determination and persistence far more than my intellectual aptitude or academic skills. I also concluded that beyond a threshold level of cognitive ability, one's work ethic could contribute substantially to academic success. However, the cost may be greater for those nearer that threshold.

Commencing College Teaching

My formal educational experiences were mere preludes to additional relevant learning, starting in the classroom as a college teacher. Learning what one does not know about the content of psychology and life and teaching students with a range of individual differences can be a humbling, yet challenging, encounter. In the early years of teaching, I noted that students varied in their motivation for being in college and for the academic component of the college experience. I came to realize that not all 18-year-olds were equally mature nor equally experienced in life events. I came to modify my goal of having "all students learn all the material" to using a variety of techniques and strategies to help students develop as much as they were capable. The reality is that not all students can achieve the same level of mastery of the same material at the same time.

I also acquired insight regarding the teacher's impact outside the classroom. I think I anticipated that I would advise students about class-related issues and that I would inform them about academic issues (i.e., curricular requirements, strategies for scheduling classes, etc.). I failed to anticipate the role I might play in students' personal lives. Issues such as boyfriend–girlfriend conflicts, family relationships, career decision making, unwanted pregnancies, and death are but a sample of experiences students described. I learned that not only did I not have the answers to their concerns, but too often I did not even know which questions to ask. Sometimes I probably gave advice when I should have listened or listened when I should have given advice. Acquiring the knowledge and resources for making appropriate referrals was probably one of the most beneficial skills for students and me that I acquired.

Experiencing Life Inside and Outside the University

I also failed to anticipate the place of faculty participation in university governance. I am confident that *faculty governance* was a concept that no one in graduate school ever mentioned. For several years, my dedication of time and effort to faculty interests in university governance was a high priority. Honing knowledge about university policy and operations and developing political skills were fundamental to affecting outcomes. The advantages of those experiences have reemerged in my role as chair.

After several years of work in university governance, I became actively involved in organized psychology at the state and national levels. In both venues, I realized considerable satisfaction and enjoyment working with professional educators who held similar values and aspirations for the quality of undergraduate education in psychology.

I discovered that there was a price to pay for investing considerable resources in professional pursuits. Reduced amount of time and energy for spouse, family, and colleagues was one such cost. Would I do it differently if I were able to turn back the clock? Perhaps, sadly, not, because reversing the clock would not change who I was. I have concluded that coping with the consequences of my choices is more adaptive than wishing I had made a different decision.

Might I advise others not to follow my path? I hope that I would not be so presumptuous to advise for or against another's decisions because I will not likely have to live with the consequences of those decisions. I believe that my contribution to persons who ask for my opinion is to help them identify and assess the advantages and disadvantages of various options and to recommend a "Plan B" should "Plan A" fail. Learning about the importance of having a Plan B has been a keen discovery. I have known many individuals who aspired to attend professional or graduate school, to pursue a particular employment option, or to have a manuscript accepted by a specific journal, but they failed to identify alternatives if they did not achieve their initial objective. I have learned to counsel others and direct myself to identify alternatives and set priorities before pursuing an objective. Fear of failure can be minimized because rejection of one objective simply leads to the pursuit of another one.

Returning to the Beginning

I return to the beginning. Why have I agreed to chair a psychology department? Would it be simplistic to say that I have been preparing for this multitask job for a lifetime? Have I reached a stage in my career in which I can contribute more to teaching and learning through administrative roles—teaching teachers so to speak? Has 35 years working with undergraduates in the classroom started to lose its luster? Do the tasks required for this department at this time in its history beckon someone with my disposition, skills, and energy? Is there even some libidinal urge compelling me to undertake this role? Perhaps the answer to several of those questions is yes. Do I have a definitive answer to the question about why I agreed to chair the department? No, but the exploration process has led me to several conclusions described in the next section.

Learning Lessons

This personal journal provides an illustration of what lifelong learning can mean and how it can relate to teaching. Lifelong learning consists of (a) encountering family, teachers, and others who stimulate and reinforce one's curiosity; and

(b) discovering life's lessons that have been successful and enhancing, as well as disappointing and painful. The accumulation of and adaptation to such experiences constitute the core of lifelong learning.

From my perspective, lifelong learning is and should be a developmental and growth process. In the academic environment, it can contribute to teaching effectiveness for teachers and learners because of the attributes of energy, development, skill (personal, interpersonal, management, and technical), direction, commitment, dedication, and sacrifice concentrated on learning for oneself and on teaching and mentoring others.

Are these attributes of lifelong learning inherent or learned? Does one's genes dispose an individual for lifelong learning? Do one's experiences mold a person to pursue lifelong learning? My answer to both questions is an unequivocal yes. My sense is that I have never had a choice to be a lifelong learner. I do not feel as if I could stop learning any more than I could stop breathing. If either happened, I believe I would die.

Have familial, social, and cultural forces shaped me to direct my energies to lifelong learning? I am quite certain they have. I had (a) parents who encouraged me to "do my best," (b) teachers who showed me the challenge and joy of discovering and understanding a more complex view of the world, and (c) events that reinforced my behavior when succeeding at a risky or novel venture.

Supporting and mentoring others in this quest is the current high point of my experience of lifelong learning. By providing empathic listening, thoughtful consideration of alternatives, reinforcement for genuine effort, and evidence of my own experience, I try to promote lifelong learning among colleagues and students. When their efforts do not succeed, I reassess the person and situation and try again—Plan B. What is left or to come, I am not sure, but if it is as stimulating and satisfying as the first part of the journey, I shall not want for enjoyment.

JOURNEY 2 (DP)

Reflecting on the First Year as Chair

Shortly after New Year's Day, I was recuperating from pneumonia when I received a phone call from the chair of my department. She said that she would not return for the spring semester. Her health had deteriorated during the fall, and under doctor's orders she had to take a medical leave and resign her position as chair.

All that I could think of was, "What now?" I had been associate chair of the department for 18 months and had been privy to only some of the chair's responsibilities. Classes were scheduled to begin in 1 week. I had a vision for the department, but had never really imagined that I would be the leader. I had chaired committees, directed a graduate program, and scoffed at the idea of being chair because I was one of the few faculty in the Education Department who lacked administration or supervision credentials.

I decided that, if asked, I would accept the position of acting chair, but I was not ready to make a commitment to be chair. Our department was relatively young. Only two faculty members were tenured, and I was not one of them. I had submitted my dossier for tenure and promotion in the fall, but 2 months would pass before the university would inform me of its decision. Meanwhile, the dean asked, and I accepted the position of acting chair.

One of the first responsibilities that I encountered was to conduct the annual evaluation. How was I to evaluate my colleagues? There were no "Cliffs Notes" for this task. I spoke with previous chairs of the department and some other chairs in the college. There was no right way to evaluate faculty—everyone seemed to have a special twist based on departmental goals and directives.

I was fortunate because our department had developed evaluation guidelines. My task was to use the experiential information I had acquired from chairs and integrate it with the guidelines and my personal beliefs to develop an evaluation format beneficial to individual faculty and the department. I successfully completed the task. Although not all agreed with my final evaluation, we gained understanding from one another about the type of leadership needed for the department.

I was tenured and promoted in March and became chair of the department in April. The associate chair, also new to her position, assumed some of the duties I had as associate chair, and we redesigned the position to fit the department's needs.

During the summer and with short notice, we moved from our office building to permit renovation and returned as classes began in the fall. Two additional faculty members experienced life-threatening illnesses. My term as chair had not been uneventful.

Many things that occurred during my first year never happen to other chairs during an entire career. I tried to remember how I managed things as a student, within the classroom, and with my clients. These life experiences and academic learnings have become the foundation for the many decisions I have made as chair.

My experiences have led me to two understandings about lifelong learning and leadership in an academic department: One leads as a servant to faculty and one mentors faculty members' goals and aspirations to guide them for professional development. Effective leadership consists of service and mentorship. I drew the same conclusion as an effective teacher and counselor. How did I arrive at this conclusion? When did I decide to mentor, serve, and teach?

Deciding to Teach

I do not really remember when I first thought about teaching. However, I remember being part of a study in graduate school when someone asked, "So when did you first decide that you wanted to be a teacher?" I remember pondering that question for a long time. The investigator appeared somewhat impatient with my delay, and I responded, "I think that I always wanted to be teacher, but I can't pinpoint the exact moment when I made the decision." That answer seemed to satisfy the investigator, and we continued with the semistructured interview.

I continued to think about the question for a long time and discovered that many events had impacted my life and led to the decision to teach and the continued decision to teach. I was the proverbial neighborhood kid who held school in the garage after school each night. We had books, tables, chalk trays, and, yes, even assignments. I had no familial models for teaching because no one in my immediate family, including grandparents, was associated with education. I also aided in Sunday school, worked the vacation church school every chance I had, and directed most of the neighborhood plays. I even assisted our Bluebird Troop Director with educational activities on field trips.

I liked these activities. I liked to teach, but most of all I loved to learn about everything. I always had my nose in a book, asked incessant questions, or went to the library to investigate some topic suggested by my teachers. By the time I was in junior high, I was interested in the field of medicine, I enjoyed science, and discovering how things changed.

During my junior high school years, teachers placed me in charge of projects so that other students would learn from my understanding about how a volcano worked, how to dissect a frog, or how embryonic changes occurred within an egg. These experiences raised my self-esteem and led me to believe that I could learn and achieve almost anything.

In addition to school activities, I became part of a mentorship program in which I was paired with a medical technologist and worked with her on Saturdays in a hospital. My interest in medicine continued, and I immersed myself in experiences that fostered growth in that area. I began college with a premed major. However, I changed my mind after one semester when I realized that I did not have the interest, motivation, or grades to pursue that goal.

In retrospect, I seemed destined to pursue education. During high school, I worked with children in Sunday school, vacation bible school, bible camps and retreats, and in the neighborhood. I became interested in children with birth defects and learning problems. I realized that a teacher, as well as a doctor, could help such children.

Pursuing a Path to Teaching and Learning

After switching majors, I felt comfortable in the education department. Everyone seemed to have the same goals, motivation, and desire to assist people in becoming all they could be, striving to achieve their potential. I spent time participating in volunteer activities with children and in field experiences in a school for special needs children. I graduated with a degree in elementary education and special education and immediately went to work. During the first few years, I meshed my idealistic understanding of how teaching should be with organizational constraints and the reality of students in the classroom. We learned much from each other.

Students helped me realize that I needed to learn more, and I returned to school and acquired a master's degree in learning disabilities.

I concluded that I had learned all I needed to know. I knew how to teach these children. I could diagnose, prescribe, implement, and evaluate their academic concerns. My students demonstrated progress. We implemented some cutting edge mentoring programs within our school, and we interacted successfully with the "normal school population."

My fall class roster arrived. The class consisted of a 12-year-old student who attempted suicide 6 weeks before the start of school. There was an 11-year-old student who suffered the death of his mother and moved from his childhood home during the 3 weeks before the start of school. Finally, there was a 10-year-old student who had been sexually abused by her mother's boyfriend for the previous 2 years. These 3 students had severe learning disabilities. I was confident about caring for the academic needs, including dyslexia, auditory or visual processing problems, and language deficits, but I had no idea about how to address the other issues.

I realized that I needed additional information and skills. I explored a counseling program to assist with the immediate need, but I also realized that if I were to assist classrooms full of students with academic issues, perhaps I could assist entire school populations with other issues (academic, peers/social, career/occupational, or crisis) that impeded their education.

After graduating with a master's degree in elementary school counseling, I worked in a private school implementing a comprehensive, developmental guidance and counseling program. Each new twist and turn in my educational path became a lifelong learning lesson for me. I found that when students identified concerns and dealt with those issues proactively, their academic progress usually improved.

However, there were a variety of issues (e.g., abuse, violence, addictions, etc.) about which I thought I needed greater knowledge and expertise. I decided to obtain a doctoral degree that combined counseling with multicultural education, but I found that trying to balance the roles of school counselor and doctoral student was not feasible.

Becoming a Residential Doctoral Student

I inquired about graduate teaching assistantships. I was immediately given a part-time teaching position that paid a meager stipend but offered tuition remission. I mention this experience because I am sure that I would still be an elementary school counselor had I not taken a risk to work for a degree on a part-time basis. Moreover, I was amazed when I realized I had never considered the university setting as a place to teach.

One of my classes, "The Art and Politics of College Teaching," offered great insight into how to maintain sanity while learning to grow in a university setting. Several topics addressed the rudiments of teaching and scholarship; others referred to how to balance personal life issues with professional demands. I have relied on many of the lessons acquired from that class while learning and growing as an adjunct faculty member, as a tenure-track faculty member, and now as a chair.

My dissertation consisted of selecting and interviewing 21 African-American girls while they were in high school. I conducted interviews with them during their junior and senior years, as well as after graduation. One goal was to identify supports for post-high school education. Of the 18 young women, 17 pursued post-high school education.

Arriving at a Destination

My greatest joy came when I found that five of the young women who participated in my dissertation research were attending the university where I had been appointed a faculty member. We began meeting about twice a month, but as their studies and service activities increased, we met less often. Currently, two of the five women are in medical school, one recently graduated with a master's degree in educational leadership, one graduated last spring from law school, and the fifth one is working on a master's degree in nursing.

You could say that we had a great impact on one another. I discovered that personal interaction and experience are required to breathe life or spirit into formal education. Each step of my journey in lifelong learning has led me to believe that formal education was necessary to my progress and performance. However, without the integration of life experiences and the learnings that I gained from others, the progress and performance would be a mere shadow of what it has been.

Learning Lessons

Well, what have I learned in this journey? What do I know about lifelong learning? Each semester, I tell students in my classes that if I have learned something and they have kept me on my toes, then it has been a great class. When I am kept on my toes, I am constantly researching the content and creating innovative presentations for students so that the information may be relevant to their goals and objectives and useful in furthering their understanding of the field of teaching.

One of the ways that students communicate if they have been intellectually stimulated and have learned valuable information is through course evaluations. Last semester, comments on a course evaluation indicated that I had assisted one student who had difficulty communicating her thoughts in writing. We made progress by the end of the semester, but I cannot truly say that her writing had improved significantly. Another student remarked that she found my class stifling, not conducive to all learning styles, and that testing was inappropriate. I believe that the student will opt to select another model for teaching.

How can I assist students with developing greater clarity in their writing? Am I really too set in my ways about evaluation of student outcomes that I ignore some learning styles? How can I keep doing what I am doing that makes students want to be teachers? Course evaluations prompt such questions, combine with the questions about what I have learned throughout my journey, and give rise to an ongoing process of reflection that I practice. After every semester, something changes in me, my courses, and my journey in lifelong learning.

What is lifelong learning for me? It includes a deep and profound curiosity. It is advocated and supported by mentors. It affords the opportunity to serve others. It is reflective.

Curiosity. I am a very curious person. I like to know the why and how of things working, people interacting, and outcomes succeeding. I was a child who always responded to a parent's statement with "Why?" I realize that this behavior must have upset many people, but others responded by mentoring me to learn and achieve at an early age.

Mentoring. Parents, other family members, and teachers have mentored me to learn throughout my life. These mentors have had a profound impact on the direction of my life and what I have achieved. I view mentoring as one of the integral parts of teaching and leadership. Everyone needs the support of another when he or she tries new strategies or options, takes risks, or even chooses a safe road.

Service. People must be at the center or focus of what I am learning for me to view the acquisition as valuable. Learning, simply because of my curiosity, is not enough. Learning must involve people. It must also involve how to assist others with acquiring a motivation or a desire to learn, to acquire a thirst that will promote further learning.

Reflection. Knowledge is acquired and through experience is expanded and reconstructed. Reflection is developmental, an experience in self-examination, is present, past, and future oriented, and offers a sense of knowing-in-action. This process aids my professional decision-making and supports my dedication to becoming a socially responsible teacher and leader.

SUMMARY

At the outset, we said that we would expose you to a glimpse of our lives and identify similarities in our experiences. Common themes in our views of lifelong learning include characterizing lifelong learning as a growth process, contributed to by a variety of formal and informal education, facilitated by the influence of affective mentors, and driven by motivations that reflect a desire for achievement or a desire to serve others. The legacy of such journeys is the discovery that despite our differences in sex, geography, institutional training, and discipline, we experienced a higher degree of similarity than dissimilarity in our views about lifelong learning.

21

Promoting the Teaching of Psychology: A History of NITOP

Douglas A. Bernstein
University of South Florida

Efforts to promote excellence in the teaching of psychology have taken innumerable forms, many of which are outlined in other chapters of this volume. Here, I focus on the one with which I am especially familiar—the psychology teaching conference. By all accounts, conferences on the teaching of psychology have had an enormous intellectual and motivational impact on psychology faculty over the last three decades. The formal presentations, poster sessions, roundtable discussions, and informal interactions that typify psychology teaching conferences have been hailed by thousands of participants as providing (a) vital content updates that inform their lectures, (b) new ideas that improve and enliven their teaching methods, (c) a forum for discussing a wide variety of issues that affect their lives as teachers, and (d) a welcome opportunity to compare notes and blow off steam about the joys and frustrations of teaching.

Today, a number of annual regional conferences on the teaching of psychology serve the interests and needs of faculty in several areas of the United States (Davis & Smith, 1992). These conferences began to appear in 1984, stimulated in part by, and largely modeled after, the National Institute on the Teaching of Psychology (NITOP), which started several years earlier. The story of the regional psychology teaching conferences has been told already (Davis & Smith, 1992). Hence, as one who was involved almost from the beginning, I eagerly accepted the editors' invitation to tell the story of NITOP—how it began, how it grew, how it almost died, and its role in promoting excellence in the teaching of psychology. I hope that this account is of interest to past and future NITOP participants, and that it provides valuable information to those contemplating the creation of new conferences promoting the teaching of psychology.

BEGINNINGS

NITOP convened for the first time on October 9–11, 1978, on the campus of the University of Illinois at Urbana–Champaign (UIUC). It was jointly sponsored by the UIUC psychology department and the University's Division of Conferences

FIG. 21.1. Frank Costin (1914–1998), founder of NITOP, maintained an abiding interest in fostering excellence in the teaching of psychology. As director of the introductory psychology program at UIUC from 1967 to 1984, he carefully selected and trained new instructors for the course and conducted research on the relative value of various methods of classroom instruction. Each year's Frank Costin Memorial Award goes to the NITOP poster presenter whose work offers the best example of promoting quality teaching methods.

and Institutes. Originally called "An Institute on the Teaching of Psychology to Undergraduates," the event was the brainchild of Frank Costin, a member of the Psychology Department at UIUC from 1948 until his death in 1998. Frank's idea for the institute was as simple and straightforward as it was important—namely, to offer psychology faculty an opportunity to get together to hear stimulating talks—and to exchange ideas and advice—about the challenges, frustrations, problems, and pleasures of teaching. The institute has grown significantly in size and scope over the years, but its purpose and goals have remained the same.

The tradition of outstanding speakers at NITOP was established in its first year with an opening address entitled "Teaching Psychology to Undergraduates: Problems, Issues, and Solutions," by Wilbert McKeachie, who was then director of the University of Michigan's Center for the Study of Learning and Teaching. The other five speakers that year included Frank Costin, along with Freda Rebelsky, a winner of the American Psychological Foundation's award for distinguished contribution to teaching; Ralph Turner, a past president of APA's Division 2 (now the Society for the Teaching of Psychology); John Ory, then coordinator of examination services for the University of Illinois' Office of Instructional Resources; and Larry Braskamp, then head of the Measurement and Research Division of that office.

Following McKeachie's opening address, the 128 participants at the 1978 institute were treated to three additional sessions on "Effective Use of Lecture and Discussion," "How to Evaluate Undergraduate Teaching and Learning," and "Innovative Methods and Techniques of Televised Instruction." The registration fee of $48 (approximately $100 in 2001 dollars) covered 11 hours of sessions, four meals, and two social hours. As a cost-cutting measure, the final morning of the institute took place three blocks from the conference hotel in the UIUC psychology building. Room rates at the hotel were $24 for a single, $34 for a double, plus tax (approximately $48 and $68, respectively, in 2001 dollars).

Participants were obviously satisfied with the institute experience. They said so on their evaluation forms, and they must have told their friends because 100 new participants—including some from Mexico and Canada—showed up in Champaign for the second annual institute on October 25–27, 1979. For their $85 registration fee, participants had the same number of meals, but heard twice as many speakers as before, including Richard Solomon, Edward Diener, Lawrence Wrightsman, William Greenough, Evelyn Satinoff, Robert Harper, John Bare, Deborah Holmes, Frank Costin, and Doug Bernstein. The institute's tradition of repeating some sessions was established that year to prevent participants from missing talks that were scheduled concurrently.

The opening talk by John Bare was a general one entitled "Developing Undergraduate Programs in Psychology: Rationale, Approaches, and Issues," but the rest of the second institute focused much more than the first one had on the teaching of specific courses. Panel discussions and workshop sessions dealt with problems and issues in teaching introductory, child/developmental, experimental/learning/quantitative, social/personality, abnormal, and physiological psychology.

As at the first institute, discussions of teaching technology focused on the use of overhead projectors and Betamax videotape players. PowerPoint and the World Wide Web were still some years away.

CHANGES IN LATITUDE, NO CHANGE IN ATTITUDE

From 1978 to 1989, NITOP was organized by staff members of the Division of Conferences and Institutes, a part of the University of Illinois' Office of Continuing Education. The first of these staffers was Carol Holden, a live wire if there ever was one, who had confidence from the beginning that the institute could grow in size and reach a far broader audience if it were moved beyond the confines of Champaign, Illinois. Early in 1980, at a planning session for the third annual institute, Carol got more specific, suggesting that the popularity of the institute might be enhanced by arranging for the next group of outstanding speakers to give their talks in a beautiful, warm place in the dead of winter. The program committee members—Doug Bernstein, Frank Costin, Bill Greenough, and John Fiore—looked out the window at the blowing snow on that February day and said, virtually in unison, "Oh, yes."

It was not long before Carol had found a new home for NITOP—the Caribbean Gulf Hotel (now the Adam's Mark) on Clearwater Beach, Florida, and the third annual institute took place there on January 8–10, 1981. The registration fee for the tropical version of NITOP went up to $185, but each of the nine speakers presented at least two talks, so the number and range of topics covered were greatly expanded. The third annual institute also included four concurrent 90-minute sessions at which participants were given the opportunity to present short papers describing their own research, innovations, or ideas on the teaching of psychology. This opportunity was obviously an important one because the number of excellent proposals submitted for these sessions in subsequent years made it impossible to accommodate all of them. That problem remained a problem until 1987, when, at the ninth annual NITOP, we scheduled our first participant poster sessions. There are now three such sessions at each institute.

To provide even more opportunity for informal interaction, the fifth annual institute, which took place on January 3–5, 1983, included two roundtable discussion sessions—one on helping students get into graduate school and the other on the use of videotapes in the classroom (16 mm film was still the most common audiovisual presentation medium at that time). The format proved popular with participants, and six roundtables were presented at the sixth NITOP on January 4–7, 1983. At the 10th annual institute, at the suggestion of program committee member Robert Hendersen, these roundtables took the form they retain today—a Participant Idea Exchange (PIE). At these PIEs, participants circulate among numerous large dining tables to take part in discussions on topics proposed and led by other participants. Bob originally envisioned these sessions as ice cream socials.

In fact, the first time we offered them, hotel employees circulated among the tables with frozen treats for everyone.

NITOP'S GROWTH—AND GROWING PAINS

The 1983 National Institute on the Teaching of Psychology to Undergraduates saw two notable changes, each brought about by the ever-increasing popularity of the institute and the expanding role of its participants. The first change was the expansion of the sixth annual meeting from 3 to 4 days. We managed to keep the previous year's $240 registration fee the same, but the new, longer format allowed for longer participant paper presentations, more repeated sessions, and a more leisurely pacing of events. It was at the sixth annual meeting, too, that the program committee began to officially recognize participants who make the most outstanding contribution to the institute's goal of promoting excellence in the teaching of psychology. This recognition took the form of the first annual Frank Costin Award, a certificate and a check for $100 given to the participant who gave what the institute program committee and invited speakers judged to be the best short paper that year. This award is still given each year, and its cash value has grown to $250. Sadly, however, in 1998, it had to be renamed the Frank Costin Memorial Award.

Three more growth-related changes appeared at the seventh annual institute. The most noticeable of these changes was the deletion of the words *to Undergraduates* from the institute's name, resulting in its present title—The National Institute on the Teaching of Psychology. The new name reflected the fact that our speakers and audiences were interested—and continue to be interested—in talking about the teaching of psychology at all levels, from secondary school through graduate school. As the years have passed, we have continued to attract participants from high schools, 2-year colleges, 4-year liberal arts colleges, research universities, and graduate colleges.

A second change at the seventh annual institute appeared in efforts to stimulate networking among participants. For the first time, we distributed the names and addresses of all participants and speakers.

Third, the program committee bowed to the wishes expressed by many of our colleagues on the West Coast of the United States that we offer NITOP in their part of the country. Thus, the seventh annual NITOP actually consisted of two institutes—one of which was held on December 27–30, 1984, in San Diego, California, and then repeated just days later, on January 2–5, 1985, at its usual location at Clearwater Beach, Florida. Most of the speakers made the transcontinental trek and gave their presentations at both NITOP-1 and NITOP-2. We expected to accommodate double the number of participants in this way, but that is not what happened. Instead, we attracted about 60 people in Florida and about 40 in California. In short, the same total number of people who normally attended NITOP chose one of the two locations, generating the same income as in the previous year, but at twice the expense to the program committee. In the hope that we simply had failed to get the word out properly, the conference committee—now comprised of Frank Costin, Doug Bernstein, Bob Hendersen, and Sandra Goss Lucas—tried the same two-meeting format again in 1985–1986, for the eighth NITOP. This time, although we tripled our publicity efforts, the outcome on the West Coast was even worse. So few people registered for the San Diego version of the institute that we were forced to cancel it. The five participants who showed up at the conference hotel were treated to dinner by a faculty member from the University of Illinois psychology department who happened to be there at the time. We lost almost $7,400 on the dual-meeting venture and, although people continue to suggest reviving the idea, we never again attempted to take NITOP on the road.

NITOP IN CRISIS

The financial losses incurred by the seventh and eighth annual institutes were absorbed by the Office of Conferences and Institutes and the Psychology Department at the University of Illinois. Both organizations made it clear, however, that further losses could not be tolerated. It was obvious to the program committee that we needed a new approach that would make NITOP self-supporting. The first step toward this new approach became obvious when, during a meeting of the program committee early in 1986, Frank Costin looked at the financial report on the eighth annual NITOP and said, "You know, our losses this year were almost exactly equal to what we paid in speaker expenses." A motion to seek a financial break-even point in future years by eliminating speakers from NITOP died for lack of a second. However, perhaps because I was working on a new textbook project at the time, it occurred to me that we could cut our speaker costs dramatically by inviting publishing companies to provide sponsoring grants to cover some of our speakers' NITOP-related travel expenses. I wrote to about 20 companies (there were a lot more of them then than there are now), and 10 agreed to be sponsors, thus beginning a partnership with publishers of textbooks and educational software that has grown over the years to benefit the publishing companies, NITOP participants, and NITOP. This continuing partnership (10 publishers provided sponsoring grants for NITOP 2002) eventually helped us minimize increases in registration fees while creating an annual surplus sufficient to invite a wide variety of speakers from all over the United States and Canada and from as far away as Britain and South Africa.

As the range and eminence of our cadre of speakers grew, so too did our reputation and the size of our audience—but not immediately. True, in 1987 the ninth annual institute attracted 121 participants, and that year we had a surplus equal to our loss the previous year. To get back to square one, however, we had been forced to charge a registration fee of $295, which in today's dollars is far more than the $395 we charged in 2002.

In short, even with publishers on board to help cut our expenses, we still had not found the right formula for NITOP. Perhaps it was the conference hotel. In 1988, at the 10th annual institute, we moved to a new and better venue—the Tradewinds Hotel and Resort on St. Petersburg Beach, Florida (where it has been held ever since), but this time only 70 of our colleagues paid the $295 fee to attend, and we lost almost $3,000.

For the 11th annual institute in 1989, we formed yet another partnership, this time with the department of psychology at the University of South Florida (USF). Louis Penner, who chaired the USF department at that time, graciously agreed to help us cut expenses by providing audiovisual equipment and several graduate student volunteers to assist in various aspects of conference administration—from registering participants to setting up slide projectors and distributing handouts. Like the partnership with publishers, the relationship with the USF psychology department turned out to be mutually beneficial, and the department, now chaired by Emanuel Donchin, remains a valued NITOP co-sponsor.

Having the support of USF certainly helped, but the institute was still in serious trouble. For the 11th annual institute, we cut the registration fee to $275, recruited more speakers than ever before (18), and sent out a record 20,000 publicity brochures. The result was the largest audience since 1978—127 participants. Unfortunately, because our publicity costs had been so great and the administrative fee we had to pay to the University of Illinois Division of Conferences and Institutes was so high, we still ended up losing $2,500.

At a NITOP program committee meeting in early 1989, a representative of the Conferences and Institutes Division proposed solving our budgetary problem by raising the registration fee to $467 for the 1990 Institute. We knew then it was time to look elsewhere for conference administration. Early in 1990, we invited Joanne Fetzner, a local meeting planner, to take a look at our conference and its budget and make recommendations for improving our financial situation. Joanne told us that we were spending far too much on poorly targeted publicity mailings and conference administration. She also outlined an plan for more focused publicity and more reasonable administrative fees. The program committee found her analysis and suggestions so impressive and compelling that we fired the Conferences and Institutes people and hired Joanne as our new NITOP coordinator. This was, to say the least, an excellent decision. With Joanne's administrative assistance, the program committee for the 12th annual institute in January 1990 was able to offer participants 21 distinguished speakers, a free 6-hour preconference workshop on "Instructional Computing for Novices," and we only had to raise the registration fee to $295. Properly focused publicity mailings describing the 1990 program brought in 240 participants—a response that allowed us to wipe out for good the deficits we had endured for several years. NITOP finally came of age.

NITOP TODAY

NITOP has continued to grow in a number of ways. The most noticeable aspect of this growth has been in the size of each year's audiences. Since 1990, as we increased the number of speakers—there were 31 at NITOP 2002—and added special events such as a dance party, a dinner/discussion evening, a social hour, up to five preconference workshops, and educational software displays, the number of participants steadily rose. When that number reached 400, in 1996, we realized that we could not allow this trend to continue unless we moved to a larger convention facility. Evaluation questionnaires made it clear, however, that participants love the Tradewinds and the atmosphere created by the relatively small audience sizes at NITOP sessions, so the program committee decided to keep the institute where it is and limit its enrollment to 400. For long-time members of the committee, the very idea of considering an enrollment cap was somewhat surreal. In 1989, we could not have imagined that the issue would ever arise, but the fact that it did confirmed that the institute is providing our colleagues with an annual event that is of great value to them.

Throughout the 1990s, the NITOP program committee worked to find new ways to build the institute's reputation for quality and to justify the continuing loyalty of its participants. For example, when the 12th annual institute achieved its unexpected financial success in 1990, we used the surplus it generated to reduce the registration fee for the 13th annual institute in 1991 to $225. That same year we were able to invite 26 speakers and, at Joanne Fetzner's suggestion, to establish the policy of giving each participant a pocket-size edition of the conference program (complete with abstracts of all presentations), along with a three-ring notepad and binder for collecting handouts and personal notes. It was at the 13th institute, too, that we started another tradition: the Laugh at Lunch feature, at which participants tell teaching-related stories involving funny student excuses, weird and/or embarrassing classroom happenings, humorous term papers, and the like.

NEW ALLIANCES, NEW DIRECTIONS

In 1993, the American Psychological Society (APS) recognized the role of NITOP in promoting excellence in the teaching of psychology by becoming an official co-sponsor of the institute. This relationship has grown to include an annual grant to the conference as well as support of a discounted registration fee for APS members. Then in 1997, NITOP formed alliances with the American Psychological Association (APA) and the Society for the Teaching of Psychology (STP). These alliances have taken the form of annual grants from APA in support of NITOP events, including preconference workshops designed for teachers of psychology in the secondary schools, and an annual STP award to an outstanding poster presenter.

The APS found its partnership with NITOP so compatible with its goal of promoting excellence in the teaching of psychology that the APS executive director, Alan Kraut, invited me to organize a 1-day preconference teaching institute at the APS convention in June 1994 in Washington, DC. This mini-NITOP consisted of an opening plenary session, concurrent sessions in the morning and afternoon, a poster session, a participant idea exchange, and a closing plenary session. As in NITOP, the APS Teaching Institute included presentations on teaching methods as well as updates on research that would help faculty improve the content of their lectures in a wide range of psychology courses. The speakers that first year included LaRue Allen, Linda Bartoshuk, Ludy Benjamin, Richard Lerner, James McGaugh, Thomas Oltmanns, Phil Zimbardo, and Elizabeth Loftus. With a line-up like that, it was no wonder that more than 400 participants attended. In fact, the first APS Teaching Institute was so successful that it has become a regular part of the APS annual convention. Over the years, participants at these mini-NITOPs have been treated to talks by distinguished researchers and teachers such as John Cacioppo, Evelyn Satinoff, Martin Seligman, Martin Fishbein, Carol Dweck, Douglas Kenrick, Carole Wade, Saul Kassin, Susan Fiske, Diane Halpern, and Gerald Davison. The tradition of outstanding speakers continued at the 8th annual APS Preconvention Teaching Institute in June 2001, when the APS Teaching Institute program included Robert Sternberg, Susan Whitbourne, Eliot Aronson, Louis Penner, Carol Tavris, and James Kalat.

Another step in the evolution of NITOP came in 1998 when NITOP became a free-standing, nonprofit educational corporation. This independent status gave the program committee additional flexibility in working with its co-sponsors on ways to make NITOP even better and to develop new projects designed to promote the teaching of psychology.

The most recent of these new projects is our annual Summer Institute on the Teaching of Psychology, which took place for the first time in July 2001. The 4-day summer institute is limited to 150 participants, and it is intended for high school teachers seeking to enrich their psychology courses, psychology graduate students preparing for academic jobs, junior faculty just beginning to develop their teaching style, and senior faculty refreshing and honing their teaching skills. The format includes speaker presentations similar to those of the January institute, but summer institute presentations are supplemented by hands-on workshops designed to give participants the opportunity to develop and practice skills relating to lecturing, classroom demonstrations, student–faculty relationship issues, and the like. Thus, participants at the first summer institute heard talks on promoting classroom discussion, creating an effective learning environment, integrating demonstrations into lectures, and teaching social, developmental, and biological psychology. They then took part in follow-up sessions at which the speakers helped them put principles into practice. As with the January NITOP, the summer institute is co-sponsored by the USF Department of Psychology and the APS and has attracted supporting grants from the APA and several textbook publishers.

What does the future hold for NITOP? Some developments are clearly in sight, including printable institute registration forms for NITOP 2002 on the NITOP Web site (www.nitop.org) and, ultimately, online registration. Other developments are harder to foresee, but they are sure to come. The program committee carefully reads the comments and suggestions submitted each year by institute participants. If the past is any guide to the future, these comments and suggestions will continue to shape NITOP. The current program committee members (Joanne Fetzner, Bob Hendersen, Sandy Goss Lucas, Lou Penner, Carole Wade, and I) are grateful for these comments and suggestions, and we thank those of you who have helped us make NITOP what it is today.

The program committee members are particularly gratified by comments from past participants suggesting that NITOP has fulfilled the vision that Frank Costin had for it nearly a quarter century ago—to get teachers of psychology together in a way that benefits their teaching and their lives as teachers. They tell us that attending NITOP helps them renew their enthusiasm for teaching, gives them new ideas for making their classes more interesting and up to date, and offers them fresh perspectives and strategies for dealing with the inevitable student–faculty problems they must face. We are gratified, too, that NITOP's impact has been amplified through its role in helping others who seek to promote the teaching of psychology. NITOP has served as a stimulus and model, not only for the many regional teaching conferences that have developed since 1984, but for the APS' efforts in the realm of teaching.

We are also pleased to have played a role in helping APS forge closer ties to the STP by inviting STP members to introduce speakers at concurrent sessions of the APS Teaching Institute. The APS–STP relationship appears to be blossoming now as STP has begun working with APS to include teaching-specific sessions throughout the APS convention program. All of these developments are good for the teaching of psychology, and the NITOP program committee is proud to have been involved in promoting them. We look forward to finding new ways to improve NITOP and expand its role in promoting excellence in the teaching of psychology.

REFERENCE

Davis, S. F., & Smith, R. A. (1992). Regional conferences for teachers and students of psychology. In A. E. Puente, J. R. Matthews, & C. L. Brewer (Eds.), *Teaching psychology in America: A history* (pp. 311–323). Washington, DC: American Psychological Association.

IV

Teaching With Technology

22

Wiring the Introductory Psychology Course: How Should We Harness the Internet?

Wayne Weiten

Santa Clara University

When Bill McKeachie and Charles Brewer began their teaching careers decades ago, mimeographs, overhead projectors, and reel-to-reel tape recorders constituted innovative educational technology. I doubt that they could have imagined the plethora of technological tools that eventually would be at their disposal. The question of how to integrate technology into the introductory psychology course has been debated for many years. Of course, issues about how to utilize educational technology transcend the introductory course, but in psychology the dialogue on technology has centered around the introductory course. This is because its huge enrollments make it easier for teachers, colleges, and publishers to justify the significant investments of time, effort, and money that are often required to launch new technologies. Hence, I reflect on how we should harness the Internet for our teaching endeavors in introductory psychology.

I hasten to acknowledge that I have no special qualifications for this mission—other than that I teach introductory psychology and have been thinking about it a lot. My fascination with new technology stems in part from my vested interest in old technology—the textbook. As an author of an introductory textbook, I must confess that I have spent the last 10 years wondering if and when new technology might make textbooks an anachronism. This anxiety has led me to spend endless hours contemplating how the textbook should be adapted for the emerging

283

digital landscape and how new technologies can be employed to bolster or supplant some of the educational functions of the traditional textbook. My anxiety initially fostered an interest in how multimedia could be used in teaching introductory psychology, and I ended up devoting 3 years to the creation of a multimedia CD-ROM (Weiten, 1998). Although I remain highly enthusiastic about the educational potential of multimedia, the astonishing growth of the World Wide Web has made it clear that the Internet is the element of new technology that will have the greatest impact on how we teach introductory psychology in the years to come.

The instructional potential of the Internet appears unlimited. The Web is a radical new medium for delivering tutorials and communicating with students that can facilitate global sharing of information and extend instruction beyond the classroom. Ross and Schultz (1999) asserted that the Internet is the most significant technological advance since the Industrial Revolution. Other enthusiasts compare the emergence of the Web to the shift from speech to writing, the invention of the printing press (Paris, 2000), and the widespread distribution of electricity (Brown, 2000). Many education experts assert that the Internet will transform and revolutionize higher education. Some pundits envision the creation of slick, sophisticated, automated instructional packages that will be delivered to students in their homes or workplaces via the Internet, making textbooks, professors, and universities obsolete (Eamon, 1999).

Although the Internet appears to have enormous potential for facilitating teaching and learning, we must avoid the common tendency to assume that technological progress will lead to improved education. New technologies may seem impressive, but they can be utilized in ineffective ways. I suspect that many faculty use the Internet in their teaching not because their educational objectives call for it, but because it is there, it seems ultramodern, and they can. As O'Sullivan (2000) put it, "Too often, the tail wags the dog: pedagogical goals, curricula, and lesson plans are made subservient to technologies" (p. 49). Other critics argue that most online educational initiatives are limited in scope, pedagogically confusing, and not transformative (Baker, Hale, & Gifford, 1997), resulting in "nothing more than digitized textbooks in cyberspace" (Navarro, 2000, pp. 282–283). Given such concerns, I think we need to subject our utilization of the Internet to critical scrutiny or we may waste time, money, and precious educational resources while accomplishing very little.

My focus in this chapter is on how we can integrate the Internet into conventional, on-campus, lecture-oriented introductory psychology classes. Although some of my comments may be relevant to online courses, I have no background in distance education, and I am sure that many of the issues and parameters are quite different. I do not intend to make recommendations about top-flight Web sites, explain how to build a Web site, or discuss arcane technical concepts. Rather, I examine the strategies available for utilizing the Internet in the introductory course and reflect on their potential value in relation to their costs and trade-offs.

For me, the key question boils down to this: Are the time, effort, money, and trade-offs likely to be worth it in terms of enhancing students' learning? Unfortunately, sound experimental research on the efficacy of Internet educational initiatives is scarce (Dillon & Gabbard, 1998). Although my evaluations have been shaped to a great degree by professional literature from both inside and outside psychology, this literature is mostly based on anecdotal evidence. Hence, this is an opinion essay, and as Charles Brewer (1998) once said, the reader should "be forewarned that my ideas may be idiosyncratic and not shared by any other biped in the galaxy" (p. 251).

So how might psychology teachers make use of the Internet in their introductory psychology classes? To get acquainted with the full range of options, I have searched the Internet extensively and read a host of journal articles, book chapters, and conference papers that describe efforts to utilize the Internet in class. The diverse educational practices I encountered basically sort into four broad categories. Teachers have used the Internet (a) for class administration, (b) for student discussion, (c) as an informational resource, and (d) as a medium for instruction.

USING THE INTERNET AS A VEHICLE FOR CLASS ADMINISTRATION

One of the simpler and easier ways to work the Internet into introductory psychology is to use the Web for class administration purposes. This strategy typically entails creating a course home page and posting your syllabus online (Baumgardner, 2000). Many instructors use their course home page to post various announcements throughout the semester about administrative trivia that often eat into class time. Some faculty also permit students to ask questions, seek advice, barter about deadlines, and so forth via e-mail, and a few hold online office hours during which they are available to respond immediately to students' inquiries. Classroom administration over the Web can extend to posting exam results, collecting instructor evaluations from students, and letting students check their current class standing.

Is class administration over the Internet a worthwhile use of time and resources? Well, it is not a bad idea, but there are not any innovations in this category that are going to alter the quality of students' learning outcomes. Insofar as a course home page can reduce class time spent on administrative trivia and make more time available for instruction, who can argue? However, if you posted all your announcements on a course home page, would you feel comfortable assuming that all your students actually visited the site and checked the announcements regularly? I doubt it. I suspect that most teachers will continue to go over everything important in class—repeatedly. So the time savings that can be realized through development of a course home page may be modest.

Moreover, I have doubts about the wisdom of shifting much student–teacher communication to the less personal, asynchronous medium of the Internet. When students have substantive matters to discuss, I am convinced that I can help them more quickly and effectively in person than via e-mail. If there is any complexity at all to their inquiry, I want the opportunity to probe and the dynamic give-and-take of real-time communication. I recognize that office hours do not always provide students with adequate access to teachers and that e-mail can expand this access, but I would hate to see e-mail become the primary medium for teacher–student interaction.

In Internet-mediated class administration, the most intriguing innovation, in my estimation, is the practice of automating the process of students obtaining feedback on their standing in class. For example, Plous (2000) described a program that allows students to enter their identification number and ascertain their cumulative point total on exams and other assignments and to see where their point total falls in the distribution for the class. Besides being available around the clock, this type of feedback is probably more precise and meaningful than the feedback teachers typically provide when they "eyeball" the data in their gradebooks and hazard a rough guess about a student's standing.

However, taken as a whole, the strategies in this category clearly will not revolutionize students' educational experiences. They probably will make school life a little more convenient for students. Is this outcome important enough to justify a great deal of effort on the part of teachers? No, but the effort required to maintain a course home page and Web syllabus has declined dramatically in recent years. A variety of commercial vendors have developed services (such as *WebCT* and *TopClass*) that make it easy for faculty who are not proficient in HTML to create course home pages and Web syllabi. Thus, I anticipate that Web-based class administration will grow.

USING THE INTERNET AS A CONDUIT FOR STUDENT DISCUSSION

A second popular strategy has been to use the Internet as a conduit for student discussion outside of class. Online discussion groups may use a variety of formats, including computer bulletin boards, Usenet newsgroups, asynchronous listserv groups, and chat rooms that allow for real-time interaction (McCormack & Jones, 1998). The instructor usually poses some questions and guides the ensuing discussion, but the goal is the same that we strive for in class—a lively, thought-provoking dialogue about issues related to the course.

Online discussion groups have some interesting strengths. Students can participate in class discussion around the clock, from work or home, when ideas or questions occur to them. No matter how much you encourage in-class discussion, the time available for it is finite, whereas online discussions are open-ended

(Bender, 2000). Faculty who have run online discussions consistently report that they can match real-time discussion in terms of depth, complexity, and vitality (Brown, 1998; Hara, Bonk, & Angeli, 2000; Poftak, 2000). Teachers who have used this approach also report that shy students seem to open up more when they do not have to speak in front of a class (Barnard, 1997). Finally, online discussions leave an archived record of everyone's contributions.

On the negative side, online discussions can feel disjointed to students (Hansen & Gladfelter, 1996), and they require quite a bit of management on the part of teachers (Brown, 1998). You need to set up rules of etiquette and decide how much irrelevant chatting to allow. You need to monitor the discussion to respond to inquiries and make sure that students are not attacking each other or engaging in other offensive behaviors. These responsibilities can consume a great deal of time. One professor reported that he checked his ongoing discussions three to five times daily (Kinney, 1998). Another professor who ran a discussion group for 50 students reported that he typically spent 4 to 5 hours per day monitoring and responding to student discussion (Barnard, 1997).

Online discussion groups are worthwhile innovations if you can afford the time. The large size of most introductory classes and the need to cover a vast range of topics usually make it difficult to allocate adequate class time to discussion. Over the years, I have cut off hundreds of wonderful discussions because of time constraints. Thus, the fact that online discussions are open-ended does not seem like a trivial advantage to me. I am also impressed by the record that an online discussion can leave behind. I usually grade students' contribution to discussion in my classes, but I have often lamented that this process is the most subjective and unreliable component of my grading because it depends much too heavily on my highly fallible memory. The ability to review a complete record of students' contributions to discussion should dramatically improve assessment in this area. Thus, online discussions appear to have rich potential.

USING THE INTERNET AS AN INFORMATIONAL RESOURCE

A third way to utilize the Internet is to require students to venture onto the World Wide Web in search of specific types of information regarding psychological issues. This type of assignment is analogous to a library assignment where students are required to work with an electronic card catalog, *Psychological Abstracts*, *PsycINFO*, and so forth to obtain specified types of information. The variations among Internet assignments that I have seen range from open-ended to precise searches where students have to locate specific resources (Field, 1997; Shackelford, Thompson, & James, 1999; Wann, 1998).

Although this assignment parallels the library assignments that we have been giving for years, we need to bear in mind that the Internet is fundamentally different from a library. The information in an academic library has been heavily screened to maximize its reliability. Academic journals have elaborate peer-review procedures. Most book publishers are discriminating about what they publish, and librarians strive to build high-quality collections. Admittedly, a great deal of questionable information still slips into our libraries, but library collections are the product of multifaceted and multilayered efforts to ensure scholarly quality.

In contrast, information on the Internet is almost completely unregulated because it reflects the uncoordinated activities of millions of people who are free to do as they please. As Wilkinson, Bennett, and Oliver (1997) put it, "When every individual can be his or her own publisher, anyone publishes—including con artists, hucksters, hate mongers, and sociopaths" (p. 53). Moreover, much of the material on the Web is self-promotional or commercial, and the line between advertising and editorial content is often blurred. Yes, there are some rating systems for Web sites, such as Magellan's star ratings system, but these ratings mostly emphasize sites' technological bells and whistles. Good ratings go to sites that are fun, entertaining, and visually attractive, as opposed to reputable, accurate, and up to date.

Given these realities, most advocates of Internet research assignments emphasize that teachers need to include a strong critical thinking component. Students should not simply be instructed to find information relevant to their topics; they should also be asked to evaluate the credibility and quality of the Web sites that they use as resources. To facilitate this process, faculty should provide students with evaluation criteria and guidelines. Fortunately, some excellent resources are available for this purpose. I highly recommend a thorough book by Alexander and Tate (1999), the previously quoted article by Wilkinson et al. (1997), and a concise, student-friendly essay by Hevern (2001).

In my opinion, Internet research assignments should be an essential component of the introductory course. I have been a long-time advocate of elaborate assignments to improve library skills in introductory psychology. I feel even more strongly about the need to teach Internet skills because the immense variations in the accuracy, objectivity, and credibility of information on the Web, coupled with its easy accessibility and relevance to students' lives, create a superb laboratory in which we can help students hone their critical thinking skills.

USING THE INTERNET AS A MEDIUM
FOR INSTRUCTION

The fourth and most sophisticated way to work with the Internet involves delivering some portion of your instruction through the Web. Among other things, faculty have delivered online lectures; posted lecture notes and summaries; distributed supplemental readings; provided chapter outlines and overviews; disseminated extra illustrations and videos; mounted interactive quizzes on course content; developed their own Web-based tutorials, simulations, and demonstrations; and provided links to external Web-based tutorials, simulations, and demonstrations (for exemplary discussions of how selected strategies have been implemented, see Forsyth & Archer, 1997; Maki, Maki, Patterson, & Whittaker, 2000; Simkins, 1999; Stith, 2000).

The diversity of the procedures in this category requires that we look at each specific strategy in turn. Online lectures typically involve PowerPoint-like slides accompanied by the audio of a lecture. One problem with this strategy is that computer-mediated approaches to instruction are usually touted as radically different alternatives to the traditional "sage on the stage" model of teaching, but online lectures simply move the sage to a new stage without altering the conventional model of education. Moreover, this format strips away the nuance, body language, and theatrics that allow some faculty to make their lectures captivating, and there is no opportunity to gaze into students' eyes and gauge whether they are getting it. Delivering lectures over the Internet may be appropriate in distance education, but in conventional classes this strategy does not make sense.

How about the posting of lecture notes? It depends on just how it is done. If the notes are posted after the lecture, they would seem to accomplish little other than providing a crutch for students who do not want to attend class. However, if skeletal outlines of lectures were provided in advance to students, these outlines could be beneficial in helping students assimilate the information covered (Couch, 1997). Obviously, lecture outlines could be composed and distributed without the Internet, but the Web permits a quantum leap in ease of distribution, which makes the whole enterprise practical enough to consider.

Anyone who has put readings on reserve at the library has heard students gripe about how the librarian could not find them, how there were not enough copies, and how the library was not open late enough. Online distribution of supplemental readings would certainly solve these problems and make life more convenient for students. However, copyright restrictions preclude the distribution of many materials over the Internet, and it is often difficult to ascertain exactly what you can and cannot do (Kuechler, 1999). Faculty can consult an article by Washburn (1998) for an overview of copyright law as it relates to the educational use of materials on the Internet.

Another common strategy is to distribute chapter outlines and overviews via the Web. Given the extensive pedagogy incorporated into most contemporary introductory psychology textbooks, these learning aids seem redundant, and this strategy strikes me as a mundane use of the Internet.

Should we use the Internet to distribute diagrams, photos, charts, and the like to students? I am a strong advocate of giving students as much information as possible in a visual format as well as a text format, so I am intrigued. Most teachers make use of many illustrations in their lectures that are not available in the particular text they have adopted. Making these illustrations available via the Internet probably would be beneficial to students. The process of digitizing illustrations is simple and inexpensive. The only significant problem with this approach is that teachers need to be cognizant of copyright restrictions.

We are fortunate to have a substantial number of videos available in psychology that can enrich students' understanding of selected concepts by showing apparatus and phenomena in ways that cannot be duplicated in class. However, few of these videos are in the public domain and available for use over the Internet. Furthermore, digitizing video is a more complex and time-consuming process than digitizing still images. Until broadband connections become more common, the Internet is a less than ideal medium for video transmission.

Online quizzes that are scored immediately can help students assess their mastery of material and identify gaps in their knowledge, and students tend to be enthusiastic about using them. Although free software is available to aid professors in developing their own Web-based quizzes (White & Hammer, 2000), I do not think it makes sense for individual professors to devote much effort to this task in introductory psychology. The publishers of introductory texts are making extensive sets of online quizzes available on their Web sites. Thus, we probably should rely on the commercial publishers for this service.

Web-based tutorials, simulations, and demonstrations clearly have enormous potential. The other materials discussed in this section—online lectures, readings, illustrations, and practice quizzes—represent straightforward extensions of teaching tools that have been around for centuries. The Web may permit more convenient delivery and hence greater usage of these tools, but the nature of the instructional material is fundamentally unchanged. In contrast, computerized tutorials, simulations, and demonstrations can give students unprecedented opportunities for active, experiential learning on their own, at their own pace. In particular, I am excited about the potential of multimedia tutorials, which can combine text, narration, photos, video, music, sound effects, animations, diagrams, and periodic quizzing with prompt feedback. I have witnessed the rich potential of multimedia tutorials in my classes. For example, in recent years, I have been using high-quality multimedia tutorials (from a CD-ROM) that have resulted in a perceptible leap in the quality of students' understanding of selected topics.

However, we do not have to rely on my anecdotal evidence because we are beginning to accumulate an empirical literature on the efficacy of multimedia. The best research, by far, has been conducted by Richard Mayer and his colleagues (Mayer & Anderson, 1991; Mayer & Gallini, 1990; Mayer & Moreno, 1998; Mayer & Sims, 1994). They have embarked on a fascinating program of carefully controlled experiments in which they manipulate specific features of multimedia presentations (such as the presence or absence of background music, sound effects, or narration) on circumscribed topics (such as the formation of lightning or the operation of hydraulic braking systems) to determine their impact on learning outcomes. In these studies, the dependent variables are measures of the ability to transfer learning to the solution of new problems that tap understanding rather than rote memory. Among other things, the results consistently demonstrate that students who receive a verbal explanation coordinated with a visual explanation perform substantially better than students who receive only a verbal explanation of the same concepts. Mayer (1997) was quick to point out that such findings cannot demonstrate that computers are superior to textbooks because the most important consideration is not the medium, but the quality of the specific instructional presentations. Mayer's caveats aside, his body of research provides impressive evidence that multimedia can enhance learning outcomes.

In light of these findings, should individual faculty start allocating lots of their time to the creation of elaborate tutorials and multimedia extravaganzas? For most of us, the wise answer probably is "no." The creation of multimedia tutorials is a complex, daunting, time-consuming task and the learning curve is steep (Taylor, 2000). According to one estimate, it takes 300 hours of work to create each hour of educational multimedia (Eamon, 1999). As Sekuler (1996) noted, "There is little doubt that even the most modest venture into educational multimedia puts demands on faculty time that nonparticipants cannot begin to imagine" (p. 285). Based on my own experience in creating a multimedia CD-ROM, I have to echo these sentiments. That said, there is a small minority among us who apparently have the skills and demeanor to enjoy software development. If you surf the Web looking for psychology tutorials, it does not take long to find excellent materials developed by individual professors. It can be done, but the vast majority of us are probably better off taking advantage of others' work.

Therein lies the beauty of the Internet, which brings us to the final strategy I mentioned—providing links to external Web-based tutorials, simulations, and demonstrations. No question, this is a sensible and potentially beneficial approach to using the Internet in class. A diverse array of tutorials suitable for introductory psychology students can be found on the Web, and the number of useful sites is growing. However, you can also find a host of tutorials on psychological topics that are inappropriate for introductory students, pedagogically unsound, or functionally unreliable. Thus, selectivity is in order. When it comes to recommending Web sites, I operate under the premise that less is more. Rather than mount links to every relevant site, I think it makes more sense to identify just a few high-quality sites that are really pertinent to your learning objectives.

CONCLUSIONS

Can I draw any broad conclusions based on my review of teachers' Internet ventures? Of course, it would not be any fun if I did not. First, we can relax. Our careers are safe. Professors, universities, and even textbooks will not vanish because of the Internet. Second, the Internet will not revolutionize teaching and learning. The vast majority of Web-based instructional initiatives are simple, direct extensions of existing educational practices that will not transform higher education. Some of them appear to have the potential to enhance learning outcomes, but much work remains before this potential is likely to be realized and documented. Third, if we expect the Internet to contribute to improved educational outcomes, teachers, schools, and publishers have to invest a great deal of time, effort, and money to develop innovative pedagogical strategies. Internet-driven progress will not unfold automatically or inevitably, as some people seem to think. Fourth, as we devise new approaches to instruction that depend on the Internet, we need to evaluate their efficacy empirically. Research suggests that both students and teachers are not accurate in judging the effectiveness of educational software programs (Bjork, 1995; Romero, Berger, Healy, & Aberson, 2000). Thus, we cannot rely on intuition as I have had to in this chapter.

REFERENCES

Alexander, J. E., & Tate, M. A. (1999). *Web wisdom: How to evaluate and create information quality on the Web.* Mahwah, NJ: Lawrence Erlbaum Associates.

Baker, W., Hale, T., & Gifford, B. R. (1997). Technology in the classroom: From theory to practice. *Educom Review, 32*(5), 42–50.

Barnard, J. (1997). The World Wide Web and higher education: The promise of virtual universities and online libraries. *Educational Technology, 37*(3), 30–35.

Baumgardner, G. (2000). *Strategies for effective online education.* New York: Forbes.

Bender, T. (2000). Facilitating on-line discussion in an asynchronous format. In R. A. Cole (Ed.), *Issues in Web-based pedagogy: A critical primer* (pp. 381–388). Westport, CT: Greenwood.

Bjork, R. A. (1995). Memory and metamemory considerations in the training of human beings. In J. M. A. P. Shimamura (Ed.), *Metacognition: Knowing about knowing* (pp. 185–205). Cambridge, MA: MIT Press.

Brewer, C. L. (1998). Predictions and retrospections. *Teaching of Psychology, 25,* 250–253.

Brown, B. M. (1998). Digital classrooms: Some myths about developing new educational programs using the Internet. *T H E Journal, 26*(5), 56–59.

Brown, J. S. (2000). Growing up digital: How the Web changes work, education, and the ways people learn. *Change, 32*(2), 11–20.

Couch, J. V. (1997). Using the Internet in instruction: A homepage for statistics. *Psychological Reports, 81,* 999–1003.

Dillon, A., & Gabbard, R. (1998). Hypermedia as an educational technology: A review of the quantitative research literature on learner comprehension, control, and style. *Review of Educational Research, 68,* 322–349.

Eamon, D. B. (1999). Distance education: Has technology become a threat to the academy? *Behavior Research Methods, Instruments, & Computers, 31,* 197–207.

Field, S. E. O. (1997, May). *Introducing the Internet into the classroom: The Netscape scavenger hunt.* Paper presented at the meeting of the American Psychological Society, Washington, DC.

Forsyth, D. R., & Archer, C. R. (1997). Technologically assisted instruction and student mastery, motivation, and matriculation. *Teaching of Psychology, 24,* 207–212.

Hansen, N. E., & Gladfelter, J. (1996). Teaching graduate psychology seminars using electronic mail: Creative distance education. *Teaching of Psychology, 23,* 252–256.

Hara, N., Bonk, C. J., & Angeli, C. (2000). Content analysis of online discussion in an applied educational psychology course. *Instructional Science, 28,* 115–152.

Hevern, V. W. (2001). Evaluating the quality of Web-based resources. In W. Weiten, *Psychology: Themes and variations* (pp. A29–A32). Belmont, CA: Wadsworth.

Kinney, N. E. (1998, January). *The use of Web conferences in psychology courses.* Poster presented at the National Institute on the Teaching of Psychology, St. Petersburg Beach, FL.

Kuechler, M. (1999). Using the Web in the classroom. *Social Science Computer Review, 17,* 144–161.

Maki, R. H., Maki, W. S., Patterson, M., & Whittaker, P. D. (2000). Evaluation of a Web-based introductory psychology course: I. Learning and satisfaction in on-line versus lecture courses. *Behavior Research Methods, Instruments, & Computers, 32,* 230–239.

Mayer, R. E. (1997). Multimedia learning: Are we asking the right questions? *Educational Psychologist, 32,* 1–19.

Mayer, R. E., & Anderson, R. B. (1991). Animations need narrations: An experimental test of a dual-coding hypothesis. *Journal of Educational Psychology, 83,* 484–490.

Mayer, R. E., & Gallini, J. K. (1990). When is an illustration worth ten thousand words? *Journal of Educational Psychology, 82,* 715–726.

Mayer, R. E., & Moreno, R. (1998). A split-attention effect in multimedia learning: Evidence for dual processing systems in working memory. *Journal of Educational Psychology, 90,* 312–320.

Mayer, R. E., & Sims, V. K. (1994). For whom is a picture worth a thousand words? Extensions of a dual-coding theory of multimedia learning. *Journal of Educational Psychology, 86,* 389–401.

McCormack, C., & Jones, D. (1998). *Building a Web-based education system.* New York: Wiley.

Navarro, P. (2000). The promise—and potential pitfalls—of cyberlearning. In R. A. Cole (Ed.), *Issues in Web-based pedagogy: A critical primer* (pp. 281–296). Westport, CT: Greenwood.

O'Sullivan, P. B. (2000). Communication technologies in an educational environment: Lessons from a historical perspective. In R. A. Cole (Ed.), *Issues in Web-based pedagogy: A critical primer* (pp. 49–64). Westport, CT: Greenwood.

Paris, D. C. (2000). Is there a professor in this class? In R. A. Cole (Ed.), *Issues in Web-based pedagogy: A critical primer* (pp. 95–110). Westport, CT: Greenwood.

Plous, S. (2000). Tips on creating and maintaining an educational World Wide Web site. *Teaching of Psychology, 27,* 63–70.

Poftak, A. (2000). Expert advice: Ted Nellen, cyber-renegade. *Technology & Learning, 21*(4), 52–53.

Romero, V. L., Berger, D. E., Healy, M. R., & Aberson, C. L. (2000). Using cognitive learning theory to design effective on-line statistics tutorials. *Behavior Research Methods, Instruments, & Computers, 32,* 246–249.

Ross, J. L., & Schulz, R. A. (1999). Using the World Wide Web to accommodate diverse learning styles. *College Teaching, 47,* 123–129.

Sekuler, R. (1996). Teaching sensory processes with multimedia: One of my teaching assistants is a mouse. *Behavior Research Methods, Instruments, & Computers, 28,* 282–285.

Shackelford, J., Thompson, D. T., & James, M. B. (1999). Teaching strategy and assignment design: Assessing the quality and validity of information via the Web. *Social Science Computer Review, 17,* 196–208.

Simkins, S. P. (1999). Promoting active-student learning using the World Wide Web in economics courses. *Journal of Economic Education, 30,* 278–291.

Stith, B. (2000). Web-enhanced lecture course scores big with students and faculty. *T H E Journal, 27*(8), 20–25.

Taylor, J. S. (2000). Using the World Wide Web in undergraduate geographic education: Potentials and pitfalls. *Journal of Geography, 99,* 11–22.

Wann, P. D. (1998, January). *Teaching students to think critically about Internet research resources.* Poster presented at the National Institute on the Teaching of Psychology, St. Petersburg Beach, FL.

Washburn, D. A. (1998). Copyright law and multimedia- or Internet-based educational applications. *Behavior Research Methods, Instruments, & Computers, 30,* 199–204.

Weiten, W. (1998). *Psyk.Trek: A multimedia introduction to psychology.* Belmont, CA: Wadsworth.

White, R. J., & Hammer, C. A. (2000). Quiz-o-matic: A free Web-based tool for construction of self-scoring on-line quizzes. *Behavior Research Methods, Instruments, & Computers, 32,* 250–253.

Wilkinson, G. L., Bennett, L. T., & Oliver, K. M. (1997). Evaluation criteria and indicators of quality for Internet resources. *Educational Technology, 37*(3), 52–59.

23

Web-Based Resources

Lonnie Yandell
Belmont University

Browser, *FAQ*, *HTML*, *URL*, *Login*, and *surfing the web* are all terms that had no meaning to psychology teachers as little as 10 years ago. Now almost all teachers in higher education (and secondary schools) are intimately aware of them. The World Wide Web (WWW) has seen remarkable growth, even for technology, in the last 10 years. In fact, in 1990, there was no such thing as the WWW. In a few short years, there has been an explosion of Web development in our culture. Business, entertainment, and education have seen unprecedented growth in Web information. A major economic indicator is the amount of sales on the Web. Many TV, magazine, and radio commercials refer to Web sites. The WWW has quickly taken its place in modern man's arsenal of technological tools along with the telephone, the TV, and the computer.

This increased importance is certainly the case for the use of the Web in education. The 2000 National Survey of Information Technology in U.S. Higher Education (Campus Computing Project, 2000) reports that

> three-fifths (59.3 percent) of all college courses now utilize electronic mail, . . . two-fifths (42.7 percent) of college courses now use Web resources as a component of the syllabus, . . . almost a third (30.7 percent) of all college courses have a Web page

[and] ... almost one-fourth (23.0 percent) of all college faculty have a personal Web
page not linked to a specific class or course. (para. 7)

Each of these categories has seen sizable gains since the 1998 survey.

More faculty are choosing to integrate Web resources into their teaching,
and many more teachers are being encouraged to do so. Kenneth C. Green,
founder/director of The Campus Computing Project and a visiting scholar at The
Center for Educational Studies of Claremont Graduate University in Claremont,
California, recently commented, "The Web has been a critical catalyst for many
faculty, offering compelling content and technology that they could bring into their
teaching and scholarly activities" (Campus Computing Project, 2000, para. 8).
However, educators have not easily absorbed this explosion of growth in informational resources. Green continued,

> But there are some real limits. The number of the faculty energized by the Web and
> willing to invest time and effort to infuse technology into their instructional activities,
> often absent adequate institutional support and recognition for their efforts, may begin
> to level off, a least for a little while. (Campus Computing Project, 2000, para 8)

Although there is likely a limit to this growth, it is not likely that the current
popularity of using the Web for teaching will subside.

The purpose of this chapter is to explore some of the major trends in Web-based
psychology resources on the WWW. The Internet includes a number of services that
make use of a variety of access protocols, such as e-mail, FTP, HTTP, Telnet, and
Usenet news. Of these services, the WWW has become popular because it includes
most of the protocols in one convenient package. This feature is especially true for
instruction because the WWW can provide not only hyperlinked text and e-mail,
but also increasingly powerful interactive multimedia.

Reviewing resources for the WWW is an enormous task because the WWW
is in constant flux. There are ever-new technological innovations, such as broader
bandwidths that allow new and more powerful plug-in programs and extend the
capabilities of Web browsers. There is a ceaseless appearance and disappearance of
Web sites with little or no advance notice or way to tell what is permanent or transitory. Commercial interests are exploring and developing ways to exploit the power
of the Web to increase the size of the educational market. The transitory nature
of the Internet will likely improve as the Web evolves. Regardless of whether this
improvement occurs quickly or sometime later, psychology teachers need to be vig-
ilant in keeping up with Web resources if they hope to make effective use of them.

PSYCHOLOGICAL INFORMATION

How has this Web information development affected education and especially the
teaching of psychology? It has arguably provided the single most information-rich
resource ever. In a 1999 book and CD-ROM combination publication, Kardas,

listed almost 1,100 psychology Web sites selected from over 10,000 Web site locations. These Web sites are arranged into 15 traditional psychology topics, much like those found in an introductory psychology textbook.

In addition to topical areas, Kardas (1999) also listed organizations, index sites, tutorial sites, quizzes, how-to-study sites, online periodicals, online texts, software, simulations, online graphics, career-related sites, data sources, and just-for-fun sites. This delineation illustrates the extensiveness of the types of psychological information that can be found on the Web.

For organizational sites, the APA (*http://www.apa.org/*) and APS (*http://www. psychologicalscience.org/*) sites are excellent examples. They contain membership information, student information, services, and links to all aspects of psychology. An example of an organizational site especially oriented to teaching psychology is the Office of Teaching Resources in Psychology [OTRP] Online (*http://www.lemoyne.edu/OTRP/*), which contains teaching and advising materials and provides services to psychology teachers at all levels on behalf of the Society for the Teaching of Psychology (STP).

Index sites, sometimes called *megalists*, are sites that contain long lists of links. They are useful for finding psychology resources. For example, *Psych Web!* (*http://www.psychwww.com/*) by Russ Dewey is one of the older and more comprehensive index sites. The site contains psychology-related information for psychology students and teachers, including lists of brochures and articles related to psychology, commercial psychology-related sites, psychology journals, other psychology megalists, scholarly psychology resources, and self-help sites.

Some of these information sites include tutorials, simulations, demonstrations, and other forms of teaching media. John H. Krantz maintains one of the more comprehensive lists of psychological tutorials and simulations (*http://psych.hanover. edu/Krantz/tutor.html*). Topics range from sensation and perception to clinical psychology and may be primarily text based or may have animations and interactive components. All types of media, such as pictures, graphics, movie clips, and sounds, are included in many of these tutorials, simulations, and demonstrations.

Along with using book- and Web-based lists of teaching resource material on the Web, searching the Web with a search engine is another effective means of exploring this vast information source. There are many search engines available, and different engines retrieve different sites for specific searches. Regardless of the search engine used, they often provide too much information. Fortunately, many helpful informational sites exist that lead you through the steps to conduct an effective online search. Kardas (1999) recommended *Finding Information on the Internet: A TUTORIAL* (*http://www.lib.berkeley.edu/TeachingLib/Guides/Internet/ FindInfo.html*) and *Conducting Research on the Internet* (*http://library.albany.edu/ Internet/research.html*) as good resources to learn about Web searching. Wienbroer (2001) also published a comprehensive guide to search for online materials, including finding, assessing, organizing, and documenting information from online sources.

EVALUATING RESOURCES

The primary challenge to finding and using Web resources as teaching resources is also one of its strengths: the shear volume of information. It is a time-consuming task to evaluate Web sites intelligently, effectively, and efficiently. This dilemma is a problem for both teachers and students.

Search engines, of course, return a list of hyperlinks or names of sites that can be downloaded with the click of a mouse. This hyperlinking feature, which makes the Web so convenient and powerful, can also lead you on time-killing chases that result in gaining little useful information. Students and teachers alike can find themselves *lost* in cyberspace if they do not use search engines and browsers effectively.

A number of Web sites (eg., see *http://www.muohio.edu/~uhlerbd/interneteval. htmlx*) are devoted to exploring the most efficient ways to evaluate Web pages. Browne and Keeley (2001) published a guide to evaluating online resources. They suggested the following eight steps:

1. What argument does the site present?
2. What is the source of the information?
3. How dependable is the authority that provided the information?
4. What does the information mean?
5. What are the primary value assumptions of the site?
6. What is the quality of the evidence?
7. Are there rival causes for the results described on the site?
8. What significant information is omitted?

Practicing critical thinking in evaluating Web sites is essential for the psychology teacher. It is also important to teach these skills to students. Evaluating Web sites is a relevant and practical venue to teach and practice critical thinking.

TEXTBOOK PUBLISHERS' SITES

Textbook publishers provide a variety of professionally developed informational Web sites targeted toward teachers and students. Because such sites are professionally produced and maintained, they provide some assurance that the material they contain is valid. The sites provide selected links, study guides, class and individual activities, and much more materials for the teacher and students.

I reviewed over 50 current textbook and teaching-oriented sites from 11 major textbook publishers. The sites were found using information from a Compendium of Introductory Psychology Texts (*http://www.lemoyne.edu/OTRP/ teachingresources.html#compendium*), which can be found on the Office of Teaching Resources in Psychology [OTRP] Online (*http://www.lemoyne.edu/OTRP/ index.html*). Although there are a small number of publisher sites that require a user id and password, most do not. A few sites allow free access to student resources, but require a password for the faculty resources. User id information is generally obtainable through the publisher's local representative. Many sites have separate sections for students and faculty. The student sites are generally oriented to links and study helps, whereas the faculty sites are more oriented to class activities, quiz materials, and lecture guides.

By far the most popular type of information (75% of the sites) for students are links to other Web psychology content. Most of the sites have various types of activities and exercises that require active input from students. Many make use of browser plugins (small programs that reside on the user's computer) to provide active animation. Online study guides, chapter objectives, and chapter reviews or outlines are available for about 25% of the texts. Most sites contain typical study guide information, including practice tests and links, and provide these aids as Web pages. However, some sites have them as text files that can be downloaded.

About a quarter of these sites provide online practice quizzes with feedback. About the same number have glossaries or lists of key words. Fewer sites have additional study aids such as crossword puzzles, essay questions, popular news items, flash cards, or frequently asked questions (FAQ). A few of the sites contain online articles, readings, or research-related items, such as how to read and evaluate research articles.

Many of the sites provide a means to increase communication among students and faculty. Chat capabilities are most often provided along with messages boards or discussion threads. At the present time, it is not clear that these communication facilitators are widely used.

Resources targeted toward faculty are found on some sites, with PowerPoint or lecture overheads found on nearly one-half of the sites. To a much lessor extent, instructor manuals, lectures, and image banks are also provided. The recent trend of making use of course management software has been adopted by some of the textbook publishers. For example, about one fourth of the sites reviewed have some relation with course management software, such as WebCT (*http://www.webct.com/*) or Blackboard (*http://www.blackboard.com/*). Most of the time, this arrangement means the publisher provides text-specific material to users of the software so it can be easily included in their Web-based courses.

Most textbook publishers who publish multiple introductory texts have established generic sites to support their texts. Sites with names such as *Psych Central*, *Psych Abilities*, *Psycafe*, *The Psychology Place*, and *Faculty Lounge* offer faculty such features as links, study helps, articles, student activities, downloadable PowerPoint lectures, and professional discussions groups and message boards. Some of the sites also provide lecture media such as animations, images, and sounds. Other sites also give support for creating Web pages with HTML tools, Web page hosting, and online syllabus-creation utilities. A few sites claim to provide a comprehensive set of Web-based materials appropriate for an entire online course.

A recent trend, which is likely to continue in the coming years, is for publishers to put entire textbooks, of course with extensive teaching and learning ancillaries, online. These sites not only include all the words, photographs, charts, and graphics found in a typical textbook, but tools that allow students to search, navigate, annotate, highlight, and bookmark their online texts. It is clear that online texts are not about just reading, but involve what Brown (2000) called *information navigation*—or the ability to deal with complex organizations of text, graphics, sounds, and animations.

UNIVERSITY INFORMATION

In the competitive environment of present-day higher education, universities and colleges seek to provide students with evermore convenient ways to enhance their educational experiences. One way to accomplish this goal is to provide services on the Web. Almost all universities and colleges have extensive Web pages. In many universities and colleges, students can look up their grades, buy their textbooks, check school policies and programs, check graduation requirements, and learn more about the faculty and staff at their schools. Often a university Web site will publish policies, such as their IRB information, in detail, including downloadable forms. Other useful information may include advice for successfully applying to graduate school, career advice, and links to other psychology sites the faculty think may be helpful to the student. The 2000 National Survey of Information Technology in U.S. Higher Education (Campus Computing Project, 2000) reveals:

> that more institutions now offer more services on their Web sites: three-fourths (76.1 percent) of the institutions participating in the 2000 Survey provide on-line undergraduate applications, up from 69.5 percent in 1999 and 55.4 percent in 1998. Over four-fifths (83.1 percent) make the course catalog available on on-line, compared to 77.3 percent last year and 65.2 percent in 1998. Course reserves are available on the Web at one-third (35.5 percent) of the institutions in the 2000 survey, up from a fourth in 1999, and 17.9 percent in 1998. And more than half (55.5 percent) of the participants in the 2000 Campus Computing Survey report that their institution currently offers one or more full college courses on-line via the Web, up from 46.5 percent last year. (para. 9)

It is clear that the Web provides students more than just a means to explore course content information.

RESEARCH ON THE WEB

There are many sites relating to the research process in psychology, including online searches of libraries and reference databases, online journals, software, statistical help, writing help, discussion groups, and e-mail. Most universities have online search capabilities for their library holdings. In addition to searching the library's holdings, you can also search selected online databases, such as ProQuest (*http://www.umi.com/proquest/*), which indexes full text of selected journal and magazine articles, or InfoTrac (*http://www.infotrac-college.com/*), a family of information databases that provides an index to and full text of selected journal and magazine articles. One of the most useful databases for psychology teachers and students is PsycINFO (*http://www.apa.org/psycinfo/*). PsycINFO, created and maintained by the APA, is a collection of bibliographic references with abstracts or summaries of journals and other literature in psychology and relevant materials from psychology. The APA maintains a Web site (*http://www.apa.org/psycinfo/training/*) that provides a number of resources for using PsycINFO, both text and online. For example, there are links to search guides that are available for using PsycINFO.

Online journal sites have greatly increased in the last 5 years. Kardas (1999) included a selected list of 10 psychology-related online journals. Most of the online sites list table of contents, instructions for authors, and editorial policies. Some sites provide sample issues, selected articles, or the full text of all articles published. The Web site Links to Psychological Journals (*http://www.wiso.uni-augsburg.de/sozio/hartmann/psycho/journals.html*) is an index of more than 1,600 online psychology and social science journals. It can be used to find out about existing journals in the field, contact publishers, browse tables of contents and abstracts, and locate online articles.

The Web has a great number of informative and useful sites related to research skills, such as using statistics, research design, and writing in an appropriate format. Kardas (1999) listed over 50 sites dealing with research and statistics. Along with general resources in research and statistics, Kardas listed sites in the following categories: experiments, mechanics of research, ethics of research, statistics, visualizing data, and just for fun. Many of the statistics and mechanics of research sites are in a tutorial format. There are also a number of sites where statistical calculations can be completed or software can be downloaded to perform various calculations.

Actual data collection via the Web is also starting to gain acceptance in psychology. For example, McGraw, Tew, and Williams (2001) compared data from classic studies on the Web to typical results reported in textbooks and found remarkable similarities in the results they obtained. They concluded, "existing technology is adequate to permit Web delivery of many cognitive and social psychological experiments" (McGraw et al., 2001, p. 502). They also maintained that "added noise of using participants for different settings and different computers is easily compensated for by the sample sizes achievable with Web delivery" (McGraw et al., 2001, p. 502).

Birnbaum (2001) suggested there are many advantages to using the Web for data collection. The advantages he listed are:

- Freedom from the constraints of testing people at a particular time and place.
- Automatic coding and construction of data files.

- Opportunity to obtain large and heterogeneous samples.
- Possibility to conduct cross-cultural research without the expense of traveling.
- Opportunity to study specific populations of rare conditions.
- Reduced costs of experimental assistants.
- Standardization of experimenter effects. (p. *ix*)

Krantz maintained a list of known psychologically related research projects (*http://psych.hanover.edu/APS/exponnet.html*). This site currently lists over 1,000 currently active research projects. The projects are categorized into 13 categories, including most of the typical subareas of psychology (e.g., social, cognitive, developmental, etc.).

ETHICS, PLAGIARISM, AND PAPER MILLS

For higher education, the power of the Web brings with it two important ethical responsibilities: copyrights and plagiarism. The first issue, copyrights, probably affects the teacher more than the student, whereas the second issue, plagiarism, is perhaps a bigger issue with students.

Copyright carries with it both ethical and legal issues for the instructor. How much of a published piece of work can be used ethically and legally in teaching and professional publications? This topic is complicated for traditional forms of publication, not including the Web. The use of the Web for publishing original information has made this issue even more obscure.

Teachers who publish their own sites must be aware of copyright policies of the material they post. Copyright laws that apply to print material also apply to Web publishing (see Brinson & Radcliffe, 1998). Of course, educators can take advantage of the fair use statue of copyright law, but interpreting this statute is not a simple matter (see *http://www.iupui.edu/~copyinfo/fairuse.html*). Determining whether certain types of media, especially graphics and animations, are subject to fair use can be confusing. Although the practice of hyperlinking to another page on the WWW seems safe from copyright infringement, this interpretation may not always be true (see Templeton, no date).

Another example of the unfortunate aspects of the WWW's power is plagiarism. Although plagiarism has always been a problem in higher education, the widespread use of the computer as a word processor and the ease of downloading editable text makes plagiarism an even greater temptation for students today. There are many related issues to consider, ranging from inappropriate citation practices to paper mills that provide entire term papers for free.

One important means of combating plagiarism is to educate students about plagiarism. When to cite sources and how sources should be quoted are examples of the kinds of information that may prevent some types of plagiarism. Many sites present this information in a convenient and useful manner (e.g., Hinchliffe, 1998; Standler, 2000).

Of course, the most blatant form of student plagiarism is downloading an entire paper and presenting it as one's own. This practice has become so common that a number of sites have popped up with names such as *Free Papers!*, *School Sucks*, *Evil House of Cheat*, and *Buy Your Paper Here!* Some sites charge for downloaded papers, and some rely on advertising for revenue and provide papers for free. One challenge to the teacher is detecting online plagiarism, and there are sites devoted to helping a teacher do just that (see Standler, 2000). Perhaps more important, teachers need to work at helping prevent plagiarism. Some sites present practical ways to prevent online plagiarism, such as discussing plagiarism with students, discussing policies and guidelines, and emphasizing process in writing assignments (see Hinchliffe, 1998).

STRENGTHS AND CHALLENGES OF USING WEB-BASED RESOURCES

What are some of the strengths and challenges to using Web-based resources? There are a number of distinct advantages to finding information on the Web. First and perhaps foremost, the Web provides a great volume of information in a convenient manner. Second, the Web provides a wide variety of information, in terms of both content and format. This true multimedia environment, easily merging text, graphics, sound, and animation, covers topics of interest to almost everyone. Topics range from cooking tips and recipes to home improvement to philosophical treatments of the relation between the mind and body. No other resource comes close to both the breadth and depth of information that the Web provides.

A third important strength of the Web as a resource is its democratic nature. Both students and teachers can equally share the Web as a resource. The Web is continually growing and being updated, and both the instructor and student can benefit. This environment is conducive to self-discovery, self-paced learning, active learning, and collaborative learning.

Brown (2000) suggested three additional positive aspects of the Web. He pointed out that the Web is a "two way push and pull" media (p. 12). Unlike text or even TV, which can only push their content at us, the Web allows us to be both the receiver (pull) and broadcaster (or pusher) of information. He also observed that the Web is the "first media that honors the notion of multiple intelligences— abstract, textual, visual, musical, social and kinesthetic" (Brown, 2000, p. 12). Of course, this situation is a direct result of the Web's power to present information in a variety of media formats. He also suggested that the Web has the distinct advantage of being able to "leverage the small efforts of the many with the large efforts of the few" (Brown, 2000, p. 12). In an informational context, once Web sites are produced (by the few), their worldwide availability can be accessed by the many in a way never before seen.

Although the strengths are impressive and encouraging, there are also some important challenges. The Web often can create tremendous frustration and anxiety as students and teachers struggle with a nonstandard, unregulated, unreliable source that can result in great amounts of wasted time. The novice Web surfer can quickly become overwhelmed with the sheer volume of information. A couple of clicks of hypertext can launch one into the dark abyss of cyberspace, only to become lost and bewildered. Brown (2000) suggested that citizens of the digital age must develop a "new literacy, beyond text and image, . . . one of information navigation" (p. 14). Students and teachers alike must be their "own reference librarian—to know how to navigate through confusing information spaces and feel comfortable doing so" (Brown, 2000, p. 14). Because anyone with a minimum of resources can publish a Web page for all to see, the quality of the information must be carefully considered.

The challenges of using the Web effectively have led some educators to warn of this diabolical maze as being too chaotic, unreliable, and expensive to ever be a positive development in higher education (Morgovsky, 1997). Every indication suggests the Web is here to stay—not only in education, but also in the fabric of our culture. Just as the telephone, TV, and computer have its detractors, so does the Web. For educators to take full advantage of this new and evolving information resource, perhaps we must slowly make a shift in our thinking. There is a need to understand the Web as a new kind of information fabric that contributes to a new learning ecology (Brown, 2000). However we view the Web, it is hard not to concede that it has changed the landscape of education. How we adapt to this change is the real challenge for psychology teachers in the 21st century.

REFERENCES

Birnbaum, M. H. (2001). *Introduction to behavioral research on the Internet.* Upper Saddle River, NJ: Prentice-Hall.

Brinson, J. D., & Radcliffe, M. F. (1998). *An intellectual property law primer for multimedia and Web developers.* Retrieved January 26, 2001 from *http://st2.yahoo.com/lib/laderapress/primer.html.*

Brown, J. S. (2000, March/April). Growing up digital: How the Web changes work, education and the ways people learn. *Change,* pp. 11–20.

Browne, M. N., & Keeley, S. M. (2001). *Psychology on the Internet: Evaluating on-line resources.* Upper Saddle River, NJ: Prentice-Hall.

Campus Computing Project. (2000, October). *The 2000 national survey of information technology in US higher education.* [Summary] Retrieved January 26, 2001 from *http://www.campuscomputing.net/summaries/2000/index.html.*

Hinchliffe, L. (1998, May). *Cut-and-paste plagiarism: Preventing, detecting and tracking on-line plagiarism.* Retrieved January 26, 2001 from *http://alexia.lis.uiuc.edu/~janicke/plagiary.htm.*

Kardas, E. P. (1999). *Psychology resources on the World Wide Web.* New York: Brooks/Cole.

Krantz, John H. (no date). *American Psychological Society: Psychology research on the net.* Retrieved September 9, 2001 from http://psych.hanover.edu/APS/exponnet.html.

McGraw, K. O., Tew, M. D., & Williams, J. E. (2001). The integrity of Web-delivered experiments: Can you trust the data? *Psychological Science, 11,* 502–506.

Morgovsky, J. (1997, June). On the Internet. *Syllabus Magazine,* pp. 47–49.

Standler, R. B. (2000). *Plagiarism in colleges in USA.* Retrieved January 26, 2001 from *http://www.rbs2.com/plag.htm.*

Templeton, B. (no date). *Linking rights.* Retrieved January 26, 2001 from *http://www.templetons.com/brad/linkright.html.*

Wienbroer, D. R. (2001). *Rules of thumb: For on-line research.* New York: McGraw-Hill.

24

Technology in the Classroom: Traditions in Psychology

Bernard C. Beins
*Ithaca College and American
Psychological Association*

Every academic discipline has traditions and characteristics that differentiate it from other philosophies and applications. In the case of psychology, we have a discipline whose philosophies and applications have led to significant contributions to education over the past century.

We have always adopted whatever tools will lead us to greater understanding of behavior and have been less entrained to a single or limited number of domains and methodological options. As such, our disciplinary heritage includes three particularly noteworthy elements that relate to education: a preeminent concentration on learning, an acceptance of a multitude of methodologies, and a creative adoption of diverse technologies.

In this chapter, it would be too easy to treat technology as consisting of *things*, most probably just computers. In reality, although psychologists have been using apparati for teaching for three quarters of a century, we should not limit our discussion to the use of implements. The content of psychology as applied to teaching truly involves the technology of behavior, which extends to the beginning of the 20th century.

EMERGING TRADITIONS

Edward Thorndike (1910) elucidated psychology's link to education early in the history of our discipline, noting that we contribute "to understanding of the means of education . . . because the influence of any . . . means, such as books, maps or apparatus, cannot be usefully studied apart from the human nature which they are to act upon" (pp. 6–7). He saw the connection between the means of teaching and learning and the psychological principles that undergird those behaviors. Interestingly, the technologies of teaching have generally reflected the theoretical orientations that have dominated the different eras. As a result, psychological techniques in teaching have taken quite different forms.

Thorndike was among the first to imply that if we were to alter the process of instruction, the outcome would differ. In what we might now see as a prophetic utterance, he asserted that, if "by a miracle of mechanical ingenuity, a book could be so arranged that only to him who had done what was directed on page one would page two become visible, . . . much that now requires personal instruction could be managed by print" (Thorndike, 1912, p. 165). In other words, learning would be better if students could not flip ahead in a book to find the answers to current questions, but were required to follow a coherent plan of exposure to material to be learned.

This suggestion influenced one of Thorkdike's contemporaries to construct a *teaching machine* that would force a student to learn certain material before advancing to subsequent lessons. Sidney Pressey (1926) developed a typewriter-like device that allowed students to input the answer to a question. If the students answered correctly, a new question appeared. As we might expect, the machine was useful when a student selected an answer from among various choices, but it could not handle answers that a learner had to generate. Nonetheless, we can recognize Pressey's machine as perhaps the first computer in the classroom.

Pressey incorporated the three basic tenets of Thorndike's model of learning as embodied in the laws of exercise, effect, and recency. In one version of Pressey's machine, students had to answer a given question correctly twice (laws of exercise and effect); the last answer that the student saw was the correct one (law of recency). Although educators seem not to have been greatly interested in Pressey's machines (Skinner, 1961) and the Great Depression in the United States forestalled implementation of Pressey's ideas, psychology was in the forefront of educational innovation since early in the century ("A Hypertext History," 2000).

B. F. Skinner (1961) developed an approach similar to Pressey's that was also derived from behavioral theory. In essence, *learning* was defined behaviorally: If a student could provide answers to questions, the student was exhibiting behaviors that defined learning. It would have been (and still is) difficult to characterize complex or abstract learning objectives precisely. Hence, the learning fostered by the teaching machines was limited to those ideas that could be simply captured.

Although the learning might have been limited to relatively simple concepts, Skinner's ideas were not. His 1961 *Scientific American* article outlined most of the complex educational issues we still deal with today: students with poor skills in math and English, teachers with low salaries, poorly developed educational materials, low student motivation, and others.

It is interesting to note that Skinner's and Pressey's teaching/learning machines evolved into paper format in the form of workbooks not unlike the study guides that accompany today's introductory psychology textbooks. In the 1950s and 1960s, students routinely worked through manuals in which major concepts appeared in a sequence of questions that differed from one another only in minor ways. The technology of psychology was thus more important than the technology of mechanical devices.

In Skinner's approach, the questions built up a series of terms and concepts in such a way that a student paying attention was not likely to make a mistake. The reinforcement history of such studying involved only positive reinforcement and virtually no punishment, which Skinner for consistency thought judicious in part because emitting any response (including a wrong answer) increased the probability of its future occurrence. Unfortunately, the exercises were often so boring that there was also considerable negative reinforcement when the learner was able to put the manual away after answering the questions correctly.

The Zeitgeist began to change in the 1960s, with cognitive approaches gaining ascendancy. The influence of behaviorism waned as a new generation of psychologists began to grapple with new psychological questions. Instead of approaching behavior from the perspective of responses to reinforcement contingencies, many psychologists decided that it was more fruitful to regard people as constructing models of the world and then acting on those models.

Approaches to teaching began to reflect the new psychological approach. One of the foremost educators who straddled the behavioral and cognitive eras was Fred Keller. Keller's (1968) Personalized System of Instruction (PSI) encouraged development of mastery in a subject matter through independent work. It had its roots in behaviorism, but anticipated the cognitive movement. The goals and objectives were clearly specified, which is consistent with the behavioral approach. At the same time, students could gain an overview of what they need to learn, which is consistent with a constructivist, cognitive approach.

With the adoption of a cognitivist perspective, many psychologists have encouraged students to take a more active role in becoming educated. Although some teachers have not yet gotten the message, the era of the student as a passive receptacle has ended. No longer do we merely have classes in which words pass from the mouth of the instructor to the pen of the student without need of a brain on either end. The stress has moved from a teacher-centered to a learner-centered environment in which the teacher may guide the students' progress, but in which the students are, in the end, responsible for creating their own learning.

EMERGING TECHNOLOGIES

Naturally, any of the traditions in teaching rely on the technology of teaching (in a psychological sense) combined with the technology of either real nuts and bolts (e.g., Pressey's or Skinner's teaching machines) or electronic nuts and bolts (e.g., the Internet). For the past century, psychologists have considered the apparatus of information delivery and accessibility. In Thorndike's era, the most advanced implement of technology was the book. He suggested that the book was probably more effective for information delivery than all but about 10% of teachers. From the mid-1920s to nearly the present, there was little advancement in the physical technology of information delivery.

Skinner's (1961) teaching machines used further refinements in behavioral theory to induce stronger learning. These newer machines allowed students to construct answers rather than simply select them. In addition, Skinner invoked two new behavioral principles: prompting and fading. Prompting involved constructing the desired response, and fading involved gradually withdrawing stimulus supports. As such, Skinner's advances in teaching machines showed considerable theoretical justification. Skinner's own aptitude for technology undoubtedly helped him refine the teaching machine.

Other psychologists have taken parallel routes to teaching, but they involved variations on the standard lecture format rather than a change in philosophy or basic approach. For example, Gaskill (1933) may have been the first teacher to usher in a form of distance learning. He presented two lectures over the radio; they involved what we would probably now call *sports psychology*. However, radio did not reappear in the literature as a medium of tutelage for 35 years (Snyder, Greer, & Snyder, 1968). Television broadcasts began at the beginning of the 1950s (Barden, 1951), and even the telephone served as a teaching tool (Cutler, McKeachie, & McNeil, 1958).

The advent of the personal computer, or the microcomputer as it was often known, signaled to psychology teachers that new possibilities for instruction loomed on the horizon. (In the early 1980s, some people avoided using the term *personal computer* because such a label suggested nonprofessional use in the minds of their administrators whose purse strings are never easily opened.) Initially, psychologists used computers primarily for teaching statistics and research methods, as reported in the journal *Behavior Research Methods and Instruments* (later renamed *Behavioral Research Methods, Instruments, and Computers [BRMIC]*). This use is not particularly surprising given the dependence on monochromatic, textual presentations in the first computers. As Figure 24.1 shows, the domains that have predominated over the past 30 years in *BRMIC* have been those that lend themselves to text (e.g., statistics, experimental modeling, etc.) and verbal stimuli (e.g., learning and cognition).

As we examine the computer applications here, we see that the innovations have involved the mode of presentation of material rather than the conceptual

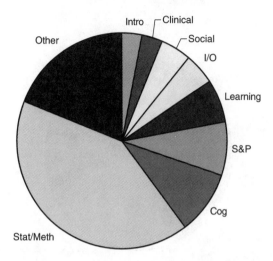

FIG. 24.1. Percentage of journal articles devoted to teaching different content areas in the journal *Behavioral Research Methods, Instruments, and Computers* over the past 30 years. (Note: *Other* refers to applications not devoted to specific courses; e.g. online testing.)

foundations of learning. As always, it is easier to get machines to deal with simple, objective materials than with abstract, complex constructs. The computers might extend the range of exercises to which students were exposed, but they were not conceptually different from Skinner's or Pressey's teaching machines.

Carpenter (1986) reported the results of a survey of computer use in small psychology departments. The numbers are obviously dated now, but his report that the most common use of computers was word processing, and that instructors used computers most frequently in experimental and statistics courses, does not seem at odds with the courses described in *BRMIC* and often quantitative topics, with content areas in the traditional experimental domains.

Another useful source of information about the impact of computers in the classroom is the journal *Teaching of Psychology (ToP)*. I served as the inaugural editor of the journal's section "Computers in Teaching," so I was privileged to communicate directly with people who provided computer innovations in their teaching. In addition, in my review of prior use of computers reported in *ToP* (Beins, 1989), I glimpsed the ongoing development of computer applications in teaching. As seen in Figure 24.2, the array of articles represents different types of applications. There is a much wider variety of courses, and the articles tend to focus more on pedagogy, content, and evaluation and less on the technical aspects that are more visible in *BRMIC*.

Throughout the past decade and a half, there has also been considerable attention paid to discussion of how to use computers most effectively in teaching. This

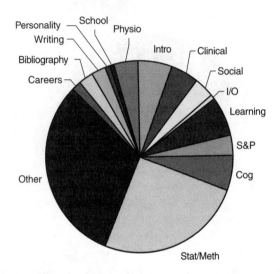

FIG. 24.2. Percentage of journal articles devoted to teaching different content areas in the journal *Teaching of Psychology* since its inception in 1974. (Note: *Other* refers to applications not devoted to specific courses; e.g. online testing.)

situation has been true both for *ToP* and for *BRMIC*. Most of the *Other* category in each graph involves such discussions.

One element that has most certainly changed is that, through the mid-1980s, many users wrote their own software. In general, many of the first nonstatistics programs were fairly simple and accomplished a single purpose—often data collection to simulate an experimental setting.

One of the first expositions of software and computer use in higher education was hosted by Gettysburg College in 1984. This forum, called the "Practicum on Computing in Undergraduate Psychology," drew a large and enthusiastic crowd of psychology teachers who had already adopted computers in their work. The software described was far from sophisticated compared with that available today, but it represented a leap into the future. Surprisingly, even at that early point, software in areas like social and developmental psychology accompanied the staple of experimental programs, although experimental psychology, statistics, and lab simulations dominated.

Porter (1984) created a computer program to reproduce Asch's conformity studies. Confederates initially drew lines on the computer monitor using a game paddle, then participants created their own lines. (These participants showed the same tendency as Asch's participants.) The goal was to have students learn about conformity by experiencing it in an experimental setting. A more complete description appears in Beins and Porter (1989).

Quite a few of the participants received their first exposure to potential uses of the modem at the Gettysburg conference. One of the most memorable aspects of the presentation, however, was that the system did not work. Yet a lot of us were impressed that the presenter's computer on his campus was hard wired to the school's computer. Many of us were not quite sure what this meant, but we believed it would be quicker and more useful than the 312 baud acoustic modems we were using. We probably would have been more impressed if the software had actually worked.

Initially, one of the problems that teachers faced was finding good programs. Into the mid-1980s, users typically wrote their own programs. My own contributions were pretty simple, but were similar to those of other teachers (Beins & Porter, 1985; Porter & Beins, 1985). However, the important point was that they served as a good vehicle for my enthusiasm for teaching. CONDUIT, a loosely knit organization of psychologists interested in pedagogical uses of computers, served as a distributor of many of the individually written programs. It seems that there was a lot of pirating of software at that point, although there was not a lot available to copy. Because most of the authors were teachers who did not expect commercial returns, many psychologists seemed to accept the practice without any bother.

Given the abundance of high-quality software distributed commercially now and the vastly greater number of teachers using them pedagogically, there has been a diminution in the proportion of users with both the knowledge and inclination to write their own code. The software available with virtually every introductory psychology text will probably work well right out of the box—something not guaranteed 20 years ago. For instance, one software package for test creation that I received from a reputable publisher led to an error message indicating that no printed test would be forthcoming. When I called the publisher's technician, he went through the same steps I had. The most help he could provide was to say, "Mine does that, too." Fortunately, we seldom encounter such problems now.

In addition, the widespread availability of programs on CD-ROM has changed the nature of the software we use. Even into the mid-1990s, CD-ROM technology was rarely used in the classroom in part because most machines did not feature CD-ROM drives. Now we can get our introductory psychology texts and study guides on CD-ROM disks, although few of us want them as such because they are not as comfortable as traditional books. Also, prior to some new technological developments, we could not take notes in the margins.

Students can also access aids to studying and learning via the Web. It is typical for publishers to include materials and resources on the Web for students, as well as teaching aids for instructors. Sometimes the Web pages not under the control of the publishers may be removed from the Internet, but as a rule the information is easily accessible when people want it.

HOW HAVE WE INTRODUCED
COMPUTERS INTO THE CLASSROOM?

With the overselling of computers as the answer to all of our educational problems, it might be useful to consider how much computers have actually entered
the classroom in postsecondary education. Many schools now have *smart classrooms* that feature the possibility of integrating true multimedia presentations of
course material. Some of the most highly developed classrooms even include the
technology that allows students to send input to a computer so that class data can
be processed on the spot.

To what extent have we begun using such facilities? The data are sparse, but
anecdotally it seems that such classrooms are in high demand, and many potential
users are closed out of participation. Because of expense, campuses are not likely to
have many of the smartest classrooms, although on a growing number of campuses
most of the classrooms are wired for computer use. In other situations, professors
may use these smart classrooms for traditional lecture-based courses because they
may be among the few large rooms on campus.

Another consideration regarding the integration of multimedia presentations is
that somebody has to create them. Administrators who tout the use of Web-based
presentation, presentation software, and other sophisticated approaches often do
not realize the amount of time required to do it well. We also have to remember
that psychology, as an empirical discipline, is evolving, so canned lectures and
presentations are not going to be very useful.

The introductory psychology class probably changes more slowly than other
offerings, so the potential for canned presentations may be greatest for this course.
Given the popularity of this course, we could probably make a solid argument
that the smart classrooms are most appropriate at this level. Introductory courses
that have laboratory components tend to use computers for data collection and
demonstrations.

After students complete the first course in psychology, they probably encounter
computers within the physical confines of the classroom less often. Still, if we expand our consideration to out-of-class computer use, there is clearly a change in the
way students gather information. For example, it would be an unusual student (or
faculty member) who would prefer using *Psychological Abstracts* over *PsycINFO*.
Computerized databases have revolutionized access to potential sources of information. Combined with the ubiquitous interlibrary loan systems that may involve
faxing requested journal articles, students can get almost immediate responses for
help. One of my most recent and unusual requests was for an article from a 1921
issue of *Chinese Students' Monthly*. I requested it online and received the fax
within a week; the slowest part was probably the trip through interoffice mail.

Naturally, the presence of the WWW has probably had the greatest immediate
impact on students. Students can remotely access course material in a great number of courses in psychology. With commercial software for course organization,

group discussions are easy, students can access their grades, and feedback between teacher and student is without apparent barrier. Over time, it is likely that boundaries of classrooms will become murky and the focus of learning will shift in location. In fact, Ehrmann (2000) believed that the most effective software will not be educationally oriented, but rather will be worldware—software that has been developed for general use, such as the WWW, and that is flexible in use.

The changes in technology are occurring quickly, so it would be hypothetically possible for educational strategies to change as well. In reality, however, it is not surprising that the education revolution in that we have expected for the past 30 years has not arrived. As Ehrmann (2000) suggested, the introduction of mainframe computers, personal computers, videodiscs, e-mail, CD-ROMS, and the Web have all had great potential, but the changes in educational structures have not occurred.

He speculated that "the revolutions have each failed because each time we have been fooled by the technology itself into making the same mistakes" (Ehrmann, 2000, p. 40). One notable problem is that we adopt and then abandon a given approach in favor of its more sophisticated, faster successor. We show remarkably poor memories about the mistakes we have made that lead to less than optimal use of any given technology. Interactive instructional software requires collaboration between experts in content and technology. The extensive time needed for development, debugging, and updating leads to prolonged delays before significant numbers of users adopt the materials. At that point, the next generation of software is set to replace the old.

"Instead of producing revolution, interactive courseware has produced barely a ripple on the stagnant surface of the instructional program. But the courseware mirage still beckons" (Ehrmann, 2000, p. 44). There may be ways to maximize our use of developing technology and software, but they will require coordination among developers and users.

WHAT ARE THE ADVANTAGES
OF COMPUTERS IN EDUCATION?

As the initial psychologists recognized, computers were excellent at the drill-and-practice exercises previous generations encountered in the original teaching machines. The big advantage of both teaching machines and computers was that students could work with the material on their own until they had achieved the degree of mastery that satisfied them. Further, there was no human teacher who would grow frustrated or surly when the students made errors. At first, the computers were probably less useful than the teaching machines because teachers had to be sophisticated technologically as well as content experts. This situation would pose a dilemma in that the newest technology was less useful in important ways than older technology, not an uncommon problem (Ehrmann, 2000).

Current technology has advantages of portability that older teaching machines did not have. Students can now carry with them more information on a 3.5-inch disk or CD-ROM disk than they could reasonably access during a semester or maybe even a lifetime. With the WWW, anyplace there is a computer, students can get relevant information. In this way, computers resemble books, which are highly portable and may have images even if they are static. (The advantage of books is that you do not have to plug them in.) In educational domains, computers are ubiquitous, so the portability of information is clearly an advantage, even if not perfect. The advent of wireless technology may solve some of the portability problems as noted later.

Most graphics-oriented software has a visual appeal that cannot be ignored. To the extent that it captures student attention, the computer image can be riveting and pedagogically useful. Textbook publishers and software developers recognize that they need such images now if only because everybody expects them. Textbooks of the 1960s and before provide a stark contrast, with their paucity or even absence of pictures and everything in black and white.

Probably the greatest advantage of computers in education involves asynchronous communication and access to course information. Interestingly, the technologies that students and faculty use for communication have arisen from sources designed for general usage, not for educational reasons. Although face-to-face office hours are still highly useful for many reasons, electronic messages provide an efficiency that is hard to beat. One person can send an inquiry to another, who can reply either immediately or after checking for relevant information. Multiple trips to an office or a meeting place are no longer required for resolving issues that cannot be settled in a single discussion. Similarly, the abundance of psychological information available on the Web provides students with the ability to get whatever information they want, whenever they want it. The linear model of information transmission is less relevant.

Some instructors maintain that distance education promotes discussion by people who would be less likely to participate in class. At the same time, there may be people who do not participate in computer discussion but would participate in class. For some people, the asynchronous discussions or synchronized chat rooms work well; for other people, they may not. In this area, we have a nice set of empirical questions begging for an answer.

As we can see from this discussion, some of the advantageous features of computers are not necessarily unique to computers. At the same time, computers show many of the positive aspects that no single other implement does.

WHAT ARE THE DISADVANTAGES
OF COMPUTERS IN EDUCATION?

Just as computers show many of the same advantages as other tools, they show some of the same disadvantages. For example, although computer studying does not require a human teacher, the result may be that students do not have access to a person when they need one. For dealing with complex, abstract concepts, students benefit from having a teacher who can guide the process of learning. Further, access to teachers who can generate ideas and create a discussion leads to the development of interest and new ideas. We have to remember that it is more important for students to learn to generate ideas that are novel to them than that the ideas actually be new.

In addition, just as the availability of information is a blessing, it can also be a problem for learners. When there is too much information to evaluate, students may accept anything on the computer as credible. Of course, this problem exists with print sources as well. Students tend to accept printed matter as valid regardless of the source. The important point is to teach critical evaluation skills no matter where we get our information.

Another concern that some people have is that reliance on the Web for information can lead to *cybersloth* (Carnie, 2001). Students at times seem to regard the Web as the most important, if not the sole, source of useful information. If what they seek is not readily available on the Web, students may flounder. This concern is important because it is the student's job to learn how to acquire knowledge. In our professional lives, we use information from the easiest good source. Students are in the position of learning how to find and evaluate sources. Some good sources still exist in paper form; there are also good human resources—often referred to as teachers.

Another perpetual problem in education involves plagiarism. Computers make it easy, with online ordering of papers and ready sources. It used to be that students had to plan ahead to plagiarize; now they can do it virtually immediately. The problem of plagiarism is the issue, not how students manage to do it. For example, once in the precomputer era, I harbored strong suspicions that a particular student of mine had plagiarized on a paper. I believed that he had paid or otherwise induced somebody simply to type a chapter from a book. The relevant clue was a sentence in his paper that read "This will be explored further in Chapter 14." Students adapt their plagiarism to whatever medium is available.

Just as computers may make plagiarism quicker and easier, computers also render the possibility of detecting plagiarism easier. Several sources on the Web have emerged recently to help teachers detect plagiarism. Sometimes when a paper seems too sophisticated for a particular student, a simple database search may locate the original source. One of my students once used an introduction section of a published paper instead of writing one. An easy search through PsycINFO® allowed me to spot the original source quickly.

Will students who have all of the information they need via computer have no need to come to class to learn? Increasingly, teachers are putting their lectures, often in the form of PowerPoint® or other presentation software, on the Web. Does this action mean that students can avoid classes? If students can get books with all the information they need, will they come to class? Ever since Gutenberg invented moveable type, we have had the opportunity for distance learning, but the educational system has worked best when people have congregated. Perhaps coming together is not absolutely essential, but it has been desirable. We will see what the future portends. Here we are asking the question in the context of computer use, but it is a relevant question about educational philosophy regardless of technology.

There are drawbacks to any medium of information exchange. Computers may change the way we approach gathering information, but they are a neutral technology: they are only as good as the uses to which we put them. Their drawbacks differ little in substance from those of other media. If we abandon our critical thinking skills when using computers, we end up with poor knowledge, but the same path also exists for traditional, paper sources.

WILL COMPUTERS FACILITATE NEW
WAYS OF TEACHING?

As we have seen, a discussion of the advantages and disadvantages of computers suggests that they can help our students learn, but that they will not necessarily show advantages or disadvantages that differ from other approaches. A critical question is how we can use computers to facilitate what good teachers have always done, which is to stimulate critical inquiry.

One of the newest approaches, Just in Time Teaching (JiTT), gives a good illustration of how to maximize what the student, teacher, and computer can achieve in combination. JiTT engages students in active learning that has come to dominate the pedagogic landscape, allows the instructor to provide good guidance and feedback, and makes effective use of time in and out of the classroom.

Using this approach, instructors pose questions or offer other preparatory assignments that students have to complete and submit within a few hours of the class meeting. The instructor reads the student responses prior to class and uses their ideas to structure class time. JiTT provides for continuous feedback between faculty and students. In some sense, class time becomes a negotiated period in which students inform the instructor (through their assignments) as to the areas in which they are weakest, and the instructor can comply with the student needs, helping to remedy any problems.

JiTT involves active learning, nearly immediate feedback, and constant updating of information. All of these features are critical elements based on current constructs in cognitive psychology. Once again, theory informs practice. JiTT is certainly possible without computers, but computers make the requisite, quick communication realistically attainable. Students work on their own, outside of class time, spending the period with the instructor either filling in the gaps in their knowledge or extending it.

Those of us who use computers extensively know that, as JiTT suggests, computers do not reduce the amount of work we do. These machines do not save time. In fact, computers often expand our work because of everything they make possible.

WHAT DOES THE FUTURE HOLD?

As the physicist Neils Bohr and the baseball player Yogi Berra both claimed, using nearly identical language, "It's tough to make predictions, especially about the future." Undoubtedly, the future of technology in teaching is going to be as unpredictable as any other feature of life.

We can get fragmentary glimpses of the future. For instance, institutions have expanded their role in distance learning. Fairleigh Dickinson University made the news when it announced that all students would have to take at least one distance learning class a year. It is not clear how cost effective this requirement will be: the time commitment by a faculty member in developing and maintaining such a course will test the system. We also need to assess how students react to distance learning. In the past, the various distance endeavors have not gained widespread acceptance.

Another emerging use of technology is the so-called *wireless campus*. With this technology, students will have access to the world of information from any point on campus. Assuming we can ignore the division between students who can afford portable computers and those students who cannot (a dubious prospect), we might welcome the idea that all students in all classes can access all information at all times. There are technical barriers to overcome, but nothing insurmountable. Interestingly, at Seton Hall University, which requires all students to have laptops, that institution has seen an increase in the demand for computer labs with desktop computers (Olsen, 2000).

As Brothen (1984) suggested nearly two decades ago, "Many children now in elementary school are 'old hands' at using computers and both they and their parents expect computers to play an important role in their elementary, secondary, and college education" (p. 105). We all encounter students for whom computers are still something of a mystery, so perhaps Brothen was a little premature in assessing student expertise. At the same time, he was correct regarding our expectations.

What is missing in many of the descriptions of future uses of technology is the role of people. Information will be accessible, but what will students and teachers do with it? The important work will still take place in the minds of members of the academic community, not in the machines. Transmitting information is not the same as understanding it; accessing information is not the same as knowing how it relates. Although the means and speed of transmission may change, we face the same psychological processes that Pressey, Skinner, Keller, and current cognitively oriented teachers have recognized as important in learning.

In describing the development of his Personalized System of Instruction, Fred Keller (1968) entitled his article "Goodbye, Teacher. . . . " Although the nature of the classroom will certainly continue to change, fortunately for those of us who teach, the demise of the teacher has been postponed.

CONCLUSION

Teachers beginning their careers in the year 2002 experience a vastly different technological environment than teachers of even a decade prior to the turn of the century. The technological tools at hand now would positively astonish one of the paragons of the teaching of psychology, Harry Kirke Wolfe (1858–1918), whose equipment needs differed from ours but who was forced by the University of Nebraska's new chancellor in 1897 to explain his budget deficit of $75.86 (Benjamin, 1991).

Wolfe was by all accounts an excellent and effective teacher. What would explain his and his students' successes? Perhaps it was his zest for teaching, which resulted in his having 35 contact hours with students each week. As Benjamin (1991) noted, "he received no teaching credit for the laboratory hours he added to his courses. Perhaps more amazing was that the students received no credit for the extra laboratory hours either. Yet enrollments in those courses continued to mushroom" (p. 62).

In the end, learning and teaching are both hard work and human-intensive. The course of the successive waves of technological revolutions suggests that it is the creativity of the teacher and the motivation of the student that are the brick and mortar of the path to learning. Technological advances provide the opportunity for greater flexibility in teaching and learning style; these advances support the revolutionary zeal of teachers. When we see the interest and excitement in technology that began in earnest in the 1970s and that recycles with each new wave, perhaps we should conclude that the teachers who remain effective constantly renew themselves. As such, the implements of teaching serve to reinforce the psychology of teaching.

REFERENCES

Barden, J. P. (1951). Instruction by television and home study. *School and Society, 74,* 374–376.

Beins, B. C. (1989). A survey of computer use reported in *Teaching of Psychology*: 1974–1988. *Teaching of Psychology, 16,* 143–145.

Beins, B. C., & Porter, J. W. (1985, October). *Computers I: A "BASIC" introduction.* Invited address to the second Mid-America Conference for Teachers of Psychology, Evansville, IN.

Beins, B. C., & Porter, J. W. (1989). A ratio scale measurement of conformity. *Educational and Psychological Measurement, 14,* 75–80.

Benjamin, Jr., L. T. (1991). *Harry Kirke Wolfe: Pioneer in psychology.* New York & London: University of Nebraska Press.

Brothen, T. (1984). Three computer-assisted laboratory exercises for introductory psychology. *Teaching of Psychology, 11,* 105–107.

Carnie, A. (2001). How to handle cyber-sloth in academe. *The Chronicle of Higher Education, 47,* B14.

Carpenter, D. L. (1986). A survey of microcomputer use in small psychology departments. *Behavioral Research Methods, Instruments, and Computers, 18,* 155–156.

Cutler, R. L., McKeachie, W. J., & McNeil, E. B. (1958). Teaching psychology by telephone. *American Psychologist, 13,* 551–552.

Ehrmann, S. C. (2000). Technology and educational revolution: Ending the cycle of failure. *Liberal Education, 86,* 40–49.

Gaskill, H. V. (1933). Broadcasting versus lecturing in psychology: Preliminary investigation. *Journal of Applied Psychology, 7,* 317–319.

A hypertext history of instructional design. (2000). http://www.coe.uh.edu/courses/cuin6373/idhistory/pressey.html (Retrieved January 18, 2001).

Keller, F. S. (1968). "Good-bye, Teacher...." *Journal of Applied Behavior Analysis, 1,* 78–89.

Olsen, F. (2000, October 13). The wireless revolution. *The Chronicle of Higher Education, 47,* pp. A59–A60, A62.

Porter, J. W. (1984, July). *Conformity research.* Presentation at the Practicum on Computing in Undergraduate Psychology, Gettysburg, PA.

Porter, J. W., & Beins, B. C. (1985, October).*Computers: II. Demonstrations in perception, statistics and experimental psychology.* Invited address to the second Mid-America Conference for Teachers of Psychology, Evansville, IN.

Pressey, S. L. (1926). A simple apparatus which gives tests and scores—and teaches. *School and Society, 23,* 373–376.

Skinner, B. F. (1961). Teaching machines. *Scientific American, 205,* 90–102.

Snyder, W. U., Greer, A. M., & Snyder, J. (1968). An experiment with radio instruction in an introductory psychology course. *Journal of Educational Research, 61,* 291–296.

Thorndike, E. L. (1910). The contribution of psychology to education. *The Journal of Educational Psychology, 1,* 5–12.

Thorndike, E. L. (1912). *Education: A first book.* New York: Macmillan.

25

The Challenges of Distance Education

Kenneth A. Weaver
Emporia State University

It is 2010, and the teacher has just finished the first class meeting with 100 students from 15 different nations. During the class, the teacher sat in a specially equipped, wireless computer chair wearing the fourth generation of i-glasses (see http://www.i-glasses.com/) with built-in microphone, which now integrated all telecommunication services including Internet access, telephone, and cable TV. Through the glasses, the instructor saw the faces of the 100 students as they *entered* the class session. The students were likewise wearing their i-glasses, seeing the other 99 students and the instructor displayed on their monitors. Thanks to iris recognition (Daugman, 2001) software built into the glasses, all students' identities were verified, and attendance was automatically taken.

The instructor began by asking the class to say two or three words and phrases describing their feelings on the first day of class (McKeachie, 1999). As they talked, the voice recognition software built into their microphone transmitted digital text versions of their responses to the teacher's home server, where a semantic recognition program processed the text to eliminate any redundancy. What replaced the other class members' faces in a matter of seconds was a column of terms describing students' current feelings.

The teacher then asked students to respond to the question, "How do you think your teacher feels on the first day of class?" Those responses appeared in a second column on the i-glass screen. The teacher verbally added comments, which the voice recognition software automatically converted to text and entered into a third column. A complete multimedia recording of the entire class session automatically stored on everyone's personal server enabled the class members to review those feelings later in the course.

The class members then engaged in problem posting (McKeachie, 1999) using the questions "What concerns do you have about the course?" and "What are your goals for the course?" The teacher opted to use small groups, so another button press on the console randomly divided the class into groups of 10. Students saw in their i-glasses the nine other students in their group, and a light diode that changed from red to green, meaning that two-way auditory communication with the other nine students was now possible. Each group selected a leader and then answered the two questions. After 5 minutes, the class reconvened, and each group leader presented the concerns and the goals, which were stored on the teacher's personal server for subsequent analysis.

With the introductory procedures completed, the teacher asked a question. The eye-tracking system built into the i-glasses detected the student whom the teacher wanted to answer. The student's light switched from red to green indicating that she was to respond orally. Her answer was partially correct. To provide the complete answer, the teacher initiated footage of a psychologist answering the question during a convention presentation. At the end of the clip, the teacher froze the footage and rotated the camera's perspective from the presenter's front to her back to show the students the audience members. The teacher zoomed in on the face of the well-known researcher who had introduced the speaker. The teacher then opened an outside channel to welcome this researcher, who started a multimedia presentation elaborating the early development of the course content.

The teacher had found the convention footage stored on a Web site belonging to the statistics Intranet section of the Internet. The creation of Intranets occurred during the 2005 iteration by The World Information Organization (WIO) of the United Nations. WIO initiated the iteration over the objections of many people who championed the egalitarianism of all information. However, epidemic information inaccuracy, search engines' continued ineffectiveness prioritizing information, and pornographic Web sites keyed to all known words in all languages (one especially enterprising entrepreneur named all entertainers after different parts of the brain) necessitated WIO's actions to certify information authenticity and importance.

THE CURRENT STATE OF AFFAIRS

Whether this or some other scenario occurs in the next decade, distance education will continue to be an "institution-based, formal education where the learning group is separated geographically, and where interactive telecommunications systems are used to connect learners, resources, and instructors" (Simonson, Smaldino, Albright, & Zvacek, 2000, p. 7). Distance education technologies encompass a variety of telecommunication systems including videotape, two-way audio, two-way audio and one-way video, two-way audio/video, Internet, and Internet with desktop teleconferencing. With convenient "24/7" access to the course, the Internet is the students' medium of choice, but other technologies are still widely used.

A variety of challenges will tax faculty effort, student connectivity, and institutional resources into the future. Will meeting the challenges result in more effective distance learning opportunities? Will teaching and learning be as effective at a distance as they are on campus?

TEACHING AND LEARNING CHALLENGES

The Dance of Mastering Technology

Who is in control, the professor or the technology? In the 20th and early 21st centuries, contemplating the future has meant contrasting visions of technological sophistication (e.g., the film *2001: A Space Odyssey*) with current reality (e.g., see Morgan, 2000). Predicting that hardware and software technology will continue to evolve requires no psychic talent, but does require the distance educator to expend considerable effort while staying abreast of technological innovations for teaching at a distance. Teachers quickly recognize that learning curves exist to master the hardware and software tools of distance education. Learning new hardware and software means additional time and effort.

Consider the ingredients for a course's Web presence. With a scanner, a teacher can easily put any image on the Internet and thus make the image readily accessible to the students. However, the teacher must first know how to use the scanner hardware and software and may need to learn additional editing software (e.g., Adobe Photoshop) to improve the image's quality or convert it to JPEG or some other format.

Although most teachers in higher education currently have little knowledge of how to develop an Internet presence, creating Web pages and downloading photographs from a digital camera are basic skills. What is *hot* is making movies! Digital video cameras and sophisticated editing software put powerful instructional tools into teachers' hands. These increasingly powerful technology tools can improve the quality of Web courses, but also require even greater investment in time and effort from the teacher new to distance education.

Web Course in a Box, Blackboard, and Web CT are software packages for creating Internet courses. In 2000, the company producing Blackboard purchased Web Course in a Box, incorporated its best features into Blackboard, and discontinued Web Course in a Box. Now the users of Web Course in a Box must either work with an unsupported product or invest time and effort learning new software. Without a profitable market, a software company will discontinue its product; without upgrades, the product will lose its utility over time.

Competently learning to use the necessary hardware and software is a daunting task, with no guarantee of product longevity or transfer of learning advantage for the upgrade or new product. Learning new technology is a steady pressure for distance educators, replete with periodic bouts of inadequacy and frustration and competing for time with staying current in their respective fields.

Reading and Writing Reign

A fascinating paradox exists in Web-based education. Although the Internet provides unlimited access to countless images and sounds that the teacher can import into the course, the primary means of communicating between teacher and students is reading the written word. Students cannot raise their hands, visit with the teacher before or after class, drop by during the teacher's office hours, or schedule an appointment. Instead, students must present all questions and concerns in writing, which means that they must write clearly, unambiguously, and to the point. These venerable qualities of writing are especially crucial in Web-based education.

Reading proficiency is as important as writing ability to fully grasp the meaning of the teacher's response. Teacher clarity is essential, as no wrinkled foreheads, pursed lips, squinting eyes, or nodding heads provide the teacher with an indication of understanding or continued confusion. Rather, the e-mailed message is *the* medium of communication. The Brewer (1985, 1997) dictum of "clarity, conciseness, and felicity of expression" must guide the crafting of the teacher's instruction, explanations, and responses.

Discussion boards, chatrooms, and listservs provide opportunities for disseminating students' questions and teachers' answers with the rest of the class members, permitting follow-up questioning. However, some students still prefer private contact to these class discussion simulations. Regardless, clear writing and astute reading are essential for successful learning.

The Straw and the Camel's Back

Keeping abreast of new technology; conceptualizing content in a distance learning format; creating Web pages, chat rooms, listservs, and other supports; and ensuring performance-based assessment require considerable investment of faculty time and resources (see SchWeber, 2000). Carefully and clearly responding to students' questions requires even more time.

Individual correspondence with each student means that enrollment will impact to a much greater degree the time spent teaching the distance course than the on-campus course. An on-campus course enrollment increase from 30 students one semester to 40 students the next semester is manageable. In contrast, an increased enrollment in a Web course from 15 to 20 students may mean an intolerable amount of additional work and misery for the teacher.

Fostering Community, Overcoming Barriers

Although the constant need to express oneself via writing is fatiguing, the resulting individual correspondence with all students produces a rich, detailed understanding of their grasp of the course content (Chamberlin, 2001). Such a "high tech-high touch" approach (Nowak, 1999) produces a faculty–student connectedness typically unmatched in an on-campus course. Paradoxically, this connectedness occurs in the absence of the professor's and students' knowing what each other looks or sounds like (Lawson, 2000).

Distance learners tend to possess attributes that foster community: highly motivated, experienced with distance education, and high achievers (Simonson et al., 2000). However, barriers impairing distance learning include personal insecurity about managing course requirements with family and job demands, lack of technical support, fear of engaging in academic discourse, and perceived lack of feedback (Grubb & Hines, 2000). Grubb and Hines (2000) proposed that offering chatrooms and listservs, creating new online content based on specific students' requests after the course has begun, promptly addressing students' requests for assistance, and encouraging students to commune or "take an active role in keeping the on-line community of learners moving forward and staying productive" (p. 375) are solutions to overcoming these barriers and creating a "virtual community of learners" (p. 367) in the process.

Similarly, Palloff and Pratt (1999) added that generating knowledge through active learning, fostering collaboration within the group and between subgroups that produces meaningful feedback, and taking responsibility for moving the learning process forward promotes community in the cyberclassroom. In addition, Web course instructors can require students to create their own Web pages containing biographical information or compose a paragraph or two about themselves as the first assignment and then post the messages to the course listserv or discussion board for practice.

Teachers' and Students' Hardware Compatibility: Sharing the Right Stuff

The teacher creates an Internet course using a 900 mHz computer with a 17-inch monitor, 128 megabytes of RAM, and a T1 384 kilobyte/second connection to the Internet. By using more sophisticated software and equipment, the teacher can post larger video- and audiofiles on course Web sites.

In contrast, the student using a 250 mHz computer with a 14-inch monitor, 32 megabytes of RAM, and a 56 kilobyte/second modem may need hours instead of minutes to download course content and may not have enough RAM to download a large file in the first place. The experience of the course will be considerably different from these two perspectives. Minimizing the hardware gap requires the students to upgrade their computers more frequently than they might otherwise do so. Teachers also need to be mindful of such disparities and use appropriate software tools that can shrink large files for their students' more efficient file access and management.

Discerning Information Quality: The Good, Bad, and Ugly

Web-based assignments are typical in distance courses. Of what quality is the information on a Web site? Does the Web site have a hidden agenda? Is this Web site attempting to market a product? Is this Web site espousing a point of view? Is it possible to obtain good (i.e., objective) information from a bad (i.e., propagandistic) Web site?

Discerning the quality of information on a Web site cognitively requires evaluation, a competency at the top of Bloom's taxonomy (Bloom, Englehart, Furst, Hill, & Krathwohl, 1956). Exercising such judgment is a difficult task for an experienced teacher but requires substantial training for many students who must first learn to look for and understand indicators of information quality embedded in a Web site before assigning value to that information.

The learner requires discipline in addition to judgment to efficiently navigate through the sheer mass of information the Internet contains. The learner must "resist delving into intriguing links containing seductive information . . . not relevant for the purpose in hand. However, a learner must . . . recognize when newfound information necessitates modifying one's original goals" (Lyman, 1999, p. 114). The teacher must model for the students the strategies to determine how objective and relevant to the instructional goal the information in a Web site is. Student practice with preselected Web sites can foster competence and increase the quality of work.

FINANCIAL CHALLENGES

Funding Technology

Technology is expensive. Providing the money for delivering distance education is an ongoing institutional challenge. Faster processors, more RAM, ethernet connections, larger monitors, equipment for compressing and decompressing video, fiberoptic cable, telephone line upgrades, servers, switches, routers, and bridges are expensive to buy. Network administrators, technicians, and service contracts add considerable maintenance expense. The hardware and support, however, do nothing unless software with expensive site licenses and programmers are present.

A round of upgrades requires considerable investment. Administrators are constantly on the alert for new funding sources to ease the financial burden. A president of a state university is quoted as having lost her appetite when she saw the governor's proposed state budget that discontinued a funding program for technology purchases (Holcomb, 2001).

Funding Support Services

Distance students expect to have the same university resources as on-campus students. Consequently, online libraries, online versions of print journals, online course catalogs, and toll-free dial-in access to universities' servers have proliferated in the past 5 years. These support services require both hardware and software investments and an ongoing institutional commitment to student access.

Paying for Convenience

Colleges and universities typically charge students enrolled in distance courses higher tuition than on-campus courses—in some cases, considerably more. However, from a cost–benefit analysis, commuting students living an hour's drive from campus, for example, can save substantial fuel costs during a semester if the course is presented over the Internet or at a local site. Additionally, eliminating *windshield time* gives students more time as well as more control over their time.

PROGRAM ACCREDITATION CHALLENGES

Accreditation is an integral part of the higher education landscape. Whether from a discipline's organization (e.g., American Psychological Association or American Chemical Society) or other professional group (e.g., National Council for the Accreditation of Teacher Education), accreditation ensures a baseline of program quality across institutions. Accrediting organizations have honed their procedures on a campus model of predominantly on-campus courses with, at best, a modicum of distance courses. How do Web-based degree programs fare in this environment?

Regional accrediting associations (e.g., North Central Association Commission on Institutions of Higher Education) have agreed on guidelines for accrediting distance-based programs (see http://www.ncacihe.org/resources/guidelines/gdistance.html), but others have not created separate guidelines. In addition, some accreditation requirements, such as requiring residency requirements, are antithetical to distance education. Accreditation is a potential flashpoint of controversy for degree programs that are delivered entirely at a distance.

COPYRIGHT CHALLENGES

Journal articles, newspaper and magazine clippings, video- and audiotapes, and CD-ROMs are common instructional aids in the on-campus course. The fair use of these copyrighted works for teaching is not an infringement of their copyright (note that the term *fair use* is determined by four criteria; see Simonson et al., 2000). However, fair use does not readily apply to distance education courses.

"Courses offered via the World Wide Web provide excellent opportunities for copyright abuse" (Simonson et al., 2000, p. 105). Whether the distance course is Web- or video-based, copyright law forbids transmitting a videotape, audiotape, photographs, graphics, or digitized images (e.g., those images produced by a scanner) for presentation. Forwarding a message to another listserv without the author's permission may also violate copyright. The distance education section of the University System of Georgia's (1997) online *Regents Guide to Understanding Copyright and Educational Fair Use* addresses some concerns. However, the issues are complex. So far, no current laws exist updating the usage of copyrighted material in distance education courses. Without clearer guidelines, faculty must err on the side of caution by seeking permission, obtaining a legal ruling, or deciding not to transmit the material.

INSTITUTIONAL CHALLENGES

A Look at the Research

Simonson et al. (2000) concluded from their review of the literature that distant and local learners achieved at the same level, had similar perceptions about the effectiveness of their instructional experiences, had their learning styles similarly provided for, and were equivalently unaffected by the amount of interaction they had in the course. Although Simonson et al. pointed to a number of methodological concerns and the lack of research in key areas, they concluded that "distance education is an effective method for teaching and learning" (p. 64). Their conclusion is consistent with the student evaluations and other assessment data obtained on distance education courses taught at Emporia State University (see http://academic.emporia.edu for a course list by semester).

The Credit Hour Bust

An emerging paradox for institutions who have viewed Web-based courses as a means of reaching a large audience and increasing student credit hour production (Chamberlin, 2001) is faculty who are adamantly establishing caps on Web course enrollments where none exists for the on-campus counterparts. Faculty cap enrollments to make the Internet course more manageable. Such caps reduce enrollments; thus more Web-based relative to on-campus sections of a course are needed to teach the same number of students. The resulting burden on faculty teaching loads can produce a host of threatening challenges, including reduced departmental offerings, reduced faculty release time for administrative and department responsibilities, reduced frequency with which courses are offered, increased time for students to finish programs, and increased pressure to hire adjuncts.

The Faculty Technology Divide

The term *digital divide* (see http://www.digitaldivide.gov/) reflects a growing dichotomy between those persons who have and those persons who do not have access to computers. In teaching Internet courses especially, an analogous technology divide is growing between those faculty with the hardware and software competencies to teach on the Internet and those faculty who do not possess them. To close that gap, institutions must entice and support novice distance educators by offering an infrastructure of training and ongoing assistance that is readily accessible and presented in understandable, user-friendly ways.

Closing the technology divide can also occur through incorporating content on teaching distance courses as part of the Preparing Future Faculty (PFF) initiative (see http://www.preparing-faculty.org/) for students finishing their doctoral programs. Several doctoral programs in psychology are already participating in the PFF program, but the PFF curricula available online show no coverage of distance education.

Easing Access to Higher Education: The Death Knell of On-Campus Instruction?

Will traditional on-campus courses eventually be replaced by distance education? Why shouldn't they? Students can now earn a variety of undergraduate and graduate degrees with (a) 24/7 access to their courses in the convenience of their homes, (b) chatrooms and listservs as learning supports, (c) timely teacher feedback, and (d) less overall expense when residence hall and meal expenses are considered. Distance education gives students a variety of institutions from which to select, fostering competition that should keep tuition costs down and course quality high.

Although distance course tuition may be higher than on-campus courses, living at home means no residential or meal plan expenses. Students can work while taking courses and can flexibly match the number of their enrolled courses to the demands of their jobs. Consequently, distance education promises a cost-effective education, providing opportunity to a significant portion of the population not previously able to afford college.

An Institutional Research Agenda

Why would anyone want to be an on-campus student and accrue considerable debt in doing so when a more cost-effective alternative exists? Why is being taught on campus better or more preferable than completing distance courses? Is there a difference between on-campus and distance learning? How do the qualities of the on-campus experience influence student learning? Are these qualities worth the substantially added expense? What impact will distance education have on maturing students, promoting citizenship, and preparing students for civic responsibility? Finding answers to these and many other questions challenge teachers and institutions for the foreseeable future.

EPILOGUE

Challenges stimulate action, and distance education is currently one of the liveliest, most invigorating entrepreneurial aspects of higher education. Virtual universities are a growth industry around the world. Teachers (e.g., Birnbaum, 2001; Stuber-McEwen, 2001) are writing psychology textbooks to maximize the Internet's use as an instructional tool. By initiating online access to their holdings, libraries are providing all students an unprecedented level of convenience and accessibility. Creative funding strategies abound for providing revenue streams to enable schools to update their technology and be competitive for both students and faculty. Colleges and universities are modernizing their classrooms to provide teachers and students access to the Internet and other multimedia tools.

Distance education is stimulating research on pedagogy (e.g., Cole, 2000; Smith & Woody, 2000) and teaching (Lawson, 2000), advancing the scholarship in our discipline (Halpern et al., 1998). Furthermore, teaching a distance course helps faculty "be a better teacher in [the on-campus] class" (Weaver; cited in Chamberlin, 2001, p. 65). The American Psychological Association's (1997) learner-centered psychological principles are equally useful to planning and implementing both distance education and on-campus courses.

McKeachie's (1999) *Teaching Tips* and Brewer's (1994) "Ten Commandments" are as relevant to distance education as they are to on-campus education. Distance educators now spawn their own lists of 10, such as Lamb and Smith's (2000) 10 facts of life for distance learning. Active learning (Lamb & Smith, 2000; McKeachie, 1999) is vital for quality distance learning, where teachers are working in unprecedented ways to bend twigs (Brewer, 1996) and hear the mermaids sing (Brewer, 1997).

REFERENCES

American Psychological Association. (1997). *Learner-centered psychological principles: A framework for school redesign and reform.* Retrieved January 31, 2001 from the World Wide Web: http://www.apa.org/ed/lcp.html.

Birnbaum, M. H. (2001). *Introduction to behavioral research on the Internet.* Upper Saddle River, NJ: Prentice-Hall.

Bloom, B., Englehart, M., Furst, E., Hill, W., & Krathwohl, O. (1956). *Taxonomy of educational goals: Handbook 1. The cognitive domain.* White Plains, NY: Longman.

Brewer, C. L. (1985). Instructions for contributors. *Teaching of Psychology, 12,* 2.

Brewer, C. L. (1994). Teaching effectively: Brewer's Ten Commandments. *Significant Difference, 4*(2), 4–5.

Brewer, C. L. (1996). A talk to teachers: Bending twigs and affecting eternity. *Platte River Review, 24*(1), 12–23.

Brewer, C. L. (1997). Undergraduate education in psychology: Will the mermaids sing? *American Psychologist, 52,* 434–441.

Chamberlin, J. (2001, January). Digital dissemination. *Monitor on Psychology, 32*(1), 64–66.

Cole, R. A. (Ed.). (2000). *Issues in Web-based pedagogy: A critical primer.* Westport, CT: Greenwood.

Daugman, J. (2001). Iris recognition. *American Scientist, 89,* 326–333.

Grubb, A., & Hines, M. (2000). Tearing down barriers and building communities: Pedagogical strategies for the Web-based environment. In R. A. Cole (Ed.), *Issues in Web-based pedagogy: A critical primer* (pp. 365–380). Westport, CT: Greenwood.

Halpern, D. F., Smothergill, D. W., Allen, M., Baker, S., Baum, C., Best, D., Ferrari, J., Geisinger, K. F., Gilden, E. R., Hester, M., Keith-Spiegel, P., Kierniesky, N. C., McGovern, T. V., McKeachie, W. J., Prokasy, W. F., Szuchman, L. T., Vasta, R., & Weaver, K. A. (1998). Scholarship in psychology: A paradigm for the twenty-first century. *American Psychologist, 53,* 1292–1297.

Holcomb, K. (2001, January 10). Schallenkamp shares vision for ESU. *The Emporia Gazette,* pp. 1, 3.

Lamb, A. C., & Smith, W. L. (2000). Ten facts of life for distance learning courses. *TechTrends, 44*(1), 12–15.

Lawson, T. J. (2000). Teaching a social psychology course on the Web. *Teaching of Psychology, 27,* 285–288.

Lyman, B. (1999). Internet-based learning: What's in it for the adult learner? In D. French, C. Hale, C. Johnson, & G. Farr (Eds.), *Internet based learning: An introduction and framework for higher education and business* (pp. 97–117). Sterling, VA: Stylus.

McKeachie, W. J. (1999). *Teaching tips: Strategies, research, and theory for college and university teachers* (10th ed.). Boston: Houghton-Mifflin.

Morgan, D. (2000). *The legacy of 2001.* Retrieved January 1, 2001 from the World Wide Web: http://abcnews.go.com/sections/scitech/DailyNews/2001_001223.html.

Nowak, S. (1999). High tech but high touch: Strategies for teaching and learning via distance. *Understanding Our Gifted, 11*(4), 26–28.

Palloff, R. M., & Pratt, K. (1999). *Building learning communities in cyberspace: Effective strategies for the online classroom.* San Francisco: Jossey-Bass.

SchWeber, C. (2000). The "time" factor in on-line teaching: Implications for faculty and their universities. In R. A. Cole (Ed.), *Issues in Web-based pedagogy: A critical primer* (pp. 227–236). Westport, CT: Greenwood.

Simonson, M., Smaldino, S., Albright, M., & Zvacek, S. (2000). *Teaching and learning at a distance: Foundations of distance education.* Upper Saddle River, NJ: Merrill.

Smith, S. M., & Woody, P. C. (2000). Interactive effect of multimedia instruction and learning styles. *Teaching of Psychology, 27,* 220–223.

Stuber-McEwen, D. (2001). *Internet psychology: Web site based exercises.* Edina, MN: Outernet.

University System of Georgia. (1997). *Regents guide to understanding copyright and educational fair use.* Retrieved February 27, 2001 from the World Wide Web: http://www. usg.edu/admin/legal/copyright/copy.html.

26

Come, Putative Ends of Psychology's Digital Future

Neil Lutsky
Carleton College

Attempts to envision the future are notoriously entertaining but rarely accurate (e.g., Corn & Horrigan, 1984/1996; but see Brewer, 1998, for an exception that is, characteristically, entertaining and accurate). Many of the great minds of the past century, Bertrand Russell included, believed that war with the Soviet Union was inevitable and advocated a "preventive" nuclear attack against the Soviets to forestall greater catastrophe (Poundstone, 1992). Thankfully, neither tragedy–the inevitable war nor the preventive attack–occurred. What emerged instead was a protracted cold war with the Soviet Union, and one result of that cold war was the development of a communications technology–packet switching on a distributed network–specifically designed to be less inviting to preemptive attack by the Soviets (Cairncross, 1997). That technology, in turn, became the foundation of another future—of what we now know as the Internet.

What does a future steeped in technology hold for the teaching of psychology? (I use the term *technology* here as an imprecise shorthand for a host of modern electronic technologies, including those employed in global information access and communications, professional networking and interaction, scientific research and research training, and course-related presentations and demonstrations.) To predict that future intelligently would require, first, more than Moore's Law (the doubling of computer power every 18 months) tells us about the growth of the technological capacities that will drive new educational applications. We know that computing power will expand, but to what ends? As Martin Trow (1997) observed:

> [T]he rapid rate of change for the technology and software makes it highly desirable to anticipate future developments, but it is almost impossible for us to do so beyond a few years or even months. During the computer's brief history, very little has been accurately predicted about its future development, either technological or social. (p. 294)

Unfortunately, neither the author nor his colleagues at that large educational retirement fund on which he relies appear to have shown any better aptitude for forecasting technological trends.

How, then, might it be possible to address technology and teaching in psychology in some grounded fashion? This chapter attempts to do so by extrapolating from three current tendencies: (a) psychologists' receptivity to new technologies, (b) psychology's attention to technology as a subject matter, and (c) teachers' experimental attitude toward applications of technology in or as the locus of teaching. The approach of the chapter is local to the teaching of psychology. The large-scale changes in education, society, and culture that technology will engender will undoubtedly continue to influence the teaching of psychology, but in modest ways the teaching of psychology will help conform that influence. The possible character of psychology teachers' impact on how technology influences teaching is what this chapter attempts to capture. How will the values, goals, interests, and conditions of the teaching of psychology address and shape uses of technology in the teaching of psychology?

In a seminal discussion of technology, culture, and higher education, James O'Donnell (1998) wrote that:

> The invention and dissemination of the personal computer and now the explosive growth in links between those computers on the worldwide networks of the internet create a genuinely new and transformative environment . . . those of us fortunate enough to live in such exciting times will be put on our mettle to find ways to adapt technology to our lives and our lives to technologies. (p. 9)

The issue of how we adapt technology to our lives as teachers, even if we do so in forms far afield from those considered in what follows, is likely to fuel continued self-reflection on our goals and purposes in teaching—on the ends in the service of which we may find technology a useful if not essential ally. Ultimately, that heightened attention to and possible expansion of our aspirations may represent one of the most important contributions technology makes to teaching.

WHY DO PSYCHOLOGISTS HAVE
AN AFFINITY FOR TECHNOLOGY?

There is sufficient reason to believe that technology will continue to figure prominently in the teaching of psychology. Base rate forces in education alone suggest so. For example, Levine (1997) identified the rise of new technologies as one of five factors likely to be responsible for dramatic changes in the academic profession as a whole. Trow (1997) agreed and identified three common motives for the investments in information technology currently being made by institutions of higher learning. Those anticipated ends are improved learning, wider access, and cost containment. Trow argued that different kinds of institutions will emphasize some of these goals over others and will attempt to select and apply technology accordingly. In his view, for example, mass institutions appear to be interested in technology as a means of transmitting knowledge efficiently, whereas elite institutions are less concerned about access and economics and rather seek to employ technology to enrich students' learning experiences. Nonetheless, although these currents may be varied and diverging ones, they all propel teachers of psychology, among others, toward a more technologically centered future.

The teaching of psychology is obviously subject to these wider forces, but there are additional reasons that technology traditionally exercises a strong gravitational pull on psychologists. One attraction has to do with the nature of research in the discipline, a second with the conditions of instruction, and a third with the mechanical interests of psychologists.

Technologies have long played an important role in psychological research. Psychology as a science has traditionally used equipment and instrumentation to support and conduct research, whether in the era of the tachistiscope and Skinner box or that of molecular genetics, magnetic resonance imagery, and personal digital assistants sampling emotion and behavior in situ. Teachers of psychological science will, where feasible, want to acquire and master those technologies for demonstration, laboratory, and independent student research purposes. The science and teaching of psychology both depend on computing for data analysis, and this use has been one of the mainstays of psychologists' involvement in computing. In addition, professional and teaching communities have developed on the Internet via e-mail-based news and discussion groups (e.g., Kelley-Milburn & Milburn, 1995) as well as educational Web sites (e.g., Plous, 2000). Finally, we should not overlook our more mundane reliance on technology for professional communication via word processing, posters, and presentational software.

Another fundamental research tool is being transformed by technology: the research library (Himmelfarb, 1997; O'Donnell, 1998). O'Donnell (1998) envisioned the development of a *virtual library* marked by the total worldwide inclusiveness of materials and immediate access to those materials. Even at present, what is in a library, how library resources are distributed in a worldwide network, and how informational resources are searched and accessed are undergoing technological change. Moreover, for many teachers and students, the Internet is serving as a more easily accessed alternate library (O'Donnell, 1998)—one that lacks key features of existing libraries. As O'Donnell noted, "one of the most valuable functions of the traditional library has been not its inclusivity but its exclusivity, its discerning judgment that keeps out as many things as it keeps in" (p. 43).

Changes in library usage are due, in part, to the technological experience and inexperience of students (Levine & Cureton, 1998). Students are far more likely than they once were to rely on an open world of digital information, often without discrimination (Floridi, 1996). Thus, teachers have to school students both on how to conduct computer based information searches and on how to strengthen their ability to evaluate the sources and claims they locate. As Himmelfarb (1997) reminded us, "It takes a discriminating mind, a mind that is already stocked with knowledge and trained in critical discernment, to distinguish between . . . the trivial and the important, the ephemeral and the enduring, the true and the false" (p. 200). O'Donnell (1998) made a similar point: "The real roles of the professor in an information-rich world will be not to provide information but to advise, guide, and encourage students wading through the deep waters of the information flood" (p. 156). In summary, the changing world of library research technology, which is so central to psychology's scholarly values, requires continued attention in the teaching of psychology.

The popularity of courses in psychology also drives teaching applications of technology. How can teachers capture and recapture the attention of students in large lecture courses? How can teachers present explicitly organized lectures? How can teachers make course materials and lecture notes available for careful review? How can teachers expose students concretely to phenomena covered in psychology courses? How can teachers maintain contact with large numbers of students? How can teachers involve large numbers of students in laboratory work in psychology or in collaborative learning activities? How can teachers accommodate the diversity of learning styles students bring to a course? How can teachers encourage student participation in informed and thoughtful discussion about course issues? Although not regarded as a panacea, technology is often cited as a resource that can be used to meet these challenges (e.g., McKeachie, 1999; Ralston & Beins, 1996/1999).

Technology is also at the heart of efforts to expand access to higher education, in psychology among other fields, via distance learning (Levine, 1997) and to replace traditional face-to-face education with alternatives such as distributed learning (Dede, 2000). As the demographic characteristics and life situations of the students we serve change (e.g., Levine & Cureton, 1998), new means of teaching are being developed that rely heavily on digital technologies.

Technology, then, may serve the goals of higher education, may be an essential component of instruction in psychological methods, and may facilitate teaching to the large numbers of students that courses in psychology attract. However, there may be a less educationally purposive reason psychologists are so involved with technology (and why students so enjoy technology): We are a science that attracts tinkerers. As Diamond (1999) observed, "[T]he greatest inventors have been tinkerers who loved tinkering for its own sake and who then had to figure out what, if anything, their devices might be good for" (p. 143). Perhaps many uses of computing in psychology are the rationalized products of such technological play. This suspicion should alert us to the dangers of technological fanaticism in the teaching of psychology, although countering this threat, I later suggest, is the constraint empirical grounding provides our possible infatuations.

In summary, technology is not merely imposing itself on the teaching of psychology. Psychologists have been drawn to technology because of the contributions it can make to psychological science, the ways it might strengthen traditional teaching and expand educational access, and the opportunities it allows for the exercise of a keen sense of play. Whether and how the end results of this fascination serve the teaching of psychology remain open questions. What is certain, however, is that technology will continue to play an increasingly important role in psychology education.

HOW WILL TECHNOLOGY CHANGE THE PSYCHOLOGY WE TEACH?

The web of reasons that psychologists may be drawn to use technology in teaching and to train students in technological applications in psychology reflects wider currents in contemporary culture. Those trends, which in small ways the teaching of psychology reinforces, alter the phenomena that psychology addresses. It may well be that the most profound effect of the proliferation of technology on the teaching of psychology will be seen in what psychologists study and, consequently, teach. Two examples illustrate this possibility.

The New Social Psychology of Interpersonal Electrons

How may the Internet affect interpersonal relationships, subjective well-being, intergroup relationships, and other psychological phenomena? How may individual differences in personality affect Internet use? Questions of this kind are redefining the objects of psychological investigation. The widespread popular attention given to initial findings on the relation between Internet usage and loneliness (Kraut et al., 1998) suggests keen public interest in the psychological study of our common digital future. Thus, both the expansion of technology in everyday affairs and human interest in the psychology of that technology may stimulate changes in what psychology emphasizes as primary topics of investigation.

McKenna and Bargh (2000) identified potential dimensions of these changes for social and personality psychology. For example, they considered how the anonymity of interpersonal relationships on the Internet may affect phenomena such as communication honesty, intergroup relationships, and social identity. Here, principles and findings in social psychology can be applied to human Internet usage to help predict the consequences of digitally mediated social behavior. McKenna and Bargh also suggested reasons that reliance on the Internet may challenge standard social psychological discoveries, including findings on the roles of physical attractiveness and proximity on relationship formation. This increased disciplinary attention to digital phenomena will influence what students learn and think about in psychology courses. It will also require new methodological strategies (McKenna & Bargh, 2000), and this shift has obvious implications for the teaching of research methods in psychology.

Goldstein (1998) provided an early example of how teaching may address new technologically based subject matters. She described an impression formation exercise in which students apply methods in implicit personality theory research to Internet home pages. Each student locates a psychologist's home page and records his or her impressions of the page's author based on the Web stimulus. The student may later contact the psychologist via an e-mail-based interview to collect additional information that might permit an assessment of the initial impression the student generated. Goldstein suggested using the exercise not only to illuminate a basic concept in person perception, but also to raise questions about how the process of impression formation may function differently in the brave new world of digital self-presentation.

The Human Factors Call of Technology Design

Recent findings (Gibbs, 1997) suggest computing has not yielded the economic productivity gains expected by its advocates, except, perhaps, in the computing industry (Cassidy, 2000). According to Gibbs (1997), the puzzle of computing's limited contribution to productivity may be explained by mismeasurement of computing's actual impact, insufficient computer presence in the current economy, a time delay until computing's impact is apparent, or the real limits of current applications of computing. Gibbs suggests that evidence makes all but the fourth possibility implausible.

Why hasn't computing done more? According to Gibbs (1997), one reason is that users spend considerable time futzing with computers and programs, organizing them, playing games with them, adjusting features, and the like. Another factor is the growing complexity of software. For example, between 1992 and 1997, the number of commands included in Microsoft's popular program Word expanded threefold, but it is unlikely that the quality of written prose has risen similarly. This *creeping featurism* in software appears to be driven more by the trade press than by the end user, and that brings us to human factors psychology.

Psychology will be required to help the digital future realize its potential. For software and hardware to work more efficiently and effectively, they have to be designed with a greater appreciation of the needs and tendencies of their human users (Gibbs, 1997). Thus, it is likely that psychology will become increasingly attentive to human factors issues in human–machine interaction and that this research area will help to define and justify psychology in the years to come. When teachers attempt to convince students and others that psychology can contribute to human health and welfare, human factors research is likely to figure prominently in the brief they offer.

The work of Richard Mayer (1997) offers a case in point. Mayer's research in psychology concerns when and why multimedia presentations may facilitate scientific understanding. His work is grounded in what he labeled "a generative theory of multimedia learning" (p. 4). Briefly, this theory holds that learning occurs when individuals are actively engaged in integrating selected features of two forms of information presentation, visual and verbal. The research results that Mayer reports are generally consistent with the theory. For example, there appears to be no general educational benefit of computer-based learning over standard text learning, although the issue is far more complex than this brief summary of Mayer's conclusions acknowledges.

What does seem to facilitate scientific understanding are verbal explanations coordinated with contiguous multimedia animations. Such a presentation facilitates active processing along the lines the generative theory highlights, as learners attempt to tie together selected features of the two concurrent information streams. Additional findings suggest that the beneficial effects of multimedia presentations constructed in this way are strongest for students who have high spatial ability (see also Smith & Woody, 2000) and little background knowledge on the topic presented. In summary, this research shows how psychology can be brought to bear on an important design problem, can assist the development of more effective digital materials, and can help specify the conditions under which those materials may be most useful. Increasingly, the kind of psychology that tackles issues of this sort may be the kind of psychology students will need and want to encounter in our courses.

WILL THE TECHNOLOGICAL METEOR EXTINGUISH THE TEACHING OF PSYCHOLOGY?

Will the impact of technology cloud and suffocate the teaching of psychology? It may, possibly, or it may extinguish intelligent life in some educational environments but not others. Apocalyptic visions of digital teaching without teachers—of homogenized optimal multimedia courses, computer grading of student work, electronic certification of mastery, and the like—are readily available for our anxious consumption. However, notwithstanding significant differences between past and currently imagined technologies, similar prospects were raised about the impact of radio, TV, and film on teaching (e.g., Cuban, 1986). Those expectations, of course, have yet to be realized. The virtues of digital interaction notwithstanding, there is something about a face-to-face encounter with a teacher's informed, nimble, and passionate mind, in the company of one's peers, that continues to attract potential students. Despite advances in home musical systems, people still want to see the Rolling Stones in concert.

We can sense that technological innovation will bring significant changes to higher education even if we do not know what those changes will be. The challenges and opportunities that technology provides, however, may be reinvigorating ones. As O'Donnell (1998) wrote, "[W]e teachers do not automatically deserve a future. We must earn it by the skill with which we disorient our students, energize them, and inculcate in them a taste for the hard disciplines of seeing and thinking" (p. 123). Technology may serve those purposes in teaching and may make teachers more purposive as they face alternative educational technologies. As Trow (1997) noted, one consequence of the technological revolution in higher education is the development of software handcrafted by teachers to serve specific educational objectives in particular educational contexts. In other words, although technology can be used to homogenize education, it can also be used quite differently to support more finely tailored educational objectives and a new age of microteaching.

I think there is reason to believe that psychology's empirical values and teachers' related commitment to assessment (e.g., Halpern, 1993) are especially likely to reinforce educational diversity via an end-driven approach to technology. Laurillard (1999) recommended that teachers of psychology apply technology in teaching experimentally, testing the effects of the innovations they develop or select. Such an experimental approach not only guards against unwarranted enthusiasms and dull uses of technology, but also requires teachers to consider their purposes in applying technology. We need to think about what our dependent goals are when seeking to assess them.

An example from my own dabbling in technology illustrates the potential for more local applications of technology. I sought means to accomplish two goals in an introductory psychology course: to involve students in psychology research and to show students how psychologists use a standard research paradigm to illuminate a general topic area. To address these goals, I developed two Web-based research modules: one on personality traits and happiness, and the other on correspondent inference (sometimes known as the *fundamental attribution error*). I briefly describe the module on correspondent inference; the interested reader is directed to both modules, which are available on the Web (Lutsky, 2000) and described at length by Lutsky (2001).

The correspondent inference module requires students to participate outside of class in a Web-based version of the standard experiment on correspondence bias (Jones & Harris, 1967). Students read an essay written to defend an assigned pro or con position on a controversial issue and then judge the actual attitude of the essay writer toward that issue. Jones and Harris's (1967) results, and the findings of almost everyone else using this research paradigm (including my classes), reliably show overattributions of the assigned position to the essayist, that is, unwarranted correspondent inference.

After discussing these results in class, students are directed back to the module to review the literature available there. The module includes summaries of the methods and results of studies using variants of Jones and Harris's (1967) paradigm. I developed this Web-based version of a literature review to show students how a series of studies in psychology employs variants of a base research method. The results reported in the reviews are not interpreted so that students have to evaluate findings. This summary literature review is initially hidden from access. (What students learn—and an interested explorer of the module should know—is that clicking on the stop sign in the module opens up the literature review.) Students are then asked to identify a question about correspondent inference, to design a study using the Jones and Harris paradigm to investigate their question, and to submit a research proposal describing their study as a regular class assignment. In summary, this module attempts to give students exposure to an extensive empirical literature based on a standard research paradigm, training in the interpretation of empirical results, and experience with experimental design and the framing of research questions.

The effects of participation in the two Web modules were assessed in a quasi-experimental study. Specifically, students ($n = 53$) in the course taught in 1997 before the introduction of the modules and students ($n = 61$) taught in 2000 with the modules completed questions on research training and their knowledge of research concepts. All other factors—including the text assigned, the course instructor, and the material covered in these courses—were approximately constant (see Lutsky, 2001).

Results of the assessment show that exposure to the modules increased students' understanding of basic methodological concepts in psychological research (e.g., correlation, reliability, and statistical significance). Moreover, the modules affected students' ratings of whether the course taught them how to think critically about research claims, how to structure a research investigation, how data are analyzed, how computers are used in research, and how research is conducted in psychology. Students completing the research modules also agreed significantly more strongly that psychology is a science. Finally, students' responses to an open-ended question about what they learned from the modules included prominent mention of psychology's grounding in lines of systematic research.

What this modest example shows is that teachers can readily use technology in attempts to achieve specific educational goals. When embraced judiciously and assessed rigorously, technology is more likely to fuel the lamp of learning than to smother it. As O'Donnell (1998) wrote, "Technology will do what it always does: provide tools. Those tools may eventually shape their owners, but they are always assuredly instruments with which their owners may pursue their own aims" (p. 148). Given the corrigible character of teaching in light of empirical assessment, there is good reason to expect that teachers will adapt and evaluate the tools technology provides in the service of the best ends of education.

CODA: WE COULD NOT PREDICT OUR MENTORS' INFLUENCE EITHER

The contributions of Bill McKeachie and Charles Brewer encompass much of what is important and meaningful in the teaching of psychology today. Technology does not readily come to mind, however, as a domain of special interest to either. Still, I hope their influence on this chapter and elsewhere in teaching is clear. By embodying and articulating the central values of our profession with discipline, grace, passion, and integrity, each man has influenced teachers and teaching in ways that could not have been anticipated and that will extend, in breadth and time, in ways we cannot foresee. Whatever the forms teaching of psychology takes now and in the future, it is and will be more caring, rigorous, effective, thoughtful, and joyful because of their good spirit.

REFERENCES

Brewer, C. L. (1998). Predictions and retrospections. *Teaching of Psychology, 25,* 250–253.

Cairncross, F. (1997). *The death of distance: How the communications revolution will change our lives.* Boston, MA: Harvard Business School Press.

Cassidy, J. (2000, November 27). The productivity mirage. *The New Yorker,* pp. 106–118.

Corn, J. J., & Horrigan, B. (1984/1996). *Yesterday's tomorrows: Past visions of the American future.* Baltimore, MD: The Johns Hopkins University Press.

Cuban, L. (1986). *Teachers and machines: The classroom use of technology since 1920.* New York: Teachers College Press.

Dede, C. (2000). Emerging technologies and distributed learning in higher education. In D. Hanna (Ed.), *Higher education in an era of digital competition: Choices and challenges* (pp. 71–92). Madison, WI: Atwood.

Diamond, J. (1999, April 18). Invention is the mother of necessity. *The New York Times Magazine,* pp. 142–144.

Floridi, L. (1996). Brave.net.world: The internet as a disinformation superhighway. *The Electronic Library, 14,* 509–514.

Gibbs, W. W. (1997). Taking computers to task. *Scientific American, 277,* 82–89.

Goldstein, M. D. (1998). Forming and testing implicit personality theories in cyberspace. *Teaching of Psychology, 25,* 216–220.

Halpern, D. F. (1993). Targeting outcomes: Covering your assessment concerns and needs. In T. V. McGovern (Ed.), *Handbook for enhancing undergraduate education in psychology.* Washington, DC: American Psychological Association.

Himmelfarb, G. (1997). Revolution in the library. *The American Scholar, 66,* 197–204.

Jones, E. E., & Harris, V. A. (1967). The attribution of attitudes. *Journal of Experimental Social Psychology, 3,* 1–24.

Kelley-Milburn, D., & Milburn, M. A. (1995). Cyberspace: Resources for psychologists on the Internet. *Psychological Science, 6,* 203–211.

Kraut, R., Patterson, M., Lundmark, V., Kiesler, S., Mukopadhyay, T., & Scherlis, W. (1998). Internet paradox: A social technology that reduces social involvement and psychological well-being? *American Psychologist, 53,* 1017–1031.

Laurillard, D. (1999). Using communications and information technology effectively. In W. J. McKeachie (Ed.), *McKeachie's teaching tips: Strategies, research, and theory for college and university teachers* (pp. 183–200). Boston, MA: Houghton-Mifflin.

Levine, A. (1997). How the academic profession is changing. *Daedalus, 126,* 1–20.

Levine, A., & Cureton, J. S. (1998). *When hope and fear collide: A portrait of today's college student.* San Francisco, CA: Jossey-Bass.

Lutsky, N. (2000). *Web-based research modules for introductory psychology.* World Wide Web: http://www.acad.carleton.edu/curricular/PSYC/classes/psych110_Lutsky/.

Lutsky, N. (2001, August). *What sticks to web-based research modules for introductory psychology?* Paper presented at the annual meeting of the American Psychological Association, San Francisco, CA.

Mayer, R. E. (1997). Multimedia learning: Are we asking the right questions? *Educational Psychologist, 32,* 1–19.

McKeachie, W. J. (1999). *McKeachie's teaching tips: Strategies, research, and theory for college and university teachers.* Boston, MA: Houghton-Mifflin.

McKenna, K. Y. A., & Bargh, J. A. (2000). Plan 9 from cyberspace: The implications of the internet for personality and social psychology. *Personality and Social Psychology Review, 4,* 57–75.

O'Donnell, J. J. (1998). *Avatars of the word: From papyrus to cyberspace.* Cambridge, MA: Harvard University Press.

Plous, S. (2000). Tips on creating and maintaining an educational world wide web site. *Teaching of Psychology, 27,* 63–70.

Poundstone, W. (1992). *Prisoner's dilemma.* New York: Doubleday.

Ralston, J. V., & Beins, B. (1996/1999). Thirteen ideas to help computerize your course. In B. Perlman, L. I. McCann, & S. H. McFadden (Eds.), *Lessons learned: Practical advice for the teaching of psychology* (pp. 73–77). Washington, DC: American Psychological Society.

Smith, S. M., & Woody, P. C. (2000). Interactive effect of multimedia instruction and learning styles. *Teaching of Psychology, 27,* 220–223.

Trow, M. (1997). The development of information technology in American higher education. *Daedalus, 126,* 293–314.

V

Teaching About
Psychology's Domains

27

Teaching the History of Psychology

C. James Goodwin
Wheeling Jesuit University

Teaching the History of Psychology course is both a great joy and an enormous challenge. It is always a pleasure to teach a course about a topic one loves, of course, but the history course presents the instructor with problems not found in other courses. For one thing, teachers of the history course seldom have been trained as historians of psychology, whereas courses in social psychology, for example, are often taught by professional social psychologists. Consequently, the level of preparation can be daunting for the person asked to teach history, and the feeling of being out of one's depth when teaching the course can be persistent. A second difficulty is student resistance. Many students come into the course having survived Western Civ or other history courses that seemed, to them at least, to involve little more than memorizing names and dates, organizing lists of the causes of war X, and placing the proper names of countries on blank maps. Then they come across the name of psychology's most prominent historian (you know who) and they just roll their eyes and prepare for what they assume will be a long and "boring" semester.

In a history course taught well, however, students end the semester in a much different frame of mind. They understand the intellectual and cultural foundations of the discipline they have chosen to study, they come to know some truly fascinating individuals, they develop a deeper understanding of how historians think, they learn to appreciate the problems associated with presentist thinking, and they understand and appreciate the interconnectedness among the various fragments of knowledge they have accumulated in their other psychology courses. This last point is especially important, I believe, because it gives students an important insight into the truth of a simple yet elegant phrase that I have heard Charles Brewer say (as only he can say it) on numerous occasions: "Everything (pause) is connected (pause) to everything else (pause and slowly scan the room)."

As a scholarly discipline, the history of psychology has changed considerably in the last 30 years. One of the goals of this chapter is to examine how the field has evolved and how these changes affect the way we teach the history course. My second goal is to describe some of the resources about psychology's history available to instructors. I close the chapter with an argument that we should make psychology's history an integral part of every psychology course, even the introductory course.

HISTORY OF PSYCHOLOGY AS A SCHOLARLY DISCIPLINE AND THE IMPACT ON TEACHING

In 1960, a brief article appeared in *American Psychologist* with the title "The History of Psychology: A Neglected Area" (Watson, 1960). Its author was Robert Watson, a clinical psychologist who became passionate about psychology's history late in his career. As is evident from the title, the article was a call to arms, a "plea for greater attention on the part of psychologists to their history" (Watson, 1960, p. 255). Over the next few years, Watson became the leader of a small but vigorous group of like-minded psychologists, the eventual result being a series of actions that professionalized history as a legitimate specialty within academic psychology (Hilgard, 1982). These events, all in 1965, included the creation of (a) a formal division within the American Psychological Association (APA Division 26); (b) an archive to collect and organize the raw materials of psychology's history, founded at the University of Akron by two other clinicians in love with history, John Popplestone and the late Marion White McPherson; and (c) a new journal, the *Journal of the History of the Behavioral Sciences*. In the late 1960s, Watson was also instrumental in the creation of the first doctoral program in the history of psychology (at the University of New Hampshire) and the formation of a second organization devoted to the history of psychology and the social sciences—the Cheiron Society.

It is not that psychologists completely ignored their history prior to Watson's activism. Courses in "history and systems of psychology" were a regular part of the psychology curriculum in Watson's time. A study conducted in the early 1960s, for instance, found that of 150 schools responding to a survey, 130 offered a course to undergraduates and/or graduate students in the history of psychology, and in most cases it was required (Nance, 1962). The Nance survey also revealed that

75% of those schools with history courses used the same textbook—E. G. Boring's *A History of Experimental Psychology* (1929, 1950). This book is appropriately recognized as one of the great books in the history of American psychology, but it also presented a portrait of psychology's history that reflected a bias that is evident from its title. Specifically, it focused on the development of psychology as an experimental laboratory science that evolved in the late 19th and early 20th centuries; had parental origins in philosophy, physiology, and Darwinian biology; and developed its identity from the conflicts among advocates of various schools of psychology (e.g., structuralism, functionalism, behaviorism).

Competing texts (e.g., Chaplin & Krawiec, 1960) were clearly influenced by Boring's work, as were texts that began to appear in the late 1960s (e.g., Schultz, 1969). Thus, a generation of psychologists learned about the history of psychology from E. G. Boring, either directly or indirectly. Students were taught a story about psychology's history that attained quasi-mythological status—the story went roughly as follows.

Philosophers asked age-old questions about human behavior, but they never bothered to subject their ideas to the purity of scientific test. Certain more enlightened 19th-century physiologists/philosophers came along (e.g., Fechner, Wundt) and corrected this egregious oversight, thereby creating psychology as a new discipline and bringing to it the bright light of scientific methodology. Wundt created the first laboratory in 1879 and founded a school of psychology called *structuralism*, the goal of which was to break consciousness into its elements using a method called *introspection*. Wundt's admiring protégé Titchener carried the master's system to the United States, but the rugged individualist do-it-their-own-way Americans had their own ideas, so they created functionalism and then behaviorism and launched an assault on structuralism, which quickly withered and died. The behaviorists were the most vigorous opponents; the functionalists were a little wishy-washy. Meanwhile in Germany, gestalt psychology came along and took up the offensive against structuralism on its home turf. It then emigrated to America, discovered that structuralism was on its last legs, looked around for a new target, and started attacking behaviorism. Outside of academia and by implication of less importance, Freud revolutionized the field of abnormal psychology and therapy.

Students in the traditional history of psychology course then learned about the attributes of the competing schools of psychology, "all with something to offer," except perhaps structuralism, tainted by the subjective (i.e., false and evil) method of introspection. Modern psychology was a culmination of the march of progress from the darkness of philosophical speculation, through the sectarian battles of the schools, to the modern era, where we are now much closer to the truth about human behavior (having corrected the errors of the past).

In the 1970s, things began to change gradually, and the mythology of psychology's history (i.e., virtually everything about the story you just read) began to be questioned. Spurred by Robert Watson and a renewed interest in the history of psychology as a scholarly discipline, articles began to appear that subjected the traditional history of psychology to intense scrutiny. For example, several articles raised serious questions about the typical portrayal of Wundt (e.g., Blumenthal, 1975; Leahey, 1979). It appeared that he was not a structuralist after all, that he was much more interested in synthesis than analysis, that his version of introspection (and his overall outlook) was very different from Titchener's (Danziger, 1980), and that he was perhaps more interested in higher level cognitive processes (e.g., language) and cross-cultural psychology than basic sensory phenomena. Historians also began to examine the life and work of E. G. Boring more closely, discovering that his view of history was influenced by his own training (he was a student of Titchener's) and by political and institutional considerations. For example, it appeared that his emphasis on the centrality of experimental psychology was motivated at least partly by his concern about the rising tide of applied psychology that occurred after World War I and by his own desire to produce an intellectual justification for his goal of creating a separate laboratory-based department of psychology at Harvard (O'Donnell, 1979).

Textbooks published during the 1980s began to reflect the new scholarship in the history of psychology. For instance, Duane Schultz's readable and popular history text kept appearing in new editions, each one reflecting changes resulting from the scholarly efforts of historians. A comparison of content in the third edition (Schultz, 1981) and fourth edition (Schultz & Schultz, 1987) provides a useful illustration of how these alterations began to occur, especially in the portrayal of Wundt. In Schultz's third edition, Chapter 4 covers Wundt and is called "The New Psychology: Structuralism and its Early Opponents" (p. 59). The chapter includes statements like these:

> ... we shall see that Titchener's position was similar to that of Wundt. (p. 59)

> Wundt mapped out the field of structural psychology. (p. 59)

> Wundt gave the larger share of his attention to the opposite of creative synthesis, to the analysis of mind, the reduction of conscious experience to its elementary component parts. (p. 68)

In the fourth edition, Schultz incorporated much of the new scholarship and the text changed its depiction of Wundt considerably. All of the prior statements disappeared, for instance, and the Wundt chapter was retitled "The New Psychology." The chapter even began with an explicit description of how new research had questioned the traditional portrayal of Wundt's ideas. Structuralism did not appear until the following chapter, when it was used as the appropriate title of the chapter on Titchener's work. The fourth edition (Schultz & Schultz, 1987) contained sentences like these:

> ... generations of students have been offered a portrait of Wundtian psychology that may be more myth than fact, more legend than truth. For 100 years after the event, texts in the history of psychology, including previous editions of this one, have been compounding and reinforcing the error. (p. 59)

E. B. Titchener altered Wundt's system dramatically while claiming to be a loyal follower. He offered his own approach, which he called structuralism, as representing the form of psychology espoused by Wundt. Yet the two systems were radically different, and the label "structuralism" cannot be applied to Wundt's work, only to Titchener's. (p. 85)

As an aside, showing students these comparisons can be a good antidote to the typical student attitude that the story has been written in stone once a historical account has been written. Rather, comparing different editions should make it clear that histories always have to be rewritten in the light of new information and new ways of looking at events.

Revised depictions of Wundt were not the only changes that occurred in history texts. As mentioned earlier, historians digging into the life and work of E. G. Boring began discovering the biases underlying the writing of his classic texts. In particular, Boring tended to overlook or downplay the importance of applied psychology. Yet historians were discovering that psychologists, at least in America, had always been interested in how their new science could be used for improving the human condition (O'Donnell, 1985). Even before World War I, psychologists were interested in mental testing, educational psychology, child study, industrial psychology, and even forensic psychology. One clear indication of textbook recognition of the rediscovered importance of applied psychology occurred in another popular history text by David Hothersall (1984). Whereas it had been customary in other texts to give Titchener and structuralism a separate chapter, Hothersall wrote a chapter that gave equal billing to Titchener and Hugo Münsterberg, one of psychology's pioneers in applied psychology. Hothersall also included a separate chapter on the applied topic of intelligence testing. More recent texts (e.g., Fancher, 1996; Goodwin, 1999; Leahey, 2001; Viney & King, 1998) routinely devote considerable space to applied psychology.

By the mid-1980s, then, scholarly work in psychology's history began to be reflected in history texts. The extent to which revised texts affected the manner in which psychology's history was taught remained unclear, however. What was needed was an explicit call for teachers of the history course to learn the new scholarship and to incorporate it into their teaching. The call arrived in the form of a G. Stanley Hall lecture delivered at the APA's annual meeting in Atlanta in 1988 by Laurel Furumoto, one of psychology's most distinguished historians.

EXCHANGING "OLD" FOR "NEW" HISTORY

Furumoto's Hall lecture appeared in print the following year, carrying the title, "The New History of Psychology" (Furumoto, 1989). If there is one article that every teacher of the history course should read, this is the one. In it Furumoto drew a sharp contrast between what she referred to as "old" history and "new" history. She described how scholarship in the history of psychology had been changing in the prior 20 years, in effect catching up with the efforts of trained historians. Yet her primary message was that it was time for those teaching the history course to both learn about the new scholarship and incorporate it into how they taught the course. According to Furumoto, old history could be described as (a) internal, (b) personalistic, (c) ceremonial and celebratory, and (d) presentist. New history, by contrast, she described as (a) external, (b) contextual, (c) critical, and (d) historicist. Let us consider each of these approaches in more detail.

Old History

By describing old history as internal, Furumoto (1989) meant that it was an approach to psychology's history that focuses on tracing the development of important concepts, theories, and research that have occurred over the years. Such histories are more likely to be written by people trained in psychology than in history, and they tend to ignore influences outside of psychology that might have played a role in historical events. In line with the prior discussion about the traditional mythological story of psychology's history, internal histories imply that cumulative progress and continued improvement characterize the evolution of ideas. For example, an internal history of cognitive psychology might concentrate on how the field developed in the wake of demonstrable problems with behaviorism such as language learning, the serial order problem (Lashley, 1951), and the problem of mediation. The history might imply that cognitive psychology represented an advance because it solved these problems. There is also an implication of inevitability—that cognitive psychology had to happen. Yet as popular historian David McCullough pointed out:

> The hardest thing to convey in writing history or teaching history is that nothing ever had to happen the way it happened. It could have gone off in any number of different directions at any point, for any number of different reasons. But the tendency in teaching history or writing history is to say, this followed this, this followed that, and that's the way it was. (cited in Snow, 1999, p. 159)

In addition to being primarily internal, old history concentrates on and celebrates the contributions of people judged to be important, sometimes ignoring forces that might have influenced the work of these individuals. Thus, a personalistic history of cognitive psychology celebrates Miller's (1956) famous 7 ± 2 paper and Neisser's (1967) famous book, said to have given the *cognitive psychology* movement its name (Baars, 1986).

It is important to note that internal histories and histories that lean toward the biographical are not necessarily flawed, just incomplete. Students in the history course, for instance, should know about Lashley as a person and about the arguments in his serial order paper (see Bruce, 1994). The old history attribute of presentism is more a problematic issue, however, and can lead to serious misunderstandings about history. To be presentist is to evaluate what happened in the past by using modern standards and values. It is a problem well known to historians. Bernard Bailyn, a noted historian of the American Revolution, considered presentism (he referred to it as *anachronism*) to be the most fundamental problem for the historian. The historian, according to Bailyn (1994), must always be conscious of "whether or not one's present views are read back into the past and, therefore, whether the past is distorted, foreshortened, and its distinctiveness lost" (p. 50). This type of vigilance is a tall order, of course, because we are products of our environment. When thinking about a historical episode, we have the advantage of knowing about the subsequent events.

One way to avoid presentist thinking, Bailyn (1994) suggested, was "to avoid assigning the heroism or villainy that was unclear at the time but that was determined by later outcomes" (p. 53). In psychology's history, for example, a good test of whether one can overcome presentist thinking comes when one first encounters Henry Goddard and his views on mental deficiency and intelligence testing. It is difficult for students to read about the Kallikak study (Goddard, 1912) and not say, "What was he thinking?" Teaching students to appreciate the dangers of presentist thinking is one of the most important goals that a teacher of the history course should have.

New History

Teaching the history of psychology from the standpoint of new history, according to Furumoto, results in a different kind of course from one dominated by old history's historiographic strategies and by psychology's traditional mythology. Rather than being internal and biographical, new history tends to be external and contextual. That is, a new history of psychology examines not just what is going within the field of psychology, but also events and developments outside of the field that might have influenced psychology. The goal is to place developments in psychology into their historical context, where this context can be socioeconomic, political, cultural, or institutional. New history also tends to be critical rather than ceremonial and tries to replace presentist thinking with *historicist* thinking—trying to re-create what it was like back then without imposing modern-day values (Stocking, 1965). A new history of cognitive psychology, for example, has to include the post-World War II history of computer science, and it has to consider wider societal events. As just one example, it is now common to refer to a cognitive revolution (e.g., Baars, 1986), although Leahey (1992) has shown rather convincingly that what happened in psychology in the 1960s and 1970s does not fit the definitions of scientific revolution held by most science historians. Furthermore, he argued that the mere presence of Kuhn's (1962) famous book, which appeared at a time of societal unrest in America (the 1960s), might have prompted young scientists and graduate students to apply contemporary revolutionary rhetoric to what was happening in experimental psychology. As a graduate student myself during that era, I can vividly recall the first reading assignment in a seminar in higher mental processes—Kuhn's book.

Teaching a history course using a new history strategy places a heavy burden on the instructor—especially an instructor not trained in history (i.e., most of us). Not only do we have to learn about events within the discipline, but we also have to learn something about the general histories of the nations involved in psychology's history, we have to learn something about the history of science, and we have to know something about historical methodology (historiography). The effort pays off, however, in a course than is both richer and closer to the truth.

RESOURCES FOR THOSE TEACHING
THE HISTORY COURSE

Fortunately for the overburdened instructor preparing to teach the new history of psychology, there is an ever-increasing supply of useful information at hand, much more than can be described adequately here. The place to start is the Web site for Division 26 of the APA (www.psych.yorku.ca/orgs/apa26). Thanks to the tireless efforts of Chris Green, a historian of psychology at York University who maintains the site, it has become invaluable to both the researcher and teacher of psychology. The resources include links to information about specific individuals, archives, journals, and apparatus collections. There are also connections to other history sites, which in turn provide multiple links. Of special note is a link on the Division 26 site to the "Classics in the History of Psychology," where Green has posted full text documents from psychology's history ranging from famous papers (e.g., Watson & Rayner's [1920] Little Albert study) to entire books (e.g., Münsterberg's [1913] *Psychology and Industrial Efficiency*).

Text-based resources also have become more abundant in recent years. These resources include a series published by the APA called *Pioneers in Psychology*, now in its fourth volume (e.g., Kimble & Wertheimer, 2000), which includes biographical sketches of 84 psychologists; an *Illustrated History of American Psychology* (Popplestone & McPherson, 1994) based on materials held by the Akron archives; a chapter in the *Annual Review of Psychology* (Hilgard, Leary, & McGuire, 1991) that includes a large section on the teaching of psychology and, like most articles in this series, has an extensive bibliography; a topically organized collection of correspondence among psychologists (Benjamin, 1993); and numerous edited books dealing with a variety of special topics ranging from psychological testing (Sokal, 1987) to experimental methodology (Morawski, 1988) to the history of APA (Evans, Sexton, & Cadwallader, 1992). In 1992, APA's centennial year, all of the APA journals carried historical articles among their usual offerings, and the *American Psychologist* had a special issue devoted to history (Benjamin, 1992).

There are several journals specialized for history, the most recognizable being *The Journal of the History of the Behavioral Sciences* and *History of Psychology*, but history articles also appear regularly in *American Psychologist* and the *American Journal of Psychology*. Articles specifically designed for the instructor in the history course can also be found. Articles in the journal *Teaching of Psychology*, for example, range from arguments about whether the course should come early or late in a student's career (Milar, 1987) to discussions about whether the course should be taught chronologically or by topic (Dagenbach, 1999) to articles that simply provide useful exercises or materials for the instructor (Goodwin, 1991; Wight, 1993).

WE'RE ALL HISTORIANS NOW: INTEGRATING HISTORY INTO THE PSYCHOLOGY CURRICULUM

There is no question in my mind that the history course is one of the two or three most important courses for undergraduates to take. There are a number of reasons for this contention, some of which are described in this chapter's opening paragraph. The most important one, I think, at least for the psychology major, is that it enables the student to connect the dots. Majors take a variety of psychology courses, but they do not often see the connections among them. I recently asked students on a take-home exam to decide whether the history course should come before they have taken a lot of psychology courses or near the end of their academic careers. Most students opted for the latter, and one student articulated the connectedness point this way: "Throughout my college career I have had many psychology classes and have never realized until now how many of these courses relate to each other" (C. Young, personal communication, December 15, 2000).

I'd like to close this chapter with an appeal that, oddly enough, might reduce the strength of the connectedness function of the history course. That is, I believe that we could do a better job of integrating history throughout the psychology curriculum. As things stand now, courses in the general topic areas of psychology usually toss a bone to history in the first week of class and in the first chapter of the book, perhaps reinforcing students' general biases about history ("Let's get it over with so we can get to the good stuff"). So an introductory lecture in a course on adolescent psychology might mention G. Stanley Hall and something about "storm and stress," the social psychology course might throw in Norman Triplett, the abnormal psychology course might mention that the insane were thought to be witches at one time, and so on. Yet considering that virtually everything taught in every class is, in effect, history, it seems to me that we could incorporate historical thinking more systematically throughout our courses. This approach would mean such things as placing the topics of our courses into their proper historical contexts and teaching students about the dangers of presentist thinking. For example, students in social psychology learning about the Asch conformity studies should learn something about the generally conservative social climate in America in the 1950s, students in the learning course should not judge Watson and Rayner with reference to today's ethics code, and students in the abnormal course should learn of the connection, via Kraepelin, between the study of schizophrenia and the early German laboratory studies of attention. It would require a different level of preparation for instructors accustomed to teaching only within their disciplinary constraints, but the outcome would be a richer course experience for students.

We could even be better at integrating history into the general psychology course, although as Benjamin pointed out (Goodwin, 1997) the ever-increasing demands on that course, and the apparent decision by publishers to favor breadth over depth, means that history might be added only at the expense of something else. Nonetheless, it should not be difficult to work psychology's history into any of the topics normally covered in the first course. Even discussing the basic definition of the field provides an opportunity to show that the inclusion of the terms behavior and mental processes reflects something of a historical compromise over the way the field should be conceptualized. More broadly, consider that the majority of students taking general psychology are not psychology majors. Thinking of general psychology as part of a liberal arts curriculum, one could imagine a course that, in Benjamin's words, "wove psychology into the broader cultural, political, social, and economic fabric of which it is a part" (Goodwin, 1997, p. 219). Hence, integrating history into general psychology could enable the student to connect the course with other courses in the wider curriculum. Who knows, perhaps some day a brave soul will even write an introductory psychology text that is truly grounded in history and some risk-taking publishing house will agree to publish it.

REFERENCES

Baars, B. J. (1986). *The cognitive revolution in psychology*. New York: Guilford.

Bailyn, B. (1994). *On the teaching and writing of history*. Hanover, NH: University Press of New England.

Benjamin, Jr., L. T. (Ed.). (1992). Special issue: The history of American psychology. *American Psychologist, 47,* 109–335.

Benjamin, Jr., L. T. (1993). *A history of psychology in letters*. Dubuque, IA: Brown & Benchmark.

Blumenthal, A. L. (1975). A reappraisal of Wilhelm Wundt. *American Psychologist, 30,* 1081–1088.

Boring, E. G. (1929). *A history of experimental psychology*. New York: Century.

Boring, E. G. (1950). *A history of experimental psychology* (2nd ed.). Englewood Cliffs, NJ: Prentice-Hall.

Bruce, D. B. (1994). Lashley and the problem of serial order. *American Psychologist, 49,* 93–103.

Chaplin, J. P., & Krawiec, T. S. (1960). *Systems and theories of psychology*. New York: Holt, Rinehart & Winston.

Dagenbach, D. (1999). Some thoughts on teaching a pluralistic history in the history and systems of psychology course. *Teaching of Psychology, 26,* 22–28.

Danziger, K. (1980). The history of introspection reconsidered. *Journal of the History of the Behavioral Sciences, 16,* 241–262.

Evans, R. B., Sexton, V. S., & Cadwallader, T. C. (Eds.). (1992). *100 years, The American Psychological Association, A historical portrait.* Washington, DC: American Psychological Association.

Fancher, R. E. (1996). *Pioneers of psychology* (3rd ed.). New York: Norton.

Furumoto, L. (1989). The new history of psychology. In I. S. Cohen (Ed.), *The G. Stanley Hall lectures* (Vol. 9, pp. 9–34). Washington, DC: American Psychological Association.

Goddard, H. H. (1912). *The Kallikak family.* New York: Macmillan.

Goodwin, C. J. (1991). Using psychologists' letters to teach about introspection. *Teaching of Psychology, 18,* 237–238.

Goodwin, C. J. (1997). The vital role of history in introductory courses: An interview with Ludy T. Benjamin, Jr. *Teaching of Psychology, 24,* 218–221.

Goodwin, C. J. (1999). *A history of modern psychology.* New York: Wiley.

Hilgard, E. R. (1982). Robert I. Watson and the founding of Division 26 of the American Psychological Association. *Journal of the History of the Behavioral Sciences, 18,* 308–311.

Hilgard, E. R., Leary, D. E., & McGuire, G. R. (1991). The history of psychology: A survey and critical assessment. *Annual review of psychology* (Vol. 42, pp. 79–107). Stanford, CA: Annual Reviews.

Hothersall, D. (1984). *History of psychology.* New York: McGraw-Hill.

Kimble, G. A., & Wertheimer, M. (Eds.). (2000). *Portraits of pioneers in psychology.* Washington, DC: American Psychological Association.

Kuhn, T. S. (1962). *The structure of scientific revolutions.* Chicago: University of Chicago Press.

Lashley, K. S. (1951). The problem of serial order in behavior. In L. A. Jeffress (Ed.), *Cerebral mechanisms in behavior: The Hixon symposium* (pp. 112–146). New York: Wiley.

Leahey, T. H. (1979). Something old, something new: Attention in Wundt and modern cognitive psychology. *Journal of the History of the Behavioral Sciences, 15,* 242–252.

Leahey, T. H. (1992). The mythical revolutions of American psychology. *American Psychologist, 47,* 308–318.

Leahey, T. H. (2001). *A history of modern psychology* (3rd ed.). Upper Saddle River, NJ: Prentice-Hall.

Milar, K. S. (1987). History of psychology: Cornerstone instead of capstone. *Teaching of Psychology, 14,* 236–238.

Miller, G. A. (1956). The magic number seven plus or minus two: Some limits on our capacity for processing information. *Psychological Review, 63,* 81–97.

Morawski, J. G. (Ed.). (1988). *The rise of experimentation in American psychology.* New Haven, CT: Yale University Press.

Münsterberg, H. (1913). *Psychology and industrial efficiency.* New York: Houghton-Mifflin.

Nance, R. D. (1962). Current practices in teaching history of psychology. *American Psychologist, 17,* 250–252.

Neisser, U. (1967). *Cognitive psychology.* New York: Appleton-Century-Crofts.

O'Donnell, J. M. (1979). The crisis of experimentalism in the 1920s: E. G. Boring and his uses of history. *American Psychologist, 34,* 289–295.

O'Donnell, J. M. (1985). *The origins of behaviorism: American psychology, 1870–1920.* New York: New York University Press.

Popplestone, J. A., & McPherson, M. W. (1994). *An illustrated history of American psychology.* Madison, WI: Brown & Benchmark.

Schultz, D. (1969). *A history of modern psychology.* New York: Academic Press.

Schultz, D. (1981). *A history of modern psychology* (3rd ed.). New York: Academic Press.

Schultz, D., & Schultz, S. E. (1987). *A history of modern psychology* (4th ed.). San Diego, CA: Harcourt Brace Jovanovich.

Snow, R. (Ed.). (1999). *American heritage: Great minds of history.* New York: Wiley.

Sokal, M. M. (Ed.). (1987). *Psychological testing and American society, 1890–1930.* New Brunswick, NJ: Rutgers University Press.

Stocking, Jr., G. W. (1965). On the limits of "presentism" and "historicism" in the historiography of the behavioral sciences. *Journal of the History of the Behavioral Sciences, 1,* 211–218.

Viney, W., & King, D. B. (1998). *A history of psychology: Ideas and context.* Boston: Allyn & Bacon.

Watson, J. B., & Rayner, R. (1920). Conditioned emotional reactions. *Journal of Experimental Psychology, 3,* 1–14.

Watson, R. I. (1960). The history of psychology: A neglected area. *American Psychologist, 15,* 251–255.

Wight, R. D. (1993). Expanding coverage in the history course by toasting significant but often overlooked contributors. *Teaching of Psychology, 20,* 112.

28

Teaching Biological Psychology to Introductory Psychology Students

James W. Kalat
North Carolina State University

Let us start with a little demonstration. Make a list of your best teachers in high school, college, or graduate school, defining *best* as the ones from whom you learned the most. Then identify what, if anything, they had in common. Any good study has a control group, so then make a list of your worst instructors, from whom you learned the least, and again identify what they had in common.

My personal list of worst instructors is short, but they have much in common: boring, disorganized, confusing, unable to explain important points, and unimaginative in their presentation. In contrast, my list of best instructors is longer, but they have little in common. Some instructors relied entirely on lecture and others on extensive class participation. Some teachers used audiovisuals regularly and others seldom even touched the chalkboard. Most of these instructors were well organized, but a few were not. You might expect me to say that they all cared deeply about their students, but I am not sure about several of them. They did, however, all care deeply about their topic. The one thing my best teachers clearly had in common, in my judgment, was that they all had important content.

Who were the world's greatest teachers of all time? (Well, besides Charles Brewer and Wilbert McKeachie!) I think most of us would include prominently on that list Jesus and Socrates. What did those two teachers have in common besides that neither of them published anything and both got executed for their efforts? Certainly they did not become famous teachers because of their excellent use of audiovisual aids, their well-organized syllabus, their well-written and promptly graded tests, or any of the other procedures we urge new teachers to adopt. Apparently class size was not the key to their success. Jesus lectured to large classes—up to 5,000 according to one account—whereas Socrates spoke to only one or two at a time. Jesus is famous for his use of analogies (parables) and Socrates for his interactive (Socratic) form of teaching, but beyond that both became famous teachers because they had something important to say. In short, I assert that the most essential element of great teaching is great content. So, in this chapter, I do not discuss *how* to teach biological psychology, but *what* to teach about it.

SELECTING CONTENT

We psychology instructors have the luxury of being able to select our topics, even in an introductory course. If I want, I can spend extra time discussing sleep and omit the topic of hearing altogether, whereas a colleague teaching another section might do the opposite. One can hardly imagine a French instructor devoting extra time to prepositions and leaving out adverbs. Our decisions necessarily reflect our judgment of what we want our students to remember.

Recently, as I was cleaning out some old files, I came across some papers left over from my college days, including a test I had taken in a freshman history course. I did well on that test, but as I looked at it decades later I realized that now I could hardly answer a single question, at least not well.

The same is true of our own students. They will dutifully memorize materials for a test—at least some of them will—but soon after they start to forget. What can we really expect them to remember from a 1-week treatment of biological psychology in their introductory psychology course? The textbooks, my own included, feature such gems as a list of the structures of the midbrain and the chemistry of the action potential. Do I really expect introductory students to learn and retain that information? Should I be distressed if they do not? I look around at my colleagues in my own department: How many of them could list the structures of the midbrain? How inconvenienced are those who cannot? If many people make successful careers in psychology without knowing about the midbrain, why do we include it in an introductory course? The same question applies to other branches of psychology. For example, when was the last time you heard a psychologist refer to the Cannon–Bard theory except when teaching introductory psychology?

However, I found when I tried once to deemphasize the listing of brain areas in my introductory psychology text that some potential adopters accused me of *dumbing down* the text. When I was working on the second edition of my introductory text many years ago, a questionnaire sent to prepublication reviewers asked whether they objected that I had omitted vestibular sensation. One reviewer replied that he had not noticed that I omitted it, but I should not have. Another reviewer said that she never mentioned the topic in class, but wanted the book to cover it anyway. (I relented and added it.) As far as I can tell, any reviewer who notices any omission protests. If you are a consistent reader of *Teaching of Psychology*, you may recall many articles over the years berating introductory psychology textbooks for less-than-complete treatments of various topics.

Nevertheless, anyone who teaches introductory psychology knows well that complete coverage of every topic would be a disaster. Just between you and me, this is how we should proceed: Textbook writers (including me) will have to include a lot of extraneous information because text reviewers and people on adoption committees insist on it. However, once we are in the classroom, we are free to ignore some topics and emphasize others.

In biological psychology (or behavioral neuroscience, or whatever else you want to call it), what are the key points worth emphasizing to introductory students? Karl Lashley (1930) wrote,

> Most of our psychology textbooks begin with an exposition of the structure of the brain and imply that this lays a foundation for a later understanding of behavior.... The chapter on the nervous system seems to provide an excuse for pictures in an otherwise dry and monotonous text. That it has any other function is not clear; there may be cursory references to it in later chapters on instinct and habit, but where the problems of psychology become complex and interesting, the nervous system is dispensed with. (pp. 1–2)

Today, almost three quarters of a century later, we would no longer say that the nervous system is "dispensed with" in later chapters, although it may still be true that some of the coverage in the biological psychology chapter "provides an excuse for pictures," especially MRI and PET scans. I suggest we take Lashley's criticism to heart and ask what content about the brain is essential for students in introductory psychology.

HIGHLIGHTS OF BIOLOGICAL PSYCHOLOGY: A PERSONAL LIST

Here are my own suggestions of key points to emphasize. Some of them actually arise in other chapters, but all are related to the biology of behavior.

The Genetics of Behavior

An understanding of how genes affect behavior is essential to dealing with the omnipresent nature–nurture issue and with many claims made on TV and in the newspapers. Behavior genetics should be addressed in the biology chapter, the development chapter, and at least briefly in many other chapters. Research over the last several decades has established that almost any aspect of behavior has some heritability, and many aspects have substantial heritability. An oft-voiced objection is that no single molecule, such as a gene, could possibly have such far-ranging implications as to control depression, sexual orientation, extraversion, or other complex behaviors. The reply is, look at the extremely far-reaching behavioral impact of ethanol, an even simpler chemical. That analogy can be pushed to useful ends: Yes, alcohol has enormous effects on behavior, and so does a gene, but neither one *forces* any particular behavior. A gene exerts its effects by producing proteins that influence the structure and function of the body. The difference between one gene and another can influence the probability of a given behavior under given circumstances, but the circumstances still matter. A superb example is that of the Pima Indians, most of whom are genetically predisposed to weight gain on a standard U.S. diet, but who had much lower weights on their traditional diet of Sonoran desert plants. So weight is a function of both the genes and the environment.

Mind–Brain Monism

Consider this simple idea that is rich in philosophical implications: Brain activity is the mind. Mind–body dualism comes naturally to almost everyone, and I do not expect to talk students out of it quickly, but the fact is that if you lose any part of your brain, you lose part of your mind. If we increase or decrease activity in any brain area, we see a corresponding change in some aspect of behavior. The key point for beginning students is not which brain area is associated with which behavior, but merely the simple idea that every aspect of behavior is associated with and dependent on brain activities. A few key examples can underscore that point, and the choice of examples is not critical.

In a large class, students may not publicly voice their misgivings about mind–brain monism, but many do believe their free will supersedes their brain and the limitations of physics. No one discards this view quickly, but the biological psychology section should at least give students something about which to think.

Brain Plasticity . . . Within Limits

Since the time of Santiago Ramon y Cajal in the late 1800s, neuroscientists believed that all vertebrate neurons formed during embryological development and that no new ones could form later. Researchers have now found that immature stem cells can differentiate into additional neurons throughout life in certain brain areas, such as the hippocampus and parts of the cerebral cortex (Eriksson et al., 1998). The additional neurons may help compensate for the loss of small numbers of cells (Magavi, Leavitt, & Macklis, 2000) and may be one mechanism of learning. The growth of new neurons is, however, ordinarily slow and limited, unlike the replacement of blood cells. Researchers may some day find ways to facilitate the production of new neurons to repair the damage of Parkinson's disease, Alzheimer's disease, and so forth.

Experience can alter the structure of axons and dendrites at any time in life, and dendritic structure is almost constantly in flux (Purves & Hadley, 1985). Specific, prolonged experiences can lead to demonstrable, if small, modifications of brain anatomy. For one human example, a study using magnetoencephalography to map brain areas found that the area of the right somatosensory cortex sensitive to fingers was larger in people who started playing stringed instruments in early childhood than in people who started later and larger in people who started in adolescence than in people who never played them at all (Elbert, Pantev, Wienbruch, Rockstroh, & Taub, 1995). The right somatosensory cortex corresponds to the left hand, and stringed instrument players finger the strings with their left hand. Evidently the extensive use of those fingers expanded their brain representation.

Similarly, nearly every adult with absolute pitch—the ability to hear a note such as $C^\#$ and identify it—has had extensive, consistent music training since early childhood (Takeuchi & Hulse, 1993). They also have larger than usual development in part of the left temporal cortex (Schlaug, Jäncke, Huang, & Steinmetz, 1995). Although we do not have a true experiment with children randomly assigned to extensive music training or not, the results suggest that the training led to a change in the brain—here, a change large enough to see with the unaided eye if one knows where to look.

We are accustomed to thinking that the infant brain is much more plastic than the adult brain, but could extensive experience modify adult brain anatomy too? One study found that posterior parts of the hippocampus, an area believed to be critical for spatial memory, are slightly larger in experienced taxi drivers than in other people matched for age, sex, and handedness. The increased size in the right hippocampus correlated .6 with years of taxi driving (Maguire et al., 2000).

A further example of brain plasticity that has clinical implications is the phantom limb. After amputation of a limb or any other body part, many people report continuing sensations as if the part were still present. Those sensations can be long-lasting and sometimes painful. An explanation has now emerged. Suppose a hand is amputated. The area of somatosensory cortex that usually responds to the hand now receives little or no input from its usual source. However, it receives other axons, representing other body parts. Previously those axons' synapses were virtually silent as the cells responded to the hand input. Now that the hand axons are inactive, the cortical cells begin responding to synapses previously ignored (Florence, Taub, & Kaas, 1998). Within the somatosensory cortex, the face area is adjacent to the hand area, and typically the hand area becomes sensitive to face axons after amputation of a hand. When face stimulation excites the hand area of the cortex, however, it is perceived not as face but as hand, and therefore produces a phantom sensation (Ramachandran & Blakeslee, 1998; Ramachandran & Hirstein, 1998).

United Consciousness Without a Central Processor

Brain functioning is a conglomerate of many separate specialized functions that somehow get united, although we do not know how. Indeed, brain research has called attention to a new problem that was virtually unidentified before the 1990s, known as the *binding problem*. That problem concerns how we bind together different experiences. When I pick up a ringing alarm clock and look at it, I perceive it as a single object that I see, hear, and feel. But how did my brain discern that unity? The visual cortex, auditory cortex, and somatosensory cortex are separate and not directly connected with one another. The brain has no central processor, and yet each of us reports a single, unified experience. One hypothesis is that sensory binding depends on exact synchrony of activity in different brain areas (Roelfsema, Engel, König, & Singer, 1997). For example, if you see a ventriloquist's dummy move its mouth in synchrony with what you hear, you attribute the sound to the dummy. If you watch a film that is badly dubbed or that has its sound track slightly out of synchrony with the picture, you immediately stop binding the sight and sound. However, although synchrony is probably necessary for binding, it cannot be sufficient. For example, in a split-brain person, something seen in the left hemisphere will not bind with something heard or felt in the right hemisphere no matter how synchronous.

The lack of a central processor also has implications for intelligence. One of the oldest and best documented phenomena in psychology is Spearman's g, the high correlation among scores on tests of different intellectual abilities. Traditionally, the most popular explanation has been that all such abilities depend on a single, general process such as working memory. However, given that brain damage can in some cases impair one ability while sparing others, we should consider an alternative explanation for g. One possibility is that all brain areas grow and develop in synchrony; the larger any one area is, the larger any other area is (Finlay & Darlington, 1995). Presumably the reason is that all brain areas depend on health, nutrition, and genes that are responsible for cell divisions and synapse formation in the brain.

Simple Synapses and Complex Behaviors

The information processing of the brain depends on synapses, but we cannot understand important behavioral processes just by looking at the activity of a synapse. Learning takes place through synaptic changes, brain plasticity depends on growth of new synapses, and drugs exert their effects on synapses. However, identifying changes at synapses is not the same as understanding corresponding behaviors. I have seen texts that listed a behavioral function for each neurotransmitter (such as dopamine-pleasure), but we have no justification for believing that any transmitter contributes only to one kind of behavior, much less that a given behavior depends only on one transmitter. For example, the drug LSD exerts its effects mainly at certain kinds of serotonin receptors, but knowing that fact does not explain why stimulating those receptors has the effects that it does. We know more about where things happen in the brain than why or how they happen.

Researchers once believed that antidepressant drugs exerted their effects by increasing activity at serotonin and dopamine synapses, and that antipsychotic drugs exerted their effects by blocking dopamine synapses. Indeed, antidepressant and antipsychotic drugs do have those effects. The problem is that the drugs exert those synaptic effects within minutes or hours (depending on the drug), but do not produce behavioral benefits until someone has taken the drugs for 2 or 3 weeks. What happens in the meantime is still uncertain.

The point extends beyond synapses. When researchers report a linkage between some behavior and increased activity at some synapse, or a particular pattern of activity as seen in an MRI or PET scan, or an aberrant gene or abnormal hormone pattern, or whatever else, it is tempting to say "now we understand the cause of the behavior." In fact, finding such a link is just a good first step toward an understanding.

CONCLUSION

Biological psychology can and should be an extraordinarily interesting topic if we start with the major issues (such as the mind–brain relationship) and the major principles. It can be boring, tedious, and difficult if we concentrate too heavily on memorizing brain structures, names of chemicals, and other arcane details. The same principle applies to teaching anything: It is possible to make any topic interesting or boring depending on whether we start with major themes or minor details.

REFERENCES

Elbert, T., Pantev, C., Wienbruch, C., Rockstroh, B., & Taub, E. (1995). Increased cortical representation of the fingers of the left hand in string players. *Science, 270,* 305–307.

Eriksson, P. S., Perfilieva, E., Björk-Eriksson, T., Alborn, A.-M., Nordborg, C., Peterson, D. A., & Gage, F. H. (1998). Neurogenesis in the adult human hippocampus. *Nature Medicine, 4,* 1313–1317.

Finlay, B. L., & Darlington, R. B. (1995). Linked regularities in the development and evolution of mammalian brains. *Science, 268,* 1578–1584.

Florence, S. L., Taub, H. B., & Kaas, J. H. (1998). Large-scale sprouting of cortical connections after peripheral injury in adult macaque monkeys. *Science, 282,* 117–121.

Lashley, K. S. (1930). Basic neural mechanisms in behavior. *Psychological Review, 37,* 1–24.

Magavi, S. S., Leavitt, B. R., & Macklis, J. D. (2000). Induction of neurogenesis in the neocortex of adult mice. *Nature, 405,* 951–955.

Maguire, E. A., Gadian, D. G., Johnsrude, I. S., Good, C. D., Ashburner, J., Frackowiak, R. S. J., & Frith, C. D. (2000). Navigation-related structural change in the hippocampi of taxi drivers. *Proceedings of the National Academy of Sciences, 97,* 4398–4403.

Purves, D., & Hadley, R. D. (1985). Changes in the dendritic branching of adult mammalian neurones revealed by repeated imaging *in situ. Nature, 315,* 404–406.

Ramachandran, V. S., & Blakeslee, S. (1998). *Phantoms in the brain.* New York: Morrow.

Ramachandran, V. S., & Hirstein, W. (1998). The perception of phantom limbs: The D. O. Hebb lecture. *Brain, 121,* 1603–1630.

Roelfsema, P. R., Engel, A. K., König, P., & Singer, W. (1997). Visuomotor integration is associated with zero time-lag synchronization among cortical areas. *Nature, 385,* 157–161.

Schlaug, G., Jäncke, L., Huang, Y., & Steinmetz, H. (1995). In vivo evidence of structural brain asymmetry in musicians. *Science, 267,* 699–701.

Takeuchi, A. H., & Hulse, S. H. (1993). Absolute pitch. *Psychological Bulletin, 113,* 345–361.

29

Teaching Statistics and Research Methods

Scott A. Bailey
Texas Lutheran University

Ware and Brewer (1999) estimated that "almost 75% of undergraduate psychology departments in the United States require their students to complete an introductory course in statistics" (p. 1). According to a recent article in the American Psychological Association (APA) Monitor, an experimental methods course is among the few required courses in most psychology curricula ("The Evolution of Experimental Psychology," 1999). In the *Handbook for Teaching Statistics and Research Methods*, Ware and Brewer (1999) underscored the importance of effective teaching of statistics and research methods. These courses are prevalent in undergraduate curricula and provide key opportunities for students to develop and sharpen their critical thinking skills. It is no wonder that they receive so much attention in periodicals such as *Teaching of Psychology* (*ToP*) and at professional meetings with forums where psychology teachers share ideas.

When considering an optimal approach to teaching statistics and research methods—one that would be characterized as both good pedagogy and interesting to students—we immediately recognize something of a chicken-and-egg problem. Students who fear statistics may be better served by introduction to research methods concepts prior to taking a statistics course. However, understanding statistics facilitates comprehension of methodological concepts. The matter is further complicated by the fact that some students resist the counsel of their academic advisors to take either course. The reputation of the courses as screening components of the department's curriculum may strengthen the aversion experienced by some students to either or both of these classes. It is regrettable that students approach statistics and research methods with such trepidation given that the desired learning outcomes for these courses will serve them well when they seek admission to graduate or professional school or to enter the job market.

There is at least one other significant obstacle to getting students to appreciate the importance of developing good design and analytic skills. Many students are attracted to psychology by an interest in an applied career, such as counseling or clinical psychology, and falsely believe that statistics and methodology courses bear little or no relationship to their career interests. Student understanding of the value of methodology courses for applied careers will likely not develop until long after the courses have been completed—a fact that threatens to stifle student responding to even the most interesting courses teachers can offer.

How, then, should we go about presenting statistics and research methods to maximize student learning and appreciation for these courses? How can we address these goals while organizing our approaches to these courses such that students will enjoy them? This chapter reviews a variety of issues and topics concerning these perennial questions.

THEMES AND VARIATIONS

A course in statistics commonly serves as a prerequisite to enrollment in a research methods class. Ideally, someone whose interests are centered on the application of statistics to psychological research and concepts teaches the course. Depending on the institution, however, someone from outside the psychology department may teach the statistics course. Irrespective of who teaches it, students may leave their first statistics course wondering why they were there in the first place. Students may not make appropriate connections between their interests in psychology and fundamental concepts in statistics, and they may not meet the goals that warrant using the statistics course as a prerequisite to studying research methods.

In other cases, the statistics course and the research methods course are taken concurrently. This approach improves the likelihood that students will see the connections between the two courses. However, it is difficult to ensure that students will be introduced to research design techniques and the associated statistical analyses with appropriate timing. A blocked course arrangement, involving faculty for the two classes that coordinate their courses well, can minimize timing problems.

Another approach involves integrating the content from the two areas in a single course or sequence of courses. The textbook market has a limited number of books that integrate the concepts of research methodology and associated statistical analyses (see e.g., Furlong, Lovelace & Lovelace, 2000; Heiman, 2001). However, the integrated approach may have some decided advantages over the statistics-first and the blocked two-course approaches to these content areas. Note that in order to address all the concepts normally covered in these courses when they are taught separately, the integrated course really has to be a two-course sequence. The advantage of integrating statistics and research methods is pedagogical rather than temporally efficient in nature.

Textbooks

Research Methods Textbooks. An APA *Monitor* article on the history of experimental psychology textbooks ("The Evolution of Experimental Psychology," 1999) reviewed the prevalent textbooks through the years since Titchener's (1905) four-volume *Experimental Psychology: A Manual of Laboratory Practice* was the mainstay. The next significantly influential text on the subject was Woodworth's (1938) book, *Experimental Psychology*, which was organized by subject with methodological issues treated secondarily. (Interestingly, Woodworth is credited for popularizing the concepts of independent and dependent variables in psychological research.) Stevens's (1951) well-known *Handbook of Experimental Psychology* was the last single-volume text to address all the major topics under the umbrella of experimental psychology. McGuigan's (1960) book, *Experimental Psychology: A Methodological Approach*, was the first to center on methodology as its primary focus. Now in its seventh edition, McGuigan's (1996) text, *Experimental Psychology: Methods of Research*, continues to be popular among research methods teachers.

Although many of the books that focus on methodology share much in common, there are some interesting examples of alternative approaches to organizing and presenting the subject. These include *Experimental Psychology: Understanding Psychological Research* (Kantowitz, Roediger, & Elmes, 2001), which is organized into two parts: Fundamentals of Research and Principles and Practices of Experimental Psychology. The first part presents basic issues in research methodology, and the second part provides an overview of several content areas in psychology, with illustrations of the ways the basic research tools are put to use throughout the broad discipline. In their text, *The Psychologist as Detective: An Introduction to Conducting Research in Psychology*, Smith and Davis (2001) incorporated student research to illustrate applications of the methodologies that are presented. Smith and Davis made copious use of citations from student journals and student presentations at professional meetings and student-oriented conferences. This approach serves to introduce students not only to the central concepts, but also to the fact that many undergraduates conduct original psychological research. The clear objectives of this approach are to make the topics match more closely the interests of students and to make the prospect of doing research less intimidating. Finally, Heiman (2001) introduced statistics and research methods together in his book *Understanding Research Methods and Statistics: An Integrated Introduction for Psychology*. This text presents the issues central to most research methodology books, but integrates design and associated statistical models as it progresses from simple to more challenging concepts. His use of psychological examples makes it easy to understand that research methods and statistics go together like hand and glove (contrast this with the disconnect experienced by some students who take statistics and research methods as separate courses).

Supplements. In addition to having students read comprehensive texts on statistics and methodology, teachers may wish to incorporate supplemental books to help convey concepts, contextualize material, and provide overviews of the steps involved in psychological report writing. Several books that can serve as excellent supplements to a primary course textbook are available. Stanovich's (2001) book, *How to Think Straight About Psychology*, provides humorous and otherwise memorable illustrations of several psychological concepts and issues. Stanovich presents arguments, examples and alternative explanations of data such that students are able to monitor development of their own critical thinking skills. Matsumoto's (1994) book, *Cultural Influences on Research Methods and Statistics*, is a brief but information-packed overview of issues that apply to cross-cultural research; it serves to reinforce what researchers generally need to know with respect to project design and analysis. Davitz and Davitz's (1996) *Evaluating Research Proposals: A Guide for the Behavioral Sciences* provides a means for assessing research proposals as well as clear summaries of important terms and their definitions and applications for psychology. Research methods teachers often require students to purchase the *Publication Manual of the American Psychological Association* (2001) to have as a resource.

Research Proposal

A common feature of research methods courses is a required research project proposal. Those faculty confined to teaching the course in a single semester, may require their students to carry out the project in addition to proposing it. Other faculty encourage students to perform their proposed projects subsequent to completing the methods course. As the time constraints of a single term limit students' abilities to perform thorough literature reviews, it is important to recognize the increased likelihood that they will unintentionally replicate others' work when they intend to do something original. However, because the primary goals for the first research project are more processes- than content-oriented this may be insignificant.

The benefits of having students design research projects are many. Perhaps most importantly, students learn to think differently and to develop appropriate questions. Many students are unaccustomed to thinking in the terms of controlled, methodological research. If the parameters of the assignment include that the research must be experimental in nature, the students will be more likely to sharpen their critical thinking skills and develop a fuller appreciation for data from systematically carried out empirical studies.

Teachers may choose to capitalize on a significant learning opportunity for their students by having them critique one another's research designs, thereby raising students' levels of awareness of both the merits and shortcomings of each proposal. Open discussion of the proposals allows teachers to underscore that there is no perfect design; an awareness of this fact can serve to liberate newcomers from their concerns about making mistakes. Another way to engage students to think about the relative merits of different research projects is to share manuscripts that are specially selected to illustrate examples of critical comparison groups, common design flaws, and so on. Ware, Badura & Davis (in press) have described a number of exercises that can be done using student (or professional) journal articles to enhance students' understanding of particular content areas, research methodology, statistics, writing style and APA format guidelines.

IDEAS AND RESOURCES FOR FACULTY

Classroom/Laboratory Exercises

Many exercises and demonstrations have been published in *ToP*, the quarterly publication of Division 2 of the APA (Society for the Teaching of Psychology). A selective set of these exercises and demonstrations has been reprinted in the *Handbook for Teaching Statistics and Research Methods* (Ware & Brewer, 1999), which is now in its second edition. The articles were written by and for teachers of undergraduate and graduate statistics and research methods. This resource is organized in two sections, Statistics and Research Methods, and has a subject index that is useful for identifying each article from the book that addresses a given topic. Examples of topics that are addressed in the statistics section of the book include generating data sets, elaborating statistical concepts with common experience, an intuitive approach to teaching analysis of variance, creating a handout of common errors in statistics, and repeated administration of exams in statistics courses. Examples from the research methods section of the book include introducing students to psychological research, avoiding subject pool contamination, teaching ethical considerations, creating guidelines for conducting literature reviews, teaching hypothesis testing, systematic observation, research design, collaborative writing, critical thinking and student presentations.

In-Class Experiments

It is often argued that the best way to learn something is by doing it. The value of having research methods students collect data, then, is clear. Although it may be optimistic to expect students to design and conduct their own research within the confines of a single semester, it is quite appropriate for students to conduct "canned experiments" on one another or on students from the school's human subjects pool. Even if students are to run their own projects, it may be desirable for them to practice by performing a canned experiment first. Although many projects are used for the purpose of getting students involved in gathering and analyzing data, a perennial favorite is a replication of the classic study by Stroop (1935).

Studying the Stroop effect is interesting for several reasons. A search of the PsycInfo database on *Stroop* reveals over 1,800 records in psychology and related periodicals. These include citations from a wide variety of journals, ranging from those that are basic to those that are applied in focus. This number and variety makes clear how significant the impact of a single finding or phenomenon can be. This exercise also helps students develop clearer pictures of how science progresses. For example, when reading the original (Stroop, 1935) article one discovers the seriousness with which research is conducted, particularly with respect to the issues of experimental control. Conducting replications serves to introduce students to the process of doing research. Depending on whether a new manipulation is made in the procedural protocol, students may be able to extend the literature on the basic phenomenon. A simple, in-class demonstration experiment on the Stroop effect can be very useful in helping students identify independent, dependent, confounding and extraneous variables. The teacher may even wish to intentionally build in design flaws for the purpose of facilitating a variables-identification exercise.

American Psychological Association Format Writing

A nearly universal goal for students of research methods courses is to learn the fundamentals of APA format writing. The APA sells books and computer-based resources that the instructor may wish to consider using to help students learn APA format. At a minimum, methods teachers should consider having students acquire a current copy of the publication manual. The fourth edition of the publication manual went through 11 printings, with substantive changes having been made along the way. The fifth edition of the manual is now available. It is important to use the most recent printing of the current edition of the manual, particularly if adherence to the manual's guidelines will be used as a criterion for evaluation and grading.

Resources

Hardcopy. Although *ToP* publishes articles concerning a host of topics and a variety of teaching domains in psychology, it frequently contains articles that pertain to the teaching of statistics and research methods. A useful index of articles that have been published in *ToP* since its inception in 1974 was prepared by Johnson (1991), and it is updated annually. The index may be downloaded from the Division 2 web page (http://www.lemoyne.edu/OTRP/index.html); it is a word processing document that is searchable via the 'find' command of any word processing software.

Online. Because Internet resources come and go, it is impossible to anticipate whether existing sites will remain available or to predict what kinds of resources may develop. As of this writing a few resources that are accessible via at the Academic Info Web site (look under Psychology: Education Materials, *http://www.academicinfo.net/psychteach.html*) deserve mention here. That site contains a directory of several useful resources for teachers—including Internet Psychology Laboratory, Office of Teaching Resources in Psychology (OTRP) Online, PsychExperiments, Psychology Tutorials and Demonstrations, Teaching Resources (hosted by the American Psychological Society [APS]), WEB Experimental Psychology Lab, and Web Interface for Statistics Education (WISE).

Conferences and Meetings. The APA, its regional affiliates, and the APS host annual conferences that include forums for psychology teachers. In addition, there are several annual regional conferences sponsored by Division 2 of the APA. These forums, including roundtable discussions, symposia, invited addresses, and presentations, often address course-relevant material.

OPPORTUNITIES AND RESOURCES FOR STUDENTS

Involving Upper Division Students and Graduate Teaching Assistants

Whether you teach in a department with graduate students or at an exclusively undergraduate institution, there are ways to obtain help with organizing canned experiments and addressing common student needs. Enlisting upper division students to help organize and carry out class exercises and serve as resources for the students enrolled in the course can be useful: Students in statistics and research methods courses appreciate having a peer resource person who has a good command of the course material. Upper division students may, by virtue of participating in the course again, sharpen their own competencies. Finally, faculty who enlist the aid of capable upper division students may facilitate student learning at times when faculty are unavailable.

A common graduate teaching assistant (GTA) assignment is as an assistant to a faculty member who teaches undergraduate psychology research methods. Graduate students who have solid grounding in statistics and research methods are good candidates for such assignments. This advantage may be used as a selling point when convincing students to invest extra efforts in class. GTAs who work with the research methods class may obviously serve the same functions mentioned earlier for upper division undergraduates, but in addition may be enlisted to teach laboratory sections of the methods class and grade homework assignments and objective test material (see chap. 11 by Davis and Huss for more information on training GTAs).

Hardcopy Psychology Journals for Students

Two hardcopy journals devoted to publishing undergraduate student research and general interest articles for psychology students can serve as tools for sharing student work and introducing students to the publication process. Psi Chi, the National Honor Society in Psychology, publishes the *Psi Chi Journal of Under-graduate Research (Psi Chi)*. *Psi Chi* is a reviewed journal and an excellent tool for encouraging students to become active in psychological science. The *Journal of Psychological Inquiry (JPI)* is published by the Great Plains Behavioral Research Association. In addition to publishing original research, *JPI* also includes a topical special features section and advise and information written particularly for undergraduates. The articles published in *Psi Chi* and *JPI* are typically fairly short and easy to read and understand, thereby making them potentially valuable for stimulating thought about research ideas and practicing critical evaluative skills for experimental design and related issues (see Ware et al., in press).

Student Conferences

Psi Chi hosts programs for students at APA (including the regional affiliate organizations) and APS meetings. In addition, students may participate in a number of other state and regional conferences held expressly for students, including meetings organized by state affiliates of the National Academy of Sciences and interdisciplinary honors societies (e.g., Alpha Chi). A significant advantage of taking students to conferences, particularly meetings that feature student research, is that beginning students can see firsthand the nature and variety of projects that have been done by their peers. Further, participation in conferences is an excellent way for students to begin to develop professional networks with students and faculty members from other institutions.

CLOSING COMMENT

Courses in the methodology domain are arguably the most significant components of psychology department curricula. Students learn to think as psychologists through experiences in courses such as statistics and research methods. Without these courses, it is impossible to fully appreciate the material from any of the content courses (e.g., animal learning, cognitive psychology, developmental psychology, psychobiology, social psychology). The skills gained in these courses help prepare students for life as consumers of information, as well as for additional training or work in psychology. Done right, these courses are enlightening for students and can thus be very rewarding to teach. There are many resources to facilitate the development of these critical components of our curricula. In a day when psychology is enjoying widespread popularity, it is perhaps more important than ever that we recognize the significance of these courses as key stepping stones on our students' paths to successful, productive lives and careers.

REFERENCES

American Psychological Association. (2001). *Publication manual of the American Psychological Association* (5th ed.). Washington, DC: Author.

American Psychological Association. (1999). The evolution of experimental psychology [11 paragraphs]. *APA Monitor Online, 30*(11). http://www.apa.org/monitor/dec99/ss5.html

Davitz, J. R., & Davitz, L. L. (1996). *Evaluating research proposals: A guide for the behavioral sciences.* Upper Saddle River, NJ: Prentice-Hall.

Furlong, N., Lovelace, E., & Lovelace, K. (2000). *Research methods and statistics: An integrated approach.* Fort Worth, TX: Harcourt College.

Heiman, G. W. (2001). *Understanding research methods and statistics: An integrated introduction for psychology* (2nd ed.). Boston: Houghton Mifflin.

Johnson, D. E. (1991). A Teaching of Psychology database: 1974–1990. *Teaching of Psychology, 18,* 49–50.

Kantowitz, B. H., Roediger, H. L. & Elmes, D. G. (2001). *Experimental psychology: Understanding psychological research* (7th ed.). Belmont, CA: Wadsworth.

Matsumoto, D. (1994). *Cultural influences on research methods and statistics.* Pacific Grove, CA: Brooks/Cole.

McGuigan, F. J. (1960). *Experimental psychology: A methodological approach.* Englewood Cliffs, NJ: Prentice-Hall.

McGuigan, F. J. (1996). *Experimental psychology: Methods of research* (7th ed.). Upper Saddle River, NJ: Prentice-Hall.

Smith, R. A., & Davis, S. F. (2001). *The psychologist as detective: An introduction to conducting research in psychology* (2nd ed.). Upper Saddle River, NJ: Prentice-Hall.

Stanovich, K. E. (2001). *How to think straight about psychology* (6th ed.). Boston: Allyn & Bacon.

Stevens, S. S. (1951). *Handbook of experimental psychology.* New York: Wiley.

Stroop, J. R. (1935). Studies of interference in serial verbal reactions. *Journal of Experimental Psychology, 18,* 643–662.

Titchener, E. B. (1905). *Experimental psychology: A manual of laboratory practice.* New York: Macmillan.

Ware, M. E., Badura, A. S. & Davis, S. F. (in press). Using student scholarship to develop student research and writing skills. *Teaching of Psychology.*

Ware, M. E., & Brewer, C. L. (Eds.). (1999). *Handbook for teaching statistics and research methods* (2nd Ed.). Mahwah, NJ: Lawrence Erlbaum Associates.

Woodworth, R. S. (1938). *Experimental psychology.* New York: Holt.

30

Teaching the Learning Course: Philosophy and Methods

Lewis Barker
Auburn University

The learning course may be considered the heart of a psychology major because a basic knowledge of psychology requires familiarity with the diverse ideas subsumed under the concepts of learning, motivation, and behavior analysis. Learning is the nurture in the interaction of how genes meet environment, and it is the acquisition process in an information-processing approach to memory. Learning concepts are implicit in the processes of development and acculturation, in educational and vocational psychology, and in distinguishing perception from sensation. Personality? Abnormal Psychology? Motivation? These areas incorporate basic associative processes and the effects of reinforcers and punishers on behavior. It is no surprise that three of four proposed models of undergraduate curricula in psychology include a course in learning (McGovern, Furumoto, Halpern, Kimble, & McKeachie, 1991). Given its central prominence in the psychology curriculum, professors should approach the teaching of learning with due consideration, humility, and passion: The stakes are high, the challenge is clear, and the task is daunting.

First, humility and passion. I have taught undergraduate learning at least twice a year from 1972 to 2000 and graduate learning about every other year. During that same time period (unbelievably, in retrospect), I taught 17 different undergraduate courses, eight graduate courses, and five laboratory courses. Second only to

379

teaching Introduction to Psychology (the Great Humbler), the teaching of learning has been my biggest classroom challenge. Arguably, the learning course presents to psychology students the most conceptual material found in the major. Hence, the learning course is one of the greatest tests for students and professors alike. After teaching 50-plus classes, I am still not satisfied that I know how to teach the best course in Learning and Behavior, the course for which I have had the most passion.

If the teaching of learning is humbling, writing a learning textbook is even more so. How does one presume to know what should be taught in a classroom, let alone how to teach it? Nevertheless, based on 20 years of classroom experience, much collaboration, and a lot of preparation, the first edition of my text on learning and behavior was eventually published (Barker, 1994).

Then well into my teaching career, something strange happened when I began to use my own textbook: The classroom experience not only was revived, but underwent a drastic change. The reason has little to do with the text's content. Rather, I found that having written what I thought was the most important content, the best integration, and the most cohesive theoretical orientation to learning, I had a new problem. What was I supposed to do in the classroom—read it to them? At that point, I became less, not more, professorial. Humility aside for the moment, under these conditions, I think I became a better teacher of learning than I had been in the preceding 22 years.

In the following 10 lessons, I share my personal experience of what I have learned about the teaching of learning. Recognizing that what has worked for me may not work for you, please think of these comments as food for thought, rather than unsolicited advice, and as a philosophy of the teaching of learning, rather than as an instructor's manual.

LESSON 1: KNOW YOUR STUDENTS' CAPABILITIES AND WORK TO EXTEND THEM

My experience best matches those of you who teach at large state universities and/or what might be considered second-tier schools. My teaching experience has been primarily at Baylor University where (best guess) the average psychology major came with about 1100 SAT scores. As at your institution, over the years, we have had some students who struggled below that level and others with perfect SAT scores.

What I ended up doing in the classroom reflected a philosophy of trying to provide learning opportunities for students of differing abilities. As such, I have little patience for colleagues who lament "the pathetic abilities of the most recent generation of students." (As an aside, I have now experienced three decades of students. It is *not* my experience that meaningful differences, in the form of secular trends, exist in the classroom abilities of students of the 1970s, 1980s, and 1990s.) Recognize that administrators set student selection standards. To the best of our abilities, professors should expend their energy responding to the challenge of teaching those who enroll in their classes. Teach, and attempt to teach well, the students you get.

How does a professor teach a class of 40 or more students of differing abilities? The recitation method, discussed later, allows me to tailor in-class questions and comments to each student. For example, rather than ask a conceptual question to a student struggling to make a C, I would be more likely to ask for a definition of a learning term. Likewise, I will not bore an exceptional student with a "gimme." From one perspective, this is not fair; I am holding different students to different standards. From another perspective, however, asking simpler questions allows a marginal student to experience success. With growing confidence, that student may be in a position later in the semester to entertain more difficult ideas.

To a lesser degree, a good lecturer does the same thing. In the words of my mentor, Dr. James C. Smith at Florida State University, a good lecturer's behavior is controlled by how students respond. Students' facial expressions and other behaviors (such as paying attention, yawning, looking around, or doodling) can be thought of as discriminative stimuli that set the occasion for a professor to either continue or change what he or she is doing. Perhaps by integrating all students' responses, a good lecturer can tell whether individual learning connections have been made. I am skeptical of that analysis. I prefer the one-on-one interactions afforded by the recitation method.

LESSON 2: KNOW AND SHARE WITH STUDENTS THE PLACE OF THE LEARNING CLASS IN THE CURRICULUM

A professor responsible for teaching the learning course should have some under-standing of why most departments of psychology include a course in learning in their curriculum (see Brewer et al., 1993). Entertaining answers to this question leads to others: What is psychology? What does it mean to major in psychology? How does the learning course fit into a student's curriculum leading to a B.A. or B.S. degree? (For discussion of these issues, see Halpern et al., 1998; McGovern, et al., 1991; McGovern & Reich, 1996.) Here the professor brings to the classroom a knowledge of psychology and a philosophy of knowledge that exceeds the course content of learning. Implicit in the professor's choice of profession and in teaching a college course is a commitment to the intellectual and social values of higher education. The learning course provides students yet another unique glimpse of what is meant by the liberal arts and sciences.

TABLE 30.1
Goals for Learning and Behavior

1. To contribute to the student's educational experience within the framework of the College of Arts and Sciences.
2. To allow the student to become a part of that small subset of the world's cultures that is literate and scientifically educated.
3. To encourage the student to entertain a scientific worldview as a meaningful alternative to a non-scientific one.
4. To enhance the student's understanding of the scientific method, which in turn allows the student to begin to engage in critical thinking.
5. To enhance the student's scientific vocabulary, which in turn allows the student to begin to enter into discourse with behavioral scientists and other learned people in our culture.
6. To enhance each student's understanding of behavior as an outcome of processes that have developed as a function of the interaction of one's unique heredity expressed in a unique environment.
7. To attain insight into the psychological concepts of learning and behavior, and to apply this knowledge to further understand oneself and others.

Your students will not necessarily see the world this way: If you think it is important information, tell them. It obviously is important to me, and I include "Goals for Learning and Behavior" in my course syllabus (see Table 30.1).

This statement of goals provides the students (and me) a context for studying learning. Ordered from most general to specific ones, these goals are followed by a statement of objectives in the course syllabus.

LESSON 3: SPECIFY COURSE OBJECTIVES AND STRATEGIES WITHIN THE CONTEXT OF A DETAILED SYLLABUS

Goals 3 and 4 in Table 30.1 inform the student that the psychology of learning is understood from a particular worldview—namely, a perspective that employs the scientific method. The syllabus further specifies that methodology and philosophy are discussed in Chapter 1 of the text and in the first few lectures.

A detailed syllabus is pedagogically sound to the extent that it sets the students' expectations for the semester. In fleshing out the course objectives for Goals 3 through 7 by reference to learning concepts found in text and lectures, the syllabus provides a contract between the student and professor. The idea is to replace ambiguity with predictability as much as possible. For example, the syllabus contains a self-test checklist of key terms, names, and concepts in learning that are useful in preparation for recitation, quizzes, and the final examination. Compulsive as it sounds, in my teaching career, I have encountered few students who complain about a nine-page syllabus that informs them, for example, that they should be ready to discuss schedules of reinforcement on October 5th and conditioning of the immune system on November 14. I also propose study strategies as follows (from the syllabus):

> Memorization is undervalued in higher education. The process of memorization prepares you for examinations, so memorize key terms in the textbook. You will be asked several key terms from each chapter in recitation and on each of 10 quizzes. To store information in long-term memory, cognitive learning theorists emphasis Rehearsal, Rehearsal, Rehearsal.

LESSON 4: PROMOTE ACTIVE LEARNING: THE RECITATION METHOD

One of the course objectives specified on the first day of class is to promote active learning in the classroom by reducing occasions for passive learning. For simplicity, I suggest to the class that traditional lectures set the occasion for passive learning, and that instead of a lecture format this class be taught by the recitation method. (Before attempting the recitation method, I used a lecture format interspersed with small-group activities.)

The recitation method has several components that collectively require a student's active participation in class to be successful in the course. The first day, I tell the students what the components are: (a) regular class attendance, (b) preparation before every class rather than just before written quizzes and examinations, (c) focused attention in the classroom, and (d) oral as well as written assessment of performance. Then the bombshell: "Throughout the semester, students will be quizzed on each chapter *before* the chapters are discussed in class." But . . . But . . .

Here is the rationale I provide to the students: You have an excellent text that has been written at a level that you will be able to read, as demonstrated both by previous students and your junior/senior status in college. I cannot explain the material any better in the classroom. (A white lie.) So, I will first quiz you over the material in a multiple-choice, short-answer identification format. Then, following the quiz and on succeeding class days, each of you will be randomly called on to describe/discuss/explain orally some content from the chapter over which you were just tested. For example, I might show you a graph of the results of an experiment from your reading (or from the test you just took) and have you interpret it to the class. Then I might ask the person sitting next to you if your interpretation was correct. (My facial expression might mislead your classmate to answer incorrectly on the odd chance she or he had not been listening.) Both your response and the next person's will be formally evaluated. I might ask you to compare and contrast *conditioned* from *latent inhibition* or tell me what are the likely response tendencies following various types of partial reinforcement. One or more of your peers may help me decide how many points to give you for your answer based on its completeness and clarity of presentation. Perhaps I will describe some specific changes in an animal's behavior following an experimental treatment and ask you whether it is an example of prepared learning and, if so, why. However, we have shared responsibility for your education, so if your answer needs fleshing out, I will provide details and explanations in a lecture format. By turning more of the responsibility over to you (reading the text to prepare for quizzes and recitation), you learn and retain more information.

LESSON 5: APPLY PRINCIPLES OF REINFORCEMENT AND PUNISHMENT IN THE CLASSROOM

Still on the first class day, I suggest to students that the distribution of available points to be earned for various activities has been carefully constructed. The idea is to reinforce differentially certain of their behaviors throughout the semester. Indeed, one can consider the university's grading system to be based on secondary reinforcers that maintain behavior. (Only later do these ideas become reframed in terms of *negative reinforcement*—a concept that takes more time and classroom discussion to develop.)

Hence, I tell students that regular attendance is important both to me and to their performance and is reinforced within a point system. Although a teacher can lecture to a half-empty classroom, she or he cannot effectively use the recitation method with absent students. Therefore, students get both attendance points and recitation points for being in class (see Table 30.2). If a randomly selected student's name comes up on a day that the student is absent, a 0 is recorded for recitation.

Table 30.2 shows how a recitation answer is evaluated. For a class of 40 students during a 15-week semester, I can ask each student four to five questions—or approximately five students each 50-minute class session. Sometimes I ask a given student two to three related questions in succession (e.g., a definition of a key term, an example, a series of questions about this and other examples) and give one recitation score for his or her collective responses.

TABLE 30.2
Evaluating Recitation (From the Syllabus)

Activity	Points
Your answer, when asked, is "I don't know" (Honesty pays)	1
You make no response for ~5 seconds	0
You make a wild guess or BS me (waste time)	0
Adequate answer	3
Good answer	4
Great answer	5

Although I do not share with a student the number of points earned for a specific answer, my immediate verbal responses, both positive and negative, provide an adequate knowledge of results that serves to reinforce or punish (sparingly) the student's recitation. The immediacy of reinforcement and punishment in the recitation procedure, plus scoring the 15-minute quizzes in class immediately after collecting them, embodies, of course, sound learning principles. In justifying to students why these activities are structured in this way, I make explicit the application of the theory of the efficacy of immediate reinforcement and punishment.

Some students express concern about being called on in class. The reasons stated are (a) not wanting to look foolish, (b) not having to do this in other classes (preferring anonymity and merely "taking the tests to pass the course"), and (c) being unfairly evaluated because they inherited a genetically determined trait of shyness. I try to be sensitive to the first and third reasons, but I am adamant with students that learning the skills of making on-the-spot oral responses to questions, and entering the give-and-take of academic discourse, are traditional, if not prevalent, goals of higher education. These behaviors also have real-world applicability. If a student is shy, recitation presents an opportunity to practice engaging in social interactions under the watchful eye of the professor qua behaviorist who uses successive approximation and the appropriate application of reinforcers in a forgiving environment. It is also the professor's job not to allow someone to look foolish. I tell students that they can pass by simply saying, "I don't know." Recitation provides students the opportunity to correct their thinking immediately. Students also find that recitation in the classroom can have a leveling effect in that the best test-taker on occasion becomes more tongue-tied in an oral exchanges than does a verbal, socially adept C student.

LESSON 6: THE WAYS IN WHICH STUDENTS ARE EVALUATED SHOULD REFLECT THE APPLICATION OF PRINCIPLES OF LEARNING

My syllabus provides students the relative point values of attendance, recitation, quizzes, and a comprehensive final exam. The various weights of each activity are carefully explained to the students. For example, attendance and recitation are worth approximately 25% of the final grade. (For each occasion a student is called on, the student earns a percentage of recitation points that, over the semester, is averaged and multiplied by 40 possible points.) Being absent subtracts 1 point from 40 attendance points (the punishment contingency is made explicit), and perfect attendance earns 5 bonus points.

Another goal of the course is high performance on a comprehensive final exam (comprised of multiple-choice, short answer essay, and key-term identification questions). To reinforce those behaviors that contribute to high performance on a comprehensive final exam, students earn about 25% of all possible points in this activity. I suggest to students that the best preparation for the final exam is the distributed learning that comes about through timely reading and testing (quizzes) over each chapter throughout the semester. Collectively, students can earn approximately 50% of the possible course points from these quizzes. Why half the points from quizzes? Students earn the most points for appropriate behavior on these quizzes because they constitute the best preparation for both recitation behavior and performance on the comprehensive final.

The learning course may be the only college class in which students can gain insight into behaviors in which they commonly engage that relate to "getting good grades." Grading reflects simple principles such as reinforcement and behavioral control, and explaining this to students helps them understand the objectives of their courses. One of the reasons that I enjoy teaching the learning class is the explicit opportunity it affords to apply principles of learning—the subject matter of the course—to an understanding of the teaching process, the learning process, and student evaluation.

LESSON 7: USE KEY TERMS TO ORGANIZE THE BREADTH OF CONTENT OF YOUR COURSE

What is the content of learning? A recent survey of learning textbooks (Epting, Saville, & Buskist, 2001) revealed diversity in both the depth and breadth of content as well as theoretical orientation. Such diversity should be neither disheartening nor surprising because learning continues to reflect the activities of a relatively young and evolving science of psychology. Nevertheless, for professors who worry about defining the core of learning as I do, Table 30.3 provides a decade-old checklist of "Top 100 Terms/Concepts in Learning and Behavior" (Boneau, 1990). A learning professor might want to compare this list with the content of the text being used and the breadth of coverage she or he chooses to teach during the semester.

The teaching goals of a given professor should be related to the terms and concepts that define learning. One way to do this in your course is to make a list of key terms (or by circling those in the text you are using and adding terms you think are important). Some professors may not think it is important for students to focus on definitions, terms, and concepts as I do, yet they may find that certain texts, each with a different emphasis, may have a collection of key terms that best reflects their interests.

In teaching my course, I cover 96 of the 100 terms on Boneau's list, plus many more terms not on the list. In general, I teach learning from an adaptive/evolutionary

TABLE 30.3

Checklist of Top 100 Terms/Concepts in Learning and Behavior
(from Boneau, 1990)

Rank	Term	Rank	Term
1	Classical conditioning	45	Spontaneous recovery
2	Operant conditioning	46	Animal cognition
3	Reinforcement	47	Skinner box
4	Positive reinforcement	48	Skinner's radical behaviorism
5	Extinction	49	Continuous reinforcement
6	Instrumental behavior	50	Negative reinforcement
7	Punishment	51	Satiation
8	Law of effect	52	Autonomic conditioning
9	Avoidance learning	53	Conditioned emotional response
10	*Origin of Species*	54	Two-factor theory, avoidance learning
11	Conditioned stimulus	55	Intervening variables
12	Discrimination learning	56	Biofeedback
13	Experimental extinction	57	Cognitive maps
14	Unconditioned response	58	Compound stimuli
15	Unconditioned stimulus	59	Preparedness
16	Contingencies of reinforcement	60	Conditioned inhibition
17	Reflex	61	Connectionism (neural modeling)
18	Schedules of reinforcement	62	Experimental analysis of behavior
19	Behavior modification	63	Learned helplessness
20	Empirical law of effect	64	Opponent process theory (Solomon)
21	Habituation	65	Second-order conditioning
22	Stimulus generalization	66	Connectionism (Thorndike)
23	Pavlov vs. Thorndike learning	67	Expectancy theory
24	Conditioned fear	68	Intertrial interval
25	Homeostasis	69	Neutral stimulus (Pavlov)
26	Generalization gradient	70	Selection by consequences
27	Stimulus control	71	Sensitization
28	Behavior therapy	72	SS vs. SR learning
29	Conditioned reinforcement	73	Successive approximation
30	Response shaping	74	Voluntary–involuntary distinction
31	Instinct	75	Insight learning (Köhler)
32	Partial reinforcement effect	76	Blocking
33	Negative transfer	77	Desensitization
34	Secondary reinforcement	78	*The Behavior of Organisms*
35	Deprivation	79	Variable-interval schedule
36	Imprinting	80	Approach–avoidance conflict
37	Learning vs. performance	81	Fixed action pattern
38	Brain stimulation	82	Superstitious behavior
39	Delay of reinforcement	83	Two-process theory of learning
40	Primary reinforcement	84	Animal concept learning
41	Species-specific behavior	85	Elicitation
42	Selective attention	86	Magnitude of reward
43	Taste-aversion learning	87	Response competition
44	Trial-and-error learning	88	Autoshaping

(Continued)

TABLE 30.3
(Continued)

Rank	Term	Rank	Term
89	Behavioral modeling	95	Circadian rhythms
90	Garcia–Koelling experiment	96	Conditioned suppression
91	Latent learning	97	Fixed ratio schedule
92	Learning sets	98	Rescorla–Wagner theory
93	Orientating reflex	99	Exploration
94	Conditioned drug tolerance	100	Generalization decrement

Source: From Boneau, C. A. (1990). Psychological literacy. A first approximation. *American Psychologist,* 45, 891–100. Copyright © 1990 by the American Psychological Association. Reprinted with permission.

perspective that includes concepts in behavioral genetics, ethology, and comparative psychology. Two applied chapters explore the role of conditioning and learning in health, drugs, eating and drinking, therapy, teaching, language acquisition, and concept formation. These areas also have key terms that help define content and objectives for students.

LESSON 8: HAVING STUDENTS MEMORIZE KEY TERMS IS PEDAGOGICALLY SOUND

One of the responsibilities of a textbook author is to identify and define key terms or glossary items. From their survey of contemporary learning textbooks, Epting et al. (2001) found wide variability in numbers of key terms and expressed concern that this number had recently declined, perhaps signaling a dumbing-down of texts. My opinion is that the decisions text writers make about "how many terms" and "which terms" is open to alternative interpretations. Here is one rationale: The third edition of my text (Barker, 2001) lists 250 key terms compared with 300 in the previous edition. Why, given similar breadth and depth of content of the two editions, did this change occur? The answer reflects what I do with key terms in my classroom. During the first few classes, I emphasize that to understand the concepts of learning and behavior students should acquire a new working vocabulary. How? They should memorize the definitions of bold-faced key terms in every chapter in the same way that they acquire new vocabulary in chemistry, biology, French, or history. To that end, I sprinkle key terms throughout quizzes and the recitation exercise: "Mr. Jaworski, what is a *gene*? Miss Hernandez, what is a *partial schedule of reinforcement*?" Then with this vocabulary in place, I can address more interesting conceptual issues: "Miss Johnson, how are *conditioned reinforcers* and *conditioned punishers* similar, and how do they differ?"

I cut back on the number of key terms to be memorized during the semester by replacing some bold-faced terms that were arguably of less importance to the learning core. Hence, by the time the comprensive final exam comes around, my students now have a core of 250 rather than 300 terms to review. At test time, they write definitions for 20 randomly selected terms. As an aside, most of the terms in Table 30.3, and about 70 terms that define operant conditioning (Buskist, Miller, Ecott, & Critchfield, 1999), are among the 250 key terms I selected to define the core of learning.

Although I have not systematically studied the results of suggesting to students that they memorize key terms, my impression is that those students who do so are more likely to understand learning concepts, and that they do *not* merely parrot the terms back at exam time. In evaluating their written identification questions, students do not earn extra credit (as more than one student has suggested) for word-for-word definitions. It is gratifying during recitation to hear students respond to a query about a key term with a memorized definition. (I suspect as an adaptive response to the classroom anxiety produced by the recitation method, these memorized responses usually begin to occur about mid-semester. Before class, in preparation for both quizzes and recitations, I have observed many students studying hand-constructed 3 × 5 flash cards with key terms on one side and printed definitions on the other.) Hence, memorizing definitions allows them to perform better on multiple-choice and short-answer essay tests as well as identification tests of terms and concepts. With this vocabulary, more students are able to appreciate the nuances of conceptual issues in learning. At a minimum, having memorized many key terms, students take away from my course a good working vocabulary of learning terminology that can help them in subsequent learning courses.

LESSON 9: USE DISCUSSION QUESTIONS
IN RECITATION

The foregoing discussion of key terms might lead the reader to think that recitation sessions in my classroom are predictable and boring—a regurgitation of definitions. It turns out recitation can set the occasion for great classroom discussions. It begins with preparation: I tell students to pay attention to the discussion questions posed throughout the textbook because I will ask students about them either during recitation or on a quiz.

Let us consider some examples. Assume a student has successfully defined the key term *generalization* during recitation. Then I call on the same or another student and read the following discussion question from the text:

> What do you suppose Dr. Spicey® tastes like? What concepts account for the fact that you think you know what a fictitious drink tastes like?

If the student who reads the question cannot get the discussion started, ask "anyone?" Should someone say "Dr. Pepper," I ask for the concept that best accounts for this answer—*generalization*. Then I ask, "which concept of Pavlov's helps us understand the generalization of the meaning of words?" Because we spend quite a lot of time with the concept, someone is likely to remember the *second signal system*. Hence, this discussion question allows for the integration of several different concepts.

Another example:

> Can you relate the typical outcomes of a *conditioned suppression* procedure to the fact that so few people volunteer to speak out in the classroom?

This discussion question is also an application of learning that illustrates classroom dynamics as they occur. Recitation in an unforgiving environment sets the occasion for punishing "speaking in a classroom," the very behavior that the recitation method is designed to facilitate. How can the environment become a forgiving one? I have found that humor, graciousness, and understanding work better than a tough love approach.

Next is a discussion question that asks students to consider the role of cognitive explanations in learning:

> Why do you think it is so hard to convince someone with a conditioned taste aversion to a specific alcoholic beverage that it really *tastes* OK, that the *taste* didn't make them sick, but rather that they drank too much and suffered alcohol poisoning? Why in this case is reasoning overridden by conditioning?

This question presents the opportunity to compare and contrast cognitive and behavioral approaches to learning. From this example, I carefully lead students to a reiteration of a major theme of the course—that at present, behavioral theories of learning better account for our empirical observations. Often this discussion question promotes one or more self-disclosures, and on occasion it turns into a serious discussion of binge drinking among college students. Although the etiology of binge drinking defies easy explanations, I attempt to lead students in a discussion of reinforcement contingencies that maintain these behaviors, examine why punishment contingencies are ineffective, and attempt to integrate Siegel's analysis of conditioned drug tolerance. Often student comments lead the way, and I do my best to follow.

A final discussion question is asked during the last couple of class days. By now, in responding to difficult personal questions for which there are no simple answers, students are more lively—they are willing to talk, discuss, argue, and apply what they have learned.

> Given the finding that children who have their noses in books most of the time do better in school, score higher on intelligence tests, and are generally smarter and have more successful careers than their less scholarly contemporaries throughout a lifetime, how are you going to raise your own children?

A theme throughout the class is the application of principles of learning in homes, schools, and society. Childrearing involves choices, and students are not neutral about how they were raised or how they will raise their children. Hence, questions of nature–nurture, free will versus determinism, the ethics of shaping behavior, the use of punishment, and other philosophical issues provide capstone-like like course-ending discussions. These discussions take on added meaning for graduating seniors.

LESSON 10: APPLY LEARNING PRINCIPLES IN A NONHUMAN ANIMAL LAB AND IN A CLASSROOM SETTING

For many years, I had the luxury of GTAs who conducted a required learning lab that accompanied the learning course. A separately graded 15-week lab met a couple hours a week for 1 hour credit. A 100-page lab manual directed students through rat lab protocol, a four-group taste aversion learning experiment that generated real data (which they collected, analyzed, and reported in an APA style paper), and through the operant conditioning of bar pressing in a rat (shaping, schedules of reinforcment, and a conditioned discrimination procedure). A lot has been written about the value of a live rat lab so I do not say much here—except for one anecdote. A student returning for a 10th-year reunion recognized me and said, "I don't remember your name, but I will never forget Alex, the rat I trained."

After much agonizing, during my last 2 years at Baylor, I changed the highly successful rat lab into an experience that took students into a kindergarten classroom. In part the agonizing concerned the hours (days, weeks) dealing with an educational bureaucracy. Fortunately, the end result proved substantially better than a traditional rat lab. Students first went through an accelerated, 3-week rat lab to familiarize them with shaping and the application of reinforcement. They then moved into an inner-city kindergarten class to work with at-risk children for 10 weeks. The task? Shaping alphabetic skills by pairing the sight of each letter with its correct pronunciation and socially reinforcing correct performance (i.e., a discriminated operant task). Each college student became a one-on-one problem solver whose job was to determine the best way to motivate, capture the attention, and arrange for reinforceable behavior. In seeking answers to these challenges, students spent a lot of time comparing notes and offering each other suggestions. They brought their training difficulties with kindergartners back into the classroom, where we jointly pursued theoretical analyses to further guide their individual efforts.

After several semesters sorting out the procedures that worked best, an experiment was designed to compare the outcomes of the specific reinforcement of alphabetic skills with a control group in which college students merely read to kindergartners (Lambdin, 2000). The results were equivocal. A few college students reported breakthroughs with their assigned child (corroborated by the child's teacher), but analyses of the differences between the two groups on a number of dependent variables were not significant. Lambdin, and students in the learning class who collected her data, proposed two reasons that they could not reject the null hypothesis: not enough reinforced trials and the confound of exposing both groups to an ongoing kindergarten curriculum (Lambdin, 2000). An unexpected outcome of this experience was that several students made unexpected career choices and began working on their teaching credentials.

A learning lab with at-risk kids takes a class in learning and the typical undergraduate experience to a new level. Indeed, compare this experience with "suggestions for an ideal curriculum" (McGovern & Reich, 1996, p. 255):

1. multiple opportunities for students to be active and collaborative learners,
2. research projects to help students learn the science of psychology,
3. fieldwork, practica, and community service experiences to help students learn the applications of psychology,
4. an emphasis on learning across the curriculum about ethical issues and values, and
5. multiple courses and research methods that heighten students' understanding of diversity in behavior.

The recitation method in the learning course and the applied laboratory in a kindergarten classroom satisfy the first three "suggestions for an ideal curriculum" and contribute to the fourth and fifth suggestions as well.

CONCLUSION

My hope is that this whirlwind tour through my learning course and lab will have some value for others who teach in this area. The recitation method, or my version of it, may be new to some readers. Teachers who try it can make it fit their teaching approach, style, and personality. I was drawn to it because of a preference for conversations over lectures and for discovery over pedantry. Recitation provides an outlet for those with a gregarious, effusive nature—students and professors alike. The discovery includes getting to know students in a way that a lecture format precludes. It is also fun to watch the wheels turn in students' minds after challenging them with an open-ended discussion question or providing opportunities to discover how one concept relates to another.

In reading this chapter, I suspect many eyebrows were raised (as they are among my students on the first day of class) at the suggestion that quizzes be given before the material is covered in class. There may be volumes published to the contrary, but my experience is that it is a pedagogically sound method. Other readers may not like the lack of structure inherent in the recitation method. In part they are right because the first semester using recitation is harrowing for students and professors alike.

After teaching more than 50 classes, I am still not satisfied that I know best how to teach learning, the course for which I continue to have the most passion. However, I eagerly await the next class of students, content in my belief that they know best how I should teach them.

REFERENCES

Barker, L. (1994). *Learning and behavior: A psychobiological perspective.* New York: Macmillan.

Barker, L. (2001). *Learning and behavior: Biological, psychological, and sociocultural perspectives* (3rd ed.). Upper Saddle River, NJ: Prentice-Hall.

Boneau, C. A. (1990). Psychological literacy: A first approximation. *American Psychologist, 45,* 891–100.

Brewer, C. L., Hopkins, J. R., Kimble, G. A., Matlin, M. W., McCann, L. I., McNeil, O. V., Nodine, B. F., Quinn, V. N., & Saundra (1993). Curriculum. In T. V. McGovern (Ed.), *Handbook for enhancing undergraduate education in psychology* (pp. 161–182). Washington, DC: APA.

Buskist, W., Miller, E., Ecott, C., & Critchfield, T. S. (1999). Updating coverage of operant conditioning in introductory psychology. *Teaching of Psychology, 26,* 280–283.

Epting, K., Saville, B., & Buskist, W. (2001). Current trends in learning texts. *The Behavioral Analyst.* 891–900.

Halpern, D. F., Smothergill, D. W., Allen, M., Baker, S., Baum, C., Best, D., Ferrari, J., Geisinger, K. F., Gilden, E. R., Hester, M., Keith-Spiegel, P., Kierniesky, N. C., McGovern, T. V., McKeachie, W. J., Prokasy, W. F., Szuchman, L. T., Vasta, R., & Weaver, K. A. (1998). Scholarship in psychology: A paradigm for the twenty-first century. *American Psychologist, 53,* 1292–1297.

Lambdin, C. L. (2000). *An investigation of the effects of specific training of alphabet skills: The alphabet project at a Waco, Texas charter school.* Unpublished master's thesis, Baylor University, Waco, TX.

McGovern, T. V., Furumoto, L., Halpern, D. F., Kimble, G. A., & McKeachie, W. J. (1991). Liberal education, study in depth, and the arts and sciences major—Psychology. *American Psychologist, 46,* 598–605.

McGovern, T. V., & Reich, J. N. (1996). A comment on the quality principles. *American Psychologist, 51,* 252–255.

31

Using Social Psychology to Teach Social Psychology: How the Field Informs the Course

Elliott D. Hammer
Xavier University of Louisiana

Elizabeth Yost Hammer
Loyola University New Orleans

Like all areas, social psychology presents a unique set of problems and opportunities for its students and instructors. Although the material is usually accessible (students seldom "just can't get it" as happens more frequently in, say, a statistics course), there is always more to the material than meets the eye. The things that make social psychology attractive to students, such as its accessibility and intuitive appeal, make it a good course to engage students and encourage critical thinking. We discuss some of the unusual opportunities that social psychology provides for the student and instructor, suggest some helpful methods instructors can employ in teaching the course that help it come alive for students, and conclude with some commentary on the nature of the critical thinking outcomes that students can take with them long after they may have forgotten material from the class.

THE AMBIVALENT COURSE

Simply put, students generally like the material in social psychology. It is rarely a course that they dread, so getting sufficient numbers for the course is almost never a problem. Nevertheless, many students find that what they thought they would like about the class turns out to be its pitfall. Because the material tends to relate to them, students can develop a false sense of security in their own mastery. We often hear students complain that the book and the class made sense, but the tests did not. Although this incongruence may be the fault of poor evaluation instruments, as students prefer to contend (an excellent opportunity to discuss attribution theory), further discussion with them usually reveals that the devil of the course is in the details. Unfortunately, the details are not the focus of a student who may understand the general idea and has better things to do than attack those details.

Such is the source of frustration for students. What seemed so easy when they first heard about it becomes confusing. The *self-serving bias* and the *fundamental attribution error* seem like the same thing. There cannot be any real difference between *self-monitoring* and *self-perception*, can there? Much of the course renders similar confusion, which can be taxing for the instructor. Only unwavering clarity and attention to specifics can maintain students' faith that the material is not tricky and keep them optimistic about their success in the course. Certain wrong multiple-choice answers seem right to many students, and their use of intuition in a critical analysis seems to be just what we were asking for despite our pleas for them to back up their points with evidence. The double-edged sword of the course's appeal requires attention to these hazards and a memory for the distinctions that seem so clear to us but remain dicey to our students.

Students quickly realize that true understanding of material requires individual reading and study. For example, some classic truisms demonstrate the fallacy of people's use of conventional wisdom. Most of us agree that "two heads are better than one," but we also agree that "too many cooks spoil the broth." "Look before you leap" sounds reasonable except in contrast to "he who hesitates is lost." Social psychology provides the resolutions to these apparent contradictions by specifying the situations in which each statement may hold. We have found that the consideration of these contradictory truisms is one of the most effective ways for students to learn the scientific nature of the field. The need for critical investigation may become clear for the first time to students who may have only recently emerged from the paradoxical era of adolescence. Their status as young adults makes them especially ripe for the lesson that things are not always as they seem—when they really think about it, they see that common sense is not always common.

At the point that students have developed a healthy appreciation for the rigors of the field, they can move on to more extensive study of the area. Students can expand their understanding of social psychology through the wealth of more specialized classes gleaned from their introduction—group dynamics, stereotypes and prejudice, attitudes, and aggression, to name a few. More than most other areas of psychology, students and teachers can see social psychology in terms of different content areas, most of which operate as topics within social psychology textbooks. Of course, all psychological areas need to be decomposed for instructive purposes, but those components rarely can exist on their own. In abnormal psychology, for example, study of only personality disorders excludes other elements of the field.

Likewise, in physiological psychology, you must study nearly all parts of the brain to have a functional knowledge base. In contrast, in social psychology, each segment of the course can be expanded to meet the goals and expertise of the individual instructor without a serious detriment to the experience.

As a field, then, social psychology presents unique opportunities and, to some extent, dilemmas for students. Perhaps the course's most prominent attribute is that it allows for a great deal of creativity and variation in its instruction.

THE VARIABLE COURSE

A number of assignments and activities lend themselves especially well to the social psychology course. Again, because the nature of the course appeals to students, in those rare instances when students have not prepared sufficiently for class, they can still get involved in discussions. Although we certainly advocate every expectation for reading and activities that encourage and reward preparation, some students on any given day will not be ready, and the sometimes intuitive nature of the course (Heider describes the lay person as a naive psychologist, after all) may include even the student with an occasional lapse in work ethic.

Still, the key to encouraging preparation is to make the reading relevant and interesting. One technique to get students to apply their burgeoning understanding of the scientific nature of psychology involves asking them to predict results of studies about which they have not yet read (because it was not assigned or is not mentioned in the textbook, rather than because they skipped the assignment). To discuss specific research findings, most instructors divulge those findings point blank or assign students to read journal articles. In a diversion from this approach, we often begin by describing a particular theory, depict a simplification of a research design for supporting this theory, and describe the methodology that a researcher has used to address the hypothesis in question. In pairs, groups, or individually, students then predict what findings would support the theory.

An example of an appropriate study for this technique is a simplification of the Schwarz and Clore (1983) study on the misattribution of affect. In it, respondents are interviewed on campus on either a pretty, sunny day or a gloomy, rainy day. The interviewer either mentions the weather, making it salient to the interviewee, or does not. The dependent variable was the self-reported mood of the respondents. Students who do not really get the theory initially predict that respondents interviewed on the sunny day will report happier moods than respondents interviewed on the cloudy day. In discussion, they may begin to realize the support that the study provides for the discounting principle in that the rainy weather is associated with worse moods only when the weather is not made salient by the interviewer. If the interviewer draws the respondent's attention to the weather, the respondent has a new attribution for his or her bad mood and thus discounts the impact that other factors have on his or her mood. Thus, the weather, if attended to, actually pushes one's bad mood in the opposite direction.

We usually take a straw poll and then ask students who predicted an incorrect outcome to explain their reasoning. Other students are then invited to explain what might be incorrect about such reasoning. Ideally, then, the entire class is drawn to the actual finding. Although this activity may seem simple for those of us familiar with the literature (hindsight is 20/20 for us too), it challenges students to reason as a scientist does, and forces prediction, rather than just after-the-fact mastery. We try to emphasize that the difficulty of the exercise demonstrates the need for up-front understanding of the material. Studies that work well in this exercise are often 2 × 2 designs even if we have to modify our description of the study to make it fit such a design. Because actual data need not be the focus, we ask our students to predict in terms of high or low levels of the DV. Examples of studies not frequently discussed in detail in social psychology texts, but that make for interesting models for this exercise, are Gilbert, Pelham, and Krull (1988), Devine (1988), and Grigg, Fletcher, and Fitness (1989).

Another helpful tool in approaching the class is to begin with a simple, specific example of a study to use as a model for the social psychological research process. Our favorite is Aronson and Mills' (1959) initial study on cognitive dissonance. In this study, college women are screened for membership in a discussion group that is billed so as to lead them to want to join it. Still, like any good group, they must be initiated to make sure that they are psychologically ready for the discussions that the group has. In their initiation, women in two of the three conditions are asked to read a list of words, ostensibly to make sure that they are comfortable with the frank nature of the discussion. In the severe initiation condition, the participants read a list of profane words; in the mild initiation condition, the words are less racy. The group ends up being a real bust for the participants. When they are asked to rate what they thought of the group (the DV), the results are surprising to many students. Participants who suffered the severe initiation report more liking for their group than do those in the mild or control conditions.

Again, the counterintuitive nature of the findings is useful for later demonstrations of the need for scientific inquiry and critical thought. It also provides a nice opportunity for students to think critically about their own experiences, such as their participation in fraternity hazing, ROTC, and the like. Throughout the semester, the teacher can refer back to the study as an example of the anatomy of a research article, the use of statistics in research, and, most important, the theoretical bases for a study. Discussions of research methods in social psychology similarly can draw on the article for identification of independent and dependent variables, research design, and the like. Revisiting a well-known study can instill confidence and allow students to communicate with expertise. A cursory introduction to the theory of cognitive dissonance provides the background for students to apply the theory to the study. Later discussions of other cognitive dissonance studies also make more sense after an in-depth examination of the Aronson and

Mills (1959) study. Of course, any simple article may provide a good example of social psychological research as long as it is one that students can comprehend and its relevance is clear to students.

Another reason that we like to use Aronson and Mills (1959) is that it is clearly flawed in ways that were largely rectified in a conceptual replication by Gerard and Mathewson (1966). The flaws addressed in the replication encourage students to critique the articles they read and recognize the importance of replication. Most students begin by taking all they read at face value. Seeing articles respectfully criticized by peers can encourage a more critical approach on the part of students. Students are able to follow along with the reasoning, not only for the original study (the story of the study's status as the first empirical test of the theory after Festinger's classic book introducing cognitive dissonance theory), but also for the replication and seeing the process. The discussion is an excellent way to demonstrate the process of imaginative theories tested through scientific methods.

The Aronson and Mills (1959) study and other classics provide a nice opportunity to consider the sociohistorical context of our field. In those cases when students have not been assigned to read (or just have not read) the article in which the words are listed, we ask whether a researcher would be able to attain the same results today as Aronson and Mills did in 1959. Most students say that reading dirty words today would hardly be an embarrassing exercise given the cultural differences that exist. At this point, we ask a student who believes that times are completely different to read the words from the study, which we have on a sheet in our pockets. Today's students (especially the bold ones who criticize the worth of the study) are willing to read the words, but they invariably look or admit to being embarrassed. We then acknowledge that a current study may need to help step up the manipulation, but the theory may hold, and it certainly was a severe initiation for those female students over 40 years ago!

Reproducing classic studies in class frequently makes for insightful examination of the field. Trying to replicate Asch's (1956) famous conformity studies is a bit contrived today, but a number of other demonstrations of conformity can be effective, such as latecomers arriving to find the entire class standing. The new arrivals stand too as they claim, "I'm not a conformist, but they must know something I didn't." A more direct replication that vividly demonstrates the evolution but not dissolution of social tendencies comes from Katz and Braly (1933). Those authors compiled the stereotypes that White students gave for various ethnic groups. Although some of them seem silly today (and many even highly prejudiced people today would avoid listing almost exclusively negative traits for African Americans and almost exclusively positive ones for Whites), the nature of agreement regarding the stereotypes is largely consistent. Also, the lists that our students generate are broader than the lists of 1933, but the difference in breadth provides further evidence of the persistence of outgroup homogeneity. Such patterns are especially interesting with different populations of students. Poll groups of African-American students today, for example, and they will come up with far more adjectives to describe their own group than White students of the 1930s did for "Negroes." Similarly, depending on one's region, perceptions of different ethnic groups may vary dramatically. In the South, for example, stereotypes of Italians are basically confined to exposure to "The Godfather" and "The Sopranos,"as opposed to the "artistic" that Katz and Braly's Princeton students reported. Examining past studies from a current perspective can help students retain the material as they gain appreciation for both the consistency and inconsistency between the original and modern replications.

As compelling as many social psychology studies are, such intuitive appeal does not always yield fruitful class time and can present problems. Unfortunately, two of the sexiest and most commonly discussed classic studies are so atypical for social psychology that they can be more confusing than helpful. In its original and most famous form, Milgram's (1963) obedience studies lack an independent variable, and Zimbardo's prison study (Haney, Banks, & Zimbardo, 1973) lacks a dependent variable in the usual sense, so they can be problematic if used for much more than a debate on ethics and the impact of social issue debates on research (as we discuss later). Instructors feel compelled at least to introduce these important studies, but they run the risk of contradicting the methodological content from the course. Discussion of more basic but typical studies may lead to a less ambiguous message for the students. By contrast, recent work in the field has often become so esoteric and methodologically and statistically complex that most students (and some of their professors) have a difficult time understanding the impact that these studies have on the field. No matter how many times you teach the course, however, you can find new material to improve and enhance the course. Such willingness to look beyond the obvious rewards us on both sides of the desk.

THE CRITICAL COURSE

A course objective that we use for many classes that is especially pertinent to the social psychology course is the objective to become *critical consumers of information*. By this phrase we mean to see the world through different eyes and not take information at face value. We assert to our students that such independence is really at the heart of the college experience. Once students learn that the literature can be criticized, they can more readily accept that the world can be criticized as well—not only from their personal objections, but also from research that calls certain views into question. Familiarity with the literature allows students to see the need for backing up their positions, and research provides a common language for the classroom.

If students disagree with a position, for example, they must back up that opposition. Inevitably, when an instructor asks for support for a position, some students claim that the professor is insisting that only his or her views merit credit. For this reason, we must make it abundantly clear that we respect students' ideas and beliefs even as we call them into question. We try to make sure that we can criticize or defend several views of a study, thus modeling a respectfully critical approach. Even when it comes to criticizing a revered paper, we find some way to call it into question. Students are especially willing to go along with such a diversion if we make the paper's findings seem contrary to common sense. Nevertheless, some other student can always be counted on to point out the error of attraction to a position merely for its intuitive appeal.

Many of today's extremely popular self-help books relate directly to social psychology. Arming students with the necessary methodological and theoretical skills enables them to critique the pop psychology they are exposed to on talk shows and in bookstores. For instance, although there is a vast literature on interpersonal relationships, attraction, and relationship satisfaction, John Gray (1992) in his Mars–Venus series does not draw from it. Instructors can use the undergraduate social psychology course to bring this omission to students' attention and discuss why this omission might be a problem. Gray and others offer very specific advice to readers that, as a classroom exercise, can be compared directly to peer-reviewed research. Guiding students through this activity—allowing them to see that some of his assertions match the research, whereas others do not—demonstrates the critical thinking approach that is beneficial to them beyond the classroom. Further, the instructor can address this theme at several points during the course, including the research methods chapter and the chapter of relevant content.

One advantage of teaching psychology in general, and social psychology specifically, is its smooth application to current events. Everyday life provides plenty of examples for theories typically covered in courses. By relating social psychological theories to current events in students' collective lives, we make the material interesting and relevant while stimulating critical thinking through application. For example, a presidential campaign and the events surrounding it provide many rich opportunities for the social psychology classroom. The applications are obvious—attitudes and persuasion, stereotyping, and attributions. After describing the traditional approach to persuasion and describing the source, message, and audience characteristics that researchers investigate, we show students the closing statements from a presidential debate. Then in small groups students discuss what characteristics they saw represented and whether they thought they were used effectively. Next, in a full-class discussion, we speculate on what characteristics the candidates might have been coached on and why. Finally, given that we are the audience, we assess who was more persuasive and why. By couching this discussion in terms of the actual election, students are able to see that social psychology is a relevant, dynamic field and research findings have practical application, all while examining a situation as a social psychologists would.

Another way we use a recent election (or another current event) is to ask students to apply any theory we have discussed in class to the event. What is one social psychological theory/concept you have noticed in the recent election mayhem (or the O.J. trial, or the public's reaction to Princess Diana's death)? We couch this activity in terms of a pop quiz, essay questions, a homework assignment, or a group activity. It allows the students to reflect on the various topics covered in the course. If shared with the whole class, it can show the interrelatedness of the different theories. Incorporating current events allows students to think critically about the events (and not just the theories), which may be a new and inspirational experience to many students.

Milgram's obedience studies allow for similar introspection, which at times can be humbling, especially when some background is available. Students should learn the circumstances and inspiration that led to the studies about which they have learned. One benefit of such context is that it allows students to see that their everyday ponderings may have merit for scientific investigation, but only if they find a critical perspective from which to address it. It also allows the study to resonate with them in their current state. Giving a context to Milgram's surprising results, such as the "evil Germans" mentality held by many Americans after World War II that Milgram questioned and the strength of social norms of obedience, helps students understand the results. Furthermore, this understanding can discount self-presentation strategies that most of us have in the classroom, freeing students to admit that they also might be capable of behavior that seems out of character as they see themselves today. Such realization and identification with the historic participants of our field can inspire students to be better experimenters and superior citizens of our future. It is the rare but unforgettable course that can truly affect our long-term perspectives and behavior.

THE PERSISTENT COURSE

Because so many students find social psychology interesting, many of them are likely to find success with their experience after the class is over. Undergraduate social psychology research, for example, is easier to conduct in an undergraduate institution than physiological (organs are expensive), animal learning (vivariums are not easy to keep), or even developmental (all that pesky parental consent) research. Practical issues are much easier to resolve when data can be collected from peers, usually with a minimum of equipment and expense. For these reasons, many students get their first research experience in social psychology, and a high proportion of articles in student journals comprise social psychological topics—a testament to the accessibility of the discipline. Because students can usually relate to the material, they may become inspired to make their own contributions to the field. This introduction to the world of research allows the teacher to take those acquired skills to other areas if the student maintains the interest.

This primary exposure can yield dividends and demonstrates the critical thinking skills that many students can acquire from a good social psychology course. Because social psychology is so broad, students learn how to take what they have learned from the course, including research methods, and consider other areas of the field with a new set of skills. Suddenly, the process of comparing training methods for maze-learning rats seems less abstract. The parenting style comparisons have new meaning. Because students can usually *get* social psychology studies, the link between theory and investigation can be strengthened, helping to produce a far more complete student.

The vividness of social psychology's principles can have a profound effect on students' lives. We have the advantage of usually showing them the process in action, and the effect may be on themselves. Allowing students to experience, for example, the immediacy behaviors—or lack thereof—in Word, Zanna, and Cooper's (1974) study can help them realize the profoundness of some of these classic studies. We like to dramatize the experiences of participants in the study. In it, participants were treated with immediacy behaviors (eye contact, forward body lean, open orientation) or without. The study demonstrated that White job applicants were more likely to experience immediacy behaviors from their interviewers than were African-American applicants. When, in a follow-up study, solely White applicants were treated with the immediacy behaviors, they performed significantly better than did White applicants denied such behaviors. This vivid demonstration of the self-fulfilling prophecy encourages students to comprehend a concept by which they might easily have been intimidated. Allowing students to do social psychology is one of the keys to their success in the social psychology course.

We find it helpful to share ways in which the material has affected our lives. The case of Kitty Genovese, for example, who was murdered within plain sight of a number of people who did nothing, minding their own business, is tragic to even the most urban-oriented student. Nevertheless, most of us would like to think that we would behave differently in the same situation. Students find it both amusing and informative that professors harbor the same rationalizations of people who perceived diffusion of responsibility in the Genovese case, but that our role as purveyors of the information presents added responsibility when we find ourselves in a similar situation. We tell of hearing shouting down the street and thinking to ourselves that it is just the neighborhood kids making their normal noises, and then remembering the study and dragging ourselves away from the newspaper or TV, realizing that if we did not, the result might be tragic, and the guilt—and irony—would be devastating. An example such as this one, of social psychology in real life, frees students to be affected by the field and admit to themselves that their education can lead to dramatic changes in their perspective and in how they conduct their lives.

Social psychology, then, is a course that can, to some extent, teach itself. Students see themselves in the studies they read even when they do not believe that they would fall for the cover story. Students with a clinical or physiological bent still can experience the social nature of their species in a new way and with a new respect for the research that allows us to look beyond common sense and assumptions. As long as teachers work to keep the material fresh for themselves and to remember the profound impact that classic studies can have on first exposure, they and their students end the semester having learned more than they knew on the day the syllabus was distributed.

REFERENCES

Aronson, E., & Mills, J. (1959). The effect of severity of initiation on liking for a group. *Journal of Abnormal and Social Psychology, 59,* 177–181.

Asch, S. E. (1956). Studies of independence and conformity: A minority of one against a unanimous majority. *Psychological Monographs, 70* (9, Whole No. 416).

Devine, P. G. (1988). Stereotypes and prejudice: Their automatic and controlled components. *Journal of Personality and Social Psychology, 56,* 5–18.

Gerard, H. B., & Mathewson, G. C. (1966). The effects of severity of initiation on liking for a group: A replication. *Journal of Experimental Social Psychology, 2,* 278–287.

Gilbert, D. T., Pelham, B. W., & Krull, D. S. (1988). On cognitive busyness: When person perceivers meet persons perceived. *Journal of Personality and Social Psychology, 54,* 733–740.

Gray, J. (1992). *Men are from Mars, women are from Venus: A practical guide for improving communication and getting what you want in your relationships.* New York: HarperCollins.

Grigg, F., Fletcher, G. J., & Fitness, J. (1989). Spontaneous attributions in happy and unhappy dating relationships. *Journal of Social and Personal Relationships, 6,* 61–68.

Haney, C., Banks, C., & Zimbardo, P. (1973). Interpersonal dynamics in a simulated prison. *International Journal of Criminology and Penology, 1,* 69–97.

Katz, D., & Braly, K. W. (1933). Racial stereotypes of 100 college students. *Journal of Abnormal and Social Psychology, 28,* 280–290.

Milgram, S. (1963). Behavioral study of obedience. *Journal of Abnormal and Social Psychology, 67,* 371–378.

Schwarz, N., & Clore, G. L. (1983). Mood, misattribution, and judgments of well-being: Informative and directive functions of affective states. *Journal of Personality and Social Psychology, 45,* 513–523.

Word, C. O., Zanna, M. P., & Cooper, J. (1974). The nonverbal mediation of self-fulfilling prophecies in interracial interaction. *Journal of Experimental Social Psychology, 10,* 109–120.

32

Teach More Than Personality in the Personality Course

Peter J. Giordano
Belmont University

The problem of self-identity is not just a problem for the young. It is a problem all the time. Perhaps the *problem. It should haunt old age and when it no longer does it should tell you that you are dead.*

—Norman Maclean (1992)

A child is born to an abusive father. We do not know much about the child's mother. The boy is eventually removed from his biological parents and enters into a series of stays in foster homes. The boy grows into an intellectually gifted young man with astonishing mathematical and verbal ability. He lacks formal education, but can talk circles around people who have had an academic silver spoon in their mouths for much of their lives. He can solve math problems that even people at the most prestigious universities cannot. This young man's intellect is both his savior and his demon. He can intellectualize any situation or personal encounter, distancing himself from real contact with others who care about him. This skill allows him to move through each day in a shell of self-protection. Every so often, this young man—let's call him Will—ends up in trouble with legal authorities. To avoid jail time, the court orders him to seek psychotherapy. No one can reach this young man until an unassuming and unpretentious counselor, someone like

Will, is able to understand his character and begins to slowly form a therapeutic alliance. Ever so slowly, Will begins to change.

If this short narrative sounds familiar, it is because it is the story of Will Hunting in the Oscar-winning film "Good Will Hunting." Will's story is powerful, and most students in some way can identify with him even if they did not grow up poor and abused in South Boston. Will's struggle for identity and his search for personal fulfillment is something that all of us wrestle with in some way, although likely not as deeply as Will.

Will's tale is also a perfect way to capture the attention of students and draw them into an examination of the wide open world of empirical and theoretical questions that make up the personality course. The greatest mistake an instructor can make in teaching this course is to focus on the particulars of specific theories and neglect the broader issues that this material churns up. Students can learn the particulars during their own study time. The instructor should introduce them to the deeper questions that have driven the thinking of Western personality theorists for over a century. The personality course is special because it connects with these fundamental questions of human experience—a topic I return to later in this chapter.

Before we discuss this course in more depth, I would like to describe the nature of this offering at my university. Your course may be different; however, the same basic issues should still apply. At my institution, personality is an upper level course, although the only prerequisite is general psychology. As a result, my class typically is composed of mostly psychology majors, with a few minors or other students with a general interest in the course material. Most students are sophomores or juniors, and many, but not all, have had at least one research methods course. Enrollment is capped at 25 and typically is full or close to full. The course emphasizes the major theoretical perspectives and is organized around them. I point out this structure to indicate that the course is not organized around topics, as is the case at some colleges and universities. The textbook I use does an excellent job of discussing empirical research in the various theoretical perspectives.

A GENERAL PHILOSOPHY FOR TEACHING PERSONALITY

Courses lend themselves to different teaching strategies. An approach that works well in one course may not be effective in another. For a number of years, I used primarily a lecture strategy in the personality course. I left room for class discussion, but believed that my primary task was to cover relevant concepts in a lecture format. Lectures have their advantages and, when used with skill, they can serve a variety of important functions. For instance, lectures can help organize complex material, present up-to-date material that is not in a textbook, motivate students to seek more information on a particular topic, and serve to model problem solving and intellectual curiosity (McKeachie, 1999).

Because of a growing discontent with the lecture format, however, my class-room has evolved from this teacher-centered approach to a subject-centered method (Palmer, 1998). In a teacher-centered classroom, the professor is the center of attention and bears primary responsibility for disseminating information. The lecture habit (Zachry, 1985) is the typical mode of content delivery in a course structured in this way. In a teacher-centered course, it is easy to fall into the mode of feeling the burden of covering the material—a phenomenon that some have called the Atlas Complex (Finkel & Monk, 1983).

The personality course is ripe for feeling overwhelmed by the volume of material and by the perceived need to cover all of it, as if one could actually accomplish this task! The number and complexity of theoretical perspectives, coupled with the vast amount of empirical research on these topics, make it easy to lecture all or most of the time. After all, you might tell yourself, "These students may be taking the GRE Psychology subject test and they need to be exposed to this material!"

In contrast to a teacher-centered approach, the subject-centered class puts a "great thing," in Palmer's (1998) words, at the center of the class discussion. Thus, attention is shifted from the skills and knowledge of the particular teacher to the importance of some aspect of the subject matter—the great thing. The great thing in the personality course may be particular issues (e.g., determinism) or specific theoretical constructs (e.g., the unconscious).

The great thing may also be a person. In recent years, I used the character of Will Hunting as the great thing around which I organized the course. I started the semester by using several class periods to view the film. Some students had already seen it and others had not. For the remainder of the semester, we connected back to Will's personality and his apparent change, and we repeatedly asked questions like, "From this particular theoretical point of view (e.g., psychoanalytic, cognitive, etc.), who is Will Hunting?" and "What made him change?" You can modify the questions to fit the vocabulary of particular theories.

The transition to using a film character as the great thing for the course was not easy. Initially, I questioned the use of class time for the purpose of viewing the film. However, after several semesters of this format, I am convinced that the time was well spent because it established a common experience for all students in the class. An instructor concerned with this use of class time could easily require students to view the film outside of class on their own time.

This subject-centered approach shifts the focus in the classroom from "delivering the content" to encouraging students to think. In making this change, therefore, I moved away from a lecture approach and its emphasis on learning specific facts. I was careful to indicate to students at the end of each class where in the reading they should be for the following class period. I assumed they would do the reading and that they would be prepared for discussion of the material during the next class. This approach made the class inherently messier. Rather than follow a specific lecture outline, I attempted to engage students in a discussion of Will via the vocabulary and constructs of different theoretical perspectives.

As one might expect, my methods of student assessment changed in accord with the shift in the classroom structure. When I first started teaching this course, I gave tests that consisted mostly of multiple-choice questions, with a few short-answer questions and essays. My tests gradually changed, however, so that eventually the tests consisted only of short-answer and essay questions. Most recently, I gave no tests in the personality course. Instead, students wrote a variety of papers throughout the semester—from short concept papers to much longer integrative papers.

In addition to these out-of-class graded writing assignments, I used a variety of in-class nongraded writing exercises to assess student understanding of topics or to allow them time to reflect on class discussion. For example, I frequently used minute papers and one-sentence summaries to assess student learning (Angelo & Cross, 1993). The minute paper asks students to respond in writing to a question that takes only a minute or two to answer. Common minute paper questions are queries like "What was the most important thing that you learned during today's class?" or "What important question remains unanswered?" The one-sentence summary encourages students to summarize the main points of the hour's discussion in, as the name implies, only one sentence. This task is not easy and requires students to be clear and concise in their responses. You may also use reflective writing exercises that take a bit longer and that give students greater freedom in how they respond. A reflective writing exercise might ask students to answer a question like, "We have been discussing the concept of unconscious determinism. How much of Will's behavior do you think is unconsciously motivated? Do you agree with the idea of unconscious determinism?" Such writing activities take students out of the mode of memorization and seek to help them understand and integrate the material at a more sophisticated cognitive level.

What did students do with all of these writing assignments? I asked them to keep a portfolio of all the materials they developed from the course. I describe the portfolio in greater detail later in this chapter.

The foregoing discussion is an overview of my general philosophy for teaching the Personality course as I currently teach it. This subject-centered method has revitalized my own interest in the course, and I think students have enjoyed it more. Embedded in this approach is also a set of key elements that augment a good atmosphere for learning.

SPECIFIC KEY ELEMENTS FOR TEACHING PERSONALITY

The personality course is unique because it links to a variety of important dimensions in the discipline of psychology. In a nutshell, this course offers a perfect opportunity to connect with the history of psychology and correct misconceptions, emphasize writing skills, teach research methods, expose students to primary sources in the field, and underscore "big potatoes."

Connect With History and
Correct Misconceptions

The Personality course provides a perfect context to help students adopt a historical frame of reference when studying psychology. In many undergraduate psychology curricula, students take a history and systems course. This course helps students integrate material from a variety of other courses and experience a more sweeping spectrum of how psychologists have built knowledge over time. However, students may not connect the history of psychology in one course (i.e., history and systems) with the content from another unless the connections are made explicit.

It is also no mystery that many of our students come into class believing that personality theorists developed their perspectives apart from any sociohistorical influences. For instance, students may believe that Freud sat down late one evening while smoking one of his cigars and, in the course of a few hours (or maybe he pulled an all-nighter), sketched out his entire theory. It comes as a surprise to them to learn that it was over the course of a lifetime that he developed, revised, and reworked his thinking. They can begin to see that his thinking was molded by important historical events such as the two World Wars, the rise of Nazi Germany, and aspects of Victorian culture.

Students are also surprised to learn that Abraham Maslow, as another example, studied with Harry Harlow and that Maslow's dissertation research investigated dominance hierarchies in monkeys (Monte, 1999). It may also interest students to learn that, early in his career, Maslow was keenly interested in Skinner's work and saw behaviorism as an answer to many perplexing questions (Engler, 1995). When this type of historical material is introduced and emphasized in the personality course, it does more than jazz up the classroom. It helps flesh out the lives and interests of the theorists. They see Freud as more than a neurotic man with strange ideas about sexuality. They come to see him as three-dimensional—as struggling with issues that have perplexed thinkers for centuries.

By adopting a historical perspective, students can also come to appreciate how our understanding of what qualifies as science has evolved over time. For example, consider Freud again (Gay, 1988). From today's perspective, he is often vilified as biased and nonscientific in his thinking. After all, the argument goes, he drew his conclusions based on a limited and highly selective set of case studies. He also clearly misunderstood women and saw them as inferior to men in important ways. Such criticism, although valid in some respects, misses an important point about the development of Freud's ideas. In his day and in the context of his thought, he was *doing* science. Indeed, Freud viewed science as the only way out of our irrational reliance on supernatural explanations for our predicament (Freud, 1928/1961). Students can understand that, in important ways, Freud embodied the scientific attitude. Over a period of decades, he scrutinized human behavior and thought, he observed the actions of masses of people, and he painstakingly revised his theoretical constructs to come in line with his observations. Were his observations systematic in the sense that we currently understand the term? Clearly not. Do we need to correct his erroneous ideas about women and their capacities? Of course. However, we oversimplify things and misrepresent Freud if we do not address popular misconceptions about his thinking and seek to show the development of his theoretical ideas in the proper context.

This discussion should not be construed as a defense of the accuracy of psychoanalytic theory. Instead, the point is to use history to take students beyond a simplistic understanding or criticism of a theory. Continuing with Freud as an example, students can then come to understand that the power of Freud's ideas stimulated others to argue against the psychoanalytic model. The clearest example of this tension, of course, is in the work of Skinner and his objection to using internal states as explanations of behavior (Skinner, 1974). However, students may not fully appreciate this tension if instructors do not help them understand the historical context that contributed to the evolution of these widely divergent theoretical approaches. Like all persons, students may think ahistorically and believe that the theories they study have always been in existence and have existed apart from a variety of social and historical forces.

Students should also examine misconceptions of theoretical ideas that have developed over time. In addition to misconceptions regarding Freud, Skinner's ideas have been distorted. As Debell and Harless (1992) noted, students commonly believe that Skinner discounted the role of physiology and genetics in behavior, believed that any behavior can be conditioned, neglected the uniqueness of the individual, viewed punishment as a preferred method of behavioral control, and denied the existence of internal states. Students can correct these misconceptions only by engaging in critical reflection regarding the assertions and implications of theorists like Skinner. If students merely memorize definitions and the like, they miss the more subtle and important aspects of the theories they study.

In a similar fashion, the teacher in the personality course can grapple with current controversies, such as genetic contributions to behavior and personality. In tracing the contemporary work of Kagan (1994), for example, on the genetics and physiology of the inhibited temperament, it can be highly productive to engage students in a discussion of the history of these ideas. In addressing this controversy, the instructor can connect to a variety of theoretical orientations, including those of Jung, Eysenck, and Costa and McCrae, which have developed during the past century.

Such historical considerations can encourage students to project into the future as well. How will this controversy continue to go forward? Will we eventually come around to agree with a rather extreme view similar to Harris' (1998) that parental influences are irrelevant in child development? Will we move to a more balanced approach similar to the assertions of Cohen (1999), who, like Kagan (1994), sees the nature versus nurture debate not as a zero sum game, but as a drama in which both nature and nurture are winners. By engaging students in this type of reasoned speculation based on historical precedent, they may come to appreciate the history that is interwoven throughout the entire personality course. In teaching the personality course, therefore, I intentionally weave in historical material to help students develop an appreciation for how theories are rooted in a specific context and evolve over time as the context changes.

Emphasize Writing Skills

The personal involvement of students in writing assignments facilitates effective composition (Britton, Burgess, Martin, McLeod, & Rosen, 1975). Conversely, students may struggle with their writing assignments because they feel disconnected from the material with which they are working. However, the fabric of the personality course puts students in direct contact with questions that are inherently interesting to them. For this reason, it is natural to include a significant writing component in this course. I am not talking about asking students to keep a personal diary or delve into their personal experiences. I have significant reservations about asking students to self-disclose in this manner. The writing assignments I use invite students to engage intellectually with important questions about personality theory and research.

In recent years, I have asked students to engage in a variety of writing assignments. This list is by no means exhaustive, and I encourage you to use your own creativity to develop other writing assignments in the course. The following is a brief outline of the assignments I have used in the recent past. Because Will Hunting was a central figure—the great thing—in the class, many assignments related to his life and personality.

Preliminary Personal Theory of Personality. This paper was a brief (3 pages) formulation or conceptualization of Will Hunting's personality. Students wrote this paper after they viewed the film and before we began discussion of any theories. I encouraged students not to worry about technical vocabulary at this point in the course; it was permissible to use folk concepts in explaining Will's personality and why he changed (or at least appeared to) at the end of the film. The purpose of this paper was to help students begin to unpack their implicit theory of personality (Anderson, Rosenfeld, & Cruikshank, 1994).

Final Personal Theory Paper. Students wrote this paper at the end of the course, and it was a more developed version of the first paper described before. The paper was longer (6–8 pages), and I asked students to use technical vocabulary and constructs from theories we discussed throughout the semester. I gave extensive guidelines for writing this paper and gave students the evaluation sheet (a checklist with ratings) that I would use to grade their papers. For this assignment, I expected students to draw from a variety of theoretical perspectives and to be internally consistent and parsimonious in their formulations.

Book Papers.   Students wrote these papers in response to reading four primary sources for the class: books by Freud (1928/1961), Skinner (1948), Frankl (1959), and Maslow (1968/1999). These papers were relatively short (3–4 pages), and I gave guidelines for the structure of the papers. In essence, these papers asked students to summarize the main ideas or arguments of the books and then react to the book's content.

Peer Review.   Students wrote peer reviews for the Freud book paper. Students masked the copy of their paper so that student peers would not know the identity of the writer. The peer reviews were about 2 to 3 pages in length, and I gave students guidelines for writing effective peer reviews.

Concept Papers.   These papers were short (2 pages), and I asked students to work with a particular construct, issue, or question we had been discussing in class. Students wrote four concept papers during the semester.

Final Portfolio.   At the end of the semester, students turned in a portfolio of course materials they had collected throughout the semester. They placed the materials in a three-ring binder, and the portfolio counted as 10% of their final grade. The portfolio included all formal written assignments including drafts, all informal in-class writing assignments, class notes, and notes from reading the primary source books. The portfolio started with a short document entitled "What I Learned in This Course." The purpose of this document was to give students the opportunity to summarize the main points they took away from the course.

Taken together, these writing assignments addressed a variety of writing skills from short, in-class, reflective pieces to formal out-of-class, integrative assignments. Grading time was significant, but it was extremely interesting to follow student thinking about the issues.

Teach Research Methods

The personality course also provides an ideal opportunity to teach research methods. Students can learn how theories are intertwined with particular research methodologies. As obvious examples, they see firsthand the connections between a case study approach and Freud's or Maslow's theory, single-subject designs and Skinner's ideas, factor analysis and Eysenck or Costa and McCrae, and a careful experimental approach in the evolution of Bandura's thinking.

By underscoring the research strategies of theorists, students see the inductive and deductive features of scientific thinking. Students can more readily comprehend how theorists make observations of behavior and, from these observations, construct theoretical assertions. Students can then understand the deductive aspect of science, in which the theoretical predictions must be subject to empirical verification. Along these same lines, you can challenge students to grasp how different perspectives seek to investigate their points of view. By seeing research methods as vehicles for the support or refutation of theoretical ideas, students gain a deeper understanding of the particular strengths and weaknesses of research strategies.

Once the complexity of these methods is understood, you have laid the groundwork for important discussions throughout the course. For example, at some point in the class, a student might indicate that she believes a particular theoretical claim because she observed the same phenomenon in her family. You can tactfully challenge her belief on the same grounds as you might challenge findings from other case study material. As these discussions unfold, students can appreciate the trade-offs that researchers make when they choose one empirical strategy over another.

An emphasis on empirical methodologies can also help students understand how a particular research method might frame the types of questions that a researcher asks. Could Freud, for example, have made such sweeping statements if he were familiar with the methods of modern science? Why is Bandura so cautious in his writing compared with a theorist like Maslow? Is it fair to construe Rogers as soft headed when he did ground-breaking research on psychotherapy processes and outcomes? Such questions challenge students to go beyond mere memorization of facts and see the interconnections between research and theory development.

Expose Students to Primary Sources

Many psychology courses are planned around textbooks. Textbooks have many advantages for presenting course material. They give a well-organized and systematic overview of important issues, theories, and empirical work. These features help students understand and learn relevant material. Textbooks also often include helpful teaching aids such as summaries, thought questions, and practice quizzes. In short, textbooks serve important pedagogical functions, especially for first exposure to course content.

However, textbooks have disadvantages as well. General overviews lose the subtleties of the material. In the personality course, textbook presentations inevitably lose the complexity of theoretical perspectives, typically do not adequately convey the sociohistorical context of the development of theoretical ideas, and may obscure the richness of thought originating from the writing of theorists. In reality, it is quite possible for undergraduates to complete their psychology major without ever reading primary theoretical sources, which are in part the basis for textbook material.

To overcome some of these limitations, I assign students primary sources to read and respond to in writing. I briefly mentioned these writing assignments earlier in this chapter. Over the years, I have used a variety of books by Freud, Jung, Skinner, Maslow, and Frankl. Obviously, you can select other authors for this purpose. My guiding principle has been to choose books that challenge students to think while also being inherently interesting. For example, students have responded favorably to reading Freud's (1928/1961) ideas about religion; Skinner's thoughts about utopian society (1948), the nature of freedom (1971), or an overview of his thinking (1974); Maslow's (1968/1999) beliefs about human potential; and Frankl's (1959) experiences in Nazi concentration camps and the development of his theory.

The ideas presented in these books are compelling and draw students into a direct conversation, if you will, with the theorists presented in their textbook. For example, if one takes seriously the arguments Freud (1928/1961) raised in *Future of an Illusion*, it becomes difficult to dismiss him merely as a quirky old man, as some students might tend to do.

If these books are students' first exposure to primary sources, they may struggle to read and comprehend the writing. The complexity of thought presented in primary sources is intrinsically more challenging than textbook reading. However, this challenge is precisely an important motivation for assigning these books. Learning does not occur without significant effort—a fact that may be new to some students (Leamnson, 1999). Students are used to textbooks, they have probably grown street-wise in how to read them, and they may view them merely as another hurdle to overcome to succeed on a test.

I have also noticed that students in the personality course who are majors in areas that typically utilize primary sources (e.g., English, history, or philosophy) seem to have less trouble working with these primary texts. For novice students, however, it is worth spending some time discussing how to read primary sources as opposed to textbooks. For example, I tell students that the organization of primary sources is often less apparent than textbooks and that the primary sources are therefore more difficult to follow. I underscore that it is important to read the primary sources in small portions and that it is useful to take notes of essential points while they are reading. I take some of my own books into class and show students the notes and comments I have written in them to suggest that effective reading takes active engagement with the books' ideas.

To further assist students in reading and discussing the primary sources, I also have scheduled times outside of class when I am available to discuss the book's content. We talk about the books in class in the context of relevant theoretical perspectives, but out-of-class time has proved useful to some students. I have tried to keep the out-of-class time informal by stationing myself at a popular coffee shop within close proximity to campus. Each week I announce the time to the class and try to vary the times from week to week to accommodate diversity in student schedules. These times are separate from regular office hours. The university cafeteria, student union, or any other popular student gathering place are good options for this purpose as well. In my experience, only a minority of students takes advantage of this discussion time, but comments regarding the idea are uniformly positive.

Skeptics might expect that students would complain about this amount of reading, and certainly some students do. However, I have found that if I stress the importance of these books and how they work with questions of fundamental importance to human experience, I can eventually win over most students. In short, these books put students face to face with the most basic and vital questions in the course.

Underscore "Big Potatoes"

Finally, and perhaps most important, the personality course should address the central questions—the "big potatoes." At the end of his personality text, Monte (1999) asked the penetrating question, "If so many of the claims of these theoretical ideas remain unsubstantiated by empirical evidence, why do they persist?" They persist, Monte concluded, because they deal with big potatoes, the penetrating questions of perennial importance to human experience. Specific techniques in psychoanalysis are small potatoes, whereas Freud's investigations into the interplay of love and hate, eros and thanatos are big ones. For Skinner, schedules of reinforcement are small potatoes; the nature of human freedom or the possibility of utopian society are big potatoes. Kagan's work can demonstrate the same phenomenon. Specific central nervous system fiber tracts are small potatoes, but issues pertaining to the *interplay* of nature and nurture generate big potato questions.

Such big questions circle back to the great thing of which Palmer (1998) spoke. Students remember the big potatoes and the great things. They may forget the ages of Freud's stages of psychosexual development, they may forget what the term *cathexis* means, but they are not likely to leave behind his inquiries into the human capacity for good and evil. They may forget the shape of response patterns associated with different schedules of reinforcement, but they likely remember Skinner's unsettling reflections on the nature of freedom. In short, students do not forget the core questions of human experience and existence.

CONCLUSION

Allport (1938) once noted that the novelist is typically more articulate than the psychologist in describing human behavior and personality. He criticized psychologists for providing thin and one-dimensional descriptions of human personality. Although Allport offered this opinion years ago, I believe his insight is still relevant today. Teachers of the personality course may fall into a similar trap by emphasizing memorization of facts and neglecting to dwell on the most significant questions that have stimulated the thinking of personality psychologists for a long, long time.

To avoid this error, personality instructors can put a great idea—a great thing—at the center of the course and orient all other material around it. Will Hunting has served this function in my class in recent years, but other possibilities are endless. Other films, novels, or historical figures could serve the same function. While keeping the great thing at the center of the class, the instructor can then move to incorporate key elements to enrich the classroom experience. I have underscored five key elements in this chapter, but you may wish to emphasize others. By connecting students to great things and perennial questions, we can certainly "bend twigs and affect eternity," as Brewer (2000) eloquently noted.

REFERENCES

Allport, G. W. (1938). Personality: A problem for science or a problem for art? *Revista de Psihologie, 1,* 1–15.

Anderson, D. D., Rosenfeld, P., & Cruikshank, L. (1994). An exercise for explicating and critiquing students' implicit personality theories. *Teaching of Psychology, 21,* 174–177.

Angelo, T. A., & Cross, K. P. (1993). *Classroom assessment techniques: A handbook for college teachers* (2nd ed.). San Francisco: Jossey-Bass.

Brewer, C. L. (2000, November). *A talk to teachers: Bending twigs and affecting eternity.* Paper presented at Creighton University, Omaha, NE.

Britton, J., Burgess, T., Martin, N., McLeod, A., & Rosen, H. (1975). *The development of writing abilities.* London: Macmillan.

Cohen, D. B. (1999). *Stranger in the nest: Do parents really shape their child's personality, intelligence, or character?* New York: Wiley.

Debell, C. S., & Harless, D. K. (1992). B. F. Skinner: Myth and misperception. *Teaching of Psychology, 19,* 68–73.

Engler, B. (1995). *Personality theories: An introduction* (4th ed.). Boston: Houghton-Mifflin.

Finkel, D. L., & Monk, G. S. (1983). Teachers and learning groups: Dissolution of the Atlas complex. In C. Bouton & R. Y. Garth (Eds.), *Learning in groups: Directions for teaching and learning* (Vol. 14, pp. 83–97). San Francisco: Jossey-Bass.

Frankl, V. E. (1959). *Man's search for meaning.* New York: Simon & Schuster.

Freud, S. (1928/1961). *Future of an illusion.* New York: Norton.

Gay, P. (1988). *Freud: A life for our time.* New York: Norton.

Harris, J. R. (1998). *The nurture assumption: Why children turn out the way they do.* New York: The Free Press.

Kagan, J. (1994). *Galen's prophecy: Temperament in human nature.* New York: Basic Books.

Leamnson, R. (1999). *Thinking about teaching and learning: Developing habits of learning with first year college and university students.* Sterling, VA: Stylus.

Maclean, N. (1992). *Young men and fire.* Chicago: The University of Chicago Press.

Maslow, A. (1968/1999). *Toward a psychology of being* (3rd ed.). New York: Wiley.

McKeachie, W. J. (1999). *Teaching tips: Strategies, research, and theory for college and university teachers* (10th ed.). Boston: Houghton-Mifflin.

Monte, C. F. (1999). *Beneath the mask: An introduction to theories of personality* (6th ed.). Fort Worth, TX: Harcourt Brace.

Palmer, P. (1998). *The courage to teach.* San Francisco: Jossey-Bass.

Skinner, B. F. (1948). *Walden two.* New York: Macmillan.

Skinner, B. F. (1971). *Beyond freedom and dignity.* New York: Knopf.

Skinner, B. F. (1974). *About behaviorism.* New York: Knopf.

Zachry, W. H. (1985). How I kicked the lecture habit: Inquiry teaching in psychology. *Teaching of Psychology, 12,* 129–131.

33

Opening Students' Eyes and Minds: Teaching the Psychology of Women

Margaret W. Matlin
SUNY Geneseo

I would like to begin this chapter by inviting you to contemplate the kinds of knowledge, skills, and perspectives that psychology majors should acquire during their undergraduate experience. At the St. Mary's Conference on Undergraduate Education, Charles Brewer and his colleagues (1993) were instructed to devise a similar list. This list, which was called "Goals for Education in Psychology," specified that the primary educational goal should be "scientific thinking about behavior" (pp. 168–169). Other more specific goals included the following items, listed in the order in which they were described in that conference summary: attention to human diversity, a broad and deep knowledge base, methodological competence, practical experience and application, effective communication skills, and sensitivity to ethical issues.

In this chapter, I argue that a course in the psychology of women provides an ideal mechanism for helping students achieve these goals—especially because the topic is inherently interesting to students and because the media frequently discuss gender issues. First, however, let us consider some descriptive information about this course. For example, a survey of U.S. undergraduate psychology courses revealed that an estimated 29% of institutions teach this course, including 42% of doctoral universities, 37% of comprehensive institutions, 22% of baccalaureate colleges, and 13% of 2-year colleges (Perlman & McCann, 1999). The Marketing

Services Group Inc. (2000) estimated that 1,036 faculty members at U.S. institutions teach a course in psychology of women or psychology of gender.

One unusual feature of the psychology of women course is that many of us who teach it had never enrolled in any formal course in psychology of women or psychology of gender. In a survey I conducted some time ago, only 27% of the respondents reported that they had taken a course of this nature (Matlin, 1989). Naturally, the percentage is higher in the current era; the number of relevant courses increased dramatically after the mid-1970s. My own background is typical of those professors who completed graduate school prior to 1970. I received my bachelor's degree in psychology from Stanford in 1966 and then went to the University of Michigan, where I earned my Ph.D. in experimental psychology in 1969. During my 7 years of formal education, I had only one woman professor in psychology, and that was Dr. Eleanor Maccoby for a course in child development. In all my academic training, I had spent about 2 hours on gender issues. Like many of my cohort, however, I was inspired by an interest in feminism in the early 1970s. I began exploring the research on the psychology of women and then decided to teach a course on the topic.

The tremendous variation in the style and content of current psychology of women classes can be partly traced to the fact that relatively few professors who teach the psychology of women had actually enrolled in a course during their undergraduate or graduate training. With no obvious model for the courses we construct, we probably feel more free to design a course that matches our own educational goals.

Because of the great variation in psychology of women courses, a professor's syllabus should take special care in describing the specific goals for the course. Drew Appleby (1999) pointed out that, for pedagogical reasons, students should be informed about the knowledge and skills they are expected to master. In addition, I would argue that, for ethical reasons, a syllabus for a psychology of women course must list the course goals. For example, I want students in my psychology of women class to know in advance that one course goal focuses on understanding emotionally sensitive diversity issues such as sexual orientation and racism. Courses such as cognitive psychology or statistics are far less likely than the psychology of women to challenge the value systems that students have learned from their families and communities.

With these considerations in mind, I would like to discuss the four goals for my own psychology of women course. As noted earlier, students' intrinsic interest in gender issues—and the salience of these issues in the media—encourage students to achieve these goals. Furthermore, these goals are generally congruent with the goals described by Brewer and his colleagues (1993). The goals include the following:

1. Acquiring basic knowledge about the discipline;
2. Acquiring skill in understanding research and in critical thinking;

3. Developing self-understanding;
4. Developing concerns about diversity and other forms of inequality.

GOAL 1: ACQUIRING THE BASIC
KNOWLEDGE ABOUT THE DISCIPLINE

When professors first began teaching psychology of women courses in the 1970s, the research was extremely limited. As Janet Hyde (1996) noted in the preface of her textbook, "Two decades ago the problem was that the field was too new and the research therefore too thin" (p. ix). Now the problem has changed from having too little research to having too much. The dilemma is no longer, "I don't trust the sample size on the only study done on this topic." Instead the dilemma is likely to be, "I cannot possibly understand the complex pattern of results in the dozens of studies on this topic, especially because no one has yet performed a meta-analysis of the research."

We need to emphasize to our students that the psychology of women has rich resources. People outside academia are often astounded that psychology of women is a scholarly area in which we have much more information than we could possibly convey in one semester. For example, in preparing the fourth edition of my psychology of women textbook (Matlin, 2000), I added more than 1,300 new references. The psychology of women is an especially rich topic of inquiry because of its interdisciplinary nature. I have pursued references in disciplines such as medicine, law, business, criminal justice, education, biology, sociology, anthropology, and literature—in addition to numerous subdisciplines within psychology.

Professors who teach psychology of women differ in the kind of research they emphasize. Those with a clinical psychology background are especially likely to focus on case studies (Kimball, 1995). Those with a background in cognitive or social psychology—like myself—are more likely to elaborate on specific studies that come out of the experimental and correlational traditions. For instance, a study that impresses my students is one by Gregory Smith (1985), who studied nursery school children. He found that attractive girls were more likely than less attractive girls to receive praise and other prosocial benefits from their classmates. These attractive girls were also less likely to be the victim of aggressive actions. In contrast, attractiveness does not matter for the little boys. That is, the boys' physical attractiveness was not correlated with the way they were treated by other children—either prosocially or antisocially. This study provides students with concrete information that boys and girls are treated differently even before they reach kindergarten. Cuteness matters for girls, whereas it is irrelevant for boys.

We need to provide our students with research findings so they can acquire a solid overview of current knowledge about the psychology of women. We also need to discuss research findings for strategic reasons so that students do not dismiss us as biased. Professors in this course are often the bearers of bad tidings because we discuss topics such as gender stereotypes, salary discrepancies, and violence against women. If the information that students receive is typically impressionistic, they may choose to discredit both the information and their professors. Interestingly, students in my course rarely write on the course evaluation sheet that I am biased or "too pro-women," and the frequent discussion of the research is essential here.

However, the emphasis on empirical research raises two important issues. First, students are invariably surprised at the complexity of most of the conclusions. They may have entered the course believing "Males are better than females at math." In about the fifth week of class, they learn that males in a certain age range may perform better than females on certain selected mathematical tasks, especially when facing a time pressure. However, gender similarities are more common, and females actually earn better grades in math classes. A course in psychology of women is especially challenging for students who prefer clear-cut information, rather than ambiguity and subtlety. What a disappointment for those students who enrolled in this class so that they could learn more about the straightforward gender differences that are emphasized on radio call-in shows! For example, just prior to preparing this chapter, I grimaced as I heard Dr. Laura Schlesinger tell a caller that her son's wrestling coach should not discourage interpersonal aggression among teammates. After all, "Boys are *supposed* to be aggressive."

Courses in the psychology of women can open students' minds about human complexity. The information should convince students that the fabric of human processes is neither a simple solid color nor an orderly plaid arrangement. Instead, the appropriate metaphor is an intricate paisley design—a design that resists a simplistic description.

The complexity of the findings is only one issue in teaching about the empirical research on the psychology of women. A second issue with respect to the empirical research is that the information keeps changing. Every professor has faced this issue in each of our courses. However, the problem is a more imposing issue in the psychology of women than in most other areas. Consider the achievement motivation literature, for instance. In the 1970s, I emphasized gender differences in "fear of success"—the notion that women would be more likely than men to be afraid that their success in an achievement situation would lead to unpopularity (e.g., Horner, 1978). Subsequent research revealed gender similarities—rather than differences—in fear of success (e.g., Mednick & Thomas, 1993; Paludi, 1984). With the next generation of students, I had to spend considerable time emphasizing that gender differences in fear of success were neither large nor consistent. Naturally, I have often worried about the previous students whom I had misinformed about a variety of topics. A metaphor occurred to me: Some years ago, I received a notice from a company that had sold me some Mexican pottery. The notice announced that the company was recalling the dishes because they contained too much lead. I often wish I could recall all those former students and tell them, "Please return to Geneseo. I need to correct some of the misinformation that has been stored in your head!"

In summary, a second problem with conveying the general information about psychology of women is that the information often changes. We need to discuss this concept with our students because psychology of women is an area that is particularly sensitive to the spirit of the times. In contrast, more biologically driven processes—such as dark adaptation in the human visual system—are immune to the political climate. The information about women does change, partly because people change in different social climates, partly because of methodological refinements, and partly because of the nature of empirical research.

GOAL 2: ACQUIRING SKILL
IN UNDERSTANDING RESEARCH
AND IN CRITICAL THINKING

Because the information changes, we do not want our students—20 years from now—to have some outdated studies as the only cognitive remnants of their psychology of women course. Consequently, another cognitive goal in this course must focus on the factor that Brewer and his coauthors (1993) called "Scientific Thinking About Behavior" (p. 169). I have translated that overarching goal into two interrelated components: (a) Students must be able to understand psychological research, and (b) They must be able to think critically about certain claims they will encounter, both in scientific journals and the popular media.

The psychology of women course provides an ideal opportunity to review important concepts in research methods. We know from the research on the spacing effect—also called the *distributed practice effect*—that students learn more effectively if their learning trials are spread over time (e.g., Cull, 2000; Dempster, 1996). The typical student in my psychology of women course is a psychology major who has taken four previous psychology courses. Even with this background, students benefit by repeated exposure to research methods. Furthermore, the recent research on situated cognition emphasizes that people often learn skills within the context of a specific situation, such as a course in research methods. As a consequence, they may fail to transfer these skills to a new situation, such as a course in the psychology of women (Kirschner & Whitson, 1997). When students see how methodological concepts can be applied in a variety of courses, they may be more likely to transfer this knowledge to the real-life settings they encounter after graduation.

One obvious way to review methodology is to begin the course with examples from the psychology of women literature on the experimental method, the correlational approach, and so on. Throughout the course, I also continue to define and use terms such as *biased sample*, *operational definition*, and *researcher (or experimenter) expectancy*. Some additional methodological issues are discussed in a book by Paula Caplan and her son Jeremy Caplan (1999), *Thinking Critically About Research on Sex and Gender*.

In addition, I often read aloud brief newspaper articles and invite students to think critically about potential methodological problems. Fortunately, the media frequently discuss gender-related topics, and the "research" they cite often suggests methodological problems. Students also point out additional information that they would find useful to decide whether the researchers' conclusions are appropriate. Students identify numerous possible flaws in the articles, including many that had not occurred to me. I specifically select examples from the popular media because our students need to become critical consumers. Twenty years from now, only one or two students in each of our classes might be in a position to browse through *Psychology of Women Quarterly* or *Journal of Personality and Social Psychology*. However, they will all be reading newspapers, and I want them to approach articles on women and gender with an open mind, prepared to ask good questions, rather than automatically accepting any conclusions that appear in print.

Furthermore, some methodological concepts are so crucial that I set aside class time for special written exercises. Two representative issues that require this focused treatment are the concept of a confounding variable and the concept that correlation does not necessarily imply causation. Before discussing confounding variables, for example, I hand out a one-page exercise that briefly describes a typical setup for a psychology of women study. The exercise lists six factors and instructs students to indicate which factors are likely to be confounding variables and which are not. They are also instructed to create their own example of another factor that could be a confounding variable. At the top of the page, students write a code name, rather than their own name. Because only a code name appears on each exercise, students know they will not be penalized for poor performance on this pretest. The code name also allows me to read their responses anonymously and correct any errors. During the next class section, students retrieve their own exercises, and we discuss the general concepts as well as common misimpressions. In the case of confounding variables, for example, students frequently believe that a confounding variable is "anything that can go wrong in a study."

Another way in which I focus on research methods is to assign two journal articles from the journal *Sex Roles*. I select articles that are accessible and interesting to undergraduates. One article has some important methodological problems, and the other is relatively problem-free. Students must independently read each article, answer a set of questions, and discuss their answers in small groups during the next class session. The questions focus on thinking critically about the design and conclusions of the study. The class discussions are especially animated if students are required to hand in a copy of their answers prior to the discussion.

Students in my psychology of women class also design and conduct an empirical research project. They report the study in standard APA format. The major advantage of the project is that, for most students, this is the first time they have had complete control over all phases of a project. They can choose any topic related to the psychology of women and gender, as long as the study is ethically appropriate.

So many choices in this research project are left up to the students that some of them are initially overwhelmed. Particularly after we have identified flaws in research studies conducted by professionals, they express anxiety about beginning the project. How could they—mere students—possibly conduct a worthwhile study? I emphasize to the class that they do not need to conduct a perfect study. In fact, an ideal study might be impossible, particularly given the difficulty of finding a representative sample of participants. Instead, I urge them to conduct the best study possible and then comment extensively in the discussion section about various factors that were less than ideal. This project is advertised as a learning experience, rather than a polished product.

Several weeks before the due date for the research project, students must turn in a brief written preview of their project, which allows me to point out potential methodological problems. I can also examine each preview for possible ethical problems. During the next class session, we discuss some of the more common problems, as well as the importance of treating participants in an ethical fashion. Also, about two thirds of the students consult with me during office hours for additional information or guidance in the statistical analysis. In these conversations, I try to act as a midwife, assisting them as they formulate their study (Belenky, Clinchy, Goldberger, & Tarule, 1986). I specifically resist the temptation to design the study for my students. They learn far more by engaging their own critical-thinking skills as they contemplate their methodological options.

Some recent research projects in my psychology of women class have included the following:

1. A Korean American student analyzed the personal advertisements in a Korean-language newspaper distributed in New York City. She found that Korean American women and men showed many of the same kinds of gender similarities and differences reported in the personal ads in mainstream English-language newspapers.

2. Inspired by a video in class about Latin-American sweatshops, a student distributed a questionnaire assessing students' knowledge about the sweatshop problem, as well as their attitudes toward the issue. She found no statistically significant gender differences on any of her measures.

3. A female student in the class had experienced a situation in which a clerk had told her she had been too aggressive. Accordingly, she designed a study in which students read a series of vignettes, each describing a potentially aggressive action. She varied the gender of the vignette's protagonist, using a between-participants design. Her results show that females were judged more harshly in some of the vignettes, although the pattern of specific findings was complex.

In short, a course in the psychology of women provides abundant opportunities for students to develop and strengthen their scientific thinking about behavior and their methodological competence. It is worth emphasizing that these activities also address several other curriculum goals emphasized by Brewer and his coauthors (1993). Specifically, projects such as the independent research paper enhance students' skills in applying their knowledge, communicating effectively, and appreciating ethical components of research.

GOAL 3: DEVELOPING
SELF-UNDERSTANDING

My third goal in teaching the psychology of women course is one not addressed in the chapter by Brewer and his colleagues (1993). As described in my course syllabus, this third goal is the "development of self-understanding, appreciating that we need not be constrained by traditional gender roles." Psychology of women courses have enormous potential for encouraging self-reflection and a thoughtful analysis of the environmental forces that affect our lives.

When teaching a course such as cognitive psychology, I often need to urge students to think of personal examples that illustrate important principles. In contrast, students eagerly engage in self-reference in a psychology of women course. As soon as we begin discussing gender stereotypes, students spontaneously bring in examples of stereotyped advertisements. When we consider gender issues during childhood, they are eager to discuss how their parents or teachers treated girls differently than boys. Many students provide more optimistic stories, such as a sensitive scout leader or relative who encouraged them to develop nontraditional talents. This enthusiasm for relating the course to personal experiences continues throughout the course—even during the last week of class—when we consider how the stereotypes about older women are markedly discrepant from the lively and competent women we know personally.

At the end of the course, I sometimes ask students to write anonymous summaries about whether their thinking has changed over the course of the semester. One student wrote, "I've never really had any interest in 'feminist issues.' Before Psychology 308, I actually had negative feelings toward feminists. This course helped me to open my eyes to what is really going on with the Women's Rights Movement." Another student reported, "As a male, the class really opened my eyes as to how much inequality (in many areas) there is present in the world. Also, the class really interested me and I'd like to explore this interest further."

The metaphor of *opening one's eyes* is frequently mentioned in students' commentaries, and so it seemed appropriate for the title of this chapter. As one student emphasized several years ago, "The problem is that once you open your eyes about gender, you can't ever shut them again, and you notice gender issues everywhere."

The problem, however, is that students may be overwhelmed and depressed when they begin to view their world with their eyes wide open. The issues become intensified later in the semester, when we consider topics such as sexual harassment, rape, and the abuse of women. Students who have lived comfortably with a just-world hypothesis now encounter situations in which life is clearly unfair.

I want students to appreciate social inequalities, but I do not want them to feel that the problems are insoluble. Accordingly, we also discuss the progress that has been made in some areas, such as the change in public opinion about violence toward women (e.g., Klein, Campbell, Soler, & Ghez, 1997). In connection with childrearing responsibilities, I talk about Deutsch's (1999) book, *Halving It All*, which explores families in which both parents share child care fairly equally.

We also discuss specific people who are making a difference in women's lives. They seem especially inspired by my reports on former students, such as Shelly's work with homeless women, Sara's job with a feminist foundation, Jody's efforts to enhance the lives of Black and Latina girls, Mark's volunteering with an anti-sweatshop campaign, and Carol's success with women who have experienced violence. During the semester, students explore small steps they can take in their own lives even if their careers do not focus specifically on women's lives. They can try to shape their own lives in a less gender-stereotyped fashion, and they can encourage other people to break free of stereotypes. Yes, the problems are daunting, but—as people of good will—we should be able to work together and dig our way out.

I also use another tactic to keep students from being overwhelmed with the pervasiveness of gender-related problems. Specifically, I try to support them as individuals and emphasize their own strengths. For example, I try to learn every student's name. When students make comments or ask questions in class, I try to be complimentary, particularly if it is an interesting comment from someone who does not ordinarily speak in class. If the comment is clearly wrong, I try to correct the misimpression as diplomatically as possible. I also acknowledge students who have brought in material to share with the class, such as an interesting cartoon, an offensive memo, or a helpful government document. I really try to encourage this behavior because it gives me an opportunity to reinforce student initiative, and it gives them the mind set that learning does not stop once they leave the classroom.

In addition, I write notes on students' exams and papers. For instance, I try to find something positive to write on each student's exam—perhaps a good point in one of the essays. I am a firm believer in the power of praise. For the poorer students, I write a supportive comment, asking them to come see me so that we can work out strategies for studying more effectively. Also, I send an e-mail to each student with a top score on an exam or a particularly impressive research paper.

However, I do not want to overemphasize professors' own roles in the students' process of self-understanding. Again, we can only act as midwives, trying to create an atmosphere in which they can feel good about women and good about themselves—an atmosphere that encourages them to contribute to the solution of difficult problems.

GOAL 4: DEVELOPING CONCERNS
ABOUT DIVERSITY AND OTHER FORMS
OF INEQUALITY

A course in psychology of women forces students to open their eyes. It also forces them to view the world from a different perspective—a perspective that values women and men equally, rather than an androcentric viewpoint in which males are normative. For example, Tavris (1992) pointed out how the normative-male principle is revealed when psychologists discuss gender comparisons, such as gender comparisons in self-confidence—an area in which gender differences are often reported (Matlin, 2000). The typical discussion assumes that males have the *normal* amount of self-confidence, whereas females are somehow defective. However, the truth may be that females are actually appropriate with respect to self-confidence, but that males are overconfident. From a normative-female perspective, the world looks different.

Once students can appreciate different perspectives on gender, they typically translate that framework into other dimensions of diversity, and they discover an entire range of social issues. Diversity dimensions that are especially relevant in a course on the psychology of women include ethnicity, social class, sexual orientation, age, and country of residence.

The chapter by Brewer and his coauthors (1993) contains a paragraph on attention to human diversity that merits quoting in its entirety:

> Education in psychology should help to prepare students for life in a heterogeneous society. Scientific understanding requires a recognition of ethnic, cultural, social, and gender diversity. Students should learn, for example, that data obtained from samples that fail to represent this diversity will have limited generalizability. Courses throughout the psychology curriculum should emphasize the sociocultural context of human behavior. In addition, students should learn about the experiences of underrepresented groups in the discipline and about their contributions to psychological scholarship. (p. 170)

During the 1970s and 1980s, almost all of the research on the psychology of women adopted the White-as-normative model, and researchers rarely commented on the limited generalizability of their sample. Most research still overrepresents European American participants, although authors customarily apologize for their limited sample. However, with effort, professors can locate research on other ethnic groups. For example, students' understanding of infertility can be enriched by reading Ceballo's (1999) research with African American women who had unsuccessfully tried to become pregnant. In addition to the expected sorrow, these women struggled against racist health care providers who thought that African-American women should be extraordinarily fertile.

To some extent, the characteristics of students in the psychology of women course can determine the emphasis on kinds of diversity. This past semester, for instance, my class of 35 students included 3 bright, verbal Black women. Fortunately, the class dynamics were favorable, and the other students learned several specific examples of racism as well as some perspectives on ethnic comparisons. Another semester, 5 of the 40 students in the class were Korean American, and these students provided information about parents favoring boys and restricting the activities of adolescent females, as well as the traditional division of power in a Korean family.

Another source of diversity is social class—a topic that psychologists typically ignore, perhaps because we feel that social class is the domain of sociologists. Again, however, information about social class enriches our perspectives. For example, I was surprised to learn that longevity is fairly similar for relatively wealthy individuals regardless whether they are female or male, Black or White (Pappas, Queen, Hadden, & Fisher, 1993). In contrast, ethnicity and gender have potent effects for low-income individuals, where the annual death rate is three times as high for a Black man as for a White woman.

Sexual orientation may be one of the most challenging diversity topics to address in the classroom, although sexual prejudice is somewhat reduced in the current era (Herek, 2000). Fortunately, the research on lesbians and gay males is now fairly extensive (e.g., Savin-Williams & Cohen, 1996). In fact, in preparing the fourth edition of my *Psychology of Women* textbook, I discovered that the file of articles on lesbian women was more extensive than the one on heterosexual married women. Typically, at least one student in each psychology of women class has told me about being gay or lesbian, but few are really "out" to their classmates. Still, many students appear to be comfortable discussing the experiences relayed to them by a gay or lesbian friend.

In contrast to sexual orientation, age and ageism are relatively easy topics to discuss with students. After all, age is the only demographic characteristic that is routinely addressed in the psychology curriculum. In a typical semester at SUNY Geneseo, for instance, my department offers 15 sections of courses in child development, adolescence, and adulthood/aging—in contrast to my one section on gender. In my psychology of women course, the discussion of women and aging comes at the end of the semester. By this time of the year—to be honest—I rarely have the luxury of exploring topics such as the *double standard of aging* in sufficient detail. However, I try to open students' eyes to an important perspective about aging: In contemporary U.S. popular culture, being youthful is normative for women. How would popular culture be different if older women were appropriately valued and if wrinkles and other signs of aging were normative?

Country of residence—the final item on my list of diversity issues—raises a different kind of challenge from the earlier issues. I try to open students' minds to the concept of U.S.-based nationalism, and I encourage them to contemplate a world in which the United States would not be the central country. From the beginning of elementary school, students have been carefully taught to be patriotic, and they learn that the United States is the best country in the world. Furthermore, students develop a perspective in which criticism of the United States is reviled as being unpatriotic. I have participated in antiwar vigils and demonstrations for 30 years now. In the 1970s, for example, protesters against the Vietnam War were told, "Go back to Russia!" Our local peace groups still elicit angry comments and obscene gestures when we hold a vigil each August to remember Hiroshima and Nagasaki. Most students arrive in my psychology of women course with the belief that the U.S. government is virtually infallible.

With respect to country of residence, my task is to have students contemplate a world in which each country—even a developing country—has sovereignty. I point out that the current international inequalities resemble gender inequalities, in which men often have more power and are allowed to dictate what women do. Similarly, the United States has more power, and we are allowed to force an embargo on Cuba, dictating that our political allies should institute a similar policy. How does that resemble the power inequalities that enraged them when we discussed domestic violence? I also point out other implications of our government's policy. The U.S. military went halfway around the world to Kuwait to *liberate* the Kuwaitis during the Gulf War. Kuwait is a country where women still cannot vote. Furthermore, the number of Kuwaitis we presumably liberated is similar to the estimated number of women who are abused and battered each year in the United States. We are willing to "free" men in another country, but we do not show the same attention to women in our own country.

I need to emphasize, however, that the discussion of international inequalities should not be overworked or a professor's credibility would be questioned. I try to choose my examples carefully, with an emphasis on current events. For example, the United States insisted that the 1990 elections in Nicaragua must be care-fully monitored by international observers—a gesture that demonstrated power inequalities. During the U.S. presidential election of 2000, many Nicaraguan ac-tivists suggested, tongue in cheek, that they should have been invited to come to the United States to monitor our elections.

Part of my focus on country of residence emphasizes adopting another point of view. The other aspect of country of residence is less controversial: Students need to learn something about women in other parts of the world. Accordingly, I show one video about girls growing up in India, Jamaica, Nicaragua, and Burkina Faso. Another video focuses on adolescent girls working in a factory in Honduras for 37 cents a day. We also discuss cross-cultural comparisons on topics such as children's gender stereotypes, adolescents' views on their mothers, and attitudes toward elderly women. Given the time constraints of the academic semester, we cannot discuss global perspectives as much as I would like. However, students need some exposure to gender issues in other cultures.

FINAL WORDS

The previous portion of my chapter emphasized adopting a flexible perspective. Accordingly, I must obey my own advice and emphasize that other professors will have equally valid alternative ways of conceptualizing their courses in the psychology of women. However, professors teaching every course—including the psychology of women—must carefully outline their goals. The chapter by Charles Brewer and his colleagues (1993) provided a useful framework from which to begin. Furthermore, from time to time, we should revisit our goals in teaching any course. Does a course feature some aspects that do not really fulfill any goals? Does this course fail to develop some goals that truly should be emphasized? A discussion about teaching techniques and pedagogy—such as this volume, *The Teaching of Psychology*—can only be successful if it changes what we do in the classroom and what our students learn.

REFERENCES

Appleby, D. C. (1999). How to improve your teaching with the course syllabus. In B. Perlman, L. I. McCann, & S. H. McFadden (Eds.), *Lessons learned: Practical advice for the teaching of psychology* (pp. 19–24). Washington, DC: The American Psychological Society.

Belenky, M. E., Clinchy, B. M., Goldberger, N. R., & Tarule, J. M. (1986). *Women's ways of knowing: The development of self, body, and mind.* New York: Basic Books.

Brewer, C. L., Hopkins, J. R., Kimble, G. A., Matlin, M. W., McCann, L. I., McNeil, O. V., Nodine, B. F., Quinn, V. N., & Saundra. (1993). Curriculum. In T. V. McGovern (Ed.), *Handbook for enhancing undergraduate education in psychology* (pp. 161–182). Washington, DC: American Psychological Association.

Caplan, P. J., & Caplan, J. B. (1999). *Thinking critically about research on sex and gender* (2nd ed.). New York: Longman.

Ceballo, R. (1999). "The only Black woman walking the face of the earth who cannot have a baby": Two women's stories. In M. Romero & A. Stewart (Eds.), *Women's untold stories: Breaking silence, talking back, voicing complexity* (pp. 3–19). New York: Routledge.

Cull, W. L. (2000). Untangling the benefits of multiple study opportunities and repeated testing for cued recall. *Applied Cognitive Psychology, 14,* 215–235.

Dempster, F. N. (1996). Distributing and managing the conditions of encoding and practice. In E. L. Bjork & R. A. Bjork (Eds.), *Memory* (pp. 318–344). San Diego: Academic Press.

Deutsch, F. M. (1999). *Halving it all: How equally shared parenting works.* Cambridge, MA: Harvard University Press.

Herek, G. M. (2000). The psychology of sexual prejudice. *Current Directions in Psychological Science, 9,* 19–22.

Horner, M. S. (1978). The measurement and behavioral implications of fear of success in women. In J. W. Atkinson & J. O. Raynor (Eds.), *Personality, motivation, and achievement* (pp. 41–70). Washington, DC: Hemisphere.

Hyde, J. S. (1996). *Half the human experience: The psychology of women* (5th ed.). Lexington, MA: Heath.

Kimball, M. M. (1995). *Feminist visions of gender similarities and differences.* Binghamton, NY: Haworth.

Kirschner, D., & Whitson, J. A. (Eds.). (1997). *Situated cognition: Social, semiotic, and psychological perspectives*. Mahwah, NJ: Lawrence Erlbaum Associates.

Klein, E., Campbell, J., Soler, E., & Ghez, M. (1997). *Ending domestic violence: Changing public perceptions/Halting the epidemic*. Thousand Oaks, CA: Sage.

Marketing Services Group Inc. (2000). *College mailing list directory*. Wilmington, MA: Author.

Matlin, M. W. (1989). Teaching psychology of women: A survey of instructors. *Psychology of Women Quarterly, 13*, 245–261.

Matlin, M. W. (2000). *The psychology of women* (4th ed.). Fort Worth: Harcourt Brace.

Mednick, M. T., & Thomas, V. (1993). Women and the psychology of achievement: A view from the eighties. In F. L. Denmark & M. A. Paludi (Eds.), *Psychology of women: A handbook of issues and theories* (pp. 585–626). Westport, CT: Greenwood.

Paludi, M. A. (1984). Psychometric properties and underlying assumptions of four objective measures of fear of success. *Sex Roles, 10*, 765–781.

Pappas, G., Queen, S., Hadden, W., & Fisher, G. (1993). The increasing disparity in mortality between socioeconomic groups in the United States, 1960 and 1986. *New England Journal of Medicine, 329*, 103–119.

Perlman, B., & McCann, L. I. (1999). The most frequently listed courses in the undergraduate psychology curriculum. *Teaching of Psychology, 26*, 177–182.

Savin-Williams, R. C., & Cohen, K. (Eds.). (1996). *The lives of lesbians, gays, and bisexuals: Children to adults*. Fort Worth: Harcourt Brace.

Smith, G. J. (1985). Facial and full-length ratings of attractiveness related to the social interactions of young children. *Sex Roles, 12*, 287–293.

Tavris, C. (1992). *The mismeasure of woman*. New York: Simon & Schuster.

34

Incorporating Cross-Cultural Perspectives into the Psychology Curriculum: Challenges and Strategies

G. William Hill IV

Kennesaw State University

Over the last two decades, there have been numerous calls for increasing the integration of diversity content in the undergraduate psychology curriculum (e.g., Brewer et al., 1993; Brislin & Horvath, 1997; Carpintero, 1992; Cole, 1984; Cushner, 1987; Enns, 1994; Flores, 1999; Goldstein, 1995; Kennedy, Scheiver, & Rogers, 1984; Kowalski, 2000; McGovern, Furumoto, Halpern, Kimble, & McKeachie, 1991; Russell, 1984; Sue, Bingham, Porché-Burke, & Vasquez, 1999). For example, McGovern et al. (1991) included among the common goals associated with the undergraduate psychology major the expectation that

> psychology students should learn to think critically about themselves, including their differences and their similarities with others; to evaluate their attitudes about people who are different from themselves; and to know how gender, race, ethnicity, culture, and class affect all human perspectives and experiences. (p. 601)

In summarizing recommendations for basic emphases and characteristics of undergraduate curricula that emerged from the American Psychological Association (APA) National Conference on Enhancing the Quality of Undergraduate Education in Psychology, Brewer et al. (1993) advocated that departments and faculty should "ensure that psychology courses more accurately reflect the diversity of humankind, including ethnic, social, cultural, and gender diversity" (p. 179).

Although I acknowledge the importance of incorporating all aspects of diversity in the curriculum (i.e., gender, ethnicity, culture, sexual orientation, disability), my primary focus here is on incorporating a cross-cultural or international perspective. Cross-cultural psychology emphasizes the central role of culture in shaping human behavior and examines the effects of both explicit and implicit aspects of culture on behavior through comparative studies of two or more cultures (Berry, Poortinga, Segall, & Dasen, 1992; Matsumoto, 2000; Shiraev & Levy, 2001).

THE IMPORTANCE OF A
CROSS-CULTURAL PERSPECTIVE

As a subdiscipline in American psychology, cross-cultural approaches are relatively recent. Although American psychology has strong international roots, with many early psychologists being trained in Germany and England and early American research strongly influenced by European psychologists (e.g., Galton, Pavlov, Wundt, and the Gestalt psychologists), the impact of European psychology on the United States declined significantly after World War I (Cole, 1984; Fowler, 2000). In the first half of the 20th century, the majority of cross-cultural research on psychological topics was dominated by sociologists and anthropologists. Although some early psychologists addressed cross-cultural issues (e.g., Wilhelm Wundt's multivolume series entitled *Volkerpsycholgie*, which attempted to relate psychology to anthropological and historical research and Carl Jung's studies of myth and rituals in various cultures), it was not until the 1960s that cross-cultural research in psychology began to become popular in America. Segall, Dasen, Berry, and Poortinga (1999) proposed that the initial emergence of cross-cultural psychology could be attributed to: (a) the ease, availability, and speed of travel to what were once isolated parts of the world; (b) the fact that many psychologists had been exposed to foreign cultures as a result of their wartime experiences; and (c) an increased availability of funding for psychological research. In addition, American psychologists began to be influenced by research conducted by European psychologists such as Piaget, Luria, and Vygotsky, and research areas that originated in Europe, such as sport psychology and clinical neuropsychology, began to have an impact on American psychology (Cole, 1984; Hogan 1996).

One common argument for the importance of including a cross-cultural perspective in psychology is that much of American psychological research presented in the undergraduate psychology curriculum has an ethnocentric bias (Lonner & Malpass, 1994; Matsumoto, 1994b). Matsumoto (1994b) stated that

American psychologists, researchers, and theorists have been primarily concerned with what has been going on in the United States and much less concerned with people and knowledge outside the United States... [and] has fostered, to a large degree, an ignorance of the psychologies of other countries and cultures. (p. viii)

Although many of the psychological theories and findings included in our curriculum are presented as if they represent universal laws and principles of behavior, the majority of findings and theories are based on research conducted by American psychologists using American participants, which does not include a non-Western perspective (Lonner & Malpass, 1994). Furthermore, much of the research is based on middle-class, White males enrolled in introductory psychology classes in American universities and neglects the experience of ethnic minority groups in the United States (African Americans, Hispanics, and Asian Americans), women, and research conducted within other cultures (Bronstein & Quina, 1988; Matsumoto, 1994b; Segall et al., 1999).

One outcome of the ethnocentric bias in American psychology is that our ability to generalize our research results and theories to different cultural groups may be limited. Unfortunately, the potential limitations of research associated with an American perspective and restricted samples have historically been left out or given superficial attention in undergraduate texts and our courses. Therefore, students may be led to believe that the research findings and theories they are learning about apply to all humans rather than representing explanations of behavior that may only apply to a particular subgroup in their own culture (Hogben & Waterman, 1997; Kowalski, 2000). To help our students obtain a complete understanding of human behavior, we need to integrate the growing body of research that documents cultural similarities and differences in behavior into the undergraduate curriculum (Goldstein, 1995; Marsella, 2000).

Another factor that argues for the importance of increasing cross-cultural content in our curriculum is the changing demographics of university students and psychologists, reflecting the increased diversity of the U.S. population (Goldstein, 1995; Segall, Lonner, & Berry, 1998). If our curriculum does not address the role of culture in human behavior, it will have decreased relevance to our ethnic minority and international students and will fail to provide all students with the knowledge and skills to interact successfully both within an increasingly pluralistic American society and with people from cultures outside the United States (Fowler, 2000; Marsella, 2000; Sue et al., 1999). Furthermore, a curriculum that lacks a multicultural perspective may contribute to decreased diversity among those students who choose to major in psychology because these students will not see the relevance of psychology to their own lives and experiences (Goldstein, 1995; Marsella, 2000; Segall et al., 1998; Sue et al., 1999).

Bronstein and Quina (1988) discussed several benefits to students associated with incorporating a multicultural perspective in the psychology curriculum. First, including a discussion of psychological research conducted with individuals living in cultures different from that of students can enable them to expand their worldview. The inclusion of culture as a variable in psychology can also contribute to an increased awareness and sensitivity to the role that a particular cultural milieu plays in shaping the behavior of its members. Finally, a discussion of cross-cultural research can help students realize how their home culture may lead to omissions and biases in their understanding and interpretation of the behavior of people from a different culture and that scientists are not immune to these biases. Addressing these factors may reduce stereotypes and ethnocentric attitudes that bias the manner in which students think about and interact with individuals from different cultures and facilitate their ability to function effectively in the global community (Bronstein & Quina, 1988; Kowalski, 2000; Segall et al., 1998).

CURRENT STATUS OF EFFORTS TO INCORPORATE A CROSS-CULTURAL PERSPECTIVE

Cole (1984) wrote that "it is not clear that psychological research making systematic use of cultural variation has penetrated very far into the undergraduate curriculum" (p. 1000). However, there is evidence that, during the 1990s, authors and publishers of psychology textbooks responded to Cole's call for increasing the cross-cultural content. Although analyses of introductory psychology textbooks by Lonner (1990; cited in Segall et al., 1998) and Weiten and Wight (1992) suggest that cross-cultural content was either absent or superficial, a recent content analysis of introductory textbooks by Hogben and Waterman (1997) found that "global diversity issues were not only addressed by many authors but integrated throughout the text as well" (p. 99). An increased inclusion of cross-cultural content is also reflected in a recent compendium of 41 introductory psychology textbooks, which notes significant coverage of diversity and cultural issues in the descriptions of 32 of the textbooks (Jackson, Griggs, Koenig, Christopher, & Marek, 2000). In addition to increased coverage of cross-cultural issues in introductory textbooks, upper level textbooks, particularly in developmental, social, abnormal, and cognitive psychology, are increasingly integrating cross-cultural material. The 1990s also saw the publication of numerous resource books to assist psychology teachers interested in increasing the coverage of cross-cultural issues including textbook supplements (e.g., Gardiner, Mutter, & Kosmitzki, 1997; Matsumoto, 1994a, 1994b, 1997; Price & Crapo, 1999), compilations of readings in cross-cultural psychology (Adler & Gielen, 2001; Goldberger & Veroff, 1995; Lonner & Malpass, 1994; Peplau, DeBro, Veniegas, & Taylor, 1999), and activities handbooks (Goldstein, 2000; Okun, Fried, & Okun, 1999; Seelye, 1996; Singelis, 1998; Whittlesey, 2001).

There are also strong indications that undergraduate psychology programs are increasingly adding separate courses in cross-cultural psychology. Although a course in cross-cultural psychology was not among the 30 most frequently listed courses in the undergraduate curriculum reported by Perlman and McCann (1999), they noted that 11% of the institutions surveyed listed a separate cross-cultural psychology course. The trend to include a separate course is also reflected in the textbook publishing field. For example, when I first offered my course on cross-cultural psychology in 1985, there were no textbooks available. Although

Marshall Segall had published a cross-cultural psychology textbook in 1979, it was out of print due to poor sales. During the 1990s, numerous undergraduate textbooks devoted to cross-cultural psychology were published (e.g., Berry et al., 1992; Brislin, 2000; Matsumoto, 2000; Segall et al., 1999; Shiraev & Levy, 2001). The number of textbooks and the fact that some are now in their second edition suggests that an increasing number of psychology departments are offering stand-alone courses in cross-cultural psychology.

The increased emphasis on incorporating a cross-cultural perspective in the psychology curriculum is also reflected in other resources available to teachers of psychology. For example, the journal *Teaching of Psychology* published only seven articles that addressed cross-cultural issues between 1974 (the year it was established) and 1989, most of which focused on faculty experiences in teaching abroad. In the 1990s, the journal published an increasing number of articles on cross-cultural and diversity issues that addressed both general curriculum reform (e.g., Enns, 1994; Gloria, Reickmann, & Rush, 2000; Golding & Kraemer, 2000; Goldstein, 1995; Hill, 2000; Hogan, 1996) and course-specific teaching techniques (e.g., Boyatzis, 1998; DeFour & Paludi, 1991; Organista, Chun, & Marín, 2000; Santos de Barona & Reid, 1992; White, 1994). Fowler (2000) also noted that several APA divisions are producing resources designed to help psychology teachers improve their coverage of multicultural issues (e.g., the Society for the Teaching of Psychology, Division 2; the Society for the Psychological Study of Ethnic Minority Issues, Division 45; and Division 52, International Psychology). For example, the Society for the Teaching of Psychology has several teaching resources that focus on multicultural issues available online through its Office of Teaching Resources in Psychology (http://www.lemoyne.edu/OTRP/teachingresources.html), including "Expanding the Psychology Curriculum: An Annotated Bibliography on Diversity in Psychology" (Caldwell-Colbert et al., 1998), "Activities and Videos for Teaching Cross-Cultural Issues in Psychology" (Hill, 1998a), and "Informational Resources for Teaching Cross-Cultural Issues in Psychology" (Hill, 1998b). Fowler (2000) also announced that APA's Committee on International Relations (CIRP) has started an initiative designed to internationalize the psychology curriculum. CIRP plans to begin by surveying psychology departments concerning texts and materials needed to teach cultural issues. Based on the survey results, CIRP will then work with other APA groups and divisions, as well as authors and publishers, to develop curriculum modules for teachers at the high school and college levels.

CHALLENGES AND SOME SOLUTIONS

Psychology teachers who wish to incorporate a cross-cultural perspective in the curriculum do, however, face several challenges. First, they may encounter resistance from colleagues. Marsella (2000) argued that many psychologists "seem to have little awareness or sympathy for altering a psychology curriculum that both reflects and supports their personal values, epistemologies, proxiologies, and training cultures" (p. 21). Some of this resistance may reflect that the academic training of most psychologists probably included little to no focus on cross-cultural perspectives (Gloria et al., 2000; Marsella, 2000; Sue et al., 1999). Such lack of training may contribute to an increased level of discomfort among faculty in taking the initiative to incorporate cross-cultural perspectives because of a lack of knowledge or fears about how it will necessitate changes in the way they teach (Flores, 1999; Kowalski, 2000). Gloria et al. (2000) and Marsella (2000) emphasized the importance of faculty taking advantage of continuing education opportunities that will increase their understanding of and appreciation for the importance of cultural factors in understanding human behavior. This goal may be accomplished through further academic course work, cultural awareness training programs, summer seminars, or initially team teaching with a colleague who is knowledgeable in cross-cultural perspectives (Gloria et al., 2000; Marsella, 2000).

Another way to expand your own cross-cultural perspective is through communicating with psychologists from other cultures. My own interest in cross-cultural psychology was originally stimulated by the opportunity to study with a Swiss psychologist as a graduate student. Later, I was given the opportunity to travel on a study tour of Russia in 1987, which included opportunities to visit Russian educational and research facilities. These experiences with non-Western psychologists exposed me to different perspectives on theories and research that strengthened my own commitment to incorporating a cross-cultural perspective into my own courses. I strongly encourage faculty interested in cross-cultural perspectives to take advantage of opportunities to communicate and collaborate with international psychologists, which is increasingly easier through the Internet as well as by getting involved in organizations that include international psychologists (e.g., Division 52 of APA, International Psychology).

Teachers who feel they lack sufficient background in cross-cultural psychology can also take advantage of resources that provide background material that can be easily incorporated into their courses. In addition to the supplemental texts and activity handbooks mentioned earlier, there are general handbooks on cross-cultural psychology that provide a wealth of information that can be integrated into any psychology course (e.g., Berry, Dasen, & Saraswathi, 1997; Berry, Poortinga, & Pandey, 1997; Berry, Segall, & Kagitçibasi, 1997; Brislin, 1990; Marsella, Tharp, & Ciborowski, 1979) and several journals devoted to cross-cultural research (e.g., *Culture & Psychology*, *Cross-Cultural Psychology*, *International Journal of Psychology*, *Cross-Cultural Research*). I have found these resources to be invaluable in broadening my own knowledge of cross-cultural research as well as providing both content for my lectures and readings for students.

Faculty should avoid presenting cross-cultural topics in a manner that communicates to the student that the material is peripheral to the main content of the course or curriculum (Brislin & Horvath 1997; Goldstein, 1995; Kowalski, 2000).

The marginalizing of cross-cultural perspectives may occur when the instructor incorporates cross-cultural findings as an aside that characterizes the research as a fascinating extension of mainstream research. Presentation of cross-cultural research in the form of supplemental readings or by choosing a textbook that presents it in a sidebar or a box presentation separate from the main text also acts to separate a cross-cultural perspective from the main core of the course (Brislin & Horvarth, 1997; Goldstein, 1995). This is a particular challenge because many textbooks still present cross-cultural psychology in a manner that separates it from the main content. I still find I must use supplementary readings and lectures to integrate cross-cultural perspectives adequately.

Once a department recognizes the importance of including a cross-cultural perspective in its curriculum, it faces the challenge of how to accomplish it. The three basic approaches that departments have used are (a) including a single survey course on cross-cultural psychology or diversity; (b) developing a set of courses that constitute an area of concentration in multicultural studies, with each course often focusing on a single topic or ethnic or cultural group; or (c) making a departmental commitment to integrate cross-cultural topics into the entire curriculum (Brislin & Horvarth, 1997; Sue et al., 1999). Most authors addressing the incorporation of cross-cultural perspectives into the curriculum advocate the curriculum integration approach (Brislin & Horvath, 1997; Kowalski, 2000; Segall et al., 1998; Sue et al., 1999).

Arguments against using separate courses or an area studies concentration include:

- the belief that a single course or set of courses is insufficient for achieving cultural understanding and awareness;
- the perception that separate course offerings are often viewed by students, administrators, and the general public as less central than traditional core courses in the discipline;
- the common practice of including these courses among the electives for the degree, which both reinforces the potential perception that the material is separate from the broader curriculum and ensures that some students will not be exposed to the content;
- and the perception by some faculty that separate courses free them from having to incorporate cross-cultural material into their own courses (Brislin & Horvath, 1997; Kowalski, 2000; Sue et al., 1999).

Despite these reservations, Brislin and Horvath (1997) noted that almost no research demonstrates that any approach is more or less effective. They recommended that research is needed to evaluate the relative benefits and weaknesses of each approach.

Currently, the majority of efforts to incorporate a cross-cultural perspective into courses primarily focus on integrating research that compares two or more cultures with respect to some psychological phenomenon (Matsumoto, 2000). However, several authors are also beginning to advocate increased attention to indigenous psychologies (e.g., Marsella, 2000; Segall et al., 1998). Although cross-cultural research focuses on identifying both behavioral universals and culture-specific behaviors through comparative research, indigenous psychology focuses on the "scientific study of human behavior (or the mind) that is native, that is not transported from other regions, and that is designed for its people" (Kim & Berry, 1993). Kim and Berry (1993) described the difference between cross-cultural and indigenous psychology in terms of the primary research focus. Cross-cultural psychology's emphasis usually originates with theories or research questions that arose in one culture and are then transported to and evaluated in other cultural contexts. In contrast, indigenous psychology focuses on research that investigates issues and concepts that are central to a particular culture, but not necessarily other cultures. Kim and Berry's (1993) *Indigenous Psychologies: Research and Experience in Cultural Context* includes chapters on indigenous psychologies in many cultures written by native psychologists and is an excellent resource for information on diversity or indigenous psychologies. Although I strongly advocate incorporating indigenous psychologies, it can be particularly challenging because they represent perspectives that are often unfamiliar and difficult to grasp for both faculty and students who have limited experience with different cultural perspectives than their own.

In addition to the more general curricular challenges cited earlier, individual instructors face several challenges in addressing cross-cultural topics in their classes. One of the most basic challenges may be simply defining the concept of culture to students. Although various disciplines (e.g., anthropology, psychology, and sociology) have extensively studied culture, there is no consensus concerning its definition. Lonner and Malpass (1994) noted that there are about 175 different definitions for culture in the social scientific literature. Brislin (2000) described culture as an amorphous concept that includes shared assumptions, values, and beliefs that guide the behavior of the members of a culture. Because most cultural beliefs and values are primarily acquired through childhood experiences and are rarely discussed overtly, members of a culture often find it difficult to communicate or identify characteristics of their native culture. An effective exercise I have used to help students understand aspects of their own culture is to have them interview sojourners from another culture and ask them to describe their perception of the values and beliefs that guide members of American culture. Alternatively, you can bring international guest speakers into class to discuss topics such as childrearing, parenting, perspectives on intelligence, or other topics relevant to your course. I have often used either students from our international student organization or faculty colleagues from other countries as guest speakers. Cushner (1987) also described a technique that uses a series of scenarios that presents sample intercultural interactions, which were originally developed by Brislin, Cushner, Cherrie, and Yong (1986) and updated in Cushner and Brislin (1996), to help students explore how implicit cultural assumptions influence their interpretation of cross-cultural interactions.

Another potential challenge is the possibility that the presentation of cross-cultural research findings may actually reinforce stereotypes of other cultural groups held by students (Goldstein, 1995; Hogben & Waterman, 1997; Kowalski, 2000). This situation may occur when instructors discuss research that compares cultures on a single dimension that leads students to oversimplifying the results and apply labels that reinforce differences and a potential perception of superiority. Faculty should also be cautious of the tendency to use terms such as *less developed* or *primitive*, which can also communicate a perception of cultural superiority (Goldstein, 1995). When discussing cross-cultural research, faculty should address similarities as well as differences between cultures and emphasize to students that within-group variability is often greater than between-group variability, focus on the characteristics of the research participants from the cultures being compared and whether they are similar or vary on dimensions other than culture that may contribute to observed differences (e.g., amount of formal schooling), and discuss the cognitive processes of stereotyping (Goldstein, 1995; Hogben & Waterman, 1997; Kowalski, 2000). I think that discussing similarities is particularly important because many textbooks seem to emphasize differences when summarizing cross-cultural research findings and pay little to no attention to similarities.

Another challenge is the fact that many of our students lack personal intercultural experiences and find it difficult to understand another culture within the context of their own personal experience (Brislin, 1997; Cushner, 1987; Gloria et al., 2000; Sue et al., 1999). One common method advocated to help increase students' appreciation for cultural differences is to use experiential exercises that promote a student's understanding of different cultural perspectives (see Brislin, 1997; Cushner, 1987). One drawback, however, may be the danger that discussions or in-class activities may elicit strong emotional responses based on the beliefs or stereotypes held by students, with which faculty may be unprepared to deal and thus contribute to increased student resistance to the material (Brislin, 1997; Gloria et al., 2000; Kowalski, 2000; Sue et al., 1999). Matsumoto (cited in Hill, 2000) suggested that, to deal with or prevent emotional reactions, instructors must model emotional regulation, encourage critical thinking, and demonstrate a nonjudgmental openness and valuing of different viewpoints through creating a classroom environment that encourages diverse student perspectives.

Faculty also sometimes struggle with the question of whether to focus on a single cultural group or multiple groups (Kowalski, 2000; Sue et al., 1999). Although it may be easier to choose one group as the focus of comparisons with American culture, Kowalski (2000) warned that this approach may act to increase ethnocentric perspectives and stereotypes and inadvertently result in inappropriately generalizing the differences to other cultural groups. Kowalski recommended a balanced presentation that includes multiple groups whose selection vary with the topic under discussion and the available cross-cultural research. I consistently try to vary the cultures I refer to in my own courses. I have found that reviewing journals such as the *Journal of Cross-Cultural Psychology* and *Cross-Cultural Research* provides me with a wealth of information on a variety of topics that incorporate research from many cultures.

SUMMARY

The last decade has been characterized by an increasing recognition of the importance of incorporating a cross-cultural perspective into the undergraduate psychology curriculum. This emphasis has been evidenced by both an increase in the publication of textbooks that include a strong multicultural perspective and recommendations for strategies and activities designed to enhance the cross-cultural perspective in individual courses as well as the curriculum as a whole. This trend is increasingly becoming an essential dimension of research and education in psychology. As Russell (1984) noted, "psychologists who are not aware of what is happening elsewhere than in their own microcosm run the risk of being left behind as psychology continues to change" (p. 1024).

REFERENCES

Adler, L. L., & Gielen, U. P. (2001). *Cross-cultural topics in psychology* (2nd ed.). Westport, CT: Greenwood.

Berry, J. W., Dasen, P. R., & Saraswathi, T. S. (Eds.). (1997). *Handbook of cross-cultural psychology: Volume 2. Basic processes and human development* (2nd ed.). Boston: Allyn & Bacon.

Berry, J. W., Poortinga, Y. H., & Pandey, J. (Eds.). (1997). *Handbook of cross-cultural psychology: Volume 1. Theory and method* (2nd ed.). Boston: Allyn & Bacon.

Berry, J. W., Poortinga, Y. H., Segall, M. H., & Dasen, P. R. (1992). *Cross-cultural psychology: Research and applications.* Cambridge, MA: Cambridge University Press.

Berry, J. W., Segall, M. H., & Kagitçibasi, C. (Eds.). (1997). *Handbook of cross-cultural psychology: Volume 3. Social behavior and applications* (2nd ed.). Boston: Allyn & Bacon.

Boyatzis, C. J. (1998). A collaborative assignment on the role of culture in child development and education. *Teaching of Psychology, 25,* 195–198.

Brewer, C. L., Hopkins, J. R., Kimble, G. A., Matlin, M. W., McCann, L. I., McNeil, O. V., Nodine, B. F., Quinn, V. N., & Saundra. (1993). Curriculum. In T. V. McGovern (Ed.), *Handbook for enhancing undergraduate education in psychology* (pp. 161–182). Washington, DC: American Psychological Association.

Brislin, R. W. (Ed.). (1990). *Cross-cultural research and methodology series: Vol. 14. Applied cross-cultural psychology.* Newbury Park, CA: Sage.

Brislin, R. W. (1997). Introducing active exercises in the college classroom for intercultural and cross-cultural courses. In K. Cushner & R. W. Brislin (Eds.), *Improving intercultural interactions: Modules for cross-cultural training programs* (Vol. 2, pp. 91–108). Thousand Oaks, CA: Sage.

Brislin, R. W. (2000). *Understanding culture's influence on behavior* (2nd ed.). Orland, FL: Harcourt College.

Brislin, R. W., Cushner, K., Cherrie, C., & Yong, M. (1986). *Intercultural interactions: A practical guide.* Newbury Park, CA: Sage.

Brislin, R. W., & Horvath, A. (1997). Cross-cultural training and multicultural education. In J. W. Berry, M. H. Segall, & C. Kagitçibasi (Eds.), *Handbook of cross-cultural psychology: Volume 3. Social behavior and applications* (2nd ed., pp. 327–370). Boston: Allyn & Bacon.

Bronstein, P., & Quina, K. (Eds.). (1988). *Teaching a psychology of people: Resources for gender and sociocultural awareness.* Washington, DC: American Psychological Association.

Caldwell-Colbert, A. T., Fassinger, R. E., Horvat, Jr., J. J., Lamas, J., Mona, L. R., Moritsugu, J. N., & Wade, C. E. (1998). *Expanding the psychology curriculum: An annotated bibliography on diversity in psychology* [On-line]. Office of Teaching Resources in Psychology [OTRP] Online. Available: http://www.Lemoyne.edu/OTRP/teachingresources.html.

Carpintero, H. (1992). International development of psychology as an academic discipline. In A. E. Puente, J. R. Matthews, & C. L. Brewer (Eds.), *Teaching psychology in America: A history* (pp. 89–121). Washington, DC: American Psychological Association.

Cole, M. (1984). The world beyond our borders: What might our students need to know about it? *American Psychologist, 39,* 998–1005.

Cushner, K. H. (1987). Teaching cross-cultural psychology: Providing the missing link. *Teaching of Psychology, 14,* 220–224.

Cushner, K. H., & Brislin, R. W. (1996). *Intercultural interactions: A practical guide* (2nd ed.). Thousand Oaks, CA: Sage.

DeFour, D. C., & Paludi, M. A. (1991). Integrating scholarship on ethnicity into the psychology of women course. *Teaching of Psychology, 18,* 85–90.

Enns, C. Z. (1994). On teaching about the cultural relativism of psychological constructs. *Teaching of Psychology, 21,* 205–211.

Flores, R. L. (1999). Teaching psychology from a cross-cultural perspective. In B. Perlman, L. I. McCann, & S. H. McFadden (Eds.), *Lessons learned: Practical advice for the teaching of psychology* (pp. 159–163). Washington, DC: American Psychological Society.

Fowler, R. D. (2000, Fall/Winter). Internationalizing the curriculum. *International Psychology Reporter, 4,* 10–12.

Gardiner, H., Mutter, J., & Kosmitzki, C. (1997). *Lives across cultures.* Boston: Allyn & Bacon.

Gloria, A. M., Reickmann, T. R., & Rush, J. D. (2000). Issues and recommendations for teaching an ethnic/culture-based course. *Teaching of Psychology, 27,* 102–107.

Goldberger, N. R., & Veroff, J. B. (Eds.). (1995). *The culture and psychology reader.* New York: New York University Press.

Golding, J. M., & Kraemer, P. J. (2000). Integrating psychology into a multidisciplinary-multicultural undergraduate program at a Research I university. *Teaching of Psychology, 27,* 169–173.

Goldstein, S. B. (1995). Cross-cultural psychology as a curriculum transformation resource. *Teaching of Psychology, 22,* 228–232.

Goldstein, S. B. (2000). *Cross-cultural explorations: Activities in culture and psychology.* Boston: Allyn & Bacon.

Hill, G. W., IV. (1998a). *Activities and videos for teaching cross-cultural issues in psychology* [On-line]. Office of Teaching Resources in Psychology [OTRP] Online. Available: http://www. Lemoyne.edu/ OTRP/teachingresources.html.

Hill, G. W., IV. (1998b). *Informational resources for teaching cross-cultural issues in psychology* [On-line]. Office of Teaching Resources in Psychology [OTRP] Online. Available: http://www. Lemoyne.edu/OTRP/teachingresources.html.

Hill, G. W., IV. (2000). Incorporating a cross-cultural perspective in the undergraduate psychology curriculum: An interview with David Matsumoto. *Teaching of Psychology, 27,* 71–75.

Hogan, J. D. (1996). International psychology and the undergraduate curriculum: A personal note. *Teaching of Psychology, 23,* 44–45.

Hogben, M., & Waterman, C. K. (1997). Are all of your students represented in their textbooks? A content analysis of coverage of diversity issues in introductory psychology textbooks. *Teaching of Psychology, 24,* 95–100.

Jackson, S. L., Griggs, R. A., Koenig, C. S., Christopher, A. N., & Marek, P. (2000). *A compendium of introductory psychology texts 1997–2000* [On-line]. Office of Teaching Resources in Psychology [OTRP] Online. Available: http://www.Lemoyne.edu/OTRP/teachingresources.html.

Kennedy, S., Scheiver, J., & Rogers, A. (1984). The price of success: Our monocultural science. *American Psychologist, 39,* 996–997.

Kim, U., & Berry, J. W. (1993). *Indigenous psychologies: Research and experience in cultural context.* Thousand Oaks, CA: Sage.

Kowalski, R. M. (2000). Including gender, race, and ethnicity in psychology content courses. *Teaching of Psychology, 27,* 18–24.

Lonner, W. J., & Malpass, R. S. (1994). *Psychology and culture.* Boston: Allyn & Bacon.

Marsella, A. J. (2000, Fall/Winter). Internationalizing the psychology curriculum: Toward new competencies and directions. *International Psychology Reporter, 4,* 21–22.

Marsella, A. J., Tharp, R. G., & Ciborowski, T. J. (Eds.). (1979). *Perspectives on cross-cultural psychology.* New York: Academic Press.

Matsumoto, D. (1994a). *Cultural influences on research methods and statistics.* Pacific Grove, CA: Brooks/Cole.

Matsumoto, D. (1994b). *People: Psychology from a cultural perspective.* Pacific Grove, CA: Brooks/Cole.

Matsumoto, D. (1997). *Culture and modern life.* Belmont, CA: Wadsworth.

Matsumoto, D. (2000). *Culture and psychology: People around the world* (2nd ed.). Belmont, CA: Wadsworth.

McGovern, T. V., Furumoto, L., Halpern, D. F., Kimble, G. A., & McKeachie, W. J. (1991). Liberal education, study in depth, and the arts and sciences major—psychology. *American Psychologist, 46,* 598–605.

Okun, B. F., Fried, J., & Okun, M. L. (1999). *Understanding diversity: A learning-as-practice primer.* Belmont, CA: Wadsworth.

Organista, P. B., Chun, K. M., & Marín, G. (2000). Teaching an undergraduate course on ethnic diversity. *Teaching of Psychology, 27,* 12–17.

Peplau, L. A., DeBro, S. C., Veniegas, R. C., & Taylor, P. L. (1999). *Gender, culture, and ethnicity: Readings in the psychology of men and women.* Mountain View, CA: Mayfield.

Perlman, B., & McCann, L. I. (1999). The most frequently listed courses in the undergraduate psychology curriculum. *Teaching of Psychology, 26,* 177–182.

Price, W. F., & Crapo, R. H. (1999). *Cross-cultural perspectives in introductory psychology.* Belmont, CA: Wadsworth.

Russell, R. W. (1984). Psychology in its world context. *American Psychologist, 39,* 1017–1025.

Santos de Barona, M., & Reid, P. T. (1992). Ethnic issues in teaching the psychology of women. *Teaching of Psychology, 19,* 96–99.

Seelye, H. N. (Ed.). (1996). *Experiential activities for intercultural learning.* Yarmouth, ME: Intercultural Press.

Segall, M. H. (1979). *Cross-cultural psychology: Human behavior in global perspective.* Monterey, CA: Brooks/Cole.

Segall, M. H., Dasen, P. R., Berry, J. W., & Poortinga, Y. H. (1999). *Human behavior in global perspective: An introduction to cross-cultural psychology* (2nd ed.). Boston: Allyn & Bacon.

Segall, M. H., Lonner, W. J., & Berry, J. W. (1998). Cross-cultural psychology as a scholarly discipline: On the flowering of culture in behavioral research. *American Psychologist, 53,* 1101–1110.

Shiraev, E., & Levy, D. (2001). *Introduction to cross-cultural psychology: Critical thinking and contemporary applications.* Boston: Allyn & Bacon.

Singelis, T. M. (Ed.). (1998). *Teaching about culture, ethnicity, & diversity.* Thousand Oaks, CA: Sage.

Sue, D. W., Bingham, R. P., Porche'-Burke, L., & Vasquez, M. (1999). The diversification of psychology: A multicultural revolution. *American Psychologists, 54,* 1061–1069.

Weiten, W., & Wight, R. D. (1992). Portraits of a discipline: An examination of introductory psychology textbooks in America. In A. E. Puente, J. R. Matthews, & C. L. Brewer (Eds.), *Teaching psychology in America: A history* (pp. 453–504). Washington, DC: American Psychological Association.

White, A. M. (1994). A course in the psychology of oppression: A different approach to teaching about diversity. *Teaching of Psychology, 21,* 17–23.

Whittlesey, V. (2001). *Diversity activities for psychology.* Boston: Allyn & Bacon.

35

Designing a Course in Industrial/Organizational Psychology to Achieve Eight Desirable Student Outcomes

Thomas P. Pusateri
Loras College

Students may leave courses in industrial/organizational (I/O) psychology with a greater understanding of the human resource functions involved in hiring, training, and evaluating employees, and a greater appreciation of the impact of organizational structure, employee attitudes, and managerial practices on work performance and organizational success. You, the instructor, can also benefit from developing and teaching courses in I/O psychology, as I would like to demonstrate from my own experiences.

PERSONAL EXPERIENCES TEACHING I/O PSYCHOLOGY

I obtained my Ph.D. in social psychology from The Ohio State University in 1984, the same year I started teaching at Loras College, a small Catholic liberal arts college. I first became interested in teaching courses in I/O psychology when one of my colleagues who regularly taught those courses resigned from the department. Because I had had no formal training in I/O psychology, the academic dean at Loras College arranged for me to enroll in three courses in the business department at the University of Iowa. By coincidence, all three of my instructors happened to have received their Ph.D.s in social psychology prior to assuming their positions teaching in the business department.

Over the past 12 years, I have developed and taught sections of a survey course in I/O psychology and upper level courses in industrial psychology, organizational psychology, and training and development in work organizations. I also collaborated with colleagues in the accounting and business department at my institution to develop a major in human resource management (HRM), the first interdisciplinary major to be offered at Loras College. The HRM major requires courses in both business and psychology, culminating in a senior thesis co-directed by a colleague in the business department and me. Over the past 10 years, my colleague and I have advised over 100 students in the successful completion of their senior theses. My experiences preparing courses in I/O psychology, particularly training and development, made me keenly aware of the importance of assessment, not only in work settings but also in higher education. As a result, I became a member of Loras College's assessment committee and I served for 2 years as the college's assessment coordinator.

I believe that teaching courses in I/O psychology may contribute to your career development in ways similar to my experiences. In addition, you have the opportunity to prepare your students for their future careers. Many of your students are unlikely to pursue graduate education in psychology and may enter careers in business, human services, education, or other related fields. If students leave your course with greater knowledge, skills, and attitudes related to sound business practices, they may be better prepared to apply psychology throughout their careers.

In this chapter, I suggest resources, classroom exercises, and sample assignments that may help you develop or enhance your course(s) in I/O psychology. Because I value the role of assessment in education, I modeled the sections of this chapter after an article that served as the foundation for the mission and goals statement of the psychology department at Loras College. McGovern, Furomoto, Halpern, Kimble, and McKeachie (1991) identified eight common goals for the psychology curriculum: knowledge base, thinking skills, language skills, information gathering and synthesis skills, research methods and statistical skills, interpersonal skills, history of psychology, and ethics and values. Each of these goals can be applied to the development of a course in I/O psychology and its role in the psychology curriculum at your institution.

GOAL 1: KNOWLEDGE BASE

McGovern et al. (1991) stated, "there are significant facts, theories and issues in psychology that a student needs to know" (p. 601). Probably the best reference for the knowledge base of I/O psychology is contained in the four-volume series of the *Handbook of Industrial and Organizational Psychology* (Dunnette & Hough,

1990–1992; Triandis, Dunnette, & Hough, 1994). This handbook is a valuable resource for both instructors and students.

Selecting Course Content

When selecting the content for a course in I/O psychology, instructors have a few options. Some instructors may choose to emphasize topics most commonly linked to personnel (industrial) psychology such as job analysis, applicant recruiting and selection, employee training and development, performance appraisal, and personnel law. Other instructors may concentrate on topics associated with organizational behavior such as theories of work motivation, employee attitudes and job satisfaction, leadership and work teams, job design, and organizational development. At the time this chapter was written, many undergraduate texts (e.g., Aamodt, 1999; Muchinsky, 2000; Schultz & Schultz, 1998) were surveying topics in both personnel psychology and organizational behavior and included coverage of other topics such as human factors/ergonomics, work conditions, labor relations, and consumer behavior. Some texts (e.g., Greenberg & Baron, 2000) focused on organizational behavior and covered few topics in personnel psychology. Other texts focused on personnel psychology with less coverage of organizational behavior (e.g., Cascio, 1998), but these texts were usually written for courses in human resource management taught in business departments.

Instructors who include coverage of topics in personnel psychology should consider whether a statistics course should be a prerequisite for enrollment. Many topics related to personnel decisions require some understanding of statistical concepts such as correlation, regression, reliability, validity, and utility. An instructor may provide undergraduates who have limited or no background in statistics a basic understanding of these concepts at appropriate times during the course. However, if an instructor desires to have students complete assignments involving statistical analyses, the instructor should consider requiring a course in statistics as a prerequisite.

I chose to develop my courses around two central concepts in I/O psychology: job analysis and work motivation. Job analysis provides the foundation for all other human resource functions (e.g., recruiting, selection, training, compensation, performance appraisal, discipline). Theories of work motivation provide the means to understand employee attitudes and performance, and they indicate appropriate practices for managing individual employees and work teams such as goal setting (Locke & Latham, 1990). In my opinion, these two concepts are intertwined in recommended business practices. A well-conducted job analysis should involve employee participation, which requires an understanding of work motivation. One outcome of a well-conducted job analysis is a set of job descriptions that should be shared with employees and used for goal setting. Throughout the course, I continually make reference to job analysis and theories of work motivation as new topics are introduced and discussed. Instructors who include discussion of

I/O psychology in an introductory psychology course may consider focusing their limited class periods on these two concepts.

Applying I/O Psychology to Teaching

Many topics in I/O psychology have implications for teaching and student learning. For example, expectancy theory (Vroom, 1964) can be applied to student motivation for success in the course. In developing this and other courses, instructors may assess student perceptions of valence, instrumentality, and expectancy as they pertain to the course. Why have students enrolled in the course and what outcomes do they value (e.g., a grade, knowledge of course content, a letter of recommendation from the instructor)? What are each student's perceptions of instrumental behaviors for achieving those outcomes (e.g., study habits, quality and promptness of submitted assignments)? What are each student's expectancies for performing those instrumental behaviors during the course (e.g., time management skills, level of self-esteem)? Leadership theories based on the principles of expectancy theory (e.g., House, 1971) have implications for instructors as they adapt their teaching strategies to the students in the course. Would students benefit from a more directive teaching approach, or are they sufficiently achievement-oriented to allow for a more collaborative course experience?

Research in goal setting (Locke & Latham, 1990) emphasizes the importance of providing employees (and students) clearly defined and challenging but achievable goals. Such goals can be articulated in a well-written course syllabus with components analogous to a job description, including a statement of employee (student) tasks and the worker requirements that contribute to successful completion of those tasks.

Topics in employee training (e.g., Goldstein, 1993) are particularly relevant to course development and assessment. Instructors should articulate their goals and desirable learning outcomes for the course (e.g., needs assessment), select appropriate teaching pedagogy to achieve those goals, and develop mechanisms for assessing achievement of those learning outcomes. Instructors should also consider appropriate methods of student performance appraisal and feedback (e.g., objective and subjective scoring, use of peer- and self-assessments after appropriate student training in such procedures).

These topics are not unique to I/O psychology, and their implications for teaching and learning have been explored in other areas of psychology and education. For more information about these and other topics as they pertain to teaching and learning, consult *Teaching Tips* (McKeachie, 1999).

GOAL 2: THINKING SKILLS

Another common goal in the psychology curriculum is to provide students with opportunities to develop skills in "learning, critical thinking, and reasoning" (McGovern et al., 1991, p. 601), which, according to the authors, may arise from work with both quantitative and qualitative data, examination of behavioral antecedents and consequences, and self-reflection particularly when relating to others of diverse origins and backgrounds. The classic method for developing critical thinking skills in an I/O course is the case study approach. Students are provided a brief description of a real or hypothetical business problem. The assignment usually requires students to (a) identify the problem, focusing on relevant details from the description of the case, (b) suggest one or more possible solutions to the problem, and (c) critically evaluate the advantages and disadvantages of the solution(s). Students may submit their analyses in written form and/or participate in a group discussion of the case. Most I/O texts and instructor's manuals accompanying these texts include case studies that can be used as course assignments.

Sample Assignment: Functional Job Analysis

For class discussion on job analysis, I developed an assignment based on the functional job analysis used in the *Dictionary of Occupational Titles* (DOT; U.S. Department of Labor, Employment, and Training Administration, 1991). I provide students with Appendix B from the DOT, which describes how jobs vary in levels of complexity along the three dimensions of data, people, and things. I also distribute copies of the DOT's job descriptions of occupations that vary in their levels of complexity (e.g., Exterminator, termite; Waiter/waitress, head; Waiter/waitress, formal; Dean of students; State-highway police officer; Elevator operator), removing the DOT codes from the job descriptions. The assignment requires students to read each job description and assign each job an appropriate level of complexity for data, people, and things with written justification for the ratings. Students bring their analyses to class and discuss their ratings in small groups, attempting to reach consensus. I evaluate the analyses based more on the logic of student arguments for each rating than on the student's accuracy in matching their ratings to those in the DOT. This assignment can lead to a discussion of the use of job analysis in job evaluation and the relative worth of jobs of varying complexities.

The U.S. Department of Labor, Employment, and Training Administration is in the process of updating the DOT to a new system known as the Occupational Information Network (O*NET; Peterson, Mumford, Borman, Jeanneret, & Fleishman, 1999). You may consider adapting this exercise to use the O*NET job characteristics. The O*NET Web site is http://www.onetcenter.org/.

GOAL 3: LANGUAGE SKILLS

McGovern et al. (1991) recommended that students develop skills in comprehending psychology texts and journal articles and writing in the scientific style of the discipline (e.g., American Psychological Association, 1994). My assignments include the following.

Sample Assignment: Reading
Journal Articles

In the *Journal of Applied Psychology*, the section entitled "Research Reports" ("Short Notes" prior to 1995) contains many articles describing a single study. Assigning one or more of these articles can provide students unfamiliar with scientific writing an opportunity to develop language skills in comprehending journal articles. These articles can also introduce students to the basic research designs used by I/O psychologists (cf. Goal 5) and how research contributes to the development of theories and applications (cf. Goal 1).

Among the articles I have assigned for students to read and discuss in class are Garland's (1982) laboratory experiment of goal setting theory, Punnett's (1986) field experiment of goal setting theory in a lesser developed country, Werbel and Gould's (1984) correlational study on how tenure moderates the correlation between organizational commitment and turnover, Weekley and Gier's (1987) correlational field study validating the use of a situational interview for a sales position, and Rodgers, Hunter, and Rogers' (1993) meta-analysis of studies correlating top management commitment to a program's success. Each of these articles spans five or fewer journal pages, discusses topics typically addressed in an I/O course, and provides a reasonably readable and straightforward example of a research design commonly used by I/O psychologists. The *Academy of Management Journal* and *Personnel Journal* are also good sources for similar articles, such as Brockner and Hess' (1986) correlational field study of self-esteem and task performance in quality circles and Montebello and Haga's (1994) case study on the utility of a training program.

GOAL 4: INFORMATION GATHERING
AND SYNTHESIS SKILLS

Students should develop skills in "gather[ing] information from a library, from computerized information and bibliographic systems, and from other sources" (McGovern et al., 1991, p. 601). The assignments in this section can be adapted to any course that has as its goal the development of information gathering skills.

Sample Assignment: Library
Scavenger Hunt

This assignment encourages students to gain familiarity with holdings and resources in your institution's library relevant to an I/O course. However, an instructor should construct the assignment so that students appreciate its value and not perceive it as simply busy work. To accomplish this objective, instructors should consider the types of library resources students might need to consult for upcoming assignments in this or future courses and then focus the assignment around those library holdings and resources. For example, I developed a scavenger hunt for my course in industrial psychology based on the knowledge that most students enrolled in the course were juniors majoring in human resource management who would write a senior thesis for their major. Therefore, I visited the library and located journals, computerized database searches, government documents, and other materials that students might need to consult in writing their theses, and I designed the scavenger hunt around these items. Here are some sample items in the scavenger hunt I developed for the course in industrial psychology.

1. Students located our library's subscription to *Annual Review in Psychology* (a useful reference for developing a historical overview of a thesis topic) and identified the years, authors, and titles of chapters relevant to an area of industrial psychology from 1980 to the most recent holding. Different students were assigned different areas (e.g., personnel selection, performance appraisal, employee training).

2. Using the most recent chapter from the first assignment, students submitted a reference in APA format. They also identified the page number in the *Publication Manual* (American Psychological Association, 1994) that included a sample reference most closely corresponding to the appropriate format for their reference.

3. Students were assigned a topic in industrial psychology (e.g., interviewing, rater training, job evaluation) and located articles relevant to the topic using the library's electronic databases, submitting a printout of one or two pages of relevant articles from the search. Part of this assignment required students to use advanced search strategies—for example, limiting their search to articles published in one journal (e.g., *Personnel Journal* or *Personnel Psychology*).

The exercises in a scavenger hunt require advance planning by instructors who should visit the library, perform each of the activities, and verify that students can find answers to each component in the hunt. One benefit of this assignment is that instructors become familiar with their library's holdings and capabilities, which enables them to serve as better academic advisors to students conducting research.

Sample Assignment: Exploring the Internet

There are several excellent Web sites related to I/O psychology that students can explore. Instructors may consider an assignment in which students report on and critically evaluate the contents of a Web site. The following are among the best Web sites for a course in I/O psychology:

Society for Industrial and Organizational Psychology: <http://www.siop.org/>
Society for Human Resource Management: <http://www.shrm.org/>
American Society for Training and Development: <http://www.astd.org/>
Bureau of Labor Statistics: <http://www.bls.gov/>
O*NET: <http://www.onetcenter.org/>
Position Analysis Questionnaire: <http://www.paq.com/>

GOAL 5: RESEARCH METHODS
AND STATISTICAL SKILLS

McGovern et al. (1991) indicated that "the skills to use experimental methods, statistics, and qualitative methods are essential" (p. 601) for psychology majors who, throughout their course work, should "develop growing sophistication about research strategies and their limitations, including such issues as the drawing of causal conclusions from experimental versus correlational results" (p. 601). The field of I/O psychology provides ample opportunities in which to explore theoretical, practical, and ethical issues of studying the behavior of people at work.

Sample Assignment: Critique
of a Scholarly Debate

One assignment I have used in I/O and other classes is to have students read and comment (through written position papers and/or discussion) on a scholarly debate relevant to the course content. An easily accessible source for such debates is the *American Psychologist*, which frequently publishes a series of comments approximately 1 year after a controversial article is published. For example, Dipboye and Flanagan (1979) wrote an article questioning the commonly held belief that I/O field studies are more generalizable than research conducted in laboratory settings, which generated two comments (Bass & Firestone, 1980; Willems & Howard, 1980) and rebuttals (Dipboye & Flanagan, 1980; Flanagan & Dipboye, 1980). This series of articles spans fewer than 18 pages and is reasonably easy to read for students who have some familiarity with basic research design. Another example appeared in the journal *Current Directions in Psychological Science*, which published an 18-page series of articles debating the validity of using intelligence tests for personnel selection (Calfee, 1993; Jensen, 1993; McClelland, 1993; Ree & Earles, 1992, 1993; Schmidt & Hunter, 1992, 1993; Sternberg & Wagner, 1993).

Sample Assignment: Validation
of Selection Tests

If a statistics course is a prerequisite for enrollment in your I/O course, I recommend enhancing students' statistical skills and awareness of the value of statistics by having them perform a validation study of one or more selection tests. One source of real data could be your I/O class (if there are at least 30 students) or a large introductory psychology class. At the beginning of the semester, obtain informed consent from students and collect information (with assurances of anonymity) such as their SAT/ACT scores, quantitative biodata such as their weight or number of siblings, and short forms of cognitive ability or personality tests. These data serve as the predictors in the validation study. The criteria would then be scores on exams, papers, or other assignments obtained later in the course. Provide students in the I/O class the data, protecting the anonymity of students who provided the data (e.g., arbitrarily assigned identification numbers). For each predictor and criterion, have students develop an expectancy chart, calculate a correlation coefficient, and draw conclusions concerning predictive validity.

If you use more than one selection test, you may introduce the concept of using multiple predictors in the selection process. I recommend selecting a few variables as potential selection tests that differ in their likelihood of correlating with the criterion. For example, if the criterion is each student's final grade in a course, some variables that might be expected to correlate with this criterion are SAT/ACT scores or scores on a cognitive ability test administered at the start of the semester. Variables that might not be expected to correlate with this criterion are body weight and arbitrarily assigned identification numbers. Sometimes significant correlations may be obtained for a variable hypothesized to be uncorrelated with the criterion. If this result occurs, it provides an opportunity for discussing spuriousness and the importance of cross-validation prior to using tests for selection. This assignment may also lead to a discussion of restriction of range: Most undergraduate institutions do not accept students below a certain SAT/ACT score, so how might the results of the validation study differ if the institution permitted open enrollment in the course?

GOAL 6: INTERPERSONAL SKILLS

Many psychology departments attempt to develop interpersonal skills in their majors, such as "the ability to monitor one's own behavior; to be sensitive to differences and similarities in the way people are treated because of gender, race, ethnicity, culture, and class; and to work effectively in groups" (McGovern et al., 1991, p. 602). Several of the assignments described in this chapter can be adapted to address this goal. For example, cases and exercises could be selected to address issues of diversity in the work force or cross-cultural comparisons. Group discussion of cases or exercises may provide students opportunities for social comparisons of their opinions and understanding of course materials. Group projects could incorporate self-assessments and peer assessments similar to those discussed in the performance appraisal chapters of I/O texts.

Sample Classroom Activity: Psychological Assessment

One way of achieving the goal of self-monitoring in students is to provide them the opportunity to take and score psychological assessments related to course content. I caution instructors to select assessment inventories that are nonthreatening to student self-concepts, so I would recommend against most selection tests, particularly cognitive ability tests, honesty tests, or clinical tests such as the MMPI unless the instructor is trained and prepared to provide appropriate interpretation of these tests to students. One option is to consider vocational counseling tests such as the Strong Interest Inventory. Your institution's career counseling center may administer and score this test for a minimal fee to students. For classroom exercises, I would recommend selecting tests that can be self-scored by students with minimal instruction, and I would allow students the option not to complete the inventory if they are uncomfortable with the activity. For example, I have administered Fiedler's (1967) Least Preferred Co-worker Scale prior to discussing contingency theory of leadership. When discussing organizational attitudes, you may want to administer a short form of a job satisfaction inventory (e.g., Weiss, Dawis, England, & Lofquist, 1967). Some textbooks (e.g., Aamodt, 1999; Muchinsky, 2000) include reproductions of these and similar psychological assessments.

GOAL 7: HISTORY OF PSYCHOLOGY

When presenting the history of psychology to majors, McGovern et al. (1991) recommended not only focusing on the contributions of historical figures in psychology, but also discussing the sociocultural influences that have contributed to developments in the field. Many psychology departments require majors to complete a course in the history of psychology. However, this requirement should not prevent us from considering how to present history within the context of other courses such as I/O psychology.

There are several sources of information concerning the history of I/O psychology. In 1992, the *Journal of Applied Psychology* published a series of articles pertaining to the history of I/O psychology in honor of the centennial of the American Psychological Association. These articles discussed Hugo Münsterberg's contributions (Landy, 1992), the history of I/O psychology in the United States emphasizing sociocultural events (Katzell & Austin, 1992), changes in the definition of performance criteria (Austin & Villanova, 1992), and the history of the Army General Classification Test, the precursor to cognitive ability tests used for screening applicants (Harrell, 1992). Each year, the *Annual Review of Psychology* includes articles summarizing theoretical developments and research in I/O psychology. Recent reviews examined human resource management (Jackson & Schuler, 1995), personnel selection (Borman, Hanson, & Hedge, 1997; Hough & Oswald, 2000), training (Salas & Cannon-Bowers, 2001), performance evaluation (Arvey & Murphy, 1998), organizational attitudes and behavior (Guzzo & Dickson, 1996; Kramer, 1999; Rousseau, 1997; Wilpert, 1995), organizational development (Weick & Quinn, 1999), and job burnout (Maslach, Schaufeli, & Leiter, 2001). These references can be valuable resources for instructors preparing classes and students writing papers or introductions to research reports.

Sample Assignment: The Hawthorne Studies

It is likely that psychology majors have learned about the Hawthorne effect in other psychology courses, but not about the original studies conducted at the Hawthorne plant of Western Electric (e.g., Homans, 1969). Instructors in I/O psychology might consider using one or more of the Hawthorne studies as case studies for classroom discussion of one historical origin of the theoretical shift from scientific management to the human relations movement. For example, I describe to my class the basic purpose of the relay assembly test room (the effects of changes in illumination on productivity) and ask the students to speculate about the results of the study. I then present the results as described in classic accounts of the study, asking students to provide some explanation for those results (e.g., the Hawthorne effect). More recent research, however, has questioned the validity of the results and interpretations (e.g., Franke & Kaul, 1975; Jones, 1992). This evaluation can lead to a discussion of critical analysis of textbook summaries of commonly accepted research findings (cf. Goals 2 and 5).

GOAL 8: ETHICS AND VALUES

Students should also develop familiarity with the *Ethical Principles of Psychologists and Code of Conduct* (American Psychological Association, 1992) "to understand conflicts, to generate alternative responses, and to act on their judgments" (McGovern et al., 1991, p. 602). There are several opportunities for discussion of ethics in a course in I/O psychology, such as nondiscrimination in personnel practices; equitable distribution of organizational resources (organizational justice); training managers and employees in diversity, sexual harassment, substance abuse and other topics; maintaining a safe and healthy work environment; resolving work–family conflicts; and managing organizational change (e.g., downsizing, mergers, job redesign). Many of these topics also raise legal issues. Most I/O texts discuss employment laws related to nondiscrimination, worker safety and health, and work–family conflict.

Sample Classroom Activity: Discussing Court Cases

Employment law texts (e.g., Sovereign, 1994) provide summaries of court cases that can serve as springboards for group discussion. Provide students the background of selected cases and the main arguments provided by the plaintiff and defendant. Then have students discuss which laws would be most relevant to the case and how the courts would likely decide the case.

CONCLUSION

A well-designed course in I/O psychology can achieve all eight of these goals, although individual instructors may wish to emphasize some goals more than others. I caution instructors developing their first courses in I/O psychology not to feel pressured to incorporate all eight goals in their first section of the course. Instead, view the development of the course as a long-term plan. Prioritize the goals most relevant for your students and your curriculum, and focus on achieving the highest priority goals in your first sections of the course. Construct assignments consistent with these goals, assess the success of those assignments (e.g., through student performance, student survey feedback, self-assessment, or assessment from a trusted colleague), and improve those assignments based on your assessments. As you gain confidence that students are achieving the most important goals for the course, you may consider introducing assignments and activities related to other goals for the course.

ACKNOWLEDGMENTS

I wish to thank Susan Davis and Stephen Milliser for their comments on early drafts of this chapter. This chapter is dedicated to Gene Steidinger, my colleague in Loras College's Department of Accounting and Business who co-directed the college's human resource management major with me for the past 10 years and who contributed significantly to my professional development.

REFERENCES

Aamodt, M. G. (1999). *Applied industrial/organizational psychology* (3rd ed.). Belmont, CA: Wadsworth.

American Psychological Association. (1992). Ethical principles of psychologists and code of conduct. *American Psychologist, 47,* 1597–1611.

American Psychological Association. (1994). *Publication manual of the American Psychological Association* (4th ed.). Washington, DC: Author.

Arvey, R. D., & Murphy, K. R. (1998). Performance evaluation in work settings. *Annual Review of Psychology, 49,* 141–168.

Austin, J. T., & Villanova, P. (1992). The criteria problem: 1917–1992. *Journal of Applied Psychology, 77,* 836–874.

Bass, A. R., & Firestone, I. J. (1980). Implications of representativeness for generalizability of field and laboratory research findings. *American Psychologist, 34,* 463–464.

Borman, W. C., Hanson, M. A., & Hedge, J. W. (1997). Personnel selection. *Annual Review of Psychology, 48,* 299–337.

Brockner, J., & Hess, T. (1986). Self-esteem and task performance in quality circles. *Academy of Management Journal, 29,* 617–623.

Calfee, R. (1993). Paper, pencil, potential, and performance. *Current Directions in Psychological Science, 2,* 6–7.

Cascio, W. F. (1998). *Applied psychology in human resource management* (5th ed.). Upper Saddle River, NJ: Prentice-Hall.

Dipboye, R. L., & Flanagan, M. F. (1979). Research settings in industrial and organizational psychology: Are findings in the field more generalizable than in the laboratory? *American Psychologist, 34,* 141–150.

Dipboye, R. L., & Flanagan, M. F. (1980). Reply to Willems and Howard. *American Psychologist, 34,* 388–390.

Dunnette, M. D., & Hough, L. M. (Eds.). (1990–1992). *Handbook of industrial and organizational psychology* (2nd ed., Vols. 1–3). Palo Alto, CA: Consulting Psychologists Press.

Fiedler, F. E. (1967). *A theory of leadership effectiveness.* New York: McGraw-Hill.

Flanagan, M. F., & Dipboye, R. L. (1980). Representativeness does have implications for the generalizability of laboratory and field research findings. *American Psychologist, 34,* 464–467.

Franke, R. H., & Kaul, J. D. (1975). The Hawthorne experiments: First statistical interpretation. *American Sociological Review, 43,* 623–643.

Garland, H. (1982). Goal levels and task performance: A compelling replication of some compelling results. *Journal of Applied Psychology, 67,* 245–248.

Goldstein, I. L. (1993). *Training and organizations: Needs assessment, development, and evaluation.* Pacific Grove, CA: Brooks/Cole.

Greenberg, J., & Baron, R. A. (2000). *Behavior in organizations* (7th ed.). Upper Saddle River, NJ: Prentice-Hall.

Guzzo, R. A., & Dickson, M. W. (1996). Teams in organizations: Recent research on performance and effectiveness. *Annual Review of Psychology, 47,* 307–338.

Harrell, T. W. (1992). Some history of the Army General Classification Test. *Journal of Applied Psychology, 77,* 875–878.

Homans, G. C. (1969). The Western Electric researches. In A. Etzioni (Ed.), *Readings on modern organizations* (pp. 99–114). Englewood Cliffs, NJ: Prentice-Hall.

Hough, L. M., & Oswald, F. L. (2000). Personnel selection: Looking toward the future—remembering the past. *Annual Review of Psychology, 51,* 631–664.

House, R. J. (1971). A path-goal theory of leader effectiveness. *Administrative Science Quarterly, 16,* 321–338.

Jackson, S. E., & Schuler, R. S. (1995). Understanding human resource management in the context of organizations and their environments. *Annual Review of Psychology, 46,* 237–264.

Jensen, A. R. (1993). Test validity: g versus "tacit knowledge." *Current Directions in Psychological Science, 2,* 9–10.

Jones, S. R. (1992). Was there a Hawthorne effect? *American Journal of Sociology, 98,* 451–468.

Katzell, R. A., & Austin, J. T. (1992). From then to now: The development of industrial-organizational psychology in the United States. *Journal of Applied Psychology, 77,* 803–835.

Kramer, R. M. (1999). Trust and distrust in organizations: Emerging perspectives, enduring questions. *Annual Review of Psychology, 50,* 569–598.

Landy, F. J. (1992). Hugo Münsterberg: Victim or visionary? *Journal of Applied Psychology, 77,* 787–802.

Locke, E. A., & Latham, G. P. (1990). *A theory of goal setting and task performance.* Englewood Cliffs, NJ: Prentice-Hall.

Maslach, C., Schaufeli, W. B., & Leiter, M. P. (2001). Job burnout. *Annual Review of Psychology, 52,* 397–422.

McClelland, D. C. (1993). Intelligence is not the best predictor of job performance. *Current Directions in Psychological Science, 2,* 5–6.

McGovern, T. V., Furumoto, L., Halpern, D. F., Kimble, G. A., & McKeachie, W. J. (1991). Liberal education, study-in-depth, and the arts and sciences major—Psychology. *American Psychologist, 46,* 598–605.

McKeachie, W. J. (1999). *Teaching tips: Strategies, research, and theory for college and university teachers* (10th ed.). Boston: Houghton-Mifflin.

Montebello, A. R., & Haga, M. (1994, January). To justify training, test, test again. *Personnel Journal,* pp. 83–87.

458   PUSATERI

Muchinsky, P. M. (2000). *Psychology applied to work: An introduction to industrial and organizational psychology* (6th ed.). Belmont, CA: Wadsworth.

Peterson, N. G., Mumford, M. D., Borman, W. C., Jeanneret, P. R., & Fleishman, E. A. (Eds.). (1999). *An occupational information system for the 21st century: The development of O*NET.* Washington, DC: American Psychological Association.

Punnett, B. J. (1986). Goal setting: An extension of the research. *Journal of Applied Psychology, 71,* 171–172.

Ree, M. J., & Earles, J. A. (1992). Intelligence is the best predictor of job performance. *Current Directions in Psychological Science, 1,* 86–89.

Ree, M. J., & Earles, J. A. (1993). g is to psychology what carbon is to chemistry: A reply to Sternberg and Wagner, McClelland, and Calfee. *Current Directions in Psychological Science, 2,* 11–12.

Rodgers, R., Hunter, J. E., & Rogers, D. L. (1993). Influence of top management commitment on management program success. *Journal of Applied Psychology, 78,* 151–155.

Rousseau, D. M. (1997). Organizational behavior in the new organizational era. *Annual Review of Psychology, 48,* 515–546.

Salas, E., & Cannon-Bowers, J. A. (2001). The science of training: A decade of progress. *Annual Review of Psychology, 52,* 471–499.

Schmidt, F. L., & Hunter, J. E. (1992). Development of a causal model of processes determining job performance. *Current Directions in Psychological Science, 1,* 89–92.

Schmidt, F. L., & Hunter, J. E. (1993). Tacit knowledge, practical intelligence, general mental ability, and job knowledge. *Current Directions in Psychological Science, 2,* 8–9.

Schultz, D., & Schultz, S. E. (1998). *Psychology and work today: An introduction to industrial and organizational psychology* (7th ed.). Upper Saddle River, NJ: Prentice-Hall.

Sovereign, K. L. (1994). *Personnel law* (3rd ed.). Englewood Cliffs, NJ: Prentice-Hall.

Sternberg, R. J., & Wagner, R. K. (1993). The g-ocentric view of intelligence and job performance is wrong. *Current Directions in Psychological Science, 2,* 1–5.

Triandis, H. C., Dunnette, M. D., & Hough, L. M. (Eds.). (1994). *Handbook of industrial and organizational psychology* (2nd ed., Vol. 4). Palo Alto, CA: Consulting Psychologists Press.

U.S. Department of Labor, Employment, and Training Administration. (1991). *Dictionary of occupational titles* (4th ed.). Washington, DC: U.S. Government Printing Office.

Vroom, V. H. (1964). *Work and motivation.* New York: Wiley.

Weekley, J. A., & Gier, J. A. (1987). Reliability and validity of the situational interview for a sales position. *Journal of Applied Psychology, 72,* 484–487.

Weick, K. E., & Quinn, R. E. (1999). Organizational change and development. *Annual Review of Psychology, 50,* 361–386.

Weiss, D. J., Dawis, R. V., England, G. W., & Lofquist, L. H. (1967). *Manual for the Minnesota Satisfaction Questionnaire.* Minneapolis: Industrial Relations Center, University of Minnesota.

Werbel, J. D., & Gould, S. (1984). A comparison of the relationship of commitment to turnover in recent hires and tenured employees. *Journal of Applied Psychology, 69,* 687–690.

Willems, E. P., & Howard, G. S. (1980). The external validity of papers on external validity. *American Psychologist, 35,* 387–388.

Wilpert, B. (1995). Organizational behavior. *Annual Review of Psychology, 46,* 59–90.

36

Psychology of Religion: Then and Now

Maureen P. Hester
Holy Names College

In July 1996, the *APA Monitor* published several articles on the rapprochement between psychology and religion. Some of the titles belie the uneasiness that psychologists have had toward religion:

- Psychologists' Faith in Religion Begins to Grow.
- Psychologists Traditionally Had Little Faith in the Importance of Religion in Mental Health. That May be Changing.
- Psychologists May Be Less Cynical of Religion.

Yet others speak more positively of the common ground that psychology and religion share:

- Religion and Psychology Share Ideals and Beliefs.
- Psychologists and Clergy Serve a Joint Constituency.
- Religion Is the Backbone of Black life. (Clay, 1996, pp. 1, 3–5)

These titles speak to the historical tension between psychology and religion. What are the current attitudes of psychologists toward religion? Does religious devotion reflect irrationality and superstition? Does a religious orientation serve as a crutch for people who cannot handle life? Do religious beliefs reflect instability? The underlying attitudes reflected in these questions can keep psychologists from investigating one of the richest topics in the field.

The current research in the psychology of religion is exciting and fertile. It is also, I suggest, little known, a bit suspect, and often treated as taboo. With 88% of people saying that religion is fairly or very important to them (Gallop Organization, 2000), psychologists should see the value of widening the circle of their tent to include the scientific study of religion in their courses. Thinking, feeling, and behavior are influenced by religion whether individuals understand it as a positive or negative factor in their lives. If we include the study of culture, sports, emotions, sexuality, and, most recently, happiness (Myers & Diener, 1996) in our courses, why not examine a subject so central to people's lives? As one colleague said, to ignore the investigation of psychology and religion is like leaving out one of the food groups in teaching cooking.

This chapter provides a brief history of the place of psychology of religion in the academic curriculum from the early 1870s to the current time. My goals are to inform teaching psychologists of a fascinating story that may be new to them, acknowledge the importance of the psychology of religion today, and encourage the inclusion of such a course in psychology programs at colleges and universities.

ORIGINS OF THE PSYCHOLOGY OF RELIGION IN THE UNITED STATES

In the 1870s, psychological science was just beginning to take root in Europe, most notably in the laboratory of Wilhelm Wundt at the University of Leipzig. In the United States, however, college presidents—often pressured by overseers of the universities—were concerned with the growing materialism found in the scientific and public arena. Many of the U.S. universities at this time were still run by religious denominations. For example, in 1893, Yale President, Noah Porter, stated the need for more rather than less Christianity at his university (see Nicholson, 1994).

During this early period, potential faculty members were scrutinized for their piety. In some institutions, prospective faculty had to pass a formal examination on religious subjects. At others, the university administration investigated the piety of the individual applying for a job (Nicholson, 1994). Within this religious context, college administrators perceived the new experimental psychology as a threat to the old philosophical traditions. As Sexton (1991) noted:

> The early or pre-Jamesian psychology in America was essentially a psychology of human conduct that had been successively nurtured in theology, moral philosophy and mental philosophy. As customarily taught in the academies and colleges by philosophy professors who invariably were Protestant clergymen and theologians, this psychology aimed to inculcate moral virtues. (p. 21)

After 1880, as Wundt's students opened psychology labs outside of Germany, the new scientifically oriented psychology began to emerge in the United States. Because the university was the research psychologist's natural home, the stage was set for the first confrontation between religion and the new psychology.

As Nicholson (1994) noted in the beginning, psychology needed to appeal to religion to "win the favor of pious university officials who controlled the resources they needed" (p. 348). Then, as well as now, psychologists need to have the support of administration to advance their careers. Further, he cited Pickren's observation that psychologists emphasized the compatibility of science and religion as a diversion tactic—to lead critics away from the conclusion that psychological research was unduly materialistic in nature (see Nicholson, 1994). By appealing to religious philosophy, early experimental psychologists strove for the support of university administrators who formulated academic policy. Tension prevailed in the climate of the academy in the 1890s. The warfare between science and religious dogma was in evidence.

In 1885, William James sought permission from Harvard President Charles Elliot to teach a course entitled "The Relation between Psychology and Physiology." According to David Leary (1987), by avoiding the title *new psychology* or *physiological psychology*, James sidestepped any controversy. Because James "neither refuted free will nor denigrated the human mind, his course was so acceptable that, one year later, he offered it to undergraduates as 'Physiological Psychology'" (Leary, 1987, p. 318). Thus, James eased psychology into the curriculum.

A product of the late 19th century, William James became the most influential contributor to psychology of religion with his *Varieties of Religious Experience*, first given as the Gifford Lectures in Edinburgh in 1901 and later published in 1902. Wulff (1997) stated eloquently about William James: "Readers from his day to ours have been struck by his brilliant and richly furnished mind, his great sympathy for his subjects and their experience, his moral sensibility, and his vivacious spontaneity, evident in a striking literary style" (p. 473). Wulff went on to describe James as "the author of a work recognized not only as the field's greatest classic but also as one of the most important writings on religion in the twentieth century" (p. 473).

Although the study of psychology of religion has had its critics and supporters, James' book has never been out of print. However, while James wrote the indisputable classic on the topic, he never mentioned religion in his *Principles of Psychology* (1890/1979).

A student of James and a major figure in the history of psychology, G. Stanley Hall also did pioneering work in the psychology of religion (see Vande Kemp, 1992, for a thorough description of Hall's work and the Clark School of Religious Psychology). Hall started out in theology, "opted instead for psychology, and in time proposed using the new discipline as a means of reconstructing religion to accord with the personal and societal needs of the modern world" (Wulff, 1997, p. 26). In his inaugural address as professor at Johns Hopkins in 1885, Hall stated that the new psychology was "Christian in its root and center and its purpose was to 'flood and transfuse the new vaster conception of the universe and man's place in it . . . with the old Scriptural sense of unity, rationality, and love beneath and above all" (Nicholson, 1994, p. 348). Thus, in contrast to James, who cited 42 definitions to illustrate his variety of religious experience, Hall sought for a common core, which he identified as "estrangement or need for reconciliation." Vande Kemp (1992) connected Hall's theme of unity and reconciliation with Menninger's (1973) *Whatever Became of Sin?* and Frankl's (1963) focus on the struggle to connect again. Hall's insistence that "health is holiness" can be found in the theologian Goldbrunner's (1964) *Holiness is Wholeness*. These themes that link psychology with religion are currently found in the research of medical psychology, which focuses on the role of religion and meditation on healing.

Hall was one of the first psychologists to publish articles, books, and journals on psychology and religion, including his 1892 article "Moral and Religious Training of Children" (cited in Paloutzian, 1996), the book chapter "Conversion" in *Adolescence* (1904), and *The American Journal of Religious Psychology and Education*, which was published irregularly between 1904 and 1915. However, Hall is not remembered for his work in the psychology of religion. Wulff (1997) suggested that this oversight could be because Hall did not "contribute influential theories such as Freud and Jung did, nor did he leave a legacy of respect and admiration akin to James" (p. 51). What Hall did contribute to the field, however, was his influence on his graduate students, who included Edwin Starbuck (1899), whose *Psychology of Religion* analyzed 192 autobiographical questionnaires on religious experience, and James Leuba, who published the results of a large scale survey on conversion in 1912.

During the early 20th century, psychology grew and became more diverse in its applications. New psychology graduates found avenues to help people outside of religious circles. Prior to this time, ministers were primarily the professional helpers to whom people turned when they were in need. Thus, you can imagine the beginning of suspicion and territoriality that emerged between psychologists and the clergy.

FROM NEAR EXTINCTION TO REVIVAL

During the Middle Period in the history of psychology of religion—from roughly 1930 to 1950—little systematic work in the field occurred. Paloutzian (1996) gave four reasons for this decline. First, by this time the philosophy of science was heavily influenced by positivism. Thus, the topics of religion and psychology had become mutually exclusive. Second, the competition for clients contributed to a tension between psychologists and religious ministers. The "cure of souls" that was the territory of the minister was now the realm of psychologists and psychiatrists using the counseling methods of the new psychology. Third, as psychology departments grew, they frequently split off from philosophy departments, where they were initially housed. With psychology following more and more the scientific model of physics, psychologists did not want to be tainted with philosophical or religious questions. Adding to the schism was Freud's (1927/1961) influential book, *The Future of an Illusion*. This work painted religion as a massive neurosis that kept people permanently in an immature parent–child relationship with what they called God. Add to this climate the growing spirit of Watson's all-pervasive behaviorism and little room was left for the inclusion of religion. The rift was most apparent in Watson's review of McDougall's instinct theory, which Watson entitled "Professor McDougall Returns to Religion" (see Paloutzian, 1996).

Despite the antipathy among psychologists toward studying religion, psychology of religion experienced resurgence in the 1950s due in no small part to the research and stature of Gordon Allport. As early as the 1940s, Allport reviewed 50 textbooks regarding the treatment of religious experience. He concluded: "About most psychological texts, there is nothing to report excepting that they contain no treatment of the religious sentiment or closely related mental functions" (cited in Wulff, 1997, p. 16). Later, Allport's work with intrinsic and extrinsic motivation regarding religion contributed to a significant body of research, including his influential book, *Individual and His Religion: A Psychological Interpretation* (Allport, 1957).

The late 1950s and early 1960s saw the publication of more scientifically oriented journals: *Review for Religious Research* and the *Journal for the Scientific Study of Religion*. In 1969, Dittes wrote a review of the research to date for the *Handbook of Social Psychology*. In 1976, The American Psychological Association (APA) initiated Division 36 devoted to the Psychology of Religion, which emerged out of an older interest group called PIRI, Psychologists Interested in Religious Issues. Twelve years later, in 1988, Richard Gorsuch summarized the history and research of the psychology of religion for the *The Annual Review of Psychology*.

In 1996, three events provided even greater exposure for the psychology of religion. For *The Journal of Social Issues*, Paloutzian and Kirkpatrick edited a special summer issue entitled "Religious Influences on Personal and Societal Well-being," which included the latest summaries of research in the psychology of religion. John Santrock developed an assemble-your-own-introductory psychology text, for which Paloutzian and Santrock wrote a chapter on the psychology of religion (Santrock, 1997). Foremost, in July 1996, the *APA Monitor* gave center stage to several articles on the rapprochement of psychology and religion (Clay, 1996).

In the past 20 years, textbooks in psychology of religion have improved in both quality and quantity. In his 1993 presidential address given to APA's Division on Psychology and Religion, Paloutzian (1994) described the changing climate in the publishing industry between the early 1980s and the 1990s. Despite the fact that there were no new texts in the field in the early 1980s, no publisher was interested in

Paloutzian's proposal for a text on the psychology of religion. He was told "that the topic was important and valid, but there was not a sufficient market" (Paloutzian, 1994, p. 7). Shortly thereafter, however, publishing houses began to publish several texts in succession: Batson and Ventis' (1982) *The Religious Experience: A Social-Psychological Perspective*; Paloutzian's (1983) *An Invitation to the Psychology of Religion*; Spilka, Hood, and Gorsuch's (1985) *The Psychology of Religion: An Empirical Approach*; and Brown's (1987) *The Psychology of Religious Belief*. In 1991, Wulff's elegant and comprehensive text, *Psychology of Religion: Classic and Contemporary Views*, added a new depth to textbook offerings. In the early 1990s, when Paloutzian wanted to publish a second edition of his work (which was available in 1996), he was astounded at the multiple opportunities offered to him by publishers (Paloutzian, 1994). By the end of the 1990s, publishers added additional texts, including second editions of Hood, Spilka, Hunsberger, and Gorsuch (1996) and Wulff (1997), among others. In considering the preparation of graduate students in clinical psychology, Shafranske (1996) made an eloquent plea for the inclusion of the study of religion in clinical practice to make up for the "lack of attention placed on the religious dimension within the training of most psychologists, psychiatrists and mental health professionals" (p. xv). The fact that APA not only was the publisher of his carefully edited book, but also published Richards and Bergan's *Spiritual Strategy for Counseling and Psychotherapy* in 1997 and their edited book *Handbook of Psychotherapy and Religious Diversity* in 2000, speaks to a changing time.

PSYCHOLOGY OF RELIGION IN THE CURRICULUM

Despite growing scholarly interest, the relation between psychology and religion in the academic curriculum remains tenuous. As Wulff (1997) noted on the content of psychology textbooks: "Although the marked decline in explicitly negative evaluations of religion in the textbooks in the 1970s is still evident in those of the 1980s, religion remains chiefly an incidental source of illustrations, not a subject matter worthy in its own right of sustained discussion" (p. 16). Similarly, Henry (1938) found in early survey work of college curricula that only 24 out of 154 psychology departments (16%) offered a psychology of religion course; 38 years later, Vande Kemp (1976) did not find a substantial change. She found that, although 190 out of 515 schools (37%) had a course relevant to the psychology of religion in either their philosophy, religion, or psychology curricula (e.g., *Psychology of Religion, Phenomenology of Religion, Religious Experience and Mysticism*, etc.), only 53 schools (10%) offered such a course specifically within the psychology department.

Since Vande Kemp's mid-1970s study, no research has specifically addressed the place of psychology of religion within college-level psychology programs in the United States. Hester and Lampert (2000, May) surveyed psychology departments nationwide to assess the current state of psychology of religion courses in their curriculum and found an increase in the number of psychology of religion courses within psychology departments since Vande Kemp's 1976 study. In her review of college catalogues, Vande Kemp found that only 10% of the psychology programs sampled offered a psychology of religion class. In contrast, 21% of the departments in the Hester and Lampert survey included such a course and offered it regularly.

In recent years, the dialogue on the role of religion has gained greater prominence within science and especially within psychology and teaching. In 1997, the Center for Theology and the Natural Sciences received a major grant for a 4-year project to study the connections between science and spirituality through international conferences and workshops (Begley, 1998; Johnson, 1998). In 1996, the National Institute on the Teaching of Psychology offered two sections on the teaching of the psychology of religion (Hester, 1996, January). The Southeastern Conference on the Teaching of Psychology and the Terman Teaching Conference included as their keynote addresses the place of religion within the psychology curriculum (Hester, 1997, 2000). *Teaching of Psychology* published an interview on "The Status of Psychology of Religion: An interview of Raymond F. Paloutzian" in its Generalist's Corner (Hester, 1998). Popular and professional publications have also shown their interest with cover stories on faith and healing (Wallis, 1996) and the mysteries of prayer (Woodward, 1997). If the recent past is any indication, the new millennium offers promise for further advancement in the integration of religion within the science of psychology.

THE MODERN PSYCHOLOGY OF RELIGION COURSE

Having given a historical perspective on the psychology of religion, let me address those readers who might be persuaded to teach it. What would you need to know? Let me frame the answer around questions I would ask about any new course that I was intrigued by, but had never taught.

1. What is the relation between spirituality and psychology? Curiosity about this question provides an excellent doorway to consider teaching the psychology of religion course. The research from Glock and Stark (1965) assisted me in making a differentiation among religious ideas. They identified the five dimensions of religious commitment: *beliefs*, *knowledge*, *feelings*, *practice*, and *effects*. Not only do these terms become associated with cognition, behavior, and emotion, but they also can be easily translated to operational definitions. As a psychologist, I can breathe easier knowing I am on familiar ground.

2. What do I know about the psychology of religion right now? To answer this question, let me relate the subject matter of psychology of religion to some topics found in the introductory psychology text.

Developmental psychology. Beyond the topic of moral development, the development of religious sensibility in children has often been the focus of study in the psychology of religion. David Elkind (1970) wrote an early article on a Piagetian stage theory of religious development. In addition, many of the current texts (to be cited later) have chapters on religion throughout the life span.

Altered states of consciousness. Meditation, altered states of consciousness, and near death experiences fit naturally in a course on the psychology of religion.

Personality theory. Freud and Jung offer rich theoretical positions on the topic of psychology of religion and are given context in David Wulff's (1997) *Psychology of Religion: Classic and Contemporary.* Wulff covered ample theoretical ground and his writing style is engaging.

Abnormal psychology. Following William James' (1902) descriptions of the depressive behaviors of St. Augustine and John Bunyon, many current authors explore the relation between religion and abnormality. Two examples serve to illustrate: "Religion, Health, and Well-Being" (Paloutzian, 1996) and "Religion and Mental Disorder" (Hood et al.,1996).

Social psychology. Research on religious attitudes benefited from the work of Allport and Ross (1967) on intrinsic and extrinsic religious orientation and its relation to prejudice. In 1995, Hunsberger's work on religion and prejudice—with a focus on the role of religious fundamentalism, quest, and right-wing authoritarianism—provided another sample of what is in store for you. Helping behavior is another topic that links naturally with psychology of religion.

Health psychology and coping. Meditation is another popular topic in psychology of religion. A notable contribution to the issue of coping is Pargament's (1997) *The Psychology of Religion and Coping: Theory, Research, Practice,* which offers a fresh perspective on the topic.

Clinical psychology. In working with clients, therapists often treat a person with a religious history. Of the current books published, the edited work by Shafranske (1996) contains articles written by the best authors in the field. In *The Birth of the Living God: A Psychoanalytic Study,* Ana-Maria Rizzuto (1979) offered a brilliant interpretation using object relation theory as her theoretical position. However, see Wulff (1997) for a thorough presentation of these theories.

Research. Methodology is discussed in many texts in psychology of religion. For instance, Wulff (1997) developed two chapters: "Religion in the Laboratory" and "Correlational Studies of Religion." Paloutzian (1996) also has a chapter on the research in psychology of religion.

3. What topics are taught in psychology of religion? From an informal survey of 21 syllabi (Hester, 1996, August), the following topics surfaced and are presented here in rank order: mysticism and prayer, conversion, mental health, development, research methods, religious experience, organization and cults, morality, death and near death experiences, and secularization of religion.

4. What texts would I use? Because the field is growing rapidly, you want to find the most recent texts in the psychology of religion. From the Hester and Lampert survey (2000), the six top-ranked texts were: Paloutzian's (1996). *The Invitation to the Psychology of Religion* offers a general overview from a social psychological perspective for undergraduates. Wulff's (1997) *Psychology of Religion: Classic and Contemporary Views* makes a significant contribution toward understanding the theories and might be better for the advanced student. Freud's (1927/1961) classic *Future of an Illusion* is next with its challenge to consider religion as a neurosis. The fourth-ranked text is Batson, Shoenrade, and Ventis' (1993) *Religion and the Individual: A Social-Psychological Perspective*, a work based on Batson's (1976) study of attitudinal and behavioral correlates of religion. Batson developed the *quest orientation*, which is defined as "the degree to which an individual involves an open-ended responsive dialogue with existential questions raised by the contradictions and tragedies of life" (Batson et al., 1993, p. 169). The Hood et al. (1996) volume *The Psychology of Religion: An Empirical Approach* offered a strong developmental section followed by the topics of mysticism, religious experience, conversion, organization, morality, adjustment, and mental disorders. In sixth place is James' (1902) *Varieties of Religious Experience*, which still offers students a challenge and a treasure.

5. What activities does one add to a psychology of religion course? In preparing for an APA symposium on the teaching of the psychology of religion (Hester, 1996, August), I obtained 21 syllabi from colleagues who teach the course. What surprised me most was the diverse activities presented. I compiled an eight-page list of them, including journaling, interviewing, paper topics, and experimentation. A sampler of these activities follows.

If you want an empirical course, you might use an idea from Susan Broderick, who asked her students to give an operational definition and quantifiable descriptions for terms such a *religiosity* and *prayer*. Alternatively, you might try Bernard Spilka's challenge presented in his syllabus. "I would like to propose a question that was asked around 1910, but never researched. Does the way one prays imply certain God images held by the prayer?" Following this question, he develops four points: "1. Need a theory: what kind of God images ought to lead to what kinds of prayers? 2. Need a method: measure of God images and forms of prayer. 3. Need to make a questionnaire. 4. Need to enter data into computer, analyze and write it up." He then suggests that if students get supportive or positive findings, they will present at a local convention.

If you are interested in an interview activity, Susan McFadden has students interview people of all ages on their religious experiences. She then includes these interviews on the day she is teaching that specific age group. Ken Pargament has prepared excellent interview directions for his students. Because his interest is in religion and coping, he gives detailed instructions for interviewing in sensitive situations such as in a hospital waiting room.

Are you beginning to see that the psychology of religion is studied, as other topics in psychology are studied, from the lens of the psychologist? My hope is that you do not relegate the psychology of religion course to an esoteric corner, but rather become excited at the prospect of teaching such a course. I hope you realize that you already know much of the framework. Teaching it can widen your thinking, deepen your knowledge, and provide a rich experience for you and your students.

FINAL THOUGHTS

Clearly, in modern society, religion and spirituality can play, and for the majority of people do play, an important role in personal development and psychological well-being. Along with the growing interest in biological and cultural considerations, the trend in modern psychology is to embrace a more holistic view of the individual. This view should include a consideration of the role of religion and spirituality on behavior. The time is ripe for the inclusion in academic curricula of the scientific study of the psychology of religion.

ACKNOWLEDGMENTS

Thanks to Doug Bernstein who originally invited me to share ideas on teaching the psychology of religion at the National Institute for the Teaching of Psychology in 1996. Thanks also to Bill Hill who challenged me to develop my thoughts more fully as the keynote speaker for the Southeastern Conference on the Teaching of Psychology in 1996. Although any errors are mine, I am grateful to Martin D. Lampert and Marcia Frideger whose editing pen brought clarity and lucidity to this work.

REFERENCES

Allport, G. W. (1957). *The individual and his religion: A psychological interpretation.* New York: Macmillan.

Allport, G. W., & Ross, J. M. (1967). Personal religious orientation and prejudice. *Journal of Personality and Social Psychology, 5,* 432–445.

Batson, C. D. (1976). Religion as prosocial: Agent or double agent? *Journal for the Scientific Study of Religion, 18,* 90–93.

Batson, C. D., Schoenrade, P., & Ventis, W. L. (1993). *Religion and the individual: A social-psychological perspective.* New York: Oxford University Press.

Batson, C. D., & Ventis, W. L. (1982). *The religious experience: A social-psychological perspective.* New York: Oxford University Press.

Begley, S. (1998, July 20). Science finds God. *Newsweek, 132,* 46.

Brown, L. B. (1987). *Psychology of religious belief.* London: Academic Press.

Clay, R. A. (1996). Psychologists' faith in religion begins to grow. *APA Monitor, 27*(8), 1, 3–5.

Dittes, J. E. (1969). Psychology of religion. In G. Lindzey & E. Aronson (Eds.), *The handbook of social psychology* (2nd ed., Vol. 5, pp. 602–659). Reading, MA: Addison-Wesley.

Elkind, D. (1970). The origins of religion in the child. *Review of Religious Research, 12*(1), 35–42.

Frankl, V. E. (1963). *Man's search for meaning: An introduction to logotherapy.* New York: Washington Square Press.

Freud, S. (1961). The future of an illusion. In J. Strachey (Ed. and Trans.), *The standard edition of the complete psychological works of Sigmund Freud* (Vol. 21, pp. 5–56). London: Horgarth. (Original work published 1927)

Gallop Organization. (2000). Poll topics: A-Z-religion [On Line]. Available: http:/gallop.com/poll/indicators/inreligiou.asp.

Glock, C. Y., & Stark, R. (1965). *Religion and society in tension.* Chicago: Rand McNally.

Goldbrunner, J. (1964). *Holiness is wholeness and other essays.* Notre Dame, IN: Notre Dame Press.

Gorsuch, R. L. (1988). Psychology of religion. *Annual Review of Psychology, 39,* 201–202.

Hall, G. S. (1904). *Adolescence: Its psychology and its relations to physiology, anthropology, sociology, sex, crime, religion, and education* (2 vols.). New York: Appleton.

Henry, E. R. (1938). A survey of courses in psychology offered by undergraduate colleges of liberal arts. *Psychological Bulletin, 35,* 430–435.

Hester, M. P. (1996, January). *Teaching the psychology of religion.* Presentation at the National Institute on the Teaching of Psychology, St. Petersburg Beach, FL.

Hester, M. P. (1996, August). Review of syllabi on psychology of religion. In M. P. Hester (Chair), *Teaching the psychology of religion.* Symposium conducted at the annual meeting of the American Psychological Association, Toronto, Canada.

Hester, M. P. (1997, February). *Psychology and/of/or religion.* Paper presented at the Ninth annual Southeastern Conference for the Teaching of Psychology, Atlanta, GA.

Hester, M. P. (1998). The status of the psychology of religion: An interview with R. F. Paloutzian. *Teaching of Psychology, 25,* 303–306.

Hester, M. P. (2000, May). *Teaching psychology of religion: If William James can do it, so can you.* Paper presented at the Terman Teaching Conference, Portland, OR.

Hester, M. P., & Lampert, M. D. (2000, May). *Psychology of religion in the academic curriculum: Current status.* Poster session presented at the annual meeting of the Western Psychological Association, Portland, OR.

Hood, Jr., R. W., Spilka, B., Hunsberger, B., & Gorsuch, R. (1996). *The psychology of religion: An empirical approach* (2nd ed.). New York: Guilford.

Hunsberger, B. (1995). Religion and prejudice: The role of religious fundamentalism, quest, and right-wing authoritarianism. *Journal of Social Issues, 51*(2), 113–130.

James, W. (1979). *Principles of psychology* (3 vols.). Cambridge, MA: Harvard University Press. (Original work published 1890)

James, W. (1902). *The varieties of religious experience.* New York: Longmans Green.

Johnson, G. (1998, June 10). Science and religion: Bridging the great divide. *New York Times,* p. B12.

Leary, D. E. (1987). Telling likely stories: The rhetoric of the new psychology, 1880–1920. *Journal of the history of behavioral sciences, 23,* 315–331.

Menninger, K. (1973). *Whatever became of sin?* New York: Hawthorn Books.

Myers, D. G., & Diener, E. (1996, May). The pursuit of happiness. *Scientific American,* pp. 70–72.

Nicholson, I. (1994). Academic professionalization and protestant reconstruction, 1890–1902: George Albert Coe's psychology of religion. *Journal of the History of the Behavioral Sciences, 30,* 348–364.

Paloutzian, R. (1983). *An invitation to the psychology of religion.* Glenview, IL: Scott, Foresman.

Paloutzian, R. (1994). Doing psychology of religion in year APA 101. *Psychology of Religion Newsletter, 19*(1), 1–7.

Paloutzian, R. (1996). *An invitation to the psychology of religion* (2nd ed.). New York: Allyn & Bacon.

Paloutzian, R. F., & Kirkpatrick, L. A. (Eds.). (1996). Religious influences on personal and societal well-being [Special Issue]. *Journal of Social Issues, 51*(2).

Pargament, K. I. (1997). *The psychology of religion and coping: Theory, research, practice.* New York: Guilford.

Richards, P. S., & Bergin, A. E. (1997). *Spiritual strategy for counseling and psychotherapy.* Washington, DC: American Psychological Association.

Richards, P. S., & Bergin, A. E. (Eds.). (2000). *Handbook of psychotherapy and religious diversity.* Washington, DC: American Psychological Association.

Rizzuto, A. (1979). *The birth of the living God: A psychoanaltyic study.* Chicago: University of Chicago Press.

Santrock, J. W. (1997). *Psychology: Content of behavior.* Madison, WI: Brown & Benchmark.

Sexton, V. S. (1991). American psychology and philosophy, 1876–1976: Alienation and reconciliation. In H. N. Malony (Ed.), *Psychology of religion: Personalities, problems, possibilities.* Grand Rapids, MI: Baker Book House.

Shafranske, E. P. (Ed.).(1996). *Religion and the clinical practice of psychology.* Washington, DC: American Psychological Association.

Spilka, B., Hood, Jr., R. W., & Gorsuch, R. L. (1985). *The psychology of religion: An empirical approach.* Englewood Cliffs, NJ: Prentice-Hall.

Starbuck, E. D. (1899). *Psychology of religion.* London: Walter Scott.

Vande Kemp, H. (1976). Teaching psychology/religion in the seventies: Monopoly or cooperation? *Teaching of Psychology, 3,* 15–19.

Vande Kemp, H. (1992). G. Stanley Hall and the Clark school of religious psychology. *American Psychologist, 47,* 290–298.

Wallis, C. (1996, June 24). Faith and healing. *Time, 147*(2), 58–62.

Woodward, K. L. (1997, March 31). Is God listening? *Newsweek, 129*(13), 56–64.

Wulff, D. (1991). *Psychology of religion: Classical and contemporary views.* New York: Wiley.

Wulff, D. (1997). *Psychology of religion: Classical and contemporary views* (2nd ed.). York: Wiley.

37

Environmental Psychology: Cognition, Affect, and Meaningful Action

Stephen Kaplan
University of Michigan

Some years ago I had a teaching assignment that threatened to be a small disaster. I was asked to give a lecture in a course required of all first-year graduate students in psychology. The teaching assistant for the course, who happened to be one of my students, came to me to express her concerns. The particular group of students taking the course that year had a passionate ideological commitment. They felt strongly that it was not meaningful to speak of people in general. Rather a person could only speak to the behavior of specific cultural and ethnic groups. The class had been aggressive in support of this position; they had, in the words of my student, been "eating guest lecturers alive." Knowing that I took a basic process approach, with a focus on mechanisms and inclinations that all people shared, she feared I was in for an experience that would be frustrating to say the least.

Despite the advance warning and my apprehensions, I decided not to change my topic. I did, however, add a brief discussion of an application at the end. As it turned out, I doubt it had much effect on the class reaction.

My topic was mental fatigue and the role of the environment in recovering from this often distressing condition. I began by pointing out that, although mental fatigue was a topic largely neglected in psychology, it was something the students presumably knew quite a bit about from first-hand experience. I discussed the attentional and inhibitory deficits associated with mental fatigue, and then described

471

the research pointing to experiences in the natural environment as particularly effective in aiding recovery (Kaplan, 1995). I ended with my appended application—a discussion of the way inner-city life could be described as engendering mental fatigue in a multitude of ways, greatly impairing the capacity of inner-city dwellers to do the things necessary to improve their circumstances.

As it turned out my concerns about the questions I would be asked were unwarranted. The first question, largely representative of the entire discussion, was "What should we do? How can we change our lives to manage mental fatigue more effectively?" The ensuing discussion was stimulating and satisfying. There was no objection to, or even mention of, the fact that I was proposing a basic, and hence, universal set of psychological mechanisms.

Why did this lecture succeed in what had previously proved to be a difficult context? Although there were a variety of factors, I would like to propose three characteristics that seem particularly important in this instance, as well as many lectures and even entire courses. This analysis is based on personal experience and intuition rather than empirical work. At the same time, however, as I try to show in the sections that follow, the analysis makes good sense in the context of what can be inferred from work on evolution, environmental psychology, and human needs. In other words, this approach provides a framework for teaching as well as for the larger topic of this chapter.

Here, then, are the three characteristics hypothesized to make a course or lecture engaging, memorable, and valued:

1. It identifies puzzles that may not have been previously acknowledged as such. It takes things students know and potentially care about and transforms them into a mystery—a puzzle worth addressing.
2. It conveys a conceptual framework—a new way of seeing so that things now make sense that did not before.
3. It has implications for action—it points to something students can do that might make a difference in their lives or in the world.

ENVIRONMENTS AND HUMAN NEEDS

To arrive at a conceptually grounded translation of what helps make a course exemplary, it is necessary to take a slight detour. Because the detour is in the realm of environmental psychology and has applications to many other areas, its content could be of interest in its own right.

The subject of this section is human needs. These are, however, a different set of human needs than those often included in psychology texts. The focus here is on *informational* needs (Kaplan, 1972). As we shall see, from an evolutionary perspective, these needs would be expected to be particularly salient to our species. In the context of teaching, being aware of these needs has interesting implications.

However, there is a third reason for this focus that is perhaps the most pivotal. Many of the needs attributed to human beings permit only modest leverage. Even with extensive knowledge of these needs, there is relatively little we can do that would improve our teaching or other contexts or environments in which people find themselves. This limitation does not apply to informational needs. An understanding of these needs can lead to opportunities for increasing human effectiveness—a central concern of the newly emerging area of positive psychology (Seligman & Csikszentmihalyi, 2000).

How It All Started

In the late 1960s, when Rachel Kaplan and I began to think about how people relate to the physical environment, not a great deal was known about people's preference for nature. Two events were responsible for moving us from interest to action. First, we were approached by John Wendt, an honors student who wanted to do a thesis that demonstrated that people liked nature. Recognizing the seriousness of the population problem, he thought that if it could be shown that people like natural settings, the potential impact of a growing world population might be taken more seriously. Remarkably, at that time, there were no data indicating what kinds of physical environments people preferred.

The other influential event involved work that did address environmental preference. It went under the name of *experimental aesthetics*. Berlyne (1960), who argued in favor of the optimal complexity hypothesis, was a prominent leader in this area. Berlyne believed that people prefer patterns that have a moderate level of complexity to patterns that are either greater or less than this optimal value. Some support for this hypothesis had been found with artificially contrived (nonsense) stimuli (Berlyne, 1960). Research had also been done with modern art. Wohlwill (1968) was the first to try to apply this theory to photographs of the physical world. Using 14 scenes that represented a range of complexity levels, he obtained a weak, but nonsignificant, inverted-U effect. By the time Wohlwill (1970) wrote an overview of environmental psychology for *American Psychologist*, the inverted-U hypothesis was treated as if it had been substantiated in the context of preference for physical environments.

The implications of this finding, if replicable, seemed to be both profound and disturbing. If complexity was indeed the primary determinant of people's preferences, then views of nature would not be missed if replaced with structures properly designed to have appropriate complexity levels. Thus motivated, we worked with John Wendt to develop an experimental design that could explore these issues. Focusing on relatively nearby environments, we decided to sample four categories of scenes: pure nature, human-influenced nature, built environments with some nature, and purely built environments. Following Wohlwill's approach, the participants used a 5-point scale to rate each of the 56 scenes for both preference and complexity.

Unbeknown to us, there was a flaw in the design. The urban scenes had been taken by a postdoctoral student who wanted to try out his new camera; he turned out to be an excellent photographer. The nature scenes were taken by a graduate student who was less skilled. Further, the scenes shown in the nature pictures, taken in fall after an exceptionally dry summer, were anything but lush. Had nature not been preferred, we would have had ample excuses readily at hand. However, that is not what happened; the preference for the nature scenes, including the human-influenced nature category, was overwhelming. All these scenes were more highly preferred than any of the urban scenes, with one exception—an urban park with several young trees. The study thus showed that the content of the scene played a substantial role in accounting for preference. Complexity, by contrast, was not a strong predictor of preference (Kaplan, Kaplan, & Wendt, 1972).

In examining the scenes within a content category (i.e., nature or urban scenes), it became clear that another factor seemed to influence preference. What was common to the more preferred instances was a feeling that people could learn more if they could walk deeper into the scene. A path that curved out of sight or a landscape partially obscured by nearby foliage were typical examples. We called this quality *mystery*, not realizing at the time that the landscape architects, Hubbard and Kimball (1917) had used the same term for a similar phenomenon in their classic volume.

What had started as an honors thesis became the forerunner of many studies of environmental preference. These studies show considerable consistency not only in the role natural settings played, but also in a set of predictors called the *preference matrix* (S. Kaplan, 1992; R. Kaplan & Kaplan, 1989). The two major components of the matrix are Exploration (of which Mystery is a prime example) and Understanding (exemplified by Legibility, features of a scene that facilitate keeping our bearings and being able to return to where we started). Conceptualizing the environment as a source of information turned out to be a useful way to understand people's preferences.

In time we came to realize that these concepts were useful in other contexts as well. The importance of providing an opportunity to explore seemed equally pertinent to structuring a lecture as to organizing a physical space. The desire to understand (and the intense frustration when one could not) applied as much to organizations (Peters & Waterman, 1982) as to landscapes.

Preference in Evolutionary Perspective

Students in environmental design learn about aesthetics in terms of the form, line, color, and texture of the landscape. Our work on preference did not show these aspects to be major factors. We puzzled over where our variables were coming from and why they seemed so readily generalizable. A breakthrough in our quest for an answer came when we discovered striking parallels in work in the area of human evolution. Anthropologists described early humans as surviving through their wits, through the acquisition of knowledge important to such essential survival activities as hunting (Lee & DeVore, 1968), gathering (Flannery, 1955), and finding one's way back home (Washburn, 1972).

In other words, the capacity to find food, avoid danger, and outwit competing species is information based (Pfeiffer, 1978). An organism that cannot depend either on speed or the sharpness of fang or claw would have to find some other survival strategy. For a variety of reasons, humans appear to have hit on information as the basis of their survival strategy. Such an organism would have to be interested in acquiring new information. It would have to be motivated to expand its knowledge of where food could be found, how various other animals behaved, and the location of alternate routes and hiding places. Thus, a preference for environments that invite exploration would be essential and adaptive. At the same time, for such an organism to leave what it knows far behind in its pursuit of new information would be risky. If survival is based on knowledge, being in an environment where one is ignorant invites trouble. Thus, environments that afford understanding would be equally important.

It is important to recognize that these characteristics are not contradictory—environments can provide opportunities for exploration while remaining understandable. Yet each mandate moderates the other. As people are pulled into new opportunities for exploration, they are likely to find themselves beyond their capacity to understand. In such cases, the need for understanding pulls them back. Likewise, as we seek the familiar and understandable, the need for exploration begins to exert a counterpressure. The result is a rather restless beast, engaged in endless rounds of venturing forth and returning home.

Exploration and understanding are thus pivotal to human functioning. From an evolutionary perspective, it is therefore not surprising that these are activities with strong affective components. Humans hate to be confused. They crave understanding, investing considerable effort into making sense of their world (Gibson, 1966; Kaplan, 1991; Kelly, 1963; Maslow & Diaz-Guerrero, 1971). Similarly, humans like to explore and gain new knowledge. These inclinations are complementary—exploration often leads to new understandings, and new understandings provide the basis for further exploration. They appear to constitute appropriate informational needs for an information-based species.

To play its adaptive role, the motivation to explore and understand must lead to knowledge. This knowledge, in turn, must not only be stored for later use, but stored in an integrated fashion, ready to support the basic informational activities of recognizing, predicting, evaluating, and acting (Kaplan, 1973). It is thus not surprising that Tolman's (1948) cognitive map concept, rescued from oblivion by urban planner Kevin Lynch (1960), has become a major construct in environmental psychology (Golledge, 1987). Although initially proposed as a way of coding spatial information, proponents of this concept quickly recognized that it could serve equally well as a general-purpose knowledge structure (Kaplan, 1973; Siegel & White, 1975). The usefulness of this broadened conception of cognitive maps is supported by the effectiveness of a tool designed to access an individual's non-spatial information. The Conceptual Content Cognitive Map (3CM) (Kearney & Kaplan, 1997) has been used in a variety of contexts, both environmental (e.g., siting of hazard waste on a Native American reservation, forest management in the Pacific Northwest) and in other domains (e.g., mothers' pre- and postnatal feelings about their first child).

The Missing Link

Understanding and exploration, even with strong affective concomitants, are essential to survival, but not sufficient. From an evolutionary perspective, information processing, no matter how skillful, has no value unless it sooner or later leads to adaptive action. Years ago, Guthrie (1935) accused Tolman (1932) of leaving the organism lost in thought. We now know that cognition does not preclude action, but neither does it guarantee it. We have seen how evolutionarily based human needs may have important implications for information processing or, more specifically, that there is a strong and constant connection between affect and cognition in an information-based organism. Likewise there must be a strong affective basis for converting information to action.

There are several interesting clues in the psychological literature as to what this bias might look like. White's (1959) concept of competence provides a good example. It suggests that people do not collect information for its own sake, but for the way it enhances their capacity to act effectively. Another useful concept is that of helplessness (Seligman, 1975). People intensely dislike being helpless—a perspective entirely consistent with an evolutionary approach. The concept of control has often been cast as the opposite of helplessness (Fry, 1989; Mikulincer, 1994; Peterson, Maier, & Seligman, 1993). Although control entails taking action, it is often not the form of action that people desire. Wanting to control things brings with it a great deal of costly overhead with which many people prefer not to deal (Little, 1987). As Antonovsky (1979) pointed out, being able to do *something* when important issues are at stake makes a great deal of difference to people; often they have no illusions that what they do controls the outcome. Thus, a rain dance is a form of participating in the functioning of the universe, not coercing it. In other words, people generally want things in control—they are easier to understand that way.

Thus, in addition to the need for exploration and understanding, there appears to be a need for meaningful action. This concept can be thought of as a need to avoid helplessness—a need to do things that matter, that make a difference. A few examples suggest both the range of possibilities here and the way meaningful action links to other needs and motives.

In some instances, meaningful action is closely related to both exploration and understanding. The process of enhancing our understanding and exploring opportunities can be a form of taking action. Many examples of meaningful action involve socially valued activities. People are motivated to do things that make them feel needed, that others perceive as useful, that gain the respect of their fellows

(Goldschmidt, 1990). Self-maintenance and enhancement constitute another domain of meaningful action. People find it meaningful to do things that concern their health, strength, competence, and appearance. They are motivated to act in ways that preserve, restore, or enhance these valued dimensions of self.

To say that these are examples of meaningful action does not imply that people will always act in this way. Motives may conflict with each other. The examples do suggest, however, that when the environment supports such activities, people are more likely to do them and gain satisfaction thereby.

THE COURSE AS AN ENVIRONMENT

So far we have looked at some key concepts I include in teaching about environmental psychology. An understanding of human needs from an informational perspective leads readily to an exploration of ways environments can be made more supportive. Unfortunately, it is all too easy to find examples of unsupportive environments and to see their cumulative costs on personal and societal levels.

In this section, I want to extend the discussion to the teaching context, not just with respect to courses on environmental psychology, but much more broadly. Informational needs are, as we have seen, motivations that guide people's cognitive relations with the environment. To facilitate connecting these needs to how the teaching process might be enhanced, it is helpful to explore the ways in which a course constitutes an environment. As will become apparent, the *environment* concept is rich with potential for generalizability.

Psychology has employed the environment concept for many years—it has long been said that behavior is a function of genetics and environment. However, what *environment* refers to in such cases is neither particularly well focused nor useful. It stands for education, stimulation, social forces, or whatever is of interest in a particular situation. By contrast, computer scientists are way ahead of us in this respect. In the concept of a software environment, they have discovered something profound. As we all know, when we sit down in front of a computer, we enter a whole world of its own. It is an interconnected set of things that, in its entirety, is far more than we can see (or even think about) at any one time. It has its own logic or characteristic patterns, and we have to build some sort of cognitive map to get where we want to go and do what we want to do. There are striking parallels to what a person has to do to function in work environments, institutional environments, social environments, and, of course, physical environments.

An environment is not simply a bundle of stimulation, a set of forces, or a series of practice trials. An environment is a coherent unit of experiences, possibilities, and implications that requires information processing and that readily elicits an evaluative reaction. It is a place that has strong cognitive and affective components. Certainly a course fits this description. As would be the case with any environment, we might expect the individual to evaluate it in the context of what it offers in terms of understanding, exploration, and meaningful action.

Let us return to the issue of what makes a course (or lecture) engaging, memorable, and valued. The intuitive description I offered focused on three themes: a puzzle, a framework, and an application. When a topic is framed as a puzzle—as something compelling that needs to be solved—there is an implicit promise that exploration will take place, that people will proceed deeper into this space and see what was only hinted at when they began. The framework speaks to the need for understanding—for achieving a coherent view of what was previously not understood. The application promises meaningful action—that a person can now do something more usefully or effectively than was possible before. Thus, the link between the informational needs and the description of what seems to work in the classroom is relatively straightforward.

In principle, these three elements—puzzle, framework, and application—can be incorporated in a broad range of courses and contexts. Admittedly, elements of the culture of college and university teaching can interfere. For example, there is the temptation to present a large number of facts and/or studies. These demonstrate the scientific status of the field and provide easy grist for exams. Unfortunately, an overemphasis on facts and data has serious pedagogic limitations. We have all been to many lectures and conference presentations where such material constitutes answers to unasked questions. In the absence of an exploratory stance, such information is often difficult to relate to prior knowledge, difficult to care about, and difficult to remember.

Furthermore, facts and studies are difficult to apply. Researchers are often frustrated that their studies have so little impact on applications. In the real world, what is typically applied is not data, but a framework—a way of thinking about something. Years of experience in applied contexts have convinced me that what works best is a portable model (Kaplan & Kaplan, 1982): a theoretical framework informed by data, but presented in a way that is sufficiently general to facilitate recognition of its applicability. The portability refers to the model's being sufficiently simplified and pared down so that it is readily remembered. To be used in the real world, an idea must be clear and memorable.

Environmental Psychology as a Broader Framework

Environmental psychology has taught us some lessons with far-ranging implications in the teaching context. Here are some examples:

1. People can manage the environment far more easily than their minds; at the same time, the management of the environment can have major consequences for well-being. For example, the social environment (e.g., the expectations of others), the physical environment (e.g., a quiet, comfortable place to work), and the natural environment (e.g., a small park where we can regain our focus and recover from mental fatigue) can have profound effects on behavior.

2. Will power tends to be overrated and leads to false expectations and disappointments. It is part of the inhibitory control mechanism that is readily overwhelmed by the chaos, distractions, and frustrations of the modern world.

3. Many unfortunate phenomena and traps can be understood in terms of the contrast between the evolutionary and modern environments. Television—that demonstrated antisocial force that people complain about but watch anyway—can be interpreted more readily and usefully in this way.

4. Ignoring people's needs does not help. By contrast, exploring environmental ways to meet them can lead to new and interesting possibilities.

An Exercise for Teachers and Students

To begin the exploration of how environmental psychology can be pertinent to a broad range of subject matters, consider the following four questions:

- What kind of environment would be good for X?
- What kind of environment would be bad for X?
- What kind of environment is typical for studying X?
- What kind of environment is typical of the way that X usually occurs?

The "X" in these questions could be learning, perceiving, processing information, recovering from mental illness, growing up, caring for a sick relative, enhancing self-esteem, acquiring competence, living a satisfying life, or some other problem, topic, or phenomenon of your choosing.

In doing this exercise, keep in mind that in the real world the environment is not noise or extraneous variance. It is a large source of influence with which people deal every day.

Some Techniques for Enhancing the Teaching and Learning Environment

In principle, the classroom provides an ideal opportunity for exploration, understanding, and meaningful action. It is less likely that these goals will be met, however, if the instructor gives in to the temptation to serve as the all-knowing expert, providing *The Answer* without engaging the students in the process. Exploration, understanding, and meaningful action are more likely to be achieved by techniques that:

- Encourage a focus on questions
- Give priority to questions for which there is no one right answer
- Require that understanding be demonstrated by using language meaningful to the student as opposed to parroting the teacher's language
- Encourage the use of personally relevant examples in the questions students ask and in writing assignments

Here are some techniques I have used to help create an environment that supports the basic information processing motives:

Agenda Setting.   Class sessions routinely begin with an agenda-setting process, in which students are asked to indicate questions they have related to the topic assigned for that class period. These agenda items, suitably rearranged, form the basis for the class discussion.

Study Questions for Review Sessions.   About 2 weeks before exams, students receive study questions and are assigned to small groups that meet outside of class. The review session provides the venue for the groups to raise issues they were not able to answer satisfactorily in working together on the study questions. This process tends to sharpen motivation, interest, and focus.

Mystery Day.   Study questions are also used for a late-in-the-term event known as Mystery Day. For this exercise, the class is again divided into small groups meeting outside of class. The format, however, is quite different from the review sessions. On the slated day, each group serves once in the capacity of Seekers—asking questions of another group, either from the study questions or other equally appropriate questions, that are intended to simulate what an interested novice might ask, and once in the capacity of Sages—answering the questions posed by the Seekers in a way that the interested novice would find understandable and helpful. A minimum of four groups is needed to ensure different combinations for the two roles. The students are apprised of the basic format ahead of time, but do not know what the pairings will be. At the end of each 30-minute segment, the participants individually record the three topics and issues they felt were dealt with least satisfactorily. A compilation of these data provides focus for each of the class sessions during the remainder of the term. Although this exercise is not graded, motivation is routinely high. Students generally evaluate the experience as being of great value.

The 5 ± 2 Paper.   Students in all my courses are assigned a one-page paper, due toward the end of the term, that identifies and explains 5 ± 2 principles that have been covered in the course in a way that makes them meaningful, useful, and exciting. The paper is to be of value to someone who has not taken the course, leaving them with a memorable take-home message. Because the students in my courses tend to represent a great diversity of fields, I encourage them to address their papers to someone in their particular area of interest. Considerable exploration goes into this effort, understanding characteristically grows in the process, and the product is often meaningful to its author in many ways.

Feedback "Open House."   Rather than simply returning these one-page papers, we have an open house session that provides students the opportunity to read not only the best papers from the current class, but from past years as well. Students quickly see that there is no right answer. They appreciate the great diversity in approach among the papers deemed excellent, including, for example, a conversation between a human and a computer (the computer was not impressed) and a Faustian drama in which a professor makes a pact with the devil in exchange for the secrets of effective presentation. Having many instances of high-quality writing, all speaking to a topic of interest and each short enough to read quickly, provides an ideal environment for exploration. The open house format is friendly and informal, encouraging comparisons of favorite papers. At the same time, reading through the many examples fosters understanding of the course material from a variety of perspectives.

CONCLUDING THOUGHTS

Environmental psychology emerged around the same time as the first Earth Day and the environmental movement of the late 1960s and early 1970s. Most psychologists before that time had taken little notice of the importance of the environment in understanding thought and action.

My psychological training preceded the days when a person was classified in terms of a subfield of psychology. Perhaps this broad training has made it easier for me to see environmental psychology as every bit as broad as psychology as a whole. The potential for applications is boundless. Not only does the work speak to fields that take the environment seriously (such as planning, natural resources, and environmental design), it also relates to areas in which information sharing can be both important and difficult (e.g., nursing and pharmacy), and to the larger field of education.

The enormous range of applications and potential usefulness of environmental psychology has taught me much that may also be valuable to colleagues in other fields. First and foremost has been the importance of developing coherent frameworks for pursuing interesting and useful applications. Having these frameworks related to a strong, guiding psychological perspective (e.g., evolution/functionalism, cognition/information processing, motivation/needs) has provided a two-way benefit. It makes available a wide range of pertinent concepts while providing a degree of integration across areas of psychology that too often are treated as distinct and unrelated.

A concern for application increases both the appeal of the course and a sense of the usefulness of psychological knowledge. The role of rigor, sometimes eschewed by persons who favor a more humanistic approach, is another important dimension. Rigor is essential if a person is to impact public policy as opposed to preaching to the choir. Cross-disciplinarity allows a person to experience and demonstrate the generality of the approach as well as break down the departmental parochialism so common in university settings. Students from widely different areas discover that they share much common ground. They also find in environmental psychology some portable models that are invaluable to their needs. I find many of these applications to be surprising, stimulating, and informative. It is particularly satisfying to teach in a context where education is a two-way process.

REFERENCES

Antonovsky, A. (1979). *Health, stress and coping.* San Francisco: Jossey-Bass.

Berlyne, D. E. (1960). *Conflict, arousal, and curiosity.* New York: McGraw-Hill.

Flannery, K. V. (1955). The ecology of early food production in Mesopotamia. *Science, 147,* 1247–1256.

Fry, P. S. (Ed.). (1989). *Psychological perspectives of helplessness and control in the elderly.* Amsterdam: Elsevier.

Gibson, J. J. (1966). *The senses considered as perceptual systems.* Boston: Houghton-Mifflin.

Goldschmidt, W. (1990). *The human career: The self in the symbolic world.* Cambridge, MA: Blackwell.

Golledge, R. G. (1987). Environmental cognition. In D. Stokols & I. Altman (Eds.), *Handbook of environmental psychology* (pp. 131–174). New York: Wiley.

Guthrie, E. R. (1935). *The psychology of learning.* New York: Harper.

Hubbard, H. V., & Kimball, T. (1917). *An introduction to the study of landscape design.* New York: Macmillan.

Kaplan, R., & Kaplan, S. (1989). *The experience of nature: A psychological perspective.* New York: Cambridge University Press. (Republished by Ann Arbor, MI: Ulrich's, 1995.)

Kaplan, S. (1972). The challenge of environmental psychology: A proposal for a new functionalism. *American Psychologist, 27,* 140–143.

Kaplan, S. (1973). Cognitive maps in perception and thought. In R. M. Downs & D. Stea (Eds.), *Image and environment* (pp. 63–78). Chicago, IL: Aldine.

Kaplan, S. (1991). Beyond rationality: Clarity-based decision making. In T. Gärling & G. Evans (Eds.), *Environment, cognition and action: An integrative multidisciplinary approach* (pp. 171–190). New York: Oxford University Press.

Kaplan, S. (1992). Environmental preference in a knowledge-seeking knowledge-using organism. In J. H. Barkow, L. Cosmides, & J. Tooby (Eds.), *The adaptive mind* (pp. 535–552). New York: Oxford University Press.

Kaplan, S. (1995). The restorative benefits of nature: Toward an integrative framework. *Journal of Environmental Psychology, 15,* 169–182.

Kaplan, S., & Kaplan, R. (1982). *Cognition and environment: Functioning in an uncertain world.* New York: Praeger. (Republished by Ann Arbor, MI: Ulrich's, 1989.)

Kaplan, S., Kaplan, R., & Wendt, J. S. (1972). Rated preference and complexity for natural and urban visual material. *Perception and Psychophysics, 12,* 354–356.

Kearney, A. R., & Kaplan, S. (1997). Toward a methodology for the measurement of the knowledge structures of ordinary people: The Conceptual Content Cognitive Map (3CM). *Environment and Behavior, 29,* 579–617.

Kelly, G. A. (1963). *A theory of personality.* New York: Norton.

Lee, R. B., & DeVore, I. (1968). *Man the hunter.* Chicago: Aldine.

Little, B. R. (1987). Personality and the environment. In D. Stokols & I. Altman (Eds.), *Handbook of environmental psychology* (pp. 205–244). New York: Wiley.

Lynch, K. (1960). *The image of the city.* Cambridge, MA: MIT Press.

Maslow, A. H., & Diaz-Guerrero, R. (1971). Adolescence and juvenile delinquency in two different cultures. In A. H. Maslow (Ed.), *The farther reaches of human nature* (pp. 369–378). New York: Viking.

Mikulincer, M. (1994). *Human learned helplessness: A coping perspective.* New York: Plenum.

Peters, T. J., & Waterman, R. H. (1982). *In search of excellence.* New York: Harper & Row.

Peterson, C., Maier, S. F., & Seligman, M. E. P. (1993). *Learned helplessness: A theory for the age of personal control.* New York: Oxford.

Pfeiffer, J. E. (1978). *The emergence of man.* New York: Harper & Row.

Seligman, M. E. P. (1975). *Helplessness: On depression, development and death.* San Francisco: Freeman.

Seligman, M. E. P., & Csikszentmihalyi, M. (Eds.). (2000). Positive psychology. *American Psychologist, 55,* 5–184.

Siegel, A. W., & White, S. H. (1975). The development of spatial representations of large-scale environments. *Advances in child development and behavior, 10,* 9–55.

Tolman, E. C. (1932). *Purposive behavior in animals and men.* New York: Century.

Tolman, E. C. (1948). Cognitive maps in rats and man. *Psychological Review, 55,* 189–208.

Washburn, S. L. (1972). Aggressive behavior and human evolution. In G. V. Coelho & E. A. Rubinstein (Eds.), *Social change and human behavior* (pp. 21–39). Washington, DC: National Institute of Mental Health.

White, R. W. (1959). Motivation reconsidered: The concept of competence. *Psychological Review, 66,* 313–324.

Wohlwill, J. F. (1968). Amount of stimulus exploration and preference as differential functions of stimulus complexity. *Perception and Psychophysics, 4,* 307–312.

Wohlwill, J. F. (1970). The emerging discipline of environmental psychology. *American Psychologist, 25,* 303–312.

VI

The Final Word

38

Ebbs, Flows, and Progress in the Teaching of Psychology

W. J. McKeachie
University of Michigan

We are fortunate to be teachers of psychology. We have a fascinating, continually developing subject to teach, and we have students in our classes who are primarily there because of their interest in the subject matter rather than because our courses are required. In this, my 55th year of teaching, I still enjoy preparing for the next week's classes, leading discussions, lecturing, presenting demonstrations, working with teaching assistants, interacting with students from diverse backgrounds, reading student journals—even commenting on and grading tests. To cap this year, I have the great honor to be associated with my good friend, Charles Brewer, in this book. I am grateful to Steve Davis and Bill Buskist for including me, and I am grateful to the authors of the preceding chapters. I have read and learned much from them.

Bill and Steve have asked us to reflect on our teaching careers. Because Eric Landrum has relieved me of the embarrassing task of reviewing my life history, I will look back on trends in three issues that ran through my years of teaching here at the University of Michigan:

- What concepts, theories, or slogans influenced our thinking about teaching and learning?

- What is the role of technology in teaching?
- How have we thought about students?

The preceding chapters are excellent representations of where we stand today, so my remarks are more in the nature of commentary than in adding substance. For each of these issues, I give my perception of the changes over the past 55 years. I wrap up with some comments about the future.

Please keep in mind that the statements I make with apparent certitude should all be prefaced by, "It seems to me...." Memory is (as we teach our students) reconstruction, and my perceptions should be checked by qualified historians of psychology.

The trends I discuss made some impression on higher education beyond the teaching of psychology, but most faculty members do not read journals in higher education or psychology so that new developments often have little impact on everyday teaching in most disciplines. Even in psychology, many teachers are relatively unaware of some of the progress in theory and practice that might influence their teaching.

WHAT CONCEPTS OR THEMES INFLUENCED OUR THINKING ABOUT TEACHING AND LEARNING?

When I became a teaching fellow in psychology at the University of Michgan in 1946, three major theoretical positions were exciting us as graduate students:

- In experimental psychology—behaviorism, particularly the theories of Hull and Tolman (Hull, 1943; Tolman, 1932).
- In clinical psychology—Rogerian nondirective counseling and client-centered psychotherapy (Rogers, 1942) (beginning to be contested by Freudian theory).
- In social psychology—Lewinian field theory and group dynamics (Lewin, Lippitt, & White, 1939).

As I noted in other memoirs (McKeachie, 1999), our group of teaching fellows debated the implications of our favorite theories so vigorously that our supervisor, Harold Guetzkow, encouraged us to carry out a research study to test the effectiveness of approaches to teaching derived from our theoretical positions. The behaviorist classes used recitation and drill with frequent testing and reinforcement, the social psychologists favored classes taught by discussion, and the nondirective approach was represented by classes in which the teacher neither lectured nor led discussions (McKeachie, Guetzkow, & Kelly, 1954).

The results of our experiment were mixed, so I followed up with my dissertation research, comparing a more directive method of discussion with student-centered discussion (McKeachie, 1954). Student-centered teaching was superior in affecting greater depth of understanding.

Student-centered teaching continued to be popular until the late 1950s when Skinnerian behaviorism became the vogue (Skinner, 1954). However, in the 1960s, sensitivity training, an early derivative of group dynamics, became the popular theme for training business executives and spilled over into college teaching, supported by the emergence of student activism centered in the civil rights and anti-Vietnam war movements. This rejuvenated student-centered approach brought to the fore motivational and affective aspects of classroom interactions (e.g., Mann et al., 1970).

Originating in the group dynamics of Lewin and his students, sensitivity training had stressed improving interpersonal communication. However, as sensitivity training spread, the emphasis shifted to the feelings of the group members. *Touchy-feely* became a term of derision. The end of the Vietnam war, a tightening job market, and the emergence of cognitive psychology led to a resurgence of more structured, content-centered approaches for the next decade or two. In the last few years, however, the air has rung with calls for learner-centered education (Barr & Tagg, 1995), active learning, and cooperative/collaborative/peer learning. Thus, once more, student-centered learning has come to the fore, this time with a stronger base in cognitive theory.

This tale may lead you to believe that education, like business, goes through phases in which particular slogans are widely proclaimed as the keys to greater effectiveness. To some extent that view may be true. Nonetheless, although the fads in business (e.g., sensitivity training, zero-based budgeting, planned program budgeting, management by objectives, mergers and acquisitions, quality circles, benchmarking, downsizing, etc.) seem to come and go with few lasting gains, what may appear to be old wine in new bottles in education is actually greatly improved not simply by aging, but by cumulative research and improved understanding of the many variables involved in effective learning and teaching. The theories of teaching of each period gave us understanding of lasting value. What did we learn?

In the post-World War II period, student-centered discussion teaching demonstrated the importance of freedom to express one's own opinions and ideas in effecting changes in attitudes, motivation, and thinking. Skinnerian behaviorism, which followed the student-centered era, had only a brief period of dominance. However, as Barker's chapter demonstrates, behaviorism still has much to offer. Concepts such as conditioning, reinforcement, and shaping continue to mold our teaching behavior.

The sensitivity training groups of the student activist period demonstrated the importance of the underlying emotional components of classroom interactions and the importance of changing teaching strategies from moment to moment and day to day to deal with the dynamics of student characteristics interacting with the development of a class as a group over an academic term. The cognitive revolution supplied depth of processing, elaboration, connectionist, and constructivist theories to enrich our understanding of what goes on in students' heads as the teacher attempts to facilitate life-long learning.

Has teaching improved? I am often asked whether teaching has improved in the last 50 years, and I answer, "Yes," with enthusiasm. There have always been excellent teachers and poor teachers, but today there are many more of the former and fewer of the latter. Moreover, the quality of teaching of the typical teacher is much better than it was a half-century ago.

I base this judgment not only on observations at my own university, but also from my visits to hundreds of colleges and universities, ranging from some of the most impoverished to some of the most elite and ranging in size from 300 to 400 students to the largest—Minnesota and Ohio State.

Why is teaching better? As the preceding chapters illustrated, we know more about characteristics of effective teachers and effective teaching. From the perspective of my value system, another factor is that we now are less likely to think of effectiveness in terms of coverage of subject matter and more likely to think of achieving goals of increased motivation for further learning, building a conceptual framework for continued learning, and developing skills for thinking. Much credit may be given to our improved understanding of the conditions that lead to better learning, memory, thinking, and motivation. More credit probably should go to the much greater frequency of systematic training and guidance of graduate students and new faculty members, which was rare when I started and is now almost universal among the large graduate training institutions (although, as Davis and Huss pointed out in chap. 11, we still need to improve).

Partly as a result of the influx of a new generation of faculty members who have already developed an interest (and found satisfaction) in teaching as graduate students and partly as a result of increased administrative and financial support for centers (or faculty committees) concerned with improving learning and teaching, cultural norms have changed. Teaching portfolios (as described by Korn in chap. 16) encourage reflection about teaching. Teaching is no longer seen as depending simply on one's knowledge of the subject matter, but recognized as an activity requiring thoughtful attention to the goals of education, the diverse needs and background of students, and the variety of teaching strategies needed to be maximally effective—an activity equally complex and challenging as disciplinary research and scholarship. Thus, as I look back, it is not with nostalgia for the good old days, but rather with gratitude for the opportunity to continue learning how to teach—and I am still learning.

WILL TECHNOLOGY BE OUR SAVIOR?

In 1946, the technology expected to have a major impact on education was film. During World War II, films had proved to be effective in training. Following the war, psychologists were in the forefront in research on educational films. The

Canadian Film Board, as well as individual psychologists and educational film companies, produced many excellent films for use in psychology classes. When I began lecturing to 500-student classes in introductory psychology, I showed a film almost every week.

It was only a few years later when a new technology became prominent— TV. In January 1951, I began teaching the first psychology course on TV—a 14-week noncredit introductory psychology series on Channel 4, Detroit (McKeachie, 1952). As TV grew in popularity, it was touted as the magical tool that would enable higher education not only to improve educational effectiveness, but also to cope with the flood of baby boomers soon to enter higher education. Master teachers would be televised to thousands of students, and the rest of us would be free to lead small-group discussions or interact with students on a one-to-one basis.

Many colleges and universities installed the equipment necessary to offer their large courses over closed-circuit TV. Films of TV lessons (kinescopes) were distributed to facilitate distance education. The Ford Foundation supported an extensive program of research on TV, and well-controlled studies were carried out in a number of universities. The results show that TV contributed to learning when students needed a good view, as in dentistry, surgery, and demonstrations in science and engineering lectures (Carpenter & Greenhill, 1955, 1958). However, master teachers on TV were not as effective as graduate students teaching small classes (Macomber & Siegel, 1960).

The excitement about educational TV was soon overshadowed by that engendered by a technology invented by psychologists—teaching machines—first suggested by Sydney Pressey in the 1926 (see Beins, chap. 24) and now made prominent by B. F. Skinner (1958, 1968). Based on the premise that the biggest barrier to effective learning is proactive interference from mistakes, teaching machines and programmed learning presented material to be learned in easy steps minimizing errors. Publishers and manufacturers rushed to get in on the enormous market expected, and teaching machines proved to be effective in teaching motivated learners. Unfortunately, the carefully sequenced, almost errorless steps were so unchallenging that most learners became bored. Simple reinforcement of getting the right answer was not enough to sustain lasting effort unless the learner had a strong need to achieve the learning objective.

Teaching machines had barely come into widespread use when an even more glamorous technology seemed to be education's salvation. In the early 1960s, Herb Simon, Nobel Prize winning psychologist and polymath, told me, "Bill, within 5 years computers will revolutionize education!"

Alas, the computer revolution sputtered. After spending millions of dollars on the Plato project for education by computers, the Department of Defense concluded that it was not cost-effective. In the last lecture I heard Herb Simon give before his death, he warned that, valuable as the computer may be, we need to keep in mind that "education takes place in the head of the person, not in some machine or network" (Simon, 1997, p. 25).

I continued to be optimistic about the potential of computers for teaching and learning. In the 1960s, while I was chairing the psychology department, I supported one of our faculty members, Dana Main, in developing computer simulations to teach research design and analysis in our core undergraduate courses. A few years later, I began using Bob Kozma's Learning Tool in my introductory psychology class.

While I was director of the Center for Research on Learning and Teaching, Karl Zinn, our technology specialist, always quick to spot new possibilities for improving education, became interested in the possibility that computer conferencing could be adapted for use in education. He hired Bob Parnes, a psychology graduate student with excellent programming skills who developed CONFER, a conferencing system adopted by universities, business, and government.

I used CONFER in my courses for a while and more recently have used e-mail and a list serve to communicate with my students. In the early years, my students who were computer buffs participated frequently (but often about social activities, dormitory food, and other issues only remotely related to the course). Most students used it infrequently, if at all. Richard Velayo, one of my doctoral students, showed that gains in learning occurred only if we required participation every week (Velayo, 1993).

More recently, our university technology group developed Course Tools, a program for teaching that looked promising. I used it for two or three terms, thinking that it would be convenient for students to submit their weekly journals by this means, but both the students and I found that hardcopy journals were more convenient. When I asked my teaching assistant, who was completing his doctorate in instructional technology, whether we should continue its use this year, he said, "No. It's more trouble than it's worth."

Although none of the technological revolutions has achieved its proponents' dreams, each has stimulated useful research and produced tools that can contribute to effective teaching. It is conventional to state that the fundamental laws of learning do not change regardless of the medium of teaching, but context is important. Both cognition and motivation will be influenced as students and faculty members become so accustomed to computers that responses are automatized and unconscious. One key to successful use will depend on whether using computers will enhance reflection and thought about the material to be learned or will simply facilitate unthinking rapid responding.

Clearly the World Wide Web (WWW) goes well beyond previous technologies in its potentiality for accessing knowledge. However, its usefulness depends on the development of new skills—not only for finding the knowledge a person needs without being overwhelmed by the plethora of information available, but also for discriminating among sound, research-based knowledge and opinions, assertions, or biases.

HOW HAS OUR THINKING ABOUT
STUDENTS CHANGED?

When I began teaching, most university introductory courses were taught in large lecture auditoria, and I suspect that most teachers thought of students as a relatively undifferentiated group. Students were students were students.

Obviously some students performed better than others, but our job was simply to present sound, up-to-date course content, and the students' job was to learn it and demonstrate their learning on course examinations. Because psychologists wanted to be objective, we used multiple-choice, true–false questions as opposed to the old-fashioned, unreliable essay exams used in the humanities and some of the other social sciences. It was only decades later that we found that students learned less when evaluated by objective tests rather than essay or open-ended methods. (Many students prepare for objective tests by rote repetition and memorization, whereas they prepare for essay tests by trying to integrate and relate materials more thoughtfully.)

At that time, we assumed that human learning conformed to general principles being identified in laboratory studies, mostly carried out with rats. Of course, individuals differed in intelligence, but admission standards in the selective institutions were intended to screen out those students whose intelligence would not enable them to learn the subject matter presented by the faculty. In state universities required to accept all high school graduates, the first year was intended to flunk out those students for whom investment in higher education would be wasted. (In fact, a similar view continued to pervade many science departments until recently, with the initial chemistry or mathematics courses designed to eliminate students who lacked the aptitude needed to become scientists, mathematicians, or physicians.)

When I followed up the students who had participated in our 1947 research on three methods of teaching (McKeachie et al., 1954), I noticed that the effects of the recitation-drill method on motivation to major in psychology differed for men and women. Thus, in all of my later research, I analyzed the results separately by sex (*gender* had not yet come into ordinary usage). Today, as Margaret Matlin (chap. 33) illustrated, it would be inconceivable to omit considerations of gender in our teaching and research.

As I became involved with the McClelland–Atkinson work on needs for achievement, affiliation, and power, I also began to look for interactions between teaching and these motivational characteristics of students. I vigorously applauded when I heard Lee Cronbach give his 1957 APA presidential address, "Beyond The Two Disciplines of Scientific Psychology," and I was highly complimented when he sent me a copy inscribed "To Bill McKeachie, who practices what I preach." I have continued to look at attribute-treatment interactions throughout my research career. Cronbach and Snow's (1977) research and writing, as well as work in personality and social psychology, on the differential effects of situations on different persons, gradually seeped into teaching so that more and more faculty members now recognize that what works for one student or group of students may not be effective for others. Moreover, research now goes beyond simple interactions such as that between gender and competition. For example, Inglehart, Brown, and Vida (1994) showed that by putting this interaction into the broader theoretical framework of stress, ways of ameliorating the negative effect of competition would be developed. As our student bodies become more diverse in age, ethnicity, and background, it is even more important that we realize that we need to vary our methods if we are to be effective for all or almost all students.

One development sensitizing teachers to individual differences was the cognitive style/learning style movement. The most significant and best validated research on cognitive style was that of Witkin (1978) on field independence and field dependence based on research on perception dating back to the 1940s. By the 1960s and 1970s, a variety of learning styles had been proposed differentiating between such characteristics as auditory versus visual, global versus analytic, sequential versus holistic, right-brained versus left-brained, abstract versus concrete, or active versus reflective learners. Although many of these styles or preferences were not demonstrated to be valid, they were useful in getting teachers to recognize the importance of varying teaching to accommodate individual differences among students.

What proved to be the most important step forward was the impact of cognitive research demonstrating that neither intelligence nor learning styles represented permanent unchanging characteristics of students. Rather researchers found that intelligence consisted of learnable skills and could be increased at any age (see Resnick, 1976). Similarly, learning styles could be changed by teaching students learning strategies (Weinstein & Mayer, 1986).

The most important variable affecting learning is prior knowledge. Intelligence tests predict educational achievement because they assess prior knowledge of domains important in education such as verbal and mathematical ability. Skinner had been right in stressing the damaging effects of incorrect prior knowledge. However, rather than following Skinner's strategy of programs designed to avoid error, contemporary educators attempt to elicit misconceptions so that they can be corrected. Rather than step-by-step responses, we try to encourage reflection and creation of meaningful conceptual structures or schemas. We recognize, as in Jane Halonen's chapter 4, that anything we do or say has different effects on different students.

The shift from a conception of education based on inherent individual differences in intelligence to one viewing human beings as natural learners has resulted in a major change in our goals as well as our methods of education. We now see teaching students in ways that will enhance their ability to continue learning as more important than differentiating between those students who should continue and those who are not capable of continuing. Student-centered/learner-centered teaching thus emerges once again as a relevant contemporary theme.

WHAT HAVE I LEARNED?

My approach to teaching has probably been more the result of learning from my students, teaching assistants, colleagues, and faculty members and friends at other institutions than from any systematic thought. Certainly group dynamics and client-centered therapy, which were two of the major theories influencing us in my graduate student days, left a lasting impression. Their emphasis on learning as an active, interpersonal, social activity seems fundamental (and contemporary).

Most teaching in other disciplines in the 1940s and 50s assumed that what was most important in teaching was the content that the teacher presented. Content certainly is important, but covering the content regardless of student attention and understanding is less important than what is going on in students' heads. In fact, the need to cover the content is one of the greatest barriers to effective teaching. I recall with a wry smile the comment of an accounting professor at the end of my workshop on teaching thinking: "These are great methods for getting students to think, but I only have time to teach accounting."

My philosophy of teaching means that I spend less time in the role of the expert dispensing information and move more toward the role of facilitating student reflecting and reacting. This philosophy does not mean that I neglect the theories, concepts, and research findings that constitute our subject matter, but it does mean that I have to be more selective in choosing what is most meaningful and of most lasting value. Facilitating student learning does not mean that the students must discover everything for themselves, but it does mean that we give them more opportunity to express their own preconceptions, curiosity, and conclusions.

Waiting for students to express their thoughts can be productive. Despite the popularity of nondirective teaching when I began teaching, I never fully implemented it. My own anxiety when there is a period of silence prevented me from becoming as nondirective as Urie Bronfenbrenner, whose office was next to mine. Urie would enter the class and sit quietly until someone said something. I could not do that.

Perhaps because I admired Urie, but could not emulate him, I have always told the teaching assistants I was training that different things work for different teachers. We can all become effective teachers, but we achieve effectiveness in ways conditioned by our own personalities.

WHAT OF THE FUTURE?

Undoubtedly, there are new challenges to meet in teaching. As early as Ted Newcomb's Bennington research in the 1930s (Newcomb & Wilson, 1966) and his application of his research results in planning the residential colleges at Michigan and the University of California campuses at Santa Cruz, Irvine, and San Diego, we recognized that most student learning goes on outside classrooms (a point mentioned in Perlman and McCann's chap. 15). Now with increased use of distance learning, we need to learn how to better incorporate the values of peer learning in nonresidential situations.

The challenges for creativity in teaching methods may be less pressing than the challenges to our identity as psychologists. In an invited address to the Canadian Psychological Association, one of psychology's wisest sages, Bandura (2001), pointed to the danger of fragmentation as interdisciplinary programs become more popular throughout higher education. Our biopsychologists are now heavily involved in neuroscience programs, and our cognitive psychologists are identified as cognitive scientists and are also heavily involved in brain imaging and neuroscience. Psychologists of all descriptions are becoming more sensitive to the crucial importance of contextual and cultural variables, and we have programs in cultural psychology, culture and cognition, environmental psychology, health psychology, engineering psychology, evolutionary psychology, psycholinguistics, information science, and many other cross-disciplinary areas.

In my APA presidential address, I suggested that cognitive psychology was providing integrative concepts across the whole range of psychological specialties, but that, even so, behavior is our ultimate dependent variable. Today, as I try to learn more about neuroscience, I see that the difference between biopsychologists and other neuroscientists is that the psychologists still are interested in the relation of neural mechanisms to psychological concepts that are tied to behavior.

As a lifelong optimist, I believe that our interest in behavioral outcomes will enable us to maintain an identity as psychologists even though more and more of us will be working with individuals in other disciplines on problems that cut across the traditional fields. Like Bandura, I believe that with the increasing need for effective human personal and collective agency, a strong core discipline of psychology is needed more than ever before. As teachers of psychology, we face the challenge of preparing ourselves and our students to bridge the differences among different fields of enquiry and application while continuing to build a solid base in the traditional core areas of psychology.

What makes psychology challenging and fascinating is the fact that we continue to confront new complexity. No research I have done ever came out with a simple answer, and what frustrates policymakers about psychologists is that we continue to point to the interactions, curvilinear relations, and contextual variables that need to be considered in policy decisions, but what is frustrating to policymakers is beguiling for us.

Although student culture changes from generation to generation, students are still intrigued with the subject matter of psychology; topics that once had little relevance to their interests, such as biopsychology, now have lots of fascinating developments, and areas such as consciousness that were once considered outside the realm of scientific psychology are now in every introductory textbook. Students still come up with new questions that make me think; they still have insights from which I learn. I know that I still have much to learn about teaching, but continued learning is part of what makes teaching fun. Thus, I anticipate that the next half century will be as much fun for the next generation of psychology teachers as the past half century has been for me.

When receiving the Canadian Psychological Association Award for Distinguished Contribution to Psychology in Education and Training, Nick Skinner concluded his address (Skinner, 2001) with words from Robert Bolt's "A Man for All Seasons." They brought tears to my eyes, and I can think of no better conclusion to these reminiscences.

Sir Thomas More assures his protege that if he becomes a teacher, he will be an outstanding teacher. "But if I were," demurs the ambitious young man, "who would know it?" More replies, "You, your friends, your students, God. Not a bad audience that." Not a bad audience indeed!

ACKNOWLEDGMENT

I am indebted to Bill Buskist, Steve Davis, Matt Kaplan, and Don Brown for helpful comments.

REFERENCES

Bandura, A. (2001). The changing face of psychology at the dawning of a globalization era. *Canadian Psychology, 42,* 12–24.

Barr, R., & Tagg, J. (1995). From teaching to learning: A new paradigm for undergraduate education. *Change, 27*(6), 12–25.

Carpenter, C., & Greenhill, L. (1955). An investigation of closed-circuit television for teaching university courses. Instructional Television Research Project No. 1. University Park: Pennsylvania State University.

Carpenter, C., & Greenhill, L. (1958). An investigation of closed-circuit television for teaching university courses. Instructional Television Research Project No. 2. University Park: Pennsylvania State University.

Cronbach, L. (1957). Beyond the two disciplines of scientific psychology. *American Psychologist, 30,* 116–127.

Cronbach, L., & Snow, R. (1977). *Aptitudes and instructional methods.* New York: Irvington.

Hull, C. L. (1943). *Principles of behavior.* New York: Appleton-Century-Crofts.

Inglehart, M., Brown, D. R., & Vida, M. (1994). Competition, achievement, and gender: A stress theoretical analysis. In P. R. Pintrich, D. R. Brown, & C. E. Weinstein (Eds.) *Student motivation, cognition, and learning: Essays in honor of Wilbert J. McKeachie* (pp. 311–329). Hillsdale, NJ: Lawrence Erlbaum Associates.

Lewin, K., Lippitt, R., & White, R. K. (1939). Patterns of aggressive behavior in experimentally created "social climates." *Journal of Social Psychology, 10,* 27–29.

Macomber, F., and Siegel, L. (1960). *Experimental study in instructional procedures* (Final report). Oxford, OH: Miami University.

Mann, R., Arnold, S., Binder, J., Cytrynbaum, S., Newman, B., Ringwald, B., Ringwald, J., & Rosenwein, R. (1970). *The college classroom: Conflict, change, and learning.* New York: Wiley.

McKeachie, W. J. (1952). Teaching psychology on television. *American Psychologist, 6,* 119–121.

McKeachie, W. J. (1954). Individual conformity to attitudes of classroom groups. *Journal of Abnormal and Social Psychology, 12,* 282–289.

McKeachie, W. J. (1999). Teaching, learning, and thinking about teaching and learning In J. C. Smart (Ed.), *Higher education: Handbook of theory and research, Vol. XIV* (pp. 1–38). New York: Agathon.

McKeachie, W. J., Guetzkow, H., & Kelly, E. L. (1954). An experimental comparison of recitation, discussion, and tutorial methods in college teaching. *Journal of Educational Psychology, 45,* 224–232.

Newcomb, T., & Wilson, E. (1966). *College peer groups.* Chicago: Aldine.

Resnick, L. B. (Ed.). (1976). *The nature of intelligence.* Hillsdale, NJ: Lawrence Erlbaum Associates.

Rogers, C. R. (1942). *Counseling and psychotherapy.* Boston: Houghton-Mifflin.

Simon, H. (1997). Technology in education, learner motivation, and the learning process. In K. R. Tedman & D. A. Goslin (Eds.), *Celebrating 50 years of research on human performance: Planning for the 21st century* (pp. 25–27). Washington, DC: American Institutes of Research.

Skinner, B. F. (1954). The science of learning and the art of teaching. *Harvard Educational Review, 24,* 86–97.

Skinner, B. F. (1958). Teaching machines. *Science, 128,* 969–977.

Skinner, B. F. (1968). *The technology of teaching.* New York: Appleton-Century-Crofts.

Skinner, N. F. (2001). A course, a course, my kingdom for a course: Reflections of an unrepentant teacher. *Canadian Psychology, 42,* 49–60.

Tolman, E. C. (1932). *Purposive behavior in animals and men.* New York: Century.

Velayo, R. S. (1993). *Computer conferencing as an instructional tool: Exploring student perceptions of use, cognitive and motivational characteristics, and frequency of interaction.* Unpublished Ph.D. dissertation, University of Michigan.

Weinstein, C. E., & Mayer, R. E. (1986). The teaching of learning strategies. In M. Wittrock (Ed.), *Handbook of research on teaching* (pp. 315–327). New York: Macmillan.

Witkin, H. A. (1978). *Cognitive styles in personal and cultural adaptation* (The 1977 Heinz Werner lectures). Worcester, MA: Clark University Press.

39

Reflections on an Academic Career: From Which Side of the Looking Glass?

Charles L. Brewer
Furman University

During 40 years of teaching, my work has received more accolades than it deserves. One of the most treasured of these is being honored with Bill McKeachie by distinguished colleagues and meritorious teachers who wrote and edited chapters for this book. All of these people have enriched my life, and I thank them very much.

When Steve Davis and Bill Buskist asked me to write a short piece for this volume, I wondered why—and I am still wondering. They suggested that I reflect on my teaching career and "not feel constrained in any way, shape, or form!" (personal communication, January 16, 2001). The implication may have been that my career has already been longer than most mere mortals can reasonably expect and that its length has exceeded tolerable limits. Their request was like a Rorschach inkblot test, intentionally unstructured so that writing about almost anything would be acceptable. Puzzling over their request, I thought that telling anyone how to teach is presumptuous and inappropriate, and I decided not to do that. This decision may surprise many readers, who consider me both presumptuous and inappropriate. I decided, instead, to emphasize a few things in my career that may relate to what the editors had in mind. Recognizing the difficulty of interpreting responses to a Rorschach inkblot, readers may never know whether what I wrote is what the editors wanted me to write.

My perspective on academic life comes from teaching at liberal arts colleges in Wooster, Ohio; Elmira, New York; and Greenville, South Carolina. Be forewarned that my comments are not constrained by one scintilla of empirical evidence. They are purely idiosyncratic and may not be shared by another person on this planet. They are not recommendations for ensuring academic success for anybody anywhere. Here, then, are my free associations to the editors' ambiguous request.

TEACHING

The banality of teaching has been recognized for a long time. A Greek proverb says that, "schoolmasters spend their lives telling the same people the same things about the same things." The eminent economist John Maynard Keynes said that education is "the inculcation of the incomprehensible into the indifferent by the incompetent," and a pedagogue is described as "one who casts false pearls before real swine." Teachers have been a sorry lot for a long time. Since Allan Bloom "closed the American mind" in 1987, however, we have seen a veritable plethora of reports about the shameful shambles in education. If we believe certain recent prognostications, the demise of teaching, alas, is imminent.

In prestige and remuneration, teachers are far below physicians, football coaches, and rock stars. I am not a physician, a football coach, or a rock star and never expect to be. I am a teacher who takes my job more seriously than some of the doomsayers seem to think. Despite being less prestigious and less lucrative than many other professions, teaching is the most exciting, challenging, rewarding, and difficult thing that I have ever done; I cannot imagine doing anything else. As you may suspect, therefore, my purpose in writing this essay is not to bury teaching, but to praise it. By doing so, I hope to counteract the pessimism that pervades our profession. I also hope to encourage young teachers who may be so disheartened by the worst of what they see that they fail to appreciate the best of what might be.

TEACHING AND RESEARCH

Higher education in the United States was experiencing unprecedented growth and prosperity during the 1960s. Enrollments were skyrocketing and funding for education, training, and research seemed unlimited. Graduate programs were highly specialized. Students were often discouraged from getting a broad background in their discipline and taking courses in other programs. This situation was considered appropriate and defensible because the Ph.D. degree was a research degree, and research was becoming more highly specialized. One critic observed that students were learning more and more about less and less. I am reminded of a comment by Mark Twain who said: "The investigations which a number of researchers have carried out have already shed a great deal of darkness on the subject and it is possible, if they continue, that we shall soon know nothing about it at all." As Ph.D. graduates moved into academic positions in large universities, they discovered that research grants and publications in the best journals were the only determinants of respectability, prestige, and advancement. Certain programs emphasized teaching in the preparation of graduate students, but not very many and not very much. Perhaps because of widespread public criticism, research universities now claim to stress quality of teaching in decisions concerning salary, tenure, and promotion. Research and publications are still necessary, but they may not be sufficient to ensure success at research universities.

When I arrived at Furman University in 1967, the situation was strikingly different. Publications by faculty members were infrequent, except by a few people in a few departments. I remember attending afternoon receptions, with cookies and Baptist punch, to celebrate the publication of an occasional article or book. Effective teaching was said to be the major criterion for academic advancement. I often thought that the only requirement for being granted tenure was that the candidate breathe sporadically enough to maintain a semblance of viability. Then, as now, the American Association of University Professors mentioned only two reasons for terminating a tenured faculty member: incompetence and moral turpitude. Then, as now, Furman did not uniformly enforce either of those guidelines, but applied them selectively in ways that remain mysterious.

With the economic downturn of the mid-1970s and the precipitous decline in academic positions, the situation changed noticeably. Many new Ph.D. graduates, who expected to get positions in large research universities, went to small liberal arts colleges where they continued the specialized research they learned to do in graduate school. Some of them made valuable contributions to the primary literature. As their research reputations spread, they insisted on receiving appropriate recognition and credit for their scholarship in considerations of salary, tenure, and promotion. Hence, Furman's recent emphasis on scholarship and academic visibility beyond the campus in Travelers Rest came from faculty members who are active scholars; it was not imposed on faculty members by administrators. This difference in judging academic performance is one striking change at Furman since 1967, and it has caused considerable consternation among certain faculty members. They insist that Furman was attractive to them because it stressed teaching and allowed them to avoid the publish-or-perish milieu of large research institutions. Having visited numerous colleges and universities as a curriculum consultant, I believe that this new stress on scholarship is widespread in American liberal arts colleges. Ironically, many research universities now claim that good teaching is more important than in the past. Will the twain ever meet?

Debating the relative importance of teaching and research has a long history. William James (1899/1939) insisted that "psychology is a science, and teaching is an art" (p. 7), and "to know psychology . . . is absolutely no guarantee that we shall be good teachers" (p. 9). More than a half century later, in an article titled "Teaching: Have Your Cake and Eat it Too?", Claude Buxton (1951), a psychologist at Yale University, highlighted the apparent conflict between subject matter specialization and teaching. He urged, "... that we value teaching as a profession in its own right, equal in importance to, not subordinate to, the life of scholarship and research" (p. 114).

Until recently, most academicians paid little attention to Buxton and his exhortation, but we are now being forced to consider certain issues that he raised. For example, Ernest Boyer (1990) commented as follows:

> A wide gap now exists between the myth and the reality of academic life. Almost all colleges pay lip service to the trilogy of teaching, research, and service, but when it comes to making judgments about professional performance, the three are rarely assigned equal merit.... The time has come to move beyond the tired old "teaching versus research" debate and give the familiar and honorable term "scholarship" a broader, more capacious meaning, one that brings legitimacy to the full scope of academic work. (p. 15)

Several professional organizations, including The Society for the Teaching of Psychology (Division 2 of the American Psychological Association), are attempting to redefine scholarship for the 21st century (see Halpern & Reich, 1999; Halpern et al., 1998). Certain disciplines, including psychology, will probably broaden their definitions of research and scholarship, and these changes may have important implications for evaluating faculty members' academic work.

On one point, let me be perfectly clear. I am not suggesting that research is an impediment to good teaching. With confidence bordering on certainty, I believe that research can improve teaching and teaching can improve research if the two appropriately complement each other in the education of students. I have been an energetic teacher and active researcher for a long time, and each of these two facets of my work has benefited the other.

Despite recent and unconvincing talk about the importance of teaching at research universities, teaching has not attained equal status with research in psychology, as Buxton (1951) hoped it would so long ago. Continuing discussions of these issues are interesting and important. Leaving this sticky wicket aside for the moment, I now highlight a few other aspects of an academic career.

THE FRANTIC FIRST YEARS

As intimated earlier, nothing in graduate school prepares one for the first few years of full-time teaching. Staying one page ahead of the students in courses you have never taught, or maybe never taken, requires more time than it does. When you teach the same course a second time, those inspired lecture notes will have lost much of their glitter. Consequently, you have to work almost as much the second time on those same lectures. As a beginning teacher, I thought that more experience would make the task less difficult and less time-consuming. I have learned, however, that once you feel more comfortable with the courses you teach, other things will take up the time that you thought would be available. For example, Furman expects faculty members to participate in faculty governance, and I did my share of that until an epiphany occurred during a general faculty meeting many years ago. On that historic day, I learned that *faculty governance* is an oxymoron, and I have since been less active in matters involving that misnomer. A former president of Furman told me to save a lot of time by not attending monthly faculty meetings, and I took him seriously. I asked Furman's next president to call me when faculty meetings were no longer a waste of time, and no call has come.

TECHNOLOGY AND TEACHING

Dramatic advances in technology have changed how teachers do their work. As one who was long called an *antediluvian Luddite*, I now use computers for more things than I knew they could do. If technological advances are used appropriately, they can enhance learning and teaching and make them more interesting. No matter how sophisticated computers become, however, the most important education will continue to be face-to-face interactions of students and teachers. Computers may supplement, but they will never supplant, these interactions as we strive to increase information, knowledge, and wisdom. I have seen far too many soporific PowerPoint presentations that had a lot of power but no point.

LESSONS FOR BEGINNING TEACHERS

I now mention 10 things about surviving and thriving in an academic career, hoping that they will be helpful for beginning teachers navigating the Scylla and Charybdis of their professional pursuits. These observations are sometimes called Brewer's Ten Commandments of Teaching, but I would never mention that. Readers who are not neophytes can stop here or read on.

Number 1

Be clear about your educational goals and objectives and be sure that your students are clear about them. Many beginning teachers may have only murky notions about their general academic goals and specific educational objectives, but how can teachers know what to do until they know what they want to do? If you do not know where you are going, the likelihood that you will get there borders on randomness.

Number 2

Know the relevant facts, but go beyond the facts. Voltaire said that some people "can think no deeper than a fact," and Thomas Huxley commented that "those who refuse to go beyond fact rarely get as far as fact." Recognize the importance of facts, but concentrate on concepts and principles that have wider applicability than isolated facts. Facts fade fast, and most students will not remember all the facts for the final examination; if they do, they will not remember them 2 weeks later. Attitudes, commitments, concepts, and principles that students learn or later discover serve them better. Emphasize Brewer's Fourth Law: Everything is related to everything else. Or, as John Muir put the same point, "when we try to pick out anything by itself, we find it hitched to everything else in the universe."

Number 3

Be willing to say "I don't know," but always strive to decrease the frequency with which you must do so. Samuel Butler observed that, "a little knowledge is a dangerous thing, but a little lack of knowledge is also a dangerous thing." As you gain experience, knowledge, and self-confidence, you will come to understand Hal Borland's point that "facts are not answers but only tools with which to fashion more questions." In addition, remember James Thurber's wise observation: "It's better to ask some questions than to know all the answers." For every complex question, there is a simple answer—and it is wrong.

Number 4

In all your speaking and writing, strive for clarity, conciseness, and felicity of expression. To paraphrase Samuel Butler, young authors are tempted to leave anything they have written through fear of not having enough to say if they go cutting out too freely. Being long is easier than being short. In the latest version of a wonderful little book titled *Elements of Style*, William Strunk and E. B. White (2000) provided excellent guidance for writing succinctly and well. Read and heed their advice. In speaking and writing, as in almost every endeavor, making things complex is simple, but making things simple is complex. Heed Henry David Thoreau's advice and simplify, simplify, simplify. Just as important, learn to recognize what Oscar Wilde called "the precise psychological moment when to say nothing." I especially like how James Russell Lowell put the same point: "Blessed are they who have nothing to say, and who cannot be persuaded to say it."

Number 5

For your learning and teaching, develop a passion that approaches religious fervor. If you are not passionate about what you are doing, your students will not be passionate about what you want them to do. I have often spoken and written about passion in teaching, which is the principal ingredient that separates adequate from exceptional teachers. Ralph Waldo Emerson insisted that "nothing great was ever achieved without enthusiasm," and he was right. The best teachers I know are as excited about learning and teaching as they were when they first started to learn and teach. The saddest people I know are teachers who have lost their passion for teaching, but they continue to teach. When teaching is no longer fun, give it up— grow geraniums, play golf, read mystery stories, help with Habitat for Humanity, watch soap operas, or become a football coach or a rock star! Your colleagues and students will rejoice.

Number 6

Be fair and friendly with all students, but familiar with none. Benjamin Franklin made a similar point when he said: "Be civil to all; sociable to many; familiar with few." Recognize, however, that you will not like some students as much as you like others. Frankly, I prefer highly capable and motivated students who work hard to learn the facts, concepts, and principles that they should know. I would be less than candid if I said otherwise. Do you favor certain kinds of students?

Number 7

Maintain appropriately rigorous academic standards despite the trend toward grade inflation that is a national travesty. Emerson probably came close to the truth when he said that "our chief want in life is someone to make us do what we can." Extrinsic motivation sometimes enhances intrinsic motivation. Do not expect instant perfection from your students, but strive for steady improvement. A common problem with beginning teachers is their almost pathological need to be liked or loved by students. Being respected is far more important. I do not know any esteemed teachers whose classes are filled with mediocre students who always get high grades without doing any serious academic work. In the obituary he wrote for his mentor and friend, Benton J. Underwood (1979) remarked:

> Extraordinary teachers are those who influence the lives of students in profound, irreversible ways. These teachers need not be nondirective; they need not take a poll among the students to determine what should be covered in a course; they need not hold hands with students in a circle in the hope that somehow, something beyond the midbrain will be stimulated. The master teacher views intellectual pursuits as tough and exacting challenges of the highest order and expects the students to view them in the same way. Art Melton was one such individual. (p. 1171)

Number 8

Maintain and cherish close ties with colleagues of all ages because you will learn a lot from them. From older ones, you learn valuable lessons about historical

perspective and Zeitgeist. From younger ones, you learn to avoid intellectual flab-
biness and to have a healthy skepticism about traditional ways of doing things.
Mark Twain put it aptly when he said: "Even if you're on the right track, you'll
get run over if you just sit there." When you agree with all of your colleagues, you
probably should change your mind.

Number 9

John Dewey suggested that "the most important attitude that can be formed is that
of desire to go on learning." Stan Ericksen agreed when he said that, "the most
important influence the teacher can have on students is to help them learn how to
learn independently." Ericksen's point can be threatening to young teachers, who
believe that students cannot learn anything that they are not taught. By contrast, I
believe that self-education is the only kind of any lasting consequence. The best
teachers are those who have no students because the students have learned how to
learn without their teachers.

Edward L. Thorndike averred that "the work of education is to make changes in
human minds." Ludy Benjamin (1991) highlighted the career of an extraordinary
teacher in his biography of Harry Kirke Wolfe. When reading about Wolfe, I was
reminded of William Arthur Ward's comment that "the mediocre teacher tells, the
good teacher explains, the great teacher demonstrates, and the truly exceptional
teacher inspires." Wolfe exemplified Thorndike's point and the qualities that make
truly exceptional teachers. Wolfe's work tells us a lot about the essence of learning and teaching, as does the career of Morrie Schwartz, a Brandeis University
sociologist, as portrayed in a moving little book titled *Tuesdays With Morrie* by
Mitch Albom (1997). We get a fuller understanding of this remarkable man from
Morrie: In His Own Words (Schwartz, 1999).

Number 10

Samuel Johnson remarked that "praise, like gold and diamonds, owes its value
to its scarcity." Teachers must be willing to work for intangible rewards that may
not come until many years after students graduate, which gives new meaning to
the "delay of reinforcement gradient." Henry Brooks Adams was right when he
said that teachers affect eternity; they never know where their influence ends.
However, you must learn to be patient with your students and especially with
yourself.

Never forget that you are still an active learner and that one of your most
important aims is to imbue your students with a passion to be lifelong learners.
Realize from the beginning, however, that one of the most frustrating things about
teaching is that you never know what you are doing. I sometimes hope to be a
house painter or a bricklayer in my next incarnation because they can more easily
quantify results of their work at the end of every day.

CODA

Teaching is more fun than most people should have. After 40 years of great fun, I cannot imagine doing anything else even for more prestige and money. (Please do not tell my president or dean that I would probably pay Furman to let me do what Furman pays me to do.)

The real reason for teaching is to make a difference—to be honorable, competent, responsible, productive, and unselfish but proud. Teaching is not a profession; teaching is a calling—delightful, invigorating, mysterious, frustrating, passionate, precious, and sacred. Good teachers stretch the mind and heart. I hope the world is a better place because we teachers make a difference to our students; after all, that is what teaching is all about.

REFERENCES

Albom, M. (1997). *Tuesdays with Morrie.* New York: Doubleday.

Benjamin, Jr., L. T. (1991). *Harry Kirke Wolfe: Pioneer in psychology.* Lincoln: University of Nebraska Press.

Bloom, A. D. (1987). *The closing of the American mind.* New York: Simon & Schuster.

Boyer, E. L. (1990). *Scholarship reconsidered: Priorities for the professoriate.* Princeton, NJ: The Carnegie Foundation for the Advancement of Teaching.

Buxton, C. E. (1951). Teaching: Have your cake and eat it too? *American Psychologist, 6,* 111–118.

Halpern, D. F., & Reich, J. N. (1999). Scholarship in psychology: Conversations about change and constancy. *American Psychologist, 54,* 347–349.

Halpern, D. F., Smothergill, D. W., Allen, M., Baker, S., Baum, C., Best, D., Ferrari, J., Geisinger, K. F., Gilden, E. R., Hester, M., Keith-Spiegel, P., Kierniesky, N. C., McGovern, T. V., McKeachie, W. J., Prokasy, W. F., Szuchman, L. T., Vasta, R., & Weaver, K. A. (1998). Scholarship in psychology: A paradigm for the twenty-first century. *American Psychologist, 53,* 1292–1297.

James, W. (1939). *Talks to teachers on psychology* (New Edition, with an Introduction by John Dewey and William H. Kilpatrick). New York: Holt. (Original work published 1899)

Schwartz, M. (1999). *Morrie in his own words.* New York: Walker.

Strunk, Jr., W., & White, E. B. (2000). *Elements of style* (4th ed.). Boston: Allyn & Bacon.

Underwood, B. J. (1979). Arthur W. Melton (1906–1978). *American Psychologist, 34,* 1171–1173.

Author Index

Subject Index

517